THE DISCOURSES OF GOTAMA BUDDHA

MIDDLE COLLECTION

THE DISCOURSES OF GOTAMA BUDDHA MIDDLE COLLECTION

New Translation in an abridged form of the Majjhima-Nikāya

Taken From the Pali Text Society Edition 1888–1902

Translated by

DAVID W. EVANS

B.A., F.L.A.

JANUS PUBLISHING COMPANY
London, England

First published in Great Britain 1992 by
Janus Publishing Company

British Library Cataloguing-in-Publication Data

Discourses of Gotama Buddha : middle collection.
I. Evans David W.
294.3823

ISBN 1 85756 025 6

Phototypeset by Intype, London

Printed & bound in England by
Antony Rowe Ltd, Chippenham, Wiltshire

Contents

Scriptural Citation xvi

Preface xvii

Introduction xviii

Untranslated Terms xxvii

Major Place Names and Territories xxviii

Major Personalities xxx

List of Discourses

All titles contain the word "discourse", but this has been omitted except in those cases where it is required to differentiate titles.

1. **A Survey of Fundamentals.** The relationship of self to the material and spiritual universe. 1

2. **All the Distractions.** Seven types of distraction and their surmounting. 3

3. **Inheritors of *Dhamma*.** Gotama and Sāriputta on the relative worthiness of different kinds of disciple. 6

4. **Fear and Dread.** The Master recalls terrifying experiences and his treatment of them: the four levels of absorption and the supernormal knowledge associated with them. 8

5. **No Blemishes.** Sāriputta and Moggallāna in dialogue concerning the temptations of the monk's life. 11

6. **What Might be Desired.** The legitimate rewards of the good life. 14

7. **The Simile of the Cloth.** The corrupt mind as a soiled cloth:the four divine abidings: the value of ritual bathing. 16

8. **Austerity.** The distinction between happiness and austerity in the *ariyan* discipline. 18

9. **Right view.** Sāriputta explains the four sustaining conditions and the eightfold path. 20

10. **The Applications of Mindfulness.** The application of mindfulness to the body, to feelings, to mental states, and to phenomena. 24

11. **Minor Discourse on the Lion's Roar.** The *ariyan* way compared with the claims of others. 27

12. **Major Discourse on the Lion's Roar.** A defecting monk has criticised Gotama, who responds by telling Sāriputta of his powers and by recalling the severity of his self-mortification in the ascetic phase of his search for enlightenment. 29

13. **Major Discourse on the Foundations of Suffering.** The satisfaction and disadvantage of normal existence and the escape from it as something beyond the capacity of other ascetics to explain. 36

14. **Minor Discourse on the Foundations of Suffering.** More on the satisfaction and disadvantage of normal existence: an encounter with the Jains recalled. 40

15. **Inference.** Moggallāna on the fractious monk. 43

16. **Barrenness of Mind.** Five forms of mental barrenness and five forms of mental constraint. 45

17. **The Forest Grove.** Progress on the Way in relation to where a monk lives. 47

18. **The Honey-Ball.** The Lord speaks briefly about obsessive ideas. Kaccāna expands on their nature and origin. 49

19. **The Dissection of Thought.** The effect of different kinds of mental pre-occupation. 52

20. **The Configuration of Thought.** Five ways of dealing with corrupting thoughts. 55

21. **The Parable of the Saw.** Patience in the face of provocation. 57

22. **The Parable of the Water-Snake.** A monk is rebuked for misinterpreting the Master: fixed opinions of various kinds and their removal. 61

23. **The Anthill.** A *deva* appears to a monk and propounds a riddle. The Lord interpretes. 66

24. **The Relay of Chariots.** A monk called Puṇṇa is much commended. Sāriputta is curious about him and seeks him out. 68

25. **Bait.** An allegory about herds of deer compared to groups of ascetics. 71

26. **The *Ariyan* Quest.** The Lord recalls his early experience with two teachers, his reaching of the goal of enlightenment, and the beginnings of his ministry. 74

27. **Minor Discourse on the Parable of the Elephant's Footprint.** Satisfaction with the teaching compared to the tracking of an elephant. 80

28. **Major Discourse on the Parable of the Elephant's Footprint.** The fivefold basis of attachment and the four great material constituents of the world. 83

29. **Major Discourse on the Parable of the Pith.** Ways of making progress but still falling short of the final goal. 87

30. **Minor Discourse on the Parable of the Pith.** More on the same theme: the formless realms. 90

31. **Minor Discourse in Gosiṅga.** The Lord visits three monks staying in a sāl-wood. They speak of their life together and their experience of the different levels of absorption. 92

32. **Major Discourse in Gosiṅga.** Various monks give their views on what kind of person would match the beauty of the sāl-wood. The Lord comments. 95

33. **Major Discourse on the Cowherd.** Eleven attributes of a cowherd: eleven attributes of a monk. 98

34. **Minor Discourse on the Cowherd.** How to cross a river – an analogy. 100

35. **Minor Discourse with Saccaka.** A debate with Saccaka, the Jain's son, about the existence and nature of self. 102

36. **Major Discourse with Saccaka.** The development of the body and of the mind: recollections of self-mortification. 107

37. **Minor Discourse on the Destruction of Craving.** The Lord speaks briefly to Sakka, king of *devas*. Moggallāna overhears and wishes to discover whether the *deva* has understood. 113

38. **Major Discourse on the Destruction of Craving.** A monk is rebuked for believing that it is consciousness that proceeds through life and that transmigrates. 116

39. **Major Discourse at Assapura.** Successive stages of the training. 120

40. **Minor Discourse at Assapura.** The externals and the essence of the good life distinguished. 123

41. **To the People of Sālā.** The roads to good and ill destinies. 125

42. **To the People of Verañjā.** Omitted – see the note following discourse 41. 127

43. **Major Discourse on the Miscellany.** A wide-ranging dialogue between Sāriputta and Koṭṭhita. 128

44. **Minor Discourse on the Miscellany.** The nun Dhammadinnā instructs a layman on the fivefold basis of attachment et alia. 132

45. **Minor Discourse on the Undertaking of *Dhamma*.** Its association with suffering and happiness in the present and in the future. 136

46. **Major Discourse on the Undertaking of *Dhamma*.** More on the same theme. 138

47. **Investigation.** How to judge the Teacher. 141

48. **At Kosambī.** The monks there quarrel and are lectured on the right way to treat one another. 143

49. **A Challenge to Brahmā.** A story about a debate with a deity who believed his heaven to be eternal. 146

50. **A Rebuke for Māra.** Moggallāna confronts the Evil One. 149

51. **To Kandaraka.** On tormenting oneself, or others, or both, or neither. 152

52. **With a Citizen of Aṭṭhaka.** Ānanda on the various levels of absorption. 155

53. **For Learners.** The Lord opens a new council-hall. Ānanda explains the stages of the Way. 157

54. **With Potaliya.** A householder describes himself as a practitioner of renunciation. The Lord sees the matter differently. 160

55. **With Jīvaka.** What a monk may and may not eat. 163

56. **With Upāli.** A debate with the Jains concerning the relative significance of mental, verbal, and physical activity: the conversion of a leading citizen. 165

57. **With the Dog Imitator.** The Lord talks with an ascetic who lives like a dog and another who lives like a cow. 171

58. **With Prince Abhaya.** Nātaputta the Jain primes the Prince with a double-edged question about right speech. 174

59. **On Much to be Experienced.** The settling of a dispute between a monk and a lay-follower about the analysis of feeling. 176

60. **On What is Certain.** Conflicting views of the fruits of asceticism analysed. 178

61. **A Talk with Rāhula at Ambalaṭṭhikā.** The evil of deliberate lying: the value of careful reflection. 181

62. **Major Discourse on a Talk with Rāhula.** The four great elements, the space element, and the divine abidings as a basis for mental discipline. 183

63. **Minor Discourse with Māluṅkyāputta.** A monk demands straight answers on questions relating to the eternity of the world, to death, and so on. 185

64. **Major Discourse with Māluṅkyāputta.** The five fetters. 187

65. **With Bhaddāli.** A monk disobeys an instruction to eat once a day: ways of dealing with an errant monk: reasons for an increase in the number of rules. 189

66. **The Parable of the Quail.** Four possible outcomes of the attempt to deal with attachment: the transcendence of all attainments. 193

67. **At Cātumā.** Some monks are sent away for being unduly noisy: a question for Sāriputta about this: hazards along the Way. 196

68. **At Naḷakapāna.** The purposes of an exemplar: reasons for disclosing the destinies of others. 199

69. **On Gulissāni.** Sāriputta on a monk who has returned from the forest. 201

70. **At Kīṭāgiri.** More problems with eating once a day: kinds and degrees of freedom. 203

71. **With Vacchagotta on the Threefold Knowledge.** Does the Lord claim omniscience? 207

72. **With Vacchagotta on Fire.** Unanswerable questions – a parable. 209

73. **Major Discourse with Vacchagotta.** The attainments of followers: the conversion of Vacchagotta. 212

74. **With Dīghanakha.** On what is pleasing, or otherwise. 215

75. **With Māgandiya.** The Lord is denounced as a suppressor of life: different kinds of happiness: misunderstanding of *nibbāna*. 217

76. **With Sandaka.** Ānanda on false teachers. 223

77. **Major Discourse with Sakuludāyin.** Why does the Lord have a reputation beyond that of other teachers? 228

78. **With Samaṇamaṇḍikā's Son.** Skilful and unskilful living and their relation to the mind. 234

79. **Minor Discourse with Sakuludāyin.** "Splendours" compared: the possibility of a world that is exclusively happy. 237

80. **With Vekhanassa.** More on "splendours": valid and invalid claims. 241

81. **On Ghaṭīkāra.** The story of a disciple of a former *buddha*. 244

82. **On Raṭṭhapāla.** An aspiring monk's problems with his parents: his encounter with a king and four declarations about *dhamma*. 248

83. **On Makhādeva.** About a dynasty of monarchs who ruled by *dhamma*. 255

84. **At Madhurā.** Kaccāna talks with King Avantiputta about caste. 258

85. **With Prince Bodhi.** The Lord visits the Prince's new palace: five qualities for exertion. 261

86. **With Aṅgulimāla.** The conversion of a mass murderer. 264

87. **On the Products of Affection.** The Lord's response to a bereaved father and an ensuing controversy. 268

88. **The Mantle.** Ānanda discusses what is skilful with King Pasenadi. 271

89. **Testimonies to *Dhamma*.** King Pasenadi conceives a longing to see the Lord. 273

90. **At Kaṇṇakatthala.** King Pasenadi interrogates the Lord on omniscience, caste, and *devas*. 276

91. **To Brahmāyu.** A leading brahman sends his pupil to investigate the thirty-two marks of a great man. 280

92. **With Sela.** A brahman and his retinue of pupils receive the going forth. 284

93. **With Assalāyana.** Another debate about caste. 286

94. **With Ghoṭamukha.** The monk Udena talks with a brahman about self-torment and torment of others. 291

95. **With Caṅkī.** The Lord and a leading brahman compared: a village welcome: tradition as a source of knowledge. 294

96. **With Esukārī.** More on caste. 299

97. **With Dhānañjāni.** Sāriputta hears that a brahman friend has fallen into bad ways. 301

98. **With Vāseṭṭha.** The true brahman. 304

99. **With Subha.** Householders and ascetics compared: brahminical claims exposed. 307

100. **With Saṅgārava.** The various grounds for the claims of ascetics and brahmans. 312

101. **At Devadaha.** A debate with the Jains on how far what is experienced is due to what was previously done. 314

102. **The Threefold Five.** A survey of views about self, death, and the world. 318

103. **On "Now What?"** How to handle disagreements. 321

104. **At Sāmagāma.** The Jain leader has just died and his followers are quarrelling. How the Order can avoid such a fate. 323

105. **With Sunakkhatta.** Claims and attainments within the Order. 327

106. **Helpful Imperturbability.** The higher realms of attainment and attachment to them. 330

107. **With Gaṇaka-Moggallāna.** The Way as a gradual training: why some succeed but not others. 333

108. **With Gopaka-Moggallāna.** Ānanda on what sustains the Order after the Lord has passed away. 336

109. **Major Discourse at the Time of the Full Moon.** The fivefold basis of attachment and the concept of self. 339

110. **Minor Discourse at the Time of the Full Moon.** The evil and the good man compared. 342

111. **The Continuous.** On Sāriputta and his attainments. 344

112. **The Sixfold Cleansing**. How to interrogate a monk who claims gnosis. 347

113. **The Good Man.** How the pride of achievement can corrupt. 351

114. **What Should and Should Not be Resorted To.** Sāriputta on the skilful and the unskilful. 353

115. **The Manifold Elements.** On the kinds of investigation that make for wisdom: the twelve factors in the cycle of existence. 356

116. **At Isigili.** Omitted – see the note following discourse 115. 359

117. **The Great Forty.** The relationship between the different elements of the eightfold path. 360

118. **Mindfulness of Breathing In and Out.** Breathing as a vehicle for contemplation. 363

119. **Mindfulness of Body.** Contemplation of the body: the four levels of absorption: ten advantages. 366

120. **On Arising Through (Mental) Characteristics.** Mental characteristics as affecting rebirth. 369

121. **Minor Discourse on Emptiness.** A progressive contemplation of emptiness. 370

122. **Major Discourse on Emptiness.** More on emptiness: misfortunes for teachers and pupils. 372

123. **Strange and Wonderful Attributes.** The special qualities of the *bodhisatta*. 376

124. **By Bakkula.** Bakkula proclaims his virtues and makes his end. 379

125. **The Tamed State.** Prince Jayasena is not convinced by the novice Aciravata. The Lord compares the training to the taming of an elephant. 381

126. **With Bhūmija.** On how the search is affected by the expectations about it. 384

127. **By Anuruddha.** Anuruddha on various realms of *devas*. 386

128. **Corruptions.** The Lord visits three monks and enquires as to their experiences. 389

129. **The Foolish and The Wise.** The consequences of being a fool and the alternative. 392

130. **The Divine Messengers.** The evil-doer finds himself in purgatory and is interrogated about his blindness during life. 397

131. **On What is Timely.** Non-attachment to past, future, or present. 400

132. **Ānanda on What is Timely.** Omitted – see the note following discourse 131. 402

133. **Kaccāna the Great on What is Timely.** More on the same. 403

134. **With Lomasakaṅgiya on What is Timely** More on the same. 405

135. **The Minor Analysis of Behaviour.** How beings inherit the fruits of their deeds. 407

136. **The Major Analysis of Behaviour.** The monk Samiddhi gives a one-sided answer to the wanderer Potaliputta: the three kinds of feeling. 410

137. **Analysis of the Six Sources (of Experience).** Delight, distress, and equanimity of the household life and of the ascetic. 413

138. **An Outline and Analysis.** Kaccāna on attachment to externals and to various attainments. 417

139. **The Analysis of Peace.** How to deal with others: the subtleties of right speech. 419

140. **Analysis of The Elements.** The Lord meets a follower who does not recognise him: the six elements, the six realms of stimulation, the eighteen mental distinctions, the four resolves. 422

141. **Analysis of The Truths.** Sāriputta on the four *ariyan* truths. 426

142. **The Analysis of Offerings.** The Lord's foster-mother brings him some garments. 429

143. **Counsel for Anāthapiṇḍika.** Anāthapiṇḍika is dying. Sāriputta offers counsel. 431

144. **Counsel for Channa.** The monk Channa is grievously sick and means to end his life: the ethics of suicide. 433

145. **A Talk with Puṇṇa.** The monk Puṇṇa is going to live in a dangerous locality and is interrogated by the Lord. 435

146. **Counsel from Nandaka.** The monk Nandaka exhorts the nuns. 437

147. **A Talk with Rāhula.** On transience. 440

148. **The Six Sixes.** Sense organs and objects, consciousness, stimuli, feeling, craving. 441

Scriptural Citation

The traditional method of Buddhist scriptural citation does not quote the name of individual discourses. Passages are indicated instead by, firstly, an abbreviation indicating the collection or work; secondly (where appropriate), a number referring to the volume of the Pali edition; and thirdly, by a numbered section within the work or volume. In the case of the Middle Collection there are three volumes within which numbering by section recommences. These are:

1. Discourses 1–76
2. Discourses 77–106
3. Discourses 107–152

Since the present work is an abridgement it has not been thought appropriate to place section numbers at precise points in the text. However, to assist in tracing citations given elsewhere, the section numbers for each discourse are given immediately below the title.

The following conventions are used in the text:

( ) editorial interpolations, paraphrases etc.

** beginning and end of verse passages

Footnotes relate to superscripts inserted in the text

PTSD in footnotes refers to the Pali Text Society Dictionary

Preface

This work is an attempt to present the most fundamental writings of Buddhism in a way which surmounts certain problems facing the modern reader. The Buddhist Canon was not compiled to be read but to be recited by monks and, for whatever reason, has become enormously inflated with repetitions as well as extremely formalised. Access to the texts for the steadily growing community of English-speaking Buddhists has therefore involved a choice between expensive multi-volume sets which offer completeness but are far too long in relation to their effective content or anthologies which are, by definition, highly selective.

The present volume is a combination of abridgement and translation which seeks to rectify this situation for one of the major collections. It is just about one third the size of Horner's translation of the same material for the Pali Text Society of London, but with well over 90% of the significant content. In consequence I believe this to be the first English version in which it is feasible to read a complete discourse to an audience. The way in which the abridgement has been achieved is discussed in detail in the introduction.

I have not provided an index. The value of one for doctrinal and psychological terms is dubious since the English equivalents vary in different translations and exhaustive indexing of names would have produced many references which merely mentioned obscure individuals in passing. I have preferred instead to give a brief indication of the nature of each discourse with the list of titles that follows this preface. The main personal and place names appearing in the text are indicated at the end of the introduction.

David Evans
Leeds, England (December 1991)

Introduction

Origins of the Buddhist Canon

According to western scholars Gotama Buddha died around 483 BC and the texts themselves indicate a teacher whose ministry had lasted between forty and fifty years. At its outset he had founded a mendicant order of wanderers which certainly numbered many hundreds by the time of his death. Hence, there was a great deal to remember and many capable of remembering some part of it. Buddhist tradition holds that a council took place within a short space of time with a view to collating the scriptures. These comprised two sections, one being the *Vinaya*, i.e. rules of monastic discipline that had evolved over the previous decades under the scrutiny of the Master himself. The other, the *Suttas* or Discourses, sought to set out what was recollected of his ministry and teaching. A third and final element of the Canon, the *Abhidhamma*, represented a detailed and abstract exegesis of the Teaching which was probably a somewhat later addition – it was not in fact accepted as canonical by all of the eighteen schools which grew up in the early centuries of Buddhism.

The earliest written records in the Indian sub-continent date from the Indus valley civilisation of the late third and early second millennium BC, but these were in the form of inscriptions on small blocks of talc, and Gotama's India still had not discovered a writing surface suitable for the production of portable documents. Some two centuries later the emperor Ashoka Maurya was to make the earliest surviving references to the religion by means of a series of edicts carved mainly on sandstone pillars. However, the scriptures themselves could hardly be preserved in such a way and it was not until Buddhism arrived in Ceylon in the first century BC that they are known with certainty to have been committed to writing. During the intervening period the monastic community handed down the Canon by systematically memorising it, and through regular recitations.

This fact is of some importance in understanding the style of the Discourses as conveyed to a twentieth-century audience. The linking of doctrines to numerical mnemonics, for instance, is one way of trying to ensure that a complex philosophy will be remembered with a degree of accuracy. Or again, the fact that converts to the Teaching embrace their new allegiance with the same form of words in narrative after narrative might well represent an attempt by the earliest compilers to simplify their task. Such factors reinforce belief in the historical basis of the material since they are unattractive in themselves and would serve no purpose if the original aim had been to produce a work of pure inspiration comparable to the great

Hindu epics such as the *Mahabharata*. On the other hand, certain elements, such as the Master's stories relating to earlier ages, and episodes involving the complex pantheon of local spirits and deities, look like an attempt to accommodate the Buddhist *dhamma* to a mass audience and to manipulate popular religion to serve its ends. This is achieved by maintaining its ancient lineage, and by representing all disembodied beings that might exist as either its disciples or as perverse and demonic. In such a connection the modern reader must realise that the early Buddhists were in competition with other sects of mendicants for the support of lay-people and of influential patrons, a circumstance particularly well illustrated in Discourse 56 of the present volume.

Two literary embodiments of the aforesaid oral tradition have come down to us intact. One, in Chinese, was a secondary translation of a version available in a form of Sanskrit when Buddhism arrived in China in the early Christian centuries, but now largely lost. The other, in Pali, was the original literary form of the Canon as copied down in Ceylon. As Pali cannot be too far removed from the language of Gotama himself it seems reasonable to view the Pali Canon as the nearest we are able to get to the origins of Buddhism.

The Discourses of the Pali Canon divide into five collections. The Long Collection (34 discourses) contains those pieces which are individually of considerable length, the Middle Collection (152 discourses) those of medium length. These two sections provide each discourse with a narrative framework, sometimes considerable, and commence with a statement of where Gotama was staying at the time. The Linked Collection (2889 pieces) is arranged on the principle of bringing together assorted statements on the same theme, the Graduated Collection (2308 pieces) by a numerical progression. These are more accurately described as collections of sayings than of discourses, being of a much more fragmented nature and carrying far less contextual information. The final section, or Minor Collection, contains fifteen independent works of a heterogeneous character including collections of birth stories and a long verse poem, the *Dhammapada*, which is the best-known work in the entire Canon.

A word remains to be said concerning the later literature of Buddhism. Half a millennium after its foundation, new trends become apparent, one of which is a re-opening of the Canon and the insertion of new texts indicating sectarian debate within the Buddhist community. Their most striking characteristic is the representation of the Buddha as a transcendental rather than a historical figure, a device allowing the authors to affirm loyalty to the religion at a basic level whilst attempting some metaphysical re-evaluation. Further discussion of such developments is beyond the scope of this introduction.

The Nature of this Edition

The Middle Collection typifies the unique problems which the Pali Canon sets for both translator and reader. These are various but two of them are central:

(1) Repetitious features occur throughout, and on a scale which enormously inflates the material. However, these are of several kinds and articulate with the structure of individual discourses in a complex manner so that any attempt to reduce the whole to a more realistic length calls for some degree of preliminary analysis. A secondary problem arising is that the process of repetition frequently breaks down even in the most complete versions so that we are confronted by "etc." or marks of omission.

(2) Individual Pali sentences translated on a word-for-word basis contain tautologies and redundancies to the point of absurdity. For instance, as many as six virtually synonymous verbs may be used in succession simply to heighten the effect. In other cases sentences are apt to turn into inventories as when a compiler making a simple statement about places where a monk may meditate offers a quite gratuitous list of some fifteen locations. Sentences may also be grammatically complex and this, when joined to the other factors mentioned, can result in something which defies an articulate rendering in English.

This edition addresses the above problems by seeking to condense the texts in a systematic but sensitive way. With this end in view, I have adopted a number of guidelines. In general these are :

- The abridgement of any particular discourse seeks to preserve the entire argument and narrative in the original words as far as possible, relying on a careful screening out of repetitions and redundancies as the principal means of shortening the piece.
- The general stylistic form and flavour of the discourses are respected and the degree of condensation is determined by this factor as well as by content.
- Parentheses are used for interpolations by the editor. These are confined to ensuring continuity of the text where a passage has been removed or to certain types of substitution e.g. pronouns for proper names (repetition of the latter *ad nauseum* being a minor but irritating problem). A third function involving the occasional insertion of a word simply to clarify a particularly ambiguous statement or passage is a normal translator's prerogative. There are no breaks or marks of omission in the text.

Two other general problems deserve mention. The first is the matter of verse passages. Although the Middle Collection is overwhelmingly a mixture of narrative and didactic prose these do occur from time to time. As most of them tend to repeat in more eloquent language a point previously made, they can, for the most part, be treated as redundant elements. However, a small number are essential for the continuity of the text, in which case they have been retained but rendered in prose form.

The other concerns material likely to be virtually meaningless to the modern reader and which I have therefore much abbreviated. This comprises passages connected with the obscurer popular beliefs of Gotama's time and with the mythological pre-history of Buddhism. To some extent these are referred to in notes. They contribute only a small proportion of the material eliminated and should not be regarded as part of any general attempt to "de-mythologise" the text.

As regards translation, I have cross-checked with Horner's existing Pali Text Society version throughout, sometimes using her renderings verbatim. However, there are also many divergences and all vocabulary and grammar has been independently checked so that this does rank as a new translation rather than an abridgement of an existing one. Detailed points connected with both the abridgement and the translation are dealt with in the ensuing sections.

The Form of the Abridgement

The major types of repetition can be fairly easily summarised together with the methods of dealing with them. I have found it possible to indicate their nature in a semi-algebraic manner and to assign names as follows:

(1) *Serial Repetitions*. These have the form A is x, B is x, C is x, etc. where A, B, and C represent specific terms and x is a general description, usually of paragraph length, which is applied to each in turn. Serial repetitions can be dealt with by simply accumulating the variables in a single description (A, B, and C are x). Exceptions to this method are situations where there are a large number of variables or where there are words in the description which correlate with them, e.g. treatments of the senses which are complicated by the correspondence of organs with faculties. Long lists of variables can be abbreviated (with footnotes as necessary), and a summarising phrase or sentence added to make quite clear that the description refers to all terms of a certain kind. Serial repetitions are by far the single largest factor making for inflation of the texts.

(2) *Reverse Repetitions*. Here the structure is A is x, B is not x. Reverse repetitions are far less pervasive than serial repetitions but are a dominant feature of some discourses. They arise because of the continual tendency to compare a desirable with an undesirable state of affairs. The second description in such cases tends to be just a point-by-point negation of the attributes named in the first and therefore adds nothing of substance overall. It can usually be omitted, though some kind of brief paraphrase may be inserted where appropriate to preserve the balance of the discourse.

(3) *Parenthetical Repetitions*. These are usually reported conversations or invitations conveyed through an intermediary, all of which tend to be repeated verbatim in the full text. The abridgement deals with all such in the obvious way, i.e. by replacing the repetition with a statement indicating that A repeated to B what he/she had been told by C.

(4) *Interactive Repetitions*. Conversational interaction produces much excess verbiage because of the highly formalised treatment of dialogue.

The most common example is the re-statement of a question in the answer, sometimes with a confirmation of the answer by the questioner so that we get "Is A x?" "Yes, A is x." "So it is agreed that A is x." The normal solution here is to delete the confirmation and reduce the answer to the simple affirmation or negation. There are also situations where a kind of interrogative version of a serial repetition is superimposed on the above problem, producing "Is A x?" "Yes, A is x." "Is B x?" "Yes, B is x." "Is C x?" (and so on). The solution is the same as for serial repetitions, i.e. to reduce the number of questions by accumulating several variables in one question.

A minor but recurring feature is the situation where Gotama asks an (apparently) rhetorical question of the monks, who politely invite him to answer it himself. This adds nothing to the discourse, so the abridgement removes it and proceeds straight to what follows.

(5) *Periodic Repetitions*. This term refers to a form of words reiterated at successive stages of a discourse and usually indicating unfulfilled purpose or constancy of endeavour in relation to otherwise changing states or circumstances. Periodic repetitions are not usually deleted as they are an important way of registering emphasis and, in so far as they indicate what factors are unaltered at various stages in a progression, are not repetitious in a sense which makes them redundant. However, it is quite important to reduce them to their essentials by removing superfluous sentences which would otherwise recur several or many times.

(6) *Layered Repetitions*. These are the most complex source of inflation of a dialogue and the most difficult to deal with. They give rise to structures such as the following – abc, adc, aec, and so on, where original material, (b,d,e), is sandwiched between repeated introductory and closing sections of a paragraph. Sometimes the repetitions may have to stand, but with the repeated elements condensed as far as possible. In other cases the number of repetitions can be reduced. It is rarely possible or desirable to eliminate them altogether.

(7) *Topic Statements*. The lengthy philosophical presentations often generate a number of sub-themes each of which is first indicated in brief, then formulated in detail, and finally referred back to as a topic that has been dealt with. This gives a structure of a1, a2, a3, b1, b2, b3, etc. where a2 and b2 are the full formulation of a topic and the other elements preliminary and concluding references. In many cases I have deleted the third element on the grounds that a change of theme is sufficiently indicated by the first, i.e. reducing the whole to a1, a2, b1, b2. This is certainly desirable in cases where the main formulation is itself relatively short, and the introductory sentences may also be abbreviated as far as possible. Occasionally the length and complexity of the main formulation make the retention of the conclusion warrantable. It seems quite possible that this very ponderous method of marking the elements of a discourse was an original feature of the Teaching

as an intended aid to the monks who were seeking to commit it to memory.

(8) *Transposed Passages*. Occasionally the sequence of material in a dialogue has been altered in a way which allows repetitious material to be removed. There is usually a note explaining this.

(9) *Standard Passages*. (1) to (7), above, refer to inflationary features of individual discourses. I have reserved the phrase "standard passage" for sections of significant length which reappear in *different* discourses throughout the collection. These are a quite distinct problem. Broadly speaking, my policy has been to translate them in full in one or two places and in abbreviated form elsewhere. However, I have avoided abbreviation in the case of passages which are very short, or in any situation where it is felt that such treatment might destroy the balance of the dialogue. Some discourses have narrative introductions which are identical except for the proper names involved and these (as opposed to doctrinal statements) are always retained.

The above are the larger structures in the text, but individual sentences or, sometimes, pairs of sentences raise just as many problems. Though these are diverse it is again possible to indicate some of the more pervasive ones.

One feature of Pali is that each one of a sequence of actions tends to be set out by means of an active verb followed by a gerundial form indicating its completion. Taking an example of a very common situation at the outset of a discourse we get the following (all subsequent examples being from Horner's translation):

"Then the venerable Ćunda the Great, emerging towards evening from solitary meditation, approached the Lord; having approached, having greeted the Lord, he sat down at a respectful distance. As he was sitting down at a respectful distance the venerable Cunda the Great spoke thus to the Lord."

Here, "having approached" and "as he was sitting down" exemplify this form of construction. The abridgement avoids such doubling of verbs and uses whatever form of the verb conveys the sense most acceptably in English. The passage quoted also brings out the undue repetition of names and epithets with three references to "the Lord" and two to Cunda the Great. For comparison the equivalent translation in the abridgement is:

"Then venerable Cunda the Great, emerging from seclusion towards evening, approached the Lord, greeted (him) and sat down at one side. Said Cunda . . ."

Another continual way of lengthening sentences is through the repetition of the same predicate or verb, e.g.:

"Material shape, monks, is impermanent, feeling is impermanent, perception is impermanent, the habitual tendencies are impermanent, consciousness is impermanent."

" . . . he fares along contemplating the body in the body internally, or he fares along contemplating the body in the body externally, or he fares along contemplating the body in the body internally and externally."

In such cases the abridgement eliminates or reduces the reiteration of "is impermanent", or "fares along contemplating" or their equivalents in other passages. (Occasionally some repetition may be retained for emphasis.)

Another common source of repetition results from a tendency to carry over verbiage from one sentence to the next in various ways such as that illustrated below:

"So I, Aggivesana, took food little by little, drop by drop, such as bean soup, or vetch soup or chick-pea soup or pea soup. While I, Aggivesana, was taking food little by little, drop by drop, such as bean soup, or vetch soup or chick-pea soup or pea soup, my body became exceedingly emaciated."

Clearly, the substitution of "(and whilst so doing)" or "(and thereby)" for the section of the second sentence preceding "my body . . ." is an effective method of abbreviation. The merging of sentences which results is a frequent occurrence in situations of this type in the abridgement. The reverse procedure, i.e. the division of a single sentence into two also occurs in a few places, though the object in these cases is to produce a manageable rendering rather than to reduce the number of words overall.

The use of direct speech in Pali leads to some strange problems. One is the number of levels of inverted commas which may confront the reader, three being common and four or even five occasional. In many cases I have converted these to reported speech. In various passages, however, we are told of someone's intentions followed by a statement in almost identical terms to the effect that the intentions were carried out, e.g.:

"But it occurred to the Lord: 'It is still too early to walk for almsfood in Vesali. Suppose I were to approach Ekapundarika, the wanderers' park, and Vacchagotta the wanderer?' Then the Lord approached Ekapundarika, the wanderers' park, and Vacchagotta the wanderer."

In this case "(And he did so.)" can be usefully substituted for the final sentence.

Practically all the above expedients illustrate ways of dealing with simple redundancy of language. The remaining points to be covered involve more subjective decisions. They relate to the thinning out of passages which are judged to be over-rhetorical, which digress into long lists of minor relevance, or that obviously impede the progress of a discourse in other ways. A frequently appearing example of the first type is:

"Herein, Ānanda, an uninstructed ordinary person, taking no account of the pure ones, [unskilled in the *dhamma* of the pure ones, untrained in the *dhamma* of the pure ones; taking no account of the true men, unskilled in the *dhamma* of the true men], untrained in the *dhamma* of the true men . . ."

I regard it as legitimate to delete the section between the square brackets in this example, though some such may be dealt with as standard passages (see above). An illustration of the inventory mentality was given in the previous section and may be handled by simply giving the first few terms and then inserting "(and so on)" if warranted. A succession of adjectives or verbs all conveying the same meaning is sometimes abbreviated.

Finally there is the important question of parables. They can be a target for condensation on two grounds. In the first place multiple parables may be used to illustrate a single point – in one case no fewer than eight are given. Generally, I have retained only the first or the most effective. Secondly, there are a few situations where the detail of a parable is expanded quite unnecessarily in relation to the point it is intended to illustrate. In such cases I have not hesitated to abbreviate it.

I have avoided over-burdening the text with footnotes explaining the abridgement process, but various of these do illustrate further the way in which condensation has been achieved.

A Note on the Translation

My approach to re-translation was conditioned by having been acquainted with the material in English for many years prior to taking up the study of Pali. During this period I had formed various definite opinions about existing translations of a range of specific terms – for example I was neither convinced that *Tathāgata* was untranslatable nor satisfied with existing renderings. On the whole this circumstance has been helpful in suggesting where particular care and thought were most needed, though inevitably in the process various of my own preconceptions have had to be revised. I have not had direct access to the ancient commentaries, though Horner's footnotes have sometimes been helpful in this respect in relation to the obscurer passages.

In translating Pali or any other language consistency is obviously important whilst not being a factor which should be allowed to override all else. As is well known, many terms in a language may not possess exact equivalents in other languages, so that it may be preferable to exercise some flexibility in rendering the same term in different contexts. That said some special considerations do seem to apply here. Key terms in the Discourses tend to appear in doctrinal formulas and clearly it *is* important that these should be invariable in their rendering. Where the same term appears in different formulas, however, variant translations may seem legitimate. Other recurring passages relate to descriptions of a broader kind, however, and minor differences of treatment in such cases have no significant effect on the interpretation whilst providing some welcome variety.

Pali syntax does not lend itself to precise translation into English without considerable distortion of normal forms of expression in the latter language – a fact which, to some extent, was indicated in the previous section. In so far as I have sometimes set aside formal linguistic constraints because of this, so as to achieve a more natural rendering, the translation can certainly be regarded as "free", though in other respects I would not so view it.

Finally, some reference to the translation is given in notes but I have largely avoided quotation of the actual Pali terms involved because of the special problems of adding diacritics to the text.

Untranslated Terms

Arahant	A follower of the Buddha who has achieved enlightenment – literally a "worthy one": also applied to the Buddha himself
Ariyan	In a Buddhist context, whatever is regarded as most truly indicative of the spiritual genius of the ariyan peoples: often translated "noble"
Bodhisatta	Literally a "wisdom being": a *buddha* prior to his enlightenment
Brahmā	A high grade of celestial being
Buddha	A being enlightened through his own efforts and a teacher of others
Deva	A celestial being
Dhamma	Truth, reality, teaching
Gandhabba	A spirit associated with conception
Māra	A malevolent spirit
Nibbāna	The blowing or dying out of all cravings: the Buddhist ultimate
Yakkha	A relatively low grade of spirit

Major Place Names and Territories

Modern equivalents are given in parentheses in the case of towns.

Bārāṇasi (Benares)	Location of the first sermon
Campā (Bhagalpur)	A town on the lower Ganges, marking the approximate eastern limits of Gotama's ministry
Gayā (Gayā)	Nearest location to the place of Gotama's enlightenment
Kapilavatthu (Kapilavastu)	Gotama's home town
Kosala	Ancient kingdom to the north-east of modern Lucknow
Kosambī	A town on the Yamuna river about 25 miles west of modern Allahabad, and marking the approximate western boundary of Gotama's ministry
Kusinārā	A village to the west of the Gandak river about 30 miles north-east of modern Gorakhpur: the place of Gotama's disease
Licchavis	A tribe inhabiting the area to the north-east of modern Patna
Magadha	Ancient kingdom to the south of modern Patna
Pāṭaliputta (Patna)	
Rājagaha (Raigir)	Capital of Magadha
Sāketa (Ayodhya)	Important town in the south of Kosala on the river Gogra
Sakyas	Gotama's tribe, with Kapilavatthu as its chief town
Sāvatthī	Capital of Kosala, situated on the Rapti river about 50 miles south-east of Kapilavatthu
Vajjis	A tribe living east of the Gandak river and north of Vesālī

Vesālī	Chief town of the Licchavi tribe, about 30 miles north of modern Patna
Videhas	A tribe living east of the Gandak river to the south of the Himālayas

Major Personalities

Ajātasattu	King of Magadha
Ānanda	Gotama's constant companion throughout his ministry, and reputedly his cousin: the narrator of the Discourses
Anāthapiṇḍika	A rich patron of the Buddhist monastic community
Gotama	The Buddha
Kassapa	A leading monk, and major narrator of the scriptures after Gotama's death
Mahāpajāpatī	Gotama's foster-mother: instigator of the nuns' order
Moggallāna	A leading monk, famed for his psychic powers
Nāṭaputta	The Jain leader
Pasenadi	King of Kosala
Sāriputta	Effectively the second-in-command of the Order

1

A Survey of Fundamentals

1–6

Thus have I heard: once the Lord dwelt near Ukkaṭṭhā in the Subhaga Grove by the great sāl-tree. There (he) addressed the monks, saying:

"I will give you a survey of the fundamentals of all things. Herein, monks, an uninformed person, heedless of the *ariyans*, untrained in the *dhamma* of good men perceives solid as solid, and having (done so) thinks about solidity, with reference to solidity, from the standpoint of solidity, (and) thinks, 'Solidity is mine.' He takes pleasure in solid (things). Why so? I say it is not well understood by him. He perceives liquid as liquid, heat as heat, the aeriform as aeriform[1], beings as beings, (and) *devas* as *devas*[2] (in the same terms). He perceives the realms of infinite space, infinite consciousness, nothingness, of neither perceiving nor not-perceiving (as such). He perceives what is seen, or heard, or (otherwise) sensed, or thought (as such). He perceives unity as unity, diversity as diversity, universality as universality. (And with regard to any of these he thinks in the same way.) Why so? I say that it is not well understood by him. He perceives *nibbāna* as *nibbāna* (and having done so) he thinks of *nibbāna*, with reference to *nibbāna*, from the standpoint of *nibbāna*. He thinks, '*Nibbāna* is for me.' He takes pleasure in (the thought of) *nibbāna*. Why so? I say it is not well understood by him.

Monks, any monk who is a trainee, of unachieved purpose, lives striving for the matchless haven from bondage. He, too, comprehends solid as solid, (and having done so) he should not think of solidity, by reference to solidity, (or) from the standpoint of solidity. He should not think, 'Solidity is for me', nor take pleasure in (it). (And likewise with all other aspects of the world and with *nibbāna* itself).

Any monk who is *arahant*, the distractions rooted out, fulfilled, who has done what needs to be done, who has shed the burden, reached the goal, finally broken the thongs of existence, and is released by true knowledge – he (will not reflect in any of these ways). Why so? I say it is well understood by him (and) because of the waning of passion, ill-will, and delusion.

The Exemplar, too, monks, *arahant*, truly enlightened, recognises (all these things for what they are, and has no attachment to any of them). Why so? I say (the matter) is well understood (by him through) seeing enjoyment as the root of suffering, birth as (arising) from coming into existence. (and that there is) old age and death for (any) being. So I say, monks, through the waning of all cravings, through dispassion, cessation, renunciation, and rejection, the Exemplar is fully enlightened with a matchless and perfect wisdom."

Thus spoke the Lord.

1. The four elements, i.e. earth, water, fire, and air if taken literally. However, they may be understood as typifying the three states of matter plus heat as the most tangible manifestation of energy.
2. Various other non-human categories are mentioned.

2

All the Distractions

6–12

Thus have I heard: once the Lord dwelt near Sāvatthī in the Jeta Grove on Anāthapiṇḍika's campus.[1] There (he) addressed the monks, saying:

"Monks, I will teach you the means of controlling all distractions. (From things) known and seen I speak of the withering of the distractions. And what (does this consist of)? There is ordered attention and there is disordered attention. From disordered attention arise distractions (previously) unconceived and (those already) arisen increase. From ordered attention unconceived distractions do not arise and (those already) arisen pass away. There are, monks, distractions to be left behind through observation, distractions to be left behind through restraint, distractions to be left behind through practice. There are (others) to be left behind through endurance, through avoidance, through removal, (or) through development.

And what are the distractions to be left behind through observation? Herein, monks, an uninformed person, heedless of the *ariyans*, untrained in the *dhamma* of good men, does not know (which) things should be given attention and (which) should not. And what are the things that should not be given attention? (If what is given attention produces a previously) unarisen distraction of worldly pursuit, of (continued) existence, or of ignorance, or if (such states) increase, then these are the things which should not be given attention.

His attention is disordered who thinks in these ways: 'Was I or was I not in the past? What was I in the past? How was I in the past? Having been what, what did I become in the past?' (Or he thinks similarly about the future or) now, in the present, (falls prey to) inner doubt thinking, 'Am I or am I not? What am I? How am I? Whence has this being come? Where is it going?'

To one whose attention is thus disordered one of six views arises as true or real: 'There is myself', or 'There is not myself', or 'I recognise self (or non-self) by means of self', or 'I recognise self by means of what is not self' Or a view occurs to him thus: 'Whatever this speaking, sentient, self of mine might be that experiences here and there the ripening of deeds both fair and foul, this (it) is that is stable, continuous, perpetual, not subject to vicissitude, and will surely be for ever more.' Monks, this can be described as going to views, as seizing on views, as the wilderness of views, as the deviousness of views, as the tortuousness of views, as the bondage of views. Enslaved by the bondage of views, I say that the uninformed person has no escape by way of birth, old age and death; has no escape from griefs and woes, from pain, distress, and trouble.

But an instructed disciple of the *ariyans*, well trained in the *dhamma* of good men, knows (which) things should be given attention and (which) should not. Thinking, 'This is suffering' he pays ordered attention. Thinking, 'This is the origin of suffering' he pays ordered attention. Thinking, 'This is the cessation of suffering' he pays ordered attention. Thinking, 'This is the way leading to the cessation of suffering' he pays ordered attention. For one who pays attention in such a way (these) three fetters pass away – views about one's own body, perplexity, adherence to convention and ritual.

And what, are the distractions to be left behind through restraint? Herein a monk, with orderly reflection, lives governed by restraint of the visual (or any other sensory or mental) faculty. (If he lives like this) the vexatious and troublesome distractions (which might arise) do not exist.

And what, monks, are the distractions to be left behind through practice? Herein a monk, with orderly reflection, utilises a robe simply for warding off the cold and the heat, (along with) gadflies, mosquitoes, wind, sun, and the contact of crawling things, (and) simply to cover his nakedness. With orderly reflection he uses almsfood, not for sport, or indulgence, or finery, or adornment, but just for sustaining and nourishing the body, for keeping it unharmed, and for furthering the good life, thinking, 'Thus do I extinguish old feeling and not create new feeling and I shall be blameless and comfortable.' With orderly reflection he uses lodgings for gaining the benefit of privacy.[2] With orderly reflection he uses medical requisites, just for warding off debilitating feelings that have arisen and for best preserving his health. (If he lives like this) the vexatious and troublesome distractions (which might arise) do not exist.

And what, monks, are the distractions to be left behind through endurance? Herein a monk, with orderly reflection, tolerates cold and heat, hunger and thirst, gadflies, mosquitoes, wind, sun, and the contact of crawling things (along with) disreputable and unwelcome ways of speaking. He is of a character to bear the onset of feelings that are painful, acute, severe, (and) harsh. (If he lives like this) the vexatious and troublesome distractions (that might arise) do not exist.

And what, monks, are the distractions to be left behind through avoidance? Herein a monk, with orderly reflection, avoids a fierce elephant, or horse, or (other such animals). (He avoids) a snake, a stake, a thorny hedge, a pit, a precipice, a dirty pond or pool. With ordered reflection he avoids an inappropriate place, an improper search (for alms), and associating with depraved friends. (For if he did such things) his intelligent associates in the good life might well imagine depraved qualities (in him). (Since he lives like this) the vexatious and troublesome distractions (which might arise) do not exist.

And what, monks, are the distractions to be left behind through removal? Herein a monk, with orderly reflection, does not yield to a worldly train of thought. He eliminates, dispels, and destroys (it), consigns (it) to oblivion, (and likewise with) thought of cruelty or in connection with (any other) unskilled states. (Since he lives like this) the vexatious and troublesome states (which might arise) do not exist.

And what, monks, are the distractions to be left behind through development? Herein a monk, with orderly reflection, cultivates mindfulness as an aspect of enlightenment sustained by solitariness, dispassion, and cessation, and consummated by surrender, (and likewise the other aspects of enlightenment, namely) examination of *dhamma*, energy, joy, repose, concentration, (and) equanimity. (If he lives like this) the vexatious and troublesome states (which might arise) do not exist.

When, in any monk, those distractions to be left behind (in these various ways) are abandoned, that monk has cut away craving, has eliminated bondage, and through fully comprehending pride will do away with suffering".

Thus spoke the Lord.

1. More broadly, the Pali term refers to a park or pleasure ground. A grant of land for the use of wandering ascetics, usually with some buildings for accommodation.
2. Other points as for robes.

3

Inheritors of *Dhamma*

12–16

Thus have I heard: once the Lord dwelt near Sāvatthī in the Jeta Grove on Anāthapiṇḍika's campus. There (he) addressed the monks, saying:

"Monks, be inheritors through me of *dhamma,* not of the things of the flesh. In me there is pity for you. And should you become inheritors of the things of the flesh not only will you thereby become (those of whom it is said): 'The disciples of the Teacher are not inheritors of *dhamma*', (but such words will also be said of me).

For example, monks, I may have eaten, and be satisfied. (The meal) complete and at an end, my surplus almsfood is about to be thrown away when two monks arrive overcome by hunger and exhaustion. I say to them: 'Eat it if you wish. If not I shall throw it away where there is no grass or drop it in water devoid of life.' One monk might think: 'These were the Lord's words – be inheritors through me of *dhamma,* not of the things of the flesh – but this, that is almsfood, is a thing of the flesh. What if, without eating this almsfood and despite this hunger and exhaustion, I were to spend the night and day like this.' (And he does so). But the second monk thinks: 'What if, having eaten this almsfood and driven out this hunger and thirst, I were to spend the night and day like that.' (And he does so). The first monk is, for me, the more to be honoured and the more praiseworthy. Why so? That (abstinence) will be conducive to the satisfaction, the contentment, the higher life, the frugality, and the arousal of energy of that monk for many a day. Therefore, monks, be inheritors through me of *dhamma,* not of the things of the flesh. In me there is pity for you.' Having spoken thus the Adept rose from his seat and entered the dwelling-place.

Thereupon the venerable Sāriputta, shortly after the Lord's departure, addressed the monks, saying 'Fellow monks, how far when the Teacher lives apart do disciples emulate his detachment? Herein, friends, the Teacher lives apart and (his) disciples do not (do this), and do not renounce the things (he) has spoken of renouncing. (They) are given over to abundance and lethargy, are soon lapsed, putting aside the responsibility of solitude.

Friends, greed is evil and ill-will is evil[1], and for the abandonment of both there exists the middle course, making for vision and knowledge, and that promotes calming, gnosis, true enlightenment and *nibbāna*. Just that is the *ariyan* eightfold path namely: right view, aim, speech, action, livelihood, effort, mindfulness, (and) concentration."

Thus spoke the venerable Sāriputta.

1. Successive paragraphs repeat what follows with reference to various other evils such as envy, hypocrisy, treachery, obstinacy, impetuosity, pride, etc.

4

Fear and Dread

16–24

Thus have I heard: once the Lord dwelt near Sāvatthī in the Jeta Grove on Anāthapiṇḍika's campus. Then the brahman Jāṇussoṇi came up to (him), exchanged greetings, and, after conversing in a friendly and polite way, sat down at one side. Said Jāṇussoṇi:

"Those sons of family who, on account of the worthy Gotama, have gone forth from home into homelessness out of faith – for these (he) is the trailblazer. (He) is of much help to them. (He) is their inspiration, and these people emulate (him)."

"That is so brahman, that is so."

"But remote forest lodgings in the wilderness are hard to bear, friend Gotama. (Such) seclusion is difficult, solitude hard to bear, and I suppose that forests overwhelm the mind of a monk who has not achieved concentration."

"That is so brahman, that is so. Before my enlightenment, being just a *bodhisatta*, (these thoughts came) to me, too. I thought: 'Any ascetics or brahmans who are not entirely pure in their deeds, words, (and thought, and pursue this kind of existence)[1], evoke (in themselves) unskilful fear and dread (because of such defilements). But I, not imperfectly pure (in this way), frequent remote forest lodgings in the wilderness.' Seeing (this) complete purity in myself I gained confidence for living in (such a place).

Concerning that I thought: 'Suppose that, on those recognised and fixed nights – the fourteenth, fifteenth, and eighth days of the half-month – I were to inhabit frightening and horrifying park shrines, forest shrines, or tree shrines so as to meet with just such fear and dread.' So, brahman, (at these appointed times I did so). And as I dwelt there an animal might come by, or a peacock make a twig snap, or the wind rustle fallen leaves (so that the thought arose): 'Is it fear and dread that comes (upon me)? Why do I live wishing only for fear? What if I were to subdue fear and dread in just that state in which (it) finds me?' And if that fear and dread came to me whilst walking I neither stood still, nor sat down, nor lay down, but subdued (it) as I walked. (If) it came as I was standing I subdued (it) just where I stood; (if) while sitting just where I sat; (if) while lying down just where I lay.

Now there are some ascetics and brahmans who see night as similar to day and day as similar to night. I say of (them) that they live in delusion. But I see night as night and day as day. Brahman, (one) can speak truly in saying (that) an undeluded being has arisen in the world, for the wellbeing and happiness of the multitude, out of pity for the world, (bringing these blessings) to *devas* and humans.

Undulled vigour was aroused in me, unconfused mindfulness was harnessed, (my) body was composed and unexcited, (my) mind was settled and focused. Aloof from worldly pursuits[2] (and from unskilled states, I entered and experienced the first (level of) absorption that is associated with thought and investigation, is born of remoteness, and is joyful and happy.

From the suppression of thought and investigation, and with mind inwardly tranquillised and focused, I entered and experienced the second (level of) absorption that is born of concentration, and is joyful and happy.

From the fading away of joy I experienced equanimity, was mindful and lucid, and felt in my body that happiness of which the *ariyans* speak. I reached and experienced the third (level of) absorption.

From the giving up of happiness and suffering, from the going down of former delight and sorrow, I reached and experienced the fourth (level of) absorption, that is entirely purified by equanimity and mindfulness.

So, with a mind composed, perfectly purified and clear, unblemished, purged of defilement, malleable, workable, steady, imperturbable, I turned (it) towards recollection and knowledge of previous existences. I recalled a diversity of former habitations – one, ten, a hundred, a thousand births, and various aeons of integration and disintegration; (that elsewhere) I was of such a name, such a lineage, such a colour, such a subsistence, and I knew happiness and suffering thus and ended my life thus; (that), passing hence, I arose in another place. (That too I remembered). (Then), passing hence, I arose here. And so I recalled various existences in all (their) characteristics and detail. Brahman, this was the first knowledge attained by me in the first watch of the night. Ignorance was vanquished, knowledge burgeoned, darkness was dispelled and light arose, even as I lived diligent, zealous, and resolute.[3]

(Then) I turned (my) mind to the knowledge of the passing away and re-emergence of (other) beings. With the purified divine eye transcending the human I beheld (them) passing away and (re-)arising. I beheld (them) as lowly or exalted, beautiful or ugly, and of good or ill destiny in accordance with their deeds. Those worthy beings possessed by evil ways of living in body, word, and thought, scoffers at the *ariyans*, given to wrong view and (ways of) acting derived from wrong view – they came to sorrow, to an evil destiny, to ruin, to purgatory[4] on the breaking up of the body at death. But those possessed by wholesome ways of living came to a good destiny, a heaven world. And so did I behold beings with the purified divine eye transcending the human. Brahman, this was the second knowledge attained by me in the second watch of the night. Ignorance was vanquished, knowledge burgeoned, darkness was dispelled and light arose, even as I lived diligent, zealous, and resolute.

(Then) I turned (my) mind to the knowledge of the rooting out of the distractions. I knew as it really is: 'This is suffering, this the origin of suffering, this the cessation of suffering, this the way leading (thereto).' I knew as it really is: 'These are the distractions, this the origin of the distractions, this (their) ending, this the way leading to (their) ending.' Having known and seen this my mind was freed from the distraction of worldly pursuits, of (continued) existence, and of ignorance. In freedom was freedom's knowledge – 'Destroyed is birth, fulfilled the good life, done what was to be done, and (there will be) no more of this world.' Brahman, this was the third knowledge attained by me in the last watch of the night. Ignorance was vanquished, knowledge burgeoned, darkness was dispelled and light arose, even as I lived diligent, zealous, and resolute.

It may be, however, that you think: 'Can it be that, even now, the ascetic Gotama is not without passion, without ill-will, without delusion, in that he frequents remote forest lodgings in the wilderness?' But you shouldn't view (the matter) like that. I (continue to live in such a way) from recognising two consequences – happiness for (my)self in this life, and out of pity for the people that come after."[5]

(Then the brahman said): "The people that come after have friend Gotama's pity through his being *arahant* and truly enlightened. Excellent, friend Gotama, excellent. It is as though one were to set upright what was overturned, or uncover what was hidden, or show a way to one who was lost, or bring an oil lamp into a dark place so that those with eyes might see. Thus in various ways is *dhamma* made evident by friend Gotama. I go to the worthy Gotama as refuge, and to the Dhamma and to the Order of monks. May the worthy Gotama accept me as a layfollower from this day forth for the rest of my life".

1. This passage recurs no fewer than fourteen times in the full text, with twelve mental attributes given (plus bodily activity and speech) as likely to evoke fear and dread, plus Gotama's claim to be free of each of them. They include such things as slothfulness, self-praise, lack of mindfulness, and so on, as well as the major passions.
2. The Pali equivalent is sometimes translated "sensuality", but the connotations here are broader.
3. I have altered the verbs from present to past tense in some parts of these passages as there are inexplicable variations.
4. Sometimes translated hell, but in Buddhism all such states are themselves impermanent.
5. i.e. as an example to followers.

5

No Blemishes

24–32

Thus have I heard: once the Lord dwelt near Sāvatthī in the Jeta Grove on Anāthapiṇḍika's campus. There the venerable Sāriputta addressed the monks, saying:

"Friends, there are these four (types of) person to be found in the world. Here some person with a blemish thinks (that he has such a blemish but)[1] fails to truly understand it. Some (other) person with a blemish (recognises it) and truly understands it. (Another) who is without blemish (knows this) but fails to truly understand it. (Yet another) who is without blemish (knows it) and truly understands.

Of those two possessed of a blemish (the first) is declared the inferior, (the second) the superior man. Of those two without blemish (the first) is (also) declared the inferior, (the second) the superior man".

When he had spoken venerable Moggallāna the Great said to the venerable Sāriputta:

"Friend Sāriputta, what is the reason, what the condition (whereby in each case) one is declared to be the inferior, one the superior?"

"Friend, of him (who has a blemish but fails to truly understand) this can be expected – that he will not manifest resolution, he will not make an effort, he will not arouse energy for the abandonment of that blemish. He will go to his death (as one) with passion, with ill-will, with delusion, with a blemish, with a corrupted mind. It is like a bronze bowl brought from a shop or a smith, and covered with dust and dirt. The owners do not even use or clean it, but leave it on one side in a dusty place. So, after a while, (it is) even filthier.[2]

Of him (who has a blemish and truly understands) this can be expected – that he will manifest resolution, he will make an effort, he will arouse energy for the abandonment of that blemish. He will go to his death (cleansed of defiling passions like one who cleans a dirty bowl).

Of him (who is without blemish but fails to truly understand) this can be expected – that he will pay attention to the pleasant aspect (of things), and from (such) attention passion will corrupt his mind. He will go to his death (as one) with passion, with ill-will, with delusion, with a blemish, with a corrupted mind. It is like a bronze bowl brought from a shop or smith and is quite pure and clean, but the owners do not even use it or (keep it) clean, and lay it on one side in a dirty place. So, after a while, (it is) even filthier.

Of him (who is without blemish and truly understands) this can be expected – that he will not pay attention to the pleasant aspect (of things).

(So) passion will not corrupt his mind. He will go to his death (still free of corrupting passions like one who keeps a bowl clean). This is the reason, this the condition friend Moggallāna why, (in each case), one is declared to be the inferior, one the superior man''.

''There is said to be a blemish friend. Of what is this a designation?''

''This is a reference to dealing in evil, unskilled impulses. It is possible that a wish such as this might come upon a monk: 'I might commit an offence and the (other) monks not find me out; (or, if they find out) they might reprimand me privately not in the midst of the Order.' (But) they might find (him) out, they might reprimand (him) in the midst of the Order. (Thereafter) he is disturbed and displeased. Such disturbance and displeasure are, each of them, a blemish.

It is possible that a wish such as this might come upon a monk: 'Should I commit an offence an equal would reprimand me, not one who is not my equal.' (But this might not happen. Thereafter) he is disturbed and displeased. Such disturbance and displeasure are, each of them, a blemish.

It is possible that a wish such as this might come upon a monk: 'Would that the Teacher might teach *dhamma* to the monks after questioning just me, not some other monk'; (or): 'Would that the monks might enter the village for food having put me at the front'; (or): 'Would that I might get the best seat, the best almsfood in the refectory'; (or): 'Would that I might be the one to give the thanks after eating in the refectory'; (or): 'Would that I might be the one to teach *dhamma* to the monks, the nuns, (and) the layfollowers who are in the park.'; (or): 'Let (all these) honour, respect, esteem, and revere me (rather than) some other monk.' (But things might not turn out as he wishes. Thereafter) he is disturbed and displeased. Such disturbance and displeasure are, each of them, a blemish.[3]

In whatever monk these dealings in evil, unskilful impulses are seen and heard to be unabandoned, whether he be a forest-dweller inhabiting a remote place, a walker on an uninterrupted almsround,[4] one clad in rags from a dust heap, or a wearer of a shabby robe – his companions in the good life do not honour, respect, esteem, or revere him. Why so? Friends, it is like a bronze bowl – the owners fill it with the remains of a snake, a dog, or a human being, enclose it within another bronze bowl and go along to the shop. People seeing it would say: 'Just look at this that has been brought as something beautiful.' Taking it up, opening it, they might inspect it. Dislike, loathing, and disgust would prevail. So it is friends with (the response to such) a monk.

(But) in whatever monk these dealings in evil, unskilled impulses are seen and heard to be abandoned, whether he be a dweller near a village, one who lives by invitations (to meals), or one who wears robes provided by householders – his companions in the good life do honour, respect, esteem, and revere him.[5] Why so? It is like a bronze bowl – the owners, filling it with fine rice, boiled rice with the black grains removed, and with various curries and vegetables, enclose it within another bronze bowl and go along to the shop. People seeing it would (find it pleasant and there would be no dislike, loathing, or disgust). So it is friends with (the response to such) a monk."

When he had spoken the venerable Moggallāna said to the venerable Sāriputta:

"Friend Sāriputta, a comparison comes to mind. Once I was living at Rājagaha at a mountain-station of cowherds. Dressing at an early hour and taking bowl and robe I went into Rājagaha for almsfood. Now at that time Samīti the carriage-maker's son was making a felloe for a chariot(-wheel) in the presence of Paṇḍuputta the mendicant,[6] formerly a carriage-maker's son. And the thought came into Paṇḍuputta's mind: 'Would that (he) might make (away with) the crookedness, the jaggedness, the fault in that felloe.' (And even as he was thinking that, so did Samīti, the carriage-maker's son remove those faults). Whereupon Paṇḍuputta the mendicant uttered a cry of pleasure saying, 'It seems he works upon the heart with knowledge of the heart.'

Likewise, friend, those people who are without faith but, lacking a living, have gone forth from home into homelessness, not with faith but crafty, hypocritical, (and) deceitful[7] – for them the venerable Sāriputta, with his survey of *dhamma* works upon the heart with knowledge of the heart. But those sons of family who have gone forth from home into homelessness out of faith – having heard (it) they drink it in and devour it, both in word and thought. Well indeed it is that a companion in the good life, turning one from the unskilled, should establish the skilful. It is like a young woman or man, in the flush of youth and fond of finery, who, washing the head and taking a garland of water-lilies or jasmine or acacia should place it upon the crown of the head. So it is (for) those sons of family who are gone forth from home into homelessness out of faith."

1. Put into direct speech in the first person in the full text.
2. The previous statement is converted from a question so as to eliminate a routine response. The simile recurs and has been abbreviated in the subsequent exchanges.
3. The full text gives further examples of the monk's wishes.
4. i.e. calling at every house.
5. A normally less well regarded group of lifestyles than those referred to in the earlier list.
6. *Ājiviko* – literally, "one finding a living". One of a selection of terms used throughout to designate the wanderers of various sects.
7. Abbreviated from a list of some twenty-five attributes.

6

What Might be Desired

33–36

Thus have I heard: once the Lord dwelt near Sāvatthī in the Jeta Grove on Anāthapiṇḍika's campus. There (he) addressed the monks, saying:

"Monks, live imbued with (right) conduct and the obligations, restrained and governed (by them), possessing the field of behaviour and fearing even slight faults. Undertaking the training persevere (with it).

If a monk wishes (to be agreeable to his) companions in the good life, liked by them, (and) esteemed and respected, he should perfect (good) conduct, be set on mental tranquillity within, not neglectful of meditation, possessed of insight, and should frequent empty places.

If (he) wishes (to obtain) the requisites of robes, almsfood, lodgings, and medicines for the sick, (he should do likewise).

If (he) wishes (for the) services of those from whom (he) enjoy(s) the requisites to be of great fruit and profit, (he should do likewise).

If (he) wishes (for the) great fruit and profit of (his) kinsfolk, who recall the dead and departed with minds that are reconciled, (he should do likewise).

If (he) wishes (to) overcome aversion and fondness (as well as) fear and dread, (he should do likewise).

If (he) wishes (to) be one who gains at (his) pleasure, (and) without problems or difficulties, the four absorptions[1] that are dependent on clearest consciousness and are states of happiness in this life,[2] (he should do likewise).

If (he) wishes (to) experience with (his) body those formless realms transcending form that are tranquil havens, (he should do likewise).

If (he) wishes (from) the final waning of the three fetters to be an enterer of the stream, not destined for a place of destruction and certain of enlightenment; (or if), from the vanishing of passion, ill-will, and delusion (he) wishes to be a once-returner coming only one more time to this world (and) making an end of suffering; (or if he) wishes, from the final waning of the five fetters that bind one to the worldly condition, to be of spontaneous rebirth, achieving *nibbāna* there, (and) not returning from that (other) world – (he should do likewise).

If (he) wishes for the diverse forms of psychic power;[3] for the purified divine ear; for comprehension (by his) mind of (those) of other beings and individuals; to remember previous existences; (or), with the purified divine eye, behold beings passing away and re-arising in accordance with their deeds – (he should do likewise).

Monks, if a monk, from rooting out the distractions, and reaching the mental freedom and the freedom of wisdom that are undistracted through (his) own gnosis in this life, wishes to abide (therein) – he should perfect (good) conduct, be set on mental tranquillity within, not neglectful of meditation, possessed of insight, and should frequent empty places."

Thus spoke the Lord.

1. More often translated "meditation".
2. Literally, "even in things seen".
3. For standard passage on psychic powers see Discourse 12.

7

The Simile of the Cloth

36–40

Thus have I heard: once the Lord dwelt near Sāvatthī in the Jeta Grove on Anāthapiṇḍika's campus. There (he) addressed the monks, saying:

"Monks, a soiled and dirty cloth dipped by a dyer into any dye would be discoloured and unclean. Why so? – because of the uncleanness of the cloth. Likewise an evil destiny can be expected for a soiled mind.

And what are the mental impurities? – acquisitiveness and petty greed, malevolence, anger, enmity, hypocrisy, spite, jealousy, stinginess, deceit, treachery, obstinacy, impetuosity, conceit, pride, intoxication, indolence – (these are they). A monk, (having recognized all these things) as defilements of the mind, abandons (them). He acquires complete confidence in the Buddha, (thinking of him as) *arahant*, truly enlightened, perfect in knowledge and conduct, adept, seer of worlds, matchless charioteer of men to be tamed, teacher of *devas* and humans, *buddha* and lord.

He acquires complete confidence in *dhamma*, (thinking of it as) well-preached by the Lord, made manifest, timeless, a come-and-see thing, ongoing, to be experienced personally by the wise.

He acquires complete confidence in the Order, (thinking that it) conducts itself well, uprightly, methodically, properly, that is to say the four pairs of men, the eight individuals;[1] (and that it) is deserving of alms, of hospitality, of gifts, of salutation, and is a matchless benefaction to the world.

At that point is his giving up, his leaving behind, his setting free, his renunciation, his forsaking. He acquires an enthusiasm for the goal and for *dhamma*. He acquires the delight associated with *dhamma*. Joy is born of delight. The body is quietened by a joyful heart. The quietened body experiences happiness. The happy mind is concentrated.

Even if he eats fine almsfood, the black grains separated, and with various curries and vegetables, that will not be a hindrance in a monk of such conduct, such *dhamma*, and such wisdom. Just as a soiled and dirty cloth becomes clean and pure with the aid of clear water, or the base metal with the aid of the furnace, so (it is with such a monk).

He lives spreading thoughts joined to goodwill in (all) directions. He lives spreading (them) everywhere, in every way, to the entire world, abundantly, boundlessly, unrestrictedly, peaceably, benevolently. He lives spreading thoughts joined to compassion, to gladness, to equanimity (in the same way).

He knows there is this, there is what is base, there is what is exalted, there is utter departure from this world of the senses. For one who knows and sees like this there is freedom from the distraction(s)[2] of worldly pursuits, of (continued) existence, (and) of ignorance. In that freedom there is the knowledge of freedom: 'Destroyed is birth, fulfilled the good life, done what was to be done, and (there is) no more of this world.' This can be described as a monk washed by an inner washing.

Now at that time the brahman Sundarika-Bhāradvāja was sitting close to the Lord (and he) said: "But does the worthy Gotama go to bathe in the river Bāhukā?"

"What is there by means of the river Bāhukā, brahman? What will the river Bāhukā do?"

"The multitude consider the river Bāhukā as (a means to) salvation, as (a way of acquiring) merit. For in (it they) wash away evil deeds."

Then the Lord addressed brahman Sundarika-Bhāradvāja in verse:

"In the Bāhukā, at Adhikakkā at Gayā, in the Sundarikā, in the Sarassatī, at Payāga, (or) in the river Bāhumatī, the fool does not purge his dark deeds by constantly plunging (into the waters). What will (any of these places) achieve for him? They do not cleanse the wrongdoer bent on evil. For the pure in heart every day is auspicious (and) sanctified. For one who acts well (his) entire practice is an observance. Just bathe like that, brahman. Forge a haven for all beings. If you do not lie, do not injure living beings, do not take what you are not given, if you have conviction and are not selfish, what would you do in going to Gayā, when Gayā is just a well for you.?"

At these words the brahman Sundarika-Bhāradvāja (praised the Lord, and having gone for refuge, sought ordination). And (he) obtained the going forth and received ordination in the Lord's presence.

Before long the venerable Bhāradvāja (was) living alone and apart, diligent, zealous, and resolute. Some time later he reached and experienced that matchless consummation of the good life for which which sons of family rightly go forth from home into homelessness, having realised it through his own gnosis. (He knew): "Destroyed is birth, fulfilled the good life, done what was to be done, and (there is) no more of this world." And so venerable Bhāradvāja became one of the *arahants*.

1. i.e. those pursuing and attaining the fruits of the four stages of progress culminating in the *arahant*
2. Literally "influxes". See particularly 2.

8

Austerity

40–46

Thus have I heard: once the Lord dwelt near Sāvatthī in the Jeta Grove on Anāthapiṇḍika's campus. Then venerable Cunda the Great, emerging from seclusion towards evening, approached the Lord, saluted (him), and sat down at one side.

Said Cunda: "Bhante, is the diversity of views that arises in the world concerning theories of the self or of the world abandoned and rejected by the monk as a consequence of (wise) attention at the outset?"

"Cunda, wherever these views arise or obsess, or are current – then, seeing (the matter) in its true nature with perfect wisdom (and thinking), 'This is not mine; I am not this; this is not myself' one abandons and rejects (them). It may be that some monk, distancing himself from worldly pursuits and unskilled states, achieves and experiences the first (and successive levels) of absorption. He may think: 'I live through austerity.' However, these are not termed 'austerities' in the *ariyan* discipline. These are called 'states of happiness in this life'.

It may be that some monk here, from the complete transcendence of the perception of form, the extinction of the perception of sensory response, and the disregard of the perception of diversity, may reach and experience the realm of infinite space. Completely transcending the realm of infinite space he reaches and experiences the realm of infinite consciousness. Completely transcending the realm of infinite consciousness he reaches and experiences the realm of nothingness. Completely transcending the realm of nothingness he reaches and experiences the realm of neither perceiving nor not-perceiving. (At each stage) he may think: 'I live through austerity.' But these are not termed 'austerities' in the *ariyan* discipline. They are termed 'peaceful states'.

This is the way austerities are to be performed Cunda. Thinking, 'Others are prone to cruelty. We shall now[1] abstain from cruelty. Others are prone to taking life. We shall now abstain from taking life. Others are prone to taking what is not given. We shall now abstain from taking what is not given. Others may not be livers of the good life. We shall now be livers of the good life. Others are prone to lying. We shall now abstain from lying.'[2] Thus are austerities to be performed.

Now I hold Cunda that the arousal of thought is of great value in relation to skilful states, not to speak of the physical and verbal (activities) that are in harmony (with thought).

Like an uneven road, though there may be another, level, road for travelling by – even so for a person prone to cruelty there is amity to go by. For a person prone to taking life there is the refraining (therefrom). For a person prone to taking what is not given there is the refraining (therefrom). For a person who is not a liver of the good life there is (such living). For a person prone to lying there is refraining (therefrom).

Cunda, all unskilled states are downward-going, all skilled states upward-leading. (And) this cannot come about – that one who is sunk in mud should pull out another (in the same state) by himself. But this may occur – that one not sunk in mud should (do that).

Such is my representation of austerity Cunda, of the arousal of thought, of (what) to go by, of (what) is upward-leading, of final *nibbāna*. What a teacher seeking the wellbeing of disciples may do out of compassion that I have done for you. Here are roots of trees, here are empty places. Meditate Cunda, be not slothful, do not be remorseful later. This is our instruction to you."

Thus spoke the Lord.

1. The Pali has spacial, temporal, and modal reference so that it might alternatively mean "here" or "herein".
2. Other kinds of wrong speech and a whole range of wrong attitudes are also listed.

9

Right View

46–55

Thus have I heard: once the Lord dwelt near Sāvatthī in the Jeta Grove on Anāthapiṇḍika's campus. There the venerable Sāriputta addressed the monks, saying:

"There is said (to be) right view, friends. Now, how far is an *ariyan* disciple of right view (so that) his view is upright, and he has complete confidence in *dhamma*, and is come to the fullness of *dhamma*?

When the *ariyan* disciple knows the unskilful, the source of the unskilful, (as well as) the skilful and the source of the skilful, to that extent (he) has (those qualities). But what are (these)?

The destruction of life is unskilful, taking what is not given is unskilful, dissolute living is unskilful, lying is unskilful, slander is unskilful, abuse is unskilful, idle prattle is unskilful, acquisitiveness is unskilful, malevolence is unskilful, wrong view is unskilful.

And what is the source of the unskilful? Greed, ill-will, and delusion are the sources of the unskilful.

And what is the skilful? Abstention (from all these things) is the skilful.

And what is the source of the skilful? Absence of greed, ill-will, and delusion is the source of the skilful.

When the *ariyan* disciple, (aware of all this), altogether casts off the propensity for passion, dispels the propensity for aversion, removes the propensity for the egocentric view 'I am', and, abandoning delusion, generates understanding, he is one who makes an end of suffering in this life. To this extent there is right view for the *ariyan* disciple."

"It is well, friend" (the monks replied). "But could there be another representation[1] of how there is right view for an *ariyan* disciple?"

"There could, friends. When (he) understands a sustaining condition,[2] the origin of a sustaining condition, the cessation of a sustaining condition and the course leading (thereto) – to that extent there is right view for the *ariyan* disciple.

But what is a sustaining condition? Friends, there are these four sustaining conditions for the maintenance of generated beings, or for the assistance of those seeking birth – material food, whether course or fine; secondly, (sensory) stimulus; thirdly, mental striving; fourthly, consciousness. The sustaining conditions have their origin in craving (and) from the cessation of craving is the cessation of the sustaining conditions. Just this *ariyan* eightfold way is the course leading to the cessation (thereof), namely: right view, aim, speech, action, livelihood, effort, mindfulness, concentration.

When the *ariyan* disciple, (aware of all this), cuts off the propensity for passion, dispels the propensity for aversion, removes the propensity for the egocentric view 'I am', and, abandoning delusion, generates understanding, he is one who makes an end of suffering in this life. To this extent there is right view for the *ariyan* disciple."

"It is well, friend" (the monks replied). "But could there be another representation of how there is right view for a monk?"

"There could, friends. When (he) understands suffering, the origin of suffering, the cessation of suffering and the way leading (thereto), to that extent there is right view for the *ariyan* disciple.

But what is suffering? Birth is suffering; old age is suffering; sickness is suffering; death is suffering; grief and woe, pain, distress, and trouble are suffering. What one wishes for but does not obtain – that is suffering. In short the five embodiments of attachment[3] are suffering.

And what is the origin of suffering? – those cravings that make for re-emergence, that are associated with delight and passion, finding pleasure here and there, namely craving for worldly pursuits, craving for (continued) existence, craving for non-existence.

And what is the cessation of suffering? – that which is the passionless cessation without remainder of just that craving, that which is renunciation, giving up, release, doing away (with craving).

And what is the course leading to the cessation of suffering? – just this *ariyan* eightfold way. When the *ariyan* disciple, (aware of all this), cuts off the propensity for passion, dispels the propensity for aversion, removes the propensity for the egocentric view 'I am', and, abandoning delusion, generates understanding, he is one who makes an end of suffering in this life. To this extent there is right view for the *ariyan* disciple."

"It is well, friend" (the monks replied). "But could there be another representation of how there is right view for a monk?"

"There could, friends. When (he) understands old age and death, the origin of old age and death, the cessation of old age and death, and the course leading (thereto) – to this extent there is right view for the *ariyan* disciple.

But what, friends, is old age and death? Whatever for this or that being in this or that realm of beings is old age, decrepitude, broken teeth, grey hair, wrinkled skin, the lessening of the life span, and the decay of the faculties – that is called old age.

And what is death? Passing away, breaking up, disappearance, death and dying, the completion of (one's) time (on earth), the breaking up of the basic components (of existence),[4] the discarding of the carcase – that is called death. Old age and death have their origin in birth, (and) from the cessation of birth is the cessation of old age and death. Just this *ariyan* eightfold path is the course leading to (such) a cessation. When the *ariyan* disciple, (aware of all this), cuts off the propensity for passion, dispels the propensity for aversion, removes the propensity for the egocentric view 'I am', and, abandoning delusion, generates understanding, he is one who makes an end of suffering in this life. To this extent there is right view for the *ariyan* disciple."

"It is well, friend" (the monks replied). "But could there be another representation of how there is right view for a monk?"

"There could, friends.[5] When (he) understands the origin of birth, (its) cessation, (and) the course leading (thereto); when he understands (similarly regarding) coming to be, attachment, craving, feeling, (sensory) stimulus, the six sources (of experience),[6] consciousness, formative tendencies, ignorance, and the distractions – to this extent there is right view for the *ariyan* disciple.

And what are (all these)? The production, appearance, entry into this or that realm of beings, the manifestation of the basic components (of existence), the taking up of the sources (of experience) – that is called birth. Birth has its origin in coming to be (and), from the cessation of coming to be, is the cessation of birth.

There are these three kinds of coming to be – the coming to be of worldly pursuits, of form, of the formless. Coming to be has its origin in attachment, (and) from the cessation of attachment is the cessation of coming to be.

There are these four attachments – attachment to worldly pursuits, to views, to convention and ritual, and to pronouncements about self. Attachment has its origin in craving, (and) from the cessation of craving is the cessation of attachment.

There are these six (types) of craving – craving for (visible) forms, for sounds, for odours, for flavours, for (physical) contact, for (mental) phenomena.[7] Craving has its origin in feeling, (and) from the cessation of feeling is the cessation of craving.

There are these six bodies of feeling – feeling due to stimulation of the (sense organs) or the mind.[8] Feeling has its origin in (sensory) stimulus, (and) from the cessation of (sensory) stimulation is the cessation of feeling.

There are these six bodies of (sensory) stimulation – (of the five senses or) of the mind. (Sensory) stimulation has its origin in the six sources (of experience, and) from the cessation of (these) is the cessation of (sensory) stimulation.

There are these six sources (of experience) – the eye, the ear, the nose, the tongue, the body, the mind location.[9] The six sources have their origin in individuality and (physical) form. From the cessation of (these) is the cessation of the six sources.

But what are individuality and (physical) form? Feeling, perception, volition, (sensory) stimulation, (and) attention – this is called individuality; the four great elements and form derived (therefrom) – that is called (physical) form. Individuality and form have their origin in consciousness, (and) from the cessation of consciousness is the cessation of individuality and form.

But what is consciousness? There are these six bodies of consciousness – (one for each of the five senses and one for the mind). Consciousness has its origin in formative tendencies,[10] (and) from the cessation of formative tendencies is the cessation of consciousness.

There are these three formative tendencies – of body, speech, and thought. Formative tendencies have their origin in ignorance, (and) from the cessation of ignorance is the cessation of formative tendencies.

But what is ignorance? Whatever is lack of understanding with regard to suffering, (its) origin, (its) cessation, and the course leading (thereto) – that is termed ignorance. Ignorance has its origin in the distractions, (and) the cessation of the distractions is the cessation of ignorance.[11]

There are these three distractions – the distraction of worldly pursuits, of (continued) existence, of ignorance.

Just this *ariyan* eightfold way is the course leading to the cessation of (all these phenomena). When the *ariyan* disciple cuts off the propensity for passion, dispels the propensity for aversion, removes the propensity for the egocentric view 'I am' and, abandoning delusion, generates understanding, he is one who makes an end of suffering in this life. To this extent there is right view for (him so that) his view is upright, and he has complete confidence in *dhamma*, and is come to the fullness of *dhamma*."

Thus spoke the venerable Sāriputta.

1. Horner has "method".
2. The root idea is of something which provides food.
3. The five elements of personality, i.e. body, feeling, perception, mental drives and patterns, and consciousness itself.
4. As (3)
5. The discourse has been slightly re-organised from this point on. The full text gives a paragraph to each of the terms subsequently discussed on the same basis as that for the previous one for old age and death. I have merged them so as to avoid further repetition of intervening passages. The meaning is in no way affected. The twelve linked terms commencing with old age and death constitute the "wheel of life" or "dependent origination".
6. The sense-organs and the physical basis of mind – covered subsequently.
7. *Dhammā* (plural) – this correlates with mind as do the specific types of sense-data with their respective organs. Its precise reference is elusive, but see Discourse 10.
8. Stimulation of the mind is presumably indirect as when a sight or sound evokes a memory.
9. No organ is specified.
10. Horner translates "formations".
11. The distractions are not normally included in the "dependent origination" formula.

10

The Applications of Mindfulness

55–63

Thus have I heard: once the Lord dwelt among the Kurus at a town called Kammāssadhamma. There (he) addressed the monks, saying:

"Monks, this is the only way for the purification of beings, for the overcoming of grief and woe, for the disappearance of pain and distress, for the attainment of the right approach, for the realisation of *nibbāna*, namely the four applications of mindfulness. What four? Herein a monk lives observing the body in terms of the body,[1] zealous, lucid, and mindful, so as to put aside the acquisitiveness and distress in the world. (And) he lives (similarly as regards) observing feeling in terms of feeling, the mind in terms of the mind, (and) phenomena in terms of phenomena.

And how does a monk live observing the body in terms of the body? Herein a monk is gone to the forest, to the root of a tree, to an empty place, and sits down cross-legged, with body upright, establishing mindfulness before[2] him as his aim. Mindful he breathes out, mindful he breathes in. Exhaling a long breath he is aware (of it).[3] Inhaling a long breath he is aware (of it). Exhaling a short breath he is aware (of it). Inhaling a short breath he is aware (of it). He trains himself, thinking, 'I will breathe out, (or in), experiencing the whole body.' (Or) he trains himself, thinking, 'I will breathe out, (or in), pacifying bodily tendencies.' Monks, it is like a skilled turner or (his) apprentice, who (is aware of making a long or short turn on a lathe). So it is with (such) a monk.

In such a way he lives observing the body in terms of the body within, or the body without, (or both together).[4] He lives observing the waxing or the waning of bodily states, (or both together). Or, aware: 'There is the body', mindfulness is present for him just to the extent necessary for knowledge and recollection,[5] and he lives ungrounded, cleaving to nothing whatsoever in the world.

Further a monk, when walking, knows: 'I walk'; when standing knows: 'I stand'; (and likewise with) sitting or lying down, so that however his body is disposed he is aware thereof.

Again, a monk is one who is lucid in his comings and goings, in looking forward and looking round, in bending and stretching, in carrying cloak or almsbowl, or robe; in eating, drinking, chewing, tasting; in excreting and urinating; in walking, standing, sitting, sleeping,[6] waking, speaking, and remaining silent.

Again a monk contemplates this very body upwards from the soles of the feet, downwards from the hair of the head. (Or he) contemplates (its) position and posture in terms of the elements. (Or he) might see a corpse (and think): 'This body, too, is such a thing, has such a destiny, cannot escape such an end.' In such (various) ways does a monk live, observing the body in terms of the body.

And how does a monk live observing feelings in terms of feelings? Herein a monk experiencing a pleasant feeling is aware (of that); experiencing a painful feeling is aware (of that and likewise for a feeling that is) neither pleasant nor painful. He is aware: 'I experience a pleasant feeling of a physical nature, (or) of a non-physical nature', (or likewise with painful and indifferent feelings as the case may be).

And he lives observing feelings in terms of the feelings within, or the feelings without, (or both together). He lives observing the waxing or waning of feelings, (or both together). Or, aware: 'There is feeling', mindfulness is present for him just to the extent necessary for knowledge and recollection, and he lives ungrounded, cleaving to nothing whatsoever in the world. In such a way does a monk live observing feelings in terms of feelings.

And how does a monk live observing the mind in terms of the mind? Herein a monk knows a mind that is passionate (as such, and) a mind devoid of passion (as such). He knows the malevolent mind, the mind without malevolence, the deluded mind, the mind free from delusion, the attentive and the inattentive minds, the mind that is or is not great, that is excelled or unexcelled, that is settled or unsettled, free or unfree.

And he lives observing the mind in terms of the mind within, or the mind without, (or both together). He lives observing the waxing or waning of the mind, (or both together, as regards these various states). Or, aware: 'There is mind', mindfulness is present for him just to the extent necessary for knowledge and recollection, and he lives ungrounded, cleaving to nothing whatsoever in the world. In such a way does a monk live observing the mind in terms of the mind.

And how does a monk live observing phenomena in terms of phenomena? Herein a monk lives (like this) in relation to the five (mental) obstacles. When there is a worldly impulse within (him) he is aware (of that, and likewise when there is not). And, in so far as there is the appearance of a (previously) unarisen worldly impulse, he is aware of that, and (likewise as regards) the abandonment of (such an impulse), and its non-arising in the future. When there is within (him) ill-will, slothfulness and sluggishness, agitation and worry, (or) uncertainty, he is (similarly) aware (of their presence, their absence, their abandonment).

Or again (he) lives observing phenomena in terms of phenomena in relation to the fivefold embodiments of attachment. Herein a monk thinks: 'Such is (physical) form, such (its) origin, such (its) disappearance. Such is the (nature), the origin, the disappearance of feeling, perception, traits and tendencies, (or) consciousness (itself).'

Or again (he) lives observing phenomena in terms of phenomena with regard to the six internal and external sources (of experience).[7] Herein a monk is aware of the eye, and is aware of (visible) forms, and is aware of the bondage that arises grounded in both (of these). And, in so far as there is abandonment of a (previously) unarisen bondage (of this nature), he is aware (of that). He is aware of (the internal and external sources of the other senses and of the mind in the same way).

Or again, (he) lives observing phenomena in terms of phenomena with regard to the seven aspects of enlightenment. Herein, when there is the aspect of enlightenment that is mindfulness within (him) he is aware (of that, and likewise when there is not). And in so far as there is the appearance of a mindfulness not (previously) arisen, (or) the complete development of a mindfulness that has arisen, he is aware (of that).

When there is the aspect of enlightenment within (him) that is examination of *dhamma*, energy, joy, concentration, repose, (or) equanimity, he is aware (of them in the same way).

Or again, (he) lives observing phenomena in terms of phenomena with regard to the four *ariyan* truths. Herein a monk, thinking, 'This is suffering, this the origin of suffering, this the cessation of suffering, this the course leading (thereto)', is aware of it as it really is.

And he lives observing (these various things) within or without, (or both together). He lives observing (their) waxing or (their) waning, (or both). Or thinking, 'There are phenomena', mindfulness is established for him just to the extent necessary for knowledge and recollection, and he lives ungrounded, cleaving to nothing whatsoever in the world. In such a way does a monk live observing phenomena in terms of phenomena. For whosoever might cultivate these four applications of mindfulness for seven years, seven months, seven days, one of two outcomes may be expected – gnosis in this life, or no return (to it) if there is a remainder (at death).

Monks, this is the only way for purifying beings, for overcoming grief and woe, for the vanishing of pain and distress, the attainment of the right approach (and) the realisation of *nibbāna*, namely the four applications of mindfulness." Thus spoke the Lord.

1. This phraseology is repeated for each application, and is probably just a way of stressing that observation not reflection is called for.
2. Usually taken to mean that his breath is physically in front of him.
3. Virtually all the material on the first application recurs in 118 and 119 in fuller form than I have given it here.
4. i.e. the bodies of others. This duality recurs for the other applications.
5. Recollection of where he is rather than memory.
6. The idea here is probably that even dreaming is subject to mindfulness.
7. The fact that an external source is indicated for the mind suggests that recognition patterns projected on to phenomena are here under consideration rather than, or as well as, imaginative constructions or memories.

11

Minor Discourse on the Lion's Roar

63–68

Thus have I heard: once the Lord dwelt near Sāvatthī in the Jeta Grove on Anāthapiṇḍika's campus. There (he) addressed the monks, saying:

" 'Here is an ascetic, here a second ascetic, here a third ascetic, here a fourth ascetic,[1] (but) devoid of ascetics are other opposing doctrines.' Thus, monks, you can rightly roar the roar of the lion. But it may be that wanderers of other persuasions will say to you: 'Whence the assurance and the authority through which (you) say (this)?' Such are to be (your) words (in reply): 'Friends, by the Lord who has known and seen – *arahant*, truly enlightened, four things have been shown us which we behold for ourselves, (and so we speak like this). There is confidence in the Teacher (and) in *dhamma*, there is fulfilment of (right) conduct, and our companions in *dhamma* as well as householders and those who have gone forth are dear and agreeable to us.'

But it may be that (these) wanderers (then) say this: 'But we too friends (are like this). So what is the distinction, what the difference, what the diversity between you and us?' (In that case) you should say: 'Friends, now is the outcome one, or is it manifold?' If they were to answer aright they would say (that it is one, not manifold).

(Then you might ask them in turn): 'Is this outcome for one of passion, of hatred, of delusion, of craving, of attachment, for the unwise, for the weak and (easily) daunted, for one devoted to obstacles, (or is it the opposite of all these)?' If they were to answer aright they would say (that it is the latter).

There are these two views, monks – the view of (continued) existence and the view of non-existence.[2] Those ascetics and brahmans that adhere to, are converted and committed to the view of (continued) existence quarrel with the view of non-existence. And those ascetics and brahmans who adhere to, are converted and committed to the view of non-existence quarrel with the view of (continued) existence. Those who do not really understand the origin and disappearance of these two views, the satisfaction (in them), (their) disadvantage, and the freedom (from them) – they are given to passion, ill-will, delusion, craving, attachment. They are the unwise, the weak and (easily) daunted, the ones devoted to obstacles. They do not escape from birth, old age, death, grief, woe, suffering, distress, and trouble. I say that they are not released from suffering.

There are these four (kinds of) attachment – to worldly pursuits. to views, to convention and ritual, to pronouncements concerning a self. There are some ascetics and brahmans who, whilst claiming comprehensive understanding of attachment, do not properly expound (such) understanding. They declare an understanding of attachment to worldly pursuits (but not of the others, or of some of the others but not all).

In that kind of *dhamma* and discipline such confidence as there is with the Teacher (and) with a *dhamma* can be described as not properly founded. (And) whatever is the fulfilment of (right) conduct, (or) regard and affection for companions in the good life, can be described as not properly founded (either). Why so? That is just how it is with a *dhamma* and discipline that is badly proclaimed, badly taught, not leading (anywhere), not conducive to peace, not taught by one who is truly enlightened.

But an exemplar, an *arahant*, one who is truly enlightened, whilst claiming comprehensive understanding of attachment, expounds (such) understanding properly. He declares an understanding of attachment to worldly pursuits, to views, to convention and ritual, and to pronouncements concerning a self. In that kind of *dhamma* and discipline such confidence as there is with the teacher (and) with *dhamma* can be described as properly founded. (And) whatever is the fulfilment of (right) conduct, (or) regard and affection for companions in the good life, can be described as properly founded. Why so? That is just the way it is with a *dhamma* and discipline that is well proclaimed, well taught, ongoing, (and) taught by one who is truly enlightened.

And what is the cause, the origin, the birth, the source of these four (kinds of) attachment? (It is) craving, monks. And of craving? – (it is response to) a stimulus. And of (that? – it is) the six sources (of experience). And of (them)? – (it is) individuality and (physical) form. And of (that? – it is) consciousness. And of consciousness? – (it is) formative tendencies. And of formative tendencies? – ignorance, monks is the cause, the origin, the birth, the source of formative tendencies.

When ignorance is left behind by a monk and gnosis has arisen he clings neither to worldly pursuits, nor to views, nor to convention and ritual, not to pronouncements concerning a self. Not clinging to anything, he is untroubled. Being untroubled, he comes by himself to final *nibbāna* knowing 'Destroyed is birth, fulfilled the good life, done what was to be done and (there will be) no more return to this world.' "

Thus spoke the Lord

1. i.e. in the Buddhist order.
2. Often referred to as eternalism and annihilationism.

12

Major Discourse on the Lion's Roar

68–83

Thus have I heard: once the Lord dwelt near Vesālī in thick jungle to the west of the town. Now at that time Sunakkhatta, the son of a Licchavi, who had recently deserted the *dhamma* and discipline spoke these words to a group (of people) at Vesālī:

"There are no superhuman states (or) true knowledge and vision characteristic of the *ariyans* in the ascetic Gotama, (and he) teaches a *dhamma* fashioned by sophistry, based on reasoning, and of his own devising. (But he claims that) that for the sake of which (his) *dhamma* is taught truly leads to the extinction of suffering for its practitioner."

Now the venerable Sāriputta, dressing at an early hour and taking bowl and robe, went into Vesālī for almsfood. (He) heard Sunakkhatta the Licchavi's speech. Having walked in Vesālī for almsfood (he) returned following the meal and approached the Lord. Saluting (him he) sat down at one side (and told the Lord of what he had heard).

"Sāriputta, Sunakkhatta is a man of wrath and folly and these words were spoken by him in anger. Thinking (of) speaking disparagingly (he) actually speaks in praise of the Exemplar. For should one speak thus of the Exemplar it is praise: '(He claims that) that for the sake of which his *dhamma* is taught truly leads to the extinction of suffering for its practitioner.' But certainly there will not be this conclusion for (him) about me that follows from *dhamma*, (namely that I am) the Lord who is *arahant*, truly enlightened, perfect in knowledge and conduct, adept, seer of worlds, matchless charioteer of men to be tamed, teacher of *devas* and men, *buddha* and lord.

(Nor will he think that I am one who) realises the diverse forms of psychic power; (who) becomes one from being many (or the reverse); (who) goes visible or invisible through a wall, a fence, or a mountain; (who) dives and rises through the ground as if in water; (who) walks on unbroken waters as though on the ground; (who) travels cross-legged through the air like a bird on the wing; (who) touches and strokes with the hand the moon and sun in all their power and splendour; and (who) extends the range of the body even as far as the *brahma*-world.

(Nor will he think that I am one who), with the purified divine ear transcending the human, hears sounds (of) both (kinds), be they far or near; or whose mind grasps and comprehends (that) of other beings and people, knowing the passionate mind, the malevolent mind, the disturbed mind, the mind become great, the unexcelled mind, the composed mind, the mind that is freed (and all contrary states for what they are).

These, however, are the ten powers of an exemplar, possessed of which (he) affirms (his) position as leader, roars the lion's roar in assemblies, and makes the *brahma*-wheel roll – (he) knows an attribute[1] (that is present) for what it is and (one that is absent likewise); (he) truly knows from its condition and its source the ripening of activities undertaken in the past, present, or future; (he) truly knows the course of all destinies; (he) truly knows the countless and varied elements of the world; (he) truly knows the diverse traits of beings; (he) truly knows the range and limits of the faculties of other beings and people; (he) truly knows the corruption, the purification, the emergence of attainment in the absorptions, in release, in concentration; (he) recalls various former existences; (he) beholds beings passing away and arising (again) with the purified divine eye transcending the human; (and) from the waning of the distractions (he) reaches and experiences the mental freedom and the freedom of wisdom that are undistracted, having realised them in this life through his own gnosis. These then, Sāriputta, are the ten powers of the Exemplar, possessed of which (he) affirms (his) position as leader, roars the roar of the lion in assemblies, and makes the *brahma*-wheel roll. If anyone knowing and seeing me thus speaks (like Sunakkhatta) then, should he not abandon that talk and that thought, should he not renounce that view, he is consigned to purgatory like a cast-off burden.

There are these four certainties of an exemplar, possessed of which (he) affirms (his) position as leader. I do not see the ground on which ascetic or brahman, *deva* or *māra* or *brahmā*, or anyone in the world can fairly reprove me saying (either): 'These things affirmed by you of a truly enlightened one are not (as you claim)'; (or): 'These distractions of which you claim the elimination are not eliminated'; (or): 'These states, described by you as obstructive, are not, when pursued, really obstructive'; (or): 'That for the sake of which *dhamma* is taught by you does not truly lead to the extinction of suffering for its practitioner.' Not seeing (such basis for reproof) I live attaining tranquillity, attaining confidence, attaining certainty.

There are these eight assemblies Sāriputta – assemblies of nobles, of brahmans, of householders, of ascetics, of the Four Great Regents, of the Thirty-Three, of Māra, and of Brahmā. Possessed of the four certainties the Exemplar approaches and goes among these eight assemblies. Now I call to mind having approached hundreds of assemblies, but prior to sitting down, prior to talking and engaging in conversation, I did not see any ground for thinking that fear or timidity might assail me. Not seeing it, I live attaining tranquillity, attaining sanctuary, attaining certainty.

There are these four modes of birth Sāriputta – birth from an egg, from a womb, from moisture, and the spontaneous mode of birth. And what is the mode of birth that is an egg? Those beings that are born by breaking through an eggshell are called the egg-born. And what is the mode of birth that is (from) a womb? Those beings that are born by breaking through a membrane are called the womb-born. And what is the mode of birth that is (from) moisture? Those beings that are born in putrid fish, corpses, or (food),[2] or in a dirty pool by a village are called the moisture-born. And what is the mode of birth that is spontaneous? *Devas*, those in purgatory, some men, and some in a place of suffering are called the spontaneous-born.

There are these five destinies Sāriputta – purgatory, birth as an animal, the realm of ghosts, men, and *devas*. I comprehend purgatory and the road leading (thereto, and how), in accordance with one's ways, one comes, at the breaking up of the body at death to sorrow, to an evil destiny, to ruin, to purgatory. I comprehend birth as an animal, the realm of ghosts, men and the world of men, and *devas* and the world of *devas* (similarly, and how), in accordance with one's ways, one comes (to each of them). And I comprehend *nibbāna* Sāriputta and the road and course leading (thereto). I comprehend that, from the rooting out of the distractions, one reaches and experiences the mental freedom and freedom through wisdom that are undistracted, having realised them in this life through one's own gnosis.

Now I Sāriputta, encompassing with my mind the mind of someone, know this – proceeding thus, behaving thus, and going down that path – on the breaking up of the body at death (he) will come to sorrow, to an evil destiny, to ruin, to purgatory. After a time, with the purified divine eye transcending the human I see (him there), experiencing feelings that are entirely painful, acute, and harsh. One might liken it to a charcoal-pit, deeper than a man is tall, and full of embers that are without flame or smoke. Then suppose a man comes along exhausted and overcome by summer's heat, weary, thirsty, and parched, taking the one road that leads to just that charcoal-pit. A man of vision, seeing (him), might well (predict that he would arrive there and), after a while, see him fallen into that charcoal-pit and experiencing feelings (of such a nature).

(In the same way I know that someone) will come to be born as an animal. After a time I see him (in that state), experiencing feelings that are painful, acute, and harsh.[3] One might liken it to a cesspool, deeper than a man is tall, and full of filth. Then suppose a man comes along exhausted and overcome by summer's heat, weary, thirsty, and parched, taking the one road that leads to just that cesspool. A man of vision, seeing (him), might well (predict that he would arrive there and), after a while, see him falling into that cesspool, and experiencing feelings (of such a nature).

(Or again I know that someone) will come to be in the realm of ghosts. After a time I see him (there), experiencing feelings of great anguish. One might liken it to a tree, growing on uneven ground with sparse leaves and foliage, (giving) patchy shade. Then suppose a man comes along exhausted and overcome by summer's heat, weary, thirsty, and parched, taking the one road that leads to just that tree. A man of vision, seeing (him), might well (predict that he would arrive there and), after a while, see him sitting or lying down in the shade of that tree, experiencing feelings (of such a nature).

(Or again I know that someone) will come to be among men. After a time

I see him experiencing feelings that are very pleasant. One might liken it to a tree growing on level ground, with abundant leaves and foliage, (giving) deep shade. Then suppose a man comes along exhausted and overcome by summer's heat, weary, thirsty, and parched, taking the one road that leads to just that tree. A man of vision, seeing (him), might well (predict that he would arrive there and), after a while, see him sitting or lying down in the shade of that tree, experiencing feelings (of such a nature).

(Or again I know that someone) will come to a good destiny, a heaven world. After a while I see him experiencing feelings that are entirely pleasant. One might liken it to a palace, gabled, smeared all round, sheltered from the wind, with bolts that are fastened, and closed windows. Therein might be a divan, spread with a wool coverlet, embroidered with flowers, a fine hide of the kadali deer, above it an awning, and with a scarlet cushion at either end. Then suppose a man comes along exhausted and overcome by summer's heat, weary, thirsty, and parched, taking the one road that leads to just that palace. A man of vision, seeing (him), might well (predict that he would arrive there and), after a while, see him sitting or lying down, and experiencing feelings (of such a nature).

(Or again I know that someone), from the waning of the distractions, reaches and experiences mental freedom and the freedom of wisdom that are undistracted, having realised them in this life through his own gnosis. After a while I see him (in that condition), experiencing feelings that are altogether happy. One might liken it to a lotus-pond, with water that is clear, sweet, cool, and limpid – with pleasant banks, close to a dense jungle-thicket. Then suppose a man comes along exhausted and overcome by summer's heat, weary, thirsty, and parched, taking the one road that leads to just that lotus-pond. A man of vision, seeing (him), might well (predict that he would arrive there and), after a while, see him, with all care and distress and fever gone, sitting or lying in that dense jungle thicket, having plunged and bathed and drunk in the lotus-pool, and experiencing feelings (of such a nature).

Sāriputta, having followed a good life[4] with four elements I am one fully versed in (such an approach). I was an ascetic, the ultimate ascetic. I was unkempt (in appearance), the ultimate in unkemptness. I was one who avoided, the foremost in avoiding. I was solitary, the furthest gone in solitude.

In that (life) there was this for me through asceticism. I was unclothed, careless of convention, licking my hands, unresponsive to greetings, not one to halt when addressed. I did not accept what was offered or (specially) provided, or (any) invitation (to a meal). I would not take (food) straight from cooking-pot or pan, nor within the threshold, nor among the faggots, nor among the pestles, nor while two people were eating, nor from a pregnant woman, nor from one giving suck, or co-habiting with a man, nor from gleanings, nor where there was a dog standing, or flies swarming, nor fish, nor meat. I drank no fermented liquor or spirits. I was a one-house man, a one piece (of food) man. I kept going on one offering. I ate once a day, or once in two days, or once in seven days. Then I lived wedded to the practice of taking food at regular fortnightly intervals. I was one for eating potherbs, or millet, or paddy, or daddula (rice), or water-plants, or husk powder, or the scum of boiling rice, or the flour of oil seeds, or grass, or cowdung. I kept going on forest roots and fruit, on fruit that had fallen. I wore coarse hempen cloth, or hemp (mixed with other materials), or grave cloth, or rags from dust heaps, or tree-bark fibre, or antelope skins, or cloaks (made from them), or grass or bark garments, or strips of wood, or blankets of human hair, or horsetails, or owl's feathers. I was one who pulled out the hair of the head and beard, and was wedded to the practice (thereof). I was one who stood upright, refusing a seat. I was one for squatting, wedded to (that) practice. I was a bed of thorns man, (making) a couch (of them). I was given to the practice of going down to bathe three times in an evening. In just these various ways did I live mortifying and afflicting the body. This then, Sāriputta, was for me through asceticism.

In that (life) there was this for me through unkemptness. There was dust and dirt of many seasons accumulated on my body and falling off in shreds, as (from) a stump of the tindukā tree. Yet it did not occur to me (that) I could surely wipe (it) away with my hand, or that others (might do so). This then, Sāriputta, was for me through unkemptness.

In that (life) there was this for me through avoidance. Mindful both in going out and returning, there was sympathy in me for even a drop of water (so that I thought): 'Let me not bring destruction upon small creatures in their various hiding-places.' This then, Sāriputta, was for me through avoidance.

In that (life) there was this for me through solitude. Entering some forest-haunt I might dwell there and, if I saw a cowherd or a cattle-herd, or someone gathering hay or firewood, or a forest forager (of any kind), I would stumble from grove to grove, from thicket to thicket, from hollow to hollow, from hill to hill. Why so? – (that) they might not see me, nor (me them), just as a deer might on seeing men. This then, Sāriputta, was for me through solitude.

Approaching on all fours the pens which were provided for the cows and from which the cowherds were gone, I fed simply on the droppings of the young suckling calves. And so far as my own urine and faeces held out I (also) ate (them). This then, Sāriputta, was for me in the great nourishment from filth.

Then I entered some terrifying forest-thicket and lived there. Of (such a place) one might say (that) whoever enters it (with a mind) not empty of passion – his hairs stand on end. During the cold winter nights between the (eight days before and after the full moon), and at a time of snowfall, I spent such nights in the open air, and the daytime in the thicket. I spent the days of the last month of the hot season in the open, and the nights in the thicket. (And the thought came) **'Now hot, now cold – alone in the terrors of the forest, naked and sitting fireless, the sage pursues his goal.'**

Next I made my bed in a cemetery with the bones of the dead for a pillow. Cowherds came up to me, spat on me, urinated on me, showered me with dirt, and stuck twigs in my ears. Yet I was not aware of generating any evil thought towards them. This then, Sāriputta, was for me through a life of equanimity.

Sāriputta, there are some ascetics and brahmans who say (that) purity is through food. They speak like this: 'We keep going on jujube fruits',[5] and they devour the jujube. They devour (it) crushed. They drink jujube juice, and they use things made of jujube in various ways. Now I have had the experience of sustaining myself on just jujube. Perhaps, Sāriputta, you think (that) at that time the jujube was very large. But it should not be viewed thus. The jujube was excellent then, just in the same way as it is now. In sustaining myself on the food of just one jujube my body became very emaciated. From eating so little all my limbs became like knotted stalks or dead creepers, my buttocks like a bullock's hoof, my protruding backbone like a string of balls, my gaunt ribs as the rotten rafters of a collapsed shed. The pupils of my eyes appeared recessed and sunken in their sockets, like sparkling water in a deep well, (and) my scalp was shrivelled and shrunk, like a bitter white gourd by a hot wind after being cut whilst raw. (When) I thought (to) touch the skin of my stomach it was my backbone that I took hold of, (and vice versa), in so far as (the one) adhered to (the other). (When) I thought (to) defecate or urinate I fell forward on my face right there. (When), soothing the body, I stroked my limbs with my hand, the body hair fell out, rotten at the roots.

Yet from that behaviour, that course, that mortification, Sāriputta, I did not come to a superhuman state or the true knowledge and vision characteristic of the *ariyans*. Why so? It is just that this is not (the way) to achieve that *ariyan* wisdom, the achievement (of which) truly leads its practitioner to the extinction of suffering.

Sāriputta, there are some ascetics and brahmans who say (that) purity is through transmigration, (or) rebirth, (or) abode. Yet the transmigration, (or) rebirth, (or) abode is not easily found that I have not at some time (experienced) during the long past, other than among the *devas* of the pure abodes. For if I had transmigrated (there) I could not have come back again to this world.

Sāriputta, there are some ascetics and brahmans who say that purity is through oblation (or) the fire-sacrifice. Yet the oblation (or) the fire-sacrifice is not easily found (that I have not made) during the long past.

Sāriputta, there are some ascetics and brahmans who say (that), as long as some worthy fellow is young, a dark-haired stripling in his early prime, just that long is he possessed of the fullest lucidity of wisdom. But when (he) is frail, old, and venerable, has lived his life and reached the end of his days, – eighty, ninety, or a hundred years of age – then he falls away from that lucidity. But it should not be viewed like this. I, too, Sāriputta, am now (come to this state). I have reached eighty, and there might be (some) of my disciples here who are a hundred years old and are possessed of the highest degree of mindfulness, (sense of) vocation, and steadfastness, and with the utmost lucidity of wisdom. One might liken each of them to a skilled archer who, as a trained, dexterous marksman, deftly shoots his winged arrow just across the shadow of a palm-tree.

Suppose these were to ask me continually about the four applications of mindfulness and I, asked time after time, were to explain, and they were to understand and not interrogate me further, (nor pause in their endeavours) except for nourishment, for food and drink, for answering the calls of nature, or expelling tiredness through sleep – still ongoing would be the Exemplar's instruction in *dhamma*, (his) characterisation of (its) stages, (his) dealing with questions, when these four aged disciples of mine might die after a hundred years. Should you carry me about in a litter still there is no alteration in the Exemplar's lucidity of wisdom. One can speak truly in saying (that) an undeluded being has arisen in the world for the wellbeing and happiness of the multitude, out of pity for the world, (bringing these blessings) to *devas* and humans."

Now at that time the venerable Nāgasamāla was standing close behind the Lord, fanning (him, and he) said "Strange, bhante, wonderful that on hearing this discourse my hair stood on end. What is its name?"

"Then remember it as the hair-raising discourse Nāgasamāla."

Thus spoke the Lord.

1. Translation here involves a pair of terms which can also refer to the possible and the impossible or to "causal occasion" (Horner), or its absence.
2. Horner gives "rice", PTSD "junket".
3. Note the absence of "entirely" as compared with the previous case.
4. This phrase has been translated "good life" in accordance with other passages. In this case, however, it represents a view subsequently abandoned. Hence I have dropped the word "good" in the ensuing paragraphs.
5. Various other foods are mentioned in the same terms.

13

Major Discourse on the Foundations of Suffering

83–90

Thus have I heard: once the Lord dwelt near Sāvatthī in the Jeta Grove on Anāthapiṇḍika's campus. Then a number of monks, dressing at an early hour and taking bowl and robe, went into Sāvatthī for alms. But it occurred to (them that it was too early to walk in Sāvatthī for alms and that they might go to the wanderer's park for a time). Having approached (the wanderers) they exchanged greetings, conversed in a friendly and polite way, and sat down at one side. Said the wanderers:

"Friends, the ascetic Gotama lays claim to full understanding of worldly pursuits. We, too, make (that) claim. (He) claims full understanding of (physical) form. We, too, make (that) claim. (He) claims full understanding of feeling. We, too, make (that) claim. So what is the distinction, what the difference, what the diversity between between (him) and us as to *dhamma*-teaching against *dhamma*-teaching, or instruction against instruction?"

Then those monks neither approved nor scorned (what the others had said to them), but rose from their seats and went away thinking:

"In the Lord's presence we shall learn the meaning of what has been said."

Having walked for alms in Sāvatthī the monks returned from the almsround after the meal and approached the Lord. (Then they told him of the discussion they had had).

'Monks, wanderers of other sects who speak like this should be asked: 'But what friends is the satisfaction of worldly pursuits, what the disadvantage, what the escape from (them)? What is the satisfaction of (physical) form (or) feeling, what (their) disadvantage, what the escape (from them)[1]?' When asked this (these) wanderers will not be able to proceed further, and will meet with difficulty. Why so? It is not within their reach monks. I do not see anyone in the world, with its *devas, māras, brahmās*, its ascetics and brahmans, or in the living universe together with its *devas* and humans, who might win one's heart with an answer to these questions, other than an exemplar, (his) disciple, or one who has heard (their teaching).

And what, monks, is the satisfaction of worldly pursuits? There are these five strands of worldly pursuits – visible forms, pleasing, welcome, enticing, voluptuous, pleasure-laden, exciting; (and sounds, smells, tastes and physical contacts of a similar nature). Whatever happiness and delight comes about on account of these five strands of worldly pursuit is the satisfaction of worldly pursuits.

And what monks is the disadvantage of worldly pursuits? Herein some son of a family earns a living through some craft, such as hand-counting, arithmetic, calculation, agriculture, trade, tending cattle, archery, service to a king, or by some other means. He is oppressed by the cold (or) the heat, and afflicted by gadflies, mosquitoes, wind, sun, and the contact of crawling things. (He) dies of hunger and thirst. This is a manifest disadvantage of worldly pursuits, a basis for suffering in worldly pursuits.

If, (on the other hand), these possessions do accrue for (him), he experiences the pain and trouble of protecting and caring for (them). (He wonders how to ensure that) kings do not take (them), or thieves steal (them), or fire consume (them), or water carry (them) off, or unloved heirs acquire (them). (Yet, despite) protecting and guarding these possessions, (such things may come about). (Then) he grieves, he wearies, he laments, he beats his breast and wails. He exhibits bewilderment declaring: 'I do not even have that which was mine.' This too is a manifest disadvantage of worldly pursuits.

Then again, monks, worldly pursuit is the reason, the pre-condition, the cause, (whereby) kings quarrel with kings, nobles with nobles, brahmans with brahmans, householders with householders, mother with son, father with son, brother with brother, brother with sister, friend with friend. Entering upon a fight, a dispute, a quarrel, those (people) attack one another with their hands, with stones, with weapons. They meet with death there, and the pain (that goes with) death. This, too, is a manifest disadvantage of worldly pursuits.

Then again, monks, worldly pursuit is the reason, the pre-condition, the cause (whereby), seizing sword and shield, fastening on bow and quiver, two sides massed for battle advance with an exchange of arrows, with daggers thrown, and with swords flashing. They wound with arrows and with daggers, they decapitate with swords, they meet with death there, and the pain (that goes with) death. (Or, again), they leap on the glistening ramparts,[2] pour boiling cowdung (on those below, or) crush (them) with a great mass.[3] This, too, is a manifest disadvantage of worldly pursuits.

Or again, monks, worldly pursuit is the reason, the pre-condition, the cause, (whereby people) break into a house, carry away plunder, act like robber(s), wait in ambush, or go to other men's wives. Kings who catch such a person mete out various punishments.[4] This, too, is a manifest disadvantage of worldly pursuits.

Or again, monks, worldly pursuit is the reason, the pre-condition, the cause (whereby) people) err in their acts, their words and their thoughts. At the breaking up of the body at death they come to sorrow, to an evil destiny, to ruin, to purgatory. This, monks, is a disadvantage of worldly pursuits, a basis for suffering.

And what, monks, is the escape from worldly pursuits? Whatever constitutes a discipline, an abandonment of the delight and intoxication with (them), is (such) an escape.

Monks, whatever ascetics and brahmans do not understand in this way, and as it really is, the satisfaction of worldly pursuits as satisfaction, the disadvantage as disadvantage, and the escape as escape, these indeed will not know their own worldly pursuits with accuracy, nor encourage another to such a state (of knowledge) as he goes his way. And what, monks, is the satisfaction of (physical) forms. Imagine a maiden of noble family, or of a brahman's family, or of a householder's family who, at the age of fifteen or sixteen, is neither too tall, nor too short, nor too thin, nor too fat, nor too dark, nor too fair – is she (not) at her most lovely and beautiful at that time?"

"Yes, bhante."

"Whatever happiness and delight comes about because of beauty and loveliness is satisfaction with (physical) form.

And what, monks, is the disadvantage of (physical) form. Well one might see that good lady, at a later time – eighty, ninety, or a hundred years old – senile, crooked as a rafter, bent, leaning on a stick, going along palsied, miserable, (long) past youth, with teeth broken, with thin grey hair, stumbling, with head bowed, wrinkled, and with skin discoloured. One might see (her) affected with illness, ailing, very enfeebled, prostrate and lying in her own excrement, rising and getting to bed (only) with the help (of others). Then again, monks, one might see her body abandoned in a cemetery, dead for one, two, or three days – bloated, discoloured, festering. What had formerly been beauty and loveliness has gone. Has (not) the disadvantage shown itself?"[5]

"Yes, bhante."

"And what, monks, is the escape from (physical) form? Whatever constitutes a discipline, an abandonment of the delight and intoxication with (it), is (such) an escape.

Monks, whatever ascetics and brahmans do not understand in this way and as it really is the satisfaction with (physical) form as satisfaction, the disadvantage as disadvantage, and the escape as escape, these indeed will not understand their own (physical) form with accuracy, nor encourage another to such a state (of knowledge) as he goes his way.

And what, monks, is the satisfaction of feelings? herein a monk, remote from worldly pursuits and from unskilled states reaches and experiences the first (and subsequent levels) of absorption. At (such) a time he simply has no thought of hurt to himself, or to others, and at just that time he experiences feelings that are untroubled. I tell you monks to be untroubled is the highest satisfaction among feelings.

And what, monks, is the disadvantage of feelings? In so far as feelings are transient, painful, and fickle states therein is (their) disadvantage.

And what, monks, is the escape from feelings? Whatever constitutes a discipline, an abandonment of the delight and intoxication with (them), is (such) an escape.

Monks, whatever ascetics and brahmans do not understand in this way and as it really is the satisfaction with feelings as satisfaction, the disadvantage as disadvantage, and the escape as escape, these indeed will not understand their own feelings with accuracy, nor encourage another to such a state (of knowledge) as he goes his way."

Thus spoke the Lord.

1. The three factors are introduced successively in the full text with the ensuing paragraph repeated three times.
2. Possibly implying smeared with a slippery substance.
3. Horner – "crush them with the (falling) portcullis."
4. A long list of punishments is given.
5. Omitted sections deal with the subsequent stages of decomposition.

14

Minor Discourse on the Foundations of Suffering

91–95

Thus have I heard: once the Lord dwelt among the Sakyans near Kapilavatthu on Nigrodha's campus. Then Mahānāma the Sakyan approached the Lord, greeted (him), and sat down at one side. Said Mahānāma:

"I have long understood the *dhamma* taught by the Lord in this way – greed is a corruption of the mind, ill-will is a corruption of the mind, delusion is a corruption of the mind. Yet at times things (rooted) in greed, in ill-will, and in delusion, encircle my mind and remain (there). Regarding that I have asked myself: 'Now what is the quality in me that, not being internally rid of it, (I succumb to these states).' "

"Indeed, Mahānāma, (it is as you say). But were you not a dweller in a house, were you not given to the indulgence of worldly pursuits, that quality in you might be internally got rid of.

Worldly pursuit offers small satisfaction, much pain, much trouble, (and) herein lies repeated disadvantage. And if this is well perceived as it really is by an *ariyan* disciple by means of true wisdom, yet he does not achieve joy or happiness or something better in separation from worldly pursuits and unskilled states, then just so long is he not unenticed by worldly pursuits.

Mahānāma, before my enlightenment, being just a *bodhisatta,* I, too, (saw the disadvantage in worldly pursuits but), in separation from worldly pursuits and unskilled states, came to no joy or happiness. Then I was conscious that, to that extent, I was not unenticed by (such things).

And what, Mahānāma, is the satisfaction of worldly pursuits? There are these five strands of worldly pursuit – visible forms, pleasing, welcome, enticing, voluptuous, pleasure-laden, exciting; (and sounds, smells, tastes, and bodily contacts of the same kind). Whatever happiness and delight comes about because of these is the satisfaction of worldly pursuits.

And what, Mahānāma, is the disadvantage of worldly pursuits? (If it fails to gain its object there is distress, if it gains its object there is the worry of protecting what has been gained. And because of it there is quarrelling, exploitation, and death).[1] This, Mahānāma, is a disadvantage of worldly pursuits that is of the future, a body of suffering with worldly pursuit as reason, as pre-condition, as cause.

Once I was living near Rājagaha on Vulture's Peak. Now at that time a number of Jains on the Black Rock on the slopes of (Mt) Isigili were standing erect, denying (themselves) a seat. They were experiencing feelings that were spasmodic, painful, acute, and harsh. Then, emerging from seclusion in the evening, I approached the slopes of (Mt) Isigili and these Jains and spoke with them:

'Now why, friends, do you, standing erect and denying (yourselves) seats, experience feelings that are spasmodic, painful, acute, and harsh?'

At (my) words the Jains said to me:

'Friend, Nātaputta the Jain knows all, sees all, (and) claims all-embracing knowledge and vision, saying: "Whether walking or standing, asleep or awake, knowledge and vision are always and fully available to me." He says (that) an evil deed committed in the past (is to be) extinguished through this painful austerity, (and that) from restraint now in body, speech, and thought there will be no performance of an evil deed in the future. Hence, from the working out and destruction of former activities and the non-performance of new activity, there will be no future effect. Because of (that) there will be a waning of activity. From the waning of activity there will be a waning of suffering. From the waning of suffering there will be a waning of feeling. Suffering in its entirety will come to an end. And since that is certainly pleasing to us and approved of by us we (feel) uplifted by it.'

'But do you know friends (that you) existed in the past?'

'Not so, friend.'

'(Or that you) did not do an evil deed in the past?'

'Not so, friend.'

'(Or that you) did not commit an evil deed like this or like that?'

'Not so, friend.'

'Then do you know (that) so much suffering is extinguished or is (yet) to be extinguished, or that in the extinction of such suffering all suffering is extinguished?'

'Not so, friend.'

'Then do you understand the abandonment of unskilled states and the acquisition of skilled states in this life?'

'Not so, friend.'

'This being so those who, on coming to a new birth among humans, are fierce, with hands that are bloodstained, and who follow a cruel occupation – they are abroad among the Jains.'

'Friend Gotama, happiness is not found through happiness, happiness is found through suffering. If happiness were to be found through happiness King Seniya Bimbisāra of Magadha would be one who lives more happily than the venerable Gotama.'

'The words of the Jain brethren are surely spoken in haste, and with lack of deliberation. Moreover, I ought to be questioned thereon (as to which) of these respected ones is the one that lives the more happily, King Seniya Bimbisāra of Magadha or the venerable Gotama.'

'(That is so, and therefore we will now put such a question to him).'

'Then I will ask you about that in turn, Jain brethren. Answer as you see fit. What do you think about this, friends? Is King Seniya Bimbisāra of

Magadha able, with unstirring body, and without uttering a word, to live experiencing nothing but happiness for seven nights and days (or even) for one night and day?'

'Not so, friend.'

'But I, friends, am able (so to do) for one night and one day, (and even) for seven nights and days. This being so, who is the one that lives more happily – King Seniya Bimbisāra of Magadha or I?'

'That being so, the venerable Gotama is certainly the happier.'"

Thus spoke the Lord.

1. Abbreviated from identical sections in the previous discourse

15

Inference[1]

95–100

Thus have I heard: once venerable Moggallāna the Great dwelt among the Bhaggas in Sumsumāragira, in the deer-park of Bhesakaḷā Grove. There (he) addressed the monks, saying:

"Fellow monks, if a monk makes a request, saying: 'Let the brethren speak to me. I should be spoken to by (them)', but he is hard to speak with and possessed of traits that render him fractious, impatient, incorrigible – then his companions in the good life consider that he should not be spoken to nor admonished, and that no trust should be placed in that person.

And what, friends, are the traits making for fractiousness? Herein a monk is of bad intentions, in the grip of evil wishes; (or) is given to exalting himself and disparaging others; (or) is bad-tempered, subject to anger; (or) to finding fault; (or) is given to taking offence;[2] (or) to speaking words associated with wrath; (or) when reproved he spills out reproof against the reprover; (or) disparages the reprover, or retorts with (another) reproof;[3] (or) prevaricates, changing the subject and manifesting anger, ill-will, and sullenness; (or) he fails to explain his movements; (or) he is harsh and spiteful; (or) envious and callous; (or) crafty and deceitful; (or) obdurate and arrogant; (or) infected with worldliness, holding to it, not readily abandoning it. These are spoken of as the traits making for fractiousness.

In this matter, friends, a monk should draw inferences about (him)self by means of (him)self thus, thinking, 'Any person who is of bad intentions and in the grip of evil wishes is not agreeable or attractive to me. So if I were (like that) I should be disagreeable and unattractive to others.' Knowing this, friends, a monk should resolve (that he) will not be of bad intentions and in the grip of evil wishes. (And he should consider and resolve similarly with regard to all the other traits making for fractiousness).

In this connection, friends, a monk should consider (him)self by means of (him)self thus, asking, 'Am I of bad intentions and in the grip of evil wishes?' If, in reflecting like that, (he) knows (that he is), he should exert himself for the abandonment of just those evil, unskilled states. But, if (he) knows (that he is not, he) should forsake (such things) in joy and gladness, training himself day and night in skilled states. (And he should proceed similarly with regard to all the other traits making for fractiousness)."

1. Horner's title – "On measuring in accordance with". The title word/phrase appears at the beginning of the fourth paragraph.

2. Following Horner; PTSD gives no help.
3. "(another)" is conjectural. Possibly the difference between the three previous situations is that the first expresses resentment at the reproof, the second is more general criticism, and the third is "tit-for-tat".

16

Barrenness of Mind

101–104

Thus have I heard: once the Lord dwelt near Sāvatthī in the Jeta Grove on Anāthapiṇḍika's campus. There he addressed the monks, saying:

"Monks, in any monk for whom five (forms of) mental barrenness are not set aside, five mental constraints not thrown off, it is certainly not possible that he will exhibit increase, growth, and maturity in this *dhamma* and discipline. What are (they)? Herein a monk has doubts about the Teacher, feels perplexity, lacks enthusiasm, is not reassured. A monk who (is like that) does not apply his mind with ardour, with application, with perseverance, (or) with effort. And so his first (form of) mental barrenness is not set aside. Then again a monk has doubts about *dhamma,* (or) the Order, (or) the training, (of the same kind). And so his second, third, (and) fourth (forms of) mental barrenness (are) not set aside. Then again a monk is offended by his companions in the good life, is uninspired, mentally afflicted, (his) barrenness grown. And so his fifth (form of) mental barrenness is not set aside. These are his five (forms of) mental barrenness.

And what are his five mental constraints that are not thrown off. In this connection a monk is not without passion with regard to worldly pursuits, not without affection, not without longing, not unconsumed, not without craving. A monk who (is like this) does not apply his mind with ardour, with application, with perseverance, (or) with effort. And so his first mental constraint is not thrown off.

Then again a monk is not without passion in relation to the body, or to (physical) form. And so his second (and) his third mental constraints are not thrown off. Then again a monk, eating as he likes and to satiety, lives wedded to the pleasure of the bed (and of) lying down, (and) of torpor. And so his fourth mental constraint is not thrown off.

Then again a monk follows the good life aspiring after some class of *devas,* thinking, 'By this conduct, or observance, or ascetic practice, or good life, I shall become a deva or one among (them).' And so his fifth mental constraint is not thrown off. These are the five mental constraints. (But for one who has overcome these various obstacles) – he develops the psychic powers endowed with concentrated resolve and concerted effort, with concentrated energy and concerted effort, (and) with concentrated consciousness and concerted effort. He develops the psychic powers endowed with concentrated examination and concerted effort, with exertion as the fifth (factor).

Monks, a monk possessed in this way of fifteen aspects of exertion is capable of breaking through, is capable of deepest wisdom, is capable of achieving the matchless haven from bondage. It is like eight, or ten, or a dozen hen's eggs, properly sat on, properly incubated, and properly hatched by the hen. For that hen (there would be no need to wish for the chicks to break out of the shell safely). (For) these chickens are capable with the claw of the foot, or the beak, of penetrating the eggshell and breaking through safely. So it is for (such) a monk." Thus spoke the Lord.

17

The Forest Grove

104–108

Thus have I heard: once the Lord dwelt near Sāvatthī in the Jeta Grove on Anāthapiṇḍika's campus. There (he) addressed the monks, saying:

"I will give you a survey (of *dhamma* in terms) of a forest grove. Herein a monk lives relying on a certain forest-grove. Whilst (so doing) mindfulness that is absent does not arise, the unsettled mind does not become composed, and unextinguished distractions do not wane. He does not reach the matchless haven from bondage that is unattained, and those requisites of life which need to be procured by a wanderer are obtained (only) with difficulty. Now that monk should reflect (that those sought-for conditions are unrealised and), whether it be night or day should quit that forest grove, not lingering further.

(In another such case those sought-for mental states are unrealised, but) those requisites of life which need to be procured by a wanderer are obtained without much difficulty. Now that monk should reflect (as follows): 'These requisites of life which need to be procured are obtained without much difficulty, but I did not go forth from home into homelessness for the sake of robes, or almsfood, or shelter, or for medicines for the sick.' Now the monk, on that count, should quit that forest grove, not lingering further.

(In another such case) a monk lives relying on a certain forest grove. Whilst (so doing) mindfulness that was absent does arise, the unsettled mind does become composed, and unextinguished distractions do wane. He does reach the matchless haven from bondage, but those requisites of life which need to be procured by a wanderer are obtained (only) with difficulty. Now that monk should reflect (as follows): 'These requisites of life which need to be procured are obtained (only) with difficulty, but I did not go forth from home into homelessness for the sake of (such things).' Then that monk, on that count, should remain in that forest grove, and not leave it.

(In another such case) a monk lives relying on a certain forest grove (and those sought-for conditions are realised), and those requisites of life which need to be procured by a wanderer are obtained without much difficulty. Monks, that monk should remain in that forest grove, not leaving it as long as life lasts."[1]

Thus spoke the Lord

1. The discourse continues with references to other types of location and to associations with people in exactly the same terms.

18

The Honey-Ball

108–114

Thus have I heard: once the Lord dwelt among the Sakyans near Kapilavatthu on Nigrodha's campus. Then the Lord, dressing at an early hour, took bowl and robe and went into Kapilavatthu for almsfood. Having walked in Kapilavatthu for almsfood and returning after the meal, he approached the Great Forest for the afternoon rest. Plunging into (it) he sat down at the foot of a young vilva tree. Daṇḍapāṇi[1] the Sakyan, who was given to wandering and roaming about, (also) plunged into the Great Forest. Approaching the Lord, he greeted (him), conversed in a friendly and polite way, and then stood on one side, leaning on a stick. Said Daṇḍapāṇi:

"What (standpoint) does the ascetic hold and preach?"

"Friend, not contending with anyone in the world, with its *devas, māras, brahmās,* ascetics and brahmans, or in the living universe of *devas* and humans, the (true) brahman[2] lives unyoked from worldly pursuits, without uncertainty, worry cut off, emptied of craving for existence or non-existence[3] (and) perceptions do not preoccupy (him). Such (a standpoint) I hold and preach."

At these words Daṇḍapāṇi the Sakyan, shaking his head and wagging his tongue, went away with a three-furrowed frown on his forehead and leaning on his stick.

Then the Lord, emerging from seclusion towards evening went to Nigrodha's campus and sat down in the place prepared (for him, where he related his encounter with Daṇḍapāṇi the Sakyan to the monks). When he had spoken a certain monk said:

"But as a holder of what (standpoint) does the Lord not contend with anyone in the world, and how does the Lord live unyoked from worldly pursuits, without uncertainty, worry cut off, emptied of craving for existence or non-existence, (so that) perceptions do not preoccupy him?"

"Monk, whatever the source of the many obsessive ideas which take hold of a man, should there be nothing there to rejoice in, welcome, or cleave to – just that is the end of the tendency to passion, to aversion, to views, to uncertainty, to pride, to the thirst for existence; just that is the end of taking a stick or sword, of quarrels, contention, dispute, strife, slander, and lies. In such a fashion do evil, unskilled states dissolve without remainder."

Saying this, the Lord, the Adept rose from his seat and entered the dwelling place. And, shortly after (his departure), these monks (asked one another): "Who can elucidate in full the meaning of that exposition set forth by the Lord in brief? The venerable Kaccāna the Great can (do so). Suppose we were to approach (him)."

Whereupon they (did so) and, having greeted (him) and conversed in a friendly and polite way, sat down at one side. (Then they explained the question that had arisen for them). (Said Kaccāna):

"Friends, like a man who walks around in need of the pith, wanting the pith, seeking the pith of a great, enduring, and pithy tree – who, passing by the root and the trunk, thinks that the pith is to be looked for in the branches and foliage – such is the brethren's behaviour in that, having been in the Teacher's presence, you pass (him) by and think to question me on the matter. Now friends, the Lord knows what is known, sees what is seen. (He) is vision-born, knowledge-born, *dhamma*-born, *brahmā*-born, enunciator, expounder, dispenser of meaning, giver of the deathless, *dhamma*-master, exemplar. This was your opportunity to question (him)."

"Certainly, friend Kaccāna. But the venerable Kaccāna is praised by the Teacher, and has the esteem of intelligent companions in the good life. Let (him) deal with (the question), if it is not inconvenient."

"Friends, I understand the meaning of that exposition set forth by the Lord in brief like this. On account of the eye, and with respect to (visible) forms, visual consciousness arises. The conjunction of the three is a (sensory) stimulus. (And the same applies to the other senses and to the mind in relation to mental phenomena). With (sensory) stimulus as a pre-condition there is feeling. What one feels, that one perceives. What one perceives, that one reflects on. What one reflects on, that one is preoccupied with, and therein is the source of the many obsessive ideas which take hold of a man. So it comes about that, given the existence of the eye, (visible) form, and visual consciousness (and their equivalents for the other senses and for mental phenomena), one will recognise the manifestation of a (sensory) stimulus. (And) it comes about that, given the manifestation of a (sensory) stimulus, one will recognise the manifestation of feeling, (and so on). (But, in the absence of the threefold conjunction, the other phenomena cannot arise). That is how I understand the meaning of that exposition set forth in brief by the Lord. But if you so wish, brethren, approach and question the Lord on the matter."

Then those monks, pleased and satisfied at what the venerable Kaccāna had said, rose from their seats and approached the Lord. Having saluted (him) they sat down at one side, (and told him of their conversation with venerable Kaccāna).

"Monks, clever and of great wisdom is Kaccāna. If you had questioned me on the matter I too would have explained (it) exactly (thus)."

At these words the venerable Ānanda said to the Lord:

"Bhante, just as a man, overcome by hunger and fatigue, might find a honey-ball, and would procure from any (part of it) he might taste a sweet and unalloyed flavour – similarly a monk of able mind might wisely examine the meaning of any (part) of this survey of *dhamma* and gain uplift and satisfaction for the mind. What is (its) name, bhante?"

"Well then, Ānanda, remember (it) as the honey-ball survey."[4]

Thus spoke the Lord.

1. The name means "Stick-in-hand".
2. i.e. with reference to himself.
3. Alternatively "any kind of existence".
4. This request for a name occurs on various occasions and may indicate a systematic method of committing the material to memory.

19

The Dissection of Thought

114–118

Thus have I heard: once the Lord dwelt near Sāvatthī in the Jeta Grove on Anāthapiṇḍika's campus. There (he) addressed the monks, saying:

"Monks, before my enlightenment, being just a *bodhisatta* it occurred to me (that) I might live dissecting thought. So whatever was thought of worldly pursuits, or harming, or cruelty – that I made into one part, and whatever was thought of renunciation, or harmlessness, or amity – that I made into a second part. Whilst I lived thus, diligent, zealous, and resolute, thought of worldly pursuits arose, and I was aware: 'This thought of worldly pursuits has arisen in me, and makes for the harming of self, the harming of others, the harming of both. It is obstructive of wisdom, troublesome, not conducive to *nibbāna*.' When I had reflected (thus) these thoughts subsided. So, as thought of (this kind) continually arose, I continually just abandoned it, just dispelled it, just made an end of it. (And I dealt likewise with thought of harming and cruelty).

Just that which a monk thinks and reflects on much determines the bias of his mind. If (he) thinks and reflects much on worldly pursuits, (or) harming, (or) cruelty, he forsakes renunciation, harmlessness, and amity. If he makes much of (them) his mind inclines towards (them). It is as though, in the last month of the rainy season in the autumn when the corn is thick, a cowherd guarding his cows might then hit and slash (them) with a stick, and check and restrain (them). Why so? (He) sees death, or imprisonment, or robbery, or blame, from such a cause.[1] Likewise did I see the disadvantage, the degradation, and the corruption of unskilful states, and the profit, the manifest cleansing, in renouncing them for skilled states.

Whilst I lived thus, diligent, zealous, and resolute, thought of renunciation arose, and I was aware: 'This thought of renunciation has arisen in me and does not make for the harming of self, the harming of others, the harming of both. It pertains to the growth of wisdom, it is not troublesome, it is conducive to *nibbāna*.' If, during night (or) day, I were to think and reflect on this I perceived no fear originating there. But I thought (that), in thinking and reflecting overlong, the body might become fatigued. From the fatigue of the body the mind might become disturbed, and the disturbed mind is far from concentration. So I inwardly settled and quietened the mind, focused and concentrated (it).

Just that which a monk thinks of and reflects on much determines the bias of his mind. If he thinks and reflects much on renunciation, harmlessness, and amity, he forsakes thought of worldly pursuits, harming, cruelty. If he makes much of (them) his mind inclines towards (them). It is as though, in the last month of the summer season with all the corn gathered in near a village, a cowherd were guarding his cows. Placing himself at the foot of a tree or in the open he calls to mind something to be done knowing: 'These cows are here.' Just so did I call to mind something to be done knowing: 'These mental states (are present).'

Monks, vigorous exertion was aroused in me, and unclouded mindfulness established. My body was at ease and unagitated, my mind composed and focused. Aloof from worldly pursuits and unskilled states I reached and experienced the first, the second, the third, and the fourth (levels of) absorption. With a mind composed, perfectly purified and clear, unblemished, purged of defilement, malleable, workable, steady, imperturbable, I turned (it) towards recollection and knowledge of previous existences, to the knowledge of the passing away and re-emergence of other beings, and to the rooting out and knowledge of the distractions.

It is like a large stretch of low-lying marshy ground in a forest wilderness which might be inhabited by a great herd of deer. Suppose some man appears, not wishing well, unfriendly, seeking their capture. Were there a safe and secure trail, enjoyable to walk in, he might block (it), opening a false trail, using a male decoy, and tethering a female. So, after a while, that great herd of deer could come to misfortune, ruin, and gradual disappearance. But if some (other) man meets with that (same) herd, a well-wisher, friendly, not seeking their capture, he can (re-)open that safe trail (and) close the false trail. He can take away the male decoy and loose the female. So, after a time, that great herd of deer could come to increase, growth, and abundance.

Monks, I have composed this parable to clarify the meaning. The large stretch of low-lying ground is a metaphor for worldly pursuits. The large herd is a name for beings. The man not wishing well is a description of Māra, the Evil One; false trail of the eightfold wrong way. The male decoy is pleasure and passion, the female ignorance. The man who is a well-wisher is a metaphor for the Exemplar; the safe trail for the *ariyan* eightfold path. Such is the secure trail, enjoyable to walk in, that I have opened. Closed is the false trail, removed the male decoy, loosed the female.[2]

What a teacher seeking the wellbeing of disciples may do out of compassion, that I have done for you. Here are roots of trees, here are empty places. Meditate, monks, be not slothful. Do not be remorseful later. This is our instruction to you."

Thus spoke the Lord.

1. The metaphor is somewhat opaque. My reading is that the crops belong to others so that the cows must be restrained from eating them.
2. I have abbreviated this passage by elimination of words contained in previous

paragraphs, by omitting the enumeration of the contents of both eightfold paths, and by avoiding tedious repetition of "This is a name for".

20

The Configuration of Thought

118–122

Thus have I heard: once the Lord dwelt near Sāvatthī in the Jeta Grove on Anāthapiṇḍika's campus. There (he) addressed the monks, saying:

"Monks, in addressing himself to the higher (aspects of) mind a monk should now and then pay attention to five qualities. What five?

Herein, if any quality that a monk has paid attention to gives rise to evil, unskilled thoughts, whether associated with desire, ill-will, or delusion, (he) should turn his attention to another quality associated with the skilful. (From doing that these states) pass away and come to an end. From their passing away the mind is inwardly settled and quietened, focused and composed. It is like a skilled carpenter who might drive out, take out, and get rid of a large pin by means of a small pin.

Monks, if having turned (his) attention to another quality (these states still persist), the disadvantage of these thoughts should be examined by the monk thinking: 'Truly these are unskilled thoughts, faulty thoughts, thoughts productive of suffering.' (From doing that these states) pass away and come to an end. From their passing away the mind is inwardly settled and quietened, focused and composed. It is like a young woman or man, in the flush of youth and fond of finery, who would be incommoded, ashamed, and disgusted to have the carcase of a snake, or a dog, or a human being hanging round his neck.

Monks, if having examined the disadvantage of these thoughts (such states still persist), forgetfulness and inattention should be generated with regard to (them) by the monk. (From doing that these states) pass away and come to an end. From their passing away the mind is inwardly settled and quietened, focused and composed. It is like a man with eyesight who take no pleasure in seeing the forms that appear (to him, and) might shut (his eyes) or look in another direction.

Monks, if having generated forgetfulness and inattention with regard to these thoughts (such states still persist, he) should address himself to (their) structure and configuration. (From doing that these states) pass away and come to an end. From their passing away the mind is inwardly settled and quietened, focused and composed. One might compare it to a man walking quickly who might ask himself: 'Why do I walk quickly? Suppose I were to walk slowly'; (then): 'Why do I walk slowly? Suppose I were to stand still', (and so on). In such a way that man, forsaking the most strenuous posture, might prepare for the most relaxed (one).

Monks, if having addressed himself to the structure and configuration of these thoughts, (such states still persist), then that monk, teeth clenched, tongue pressed against the palate, is to restrain, subdue, and dominate the mind by means of the mind. (From doing that these states) pass away and come to an end. From their passing away the mind is inwardly settled and quietened, focused and composed. It is like a powerful man who, grasping a weaker man by the head or the shoulders, restrains, subdues, and dominates (him).

By these means any quality that a monk has paid attention to which gives rise to evil, unskilled states is to be got rid of). Monks, the monk (who achieves this) is called the master of the habits and ways of thought. Anything he chooses to think, that he does think. Anything he does not choose to think, that he does not think. He has cut down craving, he has done away with bondage, and, by fully comprehending pride, has brought suffering to an end."

Thus spoke the Lord.

21

The Parable of the Saw

122–129

Thus have I heard: once the Lord dwelt near Sāvatthī in the Jeta Grove on Anāthapiṇḍika's campus. Now at that time venerable Moliyaphagguna was living in excessive contact with the nuns. If any monk spoke critically of the nuns in front of (him he) would get angry and displeased, and create a dispute.[1] Moreover, if (anyone) spoke critically of venerable Moliyaphagguna in front of the nuns (they) would get angry and displeased, and create a dispute. And so it was that (he) lived in contact with (them).

Then a certain monk approached the Lord, saluted him, and, sitting down at one side, (told him about Moliyaphagguna). Whereupon the Lord spoke to (another) monk, saying: "Go, monk, speak to the monk in my name (saying that) the Teacher would speak with (him)." (And the monk did so, and venerable Moliyaphagguna came to the Lord). Said the Lord:

"Is it true, Phagguna, that you live in contact with the nuns (like this)?"

"Yes, bhante."

"Phagguna, as a son of family, did you not go forth from home to the homeless life out of conviction?"

"Yes, bhante."

"But it is not proper that, (having done so), you should live in excessive contact with the nuns. So, if anyone speaks critically of the nuns in front of you, you should abandon mundane impulses and thoughts. As to that you must train yourself, thinking: 'My mind will not become altered, and I shall not utter evil words, and I shall live friendly and compassionate, with thoughts of goodwill, not bearing malice.' So even if someone, in your presence, should strike those nuns with their hands, or a stone, a stick, or a weapon, (still should you train yourself in this way)."

Then the Lord addressed the monks, saying:

"Once monks of mine really were mentally accomplished. I would say: 'Monks, I eat at one sitting (each day). (By so doing) I know freedom from sickness and good health. (I know) lightness, strength, and comfort. Do likewise monks, and eat at one sitting (each day).' There was nothing (further) I need do with respect to instruction of those monks. It was sufficient for me just to arouse mindfulness (in them). One might compare it to a chariot for thoroughbreds, standing harnessed on firm ground at a crossroads, and with a goad hanging down. A skilful groom, a tamer of stallions, takes the reins in his left hand on mounting, the goad in his right, and drives up and down, where and as he wishes. (And so it was for me with those monks).

Therefore, monks, you should abandon what is unskilled, and forge links with skilled states, and you too will generate increase, growth, and maturity in this *dhamma* and discipline. Monks, near to some village or town there might be a large grove of sāl-trees, overgrown by creepers. To it comes a man who is a well-wisher, friendly, seeking its wellbeing who, having cut off those sāl-tree shoots that are bent and crushed by the strength (of the creepers), takes them beyond it and thoroughly clears the inside of the wood. But those sāl-tree shoots that are straight and well-grown he takes proper care of.

At one time, monks, there was a woman householder called Vedehikā here in Sāvatthī. (This lady) had won high praise (from people who said): 'The householder Vedehikā is gentle, unassuming, and tranquil.' Now, monks, for a slave-girl she had one Kāḷī, who was able, not lazy, and a careful worker. Then Kāḷī the slave-girl said to herself: 'Now is my mistress inwardly ill-tempered, though not showing it, or otherwise. Does she perhaps not show (such) ill-temper just because of my careful work? Suppose I were to test (her).' So Kāḷī the slave-girl got up (late the next) day.[2] Whereupon Vedehikā the householder said to (her):

'Now then, Kāḷī.'

'What, mistress?'

'Why did you get up late today?'

'That's of no consequence, mistress.'

'That's nothing indeed, that you got up late, you wretched slave-girl?', and, angry and displeased, she voiced her irritation.

Then, monks, Kāḷī the slave-girl got up even (later) the next day. whereupon Vedehikā the householder, angry and displeased, took the pin for securing the cross-bar of the door and gave her a blow, splitting the head open. And Kāḷī the slave-girl, her head broken and streaming with blood, accosted the neighbours saying: 'See, sirs, the deed of the gentle one, the unassuming one, the tranquil one.' So, after a while, Vedehikā the householder earned a bad reputation.

Likewise, some monk is entirely gentle, unassuming, (and) tranquil, as long as unpleasant words do not assail him. But it is (when they do) that he is known (to possess these virtues). I do not call that monk well-spoken who is well-spoken with regard to robes, almsfood, shelter, and medicines for the sick, and who (just) shows politeness. Why so? That monk, on not getting (those things), is not well-spoken and is not polite. The monk that is well-spoken, that shows politeness, just (from) respecting, honouring, and reverencing *dhamma*, him I call well-spoken. And so, monks, should you train yourselves.

There are these five kinds of speech that others may address to you – timely or untimely, true or false, mild or harsh, profitable or unprofitable, with goodwill or bearing malice. (Likewise), monks, you might address others (in any of these ways). With regard to such things you should train yourselves, thinking, 'Our minds will not be altered, and we shall not speak evil words, and we shall live friendly and compassionate, with thoughts of goodwill, not bearing malice. And we shall live pervading that person with a mind joined to goodwill, abundantly, boundlessly, unrestrictedly, peaceably, benevolently.' Thus are you to train yourselves.

Monks, it might be compared to a man who comes along, having taken shovel and basket, saying: 'I will make this great earth earthless.' He might dig round and about, he might scatter (soil) here and there, he might spit in this or that place, he might urinate somewhere or other. What do you think about that, monks? Would he make the great earth earthless?"

"Not so, bhante. Why so? This great earth is unfathomable and boundless. It is not easy to make it earthless, to the point that that man would get exhausted and distressed (in the attempt)."

"Likewise, monks, are these five kinds of speech that others might address to you. In regard to them you should train yourselves, thinking, 'We shall pervade the entire world with a mind like the earth, abundantly, boundlessly, unrestrictedly, peaceably, benevolently.'

Monks, it is like a man who comes bringing (dyes coloured) scarlet or yellow, blue-green or crimson, saying: 'I will inscribe forms in this space. I will make forms appear.' what do you think about that, monks? Would (he achieve that)?"

"Not so, bhante. Why so? That space is formless, and without attributes. It is not easy to inscribe forms or make (them) appear, to the point that that man would get exhausted and distressed (in the attempt)."

"Likewise, monks, are these five kinds of speech that others might address to you. In regard to them you should train yourselves, thinking, 'We shall live pervading the entire world with a mind like space, abundantly, boundlessly, unrestrictedly, peaceably, benevolently.'

Monks, it is as though a man might come bringing a blazing firebrand, saying, 'I will burn and scorch the river Ganges with this firebrand.' What do you think about that, monks? Would (he achieve that)?"

"Not so, bhante. Why so? The river Ganges is deep and boundless. It is not easy to burn or scorch it with a firebrand, to the point that that man would get exhausted and distressed (in the attempt)."

"Likewise, monks, are these five kinds of speech that others might address to you. In regard to them you should train yourselves, thinking, 'We shall live pervading the entire world with a mind like the Ganges, abundantly, boundlessly, unrestrictedly, peaceably, benevolently.'

Monks, it is similar to a cat-skin bag, cured, well cured, cured all over, flexible, silky, with no hisses, no purrs. Then a man might come bringing a piece of wood or a potsherd, saying: 'I will get a hiss and a purr from this cat-skin bag with the aid of a piece of wood.' What do you think about that, monks? Would (he achieve that)?"

"Not so, bhante. Why so? (Simply because it has those properties) it is not easy (to do that), to the point that that man would get exhausted and distressed (in the attempt)."

"Likewise, monks, are these five kinds of speech that others might address to you. In regard to them you should train yourselves, thinking, 'We shall live pervading the entire world with a mind like a cat-skin bag, abundantly, boundlessly, unrestrictedly, peaceably, benevolently.'

Monks, if marauding robbers were to carve one limb from limb with a double-handled saw, even as to that, he whose mind is corrupted thereby is no follower of my teaching. Were you to attend constantly to the parable of the saw, do you (fore)see the kind of speech, whether trivial or coarse, that you could not endure?"

"No, bhante."

"Then consider (it) repeatedly, and that will be for your wellbeing and happiness for many a day."

Thus spoke the Lord.

1. Horner – "made a legal question".
2. The word used just means "by day". Possibly she would normally have risen before dawn.

22

The Parable of the Water-Snake

130–142

Thus have I heard: once the Lord dwelt near Sāvatthī in the Jeta Grove of Anāthapiṇḍika's campus. Now at that time a monk called Ariṭṭha, formerly a vulture-trainer, had conceived a pernicious view as follows: "As I understand the Lord's teaching of the *dhamma,* those states which (he) calls obstructive are not, when pursued, really obstructive at all." Now a number of monks heard (about this and) approached (him). (Then they asked him whether what they had heard was true. And the monk Ariṭṭha agreed that it was). Then those monks, with the hope of dissuading (him) from that pernicious view, cross-questioned, interrogated, and conversed with him, saying: "Friend Ariṭṭha, do not talk like that. Do not misrepresent the Lord. Misrepresentation of the Lord is not good, (for) he would not speak in such a way. Through various representations are obstructive states spoken of by (him), but their indulgence really is obstructive. Worldly pursuits are described as of little value, as (productive of) much suffering and trouble, and repeatedly as a disadvantage – as a skeleton, a piece of flesh, a firebrand, a charcoal-pit, a dream, something borrowed, the fruit of a tree, a slaughter-house, an impaling-stake, a snake's head." Yet the monk Ariṭṭha, formerly a vulture-trainer, holding and adhering to that same pernicious view with firmness, expressed (himself as before).

Being unable to dissuade (him) those monks approached the Lord. Having saluted (him), they sat down at one side (and told him of their conversation). Then the Lord spoke to a certain monk saying: "Go monk, address the monk Ariṭṭha in my name (telling him that) the Teacher would speak with him." (And the monk did so and the venerable Ariṭṭha came to the Lord). Said the Lord:

"Is it true that a pernicious view (of such a kind) has occurred to you?" (Whereupon the monk Ariṭṭha agreed that it had).

"To whom indeed do you suppose *dhamma* to have been taught by me thus, you foolish man. Have not obstructive states been described by me through various representations, and their indulgence as genuinely obstructive. Yet through your own incomprehension you misrepresent us, as well as doing much harm to yourself, and creating demerit. That will be for your misfortune and suffering for many a day."

Then the Lord addressed the monks, saying, "Do you too, monks, understand *dhamma* to have been taught by me like this?"

"Not so, bhante."

"Well (said), monks, well (said). For by diverse characterisations have I spoken of obstructive states, and their indulgence as genuinely obstructive. Certainly, this cannot be – that one should indulge worldly pursuits except through worldly pursuits themselves, through perception of worldly pursuits, and through thought (of them).

Herein, monks, some foolish men learn *dhamma*, a discourse in prose and verse, an exposition, a verse, an inspired utterance, an 'As it was said', a birth story, a supernormal occurrence, a miscellany. Having learnt this *dhamma*, they do not investigate the meaning[1] of these things with wisdom. Not being invested with wisdom, these things give them no pleasure. They learn *dhamma* just for the sake of reproaching others or just for the sake of babbling, and gain no advantage from that for the sake of which they learnt *dhamma*. Badly grasped, these things lead to their misfortune and suffering for many a day.

It is like a man walking around wanting a water-snake, seeking and searching for (one). He might see a large water-snake and take hold of it by the coil or the tail. The water-snake, turning back on him, would bite him on the hand or arm, or some other part of the body. Thereby he might come to death, or to pain like unto death. Likewise, some foolish men (come to grief through grasping *dhamma* wrongly).

(However), some sons of family learn *dhamma* (through its various forms of exposition). Having (done so), they do investigate the meaning of these things with wisdom. Well grasped, these things do give them pleasure (and) lead to wellbeing and happiness for them for many a day.

It is like a man walking around wanting a water-snake, seeking and searching for (one). He might see a large water-snake (and), pinning it with a cleft stick, successfully restrain it. (Having done so), he might grasp it properly by the neck. However much that water-snake were to encircle his hand or arm, or some other part of his body, he would not, thereby, come to death or pain like unto death. Likewise, some sons of family (come to wellbeing and happiness through grasping *dhamma* rightly). And so, monks, you can understand the meaning of what I have said, and bear it in mind in such a way. However, as to the meaning of that which you do not understand, either I or experienced monks should be questioned (about it).

Monks, I will teach you the parable of the raft, *dhamma* for crossing over, not for holding on to. Suppose that a man, journeying along the highway, sees a great flood, its near shore dangerous and fearsome, its further shore safe and unfrightening. And if there is no boat for passing over, nor a bridge across, it might occur to him (to form a raft. Now suppose he should do that and get safely across). Having crossed and arrived at the further shore, he thinks: 'This raft has been very helpful to me. What if I were to take (it) on my head, or raise it on my shoulder, and continue on my desired course.' What do you think about that, monks? Would that man, in so doing, be acting aright with regard to that raft?"

"Indeed not, bhante."

"(Monks, he would be acting aright were he to think): 'This raft has been very helpful to me. What if I were to haul (it) on dry land or drop it in the water, and continue on my desired course.' Such, monks, is the parable of the raft taught by me, *dhamma* for crossing over not for holding on to.

Monks, there are these six[2] fixed opinions. Herein an uninformed person, heedless of the *ariyan*s, untrained in the *dhamma* of good men thinks, with regard to (physical) form: 'This is mine; I am this; this is my self.' (Or he thinks this about) feeling, perception, traits and tendencies, (or) consciousness. (Or) he thinks (like that with regard to) what is seen, heard, (otherwise) sensed, cognised, attained, sought for, (or) reflected on by the mind. And this too is a fixed opinion (namely) 'This is the world; this is the self. After death I will become stable, continuous, perpetual, not subject to vicissitude, and will surely be for evermore.' All this he thinks of (in terms of): 'This is mine; I am this; this is my self.'

But, monks, an *ariyan* disciple who is heedful of the *ariyan*s, trained in the *dhamma* of good men, (rejects these fixed opinions, thinking), 'This is not mine; I am not this; this is not my self.' (By) regarding in such a way what is non-existent he will be unworried."

At these words a certain monk spoke to the Lord, saying:

"Bhante, could there not be worry about externals that are non-existent?"

"There could, monk. In such a case it occurs to someone: 'Alas that which was mine is not (any longer) mine. Alas that which could be mine, that I do not obtain.' He grieves, he is troubled, he laments, he beats his breast, he shows bewilderment."

"Bhante, could there not be worry about something internal that is non-existent?"

"There could, monk. In such a case it occurs to someone: 'This is the world; this is the self. After death I will become stable, continuous, perpetual, not subject to vicissitude, and will surely be for evermore.' He hears the *dhamma* taught by the Exemplar or a disciple (of his) for the uprooting of every predisposition, tendency, and bias towards fixed opinions. (He hears of their *dhamma*) for the calming of all tendencies, for the rejection of every attachment, for the rooting out of craving, for dispassion, for cessation, for *nibbāna*. (But) he thinks (that he) will surely be annihilated, (that he) will surely perish, (that he) will surely not be (in the future). He grieves, he is troubled, he laments, he beats his breast, he shows bewilderment.

Monks, the possession you might take hold of that would be stable, continuous, perpetual, not subject to vicissitude, and that would abide evermore – do you behold (anything of such a nature)?"

"Certainly not, bhante."

"Well (said), monks – neither do I. (And) a clinging to theories of self (by means of which) grief, woe, pain, distress, and trouble would not arise – do you see (such a thing)?"

"Certainly not, bhante."

"Well (said), monks – neither do I. (Or) a dependence on opinions (that could bring that about). Do you recognise (such opinions)?"

"Certainly not, bhante."

"Well (said), monks – neither do I. Monks, if there were a self, could one say: 'I am the possessor of a self?.'"

"Yes, bhante."

"And if there were the possession of a self could one say: 'Self is mine'?"

"Yes, bhante."

"And if, with reference to a self and the possession of a self, their reality and actuality is not established, then is not the fixed opinion (that says): 'This is the world; this is the self. After death I will become stable, continuous, perpetual, not subject to vicissitude, and will surely be for evermore' – (is not that opinion) complete and utter foolishness?"

"(What else), bhante?"

"What do you think monks? Is (physical) form enduring or transient?"

"Transient, bhante."

"But is what is transient painful or pleasant?"

"Painful, bhante."

"But as to what is transient and painful, a thing subject to vicissitude – is it appropriate to regard it (thus): 'This is mine; I am this; this is my self'?"

"Not so, bhante."

"(And) feeling, perception, traits and tendencies, consciousness?"

"Transient, bhante."

"Well then, monks, whatever is (physical) form, whether in the past, future, or present, whether internal or external, gross or subtle, foul or fair, far or near – all (such) should be seen as it is with true wisdom (in terms of): 'This is not mine; I am not this; this is not my self.' And whatever is feeling, perception, traits and tendencies, and consciousness is to be viewed (likewise in all these respects).

Monks, the informed disciple of the *ariyan*s, seeing it thus, turns away from (physical) form, turns away from feeling, perception, traits and tendencies, and consciousness. Turning away he experiences detachment. Through detachment he becomes free. In freedom there is understanding of freedom and he knows: 'Destroyed is birth, fulfilled the good life, done what was to be done and there will be no more return to this world.' Such a monk is said to have removed the obstacle, filled the ditch, pulled up (the pillar), to be unimprisoned, and to be an *ariyan* whose flag is lost, whose burden is laid down, and who is unfettered.

And how has a monk removed the obstacle? As to that, ignorance is eliminated, its root destroyed like a torn-up palm tree, annihilated for the future and taking no further hold.

And how has a monk filled the ditch? As to that, the continuum of being, the birth-cycle, is eliminated, its root destroyed.

And how has a monk pulled up (the pillar)? As to that, craving is eliminated, its root destroyed.

And how is a monk unimprisoned? As to that, the five (forms of) bondage to the worldly condition are eliminated, their roots destroyed.

And how is a monk an *ariyan*, his flag lost, his burden laid down, unfettered? As to that, the conceit of self is eliminated, its root destroyed

The monk's mind being freed in this way, the *devas* associated with Inda, with Brahmā, or with Pajāpati do not find what they seek by thinking, 'Such is the form of consciousness supporting the Exemplar.' (For) I tell you that the Exemplar is not discovered in the world of appearances. In the light of this statement and declaration some ascetics and brahmans make false, hollow, lying accusations, contrary to fact against me, saying: 'The ascetic Gotama is a nihilist. He proclaims the annihilation, the perishing, the non-existence of the essential being.' (But) as I am definitely not, and as I do not say (this), these worthies misrepresent me. Previously and now, I proclaim simply suffering and (its) cessation.

But if, concerning this, others revile, censure, and provoke the Exemplar, there is no malice, or discontent, or wrath in (his) mind thereby. And if others honour, esteem. revere, and respect (him), there is no joy, no happiness, no elation of mind. If some (adopt such an attitude) the Exemplar thinks: 'What was well understood in the past I hereby practise in such a way.' Monks, (in whatever ways others speak and act towards you, this is the manner in which you too should respond). So relinquish what is not yours, (and that) will be for your wellbeing and happiness for many a day. (Physical) form is not yours. Feeling is not yours. Perception, traits and tendencies, and consciousness are not yours.

What do you think about this, monks? If someone were to take away or burn, or do whatever he pleases with the grass, sticks, branches, and foliage of this Jeta Grove would it occur to you to think: 'He is taking, burning, and doing whatever he pleases with us'?"

"Not so, bhante. Why so? – (because) this is not our self, or what belongs to self."

"Likewise, relinquish what is not yours, and that will be for your wellbeing and happiness for many a day. (Physical) form is not yours. Feeling is not yours. Perception, traits and tendencies, and consciousness are not yours.

Thus, monks, *dhamma* is well proclaimed by me, made evident, opened up, illustrated, and stripped of its swathings. (Thereby) those monks who are *arahants*, the distractions rooted out. perfected, who have done what is to be done, shed the burden, reached their goal, the bondage of continuing existence exhausted, and who are freed by true knowledge – their rolling on is not discoverable.[3] (And) all those who have faith in me and affection for me are bound for heaven."

Thus spoke the Lord.

1. The Pali term can mean "advantage, profit" or "meaning". Both would make sense in this context.
2. The "six" are not unambiguously identified in the following list.
3. The various intermediate states of attainment, i.e. between the *arahant* and mere faith are listed in the full text.

23

The Anthill

142–145

Thus have I heard: once the Lord dwelt near Sāvatthī in the Jeta Grove on Anāthapiṇḍika's campus. Now at that time the venerable Kumārakassapa was living in Blind Men's Grove. Then, towards dawn, a certain *deva* of great beauty, shedding a radiance throughout the entire grove, approached (him). Standing at one side, the *deva* spoke:

"Monk, monk, the anthill smokes by night and blazes up by day. A brahman speaks thus: 'Take a tool o wise one, and dig it up.' Digging, the wise one saw a bolt – 'A bolt, bhaddante!' The brahman spoke thus: 'Take out the bolt, o wise one, and dig on.' Digging on, the wise one saw a frog – 'A frog, bhaddante!' 'Take out the frog, o wise one, and dig on.' Digging on, the wise one saw a forked path – 'A forked path, bhaddante!' 'Take out the forked path, o wise one, and dig on.' Digging on, the wise one saw a strainer – 'A strainer, bhaddante!' 'Take out the strainer, o wise one, and dig on.' Digging on, the wise one saw a tortoise – 'A tortoise, bhaddante!' "Take out the tortoise, o wise one, and dig on.' Digging on, the wise one saw a slaughter-house – 'A slaughter-house, bhaddante!' 'Take out the slaughter-house, o wise one, and dig on.' Digging on, the wise one saw a piece of flesh – 'A piece of flesh, bhaddante!' 'Take out the piece of flesh, o wise one, and dig on.' Digging on, the wise one saw a cobra – 'A cobra, bhaddante!' The brahman spoke thus: 'Let be the cobra, do not touch the cobra, respect the cobra.' Monk, were you to approach the Lord and question him on these matters you might bear in mind the explanation. (For) I see none in the world, with its *devas*, its *brahmās*, its ascetics and brahmans, or in the living universe together with its *devas* and humans, who can convince with his answers to these questions, other than an Exemplar, or (his) disciple, or someone who has heard their teaching." Having spoken thus, the *deva* disappeared from that place.

Then venerable Kumārakassapa, at the end of that night, approached the Lord and, saluting him, sat down at one side. (And he spoke of what had happened, and questioned the Lord on the meaning of the *deva's* message).

" 'The anthill', monk – that is a term for the body, made up of the four great elements, born of parents, nourished on gruel and sour milk, a thing subject to decay, abrasion, dissolution, and disintegration. What one thinks about and reflects on at night concerning the day's activities is 'smoking by night'. That which, having thought about and reflected on by night one engages in as bodily, verbal, or mental activity in the daytime is 'blazing up by day'. 'Brahman', monk – that is a description of the Exemplar, who is *arahant* and truly enlightened. 'Wise one' is a designation for a monk in need of training. 'Tool' is a term for the *ariyan* wisdom. 'Digging' is a reference to energetic endeavour. 'The bolt' is a simile for ignorance, (and) 'taking it out' for the abandonment of ignorance. 'Frog' is a simile for possession by anger, 'forked path' for uncertainty, 'strainer' for the five hindrances, 'tortoise' for the five embodiments of attachment, 'slaughter-house' for the five strands of worldly pursuit, 'piece of flesh' for delight and passion. (And the 'taking out' of all these means their abandonment). 'Cobra', monk – this is a term for the monk who has rooted out the distractions. Let be the cobra, do not touch the cobra, respect the cobra."

Thus spoke the Lord.

24

The Relay of Chariots

145–151

Thus have I heard: once the Lord dwelt near Rājagaha, at the squirrels' feeding ground in the Bamboo Grove. Then a number of monks native to the area, who had spent the rains in their own locality, approached the Lord, saluted (him), and sat down at one side. The Lord spoke to (them), saying:

"Who, among monks of (this locality), is honoured by (other) monks from the area who are companions in the good life as wanting little for himself, and as speaking (in such terms) to the monks? Who is content in himself and speaks of contentment? Who is secluded, ungregarious, energetically resolved, won to (right) conduct, concentration, wisdom, to the knowledge and vision of freedom, (and given to speaking of such things)? Who is given to admonishing, informing, instructing, rousing, enthusing and gladdening his companions in the good life?"

"The venerable Puṇṇa, Mantāṇi's son (is such a person), bhante."

Now at that time venerable Sāriputta was sitting quite near the Lord, and it struck him: "It is to the gain of venerable Puṇṇa, it is well for (him), that intelligent companions in the good life speak such high praise of him in the Teacher's presence. Perhaps some time or other we might meet up with (him, and) there might be some conversation."

Then the Lord, having lived at Rājagaha as long as he thought fit, set out on foot for Sāvatthī (and eventually arrived there, and) dwelt in the Jeta Grove on Anāthapiṇḍika's campus.

Venerable Puṇṇa, Mantāṇi's son, heard (of his arrival and), quitting his place of shelter and taking bowl and robe, travelled on foot (in that direction) coming, in due course, to Anāthapiṇḍika's campus. He approached the Lord, saluted him, and sat down at one side, (whereupon) the Lord instructed, roused, enthused, and gladdened (him) with *dhamma*-talk. Then venerable Puṇṇa, pleased and satisfied, rose from his seat, and, saluting with his right side, departed for the afternoon-rest in the Blind Men's Grove.

Then a certain monk (informed venerable Sāriputta of the venerable Puṇṇa's encounter with the Lord). Whereupon venerable Sāriputta, quickly taking his mat for sitting, followed closely after venerable Puṇṇa, keeping him in sight. And venerable Puṇṇa, plunging into Blind Men's Grove, seated himself at the foot of a certain tree for the afternoon-rest. Emerging from seclusion towards evening venerable Sāriputta approached venerable

Puṇṇa and, after greeting him and engaging in friendly and polite conversation, sat down at one side. Said Sāriputta:

"Friend, is the good life practised under our Lord?"

"Yes, friend."

"And is (it) lived for purity of conduct?"

"Not so, friend."

"(Or) for purity of mind?"

"Not so, friend."

"(Or) for purity of view?"

"Not so, friend."

"(Or) for the purging of doubt?"

"Not so, friend."

"(Or) for purity of knowledge and vision regarding what is and is not the Way, (or) the course (for pursuing the Way)?"

"Not so, friend."

"(Or simply) for purity of knowledge and vision?"

"Not so, friend."

"Friend, on being asked (all these questions), you say 'Not so, friend'. So to what end is the good life practised under the Lord?"

"For the goal of final *nibbāna* without attachment."

"Is purity of conduct final *nibbāna* without attachment?"

"Not so, friend."

"Is (it) purity of mind?"

"Not so, friend."

"(Or any of the other things I have referred to)?"

"Not so, friend."

"Then is it other than these states?"

"Not so, friend."

"Friend, on being asked (all these questions), you say: 'Not so, friend'. But how should the import of such words be made evident?"

"If the Lord had declared purity of conduct to be final *nibbāna* without attachment, he would, (by implication),[1] have declared (the latter state) to be accompanied by attachment, (and likewise) if he had declared (it to be identical with any of the other conditions you have mentioned). And, were it other than those states, the average person would have attained final *nibbāna*, for the average person is without (them).

Now friend, I will construct a parable, for through a parable some intelligent people grasp the meaning of what is spoken. Suppose, for King Pasenadi of Kosala, some exceptional matter arose in Sāketa whilst he was in residence at Sāvatthī. Seven relays of chariots are made ready for him between (the two places). Then King Pasenadi, leaving Sāvatthī from the palace-gate, mounts the first relay of chariots and, by means of (it), gets to the second. He (then) discharges the first and, by means of the second, gets to the third, (and so on until) he reaches Sāketa and the palace-gate (there). After his arrival friends, associates, and relatives might ask him: 'Sire, did you get (here) from Sāvatthī by means of this relay of chariots?' How would King Pasenadi answer to answer correctly?"

"Friend, (he would explain the matter as you have explained it to me)."

"In the same manner (as a relay of chariots) purity of conduct is of value for (reaching) purity of mind. Purity of mind is of value for (reaching) purity of view, purity of view for the purging of doubt, the purging of doubt for knowledge and vision of what is and is not the Way, (that in turn) for knowledge and vision of the course (for pursuing the Way, that in turn simply) for purity of knowledge and vision. Purity of knowledge and vision is of value for (reaching) final *nibbāna* without attachment. The good life under the Lord is practised for the sake of (that)."

When he had spoken venerable Sāriputta said:

"What is the venerable one's name and how do companions in the good life know him?"

"Puṇṇa is my name friend, and companions in the good life know me as Mantāṇi's son."

"Excellent friend, wonderful! – (that) profound questions should be answered in a superior way by an informed disciple, knowledgeable regarding the Teacher's doctrine, one such as venerable Puṇṇa. It is to the advantage of companions in the good life, it is well for (them) to get the opportunity to see and attend on venerable Puṇṇa. And if, (in so doing), companions in the good life were to bear (him) aloft on a cloth, it would be to their advantage and gain."

At these words venerable Puṇṇa said to venerable Sāriputta:

"What is the venerable one's name, and how do companions in the good life know (him)?"

"Upatissa is my name friend, and companions in the good life know me as Sāriputta."

"Truly I have been in conversation with the disciple likened to the Teacher, not knowing him to be venerable Sāriputta. Had I known I would not have replied at such length. Excellent friend, wonderful – that profound questions are asked in a superior way by an informed disciple, knowledgeable regarding the Teacher's doctrine, one such as the venerable Sāriputta."

In such a way did these two great ones approve of each other's well-spoken words.

1. i.e. all the previously mentioned being not without residual attachment.

25

Bait

151–160

Thus have I heard: once the Lord dwelt near Sāvatthī in the Jeta Grove on Anāthapiṇḍika's campus. There (he) addressed the monks, saying:

"Monks, a feeder of deer does not lay bait for herds of deer (with the thought): 'Let (them) enjoy the bait, and be of long life and in good condition for many days'. (He thinks, instead): 'Intruding, (they) will eagerly eat the bait (and thereby) get excited. In their excitement they will become careless. Being careless they will be at my mercy.'

Now the first herd of deer (that came along did as he had thought). So (they) did not escape the bewitchment of the deer-feeder

Then a second herd of deer (came along, and) realised (what had happened). (They thought): 'We could avoid this fodder-bait altogether and, turning from fearful enjoyment, plunge into the depths of the jungle and live there.' (And they did so). (But) in the last month of the hot season, with grass and water both consumed, and their bodies very emaciated, they returned, enfeebled, to the bait of the deer-feeder. So (they) too failed to escape the bewitchment of the deer-feeder.

Then a third herd of deer (came along, and) realised (what had happened to the other two herds). (They thought): 'We could make a refuge close (by'. And they did so. And) they ate the fodder without intrusion or eagerness, (and) did not get excited, (or) get careless. Not being careless they were not at the deer-feeder's mercy.

Whereupon the deer-feeder and (his) associates thought: 'This third herd of deer is certainly crafty and wily. (They) must be supernatural beings possessed of psychic powers, in that they enjoy the bait but we are not aware of their comings and goings. But suppose we were to surround this bait that has been laid by large snares.[1] Perhaps we could find the refuge where they might go on procuring it.' (So they resorted to that stratagem, and) the third herd of deer did not escape the bewitchment of the deer-feeder either.

Then a fourth herd of deer (came along and) realised (what had happened to the first three). (They thought): 'We could make a refuge where the deer-feeder and (his) associates do not go.' (And they did so).

Whereupon the deer-feeder and (his) associates thought: 'This fourth herd of deer is certainly crafty and wily. Perhaps we could (catch them in the same way as we caught the third herd of deer.' Then they set the snares as before. But they) did not find the refuge of the fourth herd of deer, nor where they might go on procuring (the bait). And the deer-feeder and (his) associates did not interfere with the fourth herd of deer (thereafter). So the fourth herd of deer escaped the bewitchment of the deer-feeder.

Monks, this parable was constructed by me for clarifying the meaning (of *dhamma*). 'Bait' is a description of the five strands of worldly pursuit; 'deer-feeder' of Māra the Wicked One, (and) 'associates' of Māra's associates. 'Herds of deer' is a name for ascetics and brahmans.

Herein one group of ascetics and brahmans intruded on that bait laid by Māra (in the shape of) worldly enjoyments, and consumed it with eagerness. So they did not escape Māra's bewitchment. I say (they) are like that first herd of deer.

A second (group of) ascetics and brahmans, realising this, thought: 'We could avoid this world-bait entirely, and, turning from fearful enjoyment, plunge into the depths of the jungle and live there.' (And they did so). There they were eaters of potherbs, millet, wild rice, daddula (rice), water-plants, husk-powder, the scum of boiling rice, the flour of oil-seeds, grass, or cowdung. (Or) they kept going on forest-roots and fruit. (But), in the last month of the hot season, with grass and water both dried up, and their bodies very emaciated, their strength and vigour were reduced. Because of (this) their mental freedom diminished and they returned to that world-bait laid by Māra. So they, too, failed to escape Māra's bewitchment. I say (they) are like that second herd of deer.

A third (group of) ascetics and brahmans, realising this, thought: 'We could make our abode near the world-bait laid by Māra.' (And they did so). They took nourishment there without intrusion or eagerness, (and) did not get excited, (or) display carelessness. Not being careless they were not at Māra's mercy. But they were imbued with such views as: 'The world is eternal; the world is not eternal; the world is finite; the world is infinite; the life-principle equates with the body; the life-principle is other than the body; the Exemplar survives death; the Exemplar does not survive death; (or both or neither).' So this third (group of) ascetics and brahmans did not escape Māra's bewitchment either. I say (they) are like that third herd of deer.

A fourth (group of) ascetics and brahmans, realising this, thought: 'We could make our abode where Māra and (his) associates do not come'. (And they did so). They took nourishment there without intrusion or eagerness, (and) did not get excited (or) display carelessness. I say (they) are like that fourth herd of deer.

And why, monks, do Māra and (his) associates not come. Herein a monk, remote from worldly pursuits and from unskilled states, reaches and experiences the first, the second, the third, and the fourth (realms of) absorption – and further, the realms of infinite space, infinite consciousness, of nothingness, of neither perceiving nor not perceiving, and experiences (finally) the stopping of feeling and perception.

Such a monk can be described (as one who) has made Māra blind, and having clouded Māra's eye, has gone untraced by the Evil One, transcending the entanglements of the world." Thus spoke the Lord

1. Literally "stick and net".

26

The Ariyan Quest

160–175

Thus have I heard: once the Lord dwelt near Sāvatthī in the Jeta Grove on Anāthapiṇḍika's campus. Then the Lord, dressing at an early hour, took bowl and robe and went into Sāvatthī for almsfood. Whereupon a number of monks approached venerable Ānanda and said to (him):

"Friend Ānanda, it is some time since we heard *dhamma*-talk in the presence of the Lord. It would be good to get (such) an opportunity."

"Well then, the brethren should go to the hermitage of the brahman Rammaka (where you may get your wish)."

Having walked in Sāvatthī for alms, the Lord, returning after the meal, said to venerable Ānanda:

"Let us go to the Eastern Campus, to the Migāramātu Palace, for the afternoon rest." (And they went there). Then the Lord, emerging from seclusion towards evening said to venerable Ānanda "We will go to the Eastern Porch[1] and bathe ourselves." (After they had been there) venerable Ānanda said to the Lord:

"Bhante, the hermitage of the brahman Rammaka is not far from here – a pleasant (and) lovely (place). Let the Lord go there out of compassion."

The Lord consented in silence.

Now at that time a number of monks were seated together at the hermitage, talking about *dhamma*. So the Lord stood outside the porch, waiting for the end of the conversation then, judging (it) finished, coughed and knocked upon the cross-bar. Entering he sat in the place prepared (for him and asked):

"What was (this) conversation that I have interrupted?"

"Bhante, (it) was about the Lord himself."

"Monks, this is as it should be – that you, as sons of family who have left home for the homeless life out of conviction, should sit together talking about *dhamma*. The purpose of your coming together, monks, is twofold – either *dhamma*-talk or the *ariyan* silence.

There are these two quests, monk – the *ariyan* and the *unariyan*. And what is the *unariyan* quest? As to that, one liable to birth, old age, sickness, and death because of self, seeks just what is liable to birth, old age, sickness, and death; being prone to sorrow because of self, seeks just what is prone to sorrow; being corruptible because of self seeks just what is corruptible.

And what, monks, would you say is liable to birth, old age, sickness, death, sorrow, and corruption? Son and wife, female and male servants, goat and sheep, cock and pig, elephant, cow, horse, mare, gold and silver,[2] are liable to (them). These attachments are liable to (them), wherein one who is enslaved, eager, and addicted, and liable to (them) because of self, (nonetheless) seeks just what is liable to birth, old age, sickness, and death, to sorrow and corruption.

And what, monks, is the *ariyan* quest?. Herein one liable to (these things) because of self knows (their) disadvantage, and seeks what is unborn, ageless, disease-free, immortal, unsorrowing and incorruptible – the matchless haven from bondage, (that is) *nibbāna*. Such, monks, is the *ariyan* quest.

I myself, monks, before my enlightenment, being just a *bodhisatta*, (pursued the *unariyan* quest). Then I thought: 'Why do I (live like this)?' So, after a while, being young, with jet black hair, in the flush of youth and early manhood, and with parents who were reluctant, tearful and lamenting, I cut off hair and beard, donned the yellow robe, and went from home into the homeless life. A searcher for what is skilled, seeking the matchless and excellent path to peace, I approached Āḷāra the Kālāma (and said): 'Friend Kālāma, I wish to follow the good life in this *dhamma* and discipline.' Āḷāra the Kālāma (replied): 'Live it, brother. This *dhamma* is of such a nature that an intelligent man may soon reach and experience his own teacher's (attainment), having realised it from his own gnosis.' Monks, I did indeed master that *dhamma* very soon, very quickly. In so far as mere verbal mastery and utterance goes I spoke words of knowledge, the words of an elder. And I, as well as others, claimed (that we) knew and saw. Then I thought: 'Āḷāra the Kālāma does not just speak this *dhamma* from conviction. Surely (he) proceeds with knowledge and vision.' Whereupon I approached (him and said): 'How far, friend Kālāma, do you declare this *dhamma* through achievement, having realised it from your own gnosis?' At my words Āḷāra the Kālāma proclaimed the realm of nothingness. But it occurred to me: 'It isn't only Āḷāra the Kālāma who has faith. I, too, have faith. It isn't only Āḷāra the Kālāma who has energy. I, too, have energy. It isn't only Āḷāra the Kālāma who has mindfulness, concentration, (or) wisdom. I have (them) too. Suppose I were to strive for the realisation of that *dhamma* (which he) proclaims.' And very soon, very quickly, (I came to live in that state). Then I approached Āḷāra the Kālāma (and said):

'Friend Kālāma, (is it) to this extent (that) you proclaim this *dhamma* through its achievement, having realised it from your own gnosis'

'(Yes), friend.'

'I too, friend, live in (that) realisation and experience.'

'The better for us, friend, the greater gain for us, that we see a companion in the good life such as the venerable one. So the *dhamma* that I proclaim is the *dhamma* that you have reached and experienced. As it is for me, so it is for you. Come now friend, let the two of us look after this group.' Thus did Āḷāra the Kālāma, my teacher, place me – the pupil, on the same plane as himself, and paid me the highest of compliments. (But) I thought: 'This *dhamma* is not conducive to disenchantment, to dispassion, to cessation, to calm, to gnosis, to enlightenment, to *nibbāna* – but only to the attainment of the realm of nothingness.' So, monks, not finding that *dhamma* sufficient, I wearied of (it) and went away.

Then, as a searcher for what is skilled, seeking the matchless and excellent path to peace I went to Uddaka Rāmaputta (and said): 'Friend, I wish to follow this *dhamma* and discipline.' Uddaka Ramaputta (replied) 'Live it, brother. This *dhamma* is of such a nature that an intelligent man may soon reach and experience his own teacher's (attainment), having realised it from his own gnosis.' (And it was for me with Uddaka Rāmaputta as with Āḷāra the Kālāma, except that Uddaka proclaimed the realm of neither perceiving nor not perceiving. And Uddaka Rāmaputta also raised me to equal rank with himself. But again) I thought: 'This *dhamma* is not conducive to disenchantment, to dispassion, to cessation, to calm, to gnosis, to enlightenment, to *nibbāna* – but only to the attainment of the realm of neither perceiving nor not perceiving.' So, monks, not finding that *dhamma* sufficient, I wearied of (it) and went away.[3]

So, as a searcher for what is skilled, monks, seeking the matchless and excellent path to peace and travelling on foot through Magadha, I came at length to the army village of Uruvelā. There I noticed a delightful spot, a pleasant jungle-thicket and a clear-flowing river with fine banks, and with a village (that might be useful) for the supply of food around it. And I thought: 'Surely this is a fit place for a young man desirous of striving to exert himself.' So, monks, I sat down there.

Being liable to birth, old age, sickness, and death because of self; being liable to sorrow, and corruptible because of self – and knowing the disadvantage thereof, I sought and won the unborn, ageless, disease-free, immortal, unsorrowing, incorruptible – the matchless haven from bondage, (that is) *nibbāna*. Knowledge and vision arose in me, (and I knew): 'Unshakable is (this) freedom of mine. This is the final birth. There is now no renewal of existence.'

There came the thought to me: 'This *dhamma* I have found is deep, hard to discern, difficult to understand, tranquil, exalted, not allied to sophistry, subtle, intelligible to the wise. But the living universe is given over to pleasure, to amusement, to delight. (For them) this state is hard to discern, namely the conditioned nature of (everything) here, and the originating causes. And this too is hard to discern, namely the calming of all tendencies, the renunciation of every foothold, the rooting out of craving, dispassion, cessation, *nibbāna*. And should I teach *dhamma*, others might not comprehend me, and that would be a weariness and a vexation for me.'

As I pondered in this way my mind inclined to inaction, to not teaching *dhamma*. Then, monks, Brahmā Sahampati, knowing my thoughts, (said to himself): 'Surely the world is lost, surely the world must perish, in so far as the mind of the Exemplar, (who is) arahant, truly enlightened, inclines to inaction, to not teaching *dhamma*.' So Brahmā Sahampati, just as a strong man having bent his arm might stretch it out again, vanished from the *brahmā*-world and appeared in front of me. Whereupon, arranging his robe on one shoulder and saluting with joined palms, (he) spoke thus to me:

'Let the Lord teach *dhamma*, let the Adept teach *dhamma*. There are beings that are little sullied who, through not hearing *dhamma* are degenerating. As learners of *dhamma* they will grow.

**'There has appeared in Magadha before a *dhamma* impurely and perversely conceived. Open this door to the deathless. Let the *dhamma* awakened to by the unsullied one be heard. As, on a rock on a mountain summit, one might stand seeing people on all sides – in such a way, O Wise One, ascend the palace of *dhamma*. All-seeing and emptied of grief, behold people come upon sorrow and vanquished by birth and old age. Arise hero, victorious, O leader of the caravan without a debt. Walk in the world. Let the Lord teach *dhamma*. They who learn will grow.'*

Then, monks, understanding Brahmā's entreaty and out of compassion for beings, I surveyed the world with a *buddha*'s eye. I saw beings little and much sullied, with sharp and dull faculties, well and ill-disposed, docile and intractable, a few noticing their faults in fear of a world beyond. Just as in a pond of blue, red, or white lotuses, a few (of these flowers) germinate in the water, grow in the water, or thrive immersed in the water without rising from it; a few grow in the water but breaking (its) surface; and a few grow in the water but stand up out of (it) – so, surveying the world with a *buddha*'s eye, I beheld beings (in all their diversity).

Then I responded to Brahmā Sahampati:

'Opened, O Brahmā, are the doors of the deathless for those who have ears. Let them show conviction. (Fore)seeing frustration O Brahmā I have not preached among men the *dhamma*, knowledge-laden and excellent.'

Then, monks, I asked myself: 'To whom shall I first teach *dhamma*? Who will quickly learn (it)?' And it occurred to me: 'Āḷāra the Kālāma is wise, accomplished, and intelligent, and for many a day has been unsullied. Suppose I were first to teach (it) to (him).' Whereupon *devatās* approached me, saying: 'Bhante, Āḷāra the Kālāma died seven days ago.'

(So next) I thought (of Uddaka Rāmaputta). (And again) *devatās* approached me, saying: 'Bhante, Uddaka Rāmaputta died last night.'

(Finally) it occurred to me: 'Of great service to me were a group of five monks who ministered to me when I was earnestly striving.[4] Where are (they) living now?' Then, with the purified divine eye transcending the human, I saw the five monks (to be) living in the deer park at Isipatana, near Bārāṇasī. So, having dwelt at Uruvelā as long as I felt inclined, I set out walking towards Bārāṇasī.

As I was travelling along the high road between Gayā and (the place of) my enlightenment a mendicant (called) Upaka saw me and said: 'Bright are your faculties, friend, clear and clean your complexion. For whom did you go forth? Who is your teacher? Whose *dhamma* do you profess?'

At these words I addressed Upaka the ascetic (thus):

'Overcoming all, I see everything. Unmarked amid the whole range of circumstance, abandoning all, freed through the rooting out of craving, possessing knowledge from myself, whom should I suggest? There is no teacher for me. One like me is not to be found. In the world with its *devas* I have no rival. For I am *arahant*, in the world an unexcelled teacher. I alone am truly enlightened. I am cooled and quenched. I am bound for Kāsi's city to set going the wheel of *dhamma*, beating the drum of the deathless in a blinded world.'

'In terms of what you profess, friend, you deserve conquest without end.'

'They are victors, like me, who have rooted out the distractions. Mine is the mastery of evil states, and thereby am I a conqueror, Upaka.' When I had spoken Upaka the ascetic said: 'May it be so, friend', and, shaking his head, went away by a different road.

Then, monks, travelling on foot, I at length came to Bārāṇasī, to the deer park of Isipatana, and to the group of five monks. (They), seeing me approaching some way off, agreed among themselves saying: 'Friends, it is the ascetic Gotama who comes, who lives in comfort, straying from his exertions and reverting to luxury. Let us not welcome him, nor rise from our place for him, nor accept his bowl and robe. But perhaps a seat may be made ready. If he wishes he may sit down.' However, as I approached (them, they) were unable to keep to their agreement. Some came to meet me and received my bowl and robe. Some made a place ready. Some brought water for washing the feet. Moreover, they addressed me by name and called me friend.

When they had spoken I said to (them): 'Do not address the Exemplar by name and call him "friend". The Exemplar is *arahant*, truly enlightened. Give ear monks, found is the deathless. I instruct. I teach *dhamma*. Proceeding as advised you will soon reach and experience the manifest consummation of the good life for which sons of family rightly go forth from home into homelessness, having realised it from your own gnosis.'

At these words (they) said to me: 'Friend Gotama, you did not come to a superhuman condition, (or) to the knowledge and vision that properly distinguish the *ariyans* through that lifestyle, that procedure, that practice of austerities (that you made use of previously). So how will you now reach (such a state), living in comfort, straying from your exertions, and having reverted to luxury.'

'The Exemplar does not live in comfort, stray from his exertions, or revert to luxury. The Exemplar is *arahant*, truly enlightened.' (And a second and a third time I repeated my exhortation to them. And a second and a third time they replied as before. So I said):

'Monks, are you aware that I have ever spoken like this to you before?'

'No, bhante.'

'The Exemplar is *arahant*, truly enlightened. Give ear monks, found is the deathless. I instruct. I teach *dhamma*. Proceeding as advised you will soon reach and experience the manifest consummation of the good life for which sons of family rightly go forth from home into homelessness, having realised it from your own gnosis.' And I was able to win over that group of five monks.

Monks, I now exhorted two monks (while) three walked for almsfood. What the three obtained, that, we, the band of six, kept going on. (Or) I would exhort three (while) two walked for almsfood. Then the group of five monks, being thus exhorted and instructed by me, won the uncorrupted and matchless haven from bondage, (that is) *nibbāna*.

Monks, there are these five strands of worldly pursuit – (visible) forms, pleasing, welcome, enticing, voluptuous, pleasure-laden, and exciting;

(and sounds, odours, flavours, bodily contacts, and mental phenomena likewise). Those ascetics and brahmans who enjoy these, are greedy and eager for them, not seeing their disadvantage, not wise about the escape from them – this should be understood by them, that they are fallen into misfortune and ruin, that they are at the mercy of the Evil One. One might compare it to a trapped forest deer lying enmeshed, (and say that) it has fallen into misfortune and ruin, and that it is at the mercy of the hunter.

(But) those asectics and brahmans who enjoy these five strands of worldly pursuit without being greedy and eager for them are not fallen into misfortune and ruin, or at the mercy of the Evil One. It is like a deer that roams the forest slopes in confidence, that walks and stands and sits and makes its bed in confidence. Why so? It is out of sight of the hunter. Even so a monk, remote from worldly pursuits, reaches and experiences the first, the second, the third, and the fourth (levels of) absorption. (He) reaches and experiences the realms of infinite space, infinite consciousness, nothingness, neither perceiving nor not perceiving, and the stopping of feeling and perception. Such a monk can be described (as one who) has made Māra blind, and having clouded Māra's eye, has gone untraced by the Evil One, transcending the entanglements of the world. He walks and stands and sits and makes his bed with confidence. Why so? He is out of sight of the Evil One."

Thus spoke the Lord.

1. A gateway adjoining the river Aciravatī.
2. In the light of the following sentence we must assume that it is possession of gold and silver that is referred to rather than their physical durability.
3. On the basis of other discourses the next episode does not follow for a long time – see 36.
4. See 36.

27

Minor Discourse on the Parable of the Elephant's Footprint

175–184

Thus have I heard: once the Lord dwelt near Sāvatthī in the Jeta Grove on Anāthapiṇḍika's campus. Now at that time the brahman Jāṇussoṇi went out from Sāvatthī at an early hour in a completely white carriage with a roof on it. (He) saw the wanderer Pilotika coming some way off (and spoke to him), saying:

"Now where is the good Vacchāyana coming from so early?"

"Friend, I am coming from the presence of the ascetic, Gotama."

"And what do you think, friend Vacchāyana, Is (he) accomplished in wisdom? Do you find him clever?"

"Who am I to judge the accomplishment in wisdom of the ascetic Gotama. Surely only one like him would know (about that)."

"The good Vacchāyana truly commends the ascetic Gotama with lavish praise."

"Who am I to praise (him). Praised by the praised is the worthy Gotama, the best among *devas* and humans."

"But what grounds does friend Vacchāyana see in the ascetic Gotama for being so devoted (to him)?"

"It is like a skilled elephant-hunter, who enters an elephant-forest and sees the great footprint of an elephant, long and broad. He concludes (that) it is a great animal. Likewise, from having seen the four footprints of the ascetic Gotama I have concluded (that) the Lord is truly enlightened, (his) *dhamma* is well-proclaimed, (his) Order is proceeding well. What are the four (footprints)?

Herein I see some clever nobles, subtle, and practised in disputing with others, given to hair-splitting, who go about it seems destroying opinions by their wisdom. These (people) hear (that) the ascetic Gotama would definitely visit such and such a village or town. They prepare a question thinking: 'We will approach the ascetic Gotama and ask him this question. If he answers our question thus we will refute him thus.' (But) the ascetic Gotama instructs, rouses, gladdens, and delights them with *dhamma*-talk, and they do not even ask (him) the question – whence could they refute him? On the contrary they become (his) disciples. When I saw that first footprint of the ascetic Gotama I concluded that the Lord is truly enlightened, (his) *dhamma* is well proclaimed, and (his) Order is proceeding well. (And further, I saw some clever brahmans approach him in the same way and with the same result. Then) I saw that second footprint of the ascetic Gotama.

Or again I saw some clever householders (approach him in the same way and with the same result). They asked the ascetic Gotama for permission to go forth from home into homelessness. (He) brought about their going forth. (When I saw that third footprint of the ascetic Gotama I concluded that the Lord is truly enlightened, his *dhamma* is well proclaimed, and his order is proceeding well).[1]

Or again I saw some clever ascetics (approach him in the same way and with the same result). They speak like this: 'Truly we almost perished, we almost came to ruin. For previously we professed ourselves ascetics, not being ascetics. We professed ourselves brahmans, not being brahmans. Not being *arahants* we professed ourselves *arahants*. Now indeed we are ascetics, now we are brahmans, now we are *arahants*.' When I saw that fourth footprint of the ascetic Gotama I concluded that the Lord is truly enlightened, (his) *dhamma* is well proclaimed, and (his) Order is proceeding well."

At these words Jāṇussoṇi the brahman got out of his carriage, arranged his cloak over one shoulder, and saluted the Lord with joined palms, crying out three times: 'Praise be to the Lord, *arahant*, truly enlightened! Sooner or later maybe we shall meet with the worthy Gotama. Perhaps there will be some conversation.'

Then Jāṇussoṇi the brahman approached the Lord, exchanged greetings, and, having conversed in a friendly and polite way, sat down at one side. (He) related to the Lord the entire conversation he had had with the wanderer Pilotika. When he had spoken the Lord said:

'Beyond a certain point, brahman, the parable of the elephant's footprint is incomplete. Suppose an elephant-hunter enters an elephant-forest and sees the great footprint of an elephant, both long and broad. The skilled elephant-hunter does not simply conclude (that) it is a great bull-elephant. Why so? Well there are in the elephant-forest stunted she-elephants with large footprints, (and he thinks) this might be a footprint of theirs. He follows (the trail) and notices the height of the foraging. (But still he) does not conclude (that) it is a great bull-elephant. Why so? There are tall female elephants with tushes[2] and large footprints, (and he thinks) this might be a footprint of theirs. He follows (the track further), and sees tusk marks high (on the trees). (But still he) does not conclude (that) it is a great bull-elephant. Why so? There are tall female elephants with stumpy tusks,[3] (and he thinks) it might be a footprint of theirs. He follows (the trail further) and sees rending with tusks[4] high up, and the boughs broken off, (and) beholds that bull-elephant at the root of a tree, or in the open, or moving about, or standing, or sitting, or lying down. (Then) he concludes (that) it is a great bull-elephant.

Just so, brahman, an exemplar arises in the world, *arahant*, truly enlightened, complete in knowledge and conduct, adept, seer of worlds, incomparable charioteer of men to be tamed, teacher of *devas* and humans, *buddha* and lord. He makes known this world with its *devas, māras, brahmās,* its ascetics and brahmans, (and) the living universe with its *devas* and humans, having realised gnosis for himself. He teaches, both in the meaning and the expression, a *dhamma* auspicious in its commencement, its progress, and its consummation. He makes known the good life, quite fulfilled and perfect. A householder or householder's son, or someone born into another family hears that *dhamma*. Hearing (it) he acquires faith in the Exemplar. Possessed by that faith he reflects: 'Confined and dusty is the household life, open to the skies the going forth. Suppose I give up hair and beard, don the saffron robe, and go forth from home into homelessness.' (And he does so. And in the course of time he becomes perfected in *ariyan* conduct, and rids himself of the hindrances. He reaches and experiences the first, second, third, and fourth levels of absorption. He recollects previous existences, and is aware of the minds and destinies of other beings. And by finally rooting out the distractions he reaches *nibbāna*.)[5] This, brahman, is called the Exemplar's footprint, the Exemplar's foraging, the Exemplar's rending. At this point the *ariyan* disciple comes to the conclusion: 'The Lord is truly enlightened, (his) *dhamma* is well proclaimed, (his) order is proceeding well.' At this point the parable of the elephant's footprint is complete."

At these words Jāṇussoṇi the brahman (took the refuges and became a lay-follower).

1. This is missing from my Pali text, though clearly called for.
2,3,4. Following Horner. Three different terms are here used for tusks of some kind. "Tushes" refer to vestigial tusks.
5. See 112 for detail.

28

Major Discourse on the Parable of the Elephant's Footprint

184–191

Thus have I heard: once the Lord dwelt near Sāvatthī in the Jeta Grove on Anāthapiṇḍika's campus. There venerable Sāriputta spoke to the monks, saying:

"Friends, just as among all creatures that walk all characteristics of the foot are combined in the foot of an elephant and the elephant's foot is declared to be of greatest size, so whatever states are skilled are incorporated in the four *ariyan* truths, the *ariyan* truth of suffering, of the origin of suffering, of the cessation of suffering, and of the course leading (thereto).

And what is the *ariyan* truth of suffering? Birth, old age, (and) death (are) suffering. Grief and woe, pain, distress, and trouble are suffering. Not getting what one wants is suffering. In short the five embodiments of attachment are suffering.

And what are the five embodiments of attachment? They are as follows: (physical) form, feeling, perception, traits and tendencies, and consciousness. And what is (physical) form? – the four great elements and (physical) form derived (therefrom). And what are the four great elements? – the solid, liquid, thermal and aeriform elements.

And what is the solid element? (It) might be internal[1] or external. And what is internal solidity? Whatever is internally, individually determined as rough or hardened, namely: hair of the head and of the body, nails, teeth, skin, flesh, sinews, bone, marrow, kidneys, heart, liver, pleura, spleen, lungs, intestines, mesentery, stomach, excrement, or whatever else (is describable as solid). That which is internal or external solidity, just that is the solid element. It should be seen as it is with true wisdom (in terms of) 'This is not mine; I am not this; this is not my self.' Seeing it truly thus one turns away from the solid element, one purges the mind of (it).

On occasion, external solidity is disrupted, (and) at that time external solidity dissolves. The impermanence of that so ancient external solidity will be evident. Its propensity for dissolution, decay, and alteration will be evident.[2] But what of this short-lived body gripped by craving? There is nothing here to make one say: 'I', or 'mine', or 'I am.' If others abuse, revile, annoy, or harass a monk he understands (the matter) like this: 'This painful feeling that has arisen for me is due to stimulation of the ear, and is *with* not without a cause. A (sensory) stimulus is the cause.' He recognises (sensory) stimulus as transient, (and likewise) feeling, perception, traits and tendencies, and consciousness. His mind is satisfied, reconciled, composed, and settled on the basic character (of the phenomenon).[3] If others assail him with what is unwanted, unwelcome, and disagreeable, with blows from hands, stones, sticks, or weapons he understands (the matter) like this: 'This body is so constituted that blows (of these various kinds) affect it. But it was said by the Lord in the parable of the saw (that), if marauding robbers were to carve (one) limb-from-limb with a double-handled saw, even as to that he whose mind is corrupted thereby is no follower of (the Lord's) teaching. Vigorous exertion will be aroused in me, unclouded mindfulness established, the body quietened and made undisturbed, the mind composed and focused. Now let (all these things) befall this body as they will, for this teaching of the *buddhas* is being carried out.'

If, for that monk, the Buddha, the *Dhamma*, and the Order (are) remembered thus, but the equanimity that depends on skill is not established, he is stirred, and experiences emotion, thinking (that he has failed to acquire equanimity in this way). Friends, as a daughter-in-law, seeing her father-in-law (for the first time), is stirred and experiences emotion, (so it is with that monk. But if), for that monk, the Buddha, the *Dhamma*, and the Order (are so) remembered, he is uplifted. To that extent much has been done by a monk.

And what is the liquid element? (It) might be internal or external. And what is the internal liquid, element? Whatever is internally, individually liquid or liquified, namely: bile, phlegm, pus, blood, sweat, fat, tears, grease, saliva, mucus, synovic fluid, urine, or whatever else (is describable as liquid). That which is the internal or external liquid element, just that is the liquid element. It should be seen as it is with true wisdom (in terms of): 'This is not mine; I am not this; this is not my self.' Seeing it thus one turns away from the liquid element, one purges the mind of (it).

On occasion, the external liquid element is agitated. It carries away village and town, town and countryside and district. On occasion, the waters in the great ocean recede (many miles). There is a time when (they are deep and when they are shallow). The impermanence of that so ancient liquid element will be evident. Its propensity for dissolution, decay, and alteration will be evident. (And if the monk responds to the liquid element in the same way as to the solid element and achieves equanimity) he is uplifted. To that extent much has been done by a monk.

And what is the thermal element? (It) might be internal or external. And what is internal heat? Whatever is internally, individually, heat or converted to heat, namely that through which one is warmed, hurt,[4] clothed, and through which what is eaten, drunk, consumed, and tasted is properly transformed; or whatever else (is describable as heat). That which is internal or external heat, just that is the thermal element. It should be seen as it is with true wisdom (in terms of): 'This is not mine; I am not this; this is not my self.' Seeing it truly thus one turns away from the solid element, one purges the mind of (it).

On occasion, the thermal element that is external is agitated. It burns village and town, town and countryside and district. It burns out through lack of fuel, having come to the end of a field of crops, or the edge of the highway or of rocks or water, or to a (bare) patch of earth. There is a time when (people) seek (to make) fire with the aid of a cock's wing, or with a piece of gristle. The transience of that so ancient thermal element will be evident. Its propensity for dissolution,, decay, and alteration will be evident. (And if the monk responds to the thermal element in the same way as to the solid element and achieves equanimity) he is uplifted. To that extent much has been done by a monk.

And what is the aeriform element? (It) might be internal or external. And what is the internal aeriform element? Whatever is internally, individually, aeriform or converted to the aeriform, namely: winds going up or down, bowl wind, stomach wind, winds wandering from part to part, breathing in and out, or whatever else (is describable as aeriform). That which is internally or externally aeriform , just that is the aeriform element. It should be seen as it are with true wisdom (in terms of): 'This is not mine; I am not this; this is not my self.' Seeing it truly thus one turns away from the aeriform element, one purges the mind of (it).

On occasion, the external aeriform element is agitated. It carries away village and town, town and countryside and district. There is (on the other hand) a time when, in the last month of summer, (people) seek wind with the aid of a palm-leaf fan, and a fan (for fanning the fire). The transience of that so ancient aeriform element will be evident. Its propensity for dissolution, decay, and alteration will be evident. (And if the monk responds to the aeriform element in the same way as to the solid element and achieves equanimity) he is uplifted. To that extent much has been done by a monk.

Friends, just as a space enclosed by sticks, rushes, grass, and clay is termed a hut, likewise a space surrounded by bone, sinew, flesh, and skin is termed a (living) form. If, internally, the eye is unimpaired, but externally forms do not come within range and there is not appropriate attention,[5] then there is no manifestation of the corresponding aspect of consciousness. If (the first two conditions are positive but not the third, the same is true). If (all three conditions are positive), then there is a manifestation of the appropriate aspect of consciousness. (And the same is true of the other senses and of mental phenomena).

Any form thereby produced is incorporated in the embodiment of attachment that is (physical) form. Any feeling thereby produced is incorporated in the embodiment of attachment that is feeling; any perception in the embodiment of attachment that is perception; any traits and tendencies in the embodiment of attachment that is traits and tendencies; any (arising of) consciousness in the embodiment of attachment that is consciousness. One understands it like this: 'This really is the conjunction, union, and coming together of these five embodiments of attachment. But it has been said by the Lord (that) whoever sees the conditional origin (of phenomena) sees *dhamma*, and whoever sees *dhamma* sees the conditional origin (of phenomena. Conditionally originated are these five, that is the fivefold embodiment of attachment. Whatever, with regard to the fivefold embodiment of attachment is impulse, affection, cleaving – that is the origin of suffering. Whatever, with regard to (them), is the control and abandonment of impulse and passion, that is the cessation of suffering. To that extent much has been done by a monk."

Thus spoke venerable Sāriputta.

1. Note that "internal/external" refers throughout to the contrast between one's own body and what lies outside it so that "internal" should not be taken as strictly referring to the *interior* of the former.
2. The passage that follows is repeated for each element.
3. The implication is that he makes his mind unreceptive to the offensive content by focusing on the raw sound or, possibly, on its physical source.
4. The verb used here may also mean "digested by".
5. Literally something like "consent to sustenance".

29

Major Discourse on the Parable of the Pith

192–197

Thus have I heard: once the Lord dwelt near Rājagaha on Vulture's Peak, not long after Devadatta's[1] defection. There (he) addressed the monks concerning Devadatta, saying:

"Herein monks, some son of family goes forth from home into homelessness out of faith thinking, 'I am beset by birth, old age, and death; by grief, woe, pain, distress, and trouble. Perhaps the ending of this entire body of suffering can be discovered.' Having gone forth like this he acquires gain, honour, and fame, (and is) satisfied (thereby), his purpose fulfilled. Because of (it) he exalts himself and disparages others, thinking: 'I am successful, I am famous, but these other monks are little known and of small significance.' He is exultant and careless because of (this), he exhibits negligence, and being negligent he live ill.

Monks, it is like a man who walks around in need of the pith, wanting the pith, seeking the pith of a great, enduring, and pithy tree. He overlooks the pith, the surrounding wood, the bark, and the young shoots, but cuts off and takes away the branches and foliage, imagining (he has) the pith. A man of vision, seeing him thus, might say: 'Surely this good man does not know the pith, and does not know the branches and foliage.[2] And whatever is to be done by means of the pith, that need will not be met for him.' And so it is with some son of family, who goes forth from home to homelessness (and) is satisfied with gain, honour, and fame, his purpose fulfilled. Such a monk is called one who grasps the branches and foliage of the good life. Just that is his achievement.

But, in this connection, some (other) son of family goes forth from home into homelessness out of faith (with the same thoughts as the first). Having gone forth like this he acquires gain, honour, and fame, (but is) not satisfied (thereby), his purpose being unfulfilled. He does not exalt himself and disparage others. He is not exultant and careless, nor does he exhibit negligence. Not being negligent he achieves success in (right) conduct. Because of (that) he is satisfied, his purpose fulfilled. He exalts himself and disparages others thinking: 'I am observant of (right) conduct and virtuous, but these other monks are (not).' He is exultant and careless because of that achievement in conduct, he exhibits negligence, and being negligent he lives ill.

Monks, it is like a man who walks around in need of the pith of a great, enduring, and pithy tree. He overlooks the pith, the surrounding wood, the bark, but cuts off and takes away the young shoots, imagining (he has) the pith. A man of vision, seeing him thus, might say: 'Surely this good man does not know the pith, and does not know the young shoots. And whatever is to be done by means of the pith, that need will not be met for him.' And so it is with some son of family, who goes forth from home to homelessness and is satisfied with that success as to conduct, his purpose fulfilled. Such a monk is called one who grasps the young shoots of the good life. Just that is his achievement.

But, in this connection, some (other) son of family goes forth from home into homelessness out of faith (with the same thoughts as the first). Having gone forth like this he acquires gain, honour, and fame. He achieves success as regards conduct (and is) satisfied (thereby), but his purpose is not fulfilled. He does not exalt himself and disparage others. He is not exultant and careless, nor does he exhibit negligence. Not being negligent he achieves success as regards concentration. Because of (that) he is satisfied, his purpose fulfilled. He exalts himself and disparages others, thinking, 'I am composed and mentally focused, but these other monks are (not).' He is exultant and careless because of that achievement in concentration, he exhibits negligence, and being negligent he lives ill.

Monks, it is like a man who walks around in need of the pith of a great, enduring, and pithy tree. He overlooks the pith and the surrounding wood, but cuts off and takes away the bark, (thinking he has the pith). A man of vision, seeing him thus, might say: 'Surely this good man does not know the pith, and does not know the bark. And whatever is to be done by means of the pith, that need will not be met for him.' And so it is with some son of family, who goes forth from home to homelessness and is satisfied with that achievement of concentration, his purpose fulfilled. Such a monk is called one who grasps the bark of the good life. Just that is his achievement.

But, in this connection, some (other) son of family goes forth from home into homelessness out of faith (with the same thoughts as the first). Having gone forth like this he acquires gain, honour, and fame. He achieves success as regards conduct and concentration, (and is) satisfied (thereby), but his purpose is not fulfilled. He does not exalt himself and disparage others. He is not exultant and careless, nor does he exhibit negligence. Not being negligent he achieves knowledge and vision. Because of (that) he is satisfied, his purpose fulfilled. He exalts himself and disparages others thinking: 'I live knowing and seeing, but these other monks do (not).' He is exultant and careless because of that achievement of knowledge and vision, he exhibits negligence, and being negligent he lives ill.

Monks, it is like a man who walks around in need of the pith of a great, enduring, and pithy tree. He overlooks the pith, but cuts off and takes away the surrounding wood, (thinking he has the pith). A man of vision, seeing him thus, might say: 'Surely this good man does not know the pith and does not know the surrounding wood. And whatever is to be done by means of the pith that need will not be met for him.' And so it is with some son of family, who goes forth from home to homelessness and is satisfied with that achievement of knowledge and vision. Such a monk is called one who grasps at the surrounding wood of the good life. Just that is his achievement.

But, in this connection, some (other) son of family goes forth from home into homelessness out of faith (with the same thoughts as the first). Having gone forth like this he acquires gain, honour, and fame. He achieves success in conduct, in concentration, and in knowledge and vision, (and is) satisfied (thereby), but his purpose is not fulfilled. He does not exalt himself and disparage others. He is not exultant and careless nor does he exhibit negligence. Not being negligent he achieves freedom from things temporal. But it may be that that monk falls away from that freedom from things temporal.

Monks, it is like a man who walks around in need of the pith and, having cut out and taken just the pith, goes away knowing (that he has done that). A man of vision, seeing him thus, might say: 'Surely this good man does know the pith, the surrounding wood, the bark, the young shoots, and the branches and foliage. And whatever is to be done by means of the pith, that need will be met for him.'

Just so monks, some son of family goes forth out of faith. He acquires gain, honour, and fame. He achieves success as regards conduct, concentration, and knowledge and vision. He achieves freedom with regard to things that are timeless. It cannot be, it is not possible that that monk should fall away from that freedom.

And so monks, the good life is not for the advantage of gain, honour, or fame; not for the advantage of success in conduct or concentration; not for the advantage of knowledge and vision. Whatever is unshakable freedom of mind – that is the purpose, the pith, the consummation of the good life."

Thus spoke the Lord.

1. Gotama's cousin, who is said to have created a schism in the Order. He is not referred to further so that either material is missing or he is included under one of the ensuing categories by implication.
2. The full text runs through the whole list of parts.

30

Minor Discourse on the Parable of the Pith[1]

198–205

Thus have I heard: once the Lord dwelt near Sāvatthī in the Jeta Grove on Anāthapiṇḍika's campus. Then the brahman Piṅgalakoccha approached, exchanged greetings, and having conversed in a friendly and polite way, sat down at one side. Said the brahman:

"Good Gotama, those ascetics and brahmans who are leaders of groups, and with a following, well-known, renowned, founders of sects and much-honoured by the multitude – such as Pūraṇa Kassapa, Makkhali Gosāla, Ajita Kesakambali, Pakudha Kaccāyana, Sañjaya Belaṭṭhiputta, and Nātaputta the Jain – did all these, by their own affirmation, understand fully, (or none of them), or did some understand and others not?"

"Enough brahman – let this be. I will teach you *dhamma*. It is like a man who walks around in need of the pith of a great, enduring, and pithy tree. He overlooks the pith, the surrounding wood, the bark, and the young shoots, but cuts off and takes away the branches and foliage, (thinking he has the pith). A man of vision, seeing him thus, might say: 'Surely this good man does not know the pith, and does not know the branches and foliage. And whatever is to be done by means of the pith, that need will not be met for him.' (Or he cuts off and takes away the young shoots, the bark, or the surrounding wood, and a man of vision might make the same kind of comment.)

Likewise brahman, some person goes forth from home into homelessness out of faith thinking: 'I am beset by birth, old age, death and sickness; by grief, woe, pain, distress, and trouble. Perhaps the ending of this entire body of suffering can be discovered.' Having gone forth like this he acquires gain, honour, and fame (and is) satisfied (thereby), his purpose fulfilled. Because of (it) he exalts himself and disparages others thinking: 'I am successful, I am famous, but these other monks are little known and of small significance.' Because of that gain, honour, and fame he does not arouse the desire, and does not strive for the realisation of those things which lie beyond and are more exalted. (Or he achieves success with regard to conduct, or with regard to concentration, or with regard to knowledge and vision), and does not arouse such desire and strive for (such further) realisation.

And what, brahman, are the things that lie beyond and are more exalted than knowledge and vision? Herein a monk, remote from worldly pursuits and from unskilled states, reaches and experiences the first, the second, the third, and the fourth (levels of) absorption. He reaches and experiences the realms of infinite space, of infinite consciousness, of nothingness, and of neither perceiving nor not-perceiving. Moreover, completely transcending the realm of neither perceiving nor not-perceiving, he reaches and experiences the cessation of perception and feeling, and having seen by means of wisdom, the distractions are extinguished in him. These, brahman, are the the things that lie beyond and are more exalted than knowledge and vision.

It is like a man who walks around in need of the pith and, having cut out and taken just the pith, goes away knowing (that he has done that). And whatever is to be done by means of the pith, that need will be met for him.

And so brahman, the good life is not for the advantage of gain, honour, or fame; not for the advantage of success in conduct or concentration; not for the advantage of knowledge and vision. Whatever is unshakable freedom of mind – that is the purpose, the pith, the consummation of the good life."

At these words, Piṅgalakoccha the brahman said: "Excellent good Gotama, excellent." (And he took the refuges and became a lay-follower.)

1. The detail of the dialogue is largely identical with 29. The parable is repeated twice, once in all its variations at the outset, as given in much abbreviated form here, and then again interleaved with the different levels of attainment in the same way as in the previous discourse.

31

Minor Discourse in Gosiṅga

205–211

Thus have I heard: once the Lord dwelt near Nādikā in the Brick Hall. Now at that time venerable Anuruddha, venerable Nandiya, and venerable Kimbila were living in a grove of the Gosiṅga sāl-wood. Then the Lord, emerging from seclusion towards evening, approached that grove. The keeper of the wood saw (him) coming some way off and said: "Ascetic, do not enter this wood. There are three sons of family dwelling here, seeking (the nature of) self. Do not inconvenience them." (But) venerable Anuruddha heard the keeper of the wood and said: "Do not hinder the Lord, friend. It is our teacher who has come." Then venerable Anuruddha went to (the other monks) and said: "Come, brethren. Our teacher has arrived." So they went to meet (him), one taking his bowl and robe, one making a seat ready, one providing water for his feet. The Lord sat down and washed his feet. Said the Lord:

"I hope all is well with you, that you are bearing up, and do not go short of almsfood."

"Bhante, all is well with us, we are bearing up, and do not go short of almsfood."

"(And) I hope you live in harmony, on friendly terms, without contention, becoming as milk and water, and viewing one another with affection."

"Yes indeed, bhante, we do live (together in that way)."

"And how then do you (succeed in living like this)?"

(Said Anuruddha) "Bhante, it seems to me (that) there is gain and advantage for me in living with such companions in the good life. Because of it I have (the opportunity) to offer (them) friendly deeds, friendly words, friendly thoughts, both in public and private. I proceed under the influence of (their) minds, having surrendered my own. Bhante, we are different in our bodies, but our minds are as one." (And venerable Nandiya and venerable Kimbila spoke in the same terms).

"Good. And I hope that you live diligent, zealous, and resolute."

"Indeed we (do)."

"And how do you live (like that)?"

"Whichever of us returns first from the village almsround prepares seats, and gets drinking and washing water ready, (as well as) a refuse-bowl. Whoever returns later eats any remaining food, should he so desire. If not, he throws it away in a place without (growing) corn, or into water where there are no living things. He puts (everything) away, washes the refuse bowl, and sweeps the eating area.[1] And every fifth night we settle down for a discussion on *dhamma*. This is how we live diligent, zealous, and resolute."

"Good. But have you achieved superhuman states, the true knowledge and vision characteristic of the *ariyans*, a state of ease?"

"How could it be otherwise, bhante. Herein, to the extent that we wish, we reach and experience the first (level of) absorption."

"Good. But, by the surpassing and subsiding of that experience, have you achieved another superhuman state?"

"How could it be otherwise, bhante. Herein, to the extent that we wish, we reach and experience the second, third, and fourth (levels of) absorption. To the extent that we wish we reach and experience the realms of infinite space, of infinite consciousness, of nothingness, and of neither perceiving nor not-perceiving. Completely transcending the realm of neither perceiving nor not-perceiving we, to the extent that we wish, reach and experience the cessation of perception and feeling, and having seen by means of wisdom, the distractions are completely extinguished in us. By the overcoming and subsiding of that experience another superhuman state, a true knowledge and vision characteristic of the *ariyans* is obtained, a state of ease. And we do not perceive another state of ease surpassing or more exalted than that."

"Good, Anuruddhas. There is no other state of ease surpassing or more exalted than that."

Then the Lord, having instructed, aroused, gladdened, and delighted (these three monks) with *dhamma*-talk rose from his seat and departed. Anuruddha (and his two brethren) escorted (him) and, returning thence venerable Nandiya and venerable Kimbila said to venerable Anuruddha:

"Did we tell (you that) we were winners of this or that state of attainment?"

"Not (so). But my mind encompassed and knew the minds of the brethren. And *devatās* also related this thing to me. Thus were the questions put by the Lord answered."

Then Dīgha Parajana, a *yakkha*, came to the Lord, greeted (him), and sat down at one side. Said Dīgha Parajana:

"It is gain for the Vajjis, it is well-gotten and profitable for the Vajji people that the Exemplar, *arahant*, and truly enlightened, is staying (here), and these three sons of family."

"That is so, Dīgha. And should that family from which these three went forth from home into homelessness recollect them with a trusting mind, it will be to their benefit and wellbeing for many a day. See, Dīgha, how (they) are proceeding for the wellbeing and happiness of the multitude, out of compassion for the world, for the profit, the wellbeing and happiness of *devas* and humans."

Thus spoke the Lord.

1. A short and slightly obscure passage intervenes relating how certain mundane tasks were carried out without conversation.

32

Major Discourse in Gosiṅga

212–219

Thus have I heard: once the Lord dwelt in a grove in Gosiṅga sāl-wood, along with many well-known disciples who were elders, with venerable Sāriputta, Moggallāna the Great, Kassapa the Great, Anuruddha, Revata, Ānanda and others.

Whereupon venerable Moggallāna, emerging from seclusion towards evening, approached venerable Kassapa, and said: "Come, friend Kassapa, we will approach venerable Sāriputta to hear *dhamma*." (And they and venerable Anuruddha did so, and venerable Ānanda, seeing them, likewise approached venerable Revata and they also joined the company).

Now venerable Sāriputta saw venerable Revata and Ānanda coming some way off, and said to (the latter):

"Welcome to venerable Ānanda, greetings to the Lord's attendant and companion. Pleasant is Gosiṅga sāl-wood, friend Ānanda, (and) it is a clear night, (with) the sāl-trees in full blossom. Divine indeed are the scents that circulate. By what kind of monk would the Gosiṅga sāl-wood be illuminated?"

"As to that, friend Sāriputta, a monk is one who is well-informed, remembering and retaining what he has heard. Those things that are auspicious at the outset, in their progress, and in their consummation, and that proclaim, in the meaning and the expression, a good life quite fulfilled and purified – he is well-informed about such things, (and they are) kept in mind, given utterance to, augmented, pondered over, and properly penetrated by (right) view. He teaches *dhamma* to the four assemblies, with well-turned and fluent phrases and expressions for the uprooting of bias. By such a monk would the Gosiṅga sāl-wood be illuminated."

When he had spoken, venerable Sāriputta said to venerable Revata:

"Venerable Ānanda has explained (the matter) according to his own understanding. Now we would ask venerable Revata about it."

"Herein, friend Sāriputta, a monk is fond of solitude, devoted to (it), set upon mental tranquillity within. His absorption is not neglected, he is possessed of insight, he is a frequenter of empty places. By such a monk would Gosiṅga sāl-wood be illuminated."

This said, venerable Sāriputta addressed venerable Anuruddha (in the same terms):

"In this regard, friend Sāriputta, a monk surveys a thousand worlds with the purified divine eye transcending the human. Just as a man who had gone to the top of some splendid palace might observe the boundaries of a thousand enclosures. By such a monk Gosiṅga sāl-wood would be illuminated."

(Next) venerable Sāriputta spoke to venerable Kassapa (as to the others):

"In this matter, friend Sāriputta, a monk is a forest-dweller, is given to alms-gathering; is one who robes himself in rags; is one who wears three robes; is of few desires; is happy; is detached; is not gregarious; is of aroused energy; is successful in conduct, in concentration, and in wisdom; (and) has won freedom and the knowledge and vision of freedom. (All these things he both practises himself and commends to others.) By such a monk would Gosiṅga sāl-wood be illuminated."

When he had spoken venerable Sariputta (put his question to) venerable Moggallāna:

"Friend Sāriputta, two monks discuss the higher *dhamma*. They ask each other questions. They reply to each other and do not fail (in their answers). Their talk is of a nature to progress. By such monks would Gosiṅga sāl-wood be illuminated."

Then venerable Moggallāna said to venerable Sāriputta:

"All of us have declared ourselves in the light of our own understanding. Now we will ask venerable Sāriputta (this very same question)."

"Herein, friend Moggallāna, a monk exerts control over the mind, and is not ruled by the mind. Whatever (mental) state he chooses to attain in the morning that is the state he attains in the morning, (and likewise at midday and in the evening). It is as though there were a clothes-chest full of clothes of various colours for a king or a king's minister. Whichever set of clothes he chooses to wear in the morning, just that is the set of clothes that he does wear, (and likewise at midday and in the evening). By such a monk would Gosiṅga sāl-wood be illuminated."

Then venerable Sāriputta said to the (others):

"We have all pronounced according to our own understanding. Come, brethren, we will go to the Lord and relate this matter to (him). As the Lord answers us, so we will remember it."

(So they approached the Lord and related their conversation to him. Said the Lord):[1]

"It is well, Sāriputta. In replying like that Ānanda replies rightly. For Ānanda is one who is well-informed, (and) has learnt and retained what he has heard. Revata is one who is fond of solitude, devoted to solitude, set upon mental tranquillity within. (And similarly the rest of you spoke each in accordance with his own characteristics.)

You all spoke well in your turn, Sariputta. And now hear from me by what kind of monk Gosiṅga sāl-wood would be illuminated, Returning from the almsround after the meal, (he) sits down cross-legged, with body upright, establishing mindfulness before him as his aim, and thinking: 'I will not abandon this cross-legged (position) as long as my mind is not released from the distractions without remainder.' "

Thus spoke the Lord.

1. From here on the full text virtually repeats the foregoing, interleaving Gotama's comments on each monk's reply.

33

Major Discourse on the Cowherd

220–224

Thus have I heard: once the Lord dwelt near Sāvatthī in the Jeta Grove on Anāthapiṇḍika's campus. There (he) addressed the monks, saying:

"Monks, a cowherd possessed of (these) eleven qualities cannot look after a herd of cows, nor make it prosper. Herein (he) is not knowledgeable about (physical) form; he is not skilled in distinguishing features; he does not remove flies' eggs; he does not dress a sore; he makes no fumigation; he does not recognise a fording-place, (or) a watering-place, (or) a track; he is not skilled about grazing; he is one who milks dry; (and) he pays no particular attention to those bulls who are protectors and leaders of the herd.

In the same way a monk possessed of (these) eleven attributes cannot exhibit progress, growth, or full development in this *dhamma* and discipline. Herein a monk is not knowledgeable about (physical) form; he is not skilled in distinguishing features; he does not remove flies' eggs; he does not dress a sore; he makes no fumigation; he does not recognise a fording-place, (or) a watering-place, (or) a track; he is not skilled about grazing; he is one who milks dry; (and) he pays no particular attention to those monks who are elders, of long standing, who are long gone forth, and who are protectors and leaders of the Order.

And how is a monk without knowledge of (physical) form? Herein (he) does not understand as it truly is, that whatever is (physical) form is entirely the four elements and (what) is derived (therefrom).

And how is (he) not skilled in distinguishing features? Herein (he) does not understand as it truly is, (that) a fool and a wise man are characterised by their behaviour.

And how does (he) fail to remove flies' eggs? In this connection he gives in to thoughts about worldly pursuits that have arisen. He does not abandon, or dispel, or destroy, or consign them to oblivion. (Or he fails to deal similarly with ill-will, cruelty, or other harmful conditions).

And how does (he) not dress a sore? As to this, having seen a form with the eye, (he) is preoccupied with its attributes, (or) with its detail. Because of living uncontrolled as regards the eye, longing and distress, wretched and unskilled states, may intrude on one who proceeds without restraint, who does not guard the eye, who does not undergo the discipline of the eye, (and who similarly fails to discipline the other senses and mental imagery).

And how does (he) make no fumigation? Herein (he) does not teach *dhamma* to others in detail as he has heard and mastered it.

And how does (he) not recognise a fording-place? Regarding that, when (he) now and then approaches those monks who have heard much, who are custodians (of the tradition), learned in *dhamma*, learned in the summaries, he does not question or interrogate them. The brethren do not disclose the undisclosed to him, they do not declare the undeclared, they do not dispel doubt on various doubtful matters concerning *dhamma*.

And how does (he) not recognise a watering-place? As to this (he) does not acquire an enthusiasm for the goal nor for the *dhamma* when the *dhamma* and discipline proclaimed by the Exemplar are being taught, nor does he gain the joy associated with *dhamma*.

And how does (he) not recognise a track? As to this (he) does not comprehend the *ariyan* eightfold way for what it is.

And how is (he) unskilled about grazing? As to this (he) does not comprehend the four applications of mindfulness for what they are.

And how is (he) one who milks dry? As to this, when householders out of faith bring and offer him the requisites of robes, almsfood, shelter, and medicines for the sick, he does not know moderation in the acceptance (thereof).

And how is (he) one who pays no particular attention to monks who are elders. As to this (he) does not minister to (them) in public and private with activities that are friendly in body, word, and thought.

Monks, a monk possessing these eleven attributes cannot exhibit progress, growth, and full development in this *dhamma* and discipline."

Thus spoke the Lord.

34

Minor Discourse on the Cowherd

225–227

Thus have I heard: once the Lord dwelt among the Vajjis at Ukkācelā on the banks of the river Ganges. There (he) addressed the monks, saying:

"Once upon a time monks (there was) an incompetent cowherd of Magadha. In the last month of the rains during the Autumn, and without examining the near bank (or) the far bank, (he) simply drove (his) cattle across to the north side in Suvidehā, (at a place) without a ford. Whereupon the cattle crowded into a circle in the midst of the torrent and came to grief and trouble there.

Likewise (there are some) ascetics and brahmans who are unskilled about this world or the next, unskilled about what is Māra's realm and what is not, unskilled about what belongs to Death and what does not. For those who think these (people) are to be listened to or believed there will be disadvantage and unhappiness for many a day.

Once upon a time monks (there was) a competent cowherd. Examining the near bank (and) the further bank, he drove (his) cattle across to the north side in Suvidehā (at a place) with a ford. First he made the bulls who are protectors and leaders of the herd go across. They, breasting the Ganges current, came safely to the other side. Then he sent the sturdy bullocks and steers, then the half-grown bullocks and heifers, then the weaker calves. (And) there was a new-born calf that, by just following the bellowing of its mother, (also) came safely to the far side.

In the same way (there are some) ascetics and brahmans who are skilled about this world and the next, skilled about what is Māra's realm and what is not, skilled about what belongs to Death and what does not. For those who think these (people) are to be listened to and believed there will be wellbeing and happiness for many a day.

Monks, as are those bulls who are protectors and leaders of the herd, so are those monks who are *arahants*, their distractions rooted out, fulfilled in their aims, having done what was to be done and put down the burden, reached the goal, finally broken the thongs of (continued) existence, and are truly freed by knowledge. They, breasting the torrent of Māra, have gone safely to the further shore.

As are the sturdy bullocks and steers, so are those monks who, through eliminating the five fetters of the worldly condition, are of spontaneous uprising, achieving *nibbāna* there without return from that world. They too, breasting the torrent of Māra, will go safely to the further shore.

As are the half-grown bullocks and heifers, so are those monks who, through the elimination of the three fetters and the waning of passion, ill-will, and delusion, are ones who will return once to this world and who, having come, will make an end of suffering. They, too, breasting Māra's torrent, will go safely to the further shore.

As are the weaker calves, so are those monks who, through the elimination of the three fetters are enterers of the stream (of *dhamma*), not destined for a place of destruction, assured, and bound for the highest wisdom. They, too, breasting Māra's torrent, will go safely to the further shore. As is that new-born calf, so are those monks who are acting in accordance with *dhamma* and conviction. They, too, breasting Māra's torrent, will go safely to the further shore.

But I, monks, am skilled about this world and the next, skilled about what is Māra's realm and what is not, skilled about what belongs to Death and what does not. For those who think I am to be listened to and believed, there will be wellbeing and happiness for many a day."

Thus spoke the Lord.

35

Minor Discourse with Saccaka

227–237

Thus have I heard: once the Lord dwelt at Vesālī in the Great Grove in the hall of the Gabled House. Now at that time Saccaka, the son of a Jain (of the Aggivessana clan), was living in Vesālī, a controversialist, a skilled debater, and much esteemed by the people. He made this declaration throughout Vesālī:

"I see no ascetic or brahman, no leader of a group with a following, even though he claims to be *arahant* or truly enlightened, who will not shake and tremble and be perturbed on being assailed by me argument by argument, and who will not drip sweat from his armpits. Even a pillar without a mind would shake and tremble, let alone a human being."

Then venerable Assaji, dressing at an early hour and taking bowl and robe, went into Vesālī for almsfood. Saccaka the Jain's son, who was given to wandering and roaming about Vesālī, saw venerable Assaji coming some way off. He approached (him) and, having exchanged greetings and conversed in a friendly and polite way, stood at one side. Said Saccaka:

"How, good Assaji, does the ascetic Gotama train disciples, and how does (his) full instruction proceed from the element(s)?"

"In this way Aggivessana – (physical) form is transient, (likewise) feeling, perception, traits and tendencies, (and) consciousness. (Physical) form is not self, (neither are any of the others). All compounded things are impermanent, all states are devoid of self."

"Good Assaji, those of us who heard that the ascetic Gotama spoke like this were truly disappointed. Maybe we could meet with (him) sooner or later (and hold) some conversation. Perhaps we could dissuade him from that pernicious view."

Now at that time some five hundred Licchavis were assembled in a council hall on some kind of business. Whereupon Saccaka the Jain's son went up to (them) and said:

"Come, worthy Licchavis. This very day there will be some talk between me and the ascetic Gotama. If (he) takes the position against me that a certain well-known disciple, the monk Assaji, has done, (then), just as a strong man, seizing a long-haired ram by its fleece, might pull, drag, and draw it along, just so shall I, argument by argument, (deal with) the ascetic Gotama."

Then some Licchavis said: "How can the ascetic Gotama refute Saccaka the Jain's son?", (and) some said: "How can Saccaka the Jain's son refute the Lord?" Then Saccaka, surrounded by (some) five hundred Licchavis, went to the Great Grove and the hall of the Gabled House.

On that occasion a number of monks were walking about in the open air. Approaching (them) Saccaka the Jain's son said: "Where, friends, is the worthy Gotama staying now? We should like to see (him)."

"Aggivessana, the Lord has gone into the Great Grove and is seated at the root of a tree for the afternoon rest." Then Saccaka (and the) Licchavis entered the Great Grove and approached the Lord. Having greeted (him) and conversed in a friendly and polite way, (Saccaka) sat down at one side. The Licchavis too sat down at one side, some (just) greeting (him), some conversing in a friendly and polite way, some saluting with joined palms, some making known their name and lineage, some in silence. Said Saccaka:

"I would ask the worthy Gotama about a small point if he will give me the opportunity."

"Ask whatever you wish, Aggivessana."

"How does good Gotama train disciples, and how does (his) full instruction proceed from the element(s)?"

"In this way, Aggivessana – (physical) form is transient; (likewise) feeling, perception, traits and tendencies, (and) consciousness. (Physical) form is not self, (neither are any of the others). All compounded things are impermanent, all states are devoid of self."

"A parable occurs to me good Gotama."

"Speak it forth, Aggivessana."

"Good Gotama, as everything (connected with) the growth of seeds and plants shows increase, development, and maturity on account of the earth, and is rooted in the earth, and as all those occupations calling for strength are (also) based on and rooted in the earth – so likewise the self of (physical) form – that is the person. Rooted in (physical) form it produces merit and demerit. The self of feeling – that is the person. Rooted in feeling it produces merit and demerit. The self of perception – that is the person. Rooted in perception it produces merit and demerit. The self of traits and tendencies – that is the person. Rooted in traits and tendencies it produces merit and demerit. The self of consciousness – that is the person. Rooted in consciousness it produces merit and demerit."

"Aggivessana, can it be that you speak like this – (physical) form is my self; feeling is my self; (likewise) perception, traits and tendencies, (and) consciousness."

"Indeed I do speak thus, good Gotama, and so does this great assembly."

"What can this great assembly do for you, Aggivessana! Just make clear your own words. Now I will ask you about this in turn. As you see fit, so you can explain it. What do you think about this? Would an anointed warrior king have the power, in his own realm, to put to death those deserving death, to plunder those deserving to be plundered, to banish those deserving banishment – such kings as Pasenadi of Kosāla (or) Ajātasattu of Magadha."

"(Certainly), good Gotama. Why, even for an assembly or meeting such as that of the Vajjis or Mallas (such powers exist). How much more for (these two kings)."

"Then what do you think about this, Aggivessana? When you say this: '(Physical) form is my self' – do you have control over that (physical) form (so as to be able to say): 'Let my (physical) form be like this' or: 'Let my (physical) form be other than this?''

At these word Saccaka the Jain's son was silent.

(And twice more the Lord asked him that question. And again Saccaka the Jain's son was silent). Then the Lord said to (him):

"Answer now. This is not the moment for silence. Whoever fails to answer a question concerning *dhamma* which has been asked three times by the Exemplar will have his skull split in seven pieces."

Now at that time a *yakkha* bearing a thunderbolt of iron took (it), blazing, flaming, and glowing, and stood in the sky above Saccaka the Jain's son. But only the Lord and Saccaka saw (this). Then Saccaka, terrified, agitated, (and) with his hair standing on end, and seeking shelter, protection, and refuge in the Lord said: "Let good Gotama ask me. I will answer."

"Then what do you think about this, Aggivessana? When you say this: '(Physical) form is my self' – do you have control over that (physical) form (so as to be able to say): 'Let my (physical) form be like this.' or 'Let my (physical) form be other than this?'

"Not so, good Gotama."

"And feeling, perception, traits and tendencies, and consciousness?"

("The same applies, good Gotama")

"And what do you think, Aggivessana – (physical) form, feeling, perception, traits and tendencies, consciousness – (are they) enduring or transient?"

"Transient, good Gotama."

"But is what is transient painful or pleasant?"

"Painful, good Gotama."

"But regarding what is transient, painful, (and) a thing subject to vicissitude, is it suitable that one should see it thus: 'This is mine; I am this; this is my self?' "

"Not so, good Gotama."

"And whoever is soiled by suffering, undergoing suffering, bent on suffering – does he perceive (it) thus: 'This is mine, I am this, this is my self', and could he comprehend his own suffering, or live containing (it)?"

"How could that be, good Gotama?"

"Aggivessana, it is like a man who walks around in need of the pith, wanting the pith, seeking the pith, and who might enter a wood taking a sharp knife. Suppose he sees there the trunk of a great plantain tree, upright, young, and of immense height. He severs it at the root, he cuts the crown, he removes the peripheral foliage, (but in so doing) he does not acquire the softwood, let alone the pith. Similarly you, Aggivessana, on being interrogated, asked for reasons, and debated with by me, are hollow, vain, and found wanting. Yet you spoke like this to the crowd at Vesali: 'I see no ascetic or brahman, no leader of a group with a following, even though he claims to be *arahant* or truly enlightened, who will not shake and tremble and be perturbed on being assailed by me argument by argument, and who will not drip sweat from his armpits.' But it is from your brow that drops of sweat are dripping and, soaking through your outer cloak, are settling on the ground. On my body however there is now no perspiration." And the Lord showed his golden body to that assembly.

At these words Saccaka the Jain's son sat silent and troubled, his shoulders drooping, face lowered, downcast and bewildered. Then Dummukha the son of a Licchavi, observing (this), spoke to the Lord.

"Bhante, it is like a lotus pond[1] close to a village or a town where there might be a crab. Then a number of boys and girls might go (there) and plunge in, taking the crab from the water and putting it on the dry land. And whatever claw the crab directs (at them, they) destroy, break, and smash with a piece of wood or a potsherd. With all its claws (in that state) it is not possible for the crab to go back down into the lotus-pond in the same way as before. Likewise, whatever may be the distortions, the disagreements, the prevarications, of Saccaka the Jain's son, they are all destroyed, broken, and smashed by the Lord, and Saccaka the Jain's son cannot now approach the Lord further with a desire for (such) talk."

Then Saccaka said to Dummukha, the Licchavi: "Wait, Dummukha, wait. I am conferring with the worthy Gotama, not with you. Let be these words of ours, good Gotama, and of various other ascetics and brahmans, idle talk no doubt. Now how far is a disciple a follower of the teaching, a follower of the admonitions, (who has) transcended doubt, banished perplexity, and lives in complete confidence, not reliant on others with regard to the teacher's instruction?"

"Herein a disciple of mine, as regards whatever is (physical) form, be it in the past, the future, or in the present, be it internal or external, gross or subtle, foul or fair, far or near thinks: 'This is not mine; I am not this; this is not my self', seeing all (physical) form as it is with true wisdom. (And he thinks likewise as regards feeling, perception, traits and tendencies, and consciousness).

And how far is a monk *arahant*, the distractions rooted out, fulfilled, having done what was to be done, unburdened, the goal reached, the thongs of existence wholly destroyed, truly freed by knowledge?

Herein, Aggivessana, a monk, having seen all (physical) form, feeling, perception, traits and tendencies, and consciousness for what they are, and not being ongoing, is freed. Freed in this way a monk is possessed of three matchless things – vision, the Way, and freedom. Freed in this way a monk respects, honours, esteems, and reveres only the Exemplar. (He proclaims): 'The Lord is enlightened and teaches *dhamma* only for enlightenment. (He) is restrained and teaches (it) for restraint. (He) is tranquil and teaches (it) for tranquillity. (He) has gone across and teaches (it) for going across. (He) has attained *nibbāna* and teaches (it) for the attainment of *nibbāna*.' "

When he had spoken, Saccaka the Jain's son said: "Good Gotama, I was arrogant, I was reckless in thinking to assail the esteemed Gotama argument by argument. In assailing a furious elephant, or a blazing fire, or a venomous snake, there might be safety for a man, but not in assailing the esteemed Gotama. May (he) accept (the invitation to) a meal with me on the morrow, along with the Order of monks." The Lord consented in silence.

Then, aware of the Lord's consent, Saccaka the Jain's son addressed the Licchavis, saying: "Hear me good Licchavis. The ascetic Gotama is invited to a meal with me on the morrow, along with the Order of monks. Bring me whatever you think is suitable." Then the Licchavis, towards dawn, brought five hundred cooked dishes as gifts of food. And Saccaka the Jain's son, having got ready abundant food, both hard and soft, in his own park, made known the time (of the meal) to the Lord. The Lord, dressing at an early hour, took bowl and robe and went (there), sitting in the place provided along with the Order of monks. Then Saccaka, the Jain's son, satisfied and served the Order of monks led by the Buddha with his own hand. When the Lord had eaten and put aside the bowl Saccaka the Jain's son took a low seat, and sat down at one side. Said Saccaka:

"Whatever is favourable and accompanied by merit in (this) gift, may it be for the happiness of the donors."

"Aggivessana, there will be for donors whatever is appropriate for the kind of recipient who, like you, is not without passion, hatred, or delusion. There will be for you whatever is appropriate for a recipient such as I who am (without these faults)."

1. The term apparently means an artificial pond. Horner has "tank".

36

Major Discourse with Saccaka

237–251

Thus have I heard: once the Lord dwelt at Vesālī in the Great Grove in the hall of the Gabled House. Now at that time the Lord, being fully dressed at an early hour, took bowl and robe with the intention of entering Vesālī for almsfood. Then Saccaka, the son of a Jain, who was given to wandering and roaming about, approached the Great Grove and the hall of the Gabled House. Seeing (him) coming whilst some way off, venerable Ānanda said to the Lord:

"Bhante, this Saccaka who comes is a controversialist, a skilled debater, and one much esteemed by the people. He intends dispraise of the Buddha, of the *Dhamma*, and of the Order. Would that the Lord might sit awhile out of compassion." The Lord sat in the place provided.

Whereupon Saccaka the Jain's son came up to the Lord, exchanged greetings and, having conversed in a friendly and polite way, sat down at one side. Said Saccaka:

"Good Gotama, there are some ascetics and brahmans who live intent on the development of the body, not of the mind. They encounter a physical feeling that is painful. From the previously acquired painful physical feeling there can come paralysis of the legs, bursting of the heart, hot blood gushing from the mouth, madness, mental disturbance. Such is (the fate) of one whose mind obeys the body, who proceeds under the control of the body. Why so? It is for want of development of the mind.

However, good Gotama, there are some ascetics and brahmans who live intent on the development of the mind, not of the body. They encounter a physical feeling that is painful. From the previously acquired painful physical feeling there can come paralysis of the legs, bursting of the heart, hot blood gushing from the mouth, madness, mental-disturbance. Such is (the fate) of one whose mind obeys the body, who proceeds under the control of the body. Why so? It is for want of development of the mind. However, good Gotama, there are some ascetics and brahmans who live intent on the development of the mind, not of the body. They encounter a mental feeling that is painful. From the previously acquired painful mental feeling there can come paralysis of the legs (and the other conditions I have referred to). Such is the fate of one whose body obeys the mind, who proceeds under the control of the mind. Why so? It is for want of development of the body.

Concerning (all) this it occurs to me – surely the disciples of the worthy Gotama live intent on the development of the mind, not of the body."

"But what have you heard about the development of the body, Aggivessana?"

"The following – Nanda Vaccha, Kisa Saṅkicca, Makkhali Gosāla – these, good Gotama, are unclothed, careless of convention, licking their hands, unresponsive to greetings, not halting when addressed. They do not accept what is offered, or (specially) provided, or (any) invitation (to a meal). They do not take (food) straight from cooking-pot or pan, nor within the threshold, nor among the faggots, nor among the pestles, nor while two people are eating, nor from a pregnant woman, nor from one giving suck, nor from one co-habiting with a man, nor from gleanings, nor where there is a dog standing, or flies swarming, not fish, not meat. They drink no fermented liquor or spirits. They are one-house men, one piece (of food) men. They keep going on one offering. They eat once a day, or once in two days, or once in seven days. (Or) they live wedded to the practice of taking food at regular fortnightly intervals."

"But do they keep going on so little, Aggivessana?"

"Not so, good Gotama. Sometimes they consume rich solid food, or eat good soft food, or savour fine savoury food, or drink excellent drinks. By such means they build up the strength of the body, they grow, they become fat."

"So, Aggivessana, what these (people) at first abandon, they subsequently pay attention to. In such a way there is both increase and loss for the body. But what have you heard about the development of the mind?"

Saccaka the Jain's son did not succeed in answering the Lord's question (on this point). Then the Lord said to (him):

"What you first described as the development of the body is not the true development of the body according to the *ariyan* discipline. You do not understand the development of the body, so how could you understand the development of the mind. But hear how there is not development of (either) and how there is development of (both).

And how, Aggivessana, is there not development of (either)? Herein a pleasant feeling arises for an uninformed worldling and he, being affected by (it), thirsts for pleasure and exhibits (that) thirst. Should his pleasant feeling dissolve, from (that) dissolution comes a painful feeling. Being affected by (that in turn) he grieves, he wearies, he laments, he beats his breast, he becomes disillusioned. Because of the non-development of the body this pleasant feeling that has arisen (and) taken hold of the mind persists in him. From the non-development of the mind the painful feeling that has arisen (and) taken hold of the mind persists in him. (Anyone like this is said to be) undeveloped in body and undeveloped in mind.

And how is there development of the body and development of the mind? Herein a pleasant feeling arises for an informed disciple of the *ariyans* (and) he, being affected by (it), does not thirst for pleasure nor exhibit (such) thirst. Should his pleasant feeling dissolve, from (that) dissolution comes a painful feeling. Being affected by that (in turn) he does not grieve, or weary, or lament. Because of the development of the body this pleasant feeling that has arisen and taken hold of the mind does not persist in him. From the development of the mind the painful feeling that has arisen (and) taken hold of the mind does not persist in him. (Anyone like this is said to be) developed in body and developed in mind."

"Such is my trust in the good Gotama. For the worthy Gotama is developed (in both respects)."

"Aggivessana, this comment of yours is indeed offensive and challenging. Nonetheless I will answer you. When I, shaven of hair and beard and donning the yellow robe, went forth from home into homelessness, it was not possible that either a pleasant feeling or a painful feeling that arose and took hold of the mind should have persisted in me."

"Oh! Then does the kind of pleasant and painful feeling that takes hold of the mind and persists not arise for the worthy Gotama?"[1]

"Why shouldn't it be so, Aggivessana? Suppose a dry piece of sapless wood is lying on dry ground, far from water.[2] Along comes a man bringing a superior piece of kindle-wood and thinks: "I will produce fire. I will make heat appear." (Would he succeed)?"

"Certainly! Why so? Because the wood is dry and sapless, and lying on dry ground far from water."

"Aggivessana, for those ascetics and brahmans who live withdrawn from the worldly pursuits of the body, and for whom everything relating to worldly pursuits (or their concomitants) is properly abandoned and allayed, then, whether (they) experience feelings that are spasmodic, painful, acute, and harsh (or otherwise, they) are capable of knowledge, vision, and matchless enlightenment.

(Once) I thought: 'Suppose, taking hold of the mind by means of the mind I were to restrain, subdue, and dominate it, with my teeth clenched and tongue pressed against the palate.' Sweat dripped from my armpits (as I did so). Just as a strong man, seizing a weaker man by by the crown of the head or by his shoulders might dominate him, so did I, taking hold of the mind by means of the mind, dominate it. Vigorous exertion was aroused by me, unclouded mindfulness established, yet my body was wracked rather than allayed, being overwhelmed by the pain of the exertion. In such a way did the painful feeling aroused in me persist though without taking hold of my mind.[3]

(Then) it occurred to me: 'Suppose that I were to pursue the breathless (states of) absorption.' So I stopped the passage of the breath to and from the mouth and nose. (When I did so) there was an extraordinary noise of winds escaping through the auditory passages, just like (that) of a smith's bellows. Vigorous exertion was aroused by me, unclouded mindfulness established, yet my body was wracked rather than allayed, being overwhelmed by the pain of the exertion. In such a way did the painful feeling aroused in me persist without taking hold of my mind.

(Next) I thought: 'Suppose I pursue the breathless (states of) absorption (further).' I stopped the passage of the breath to and from the mouth, the nose, and the auditory passages. (When I did this) extraordinary winds disturbed my head, as though a strong man had cleaved (it) with a sharp sword.[4] There were extreme headaches. Strong winds rent my belly. There was great heat in my body. Vigorous exertion was aroused by me, unclouded mindfulness established, yet my body was wracked rather than allayed, being overwhelmed by the pain of the exertion. In such a way did the painful feeling aroused in me persist without taking hold of my mind. Moreover *devatās*, seeing me, thought: 'The ascetic Gotama is dead.' Other(s) thought: 'He is not dead, but he is dying.' Other(s) thought: 'He is neither dead nor dying, he is *arahant*. The life of an *arahant* is just like this.'

(Next) I thought: 'Suppose I were to undertake the cutting off of all nourishment.' Whereupon *devatās* came to me and said: ''Sir, do not (do that). (But) if you (do so) we will take divine essences through the pores of your skin. You will keep going on that.' (However) I spurned those *devatās*.

(Next) I thought: 'Suppose I were to take food in very small amounts, in handfuls, whether it be bean soup, vetch soup, chick-pea soup, or pea soup.' (And I did so). My body became very emaciated. From eating so little all my limbs became like knotted stalks or dead creepers, my buttocks like a bullock's hoof, my protruding backbone like a string of balls, my gaunt ribs as the rotten rafters of a collapsed shed. The pupils of my eyes appeared recessed and sunken in their sockets, like sparkling water in a deep well, and my scalp was shrivelled and shrunk as a bitter white gourd is shrivelled and shrunk by a hot wind, after being cut whilst raw. (When) I thought to touch the skin of my stomach, it was my backbone I took hold of (and vice versa), in so far as (the one) adhered to (the other). (When) I thought to defecate or urinate I fell forward on my face right there. (When), soothing the body, I stroked my limbs with my hand, the body hair fell out, rotten at the roots. Moreover, men seeing me thought (that I was black or some other abnormal colour). To that extent was my clear and pure skin colour spoilt because I ate so little.

It occurred to me: 'Any ascetics and brahmans who, in the past, experienced feelings that were spasmodic, painful, acute, and harsh knew nothing beyond this, (and likewise any who might be in the future or are now alive). Yet by these severe austerities I am not come to superhuman states, to the true knowledge and vision characteristic of the *ariyans*. Is there some other road to enlightenment?'

(Then) I thought: 'I am aware that, (once), whilst my father the Sakyan was ploughing, I was seated in the cool shade of a rose-apple tree, remote from worldly pursuits and from unskilled states. I reached and experienced the first (level of) absorption, linked to thought and investigation, to equanimity, joy, and happiness. Could this be the road to enlightenment?' Following that recollection I was aware: 'This is the road to enlightenment. Am I afraid of happiness, that happiness that is remote from worldly pursuits and from unskilled states? No, I am not (thus) afraid. (But) it is not easy to reach that happiness through a body brought to (such) a wasted (condition). Suppose I were to take substantial nourishment, some boiled rice and junket.' (And I did so). Now at that time five monks were attending me (and they thought): 'The ascetic Gotama will tell us of whatever *dhamma* he finds.' Because I took substantial nourishment these five monks left me in disgust saying: 'The ascetic Gotama is living in comfort and straying from his exertions, having reverted to luxury.'

Then, Aggivessana, having taken substantial nourishment, having gained strength, I reached the first, second, third, and fourth (levels of) absorption. In such a way feelings of happiness were aroused in me and persisted, without taking hold of my mind.

So, with a mind composed, perfectly purified, and clear, unblemished, purged of defilement, malleable, workable, steady, imperturbable I turned (it) towards recollection and knowledge of previous existences, to the passing away and (re-) emergence of (other) beings, to the rooting out and knowledge of the distractions. In such way(s) feeling(s) of happiness (were) aroused in me and persisted, without taking hold of my mind.

I am well aware, Aggivessana, that in teaching *dhamma* to groups of several hundred each one thinks this of me: 'The Exemplar has taught *dhamma* especially for me.' But it should not be understood like that Aggivessana. The Exemplar teaches *dhamma* to others for the sake of (general) instruction. And at the end of that talk I settle, compose, focus, and concentrate the mind inwardly into that first attribute of concentration wherein I continually dwell."

"This is to be believed of the worthy Gotama as *arahant* and truly enlightened. But does the worthy Gotama acknowledge that he has slept during the daytime?"

"I acknowledge that, in the last month of the summer, having come back from the almsround after the meal, I spread out my outer robe (folded) into four, and, mindful and lucid, I fall asleep on my right side."

"Good Gotama, some ascetics and brahmans describe this (state) as living in confusion."

"As far as that goes there is neither confusion nor absence of confusion. But with regard to confusion and non-confusion hear this:

I say he is confused in whom those distractions that corrupt, that make for renewal of existence, that are fearful and end in suffering, and that make for birth, old age, and death in the future are not abandoned. Not to abandon the distractions – (that) is confusion. For the Exemplar (they) are left behind, (their) foundation destroyed, (like) a torn up palm-tree, annihilated for the future, and taking no further hold."

When he had spoken Saccaka the Jain's son said to the Lord:

"Excellent, good Gotama, wonderful – in that, while being spoken to so offensively and being subjected to such a challenging form of speech his skin colour remains clear and his countenance happy, like that of an *arahant*, truly enlightened. I know that Pūrana Kassapa, when drawn into argument by me, prevaricated and got off the point, evincing anger, ill-will and lack of confidence. (Likewise) Makkhali Gosāla, Ajita Kesakambaliī, Pakudha Kaccāyana, Sañjaya Belaṭṭhaputta and Nātaputta the Jain.

But alas, now we must be going good Gotama, for we are very busy, and there is much to do."

"Do whatever you think is timely, Aggivessana."

And Saccaka the Jain's son, pleased and satisfied at what the Lord had said, rose from his seat and went his way.

1. A difficult sentence which Horner translates with a double negative. The answer unfolds very slowly.
2. Three parables are offered. I have omitted the others.
3. The precise translation of this statement and its variants is elusive. "Persists" presumably refers to its continuation in the body.
4. This set of symptoms spreads over successive paragraphs with repetition of the remainder.

37

Minor Discourse on the Destruction of Craving

251–256

Thus have I heard: once the Lord dwelt near Sāvatthī at the Migāramātu Palace on the Eastern Campus. Then Sakka, lord of *devas*, approached the Lord and, greeting (him), stood at one side. Said Sakka:

"In brief, bhante, how far is a monk freed by the destruction of craving, (how far) entirely fulfilled (in his purpose), completely safe from bondage, altogether a follower of the good life, fully consummated, best among *devas* and humans?"

"Herein, lord of *devas*, a monk hears (that) no (psychological or material) conditions warrant adherence. If (he) hears (that) he knows every condition thoroughly, (and) with (such) knowledge he recognises every condition with certainty. Because of (that) whatever feeling he experiences – be it pleasant, painful, or (neither) – he lives observing those feelings in terms of impermanence, dispassion, cessation, and renunciation. (Thereby) he cleaves to nothing whatsoever in the world. Being unattached he is untormented, and being untormented he comes of himself to final *nibbāna* knowing: 'Destroyed is birth, fulfilled the good life, done what was to be done, with no further return to this world.' To that extent, lord of *devas*, is a monk freed by the destruction of craving." Then Sakka, lord of *devas*, pleased and satisfied at what the Lord had said, and saluting (him), disappeared from that place with his right side towards him.

Now at that time venerable Moggallāna the Great was seated not far from the Lord. And it occurred to (him): "Did that *yakkha* find satisfaction in what the Lord said on the basis of understanding or not? Suppose I were to find out." Whereupon venerable Moggallāna, like a strong man who flexes his arm and then stretches it out, vanished from the Migāramātu Palace on the Eastern Campus and appeared among the *devas* of the Thirty-Three. On that occasion, Sakka, lord of *devas*, equipped and provided with five hundred divine musical instruments, was enjoying himself in the One-Lotus pleasure garden. (He) saw venerable Moggallāna coming some way off and, sending away those instruments, approached (him), saying: "Greetings, sir, welcome. It is some time since the esteemed Moggallāna took the opportunity to come here. Be seated." Venerable Moggallāna sat in the place provided (whilst) Sakka, lord of *devas*, took a low seat at one side. Said Moggallāna:

"As to the talk the Lord gave you in brief about freedom through the destruction of craving, it would be good if we could share in (its) hearing."

"We are busy, we have much to do, esteemed Moggallāna, for myself as well as for the Devas of the Thirty-Three. Moreover, it was properly heard, grasped, attended to, and born in mind, and so will not quickly vanish (from memory). Once upon a time *devas* and demons were engaged in battle. In (it) the *devas* conquered and the demons were defeated. Having won that battle, and returning victorious, I created the Vejayanta Palace. There are a hundred towers in Vejayanta Palace, in each tower seven gabled houses, in each gabled house seven nymphs, for each nymph seven handmaidens. You might like to behold the loveliness of the Vejayanta Palace." Venerable Moggallāna consented in silence.

Then Sakka, lord of *devas*, and the great king (of *devas*) Vessavana, putting venerable Moggallāna to the fore, approached the Vejayanta Palace. The handmaidens of Sakka, lord of *devas*, saw venerable Moggallāna coming some way off and, shrinking and shy, went to their own inner rooms. Like a daughter-in-law who shrinks and is shy on seeing her father-in-law (for the first time), so (were those) handmaidens on seeing venerable Moggallāna.

Then Sakka, lord of *devas*, and the great king Vessavana led (him) into the palace and (permitted him) to explore it, saying: "Behold this loveliness of the Vejayanta Palace. This has the splendour of the former meritorious deed of venerable Kosiya,[1] and humans seeing anything so lovely think: 'Indeed it has the splendour of the Devas of the Thirty-Three.' "

Then venerable Moggallāna thought: "This *yakkha* lives too indolently. Suppose I were to stir (him) up." So venerable Moggallāna performed (such) a feat of psychic power with his toe as to make the Vejayanta Palace tremble, shake, and quiver. And the minds of Sakka, lord of *devas*. the great king Vessavana, and the *devas* of the Thirty-Three were filled with awe and wonder and they thought: "Strange and wonderful indeed is the great psychic feat, the great majesty of the worthy ascetic, in causing the divine realm to tremble, shake, and quiver with his toe." Whereupon venerable Moggallāna, seeing Sakka, lord of *devas*, to be shaken and astonished said:

"As to this talk the Lord gave you in brief about freedom through the destruction of craving, it would be good if we could share in its hearing." (And Sakka, lord of *devas*, related his conversation with the Lord just as it had taken place).

Then venerable Moggallāna, pleased and satisfied with what Sakka, lord of *devas*, had said, and like a strong man who flexes his arm and then stretches it out, vanished from among the Devas of the Thirty-Three and appeared in the Migāramātu Palace. And not long after (his) departure the handmaidens of Sakka, lord of *devas*, said to (him):

"Sir, is not this Lord your teacher?"

"Not (so), ladies. This is a companion of mine in the good life."

"It is gain for you, sir, whose companion in the good life is of such great psychic power and majesty. Surely the Lord is your teacher."

Then venerable Moggallāna approached the Lord, saluted (him), and sat down at one side. Said Moggallāna:

"Is the Lord aware that he spoke just now in brief of freedom through the destruction of craving to a certain *yakkha* of great power?"

"I know, Moggallāna, that Sakka, lord of *devas* came to me here (and asked me a question about that." (And the Lord recounted his answer just as Sakka, lord of *devas* had explained it to venerable Moggallāna).

1. Another name of Sakka.

38

Major Discourse on the Destruction of Craving

256–271

Thus have I heard: once the Lord dwelt near Sāvatthī in the Jeta Grove on Anāthapiṇḍika's campus. Now at that time a monk called Sāti, a fisherman's son, had conceived a pernicious view as follows:

"As I understand the Lord's teaching of *dhamma* it is just this consciousness that proceeds onward and transmigrates, not another." Now a number of monks heard (about this and) approached (him. Then they asked whether what they had heard was true. And the monk Sāti agreed that it was). Then those monks, with the hope of dissuading the monk Sāti from that pernicious view, cross-questioned, interrogated, and conversed with him, saying: "Friend, do not talk like this. Do not misrepresent the Lord. Misrepresentation of the Lord is not good (for) he would not speak in such a way. Through various representations, friend Sāti, has the contingent nature of consciousness been referred to by (him, to the effect that) "There is no origin of consciousness other than from (some) condition." ' Yet the monk Sāti, clinging and inclining to that same pernicious view with firmness, expressed (himself as before).

Being unable to dissuade the monk Sāti, those monks approached the Lord. Having greeted (him) they sat down at one side (and told him of their conversation). Then the Lord spoke to a certain monk, saying: "Go, monk, address the monk Sāti in my name, saying the Teacher would speak with (him)." (And the monk did so and venerable Sāti came to the Lord). Said the Lord:

"Is it true that a pernicious view of such a kind has occurred to you?" (Whereupon the monk Sāti agreed that it had).

"What is this consciousness, Sāti?"

"Whatever it is that speaks and feels and experiences somewhere or other the result of auspicious or evil activities."

"To whom indeed do you suppose *dhamma* to have been taught by me thus, you foolish man? Has not the contingent nature of consciousness been described by me through various representations (to the effect that) 'There is no origin of consciousness other than through (some) condition.' Yet through your own incomprehension you misrepresent us, as well as doing much harm to yourself and creating demerit. Foolish man, that will be for your misfortune and suffering for many a day."

Then the Lord addressed the monks, saying:

"Do you too, monks, understand *dhamma* to have been taught by me like this?"

"Not so, bhante."

"Correct, monks. Any (form of) consciousness that arises dependent on (some) condition goes by just that name. (It) arises dependent on the eye and upon (visible) forms, and goes by the name of visual consciousness. (Or it) arises dependent on the ear and sounds, and goes by the name of auditory consciousness, (and so on for the various senses and for mental imagery). Similarly, a fire that burns dependent on some condition goes by just such a name, (for example) as a stick fire, a chip fire, a grass fire, a cowdung fire (and so on). Monks, do you recognise: 'This has come to be.' "

"Yes, bhante."

"Do you recognise the origin of that sustaining (condition)?"

"Yes, bhante."

"Do you recognise that, from the ending of that sustaining condition, what has come to be (as a result) is of a nature to cease?"

"Yes, bhante."

"From perplexity (as to whether) what has come to be might not exist, does uncertainty arise?"

"Yes, bhante."

"From perplexity (as to whether) an origin of that sustaining condition might not be, does uncertainty arise?"

"Yes, bhante."

"From perplexity (as to whether), from the cessation of that sustaining (condition), what has come to be (as a result) might not (also) be of a nature to cease, does uncertainty arise?"

"Yes, bhante."

"Seeing: 'This has come to be' as it is and with true wisdom, is such uncertainty left behind?"

"Yes, bhante."

"Seeing the origin of a sustaining (condition) as it is, and with true wisdom, is such uncertainty left behind?,"

"Yes, bhante."

"Seeing that, from the ending of that sustaining (condition), what has come to be (as a result) is of a nature to cease, is such uncertainty left behind?"

"Yes, bhante."

"Monks, if you adhere to, take pride in, cherish, or foster that view, thus purified and unclouded, could you understand the parable of the raft – *dhamma* taught for crossing over not for holding on to?"

"Not so, bhante."

"Monks, there are these four sustaining (conditions) for the maintenance of generated beings, or for the assistance of those seeking birth – edible food, whether coarse or fine; secondly, (sensory) stimulus; thirdly, mental striving; fourthly, consciousness. And what is the cause, the origin, the bringing forth, the source of these four sustaining conditions. Craving is the cause, the origin, the bringing forth, the source. And (similarly) feeling of craving, (sensory) stimulus of feeling, the six sources (of experience) of (sensory) stimulus, individuality and form of the six sources, consciousness of individuality and form, formative tendencies of consciousness, ignorance of formative tendencies.

With ignorance as pre-condition, the formative tendencies; with formative tendencies as pre-condition, consciousness; with consciousness as pre-condition, individuality and form; with individuality and form as pre-condition, the six sources (of experience); with (those) as precondition, (sensory) stimulus; with (sensory) stimulus as pre-condition, feeling; with feeling as pre-condition, craving; with craving as pre-condition, attachment; with attachment as pre-condition, (continued) existence; with (continued) existence as pre-condition, birth. With birth as pre-condition, decay and death, grief, woe, pain, distress, and trouble are ongoing. Such is the origin of this entire body of suffering.

But from the fading away and destruction without remainder of just this ignorance is the cessation of formative tendencies. From the destruction of formative tendencies is the cessation of consciousness, (then in turn of) individuality and form, the six sources (of experience), (sensory) stimulus, feeling, craving, attachment, (continued) existence, (and) birth. From the cessation of birth decay and death, grief, woe, pain, distress, and trouble are brought to an end. Such is the termination of this entire body of suffering.

Now, monks, knowing and seeing (things) in this way, would you run back to earlier times, wondering: 'Were we (or) were we not in the past; what were we in the past; how were we in the past; having been what, what did we become in the past?' "

"Not so, bhante."

"And would you run forward to times yet to come or now debate inwardly about the present, (asking similar questions)?"

"Not so, bhante."

"And would you talk in this way: 'The Teacher is oppressive, and we speak (only) from respect for (him)?' "

"Not so, bhante."

"And would you talk like this: 'An ascetic and ascetics have said such and such to us, but we do not speak like that?' "

"Not so, bhante."

"And would you propose another teacher?"

"Not so, bhante."

"And would you return to those observances and celebrations of various ascetics and brahmans as the heart (of things)?"

"Not so, bhante."

"Monks, do you speak of just that which you yourselves have known, seen, and found?"

"Yes, bhante."

"It is well, monks. You have been presented by me with this *dhamma* that is visible, timeless, verifiable, ongoing, and to be experienced individually by the wise. What has been said has been said because of this.

Monks, through the conjunction of these three things there is conception. There is union of mother and father, it is the mother's season, and the *gandhabba* is present. Then, for nine or ten months, the mother carries the foetus about in the womb with great anxiety for the heavy burden. Then (she) gives birth with great anxiety. When it is born she nourishes it with her own life-blood. For in the *ariyan* discipline this is life-blood, namely mother's milk. And when that boy has grown and developed his faculties he makes sport with the playthings of small boys – with a toy plough, with a game of sticks, with somersaults, with a toy windmill, or piles of leaves, or a cart, or a bow. Endowed with and possessing the five strands of worldly pursuit, he enjoys himself – with forms visible to the eye, sounds audible to the ear, and odours, tastes, and bodily contacts (similarly).

Seeing a form with the eye, he is drawn to pleasant forms, he reacts against unpleasant forms, (and likewise with experience through other senses). He lives not attending to mindfulness of the body, and with a limited mind. He does not know for what they are that freedom of mind, that freedom through wisdom, whereby those states of his which are evil and unskilled (could) subside without remainder. Having gained satisfaction and dissatisfaction in that way, he approves and welcomes whatever feeling he feels, whether pleasant, unpleasant,[1] or (neither), and persists in his indulgence (of it). (As a result) enjoyment arises. Whatever enjoyment comes about with regard to feeling, that is attachment. With attachment as pre-condition, there is (continued) existence; with (continued) existence as pre-condition, there is birth; with birth as pre-condition, decay and death, grief, woe, pain, distress, and trouble come about. Such is the origin of this entire body of suffering.

Monks, bear in mind this freedom through the destruction of craving, taught by me in brief. But the monk Sāti, the fisherman's son, is enmeshed in the great net, the tangle, of craving."

Thus spoke the Lord.

1. Welcoming what is unpleasant is presumably a reference to masochistic impulses or to the kind of austerities that Gotama had once practised and then discarded.

39

Major Discourse at Assapura

271–280

Thus have I heard: once the Lord dwelt among the Aṅgas (at) a town called Assapura. There (he) addressed the monks, saying:

" 'Ascetic, ascetic' – so the people recognise you and, being asked: 'Who are you?', you agree: 'We are ascetics.' (In the light) of such descriptions and such avowals as these you (might say): 'We have taken upon ourselves, and will proceed by those things that are the activities of ascetics and brahmans. Thus will this description of us become a reality and the avowal a fact. These requisites we use – robe, almsfood, shelter, medicine for the sick – will be of great fruit and merit. And this, our going forth, shall not be barren, but fruitful and efficacious.' In this way, monks, must you train yourselves.

And what are the things that are the activities of ascetics and brahmans? Thinking: 'We will become conscientious and scrupulous.' – thus must you train yourselves. But maybe you think 'We are (like that). It is enough, It is done. We have achieved the goal of the ascetic and there is nothing further to be done.' Just to that extent you might experience satisfaction. I tell you, I exhort you – do not fall away from the goal of the ascetic as long as there is something further to do.

And what is there further to be done? Thinking: 'Our bodily conduct will become pure, manifest, and open; without fault and under restraint. Yet we will not exalt ourselves nor disparage others (on that account).' Thus must you train yourselves. But (again) maybe you think: 'We are (like that). It is enough. It is done.' I tell you, I exhort you – do not fall away from the goal of the ascetic as long as there is something further to do.

And what is there further to be done? Thinking about mode of speech and manner of subsistence (in the same way) – thus must you train yourselves. But (again) maybe you think: 'We are (like that). It is enough. It is done.' I tell you, I exhort you – do not fall away from the goal of the ascetic as long as there is something further to do.

And what is there further to be done? Thinking: 'We will guard the doors of the faculties and, seeing a form with the eye, be infatuated neither with the appearance nor the attributes. For longing and distress, and wretched and unskilled states, may intrude on the eye that is wayward. So we will proceed with restraint. We will guard the eye, undergo the discipline of the eye, (and likewise of the ear, the nose, the tongue, the tactile sense, and mental images).' But (again) maybe you think: 'We are (like that). It is enough. It is done.' I tell you, I exhort you – do not fall away from the goal of the ascetic as long as there is something further to do.

And what is there further to be done? Thinking: 'We will be moderate in eating, reflecting thoroughly. We will not eat for sport, not for indulgence, not for finery, not for ornament, but in the measure needed for the endurance and sustenance of the body, for its protection, and for furtherance of the good life. (We) will make an end of old feeling, and not create new feeling, and there shall be continuance, and blamelessness, and comfort for (us).' Thus must you train yourselves. But (again) maybe you think: 'We are (like that). It is enough. It is done.' I tell you, I exhort you – do not fall away from the goal of the ascetic as long as there is something further to do.

And what is there further to be done? Thinking: 'We will be set on vigilance. In a day of walking about and sitting down we will clear the mind of obstructive things. In the first watch of the night we will (do likewise). In the middle watch we will lie down on the right side with one foot resting on the other, mindful and lucid, attending to the thought of getting up. In the last watch of the night we will arise (and continue as before).' Thus, monks, must you train yourselves. But (again) maybe you think: 'We are (like that). It is enough. It is done.' I tell you, I exhort you – do not fall away from the goal of the ascetic as long as there is something further to do.

And what is there further to be done? Thinking: 'We will be mindful and lucid; in coming and going; in looking forward and looking round; in bending and stretching; in carrying cloak or almsbowl, or robe; in eating, drinking, chewing, tasting; in excreting and urinating; in walking, standing, sitting, sleeping, waking, speaking and remaining silent.' Thus must you train yourselves. But (again) maybe you think: 'We are (like that). It is enough. It is done.' I tell you, I exhort you – do not fall away from the goal of the ascetic as long as there is something further to do.

And what is there further to be done? As to that a monk resorts to some solitary abode in a forest, at the root of a tree, on a rock, in a glen, a mountain cave, a cemetery, a woodland grove, in the open, or on a heap of straw. On returning from the alms-gathering, he sits down cross-legged, body upright, establishing mindfulness before him as his aim. Abandoning longing for the world he lives with mind purged (thereof). Abandoning the taint of ill-will he lives without malevolence, and with friendship and mercy to all living things. Abandoning sloth and torpor he lives emptied (thereof), perceiving light, mindful and lucid. Abandoning agitation and worry he lives inwardly calm and composed. Abandoning perplexity he lives beyond doubt, untroubled as to skilful things.

Monks, it is like a man who has incurred a debt and who engages in business. (He) might prosper (therefrom, and then) repay those old debts. And there might be a surplus for maintenance of his wife. For that reason he becomes joyful, he obtains happiness.[1]

Abandoning these five hindrances which blemish the mind and are injurious to wisdom, removed from worldly pursuits and unskilled states, he reaches and experiences the first, the second, the third, and the fourth (levels of) absorption.

With a mind thus composed he recalls a variety of previous existences in all their characteristics and detail. One might liken it to a man who goes from his own village to another village, (thence to a third), and then back to his own, (and remembers how) he stood, sat, spoke and remained silent, and went from (place to place).

And he beholds beings passing away and re-arising with the purified divine eye transcending the human. It is as though there were two houses with doors, and a man standing in between were to see people entering, leaving, walking, and wandering about.

And he turns his mind to the rooting out of the distractions. It is like a lake near the top of a mountain, clear, limpid, and calm – and a man standing on the bank there sees oysters and shells, gravel and pebbles, and shoals of fish, swimming about or motionless.

This is a monk who is called an ascetic. And how is a monk an ascetic? In him are pacified (those) wretched and unskilled states, of a nature to corrupt, renewing existence, unhappy, resulting in suffering, that relate to future birth, ageing, and death. In such a way a monk is *arahant*."

Thus spoke the Lord.

1. There are four other similes.

40

Minor Discourse at Assapura

281–284

Thus have I heard: once the Lord dwelt among the Aṅgas (at) a town called Assapura. There (he) addressed the monks, saying:

" 'Ascetic, ascetic' – so the people recognise you and, being asked: 'Who are you?', you agree: 'We are ascetics.' (In the light) of such descriptions and such avowals as these you (might say): 'Whatever is the right course for an ascetic, that is the course we will proceed by. Thus will this description of us become a reality and the avowal a fact.

These requisites we use – robe, almsfood, shelter, medicine for the sick – will be of great fruit and merit. And this, our going forth, shall not be barren, but fruitful and efficacious.' In this way, monks, must you train yourselves.

And how does a monk not follow the right course for an ascetic? I declare that the right course for an ascetic is not followed by any monk who is covetous, malevolently disposed, wrathful, hypocritical, spiteful, jealous, selfish, treacherous, deceitful, of evil desires, (or) of mistaken views, (and in whom) are not abandoned these blemishes, faults, (and) vices of an ascetic (conducive to) the sorrowful states to be experienced in an evil destiny. I say that the going forth of that monk is to be likened to a weapon, double-edged and whetted sharp, that is covered up and enveloped by a cloak.

Monks, I do not say that the ascetic's vocation for one who wears a cloak is measured by (its) wearing; (nor) for one unclothed by (being so); (nor likewise) for one living in dust and dirt; (or) given to ceremonial bathing; (or) living at the root of a tree (or) in the open; (or) standing upright; (or) feeding at intervals; (or) who meditates on mantras, (or) has matted hair.

(If any corrupt state could be brought to an end by the wearing of a robe) friends, associates, and relatives would make (a man) wear an outer robe from birth. But since I see in this place[1] some wearers of a cloak (who are possessed of these various faults), I do not say (this. Nor for the same reasons do I say that about living unclothed, living in dust and dirt, ceremonial bathing, and those other practices).

And how does a monk follow the right course for an ascetic? I declare that the right course for an ascetic is followed by any monk who, being covetous, rids himself (of that condition), being malevolently disposed, throws off (that state, and deals similarly with wrath, hypocrisy, spite, jealousy, selfishness, treachery, deceit, evil desires, and mistaken views, and in whom) are abandoned these blemishes, faults, (and) vices of an ascetic (conducive to) the sorrowful state experienced in an evil destiny. He perceives (him)self purified of all these wretched and unskilled states. He perceives (him)self freed (and thereby) delight is born. Joy is born of delight. The joyful heart quietens the body. The quietened body experiences happiness. Being happy the mind is concentrated.

He lives spreading thoughts joined to goodwill in (all) directions. He lives spreading (them) everywhere, in every way, to the entire world, abundantly, boundlessly, unrestrictedly, peaceably, benevolently. He lives spreading thoughts joined to compassion, thoughts joined to gladness, thoughts joined to equanimity (in the same way). One might liken it to a lotus-pond, with water that is limpid and sweet, cool and clear, that has pleasant banks and is delightful, and close to a dense jungle thicket. Suppose a man should come, (whether) from east, west, north, south, or wherever, exhausted and overcome by summer's heat, weary, thirsty, and parched. Then, having come to that lotus-pond, he could quench his thirst, could end his summer's fever. Just so, monks, if the son of a nobleman, a brahman, a merchant, a worker, or whatever (kind of) person goes forth from home into homelessness and comes to the *dhamma* and discipline made known by the Exemplar. Having thus developed goodwill, compassion, gladness, and equanimity, he gains inner tranquillity. It is by (that) I declare that the right course for an ascetic is followed. And if one has gone forth from home into homelessness (from whatever kind of family) and, from the rooting out of the distractions, reaches and experiences the mental freedom and the freedom of wisdom, having realised them from one's own gnosis in this life – then one is an ascetic."

Thus spoke the Lord.

1. This may be partially a reference to the audience, but most of the lifestyles, e.g. nakedness, are not those of a Buddhist monk. "In this place" probably refers to the neighbourhood.

41

To the People of Sālā

285–290

Thus have I heard: once the Lord, whilst travelling on foot among the Kosalans together with a large company of monks, came to a brahman village called Sālā. Now the brahman householders of Sālā heard (that) the ascetic Gotama, a son of the Sakyans gone forth from the Sakya clan, (was among them, and that he was of high renown).

Then the brahman householders of Sālā approached the Lord. Some greeted him and sat down at one side, some (after) exchanging courtesies and conversing in a friendly and polite way, some saluting with joined palms, some having announced their names and lineage, some in silence.

(Then they) spoke thus to the Lord:

"What is the reason, good Gotama, what the condition, whereby some beings at the breaking up of the body on death come to sorrow, to an evil destiny, to ruin, to purgatory, (whilst others) come to a good destiny, a heaven world?"

"Householders, the reason (for this) is the errant way that does not go by *dhamma*, (and) the steadfast way that does go by *dhamma*."

"We do not understand the complete meaning of what the good Gotama has spoken of in brief. Would that (he) might teach us." Said the Lord:

"Householders, the errant way that does not go by *dhamma* is threefold in terms of the body, fourfold in terms of speech, threefold in terms of the mind. And how (is this so) as to body? Herein someone is a taker of life, cruel, with blood on his hands, set on injuring and overcoming, bereft of kindness towards living things. He is a thief (and), whether gone to a village or to the forest, takes by stealth what is not given him. He is a libertine, (and) has intercourse with (girls) who are under the protection of mother or father or brother or sister (or other) relatives, who have husbands, whose use involves punishments, or even who are garlanded (for betrothal). Householders, this is the threefold errant way that does not go by *dhamma* with regard to the body.

And how is there a fourfold errant way in terms of speech? Herein someone is a liar. Called upon to testify, whether in an assembly or in a crowd, or amid his relations, or in a guild, or the king's court, (he is told): 'Say what you know, friend.' Not knowing, he replies: 'I know'; knowing, he replies: 'I do not know.' Not having seen, he replies: 'I saw"; having seen, he replies: 'I did not see.' So a deliberate lie is told either on his own account or someone else's, or for some gain. Also he is a slanderer. Hearing (something) in one place he relates it elsewhere to sow dissension. So he is a breaker of harmony and a bringer about of disagreements, delighting in discord, intent on discord, finding enjoyment (therein), with discord as the motive of his speech. He is abusive, and his words are insolent, hard, bitter towards others, cursing others, close to anger, not conducive to concentration. He is a driveller, of untimely speech, at variance with reality, an unprofitable speaker, a talker about what is not *dhamma*, not discipline. He speaks words that are not worth bearing in mind, that being untimely are not to the point, undiscriminating, useless. Householders, such is the fourfold errant way that does not go by *dhamma* with regard to speech.

And how is there a threefold errant way in terms of the mind? Herein someone is envious, thinking: 'Would that that which belongs to others were mine.' He is malevolently disposed, corrupt in thought and character, thinking: 'Let these beings be killed, destroyed, exterminated, made to perish, so as not to have been.' He holds false views and is of perverted outlook, thinking: 'There is neither gift, nor offering, nor sacrifice, nor ripening and result of good deeds and bad; neither this world nor another; neither mother nor father nor spontaneous uprising; no ascetics or brahmans living rightly, proceeding rightly, who make known this world and the next, having realised them through their own gnosis.' Householders, such is the threefold errant way that does not go by *dhamma* with regard to the mind. (And because of all this) some beings, at the breaking up of the body on death, come to sorrow, to an evil destiny, to ruin, to purgatory.

Threefold (however) is the steadfast way that does go by *dhamma* in terms of the body, fourfold in terms of speech, and threefold in terms of the mind. Herein someone (simply desists from all these actions with regard to the body, all these ways of talking with regard to speech, and all these ways of thinking with regard to the mind).

Householders, should one who goes by *dhamma* and who is steadfast desire (to gain companionship with rich nobles or brahmans, or householders or *devas*)[1] on the breaking-up of the body at death – that situation can occur. Why so? – because he is one who goes by *dhamma* and is steadfast.

Should (such a person) wish (for the companionship of *devas* who experience the realm of infinite space, infinite consciousness, nothingness, and of neither perceiving nor not perceiving) – that situation can occur. Why so? – because he is one who goes by *dhamma* and is steadfast.

Should (such a person) wish: 'From the rooting out of the distractions may I reach and experience freedom of mind, the freedom of wisdom that is undistracted, having realised them through my own gnosis in this life' – that situation can occur. Why so? – because he is one who goes by *dhamma* and is steadfast."

When he had spoken, the brahman householders spoke thus to the Lord: "Excellent, good Gotama, excellent." (And the brahman householders of Sālā were well pleased and took the refuges).

1. All the categories are given separate statements and a long list of classes of *deva* is given in the complete text.

42

To the People of Verañjā

290–291

(This discourse is omitted as the content is identical with 41 except for the first three sentences which refer to the venue).

43

Major Discourse on the Miscellany

292–298

Thus have I heard: once the Lord dwelt near Sāvatthī in the Jeta Grove on Anāthapiṇḍika's campus. Then venerable Koṭṭhita the Great, emerging from seclusion towards evening, approached venerable Sāriputta, greeted him, and having conversed in a friendly and polite way, sat down at one side. Said Koṭṭhita:

"Friend, one is called 'poor in wisdom, poor in wisdom'. In what sense is one (so) described?"

"One does not know friend, one does not know. Therefore one is called 'poor in wisdom'. One does not know: 'This is suffering, this the origin of suffering, this the cessation of suffering, this the course leading (thereto).' "

"One is called 'wise', friend, one is called 'wise'. In what sense is one (so) described?"

"One knows friend, one knows. One knows: 'This is suffering, this the origin of suffering, this the cessation of suffering, this the course leading (thereto).' "

"It is called 'consciousness', friend, 'consciousness'. In what sense is it (so) described?"

"One distinguishes, friend, one distinguishes. Therefore it is called 'consciousness'. One distinguishes pleasure, one distinguishes pain, one distinguishes (that which is neither)."

"That which is wisdom and that which is consciousness – are these (two) things associated or dissociated, and is it possible to indicate the diversity between (them) after thorough analysis?"

"(They) are associated, friend, not dissociated. What one knows, that one distinguishes."

"(Then) wherein is the difference of these (two) states that are associated not dissociated?"

"Wisdom should be cultivated, friend, consciousness should be understood."

"It is called 'feeling', friend, 'feeling'. In what sense is it (so) described?"

"One feels, friend, one feels. Therefore it is called 'feeling'. One feels pleasure, one feels pain, one feels (that which is neither)."

"It is called 'perception', friend, 'perception'. In what sense is it (so) described?"

"One perceives, friend, one perceives. Therefore it is called 'perception'. One perceives what is black, yellow, red, or white."

"That which is feeling, that which is perception, that which is consciousness – are these (three) things associated or dissociated, and is it possible to indicate the diversity between them after thorough analysis?"

"(They) are associated, friend, not dissociated, and it is not possible to indicate a diversity between them after thorough analysis. What one feels, that one perceives. What one perceives, that one distinguishes."

"What can be apprehended by purified cognition when the five senses are in abeyance?"

"The realm of infinite space may be (thus) apprehended, (likewise) the realm of infinite consciousness and the realm of nothingness."

"But by what means does one know a state that can be apprehended?"

"One knows it with the eye of wisdom."

"But to what end is wisdom, friend."

"Wisdom is for the sake of gnosis, for the sake of (complete) understanding, for the sake of abandonment."

"How many conditions are there for the arising of right view, friend?"

"Two, friend – the utterance of another (person) and proper attention."

"And how many factors contribute to right view (so that) there is the fruit of mental freedom, and of freedom through wisdom, and the advantages (belonging to these)?"

"Five, friend – herein there is the contribution of conduct, of having heard (*dhamma*), of discussion, of calmness, and of insight."

"And how many (planes of) existence are there?"

"Three, friend – of worldly pursuit, form, and the formless."

"And how is there further existence via future renewal?"

"For beings obstructed by ignorance and fettered by craving there are delights here and there, (and) thus there is (such) renewal."

"And how is there no further existence via future renewal?"

"From the waning of ignorance, the arising of knowledge, and the cessation of craving."

"And what, friend, is the first (level of) absorption?"

"As to that a monk, remote from worldly pursuits and from unskilled states, reaches and experiences the first (level of) absorption, associated with thought and investigation, born of remoteness, joyful and happy."

"And how many factors are there in the first (level of) absorption?"

"Five, friend – herein, for a monk attaining the first (level of) absorption, there is thought and investigation, joy, happiness, and focusing of the mind."

"But how many factors are given up and how many possessed in the first (level of) absorption?"

"Five are given up, five possessed, friend. Worldly pursuits and impulses, ill-will, sloth and torpor, agitation and worry, and uncertainty are abandoned. (Those I have just referred to) are possessed."

"Friend, these five sense-faculties, of diverse ranges and fields, do not encounter one another's fields and ranges, namely the faculty of the eye, the ear, the nose, the tongue, and the body. What is (their) repository and what encounters their fields and ranges?"

"The mind, friend."

"On what do these five faculties depend?"

"On the life-principle."

"On what does the life-principle depend?"

"On heat, friend."

"On what does heat depend?"

"On the life-principle."

"We now understand the words of venerable Sāriputta like this: 'The life-principle depends on heat, heat on the life-principle.' How is their meaning to be viewed?"

"I will construct a parable for you, friend. As in the burning of an oil-lamp the light is perceived because of the flame (and vice versa), just so the life-principle depends on heat, heat on the life-principle."

"Now are these life processes things that may be felt or (otherwise)?"

"These life processes are not things that may be felt. Were they (of such a nature) no emergence would be evident for a monk attained to the cessation of perception and feeling."

"After how many things have left this body does (it) lie like some mindless piece of wood, forsaken and cast aside?"

"After three things have left (it) – the life principle, heat, and consciousness."

"What is the difference between one who is dead and gone, and a monk attained to the cessation of perception and feeling?"

"The bodily processes of the one who is dead and gone have ceased, and (likewise) the verbal and mental processes. Life is extinct, the heat (of the body) is allayed, the faculties dissolved. But the monk attained to the cessation of perception and feeling, whose bodily, verbal, and mental processes have subsided – his life is not extinct, the heat (of the body) is not allayed, his faculties are clear."

"And how many conditions are there for the achievement of mental freedom devoid of both pain and pleasure?"

"Four, friend – herein a monk, from the giving up of happiness and suffering, from the going down of former delight and sorrow, reaches and experiences the fourth (level of) absorption, devoid of pain and happiness, and purified by equanimity and mindfulness."

"And how many conditions are there for the achievement of the mental freedom that is without attribute?"

"Two, friend – paying no attention to any attribute, and paying attention to the element devoid of attribute."

"And how many conditions are there for the endurance of the mental freedom that is without attribute?"

"Three, friend – paying no attention to any attribute, paying attention to the element devoid of attribute, and previous preparation."

"And how many conditions are there for emergence from the mental freedom that is without attribute?"

"Two, friend – paying attention to all attributes and paying no attention to the element devoid of attribute."

"And (as regards) the freedom of mind that is limitless, the freedom of mind that is nothingness, the freedom of mind that is empty, and the freedom of mind that is without attribute – are these things different both in meaning and expression, or one as to meaning and only different as to expression?"

"Friend, there is (one) analysis according to which (they) are different both in meaning and expression, and there is (another) according to which (they) are one as to meaning but different as to expression."

"And what is (the first analysis)? Herein a monk lives spreading thoughts joined to goodwill in (all) directions. He lives spreading (them) everywhere, in every way, to the entire world, abundantly, boundlessly, unrestrictedly, peaceably, benevolently. He lives spreading thoughts joined to compassion, to gladness, to equanimity (in the same way). This is termed 'limitless mental freedom'. Herein a monk, transcending the realm of infinite consciousness, reaches and experiences the realm of nothingness. This is termed 'mental freedom that is nothingness'. Herein a monk is forest-gone, gone to the root of a tree, gone to an empty place, and reflects: 'This is void of self or anything of the nature of self.' This is termed 'mental freedom that is empty'. Herein a monk, paying no attention to any attribute, reaches and experiences a concentration of mind devoid of attribute. This is termed 'mental freedom devoid of attributes'.

And what, friend, is (the second analysis)? Passion is limiting, hatred is limiting, delusion is limiting. As regards freedoms of mind that are limitless, unshakable freedom of mind is declared foremost, and (such) freedom is empty of passion, hatred, and delusion. As regards freedoms of mind that are nothingness, unshakable freedom of mind is declared foremost, and (such) freedom is empty of passion, hatred, and delusion. As regards freedoms of mind that are devoid of attribute, unshakable freedom of mind is declared foremost, and (such) freedom is empty of passion, hatred, and delusion. For a monk in whom the distractions are rooted out these (states) are abandoned, destroyed at source, made like a torn-up palm-tree annihilated for the future and taking no further hold."[1]

This was said by venerable Sāriputta. Venerable Koṭṭhita, uplifted, found satisfaction in what (he) had said.

1. The final passage on the second analysis is rather rambling and incoherent in the full version with the sentence about the palm-tree recurring four times. I have moved this statement to the end where it seems to fit better.

44

Minor Discourse on the Miscellany

299–305

Thus have I heard: once the Lord dwelt near Rājagaha in the Bamboo Grove at the squirrels' feeding ground. Then the lay-follower Visākha approached the nun Dhammadinnā and, saluting her, sat down at one side. Said Visākha:

"Lady, it is called 'own body, own body'. What is 'own body', as spoken of by the Lord?"

"Friend Visākha, these five embodiments of attachment are spoken of as 'own body' by the Lord, namely attachment to (physical) form, feeling, perception, traits and tendencies, and consciousness."

"Lady, it is called 'origin of own body, origin of own body'. What is 'origin of own body', as spoken of by the Lord?"

"Whatever is craving, leading to further renewal, accompanied by pleasure and passion, finding enjoyment here and there, namely desire for worldly pursuits, for existence, or for non-existence – this is 'origin of own body]' as spoken of by the Lord."

"Lady, it is called 'cessation of own body, cessation of own body'. What is 'cessation of own body', as spoken of by the Lord?"

"Friend Visākha, whatever is the fading away and cessation without remainder, the renunciation, giving up, freedom, and doing away with just that craving – that is 'cessation of own body', as spoken of by the Lord."

"Lady, it is called 'the course leading to the cessation of own body'. What is (this) as spoken of by the Lord?"

"Friend Visākha, this *ariyan* eightfold path is (such) a course as spoken of by the Lord."

"So is attachment just these five embodiments of attachment or is there another embodiment of attachment?"

"Attachment is not just these five embodiments of attachment, but neither is there another embodiment of (it). Whatever is impulse and passion with regard to the five embodiments of attachment, just that is the attachment therein."

"And how is there view of 'own body', lady?"

"Herein, friend Visākha, an uninformed worldling, heedless of the *ariyans*, untrained in the *dhamma* of good men, regards (physical) form from the standpoint of self, or self as having (physical) form, or self as in (physical) form; (or he views feeling, perception, traits and tendencies, or consciousness in any of these ways). In that way is there a view regarding 'own body, own feelings,' (and so on)."

"And what is the *ariyan* eightfold path, lady?"

"Right view, aim, speech, action, livelihood, effort, mindfulness, concentration, friend Visākha."

"And is this *ariyan* eightfold path compound or uncompounded?"

"Compound, friend Visākha."

"Lady, is the threefold basis brought within the *ariyan* eightfold path, or (vice versa)?"

"(The latter), friend Visākha. Whatever is right speech, action (and) livelihood is brought under the basis that is conduct. Whatever is right effort, mindfulness (and) concentration is brought under the basis that is concentration. Whatever is right view or aim is brought under the basis that is wisdom."

"But what, lady, is concentration, what (its) attributes, what (its) requisites, what (its) cultivation?"

"Whatever is focusing of the mind, friend Visākha – that is concentration. The four applications of mindfulness are (its) attributes, the four exertions (its) requisites, and whatever is just the pursuit, the development, the making much of these things is the cultivation of concentration."

"And how many (kinds of habitual human) process are there?"

"Three, friend – processes of the body, of speech, and of the mind?"

"And what are (each of these), lady?"

"Breathing in and out is a process of the body, thought and investigation of speech, perception and feeling of the mind."

"And why is (this so)?"

"Breathing in and out – these are things of the body and dependent on the body. After thought and investigation one (may) then erupt into speech. Perception and feeling – these are things of the mind, and dependent on the mind."

"And how, lady, is there the attainment of the cessation of perception and feeling?"

"The monk attaining the cessation of perception and feeling does not think in terms of: '(It is) I (who) will attain, am attaining, or have attained (this state)', for his mind, previously cultivated in such a way, brings him to such (a state)."

"And, for a monk attaining the cessation of perception and feeling, what things disappear first?"

"Processes of speech disappear first, friend Visākha, then of body, then of mind."

"And how, lady, is there emergence from (this) state?"

"The monk emerging from (it) does not think in terms of: '(It is) I (who) will emerge, am emerging, have emerged from (this state)', for his mind, previously cultivated in such a way, brings him to such (a state)."

"And, for a monk (so) emerging, what things arise first?"

"Mental processes arise first, then bodily processes, then (those) of speech."

"And how many contacts impinge on a monk (so) emerging?"

"Three, friend Visākha – the contact that is empty, the contact that is attributeless, the contact that is without any bias."

"What does the mind of a monk (so) emerging incline, tend, and gravitate to?"

"To detachment, friend Visākha."

"How many feelings are there, lady?"

"There are these three feelings – pleasant feeling, painful feeling and neutral[1] feeling."

"And what is (each of these)?"

"Anything of the body or mind that is experienced as pleasant or agreeable – that is pleasant feeling. Anything of body or mind that is experienced as painful – that is painful feeling. Anything experienced as neither is neutral feeling."

"And what is the pleasant, what the painful in pleasant feeling. What is the painful, what the pleasant in painful feeling. What is the pleasant, what the painful, in neutral feeling?"

"In pleasant feeling the pleasant is continuous, the painful intermittent; in painful feeling (the reverse). In neutral feeling the known is pleasant, the unknown painful."

"And what is the proclivity that informs (each kind of feeling)?"

"Passion is the proclivity that informs pleasant feeling, revulsion the proclivity that informs painful feeling, ignorance the proclivity that informs neutral feeling."

"Does a proclivity for passion, revulsion, or ignorance inform every feeling (of the relevant kind)?"

"No, friend Visākha."

"And what should be abandoned in (each kind of feeling)?"

"(Its proclivity), friend Visākha."

"Should (each) proclivity be abandoned in every feeling (of the relevant kind)?"

"No, friend Visākha.[2] Herein a monk, remote from worldly pursuits and from unskilled states, achieves and experiences the first (level of) absorption, associated with thought and investigation, born of remoteness, joyful and happy. Thereby he abandons passion (so that) no (such) proclivity informs that (state of absorption). In this connection (he) reflects: 'When shall I reach and experience that realm which the *ariyans* now reach and experience?' In such a way, and from the establishment of longing for the matchless freedoms, distress arises as a result of that longing. Thereby he abandons revulsion, (so that) no (such) proclivity informs that (state of absorption). Herein a monk, from the giving up of happiness and suffering, from the going down of former delight and sorrow, reaches and experiences the fourth (level of) absorption, devoid of pain and happiness, and purified by equanimity and mindfulness. Thereby he abandons ignorance, (so that) no (such) proclivity informs that (state)."

"What is the counterpart of pleasant feeling, lady?"
"Painful feeling, friend Visākha."
"And of painful feeling?"
"Pleasant feeling, friend Visākha."
"And of neutral feeling?"
"Ignorance, friend Visākha."
"And of ignorance?"
"Knowledge, friend Visākha."
"And of knowledge?"
"Freedom, friend Visākha."
"And of freedom?"
"*Nibbāna*, friend Visākha."
"And of *nibbāna*?"

"That question is beyond the limits (of understanding), friend Visākha. One cannot set bounds to (it). The good life is a plunging into *nibbāna*, has *nibbāna* as consummation and goal. But if you wish friend, approach the Lord and question (him) and, however he explains, bear it in mind."

Whereupon the layfollower Visākha, pleased and satisfied with what the nun Dhammadinnā had said, rose from his seat, and saluting with right side towards (her), approached the Lord. Saluting (him) he sat down at one side (where he related the whole conversation). Said the Lord:

"Clever and of great wisdom is the nun Dhammadinnā. Were you to question me, just thus would I explain, and such is the meaning of it. Remember it so."

Thus spoke the Lord.

1. Literally "not painful, not pleasant".
2. The ensuing passage is very difficult. My interpretation is that, whilst the proclivities that inhere in each type of feeling are generally to be abandoned, the desire to achieve the pleasant feelings associated with the first level of absorption is necessary in order to achieve it. Likewise the dissatisfaction with that state is necessary in order to promote striving for a higher state.

45

Minor Discourse on the Undertaking of *Dhamma*

305–309

Thus have I heard: once the Lord dwelt near Sāvatthī in the Jeta Grove on Anāthapiṇḍika's campus. There (he) addressed the monks, saying: "Monks, there are these four (ways of) undertaking *dhamma*: (with) present happiness but productive of future suffering; (with) present suffering and productive of future suffering; (with) present suffering but productive of future happiness; (and with) present happiness as well as future happiness.

And what is the way of undertaking *dhamma* that is happiness in the present, but productive of future suffering? There are, monks, some ascetics and brahmans who speak and think like this: 'There is no harm in worldly pursuits.' They succumb to worldly pursuits. (They) amuse themselves with female wanderers with their hair tied in topknots and think in this way: 'How can these worthy ascetics and brahmans, perceiving a future danger in worldly pursuits, think of giving (them) up or proclaim the understanding of (them).' Thinking: 'Happiness is in the young, soft, and downy arms of this female wanderer', they succumb to worldly pursuits. (Having done so) they come to an evil destiny, to ruin, to purgatory, at the breaking up of the body on death. They experience there feelings that are painful, acute, and harsh. (Then) it occurs to them: 'These worthy ascetics and brahmans proclaimed (such things) but we, because of worldly pursuits and with worldly pursuits as the cause, are experiencing feelings that are painful, acute, and harsh.'

It is as if, in the last month of the hot season, the seed-pod of a creeper breaks open and a seed falls at the foot of a sāl-tree. Then the *devatā* inhabiting that sāl-tree, fearful and excited, falls atrembling. But friends, associates and relations of the devatā, *devatās* of parks, of forests, of trees; *devatās* inhabiting herbs, grasses, and woods, having assembled and met together reassure (him) like this: 'Be not afraid brother, be not afraid. Perhaps a peacock will devour it, or a deer consume it, or a forest-fire burn it, or those who work in the forest remove it, or termites eat it, or it might not even germinate.' (However, none of these things come about), and the seed does germinate. Rained on by a thunderstorm it grows normally and a young, soft, downy, sinuous tendril of the creeper takes hold of that sāl-tree. Then the *devatā* inhabiting that sāl-tree (asks himself why the others had foreseen a peril) and thinks: 'Pleasant is the touch of this young, soft, downy, and sinuous tendril.' (Then the creeper) embraces that sāl-tree and makes a canopy above (it). Having made a canopy it produces dense undergrowth, and (then) strangles all the great limbs of that sāl-tree. Then it occurs to the *devatā*: 'This (is the reason they foresaw a peril), in that I now experience feelings that are painful, acute, and harsh because of the creeper's seed.' And so it is (with those ascetics and brahmans who proclaim that) there is no harm in worldly pursuits. This, monks, is what is called the undertaking of *dhamma* that is happiness in the present but productive of future suffering.

And what is the undertaking of *dhamma* that is suffering in the present and productive of future suffering? Herein someone is a naked ascetic, careless of convention, and lives mortifying and afflicting the body (in a variety of ways).[1] At the breaking up of the body at death he comes to sorrow, to an evil destiny, to ruin, to purgatory. This, monks, is what is called the undertaking of *dhamma* that is suffering in (both) present and future.

And what is the undertaking of *dhamma* that is suffering in the present but productive of happiness in the future. Herein someone is very passionate, malicious, or stupid by nature, and experiences repeated suffering and distress (because of that). He follows, to the accompaniment of suffering and distress, and tearful and weeping, the good life that is perfect and purified. At the breaking up of the body upon death he comes to a good destiny, a heaven world. This, monks, is what is called the undertaking of *dhamma* that is suffering in the present, but productive of future happiness.

And what is the undertaking of *dhamma* that is happiness in the present and productive of future happiness. Herein someone is not very passionate, malicious, or stupid by nature. He does not repeatedly experience suffering and distress. Remote from worldly pursuits and from unskilled states he reaches and experiences the first, the second, the third, and the fourth (levels of) absorption. At the breaking up of the body upon death he comes to a good destiny, a heaven world. This, monks, is what is called the undertaking of *dhamma* that is happiness in (both) present and future. These are the four ways of undertaking *dhamma*."

Thus spoke the Lord

1. For detail see 12.

46

Major Discourse on the Undertaking of *Dhamma*

309–317

Thus have I heard: once the Lord dwelt near Sāvatthī in the Jeta Grove on Anāthapiṇḍika's campus. There (he) addressed the monks, saying:

"Normally, monks, beings desire, wish, and intend like this: 'Would indeed that unwelcome, unpleasant, disagreeable things might diminish (and that) welcome, pleasant, agreeable things might increase.' (But) for beings (like that the opposite may well occur). Herein an uninformed worldling, heedless of the *ariyans*, untrained in the *dhamma* of good men, does not know what things are to be embraced and what are not, does not know what things are to be followed and what are not – (so) unwelcome, unpleasant, disagreeable things increase for him (whilst positive states) diminish. And why? That is how it is, monks, for one who is foolish in (such matters).

But an *ariyan* disciple, heedful of the *ariyans*, trained in the *dhamma* of good men, does understand (these things correctly, so) unwelcome, unpleasant, disagreeable things diminish for him (whilst positive states) increase. And why? That is how it is, monks, for one who is wise in (such things).

Monks, there are these four (ways of) undertaking *dhamma*: with present suffering and productive of future suffering; with present happiness but productive of future suffering; with present suffering but productive of future happiness; and with present happiness and productive of future happiness.

As to that the undertaking of *dhamma* that is present suffering and productive of future suffering, or that is present happiness but productive of future suffering, (may not be understood by someone for what it is). Unknowing, ignorant, he embraces (that approach), he does not avoid it. (Through so doing) unwelcome, unpleasant, disagreeable things increase for him (whilst positive states) diminish. Why so? That is how it is for one who is foolish in (such matters).

The undertaking of *dhamma* that is present suffering but productive of future happiness, or that is present happiness and productive of future happiness, (may not be seen by someone for what it is). Unknowing, ignorant, he does not embrace (that approach), he avoids it. (Through so doing) unwelcome, unpleasant, disagreeable things increase for him (whilst positive states) diminish. Why so? That is how it is for one who is foolish in (such matters).

(But) the undertaking of *dhamma* that is present suffering and productive of future suffering, (or) that is present happiness but productive of future suffering, (may be seen by someone for what it is). Perceptive, knowledgeable, he does not embrace (that approach), he avoids it. (Through so doing) unwelcome, unpleasant, disagreeable things diminish for him (whilst positive states) increase. Why so? That is how it is for one who is wise in (such matters).

(Likewise) the undertaking of *dhamma* that is present suffering but productive of future happiness, (or), that is present happiness and productive of future happiness, (may be seen by someone for what it is). Perceptive, knowledgeable, he embraces (that approach), he does not avoid it. (Through so doing) unwelcome, unpleasant, disagreeable things diminish for him (whilst positive states) increase. Why so? That is how it is, monks, for one who is wise in (such a matter).

And what, monks, is the undertaking of *dhamma* that is present suffering and productive of future suffering? Herein someone is a destroyer of life, though with suffering and distress, and because of that destruction of life experiences suffering and distress; (or he acts likewise because of theft, dissolute living, lies, slander, abuse, idle prattle, envy, malevolence, or perverse views). At the breaking up of the body on death he comes to sorrow, to an evil destiny, to ruin, to purgatory.

[1]Monks, suppose there to be a bitter white gourd mixed with poison. Along comes a man desiring sustenance, unwilling to die, wanting happiness, averse to suffering, and (people) tell him: 'Good fellow, here is a bitter white gourd mixed with poison. Drink if you wish, but it will please neither in its colour, nor its aroma, nor its taste, and having drunk it you will come to your death, or pain like unto death.' Unreflecting, he drinks, he does not renounce it, (and what they have told him comes about). I say that (such a) way of undertaking *dhamma* is comparable (to this).

And what, monks, is the way of undertaking *dhamma* that is present happiness but productive of future suffering? Herein someone destroys life with pleasure and satisfaction, and because of that destruction of life experiences pleasure and satisfaction; (or likewise because of any of the other aforesaid evil practices. His fate is similar.)

Monks, suppose there to be a bronze goblet, (its contents) perfect in colour, aroma, and taste, but mixed with poison. Along comes a man (of the same kind) and (people) tell him: 'Drink if you wish and it will please you in its colour, aroma, and taste, but having drunk it you will come to your death, or pain like unto death.' Unreflecting, he drinks, he does not renounce it, (and what they have told him comes about). I say that (such a) way of undertaking *dhamma* is comparable (to this).

And what, monks, is the way of undertaking *dhamma* that is present suffering but productive of future happiness? Herein someone desists from destroying life, though with suffering and distress, and because of (that) abstinence experiences suffering and distress; (or likewise because of any of the other aforesaid evil practices). At the breaking up of the body on death he comes to a good destiny, a heaven world.

Monks, suppose cattle urine to be mixed with various medicines. Along comes a man with jaundice, and (people) tell him: 'Good fellow, here is cattle urine mixed with various medicines. Drink if you wish, and it will please neither in its colour, nor its aroma, nor its taste, but having drunk you will be at your ease.' After reflection he drinks, he does not renounce it, (and what they have told him comes about). I say that (such a) way of undertaking *dhamma* is comparable (to this).

And what, monks, is the way of undertaking *dhamma* that is present happiness and productive of future happiness? Herein someone desists from destroying life (or any other form of wrongdoing) with pleasure and satisfaction, and because of (that) abstinence experiences pleasure and satisfaction. (His fate is similar.)

Monks, suppose curds and honey and ghee and molasses were mixed together. Then along comes a man with dysentery and (people) tell him: 'Drink if you wish and it will please in its colour, its aroma, and its taste, and having drunk you will be at ease.' After reflection he drinks, he does not renounce it, (and what they have told him comes about). I say that (such a) way of undertaking *dhamma* is comparable to this.

Monks, as, in the last month of the rainy season, in the clear and cloudless sky of autumn, the sun, rising above the mist and banishing darkness from all the sky, shines forth and is bright and brilliant – like that is the way of undertaking *dhamma* that is present happiness and productive of future happiness and that, banishing the challenge of various other ascetics and brahmans, shines forth and is bright and brilliant.''

Thus spoke the Lord.

1. The ensuing parables are all at the end in the full text. I have re-arranged them under the situations to which they refer.

47

Investigation

317–320

Thus have I heard: once the Lord dwelt near Sāvatthī in the Jeta Grove on Anāthapiṇḍika's campus. There (he) addressed the monks, saying:

"For an enquiring monk learning about the mental traits of another the Exemplar is to be sought in two (kinds of) thing, things knowable through the eye and through the ear. (He asks himself whether) those corrupt states that are knowable through eye and ear exist in the Exemplar or not, (and he finds that they do not). Thereafter he explores further, (asking whether) those mingled states that are knowable through eye and ear exist in the Exemplar or not, (and he finds that they do not). Thereafter he explores further, (asking whether) those unsullied states that are knowable through eye and ear exist in the Exemplar or not, (and he finds that they do).

Then he explores further, (asking whether a certain) monk[1] has attained to (a certain) skilled state for a long or a short time. From such examining he is aware: 'This brother has attained to this state for a long time.' Then he explores further, (asking whether) any dangers exist for the monk who has experienced fame and won renown. Monks, to the extent that a monk has not experienced fame or won renown here there are some dangers that do not exist for him, but after (this has come about) there are (such) dangers. Investigating thus (the enquiring monk) knows (of a certain) monk (that), having experienced fame and won renown, there are some dangers which do not exist for him. Then he explores further, (asking whether a certain) monk restrains (himself) without fear, not with fear, (and whether) it is because he is passionless from the rooting out of passion that he does not resort to worldly pursuits, (and he finds that it is so). If others should ask: 'What are the grounds, what the inferences by which (you) say that?' a monk, answering aright, would reply: 'Whether living in company or alone this brother does not spurn those who proceed well or those who proceed badly, (does not spurn) those who instruct a group, (does not spurn) any who consort with the things of the flesh or any who are unsullied by (them). Moreover, in the Lord's presence I learned (that he is) restrained without fear, not with fear and, passionless from the rooting out of passions, does not resort to worldly pursuits.'[2]

In this connection the Exemplar should be questioned further (as to whether) those corrupt states knowable through eye and ear, (or) those mingled states (likewise) knowable, exist in him, (and the Exemplar will reply that they do not). (And he) should be questioned (as to whether) those unsullied states knowable through eye and ear exist in him, (and he will reply that they do), saying: 'I am that path and that pasture and none is like me in this.' Monks, a disciple is warranted in approaching a teacher who speaks like this so as to hear about *dhamma*. In whatever way the Teacher instructs (him) in a *dhamma* that is supreme, beyond excellence, (and relating to) darkness and light and their conflicting attributes,[3] so he brings to fruition some (part of) *dhamma* through (personal) knowledge here (on earth). He is satisfied with the Teacher, saying: 'The Lord is truly enlightened, (his) *dhamma* well-proclaimed, the Order proceeds well.'

Monks, if others should ask that monk (his grounds for speaking thus), he can reply (by pointing to the personal knowledge he has gained through the Teacher's instruction). For whomsoever faith is established, rooted, and settled in the Exemplar on these grounds, in this way, and with these signs, that faith can be described as reasonable, rooted in vision, steadfast. (It) cannot be demolished by ascetic, or brahman, or *deva*, or *māra*, or *brahmā*, or anyone in the world. Such, monks, is the examination of *dhamma* with respect to the Exemplar, and thus is (he) properly examined."

Thus spoke the Lord.

1. It is not entirely clear whether the same monk is referred to throughout the next section – presumably not.
2. This is knowledge "by ear", i.e. the original gives it in the first person as a statement of the Exemplar about himself.
3. Horner has: "what is dark and what is bright with their counterparts.", taking counterparts as referring to their respective consequences.

48

At Kosambī

320–325

Thus have I heard: once the Lord dwelt at Kosambī on Ghosita's campus. But at that time the monks of Kosambī lived disputing, quarrelsome, and contentious, indulging in mutual recrimination. They neither convinced nor were convinced. They neither made one another well disposed nor were well disposed themselves. Then a certain monk came to the Lord, saluted him, (and told him about their behaviour. Whereupon the Lord told another monk): "Go, monk, address those monks in my name saying (that) the Teacher would speak with (them)." (Then) those monks came to the Lord, saluted him, and sat down at one side. (And he asked them whether what had been reported about them was true. And they admitted that it was).

"Then what do you think about this, monks. (When you treat one another like this), is a kindly action, or word, or thought offered to your companions in the good life, either in public or private."

"Not so, bhante."

"Then knowing and seeing what do you live (in such a manner), you foolish men? This will be for your misfortune and suffering for many a day.

Monks, there are these six courtesies that make for affection and esteem, that lead to amity, harmony, concord, and unity, (namely a kindly deed, word, or thought offered in public or private). And moreover a monk should enjoy sharing any legitimate possessions, properly acquired, though they be only what is encompassed by an alms-bowl, and should enjoy them in common with his worthy companions in the good life. Then again, whatever conduct is unimpaired, faultless, spotless, unblemished, cleansed, not defective, untarnished, conducive to concentration – he should live united in virtues such as these with his companions in the good life, both in public and in private. But further, (he) should live united with (them) in whatever view is *ariyan*, profitable, and leading whoever acts upon it to the complete waning of suffering. These, monks, are the six courtesies that make for affection and esteem, (and) that lead to amity, harmony, concord, and unity. And of these this is the apex, the cement, the support, namely that *ariyan* view.

And how, monks, is this *ariyan* view profitable and leading whoever acts upon it to the complete waning of suffering? Herein a monk who is forest-gone, gone to the root of a tree, gone to an empty place reflects: 'Perhaps I have here some unrenounced inner obsession because of which, my mind being possessed by it, I cannot understand and perceive (things) as they are.' If a monk is possessed by worldly impulses his mind is (so) possessed, (or) by malevolence, (or) by sloth and torpor, (or) by agitation and worry, (or) by uncertainty, or by pursuit of this world in his thoughts, (or) by pursuit of a world beyond in his thoughts, (or) by quarrel, dispute, contention, recrimination. (But when) he knows: 'I do not have an unrenounced inner obsession', that is the first (level of) knowledge attained by him, beyond the ordinary, not shared with the masses.

But further, monks, an *ariyan* disciple reflects like this: 'Perhaps in following, cultivating, and making much of this view I can obtain peace (and) satiety.' (When) he knows (this to be the case), that is the second (level of) knowledge attained by him, *ariyan,* beyond the ordinary, not shared with the masses.

But further, monks, an *ariyan* disciple reflects like this: 'Perhaps there is some other ascetic or brahman beyond this place who has acquired a view such as mine.' (When) he knows (that this is not so), that is the third (level of) knowledge attained by him, *ariyan,* beyond the ordinary, not shared with the masses.

But further, monks, an *ariyan* disciple reflects like this: 'Am I also endowed with that (first) kind of conformity to *dhamma* possessed by a man of right view?' And what is (this)? For any kind of fault that he commits of which the source is evident, he quickly points out, uncovers, and declares (it) to the Teacher or to wise companions in the good life, and (having done so) exhibits restraint subsequently? Just as a tiny, tender, child, lying on his back, on encountering a live ember with his hand or foot quickly withdraws it, (so it is with such a person). (When the *ariyan* disciple knows himself to be so endowed), that is the fourth (level of) knowledge attained by him, *ariyan,* beyond the ordinary, not shared with the masses.

Then again, monks, an *ariyan* disciple reflects in this way: 'Am I also endowed with that (second) kind of conformity to *dhamma* possessed by a man of right view?' And what is (this)? Having shown zeal in whatever are his various duties to his companions in the good life, he is then keen in his aspiration to train (himself) in the higher morality, the higher contemplation, the higher wisdom. Just as a cow with a young calf both crops the grass and attends to the calf, (so it is with such a person). (When the *ariyan* disciple knows himself to be so endowed), that is the fifth (level of) knowledge attained by him, *ariyan,* beyond the ordinary, not shared with the masses.

But further, monks, an *ariyan* disciple reflects: 'Am I also endowed with that (first) kind of strength possessed by a man of right view?' And what is (that)? He listens attentively whilst what is proclaimed by the Exemplar about *dhamma* and discipline is being taught, making it his object, paying attention, concentrating his entire mind. (When) he knows (himself to be so endowed), that is the sixth (level of) knowledge attained by him, *ariyan,* beyond the ordinary, not shared with the masses.

But further, monks, an *ariyan* disciple reflects: 'Am I endowed with that (second) kind of strength possessed by a man of right view?' And what is (that)? Whilst what is proclaimed by the Exemplar about *dhamma* and discipline is being taught he gains the enthusiasm of the goal and of *dhamma*, and the delight associated with *dhamma*. (When) he knows (himself to be so endowed), that is the seventh (level of) knowledge attained by him, *ariyan*, beyond the ordinary, not shared with the masses.

And so, monks, is conformity to *dhamma* well sought by an *ariyan* disciple endowed with seven factors for realising the fruit of entering the stream (of *dhamma*)."

Thus spoke the Lord.

49

A Challenge to Brahmā

326–331

Thus have I heard: once the Lord dwelt near Sāvatthī in the Jeta Grove on Anāthapiṇḍika's campus. There (he) addressed the monks, saying:

"Once, monks, I was staying at Ukkaṭṭhā in the Subhaga Grove at the foot of the great sāl-tree. Now at that time Baka the Brahmā was given over to a pernicious view of this nature: 'This is a stable, continuous, and perpetual (state), this is complete, this is not a transient condition, this is not born, does not age, does not die, does not pass away, does not re-arise and there is no going beyond (it).'

Then, knowing in my mind the reasoning of Baka the Brahmā, I vanished from the foot of the sāl-tree in the Subhaga Grove and, just as a strong man might straighten his bent arm, I appeared in the *brahmā*-world. Baka the Brahmā saw me coming some way off, and said: 'Welcome sir, greetings! At last you have taken the opportunity to come here. This is a stable, continuous, and perpetual (state), this is complete, this is not a transient condition, this is not born, does not age, does not die, does not pass away, does not re-arise and there is no going beyond (it).'

At these words I said to (him): 'Truly given over to ignorance is Baka the Brahmā in as much as he declares (such views).' Then, monks, Māra the Evil One, having come among a certain company of *brahmās* spoke to me thus:

'Monk, monk, do not concern yourself with this, for this *brahmā* is a great *brahmā*, a victor, unmastered, all-seeing, omnipotent, lord, creator, most exalted, disposer, master, father of what is and is to be. Monk, there were ascetics and brahmans before you spurning and contemptuous of things solid, liquid, thermal, and aeriform, spurning and contemptuous of beings, of *devas*, of Pajāpati, of *brahmās*; and these, on the breaking-up of the body, the dissolution of the living being, became established in an inferior group. But there were also ascetics and brahmans before you who were praisers of (all these), rejoicers in (all these); and they, on the breaking up of the body, the dissolution of the living being, became established in an excellent group. Therefore, I say to you, monk – come now, good sir. What Brahmā has said to you, that you should do. Do not overstep the words of Brahmā. If you (do so) it will be like that of a man who wards off the approach of glory with a stick, or of a man falling down the slopes of purgatory who might miss hand and foothold. Monk, do you not see the company of Brahmā seated together?'

(And I replied) to Māra, the Evil One: 'I know you, Evil One, do not imagine (you are not known to me). Māra, you are evil. And whoever, Evil One, is a *brahmā,* or whatever is a *brahmā* assembly or company – all are possessed by you and in your power. But I am not possessed by you or in your power.'

At my words Baka the Brahmā said: 'But I sir say (all these things because they are true). Monk, there were ascetics and brahmans in the world before you who practised austerities for as long as your entire lifespan. They would be aware (that), either there is another existence going beyond (this, or that) there is no existence going beyond (this state). There is not. So I say to you monk that you will not see such a going beyond, however much you exhaust and vex yourself. But if you cleave to solid, to liquid, to heat, to the aeriform, to beings to *devas,* to Pajāpati, to Brahmā – then you will become close to me, resting on my substance, my plaything, guarded (from sin).''[1]

''I too, Brahmā, know (all this). Moreover, I understand your destiny, your splendour, such is the great psychic power of Baka the Brahmā, such the great majesty, such the great fame. But in what manner do I understand (such things)? **As far as moon and sun revolve in splendour, lighting all quarters, so extends the thousand-world system, (and) here your authority runs, but do you then know the far and near of passion and dispassion, the here and there existence, the comings and goings of beings.**

Lo, Brahmā, there are three other groups that you neither know nor see, but that I (do). There is the group called the radiant ones from which, passing away, you arose in this place, but because of your long sojourn here have lost the memory. There is, Brahmā, the group called the lustrous ones and the group called Vehapphalā. So, Brahmā, I am not identical to you in knowledge. I am superior to you. Knowing what is solid as solid, to the extent of knowing that which is not enjoyed through the solidity of what is solid, (I do not think in terms of): 'There is solidity; there is (such and such) with reference to solidity; there is (such and such) arising from solidity; (or) solidity is mine.' I do not proclaim solidity. (Likewise) I do not proclaim liquid, or heat, or the aeriform. I do not proclaim beings, *devas,* Pajāpati, *brahmās,* the radiant ones, the lustrous ones, the Vehapphalas, (or) a Lord (in such terms). Knowing totality as totality, to the extent of knowing that which is not enjoyed through the totality of totality, (I do not think in terms of): 'There is totality; there is (such and such) with reference to totality; there is (such and such) arising from totality; (or) totality is mine.' I do not proclaim totality.[2] Again then, Brahmā, I am not identical to you in knowledge. I am superior to you. If, sir, through the totality of totality, you have not experienced (that), let it not be empty and vain for you. Consciousness that is attributeless and infinite, lucid in every respect – that is not enjoyed through (any of those kinds of experience which I have referred to). And now, sir, I shall become invisible to you, and you shall become invisible to me if you are able.

Then Baka the Brahmā, saying: 'I shall become invisible to the ascetic Gotama', was yet unable (to become so). At these words I said to Baka the Brahmā: 'And now, lo, I will become invisible to you, Brahmā.' Then, monks, I put forth a manifestation of supernormal powers, thinking: 'May

Brahmā, together with (his) assembled company and retinue, hear the sound of me whilst not seeing me.' Having vanished I composed this verse:

'Having seen the disadvantage of coming into being and existence seeking non-existence I did not proclaim existence nor become attached to whatever is pleasing.'

Then, monks, Brahmā and (his) company and retinue, wonder and astonishment having come into their minds, said: 'Wonderful and strange indeed is the great supernormal manifestation, and great the power of the ascetic Gotama. And no other ascetic or brahman as great has been seen or heard by us before as this Gotama, son of the Sakyans, gone forth from the Sakya clan. In a world in love with (its) existence, devoted to (its) existence, delighting in (its) existence, he has truly drawn out the root of existence.' Then, monks, Māra the Evil One, having entered a great company of *brahmās*, spoke to me thus:

'If you know this, if you are thus enlightened, do not offer it to disciples and wanderers, do not teach *dhamma* to (them), do not become ambitious in relation to (them). There were ascetics and brahmans before you in the world claiming to be *arahants* and truly enlightened. They (had such ambitions but), at the breaking up of the body upon death, on the dissolution of the living being, they become established in an inferior group. (But those) claiming to be *arahants* and truly enlightened, (who did not seek disciples or cherish the ambition to teach), became established in an exalted group on the breaking up of the body. So I say this to you, monk – come, live unconcerned, given over to a state of ease in this life. Not to tell is skilful. Do not instruct others.'

At these words I spoke thus to Māra the Evil One: 'I know you, Evil One, do not imagine (you are not known to me). Māra, you are evil. You do not speak to me as one who is friendly and compassionate, (but) as one who is hostile and merciless, thinking (that) those to whom the ascetic Gotama teaches *dhamma* will go beyond (your) reach. But, Evil One, those ascetics and brahmans who claimed (that they were) truly enlightened (were not so). However, I, (who also) claim (it), am indeed truly enlightened. Whether teaching *dhamma* to disciples, or not (so) doing, whether offering (it) among (them) or not, an exemplar is of that nature. Why so? Evil One, those distractions that corrupt, that lead to renewal, that are fearful, productive of suffering, leading to birth, ageing, and death in the future – for the Exemplar they are abandoned, their roots destroyed, like a torn-up palm tree, annihilated for the future, and taking no further hold.' "

And so, through Māra's failure to persuade and the challenge to Brahmā, the name of this exposition is 'a challenge to Brahmā'."

1. Horner has "dwarfed".
2. i.e. presumably meaning that the ultimate condition is not the experience of totality.

50

A Rebuke for Māra

332–338

Thus have I heard: once venerable Moggallāna the Great dwelt among the Bhaggas at Sumsumāragira, in the Bhesakaḷā Grove of the deer park. Now at that time (he) was walking about in the open (and) Māra, the Evil One, entered (his) belly and got into (his) stomach. Then venerable Moggallāna said to himself: "Now why should my belly be heavy as though filled up?" Having descended from the place where he was walking he entered the dwelling-place, sat down on a prepared seat, (and) directed careful attention to himself. (He) saw (what had happened) and said:

"Be gone, Evil One, be gone. Do not annoy the Exemplar or (his) disciple, or there will be misfortune and unhappiness for you for many a day."

Whereupon Māra, the Evil One thought: "The ascetic speaks (like this) without knowing or seeing me. Even his teacher could not know me so quickly." Then venerable Moggallāna said "Yet I do know you, Evil One. Do not think (otherwise). Māra you are evil."

Then Māra the Evil One thought: "Indeed this ascetic spoke thus, knowing and seeing me." So Māra the Evil One, coming out through (his) mouth, stood behind the door. Seeing (him there), venerable, Moggallāna said:

"I see you here too, Evil One. Do not think (otherwise). You it is who stands behind the door. Once upon a time I was the *māra* called Dūsī, and my sister was called Kāḷī. You, as her son, were thus my nephew. Now at that time Kakusandha, lord, *arahant*, truly enlightened, had arisen in the world. Vidhura and Sañjīva were (his) two leading disciples, a noble pair.

Among the Lord's disciples there were none like venerable Vidhura as regards the teaching of *dhamma*. By this instruction of venerable Vidhura the name Vidhura, the 'Peerless'[1] came about. But venerable Sañjīva, forest-gone, gone to the root of a tree, to an empty place, entered upon the cessation of perception and feeling. On one occasion (he) was sitting (there in that state). Ox and cattle herdsmen and tillers of the soil saw (him) and thought: 'Strange, wonderful! – this seated ascetic is surely dead. Well then, we will cremate him.'

Then (they) collected grass, sticks, and cowdung, heaped it up on the body of venerable Sañjīva and, having lit the fire, went their way. And venerable Sañjīva, emerging from that attainment at the end of the night, beat his robes, dressed at an early hour and, taking bowl and robe, went to the village for almsfood. Those (who had made the fire) saw (him) and thought: 'Strange, wonderful – that ascetic who was sitting (there) dead has come back to life.' By this means venerable Sañjīva's name came to be Sañjīva, the 'Resuscitated.'

Then Dūsī the Māra thought: 'I do not really know the comings and goings of these virtuous, well-behaved monks. Suppose I were to visit[2] brahman householders and (urge them to) revile, censure, provoke, and insult the virtuous, well-behaved monks. (Thereby) there might be a change of attitude giving Dūsī the Māra his chance (to test) them.' (And he did so, and the brahman householders acted upon his suggestion), saying: 'These shaven ascetics, menial, black, the foot droppings of a kinsman – (they are) drooping, stooping, stupefied. They meditate, are mournful, thoughtful, (ever) pondering, like an owl in the branch of a tree tracking a mouse.' (In consequence of that abuse) nearly all the people at that time came to sorrow, to an evil destiny, to ruin, to purgatory, on the breaking up of the body upon death.

Whereupon Kakusandha, lord, *arahant*, truly enlightened, addressed the monks, saying: 'Monks, the brahman householders are possessed by Dūsī the Māra, (who incites them to censure you). Come, monks, live spreading thoughts joined to goodwill in (all) directions. Live spreading (them) everywhere, in every way, to the entire world, abundantly, boundlessly, unrestrictedly, peaceably, benevolently. Live spreading thoughts joined to compassion, to gladness, to equanimity (in the same way).' And those monks, thus exhorted and admonished, having gone to the forest, to the roots of trees, to empty places, (applied themselves in just those ways).

Then Dūsī the Māra thought: 'By this means I still do not know the coming and going of these virtuous, well-behaved monks. Suppose I were to visit the brahman householders and (urge them to) honour, esteem, revere, and respect the virtuous, well-behaved monks.'[3] (And he did so, and the brahman householders acted upon his suggestion). (In consequence of this) nearly all the people at that time came to a good destiny, a heaven world, on the breaking up of the body at death.

Whereupon Kakusandha, lord, *arahant*, truly enlightened, addressed the monks, saying: 'Monks, the brahman householders are possessed by Dūsī the Māra. Come, monks, live observing the impurity of the body, perceiving the unpleasantness in food, perceiving no delight in the entire world, and observing the transience of all compounded things.' And those monks, thus exhorted and admonished, and having gone to the forest, to roots of trees, to empty places, (applied themselves in just those ways).

Then Kakusandha, lord, *arahant*, truly enlightened, dressed at an early hour and, taking bowl and robe, went to the village for almsfood with venerable Vidhura in attendance. And Dūsī the Māra, having taken possession of a certain youth, seized a stone, striking and splitting the head of venerable Vidhura (with it). And venerable Vidhura, his head broken and with blood pouring, just followed closely after Lord Kakusandha. Then Lord Kakusandha looked round with the elephant-look[4] and said: 'This Dūsī the Māra knows no limits.'' At his looking-round Dūsī the Māra fell from that place and arose in the great purgatory. And the guardian of purgatory approached me, saying: 'When spike meets spike in your heart then you may know (that) there will be a thousand years in purgatory (for you).[5] ''

1. In both cases, i.e. Vidhura and Sañjīva, the epithets are translations of the names.
2. The Pali term here means either "visit" or "possess", suggesting two slightly different scenarios. In the stone-throwing episode later on, where the same word is used, the idea of possession is clearly the right one.
3. i.e. hoping that the monks will become conceited through the respect shown them.
4. i.e. with the whole of his body.
5. The full text assigns Dūsī to a spell in another purgatory and ends with a long verse passage.

51

To Kandaraka

339–349

Thus I have I heard: once the Lord dwelt at Campā by the shore of the Gaggarā lotus-pond together with a great company of monks. Then Pessa, the mahout's son, and the wanderer Kandaraka approached the Lord. Pessa, saluting (him), sat down at one side, (while) Kandaraka exchanged greetings and conversed in a friendly and polite way before standing at one side. Looking round at the Order of monks, which had grown silent (he) said:

"Strange, good Gotama, wonderful, in as much as the Order of monks is well led by by (him). And did those who in past ages were *arahants*, truly enlightened, also lead such an excellent order of monks, (and will this also be the case in the future)."

"Even so, Kandaraka, even so. Kandaraka, there are monks in this order of monks who are *arahants*, the distractions rooted out, fulfilled, having done what was to be done, laid down the burden, reached the goal, the thongs of existence utterly destroyed, and who are truly freed by knowledge. Moreover, there are monks in this order of monks who are in training, unwavering in conduct and practice, clever, intelligent in their ways. They live with minds well established in the four applications of mindfulness. What four? Herein, Kandaraka, a monk lives observing the body in the body, zealous, lucid, and mindful, that he might put aside the longing and distress in the world. (Likewise) he lives zealous, lucid, and mindful, observing feelings in feelings, the mind in the mind, and phenomena in phenomena."[1]

At these words Pessa the mahout's son said "Strange, bhante, wonderful, in as much as these four applications of mindfulness are well indicated by the Lord for the purification of beings, for the transcending of griefs and sorrows, for the going down of suffering and distress, for the realisation of *nibbāna*. We householders dressed in white also, on occasion, live with minds well established in the four applications of mindfulness. Strange, bhante, wonderful, how, amid the continuing deviousness, viciousness, (and) treachery of men, the Lord knows the good and the ill for beings. Now this is a thicket, namely men, and this is an open clearing, namely animals. For I am able to make an elephant in training remember so that, no matter what the interval between his comings and goings at Campā, he will display all (manner of) tricks, deceits, cunning, and wiles. But those (supposedly) our slaves, or servants, or workpeople – they practise one thing with their body, something else through their speech, and their mind is yet another. (And yet) the Lord, amid the continuing deviousness, viciousness, (and) treachery of men, knows the good and the ill for beings."

"That is so, Pessa, that is so. Pessa, there are these four (types of) person to be found in the world. Herein someone is a tormentor of himself, intent on and devoted to (such practices), but someone (else) is (likewise) a tormentor of others. Herein someone is both a tormentor of himself and a tormentor of others, but someone (else) is neither a tormentor of himself nor a tormentor of others. He, satisfied, cooled, and become tranquil, in this life experiences happiness, and lives with a self become like Brahmā. Of these four (types of) person Pessa, which pleases your mind?"

"He that lives with a self become like Brahmā – that person pleases my mind."

"But why, Pessa, do these (other) three not please your mind?"

"Bhante, he that is a tormentor of himself (nonetheless) torments a self that is desirous of happiness and averse to pain. He that is a tormentor of others (does likewise, as does) he that is both a tormentor of himself and of others. Therefore (these) do not appeal to my mind. But now, bhante, we must go. We are busy and there is much to be done."

"Do whatever you think is timely, Pessa."

Then Pessa, the mahout's son, pleased and satisfied with the Lord's words, rose from his place, saluted, and with right side towards (him) went his way. Not long after (his) departure the Lord addressed the monks, saying:

"Clever, monks, is Pessa the mahout's son, and great in wisdom. If (he) had remained seated briefly whilst I analysed these four (kinds of) person in detail for him, he would have found great advantage. But even as it is Pessa the mahout's son has found great advantage.

And what, monks, is the (kind of) person who is a tormentor of himself, intent on and devoted to (such practices)? Herein someone is unclothed, careless of convention, (given to) mortifying and afflicting the body. This is the (kind of) person who is called a tormentor of himself.

And what, monks, is the (kind of) person who is a tormentor of others, intent on and devoted to (such practices)? Herein someone is a sheep-killer, a pig-killer, a fowler, a deerslayer, a huntsman, a fisherman, a robber, a gaoler, an executioner, or (one of) those others who are of a bloody occupation. This is the (kind of) person who is called a tormentor of others.

And what, monks, is the (kind of) person who is both a tormentor of himself and a tormentor of others? Herein someone is a noble warrior king, or a brahman with great property. Having brought about the erection of a new conference hall in the east of the city he has hair and beard shaved off, dons a rough (antelope) skin, anoints his body with ghee and oil and, scratching his back with a deer-horn, enters the conference hall together with his first consort and chief priest. There he makes his bed on the bare but grass-covered ground. The king sustains himself on the milk in the udder of a cow with a calf of like colour. The first consort sustains herself on the milk from the second udder, the chief priest on the milk from the third udder, and such milk as is in the fourth udder they sacrifice to the fire. The calf lives off the remainder. He talks like this: 'Let so many bulls be slain for the sacrifice, (likewise) so many bullocks, so many heifers, so many goats, so many wethers. Let so many trees be felled, so many bunches of kusa grass reaped for a sacrifice of grass.' Scared of a thrashing and fearful, those termed servants, slaves, and workpeople make the arrangements, tearful and wailing. This is the (kind of) person who is called both a tormentor of himself and a tormentor of others.

And what, monks, is the (kind of) person who is neither a tormentor of himself nor a tormentor of others, and is not intent on or devoted to (such practices). Herein a householder or householder's son hears the *dhamma,* (embraces it, and brings it to fulfilment).[2] This, monks, is the (kind of) person who is called neither a tormentor of himself nor a tormentor of others. He, satisfied, cooled, and become tranquil, in this life experiences happiness, and lives with a self become like Brahmā."

Thus spoke the Lord.

1. See 10 for detail on the applications of mindfulness.
2. A lengthy account – detail as 112.

52

With a Citizen of Aṭṭhaka

349–353

Thus have I heard: once venerable Ānanda dwelt near Vesālī at Beluva village. Now at that time the householder Dasama, a citizen of Aṭṭhaka, had come to Pāṭaliputta on some business. Then (he) approached a certain monk on Cock's campus and, saluting him, sat down at one side. Said Dasama:

"Bhante, where is venerable Ānanda living at this time, for we are desirous of seeing (him)." (And the monk told him). So Dasama the householder, having completed his business in Pāṭaliputta, approached venerable Ānanda in Beluva village and, saluting him, sat down at one side. Said Dasama:

"Bhante, is there one thing declared by that Lord who has known and seen, who is *arahant*, truly enlightened, whereby for a monk who lives diligent, zealous, and resolute the unfreed mind is freed, the undissolved distractions meet their end, and he finds the matchless haven from bondage?"

"There is, householder. Herein a monk, remote from worldly pursuits and from unskilled states, reaches and experiences the first (level of) absorption, associated with thought and investigation, born of remoteness, joyful and happy. He reflects on this and understands: 'This first (level of) absorption is brought about and planned for. But (anything like that) is transient, a state that must come to an end.' Established in that (understanding) he achieves the rooting out of the distractions (or), if he does not, then by that passion for *dhamma*, that delight in *dhamma*, there is spontaneous rebirth through the dissolution of the five fetters that bind (him) to the worldly condition, with final *nibbāna* there and no return from that world.

Further, householder, a monk reaches and experiences the second, the third, and the fourth (levels of) absorption; (or) lives with thoughts joined to goodwill, compassion, gladness, or equanimity; (or), entirely transcending perception of form (reaches and experiences) the realm of infinite space, of infinite consciousness, and of nothingness. (In each case) he reflects that (such a state) is brought about and planned for (and that all such) are transient, and must come to an end. Established in that (understanding) he achieves the rooting out of the distractions (or), if he does not then, by that passion for *dhamma*, that delight in *dhamma*, there is (likewise) spontaneous rebirth, with final *nibbāna* there and no return from that world?"

At these words Dasama the householder, a citizen of Aṭṭhaka spoke thus to venerable Ānanda:

"Bhante, it is as though a man searching for just one opening to a treasure-trove were to come upon eleven (such) openings. Likewise, in seeking just one door to the deathless I come to hear of eleven at once. And it is like a man whose house has eleven doors and could make himself safe, if (it) were burning by (going through) any one. Likewise, I could make myself safe by any of these eleven doors to the deathless. Those who are adherents of other sects would expect a teacher's fee, but why should I not pay respect to venerable Ānanda."

Whereupon Dasama the householder, citizen of Aṭṭhaka, bringing together the Order of monks at Pāṭaliputta and Vesālī, satisfied and served (them) with abundant food, both hard and soft, from his own hand. Also he presented (them) individually with a set of garments, and venerable Ānanda with three robes, as well as constructing a dwelling-place (for him) costing five hundred pieces.

53

For Learners

353-359

Thus have I heard: once the Lord dwelt among the Sakyans on Nigrodha's campus in Kapilavatthu. Now at that time there was a new council hall of the Sakyans not long constructed, and unoccupied by ascetic or brahman or any human being. Then the Sakyans of Kapilavatthu approached the Lord, saluted (him), and sat down at one side. Said the Sakyans:

"Let the Lord be the first to make use of (the new conference hall). (That) would be for the wellbeing and happiness of the Sakyans of Kapilavatthu for many a long day." The Lord consented in silence. And the Sakyans, recognising (his) consent, rose from their seats, saluted (him), and with their right side towards him, approached the conference hall.

They spread the conference hall with all the spreadings, made seats ready, set up a water pot, and prepared an oil lamp. Then they approached the Lord, saying: "Now is the time for whatever the Lord thinks (appropriate)." And the Lord, having dressed and taking bowl and robe, went to the conference hall together with the Order of monks.

After washing (their) feet they entered (it), and (the Lord) sat against the central pillar facing east, the Order of monks against the western wall facing east, with the Lord in front of them. The Sakyans of Kapilavatthu sat down against the eastern wall facing west, with the Lord facing them. Then the Lord, having instructed, roused, gladdened, and delighted (them) far into the night with *dhamma*-talk addressed venerable Ānanda, saying: "Ānanda, bring to mind a learner's course for the Sakyans of Kapilavatthu. My back aches. I will stretch it." Whereupon, folding his outer robe into four, (he) lay down on his right side in the lion posture, foot upon foot, mindful and lucid, attending to the thought of getting up.

Then venerable Ānanda addressed Mahānāma the Sakyan, saying:

"Now, Mahānāma, an *ariyan* disciple is successful in terms of conduct, guards the doors of the faculties, is moderate in eating, set on vigilance, possessed of seven good states, and is one who attains as he pleases, and without distress or trouble, the four (levels of) absorption that are dependent on the clearest consciousness, and are the experience of happiness in this life.

And how, Mahānāma, is an *ariyan* disciple successful as to conduct? Herein (he) is virtuous, he lives governed by the restraint of the obligations, successful in the field of behaviour and perceiving danger in the smallest faults. Undertaking them he trains himself in regard to the precepts.

And how does (he) guard the doors of the faculties? Herein, seeing a form with the eye, he is not infatuated with the appearance nor with the attributes. For longing and distress, and wretched and unskilled states, may intrude on the eye that is wayward. So he proceeds with restraint, guarding the eye, undergoing the discipline of the eye. (And he proceeds likewise with regard to the ear, the nose, the tongue, the tactile sense and mental images).

And how is (he) moderate in eating? Herein an *ariyan* disciple takes food reflecting thoroughly, not for sport, not for indulgence, not for finery, not for ornament, but in the measure needed for the endurance and sustenance of the body, for its protection, and for the furtherance of the good life, thinking: 'I will make an end of old feeling and not create new feeling, and there shall be continuance and blamelessness and comfort for me.'

And how, Mahānāma, is an *ariyan* disciple one set on vigilance? In a day of walking about and sitting down he clears the mind of obstructive things. In the first watch of the night (he does likewise). In the middle watch of the night he lies down on the right side in the lion posture, with one foot resting on the other, mindful and lucid, attending to the thought of getting up. In the last watch of the night he arises and (continues as before).

And how is an *ariyan* disciple possessed of seven good states? Herein (he) has faith, (and) is convinced of the wisdom of the Exemplar, thinking: 'Indeed he is Lord, *arahant*, truly enlightened.' He is conscientious, he is ashamed of ill-living, whether in body, word, or thought, or in reaching evil, unskilled states. He is scrupulous (in all these matters). He is well-informed, retaining and accumulating what he has heard. Those things that are auspicious at the outset, during the progress, and in the consummation, and that proclaim the good life entirely fulfilled and purified in both meaning and expression – things of that nature are well absorbed by him, kept in mind, talked about, carefully considered and properly penetrated as to view. He lives with energy aroused for the abandonment of unskilled states and the arising of skilled states, steadfast, of strong effort, persevering in skilled states. He is mindful, endowed with the greatest mindfulness and discrimination, remembering and recollecting (things) done and said long before. He is wise, possessed of the wisdom of what makes for rise and fall, and of the *ariyan* penetration leading to the complete waning of suffering. In such a way is an *ariyan* disciple possessed of seven good states.

And how, Mahānāma, is an *ariyan* disciple one who attains as he pleases, and without distress or trouble, the four (levels of) absorption that are dependent on the clearest consciousness and are states of happiness in this life? Herein, remote from worldly pursuits and from unskilled states, he reaches and experiences the first, second, third, and fourth (levels of) absorption.

When an *ariyan* disciple has achieved (all these characteristics), that (person) is called (one) who, on a learner's course, has come to a state of health, capable of breaking through, of highest wisdom, of reaching the matchless haven from bondage. It is like eight, ten, or a dozen hen's eggs that have been properly sat on, properly incubated, and properly hatched. For that hen (there would be no need to wish for the chicks to break out of the shell safely). (For) those chickens are capable, with the claw of the foot or the beak, of penetrating the eggshells and breaking through safely.

(Then) this *ariyan* disciple, owing to just this matchless purification through equanimity and mindfulness, recalls a variety of previous existences. With the purified divine eye transcending that of men (he) beholds the passing away and re-emergence of (other) beings. From the rooting out of the distractions he reaches and experiences freedom of mind and the freedom of wisdom, having realised them from his own gnosis in this life. (These are the three) breakings through like a chick from the egg-shell.

Such success as the *ariyan* disciple achieves in conduct, the guarding of the doors to the faculties, moderation in eating, intention for vigilance, possession of the seven good states, and the attainment of the four (levels of) absorption – (all these) have reference to behaviour. Such recollection of previous existences, the vision of the passing away and re-emergence of (other) beings, and freedom of mind and freedom of wisdom (as he achieves – all these) have reference to knowledge. This is called an *ariyan* disciple successful as to behaviour and knowledge. Mahānāma, this verse was spoken by primaeval Brahmā **'The nobleman is best among people who rely on lineage. Among *devas* and humans he is best that is successful in knowledge and behaviour.' "**

Then the Lord, having risen, addressed venerable Ānanda saying: "Well (said), Ānanda, well (said)."

This was spoken by venerable Ānanda, and obtained the Teacher's approval.

54
With Potaliya

359–368

Thus have I heard: once the Lord dwelt in Aṅguttarāpa (at) a town called Āpaṇa. Then the Lord, dressing at an early hour and taking bowl and robe, went into Āpaṇa for almsfood. When he (had done so) and was returning after the meal, he approached a certain jungle-thicket for the afternoon rest. Plunging into (it) he sat down at the foot of a tree. But the householder Potaliya, who was given to walking and roaming about, and was fully dressed and clothed and equipped with a parasol and sandals, approached the Lord. Having exchanged greetings and conversed in a friendly and polite way he stood at one side. Said the Lord: "There are seats, householder. Sit down if you wish."

At these words Potaliya the householder thought: "The ascetic Gotama addresses me with the term 'householder'," and becoming angry and depressed, was silent. (Then a second and a third time the Lord spoke to him in the same terms, whereupon) Potaliya the householder said:

"It is not proper, good Gotama, nor fitting that you should call me 'householder'."

"But, householder, you have the attributes, the marks, the characteristics of (one)."

"However, good Gotama, all (such) activities have been rejected by me, all (such) transactions set aside."

"In what way?"

"Herein I made over to my sons, as their inheritance, all my wealth, grain, silver, and gold. I live neither advising nor blaming in these matters, and with the minimum of food and clothing."

"Householder, you speak of setting aside of transactions in one way, but the setting aside of transactions in the discipline of the *ariyan* is something else."

"How so, bhante? Would that the Lord might teach me *dhamma* (concerning this)."

"Householder, these eight things lead to the setting aside of transactions in the discipline of the *ariyan*. Through not taking life the destruction of life is to be abandoned. Through not taking what is not given theft is to be abandoned. Through speaking truth lying is to be abandoned. Through not speaking slander (that too) is to be abandoned, (and similarly with) greed and covetousness, irritation and fault-finding, anger and agitation, and conceit. Briefly stated, householder, these are the eight things that lead to the setting aside of transactions in the discipline of the *ariyan*."

"Would that the Lord, out of compassion, might analyse these eight things in detail."

"Herein an *ariyan* disciple reflects: 'I am practising for the abandonment and setting aside of that bondage of which the taking of life may be a cause. And were I to take life I might reproach myself (for so doing). The wise, on finding out, might censure me and, on the breaking up of the body at death, an evil destiny might be expected. This is certainly a bond, this is a hindrance, namely the taking of life. And whatever troublesome and consuming distractions arise from the taking of life (do not arise for one not given to such practice.' And he reflects similarly on the other seven forms of abstinence). These eight things, householder, referred to in brief and (now) fully analysed, lead to the setting aside of transactions in the discipline of the *ariyan*. But not yet is there completely and in every way a setting aside of transactions in the discipline of the *ariyan*."

"How so, bhante? Would that the Lord might teach me *dhamma* (about this)."

"Householder, it is as though a dog that was weak and debilitated from hunger were to find himself in a slaughter-house, and a skilled butcher were to throw him a scraped and fleshless skeleton, with but a smear of blood on it. What do you think? Would that dog overcome his hunger and weakness (thereby)?"

"Not so, bhante. That dog would become exhausted and distressed."

"Likewise, householder, an *ariyan* disciple reflects (as follows): 'Worldly pursuit is spoken of by the Lord as like a skeleton in the greatness of its suffering and tribulation, as more wretched in fact.' Having seen this as it truly is with perfect wisdom, and having rejected that equanimity that is a diversity and founded on diversity, he cultivates that equanimity that is a unity[1] and founded on unity, and where attachments to the things of the flesh have entirely waned.[2]

The *ariyan* disciple who has come to this incomparable purity through equanimity and mindfulness recalls a variety of previous existences. With the purified divine eye transcending the human he beholds the passing away and re-emergence of (other) beings. He lives with the distractions rooted out, reaching and experiencing freedom of mind and the freedom of wisdom, having realised them in this life from his own gnosis. To that extent is there, completely and in every way, a setting aside of transactions in the discipline of the *ariyan*. What do you think about that, householder? Do you recognise such a setting aside of transactions in yourself?"

"Bhante, who am I (to make such a claim). Up to now we had thought the ill-bred wanderers of other sects to be thoroughbreds. We have given (them) food for thoroughbreds. We have offered (them) places for thoroughbreds. But now we know (otherwise and shall act accordingly). The Lord's monks, however, we shall know as thoroughbreds. Indeed, bhante, the Lord has induced in me affection for ascetics, satisfaction and esteem for (them). Wonderful, bhante, wonderful." (And Potaliya the householder took the refuges and became a lay-follower).

1. "diversity" i.e. worldly experience; "unity" i.e. the absorptions.
2. No fewer than seven other parables are used to make the same point.

55

With Jīvaka

368–371

Thus have I heard: once the Lord dwelt at Rājagaha in Jīvaka Komārabhacca's Mango Grove. Then Jīvaka Komārabhacca approached the Lord, saluted (him), and sat down at one side. Said Jīvaka:

"Bhante, I have heard this – (that) they seize a living thing on account of the ascetic Gotama, and that (he) knowingly partakes of flesh meant for him and prepared for him. Do those who think thus speak the words of the Lord and not accuse him falsely, and do they explain the truth of *dhamma*, and does no doctrine according with *dhamma* incur blame?"

"Jīvaka, (they) do not speak my words, but accuse me in error and falsely. I say that in three situations flesh is not to be partaken of – when it is seen, heard, or suspected (that an animal has been killed for a monk). I say that in three situations flesh can be partaken of – when it is not seen, heard, or suspected (that this is so).

Herein, Jīvaka, a monk lives relying on some village or town. He lives spreading thoughts joined to goodwill in (all) directions. He lives spreading them everywhere, in every way, to the entire world, abundantly, boundlessly, unrestrictedly, peaceably, benevolently. A householder or (his) son approaches, and invites him for a meal the following day. If the monk so wishes he consents. When the night has waned he dresses at an early hour and, taking bowl and robe, goes to the house of that householder or (his) son, and sits in the place prepared (for him). (They) serve him with abundant almsfood. He does not think to himself: 'It is well that the householder or (his) son waits upon me (like this), or might (do so again) in the future.' He partakes of the almsfood without greed, or enthusiasm, or relish, but perceiving the disadvantage, wise as to the outcome.[1]

What do you think about that, Jīvaka? Would that monk, on that occasion, intend harm towards himself, or others, or both?"

"Not so, bhante."

"Does (he), at that time, take sustenance blamelessly?"

"Indeed, bhante. Bhante, I have heard this, (that) the abode of goodwill is sublime. The Lord is seen as my witness for this. Indeed the Lord is abiding in goodwill."

"Jīvaka, the passion, ill-will, or delusion through which there might be the will to injure, they are abandoned, destroyed at the root by the Exemplar, like a torn up palm-tree, annihilated for the future, and taking no further hold. If that is what your words refer to I agree with you."

"Indeed, such is the meaning of my words, bhante."

"Herein, Jīvaka, a monk lives depending on some village or town. He lives spreading thoughts joined to compassion, gladness, equanimity. Would that monk, at (such) a time, take food blamelessly?"

"Indeed, bhante."

"Jīvaka, whoever seizes a living thing (to kill it) on behalf of the Exemplar or (his) disciple produces much demerit in five situations; when he speaks thus: 'Go and bring that creature'; when (it) is being fetched, and experiences pain and distress through (the thong) that afflicts its throat; when he speaks thus: 'Go and seize that animal (and kill it)'; when (it) is seized and experiences pain and distress; and when he improperly offends the Exemplar or (his) disciple (by offering the meat)."

"Excellent, bhante, wonderful. Properly indeed does the monk take sustenance." (And Jīvaka took the refuges and became a lay-follower).

1. "disadvantage" – presumably of attachment to food; "outcome" – possibly awareness of its value in providing sustenance. However Horner translates "escape", implying rather awareness of the general goal.

56

With Upāli

371–387

Thus have I heard: once the Lord dwelt at Nāḷandā in Pāvārika's Mango Grove. Now at that time Nātaputta the Jain was (also) living at Nāḷandā, together with a large company of Jains. Then Dīghatapassin the Jain, having walked through Nāḷandā for almsfood, returned after the meal and approached Pāvārika's Mango Grove (and) the Lord. (Then), having exchanged greetings and conversed in a friendly and polite way, he stood at one side. Said the Lord: "There are seats, Tapassin. Sit down if you wish." At these words Dīghatapassin the Jain, taking a low seat, sat down at one side, (whereupon) the Lord said (to him):

"Tapassin, how many activities does Nātaputta the Jain recognise in the performance and execution of an evil deed?"

"Friend Gotama, Nātaputta the Jain is not given to recognising 'activity'. He is given to recognising 'wrong'."

"Tapassin, how many wrongs does Nātaputta the Jain recognise in the performance and execution of an evil deed?"

"Three friend, namely wrong of body, wrong of speech, wrong of mind."

"But is wrong of body one thing, wrong of speech another thing, and wrong of mind yet another thing?"

"(That is so), friend Gotama."

"But of these three wrongs as analysed and specified, which wrong does Nātaputta the Jain declare to be most blamable in the performance and execution of an evil deed."

"Nātaputta the Jain declares the most blamable to be the wrong of body."

"You say 'wrong of body', Tapassin?"

"I (do), friend Gotama."

"At these words Dīghatapassin the Jain said to the Lord."

"But how many wrongs do you recognise, friend Gotama, in the performance and execution of an evil deed?"

"Tapassin, the Exemplar is not given to recognising 'wrong'. (He) is given to recognising 'activity'."

"How many activities do you recognise, friend Gotama, in the performance and activity of an evil deed?"

"Three, Tapassin, namely bodily activity, verbal activity, mental activity."

"But is bodily activity one thing, verbal activity another thing, and mental activity yet another thing?"

"(That is so), Tapassin."

"Of these three activities thus analysed and specified, friend Gotama, which activity do you declare to be the most blamable in the performance and execution of an evil deed?"

"I declare mental activity to be the most blamable, Tapassin."

"You say 'mental activity', friend Gotama?"

"(I do), Tapassin."

(Upon that) Dīghatapassin the Jain rose from his seat, (went away, and) approached Nātaputta the Jain. Now at that time Nātaputta the Jain was seated with a large assembly of householders, with Upāli of Bālaka village at their head. Nātaputta the Jain saw Dīghatapassin the Jain coming some way off and said to (him):

"Well now, Tapassin, whence have you come so early?"

"I have come from the presence of the ascetic Gotama, bhante."

"And what was the talk between you?"

Then Dīghatapassin the Jain related the whole of the conversation that had passed with the Lord. When he had spoken Nātaputta the Jain said:

"It is well, Tapassin, that the ascetic Gotama should have been answered thus by Dīghatapassin the Jain, a well-instructed disciple who understands the Teacher's instruction correctly. How can the trivial wrong of mind signify[1] compared to that weighty wrong of body. Hence wrong of body is the most blamable in the performance and execution of an evil deed."

At these words Upāli the householder said to Nātaputta the Jain: "Well then, I will go to the ascetic Gotama, and refute him on the point at issue. If (he) stands fast (in response) to me as he was made to stand fast by venerable Tapassin, then, just as a strong man, seizing a long-haired ram by its fleece, might pull, drag, and draw it along, just so shall I, argument by argument, (deal with) the ascetic Gotama. And now, bhante, I shall go (and do so)."

"Go, householder, and refute the ascetic Gotama. For I, or Dīghatapassin the Jain, or you could (equally well do so)."

At these words Dīghatapassin the Jain said to Nātaputta the Jain: "I am not happy that Upāli the householder should (seek to) refute the ascetic Gotama. Bhante, the ascetic Gotama is deceitful. He has the trick of turning (things) round, thereby converting disciples of other sects."

"It cannot be, there is no chance, Tapassin, that Upāli the householder should come to be a disciple of the ascetic Gotama, (but the reverse might well happen). Go (therefore), householder, and refute the ascetic Gotama."

"Very well, bhante", (said) Upāli the householder, rising from his seat and saluting Nātaputta the Jain. (Then), keeping his right side towards (him, he went away) and approached Pāvārika's Mango Grove and the Lord. Saluting the Lord, he sat down at one side. Said Upāli: "Has Dīghatapassin the Jain been here, bhante?"

"(He has), householder."

"But what was the talk between you, bhante?" Then the Lord related the whole of (that) conversation. At his words Upāli the householder said:

"It is well, bhante, that the Lord should have been answered thus. How can the trivial wrong of mind signify compared with that weighty wrong of body. Hence wrong of body is the most blamable in the performance and execution of an evil deed."

"Were you to speak with a grounding in truth, householder, there might be some conversation between us in this matter."

"I do speak with a grounding in truth, bhante. Let there be conversation in this matter."

"Then what do you think, householder? There might be some Jain who is sick, ailing, very ill, and who, refusing cold water, takes only hot water. Not obtaining cold water he might come to his death. Where, householder, does Nātaputta the Jain declare his re-emergence to be?"

"Bhante, there are *devas* called 'the mind-attached (ones)'. He arises there. Why so? – because, when that (person) died, he was in bondage to the mind."

"Householder, householder, take care how you explain. Your later (comments) do not follow from the earlier ones."

"Although the Lord speaks thus, (still) wrong of body is the most blamable in the performance and execution of an evil deed."

"Then what do you think about this, householder? Some Jain is controlled by the fourfold restraint,[2] wholly restrained as to water, wholly involved with (it), shaking (it) entirely off, completely permeated with (such restraint), but, whilst coming and going, brings about the destruction of many small creatures. What does Nātaputta the Jain declare to be the consequences of that for him?"

"If unintentional (he) asserts that there is no great blame."

"And if he intends it, householder?"

"Then there is great blame, bhante."

"But in what (division) does Nātaputta the Jain hold 'intention' to be?"

"In wrong of mind, bhante."

"Householder, householder, take care how you explain. Your later (comments) do not follow from the earlier ones."

"Although the Lord speaks thus (still) wrong of body is the most blamable in the performance and execution of an evil deed."

"Then what do you think about this, householder. Is this Nāḷandā rich and prosperous, crowded and populous?"

"Indeed, bhante."

"Then what do you think about this? A man comes along with a drawn sword, saying: 'In the space of a second, in a trice, I will reduce all such creatures as there are in this Nāḷandā to one mass of flesh, to one heap of flesh.' Could (he do that)?"

"Even fifty men (could not accomplish it), bhante."

"Then what do you think about this, householder? An ascetic or brahman, possessed of psychic powers and mastery of the mind comes here saying: 'I will reduce this Nāḷandā to ashes through one (surge) of ill-will.' Could (he do that)?"

"Even fifty Nāḷandās, bhante."

"Householder, householder, take care how you explain. Your later (comments) do not follow from the earlier ones."[3]

"Bhante, I was pleased and satisfied by the Lord's first example. Nonetheless, wishing to hear a diversity of responses, I thought to become his adversary. Excellent, bhante, excellent." (Whereupon Upāli the householder took the refuges and became a lay-follower. Then the Lord said):

"Make a thorough investigation, householder. (Such a procedure) is proper for well-known people such as yourself."

"I am very pleased and satisfied by that (statement), bhante. For, if adherents of another sect had made a convert of me, they would have paraded a banner through Nāḷandā for ages."

"For a long time, householder, your family has been a provider for the Jains. You will remember to give almsfood to those who approach you?"

"I am very pleased and satisfied by that (statement), bhante. (For) I had heard (it said that) the ascetic Gotama speaks thus: 'Hospitality is to be given just to me not to others, to my disciples not to the disciples of others. What is given to me (and) my disciples is alone of great fruit, (not so) what is given to others.' Yet the Lord exhorts me concerning hospitality for the Jains also."

Then the Lord gave a progressive exposition to Upāli the householder, namely a talk on hospitality, on conduct, on the next world, on the disadvantage, vanity, and corruption in worldly pursuits, and illustrated the merit of dispassion.

When the Lord knew the mind of Upāli the householder to be prepared, soft, unobstructed, upraised and clear, he made known to him the exalted teaching of the *buddhas* – suffering, (its) origin, (its) ceasing, and the Way. And, as a clean cloth free from dirt can easily absorb dye, so there arose for Upāli the householder just where he sat the spotless, unstained eye of *dhamma*. That whatever is of a nature to originate is entirely of a nature to perish. Then Upāli the householder, seeing the *dhamma*, obtaining (it), knowing (it), immersed in (it), crossing over uncertainty, emptied of doubt, achieving satisfaction, and not (any longer) dependent on others with respect to the Teacher's message, said to the Lord: "Well now, bhante, we must go. We are busy, and there is much to be done."

"Do whatever you think is timely, householder."

Then Upāli the householder, pleased and satisfied with the Lord's words, rose from his seat and saluted. (Then), keeping his right side towards the Lord, he went his way towards his own house, (where) he addressed the gatekeeper saying: "Henceforth, good gatekeeper, I am keeping male and female Jains beyond the gate, but (it) is open to the Lord's monks and nuns, and his male and female lay-followers. If any Jain should come you are to say: 'Stand there, bhante, do not enter. If you have need of almsfood remain here, and they will bring it to you.' "

Now Dīghatapassin the Jain heard (that) Upāli the householder had come to discipleship under the ascetic Gotama, whereupon (he) went to Nātaputta the Jain and (told him).

"This cannot be, Tapassin, there is no chance of (it), but it is possible that the ascetic Gotama should have come to discipleship under Upāli the householder."

"Well then, bhante, I shall go and find out."

Then Dīghatapassin the Jain went to the house of Upāli the householder. Seeing him coming some way off the gatekeeper (spoke as instructed). (So Dīghatapassin the Jain) turned back, and went (once more) to Nātaputta the Jain, saying: "It is true, bhante, that Upāli the householder has come to discipleship under the ascetic Gotama." (And he reminded him of the warning he had given. But Nātaputta the Jain would not believe him and said): "Well then, Tapassin, I shall go and find out for myself."

Then Nātaputta the Jain, accompanied by a large company of Jains, approached the house of Upāli the householder. (Whereupon the gatekeeper spoke to him as to Dīghatapassin. Said Nātaputta):

"Now, worthy gatekeeper, go to Upāli the householder and say (to him that) Nātaputta the Jain, with a great company of Jains, stands beyond the gateway, and wishes to see (him)." (And the gatekeeper did so. Replied Upāli the householder):

"Now, good gatekeeper, prepare places in the middle hall.[4]"

(When this had been done) Upāli the householder went to the middle hall and, seating himself on the highest, best, finest, and most excellent seat, addressed the gatekeeper, (telling him to bring Nātaputta the Jain and his company).

Then Upāli the householder, who was there first, saw Nātaputta the Jain coming some way off. (Returning with him) he dusted the highest, best, finest, and most excellent seat with his outer robe, possessed himself of it, and sat down, saying to Nātaputta the Jain:

"There are seats, bhante. Sit down if you wish."

At these words Nātaputta the Jain said (to him): "You are out of your mind, householder. You are an imbecile. (Having said you would) go to the ascetic Gotama and refute (him) you have come back enmeshed by a great tangle of words. It is as though a man should go out, and come back with his testicles removed. You are turned about, householder, by the trickery of the ascetic Gotama."

"The trickery is valuable, bhante, the trickery is helpful. Were my close relatives (or, for that matter, any being in the world) to be turned by this turning about, it would be for their wellbeing and happiness for many a day. Now I will make a parable for you and, through it, a few men of intelligence will understand the meaning.

Once upon a time the tender young wife of a certain frail, aged, and venerable brahman was pregnant and nearing her time.[5] Said (she) to (him): 'Go, brahman, and buy a young, male monkey. Bring him as playmate for my little boy.' Then the brahman, being devoted to (her), and under (her) sway, (bought a male monkey). (Whereupon she said to him): 'Take this young, male monkey and go to Rattapāṇi the dyer's son. Say to (him that you wish) this young, male monkey to be dyed a golden colour, flattened and pressed all round, and made smooth on both sides.' (And the brahman conveyed her request to Rattapāṇi, the dyer's son). Said Rattapāṇi: 'This young, male monkey of yours will sustain colouring, but not (the rest).

Similarly the doctrine of the Jains will sustain the colouring of the foolish, but not of the wise, will not bear questioning or smoothing.'

Then, bhante, the brahman, on another occasion, took a suit of new garments and approached Rattapāṇi the dyer's son (with the same request) Said Rattapāṇi: 'This new suit of garments of yours will sustain colouring, flattening and pressing, and smoothing.' Likewise the doctrine of the Lord who is *arahant*, truly enlightened, that takes its colouring (only) from the wise, and will bear questioning and smoothing."

"Householder, this company, together with the rulers, understand (that) Upāli the householder is a disciple of Nātaputta the Jain. Whose disciple do we (now) take you to be?"

At these words Upāli the householder rose from his place, arranged his outer robe over one shoulder, and saluted the Lord with joined palms saying: "Well, bhante, hear whose disciple I am." (And he spoke a great eulogy in praise of the Lord).[6]

(When he had finished Nātaputta the Jain asked): "But when, householder were these splendours of the ascetic Gotama gathered by you?"

"Bhante, it is as though there were a diversity of flowers, a great heap, and a skilled garland-maker were to bind them into an ornamental garland. Just so the Lord has many splendours, hundreds of splendours. And who, bhante, will not praise the praiseworthy?"

But Nātaputta the Jain, being unable to endure such honour for the Lord, spilled hot blood from the mouth on that very spot.

1. Literally "shine forth".
2. A standard Jain practice. The point of the passage appears to be that water may be studiously filtered to prevent the destruction of small organisms, but that such may be killed by the Jain's comings and goings.
3. Further exchanges occur but the additional examples add very little.
4. The full text gratuitously adds "with doors."
5. The ensuing parable gets off the point with irrelevant detail in the original. Hence I have considerably abbreviated it.
6. The eulogy takes the form of a lengthy verse passage.

57

With the Dog Imitator

387–392

Thus have I heard: once the Lord dwelt among the Koḷiyans, (at) a town (of theirs) called Haliddavasana. Then Puṇṇa, a naked ascetic given to imitating a cow, and Seniya who was given to imitating a dog, approached the Lord. Puṇṇa the cow-imitator saluted the Lord and sat down at one side. But Seniya exchanged greetings and conversed in a friendly and polite way, and (then) sat down at one side, curling up like a dog. Said Puṇṇa:

"Bhante, this ascetic Seniya given to imitating a dog is a practitioner of a difficult austerity. He eats lying on the ground, a canine practice undertaken by him in full for a long time. What is his destiny, what his future state?"

"Enough, Puṇṇa. Let that be. Do not ask me about it." (But Puṇṇa persisted with his question).

(Said the Lord): "Really, Puṇṇa I did not allow (your question, but since you press me) I will nevertheless explain to you. Herein, someone develops the canine practice completely and constantly (in terms of) canine behaviour, a canine attitude, a canine norm. At the breaking up of the body he comes to be in companionship with dogs. But if he has the belief: 'By this behaviour, or practice, or austerity, or chastity, I shall become a *deva*, or of a *deva*'s retinue.' – that is a wrong view on his part. For wrong view I say there is one of two destinies Puṇṇa – purgatory or the world of animals. If successful, the canine practice leads to companionship with dogs, if unsuccessful to purgatory."

At these words Seniya the dog-imitator cried out and wept. Then the Lord said to Puṇṇa, the cow-imitator: "I did not allow this (question) Puṇṇa." Said Seniya: "I am not crying because the Lord has spoken of me in this way. Nonetheless this canine practice has been undertaken by me in full for a long time. Bhante, Puṇṇa who is given to imitating a cow – that bovine practice (of his) has been undertaken in full for a long time. What is his destiny, what his future state." (And the Lord answered Seniya in the same terms as Puṇṇa, whereupon Puṇṇa also wept). Then the Lord said to Seniya: "I did not allow this question of yours, Seniya."

(Said Puṇṇa): "I am not crying because the Lord has spoken of me in this way. Nonetheless this bovine practice has been undertaken by me for a long time. I have trust in the Lord. He is able to teach *dhamma* so that I might give up this bovine practice and Seniya that canine practice."

Said the Lord: "There are these four activities Puṇṇa, realised through my own gnosis, that I make known. There is the activity that is dark and with dark result. There is the activity that is fair and with fair result. There is the (one) that is both dark and fair, and with (both kinds of) result. There is the (one) that is neither dark nor fair and that leads to the termination of activity.

And what is the activity that is dark and with dark result? Herein, Puṇṇa, someone creates bodily, verbal, and mental tendencies that are injurious. (Having done so), he arises in a world that is injurious. Having arisen in (such) a world, injurious sensations envelope him. (In consequence) he experiences an injurious feeling, (one) entirely painful, as do beings in purgatory. Such is the re-emergence of a being out of what has been. As one does so one comes to be. And so I say Puṇṇa that beings are heirs to their deeds.

And what is the activity that is fair and with fair result? Herein, someone creates bodily, verbal, and mental tendencies that are harmless (and that have corresponding results). Having arisen in a world that is harmless, harmless sensations envelope him. (In consequence) he experiences a harmless feeling, (one) entirely happy, as do the shining *devas*. Such is the re-emergence of a being out of what has been. As one does so one comes to be. And so I say Puṇṇa that beings are heirs to their deeds.

And what is the activity that is both dark and fair, and with (both kinds of) result? Herein, Puṇṇa, someone creates (tendencies of both kinds and with both kinds of result). Having arisen in a world that is (of a mixed nature, both kinds) of sensation envelope him. (In consequence) he experiences a feeling in which happiness and pain combine, as do human beings, some *devas*, and some in the realm of sorrows. Such is the re-emergence of a being out of what has been. As one does so one comes to be. And so I say Puṇṇa that beings are heirs to their deeds.

And what is the activity that is neither dark nor fair and that leads to the termination of activity? As to that Puṇṇa, whatever intention there is to abandon the activity that is dark, the activity that is fair, and the activity that is (both) – that is called the activity that leads to the termination of activity. These, Puṇṇa, are the four activities that I make known, having realised them through my own gnosis.".

At these words Puṇṇa the cow-imitator said to the Lord: "Excellent, bhante, excellent." (And, taking the refuges, he became a lay-follower. But Seniya the dog-imitator sought ordination).

(Said the Lord): "Anyone who is a former member of another sect and wishes for the going forth in this *dhamma* and discipline, and for ordination, lives on probation for four months. At the end of four months the monks, if they are so minded, permit the going forth and ordination as a monk. Nevertheless differences between individuals are known to me."

"(The Lord speaks of four months, but) I will live on probation for four years and (then) let the monks, if so minded, permit the going forth and ordination as a monk." But Seniya, the naked ascetic who was a dog-imitator, obtained the going forth and ordination in the Lord's presence. Before long venerable Seniya (was) living alone and apart, diligent, zealous, and resolute. Some time later, having realised it from his own gnosis in this life, he reached and experienced that consummation of the good life for which sons of family rightly go forth from home into homelessness. (He knew): "Destroyed is birth, fulfilled the good life, done what was to be done, and no further return to this world." And so venerable Seniya became one of the *arahants*.

58

With Prince Abhaya

392–396

Thus have I heard: once the Lord dwelt near Rājagaha in the Bamboo Grove at the squirrels' feeding-ground.

Then Prince Abhaya approached Nātaputta the Jain, saluted him, and sat down at one side. Said Nātaputta the Jain: "Go, Prince, and refute the ascetic Gotama, and then a fine reputation will circulate concerning you."

"But in what way, bhante, can I refute (one) of such great power and eminence as the ascetic Gotama?"

"Approach (him) and say: 'Is it possible for the Exemplar to speak such words as will be unpleasant and disagreeable to others?' If, thus questioned, (he) should answer (that it is possible), then you should say this to him: 'Then what is the difference between you and an ordinary person (who might well speak like that)?' But if (he) replies (that it is not possible), then you should say this to him: 'In that case why was Devadatta angered and displeased when declared by you (to be) destined for a woeful state, for purgatory, to be stuck for an aeon, and to be beyond help?' If, Prince, you ask the ascetic Gotama such a double-edged question, (he) will neither be able to spit (it) out nor to swallow (it), just like a man with an iron ring stuck in his throat."

"Very well, bhante", said Prince Abhaya in assent and, rising from his place, he saluted Nātaputta the Jain, and with his right side towards him (departed). (Then) he approached the Lord and, after saluting (him), sat down at one side. But, after observing the sun, Prince Abhaya decided (that the time was not ripe and instead invited the Lord to a meal on the morrow).

Then the Lord, when the night had waned, dressed at an early hour and, taking bowl and robe, went to Prince Abhaya's dwelling, where he sat in the place prepared for him. Whereupon Prince Abhaya served and satisfied the Lord from his own hand with plentiful food, both hard and soft. When the Lord had eaten and set aside the bowl (the Prince) sat down at one side on a low seat.

Said Prince Abhaya: "Is it possible for the Exemplar to speak such words as will be unpleasant and disagreeable to others?"

"(The answer to this is) indefinite, Prince."

"Now the Jains are undone, bhante."

"Now why do you say (that), Prince?"

(Then Prince Abhaya related the whole of his conversation with Nātaputta the Jain). Now at that time a small and tender boy was lying on his back in Prince Abhaya's lap. Said the Lord: "Now what do you think about this, Prince. If this boy were to suffer carelessness at your hands or that of his wet-nurse, and were to get a splint or pebble in his mouth, how would you treat him?"

"I would take it out of him, bhante. If I could not (do so) at once I would grasp his head with my left hand and, crooking a finger, would get it out with my right hand, even at the cost of drawing blood. Why so? There is compassion in me for the boy."

"Likewise, Prince, the Exemplar does not speak (what) he knows to be false, unjustified, and unprofitable, as well as unpleasant and disagreeable to others. (He) does not speak (what) he knows to be true and justified, but unprofitable, as well as unpleasant and disagreeable to others. Whatever (he) knows to be true, justified, and profitable, as well as unpleasant and disagreeable to others – (he) is aware of the proper occasion for (saying that). (He) does not speak (what) he knows to be false, unjustified, and unprofitable, even though pleasant and agreeable to others. (He) does not speak (what) he knows to be true and justified, but unprofitable, though pleasant and agreeable to others. And whatever (he) knows to be true, justified, and profitable, as well as pleasant and agreeable to others – (he) is aware of the proper occasion for (saying that). Why so? It is because of the Exemplar's compassion for beings, Prince."

"Bhante, when clever nobles, or brahmans, or householders, or ascetics prepare a question and come to the Exemplar and ask it, has it been previously reflected on in the Lord's mind (like this): 'To any who approach and question me thus I will answer thus', or does such (an answer) occur to him spontaneously?"

"Well now, Prince, I will ask you a question in return. Answer as you see fit. What do you think about this? Are you knowledgeable as to the parts of a chariot?"

"Yes indeed, bhante."

"(And) should those who approach you ask (about such matters), would it have been previously reflected on in your mind, or would such (an answer) occur to you spontaneously?"

"Bhante, I am a skilled charioteer, knowledgeable as to the parts of a chariot. Such (an answer) would occur to me spontaneously."

"Just so, Prince, when (various people) prepare a question (for the Exemplar the answer) occurs to him spontaneously. Why so? It is that the nature of *dhamma* is well penetrated by (him, and thus the answer) occurs to (him) spontaneously."

At these words Prince Abhaya said to the Lord: "Excellent, bhante, excellent". (And Prince Abhaya took the refuges and became a lay-follower).

59

On Much to be Experienced

396–400

Thus have I heard: once the Lord dwelt near Sāvatthī in the Jeta Grove on Anāthapiṇḍika's campus. Then Pañcakaṅga the carpenter approached venerable Udāyin and, saluting him, sat down at one side. Said Pañcakaṅga:

"How many (kinds of) feeling are spoken of by the Lord, bhante?"

"Three, householder: pleasant feeling, painful feeling, and feeling which is neither."

"(Not so), bhante – two (kinds of) feeling are spoken of by (him): pleasant feeling and painful feeling. The feeling that is neither is referred to as exalted happiness by (him)."

"(Not so), householder – three (kinds of) feeling are spoken of by (him): pleasant feeling, painful feeling, and feeling that is neither."

(Thus did Pañcakaṅga the carpenter and venerable Udāyin dispute the matter, neither being able to convince the other).

Now venerable Ānanda overheard that conversation. Whereupon (he) approached the Lord, saluted (him), and sat down at one side. (Then he) related the whole of (that) conversation to the Lord.

At these words the Lord said: "The analysis of venerable Udāyin was correct, though Pañcakaṅga the carpenter was not satisfied. The analysis of Pañcakaṅga was correct, though venerable Udāyin was not satisfied. Ānanda, two (kinds of) feeling are spoken of by me in terms of (one) analysis, but also three, five, six, eighteen, thirty-six, and one hundred and eight (kinds). Such is the method (used) by me in teaching *dhamma*. For those who do not allow, approve, or find satisfaction in one another's well-spoken words this is to be expected – that they will live disputing, quarrelsome, and contentious, indulging in mutual recrimination. For those who do, this is to be expected – that they will live in unity, on friendly terms, not quarrelling, blending as milk with water, and looking on one another with the eye of affection.

There are these five strands of worldly pursuit, Ānanda: visible forms, pleasing, welcome, enticing, voluptuous, pleasure-laden, exciting; (and sounds, smells, tastes, and contacts of a similar nature). Whatever happiness and delight comes about on account of these is called the happiness of worldly pursuit.

Ānanda, whoever might say (that) this is the supreme happiness and delight that beings experience – that I do not concede to him. Why so? There is another happiness more excellent and exalted than that happiness. And what (is that)? Remote from worldly pursuits and from unskilled states, a monk reaches and experiences the first, the second, the third, and the fourth (levels of) absorption, (and subsequently) the realms of infinite space, infinite consciousness, nothingness, of neither perceiving nor not perceiving, and the cessation of perception and feeling. This is another happiness more excellent and exalted.

But it is possible, Ānanda, that wanderers of other sects will say this: 'The wanderer Gotama speaks of the cessation of perception and feeling, and talks about it with reference to happiness. What can that mean? How can it be so?' (Such people) are to be answered thus: 'With reference to happiness the Lord did not only speak in terms of happy *feeling*. Whenever and wherever happiness is to be found – just that he talks about in terms of happiness.' "

Thus spoke the Lord.

60

On What is Certain

400–413

Thus have I heard: once the Lord, whilst travelling on foot amongst the Kosalans together with a large company of monks, came to a brahman village of (theirs) called Sālā. Now the brahman householders (there) heard that the ascetic Gotama, a son of the Sakyans, gone forth from the Sakya clan (was among them, and that he was of high renown). Then the brahman householders of Sālā approached the Lord. Some greeted (him) and sat down at one side, some having exchanged greetings and conversed in a friendly and polite way, some after saluting with joined palms, some after announcing their names and lineage, some in silence. Said the Lord:

"Now, householders, is there a satisfactory teacher in whom you have well-founded conviction?"

"(Not so), bhante."

"Then you should undertake and practise this *dhamma* that is certain. Certain is the perfected *dhamma* and, if undertaken by you, will be for your wellbeing and happiness for many a day. And what, householders, is the *dhamma* that is certain?

There are some ascetics and brahmans who speak and think like this: 'There is neither gift, nor offering, nor sacrifice, nor ripening and result of good deeds and bad; neither this world nor another; neither mother nor father nor spontaneous uprising; no ascetics or brahmans living rightly, proceeding rightly, who make known this world and the next, having realised them through their own gnosis.'

There are (also), householders, some ascetics and brahmans who speak and think like this: 'From performing or causing action, from mutilating or causing mutilation, from torturing or causing torture, from causing grief, from causing misery, from tormenting or causing torment, from the destruction of living things, from stealing, from breaking and entering, from plundering, from robbery, from lying in ambush, from going to other men's wives, from lying – from acting in (all these ways) no evil is brought about. (And) in giving, in making offerings, in self-control, abstinence, truthfulness, (and persuading others to live in the same way) there is no virtue, no virtuous outcome.' (Then again) there are, householders, some ascetics and brahmans who speak like this: 'There is no reason, no condition, for the corruption of beings. Without reason or condition (are both these states). There is no strength, no energy, no individual steadfastness or endeavour. All beings, all living things, all existence, all creatures, are devoid of (these characteristics). (They) are confined by fate, accident, and (their) natures. (They) experience pleasure and pain amid the six races[1] (of mankind).'[2]

(But in respect of all the views I have just outlined) there are some ascetics and brahmans who (declare the opposite). What do you think about this, householders? Are not these (groups of) ascetics and brahmans in direct conflict with one another?"

"Yes indeed, bhante."

"With regard to those (who deny a world beyond, who deny effective action, and who deny any reason for the corruption of beings) this is to be expected for them – that they will take upon themselves and practise these three unskilful conditions, (namely), ill-conduct in body, word, and thought. Why so? These worthy ascetics and brahmans fail to see the disadvantage, the folly, the corruption of unskilful conditions, and the profit, the alternative of purity, in renouncing (them).

For, since there is a world beyond; since there is (effective) action; and since there is a reason for the corruption of beings (to think, imagine, or speak otherwise is wrong). (It) stands in opposition to those who, as *arahants,* are exponents of (the truth in these matters). If (anyone) convinces others (to the contrary, that) is in conflict with true *dhamma,* though by means of (such conversions) he exalts himself and disparages others. So, (even) before one has set aside good conduct, bad conduct is present, (as well as) wrong views, imaginings, and speech, antagonism to the *ariyans,* self-praise and denigration of others. In such a way these various evil and unskilled states follow from wrong view.

An intelligent person reflects like this: 'If (those who deny these things are correct) this worthy individual will make himself safe on the breaking up of the body at death. If (they are not he) will come to sorrow, to an evil destiny, to ruin, to purgatory (thereafter). But, if it be granted that (they are right), yet this worthy individual is censured by the wise in this life (on the grounds that he is of) bad conduct, (and of) wrong view. And, if (they are wrong), there is defeat for him on two counts. So this (supposedly) certain *dhamma* undertaken by him comes to a bad end. He remains absorbed in one aspect, and gives up the skilful position."

(But) there are some ascetics and brahmans who (declare the opposite). For them this is to be expected – that they will take upon themselves and practise these three skilful conditions, (namely), good conduct in body, word, and thought. Why so? These worthy ascetics and brahmans see the disadvantage, the folly, the corruption of unskilful conditions, and the profit, the alternative of purity in renouncing (them).

There are, householders, some ascetics and brahmans who speak and think like this: 'There is no (state) which is formless throughout.' (But) there are some ascetics and brahmans who (declare the opposite). There are (also), householders, some ascetics and brahmans who speak and think like this: 'There is no complete cessation of (continued) existence.' (But) there are some ascetics and brahmans who (declare the opposite). What do you think about this, householders? Are not these (groups of) ascetics and brahmans in direct conflict with one another?"

"Yes indeed, bhante."

"An intelligent person reflects like this: '(The truth with regard to these matters) is not seen by me, not known to me. And were I, without seeing or knowing, to take up and express a one-sided position – that would be improper. If (those who deny that there is any state that is formless throughout speak the truth) it is possible that my arising among the *devas* that have form and are mind-made is assured. But, because of form, seizing of stick and sword is seen (together with) quarrel, dispute, contention, strife, lying, and slander. But, in what is formless throughout, this does not occur.' By reflecting in this way he proceeds to weariness with forms, dispassion (towards them), and towards (their) dissolution.

And (he further) reflects: 'If those (who deny the complete cessation of continued existence speak the truth) it is possible that my arising among those *devas* that are without form and are made by perception is assured. (But if the others speak the truth) it is possible I shall reach *nibbāna* in this present existence. (If the first group are right) this view of theirs is an accompaniment of infatuation, of bondage, of enjoyment, of clinging, of attachment. (If the second group are right) this view of theirs is an accompaniment of dispassion, of freedom from bondage, of disenchantment, of freedom from clinging, of detachment.' By reflecting in this way he proceeds to weariness with (continued) existence, dispassion towards (it), and towards (its) dissolution."

At these words the brahman householders of Sālā said to the Lord: "Excellent, good Gotama, excellent" – (and they took the refuges, becoming lay-followers).

1. Non-Buddhist teachers divided mankind into six races.
2. In the full text the material in the next five paragraphs takes the form of a sixfold repetition interleaved with the previous threefold statement of views, i.e. there are three sets of deniers and three sets of affirmers discussed in identical terms. The final sections, beginning with the reference to the formless realms have been similarly condensed.

61

A Talk with Rāhula at Abalaṭṭhikā

414–420

Thus have I heard: once the Lord dwelt at Rājagaha in the Bamboo Grove at the squirrels' feeding-place. Now at that time venerable Rāhula was living at Ambalaṭṭhikā. Then the Lord, emerging from seclusion in the evening, approached Ambalaṭṭhikā and venerable Rāhula. Seeing the Lord coming some way off, venerable Rāhula prepared a seat and water for the feet. The Lord sat down and bathed his feet (whilst) venerable Rāhula, after saluting (him), sat down at one side. Then the Lord, putting a small quantity of remaining water into a water-vessel, said:

"Rāhula, do you see this small amount of water?"

"Yes, bhante."

"Just as little is (the value of) the ascetic's life[1] for those without shame in respect of deliberate lying." Then the Lord, throwing away the small amount of water that was left over, said:

"Rāhula, do you see this small amount of water that has been thrown away?"

"Yes, bhante."

"Equally thrown away is the ascetic's life for those without shame in respect of deliberate lying." Then the Lord, turning the water-vessel upside down, said:

"Rāhula, do you see this overturned water-vessel?"

"Yes, bhante."

"Equally overturned is the ascetic's life for those without shame in respect of deliberate lying." Then the Lord, righting the water-vessel, said:

"Rāhula, do you see this water-vessel that is empty and void?"

"Yes, bhante."

"Equally empty and void is the ascetic's life that is without shame with respect to deliberate lying. Rāhula, it is like a king's elephant with tusks as long as a plough-pole, strong, of high pedigree, at home on the battle-field. When engaged in battle he uses both forelegs and hindlegs, both the front and rear (parts) of his body, (as well as) his head, his tusks, his tail, protecting just his trunk. It occurs to the mahout (that) the king's elephant, in protecting only his trunk, has not forfeited his life. But when the king's elephant (also) uses his trunk it occurs to the mahout (that he) has forfeited his life, (and that) now nothing can be done for (him). Just so, Rāhula, I declare any evil can be perpetrated by one who is without shame in respect of deliberate lying. And so you are to train yourself thinking: 'I shall not tell lies, even in jest'."

"What do you think about this, Rāhula? What is the function of a mirror?"

"Its function is to reflect, bhante."

"Even so, bodily activity is to be resorted to (only) after reflection. Verbal activity is to be resorted to (only) after reflection. Mental activity is to be resorted to (only) after reflection. Rāhula – that bodily activity which you are desirous of performing – just that you should reflect on, thinking: 'Should this bodily activity tend to produce harm for self, or others, or both, (then it) is unskilful, of painful outcome and result', and you should desist from such activity. (Also), whilst performing bodily action you should reflect (similarly), and should you know that it is tending to (such) harm, you should abandon (it). After performing an action with the body you should reflect (similarly). If, reflecting, you should know (that it) has tended to produce harm for self, or others, or both, you should confess, disclose, and declare (that) to the Teacher, or to intelligent companions in the good life. (Having done so) you should show restraint in the future. But if you know that (it) did not produce harm, then you may live in joy and gladness, training yourself day and night in the states that are skilled.

(And, Rāhula, with regard to verbal activity, whether future, present, or past, you should train yourself likewise. And with regard even to future and present mental activity you should do the same. And if, reflecting on past mental activity, you deem it to have been harmful), you should be concerned, ashamed, and disgusted, (and then) show restraint in the future.

Rāhula, all those ascetics and brahmans who, throughout the past, purified bodily, verbal, and mental activity; who, in the fullness of time will do so; or who are now (doing so, do so only) after reflection. And thus must you train yourself, Rāhula."

Thus spoke the Lord.

1. Abstract noun – Horner renders "recluseship".

62

Major Discourse on a Talk with Rāhula

420–426

Thus have I heard: once the Lord dwelt near Sāvatthī in the Jeta Grove on Anāthapiṇḍika's campus. Then the Lord, dressing at an early hour, and taking bowl and robe, went into Sāvatthī for almsfood. Venerable Rāhula followed close behind. Then the Lord, looking round, said:

"Whatever is (physical) form, Rāhula, be it past, future, or present; internal or external; gross or subtle; foul or fair; far or near – (it) is to be seen with true wisdom for what it is (in terms of): 'This is not mine; I am not this; this is not my self'."

"Only (physical) form Lord, only (physical) form?"

"(Physical) form, Rāhula – also feeling, perception, traits and tendencies, and consciousness."

Then venerable Rāhula thought to himself: "Who would enter a village for almsfood today on being instructed (thus) in the Lord's presence." And turning thence he sat down cross-legged at the root of a tree with body upright, and establishing mindfulness before him as his aim. (Now) venerable Sāriputta saw (this) and said to venerable Rāhula: "Cultivate awareness of breathing in and out, Rāhula. (Such) awareness, when much practised, is highly fruitful and profitable." Then venerable Rāhula, emerging from seclusion in the evening, approached the Lord and, saluting (him), sat down at one side. Said Rāhula:

"How, bhante, if cultivated and much practised, is awareness of in and out breathing highly fruitful and profitable?"

"Whatever (belongs to the four great elements, namely whatever is the internal or external solid, liquid, heat, or aeriform elements)[1] is to be seen with true wisdom for what it is (in terms of): 'This is not mine; I am not this; this is not my self.' And (likewise with regard to whatever is) the element of space. The space element may be internal or external. And what, Rāhula, is the internal space element? Whatever is internally, individually space, become space, and of a secondary nature,[2] namely the ear and nasal orifice, the mouth opening, and that by which one swallows what is eaten, drunk, consumed, and tasted, (the place) where one contains (it), and that by which (it) is evacuated from the lower part (of the body); or whatever else, internal to the individual, is the space element, or converted to space, (and) is of a secondary nature. Seeing it thus one turns away from (all the elements), one purges the mind of (them).

Apply the (mental) development that is earth-like, Rāhula, for (by this means) seductive and repulsive impressions that have arisen and taken hold of the mind will not persist. As (people) discard both the clean and the filthy on the earth, as they discard both excrement and urine on to (it, as well as) phlegm, pus, and blood – and yet the earth is neither troubled, nor vexed, nor disgusted – just so apply the (mental) development that is earth-like.

Apply the (mental) development that is as liquid, Rāhula, for (by this means) seductive and repulsive impressions that have arisen and taken hold of the mind will not persist. As (people) immerse both the clean and the filthy in water – yet the water is neither troubled, nor vexed, nor disgusted – just so apply the (mental) development that is as liquid.

Apply the (mental) development that is like heat, Rāhula, for (by this means) seductive and repulsive impressions that have arisen and taken hold of the mind will not persist. As fire consumes both the clean and the filthy – yet the fire is neither troubled, nor vexed, nor disgusted – just so apply the (mental) development that is like heat.

Apply the (mental) development that is like air, Rāhula, for (by this means) seductive and repulsive impressions that have arisen and taken hold of the mind will not persist. As the wind blows on both the clean and filthy – yet the air is neither troubled, nor vexed, nor disgusted – just so apply the (mental) development that is like air.

Apply the (mental) development that is like space, Rāhula, for (by this means) seductive and repulsive impressions that have arisen and taken hold of the mind will not persist. As space is located nowhere, just so apply the (mental) development that is like space.

Apply the (mental) development that is goodwill, Rāhula, for (by this means) ill-will will be abandoned. Apply the (mental) development that is compassion, Rāhula, for (by this means) injuring will be abandoned. Apply the (mental) development that is gladness, Rāhula, for (by this means) discontent will be abandoned. Apply the (mental) development that is equanimity, Rāhula, for (by this means) reaction will be abandoned. Apply the (mental) development that relates to the ugly, Rāhula, for (by this means) passion will be abandoned. Apply the (mental) development that is the perception of what is transient, Rāhula, for (by this means) self-exaltation will be abandoned."

Thus spoke the Lord.

1. The description of the four elements is greatly condensed. The detail is identical to that in other discourses.
2. i.e. presumably with space in its entirety as "primary".

63

Minor Discourse with Māluṅkyāputta

426–432

Thus have I heard: once the Lord dwelt near Sāvatthī in the Jeta Grove on Anāthapiṇḍika's campus. Then to venerable Māluṅkyāputta in solitude and seclusion came the thought: "Those opinions not clarified by the Lord, (but) set aside and rejected (by him, namely) that the world is eternal; that the world is not eternal; that the world is finite; that the world is infinite; that the life principle is (the same as) the body; that the life-principle is one thing, the body something else; that the Exemplar exists after death; that the Exemplar does not exist after death; (or both, or neither). These matters have not been made plain to me by the Lord, (and that) does not please me, that does not satisfy me. I shall go and ask (him) the significance of this. If (he) explains to me (by means of definite answers) I will pursue the good life under the Lord. If (not) I shall repudiate the training and return to the worldly condition."

Then venerable Māluṅkyāputta, emerging from seclusion towards evening, approached the Lord, saluted (him), and sat down at one side. (Having explained the train of thought that had occurred to him, venerable Māluṅkyāputta said): "If the Lord does not know (the answers to these questions)) this would be honest, namely (to say): 'I do not know, I do not see.' "

"Māluṅkyāputta, have I spoken to you like this: 'Come, Māluṅkyāputta, pursue the good life under me and I will explain that the world is eternal, (or) that the world is not eternal, (and so on)?' "

"Not so, bhante."

"And did you say to me: 'I will pursue the good life under the Lord (provided that he satisfies me on such matters)?' "

"Not so, bhante."

"That being so, foolish man, who are you and what do you repudiate? Māluṅkyāputta, anyone who should say: 'I will not pursue the good life under the Lord until (he has explained these matters)' would die before that was explained to him by the Exemplar.[1] It is as though a man had been pierced by an arrow thickly smeared with poison, and friends, companions, and relations were to procure a physician and surgeon. (But then) he says: 'I will not draw out this arrow until I know the man by whom I am hurt; whether he be noble or brahman, or merchant, or artisan; until I know his name and lineage; until I know whether he is tall, or short, or middling, (and so on). I will not draw out the arrow until I know (what kind of bow, what kind of bow-string, what kind of shaft was used, and so on).' Māluṅkyāputta, that person would die before (all) that had been learnt by (him).[2]

Māluṅkyāputta, the living of the good life could not be said to depend on the view that the world is eternal, (or) on the view that the world is not eternal, (or on answers to any of the other questions which you raise). Whether there is (the one or the other of these views) there remains birth, old age, and death, and there are grief, woe, pain, distress, and trouble – of which I declare the overcoming in this life.

Therefore Māluṅkyāputta, bear in mind what I have explained, and what I have not explained. I have not explained (those matters on which you have questioned me). And why have I not (done so)? Because this is not useful, not the starting-point of the good life, not conducive to disenchantment, dispassion, becoming tranquil, cessation, gnosis, enlightenment, *nibbāna*.

And what have I explained, Māluṅkyāputta? I have explained: 'This is suffering.': I have explained: 'This is the origin of suffering.' I have explained: 'This is the cessation of suffering.' I have explained: 'This is the way leading to the cessation of suffering.' And why have I (done so)? Because this is useful, this is the starting-point of the good life, and conducive to (those states I have mentioned)."

Thus spoke the Lord.

1. Generally assumed to mean simply that the Master would set aside all such questions but maybe also hinting at the absurdity of expecting *brief* answers on such imponderables.
2. Detail of the parable considerably abbreviated.

64

Major Discourse with Māluṅkyāputta

433–437

Thus have I heard: once the Lord dwelt near Sāvatthī, in the Jeta Grove on Anāthapiṇḍika's campus. There (he) addressed the monks, saying:

"Monks, do you recall me teaching the five fetters that bind (one) to the worldly condition?" At these words venerable Māluṅkyāputta said to the Lord:

"I recall (them), bhante. I recall the view of one's own body (as such a fetter, and also) uncertainty, the influence of convention and ritual, worldly impulses, (and) malice. Thus do I recall the Lord's teaching of the five fetters that bind (one) to the worldly condition."

"To whom, Māluṅkyāputta, do you recall the five fetters being taught by me like that? Will not wanderers of other sects chide you with the analogy of a young child. For if there is not (his) own body for a baby boy lying on his back, how could the view of own body come about for him? The view of own body is, in fact, innate in him. If there are not phenomena[1] (for such a baby) how could uncertainty regarding phenomena arise for him. If there are not habits[2] how does the influence of convention and ritual arise? If there is not worldly pursuit how could the impulse to worldly pursuit arise? If there are not beings how could ill-will towards beings arise? Uncertainty, habits, impulse towards worldly pursuits, and ill-will are (therefore likewise) innate in (a small baby). What if the wanderers of other sects chide you (by means of such an analogy)?"

At these words venerable Ānanda said to the Lord: "The time is right for the Lord to teach the five fetters that bind (one) to the worldly condition."

"As to this, Ānanda, some uninformed worldling, heedless of the *ariyans*, untrained in the *dhamma* of good men, lives with a mind possessed and overcome by the view of 'own body', and unaware of the true nature of deliverance from (such a view). For him the rooted, undispelled view of 'own body' is a fetter binding (him) to the worldly condition. (Similarly) he lives with a mind possessed and overcome by uncertainty, the influence of convention and ritual, impulse towards worldly pursuit, and malice, unaware of the true nature of deliverance from (such things). But, Ānanda, an informed disciple of the *ariyans*, heeding (them), does not live with a mind (thus) possessed and overcome.

Ānanda, whatever the way and the course for the abandonment of the five fetters that bind (one) to the worldly condition, it is not possible that one will know, or see, or give (them) up without recourse to that way – just as it is not possible that there can be the cutting out of the pith from a great, enduring, and pithy tree without (first) stripping the bark and the accessory wood.

(And), just as a weak man might come along (thinking to swim across the river Ganges, but fail to do so), likewise anyone whose mind is not satisfied, pleased, and composed, when states for the cessation of 'own body' are taught him is not freed (thereby).

And what, Ānanda, is the way and the course for the abandonment of the five fetters that bind (one) to the worldly condition? Herein a monk, distancing (himself) from attachment, abandoning unskilled states, and with the total subsiding of the unwholesome lusts of the body, reaches and experiences the first, the second, the third, and the fourth (levels of) absorption. Further, Ānanda, by completely transcending the perception of (physical) form, he reaches and experiences the realm of infinite space, infinite consciousness, and of nothingness. Whatever (in any of those states) is become (physical) form, feeling, perception, traits and tendencies, or consciousness – he recognises these things as transient, painful, an illness, an abscess, a dart, a misfortune, an affliction, as alien, as in decay, as empty, and as devoid of self. He turns his mind from these things and focuses (it) on the element of the deathless. This is the real, this is the exalted, namely the quietening of all tendencies, the giving up of every attachment, the rooting out of craving, dispassion, cessation, *nibbāna*. Steadfast he achieves the rooting out of the distractions at that point. If he does not achieve (that), then by his passion for *dhamma*, and his delight in *dhamma*, and by the final disappearance of the five fetters that bind (one) to the worldly condition, he is one of spontaneous uprising, reaching *nibbāna* there and without return from that world. Ānanda, this is the way and the course for the abandonment of the five fetters."

"Bhante, if this is the way and course for the abandonment of the five fetters that bind (one) to the worldly condition, why are some monks here freed through the mind,[3] some through wisdom?"

"In this matter, Ānanda, I speak of differences in their faculties."

Thus spoke the Lord.

1. Could mean either mental or physical phenomena or both in this context.
2. The same Pali word has here been translated both "convention" and "habit".
3. Horner notes that "freed through the mind" here refers to a predominance of concentration or one-pointedness.

65

With Bhaddāli

437–447

Thus have I heard: once the Lord dwelt at Sāvatthī in the Jeta Grove of Anāthapiṇḍika's park. There (he) addressed the monks, saying:

"Monks, I eat at one sitting (each day). (By so doing) I know freedom from sickness and good health. (I know) lightness, strength, and comfort. Do likewise monks, and eat at one sitting."

At these words venerable Bhaddāli said to the Lord: "I am not able to eat at one sitting, bhante. (In doing so) I might have scruples and misgivings."

"Well then, Bhaddāli, after consuming one portion at the place to which you were invited, you could take another portion away and eat that too. Eating in that way you could keep going." (But venerable Bhaddāli just repeated what he had said at first. And), subsequently,[1] (he) declared his inability with regard to the instruction laid down by the Lord among the Order of monks, and with reference to the understanding of the training. Whereupon (he) did not see the Lord face-to-face for three months, not being one who lived up to the Teacher's admonition.

Now at that time a large number of monks were engaged in robe-making for the Lord, thinking: "When the robe is completed, then the Lord will go on a three months walk." Then venerable Bhaddāli went up to these monks, exchanged greetings and, after conversing in a friendly and polite way, sat down at one side. (The monks told him of the Lord's approaching departure, implying that he should approach the Lord, and saying): "Come on, friend Bhaddāli. Take full heed of this advice. Do not be remorseful later." (Accepting their reproof) venerable Bhaddāli approached the Lord, saluted him, and sat down at one side. Said Bhaddāli:

"I am at fault bhante in that, ignorant, erring, and unskilled, I declared (my) inability in regard to (that) instruction. May the Lord acknowledge the fault as a fault, that there may be restraint in the future."

"Bhaddāli, a fault did indeed overcome you. (During) this time,[2] you were unaware (that I dwelt at Sāvatthī, and would know that) the monk Bhaddāli was not one who lived up to the Teacher's admonition. (Likewise) you were unaware that many monks who were come to Sāvatthī for the rains, many nuns, many lay-followers (also knew it)."

"May the Lord acknowledge the fault as a fault, that there may be restraint in the future."

"What do you think about this, Bhaddāli? I might say to a monk who is liberated in both ways, (or to many of lesser attainment):[3] 'Be a bridge for me in the mire.' Would he make a bridge (of himself) – or would he shift his body about, or would he say no?"

"Not so, bhante."

"And what do you think about this, Bhaddāli. At this time were you one who was liberated in both ways, (or even) striving out of faith?"

"Not so, bhante."

"At this time were you not empty, vain, and found wanting?"

"Yes, bhante. May the Lord acknowledge the fault as a fault, that there may be restraint in the future."

"Because you see the fault as a fault Bhaddāli, and confess it in accordance with *dhamma*, we accept it from you.[4] For this is growth in the discipline of the *ariyans* that, seeing a fault as a fault, and confessing it in accordance with *dhamma*, one then shows restraint in the future.

Herein, Bhaddāli, some monk is one who does not live up to the Teacher's admonition, thinking: 'Supposing I were to resort to a remote dwelling, to a forest, I might well reach superhuman states, the knowledge and vision truly characteristic of the *ariyans*.' (Whereupon he seeks out such a place). Having lived remote in such a way the Teacher criticises him, or, after investigation, his intelligent companions in the good life criticise him, or *devas* do so, or he reproaches himself. (Thereafter), he fails to reach (those states). Why so? That is how it is, Bhaddāli, for one who does not live up to the Teacher's admonition.

Herein, Bhaddāli, some (other) monk is one who does live up to the Teacher's admonition. He, too, (finds a remote and secluded place, but having lived there), the Teacher (and others) do not criticise him. (Thereafter) he does reach (such states). Remote from worldly pursuits and from unskilled states he reaches and experiences the first, the second, the third, and the fourth (levels of) absorption. He turns the mind towards recollection and knowledge of previous existences, and to the knowledge of the passing away and re-emergence of (other) beings. (And) he turns (it) to the rooting out and knowledge of the distractions."

At these words venerable Bhaddāli said: "Bhante, what is the reason, what the condition, whereby they act against some monk here repeatedly, (but not against another)."

"Herein, Bhaddāli, some monk is frequently guilty of an offence, is much offending. On being spoken to by the monks he answers evasively, he gets off the point, he shows irritation, anger, and discontent. He does not comport himself properly, he is not subdued. He is not acquitted, (and it does not occur to him to ask what he can do to please the Order). Then the monks think (that that monk is found wanting in those ways, saying to one another): 'It would surely be well if the brethren were to investigate this monk in such and such a way. Thus his case might not be settled quickly.'

Herein (however), Bhaddāli, some (other) monk is (likewise a constant offender but), on being spoken to by the monks, he (is open and unresentful). Then the monks (say to one another): 'It would surely be well if the brethren were to investigate this monk in such and such a way. Thus his case might be settled quickly.'

Herein (however), Bhaddāli, some (other) monk is not an intentional offender, not much offending (but), on being spoken to by the monks, (he behaves like the first, is evasive and resentful). Then the monks say to one another: 'It would surely be well if the brethren investigated this monk in such and such a way. Thus his case might not be settled quickly.'

Herein (however), Bhaddāli, some (other) monk is not an intentional offender, not much offending (and), on being spoken to by the monks, (he is open and unresentful). Then the monks say to one another: 'It would surely be well if the brethren investigated this monk in such and such a way. Thus his case might be settled quickly.'

Herein (however), Bhaddāli, some (other) monk proceeds with (only) a certain degree of faith and enthusiasm. (And the monks recognise this and say to one another): 'If we act constantly against this monk even such faith and enthusiasm as he has may deteriorate.' Bhaddāli, it is like a one-eyed man whose friends, companions, and relatives might shelter that one eye thinking: 'Let not that one eye of his deteriorate.'

This, Bhaddāli, is the reason, this the condition, whereby they act repeatedly against one monk, (but not another)."

"What is the reason, bhante, what the condition, whereby formerly there were fewer rules of training and more monks established in knowledge, (as compared with the present)?"

"This is how it is, Bhaddāli. When beings are falling away and true *dhamma* is vanishing there are a greater number of rules and fewer monks established in knowledge. Only in so far as conditions rooted in the distractions appear here, amid the Order, does the Teacher lay down a rule of training for disciples. (And) only when the Order has reached large proportions do some conditions rooted in the distractions appear, (or when it has reached its zenith in terms of) possessions, fame, great learning, or is (simply) long established. Because of (any of these factors) the Teacher (may) declare a rule of training for disciples, so as to ward off those conditions rooted in the distractions.

Bhaddāli, there were few of you when I taught the parable of the young thoroughbred as a way of representing *dhamma*. Do you recall it?"

"No, bhante."

"How do you account for that?"

"Indeed that for a long time I did not live up to the training in respect of the Teacher's admonition."

"That is not the only reason and explanation, Bhaddāli. Even for a long time I have grasped and known your mind with (mine, realising): 'When I am teaching this foolish man hears *dhamma* without evaluation, or attention, or applying his entire mind, or with ready ear.' Nevertheless I shall teach you the parable of the young thoroughbred.

Bhaddāli, it is like a skilful horse-trainer who, on acquiring a fine thoroughbred, first imposes the bit. Whilst getting used to the bit, and (despite) whatever irritations, tricks, and struggles there are (in the horse), he becomes proficient in that respect through repeated and gradual training. (Then) the horse-trainer imposes the harness (similarly). (After that he) trains it (to go) straight, in a circle, (to make use of) its hooves, and with respect to galloping, neighing, the royal trick, the royal acrobatic feat, incomparable speed and swiftness, and incomparable temperament. (The horse) becomes proficient in (each) respect through repeated and gradual training. (Finally) the horse-trainer gives him the utmost (grooming).[5] Possessed of these ten attributes a fine thoroughbred befits a king, is serviceable to a king, and is deemed a royal asset. Likewise a monk possessed of ten qualities is worthy of offerings, of hospitality, and of gifts, of salutation with joined palms, (as) a supreme source of good for the world. What ten? Herein, Bhaddāli, a monk is endowed with proficiency as regards right view, aim, speech, action, livelihood, effort, mindfulness, concentration, true knowledge (and) freedom. Possessed of these ten attributes a monk is worthy (of such courtesies)."

Thus spoke the Lord.

1. Normally the Pali word means "then", but there is clearly some lapse of time involved here.
2. Normal translation would be "at this time", but this can only refer to the three-month interval.
3. A list of lesser attainments is given, "faith" being the least of them.
4. Bhaddāli's confession is accepted only at the third protestation. Clearly he is regarded as a hard case.
5. Two words, one meaning "colour", the other of doubtful meaning, but clearly having reference to what the trainer does for the horse.

66

The Parable of the Quail

447–456

Thus have I heard: once the Lord dwelt in Aṅguttarāpa (at a town called) Āpaṇa. Then the Lord, dressing at an early hour and taking bowl and robe, went into Āpaṇa for almsfood. (Having done so), and returning after the meal, he approached a certain jungle-thicket for the afternoon rest. Plunging into (it) he seated himself at the root of a tree.

(Now it so happened that venerable Udāyin had resorted to that same jungle-thicket) where the thought came to him: "Truly the Lord is the remover of many painful conditions and the bringer of many happy conditions for us; a remover of many unskilful states and a bringer of many skilful states." Whereupon venerable Udāyin, emerging from seclusion in the evening, approached the Lord, saluted (him), and sat down at one side. (Telling the Lord of his train of thought), Udāyin said:

"Formerly, bhante, we ate in the evening and in the morning, and during the day – at a wrong time. (Then) there was the occasion when the Lord addressed the monks, saying: 'Now then, monks, give up this wrong practice of eating during the daytime.' I was affected by this. I was distressed, thinking: 'What householders give us out of faith, but at a wrong time during the day, that the Adept enjoins us to reject.' We, who look to the Lord with affection and respect, with shame and fear (with regard to wrongdoing), thus forsook that wrong mealtime. (After this) we would eat in the morning and in the evening, (but then) the Lord addressed the monks, saying: 'Now then, monks, give up this wrong practice of eating during the night.' I was affected by this. I was distressed. For that which was accounted more excellent of these two meals, that the Lord enjoined us to abandon, that the Adept enjoined us to reject.

Formerly, bhante, a certain man obtained a curry during the day and said: 'Now put this aside, and we will all eat it together come evening.' And whatever cooking there might be is largely at night. We, who look to the Lord with affection and respect, with shame and fear (with regard to wrongdoing), thus forsook that wrong mealtime. Formerly, bhante, monks walking for almsfood in the pitch darkness of night would walk into a pool at the entrance to a village, or fall into a dirty pond, or run into a thorn hedge, or a sleeping cow, or meet with youths – some committing a crime, or womenfolk who would divert them from true *dhamma*.

Once, bhante, I walked for almsfood in the pitch darkness of night. A certain woman saw me during a flash of lightning as she washed a bowl, and let out a scream of fear, crying: 'Help – a demon is upon me!' I spoke to (her) saying: 'I am not a demon, sister, but a monk waiting for almsfood.' (She replied): 'The father or mother of a monk must be dead. Monk, you would do better to slash your belly with a sharp butcher's knife than to walk for almsfood for the sake of your belly in the pitch darkness of night.' Recalling that I think: 'Truly the Lord is the remover of many painful conditions and the bringer of many happy conditions for us; a remover of many unskilful states and a bringer of many skilful states.' "

Herein however, Udāyin, some foolish people, on being told by me (to) give this up, think: 'What of this insignificant and mundane matter. This ascetic overdoes austerity.' They do not give it up, and they sow discontent with regard to me and those monks who desire the training. Udāyin, that is a powerful, firm, tough, and lasting bond for them, a gross piece of lumber. It is like a quail, a hen bird, caught in the coils of a rotten creeper, who is killed, or captured, or dies there. If someone were to say: 'This is not a strong, or serious, or lasting, or real bond for that quail', would he be speaking the truth?"

"Not so, bhante."

"Likewise, Udāyin, (for those who regard my words on this matter as of little significance), that is a powerful, firm, tough, and lasting bond for them, a gross piece of lumber. But some sons of family, on being told by me (to) give this up, think: 'What of this insignificant and mundane renunciation which the Lord tells us to make, (this small thing) which the Adept enjoins us to reject.' They give it up and do not sow discontent with regard to me and those monks who desire the training. Having abandoned it they live unconcerned, pacified, finding pleasure in constraint, with a mind like a wild thing. For them, Udāyin, there is no strong, or serious, or lasting, or real bond. It is like a king's elephant, with tusks as long as a plough-pole, immense, well-sired, at home on the battlefield who, if held fast by leather thongs, easily bends his body and, having destroyed and torn apart those bonds, goes away at his pleasure. Would anyone be speaking aright, Udāyin, who said: 'That was a strong, a serious, a lasting, a real bond for him, a gross piece of lumber.' "

"Not so, bhante."

"And so it is, Udāyin, (for those who do not regard my words on this matter as of little significance). Udāyin, there are these four kinds of person to be found in the world. Herein, some person is practising for the abandonment of attachment, for (its) rejection, (but) memories and aspirations connected with attachment assail him. He gives in to them, does not renounce them, does not rid himself of them, does not consign them to oblivion. I declare that person to be in bondage, not free from bondage. Why so? The specific faculties of that person are known to me.

Herein, Udāyin, some (other) person is practising (in the same way), and is (similarly) assailed. He does not give in, he renounces (these memories and aspirations connected with attachment), rids himself of them, consigns them to oblivion. I declare that person also to be in bondage, not free from bondage. Why so? The specific faculties of that person are known to me.

Herein, Udāyin, some (other) person is practising in (such a way) and, sooner or later, through want of mindfulness, memories and aspirations connected with attachment assail him. (After the) slow (re)-arising of mindfulness he then quickly renounces them, rids himself of them, consigns them to oblivion, It is as though a man were to let fall two or three drops of water into a pot heated for a whole day. Slow might the drops of water have fallen, but quickly would they then be destroyed and consumed. Likewise for the person (who suffers a momentary loss of mindfulness). I declare that person also to be in bondage, not free from bondage. Why so? The specific faculties of that person are known to me.

Herein however, Udāyin, some (other) person thinks: 'Attachment is the root of suffering' and having seen this, there is a waning of attachment, there is freedom in terms of the ending of attachment. I declare that person not to be in bondage, to be free from it. Why so? The specific faculties of that person are known to me.

There are these five strands of worldly pursuit, Udāyin: visible forms, pleasing, welcome, enticing, voluptuous, laden with pleasure, exciting; (and likewise for the other senses). The happiness and delight that come about because of these is called worldly happiness, vile, plebeian, un*ariyan*. Of these pleasures I say they are not to be indulged, cultivated, nor made much of, (but) to be feared.

Herein, Udāyin, a monk, remote from worldly pursuits and from unskilled states, reaches and experiences the first, the second, and the third (levels of) absorption. I say that (each of these) belongs with what is unstable (by virtue of the thought and investigation, the joy, the suffering, and the happiness they contain. But) a monk, by abandoning happiness and suffering, reaches and experiences the fourth (level of) absorption, that is completely purified by equanimity and mindfulness. I say that this belongs to what is stable.

(But of all these) I say (that they are) insufficient. I say (that they should be renounced). And wherein is (their) transcendence? Herein a monk, by completely transcending the perception of (material) form, reaches and experiences the realm of infinite space, of infinite consciousness, of nothingness, and of neither perceiving nor not-perceiving. (But of all these) I say (that they should be renounced). And wherein is (their) transcendence? Herein a monk, by completely transcending the realm of neither perceiving nor not-perceiving, reaches and experiences the cessation of perception and feeling. Therein is (their) transcendence. Udāyin, do you see the bond, be it subtle or gross, of which I have not told the abandonment."

"Not so, bhante."

Thus spoke the Lord.

67

At Cātumā

456–462

Thus have I heard: once the Lord dwelt at Cātumā in the Myrobalan Grove. Now at that time Sāriputta and Moggallāna, at the head of as many as five hundred monks, had arrived at Cātumā to see the Lord, and there were loud noises and great tumult as the newcomers exchanged greetings with the resident monks, and lodgings were assigned, and robes and bowls sorted out.[1] Then the Lord addressed venerable Ānanda, saying: "What are those loud noises, Ānanda? One might think fishermen were hauling in a catch." (Whereupon venerable Ānanda told him what was happening).

"Go and speak to those monks in my name, Ānanda, saying: 'The Teacher would have words with the brethren.' " (And venerable Ānanda went and summoned those monks to the Lord's presence. Then) the monks approached the Lord, saluted (him), and sat down at one side. Said the Lord:

"Monks, isn't this loud din and great tumult like fishermen hauling in a catch?" (And they explained the reason for it).

"Go, monks. I dismiss you. Keep away from me."

"Yes, bhante", replied those monks. Then they rose from their seats, saluting the Lord, and keeping their right sides towards him. After tidying their lodgings they went away, taking (only) bowls and robes.

Now at that time the Sakyans of Cātumā had come together in a council-hall on some business. (They) saw those monks some way off and went up to (them), saying: "Well now, brethren. Where are you going?"

"Friends, the Order of monks has been dismissed by the Lord."

"Then sit down for a while, venerable ones. Perhaps we can pacify the Lord." Then the Sakyans of Cātumā went to the Lord, saluted (him), and sat down at one side. Said (they):

"Rejoice in the Order of monks, bhante, greet (them). Just as the Order of monks has been helped by the Lord on former occasions let (it be so) now. There are monks here not long gone forth, newcomers to this *dhamma* and discipline. Having lost the chance of seeing the Lord then, just as young seeds might be altered and suffer reverse if denied water, (or) a young calf (similarly) if not seeing its mother – (such might be their fate)."

Then Brahmā Sahampati, knowing with his mind the Lord's train of thought, and just as a strong man might stretch out his arm and then bend it) back, disappeared from the *brahmā-* world and appeared before the Lord. Arranging his robe over one shoulder, and saluting the Lord with joined palms, (he) said:

"Rejoice in the Order of monks, bhante. Just as the Order of monks has been helped by the Lord on former occasions let (it be so) now."[2]

The Sakyans of Cātumā and Brahma Sahampati succeeded in pacifying the Lord with the aid of the parables of the seeds, and of the young calf.

Then venerable Moggallāna the Great addressed the monks, saying: "Arise, friends. Take your bowls and robes. The Lord has been pacified." (Whereupon) the monks, rising from their seats and bringing their bowls and robes, went to the Lord, saluted (him), and sat down at one side. Said the Lord to Sāriputta: "What did you think, Sāriputta, when the Order of monks were dismissed by me?"

"I thought: 'The Lord will now dwell unconcerned, and given over to a state of ease in this life, and we will (do likewise).' "

"Wait, Sāriputta, wait! Don't let such a thought come to you again." Then the Lord (put the same question to venerable Moggallāna). Said Moggallāna:

"I thought: 'The Lord will now dwell unconcerned and given over to a state of ease in this life. I and venerable Sāriputta will now look after the Order of monks.' "

"Well (said), Moggallāna, well (said). For either I could look after the Order of monks, or Sāriputta and Moggallāna."

Then the Lord addressed the monks, saying:

"Monks, these four hazards might be anticipated for those going down to the water – waves, crocodiles, whirlpools, fierce fishes.[3] Likewise four hazards are to be anticipated for some people going forth from home to the homeless life.

And what, monks, is the hazard of waves? Herein some son of family, gone forth from home into homelessness, thinks: 'I am beset by birth, old age, and death; by grief, woe, pain, distress, and trouble; beset and overcome by suffering. Perhaps some means can be found for bringing this entirety of suffering to an end.' His companions in the good life exhort and advise the one gone forth like this: 'Thus you should go out, thus you should return. Thus you should look forward, thus you should look round. Thus you should bend, thus you should straighten up. Thus you should carry cloak, bowl, and robe.' He thinks: 'When we were in the position of householders we used to exhort and advise others. But these who might be our sons, or grandsons, think they should advise and exhort us.' Repudiating the training, he returns to the worldly condition. The hazard of waves is an expression for being pervaded with anger.

And what, monks, is the hazard of crocodiles? Herein some (other) son of family, gone forth from home into homelessness, thinks (as the first). His companions in the good life exhort and advise him like this: 'You can eat this (but) not this. You can enjoy this (but) not this. You can savour this (but) not this. You can drink this (but) not this. (Or), you can do (all these things) in a proper way (but) not in an improper way, (or) at a proper time (but) not at an improper time.' He thinks: 'When we were in the position of householders we (enjoyed what we wanted, in the way we wanted, and when we wanted). But when householders, during the day, give us excellent food, both hard and soft, out of faith – but at a wrong time, they seem to muzzle the mouth.' Repudiating the training, he returns to the worldly condition. The hazard of crocodiles, monks, is an expression for gluttony.

And what, monks, is the hazard of whirlpools? Herein, some (other) son of a family, gone forth from home into homelessness, thinks (like the first two). Dressing at an early hour, and taking bowl and robe, he enters the village or town for almsfood with body unguarded, with speech unguarded, with mindfulness not established, and with unrestrained faculties. There he sees a householder or (his) son possessing, indulging, and ministering to the five strands of worldly pursuit. He thinks: 'When we were in the position of householders we (were like this). There being possessions in the home it is possible both to enjoy (them), and to perform deeds of merit.' Repudiating the training, he returns to the worldly condition. The hazard of whirlpools, monks, is an expression for the five strands of worldly pursuit.

And what, monks, is the hazard of fierce fishes? Herein some (other) son of family, gone forth from home into homelessness, thinks (like the first three). Dressing at an early hour, and taking bowl and robe, he enters the village or town for almsfood, with body unguarded, with speech unguarded, with mindfulness not established, and with unrestrained faculties. He sees there women scantily covered, improperly clothed. (Thereupon) passion corrupts his mind and, repudiating the training, he returns to the worldly condition. The hazard of fierce fishes, monks, is an expression for womenfolk.

These, monks, are the four hazards to be anticipated for some persons going forth from home into homelessness in this *dhamma* and discipline."

Thus spoke the Lord.

1. Horner has "put away".
2. Brahmā's exhortation continues as an exact repetition of the Sakyans.
3. I am not sure of the source of Horner's translation for the last term, but have preferred it to PTSD which gives "alligators".

68

At Naḷakapāna

462–468

Thus have I heard: once the Lord dwelt near Naḷakapāna among the Kosalans in the Judas-tree Grove. Now at that time many sons of family had gone forth from home into homelessness out of faith – venerable Anuruddha, Nandiya, Kimbila, Bhagu, Kuṇḍadhāna, Revata, and venerable Ānanda, and many other well-known sons of family. At that time the Lord was seated in the open air surrounded by a group[1] of monks. Then the Lord addressed the monks with reference to these sons of family, saying: "I trust that these sons of family are finding enjoyment in the good life, monks." At these words the monks were silent.

Then the Lord thought: "What if I were to question these sons of family themselves." Whereupon (he) addressed venerable Anuruddha, saying:

"I trust you are finding enjoyment in the good life, Anuruddhas."[2]

"Certainly we are, bhante."

"It is well. That is fitting for sons of family such as you, gone forth from home into homelessness out of faith. At a time that you, with your happy youth, in your early prime, and with jet black hair, might indulge in worldly pursuits, you (choose this life instead). Moreover you are not (thus) gone forth as obliged by kings,[3] or robbers, or because of debt, or through fear, or through loss of livelihood. (Was it rather) with the thought: 'I am beset by birth, old age, and death; by grief, woe, pain, distress, and trouble; beset and overcome by suffering. Perhaps some means can be found for bringing this entirety of suffering to an end', (that you did so)?."

"Yes, bhante."

"But, for a son of family gone forth in this manner, what is his task? Remote from worldly pursuits and unskilled states, should he not obtain joy and happiness, or something better than that, (worldly) desire continues to take hold of his mind, (or) ill-will, sloth and torpor, agitation and worry, uncertainty, discontent, or weariness. (But if he does reach such states, these defilements of the mind do not persist).

What is there for you in me, Anuruddhas? Those distractions that are corrupting, leading to renewal, fearful, culminating in suffering, and birth, old age and death in the future – (do you think) that these are unabandoned by the Exemplar and that therefore, after reflection, he pursues one thing, endures another, avoids another, and eliminates something else?"

"Not so, bhante. We think that (they) *are* abandoned by (him), and that therefore, after reflection, he pursues one thing, endures another, avoids another, and eliminates something else?"

"Well (said), Anuruddhas. (And so indeed it is). It is like a torn up palm-tree, annihilated for the future, and taking no further hold. (So it is for the Exemplar).

What do you think about this, Anuruddhas? For what reason does the Exemplar, in connection with the rebirths of dead and departed disciples, declare: 'This one has arisen in this place, this one in that place'?"

"For us realities are rooted in the Lord, have the Lord for conduit, have the Lord for protection. Would that the meaning of these words were made evident. Having heard, the monks will bear it in mind."

"Anuruddhas, the Exemplar has no intent of deceiving people, of cajoling people; nor (does he seek) gain or honour, fame or profit; nor does he think: 'Let people know me thus' – (when he explains these things). But there are sons of family with faith, greatly uplifted, greatly joyful. They, on hearing those things, focus their minds on reality.[4] That is for their wellbeing and happiness for many a day.

Herein, Anuruddhas, a monk, or a nun, or a layfollower hears that[5] (a person) of a certain name has died, and it is declared by the Lord (that) he or she is established in profound knowledge; or is of spontaneous uprising through bringing to an end the five fetters that bind one to the worldly condition; or has brought to an end the three fetters of passion, ill-will, and delusion; or is an enterer of the stream (of *dhamma*), not destined for a place of destruction. If that venerable one, or sister, or layfollower, has seen for him or herself, or heard reports that (that person referred to by the Lord) was of such a kind in his conduct, in (mental) states, in terms of wisdom, in mode of living, and in terms of freedom, (then the hearer) focuses his or her mind on reality. And so, Anuruddhas, there is reassurance[6] for (such a person).

Anuruddhas, the Exemplar has no intent of deceiving people, of cajoling people; nor (does he seek) gain or honour, fame or profit; nor does he think: 'Let people know me thus' – (when he explains these things). But there are sons of family with faith, greatly uplifted, greatly joyful . They, on hearing those things, focus their minds on reality. That is for their wellbeing and happiness for many a day."

Thus spoke the Lord.

1. There is an ongoing problem regarding the translation of "sangha" as "the Order" or as "a group". Clearly, at the outset the entire Order constituted a small group, the whole of which may have been present for a particular discourse.
2. Refers to three monks.
3. i.e. as alternative to punishment for some wrong.
4. Literally "on suchness' or "on thusness".
5. Much condensed – the full text repeats the various attainments separately for monks, nuns, and for layfollowers of each sex.
6. Literally "living at ease".

69

On Gulissāni

469–473

Thus have I heard: once the Lord dwelt near Rājagaha in the Bamboo Grove at the squirrels' feeding-place. Now at that time a monk called Gulissāni, (who had been) forest-gone and was crude in his behaviour, had come into the midst of the Order for some purpose or other. In that connection venerable Sāriputta, with reference to the monk Gulissāni, addressed the monks, saying:

"Friends, a monk (who has been) forest-gone, and (then) returns among the Order, should be respectful and show deference towards his companions in the good life. If (he does not so behave) there will be those who say of him: 'What (price) then this venerable one, who has been forest-gone, living as he chooses, but who (now acts like this).' So (such a person) should be respectful and show deference towards his companions in the good life.[1]

Friends, (he) should be skilful with regard to seats, thinking: 'I will not intrude among monks who are elders, and I will not refuse novice monks a seat.'[2] (He) should not enter a village too early, nor return during the day (to the campus).[3] (He) should not mix with families before and after a meal. (He) should not be conceited or fickle; not garrulous or of loose talk. (He) should be of pleasant speech and a friend to what is helpful;[4] guarded as to the doors of his faculties; moderate in eating; intent on vigilance; of resolute endeavour; of established mindfulness; composed; and possessed of wisdom. (For, if he is lacking in any of these respects, he may provoke adverse comment).

Friends, (he) should apply himself to the highest *dhamma* and discipline; to those (states) that are peaceful freedoms and formless, having transcended form; (and) to superhuman states. (For) there are those who will question a monk who has been forest-gone (on these matters, and will comment adversely if he cannot answer properly)."

At these words venerable Moggallāna the Great spoke thus to venerable Sāriputta: "Friend Sāriputta, are these things to be undertaken and practised just by a monk who (has been) forest-gone, or also by one living near a village?"

"By a monk who (has been) forest-gone, friend Moggallāna – even more by one living near a village."

1. There are sixteen paragraphs in all with the same form as the foregoing. I have condensed the material into the two that follow.

2. i.e. people who might feel obliged to remain standing unless invited to sit down.
3. A minor infringement. Various items in the list are obviously the kind of thing that a forest-gone monk could usefully be reminded of on returning to communal life.
4. The remainder of the admonitions are more concerned with his task whilst forest-gone.

70

At Kīṭāgiri

473–481

Thus have I heard: once the Lord was travelling on foot in Kāsi, together with a large company of monks. There (he) addressed the monks, saying:

"Monks, I do not eat at night (and, so doing), I am aware of little illness or disease, of buoyancy, strength, and of living at my ease. In this you (should follow my example)."

Then the Lord, (continuing his travels), arrived at a town called Kīṭāgiri (and stayed there). At that time the monks called Assaji and Punabbasuka were in residence at Kīṭāgiri. Whereupon several monks went to (them and told them of the Lord's instruction).

At these words the monks Assaji and Punabbasuka said:

"Friends, we eat in the evening, in the early morning and during the day – at a wrong time. (So doing) we are aware of little illness or disease, of buoyancy, strength, and of living at our ease. Why should we give up our actual (course) and follow (something) hypothetical? We shall (continue to eat as at present)."

Being unable to convince the monks Assaji and Punabbasuka, those (other) monks approached the Lord, saluted (him), and sat down at one side, (where they told him of the conversation they had had). Then the Lord addressed a certain monk, saying: "Go monk, summon the monks Assaji and Punabassuka in my name, saying the Teacher would speak with (them)."

(And so the monks Assaji and Punabbasuka came to the Lord). Said the Lord: "Is (what has been reported to me) true?"

"Yes, bhante."

"Monks, do you understand me to have taught *dhamma* like this – whatever the individual experiences, be it pleasant, painful, (or neither), unskilful states diminish and skilful states increase for him?"

"Not so, bhante."

"Have you not understood me to have taught *dhamma* like this – for someone here experiencing a pleasant feeling of one kind, unskilful states increase and skilful states diminish, (whereas), for someone experiencing a pleasant feeling of another kind, unskilful states diminish and skilful states increase. (And likewise with painful and neutral feelings)?"

"Yes, bhante."

"Well (said), monks. And, had I not known, seen, understood, realised, and ascertained through wisdom that, for someone here experiencing a pleasant feeling of one kind, unskilful states increase and skilful states diminish, would it be proper for me, in that (absence of) knowledge to say: 'Renounce such a kind of pleasant feeling'?"

"Not so, bhante."

"And would it be proper for me to say (in the opposite case): 'A pleasant feeling of such a kind having arisen, experience it'?"[1]

"Not so, bhante."

"Monks, I do not say of all monks (that) there is something to be done through alertness. Of those monks who are *arahant*, with the distractions rooted out, fulfilled, who have done what was to be done, who have put down the burden, reached the goal, have utterly destroyed the thongs of existence, and are truly freed through knowledge – I say (of them) that there is nothing to be (so achieved). Why so? It is impossible for them to be neglectful. But of those monks still under training, of unachieved purpose, and living aspiring for the matchless haven from bondage – I say (of them that there is something to be so achieved). Why so? Perhaps in resorting to suitable lodgings, in keeping company with helpful friends, in controlling the faculties, they may reach and experience that matchless conclusion of the good life for which sons of family rightly go forth from home into homelessness, having reached it through their own gnosis in this life. So, in considering the fruits of alertness, for these monks I say (that) there is something to be done by means (of it).

Monks, there are these seven (kinds of) person to be found in the world – the one who is liberated in two ways, the one who is freed through wisdom, the one who bears witness through the body, the one who has gained (right) view, the one freed through faith, the one striving for *dhamma*, and the one striving for faith.

And who is the person who is liberated in two ways? Herein, someone lives encountering through his body those peaceful freedoms that transcend forms and, having (also) seen by means of wisdom, the distractions are extinguished in him. For that monk I say there is nothing to be achieved by alertness.

And who, monks, is the person that is freed through wisdom? Herein, someone does not live encountering through his body those peaceful freedoms that transcend forms, but having ascertained (the truth) by means of wisdom, the distractions are extinguished in him. For that monk I say there is nothing to be achieved by alertness.

And who, monks, is the person who is witness through the body?[2] Herein, someone lives encountering through his body those peaceful freedoms that transcend forms, but having seen by means of wisdom, some distractions are extinguished in him. For that monk I say there is something to be achieved by alertness. Why so? Perhaps, in resorting to suitable lodgings (and the other activities I mentioned), he may reach and experience that matchless conclusion of the good life. For that monk I say there is something to be achieved by alertness.

And who, monks, is the person who has gained (right) view? Herein, someone does not live encountering through his body those peaceful freedoms that transcend forms, but having seen by means of wisdom, some distractions are extinguished in him. The matters declared by the Exemplar are fully understood and investigated in him by means of wisdom. For that monk I say there is something to be achieved by alertness (for the same reason).

And who, monks, is the person freed through faith. Herein, someone does not live encountering through his body those peaceful freedoms that transcend forms, but having seen by means of wisdom, some distractions are extinguished in him. His faith in the Exemplar is firm, properly rooted and settled. For that monk I say there is something to be achieved by alertness (for the same reason).

And who, monks, is the person who is striving for *dhamma*. Herein, someone does not live encountering through his body those peaceful freedoms that transcend forms and, (though) seeing by means of wisdom, the distractions are not extinguished in him. The matters declared by the Exemplar are only partly appreciated by him through wisdom, yet these states are his, namely the faculties of faith, vigour, mindfulness, concentration, and wisdom. For that monk I say there is something to be achieved by alertness (for the same reason).

And who, monks, is the person who is striving for faith? Herein, someone does not live encountering through his body those peaceful freedoms that transcend forms, and, (though) seeing by means of wisdom, the distractions are not extinguished in him. If faith in and affection for the Exemplar are sufficient these states will be his, namely the faculties of faith, vigour, mindfulness, concentration, and wisdom. For that monk I say there is something to be achieved by alertness (for the same reason).

Monks, I do not maintain the attainment of complete knowledge at the outset. Nonetheless, from a gradual training, a gradual performance, a gradual method is (such) attainment. And how (does this come about)? Herein, with the arising of faith one draws near, and having drawn near one remains in attendance. (Then, successively), one lends an ear, one listens, one commits *dhamma* to memory, one investigates the meaning of *dhamma* thus remembered, and (these) matters are found satisfactory. (Whereupon) one finds resolve, (then) one is able (to make a beginning), (then) one evaluates, (then) one strives, (then) through one's own resolution, one reaches the highest truth, and one penetrates and sees it by means of wisdom. But if that faith had been absent, then there would have been no drawing near, no remaining in attendance (and so on). Monks, you have gone astray, you are on a wrong course. How far, monks, have these foolish people departed from this *dhamma* and discipline.

Monks, there is a fourfold exposition the meaning of which, when set out, an intelligent person should soon understand. Even a teacher who puts value on the things of the flesh, is (their) heir, and lives in association with (them), does not put up with this kind of carping and quibbling, (whereby some say): 'Now, we should act on this (instruction) of his to us, but not on that (instruction).' And does not the Exemplar live wholly dissociated from the things of the flesh? For the believing disciple proceeding in the closest conjunction with the Teacher's doctrine, there is (only) this accord with *dhamma*, (whereby he thinks): 'The Lord is the Teacher, I am the disciple. The Lord knows, I do not know.' For (such a person) the Teacher's doctrine represents the furtherance of growth and a source of strength. For (such a person) there is only this accord with *dhamma*, (whereby he thinks): 'Let only skin, sinews, and bone remain; let the body's flesh and blood dry up, if thereby will be generated the fuel of energy without which what is to be gained through human strength, vigour, and exertion remains ungained.' For (such a person), monks, either of two fruits is to be anticipated – gnosis in this life or the state of no return, should there be some residual existence."

Thus spoke the Lord.

1. The other types of feeling are given parallel treatment.
2. Horner translates "who is a mental-realiser", and goes on to suggest that it is, in fact, the three mental aspects of feeling, perception, and psychological tendencies that are being referred to as something fully comprehended. This would mean that "body" is here being used figuratively in the way that we might talk about a "body" of opinion. However, in the light of the sentence that follows I find the more straightforward interpretation more convincing.

71

With Vacchagotta on the Threefold Knowledge

481–483

Thus have I heard: once the Lord dwelt at Vesālī in the Great Grove in the hall of the Gabled House. Now at that time the wanderer Vacchagotta was living on the wanderers' park at Ekapuṇḍarīka. Then the Lord, dressing at an early hour and taking bowl and robe, went into Vesālī for almsfood, (but on his way it struck him): "It is too early to walk round Vesālī for almsfood. Suppose I were to approach the wanderers' campus at Ekapuṇḍarīka and the wanderer Vacchagotta." (And he did so). Vacchagotta saw the Lord coming some way off and said to (him):

"Welcome, bhante, greetings. It is some time since the Lord took the opportunity to come here. Let the Lord be seated. This place is made ready." The Lord sat down and the wanderer Vacchagotta took another lower seat at one side. Said Vacchagotta:

"Bhante, I have heard (that) the ascetic Gotama knows all, sees all, and claims all-embracing knowledge, saying: 'Whether walking or standing, asleep or awake, knowledge and vision is always and fully available to me.' Do those who speak thus speak the words of the Lord and not accuse him falsely, and do they explain the truth of *dhamma*, and does no truth in accordance with *dhamma* incur blame?"

"Vaccha, those who say (this) are not speaking (aright). (How so)? Saying: 'The ascetic Gotama has a threefold knowledge', they would be speaking in accordance with what I have said. To the extent that I desire, Vaccha, I recall a diversity of previous existences. With the purified divine eye transcending the human I behold beings passing away and re-arising. And, Vaccha, I reach and experience the mental freedom and the freedom through wisdom that are undistracted, having realised them in this life through my own gnosis."

At these words the wanderer Vacchagotta said to the Lord: "Worthy Gotama, is there any layman who, without abandoning the layman's fetters, has made an end of suffering on the breaking up of the body after death?"

"There is not, Vaccha."

"But is there (such a person) who has reached heaven?"

"Not one, not two, Vaccha, not five hundred – even more." "And is there any mendicant (among other sects) who has made an end of suffering on the breaking up of the body at death?"

"There is not, Vaccha."

"But is there (such a person) who has reached heaven?"

"I recall ninety-one aeons, and am not aware of any, except one, and he was an exponent of activity and of the effectiveness (of activity)."[1]

"That being the case, good Gotama, the realm of the sects is empty, even as regards the reaching of heaven."

"(Even so), Vaccha."

Thus spoke the Lord.

1. The negative form of this word means without outcome or significance i.e. this man agreed with the Buddhists in broad terms in accepting that activity has a result.

72

With Vacchagotta on Fire

483–489

Thus have I heard: once the Lord dwelt at Sāvatthī in the Jeta Grove of Anāthapiṇḍika's park. Then the wanderer Vacchagotta approached the Lord, exchanged greetings, and having conversed in a friendly and polite way, sat down at one side. Said Vacchagotta:

"What say you, good Gotama – (that) the world is eternal, and that just this is the truth, all else foolishness?"

"Such is not my view, Vaccha."

"Well then, good Gotama, do you say (the opposite)?"

"Such is not my view, Vaccha."

"Well then, good Gotama, do you say (that) the world is finite, that this is the truth, all else foolishness?"

"Such is not my view, Vaccha."

"Well then, good Gotama, do you say (the opposite)?"

"Such is not my view, Vaccha."

"Well then, good Gotama, do you say (that) the life-principle is identical with the body, that this is the truth, all else foolishness?"

"Such is not my view, Vaccha."

"Well then, good Gotama, do you say (the opposite)?"

"Such is not my view, Vaccha."

"Well then, good Gotama, do you say that the Exemplar exists after death, that this is the truth, all else foolishness?"

"Such is not my view, Vaccha."

"Well then, good Gotama do you say (the opposite)?"

"Such is not my view, Vaccha."

"Well then, good Gotama, do you say (that) the Exemplar both exists and does not exist after death?"

"Such is not my view, Vaccha."

"Well then, good Gotama, do you say (that) the Exemplar neither exists nor does not exist after death?"

"Such is not my view, Vaccha."

"On being asked (all these questions) the ascetic Gotama replies: 'Such is not my view, Vaccha.' So what disadvantage does the worthy Gotama see, that thus leads him to avoid these standpoints altogether?"

"Vaccha – that the world is eternal – this standpoint is seizing on a view, getting bogged down in a view, manoeuvring with a view, fencing with a view, bondage to a view, and is connected with suffering, vexation, trouble, and feverishness. It does not make for disenchantment, dispassion, cessation, gnosis, enlightenment, *nibbāna*. (And the same is true of all the other standpoints you have mentioned). This is the disadvantage that I see, Vaccha, and leads me thus to avoid these standpoints altogether."

"But is there any standpoint whatsoever for the worthy Gotama?"

"'Standpoint' is abandoned by the Exemplar. For this is seen by (him) 'Here is (physical) form. Here is the origin of (physical) form. Here is the disappearance of (physical) form. Here (are) feeling, perception, traits and tendencies, and consciousness; here (their) origin; here (their) disappearance.' Therefore I say, the Exemplar, from dispassion, cessation, abandonment, renunciation, non-attachment, is freed of every illusion, every disturbance of mind, every bias towards: 'I the doer, mine the deed'."

"And thus freed in his mind, good Gotama, where does a monk arise?"

"'Arise' is not applicable, Vaccha."

"Well then, good Gotama, does he not arise?"

"'Not arise' is not applicable, Vaccha."

"Well then, good Gotama, does he both arise and not arise?"

"(This too) is not applicable, Vaccha."

"Well then, good Gotama, does he neither arise nor not arise?"

"(This too) is not applicable, Vaccha."

"But, on being asked (all these questions) you said 'not applicable, Vaccha.' I was mystified and confused at this, and that measure of satisfaction gained through a previous conversation with the worthy Gotama is now gone."

"Certainly there is mystification and confusion for you, Vaccha. For this *dhamma* is deep, hard to discern and fully comprehend, peaceful, excellent, transcending logic, subtle, intelligible (only) to the wise. It is difficult to understand for you, who subscribe to a different view, a different allegiance, a different persuasion, whose links are elsewhere, and who follow another teacher. Now, Vaccha, I shall question you on the matter like this. Answer as you see fit. What do you think about this – if a fire were burning in front of you would you be aware (of that)?"

"I would be aware (of it), good Gotama."

"But if someone were to put the question: 'This fire that burns in front of you – on account of what does (it) burn?' – how would you answer?"

"I would answer (that it) burns on account of being fuelled by grass and sticks."

"And if the fire in front of you were to die out would you be aware (of that)?"

"I would be aware (of it), good Gotama."

"But if then someone were to put the question: 'This fire extinguished in front of you – in which direction has it gone?' – how would you answer?"

"(The question) is inapplicable, good Gotama. The fire burnt because of being fuelled by the grass and sticks, and from the consumption of that together with the unavailability of any further (fuel), then being unreplenished, it is simply referred to as 'extinguished'."

"Just so, Vaccha, the (physical) form by which one recognises the Exemplar is abandoned for (him), destroyed at the root, like a torn up palm-tree, annihilated for the future, and taking no further hold. The Exemplar is freed from the designation of (physical) form, Vaccha. Deep, immeasurable, unfathomable as the great ocean, neither 'arises' nor 'does not arise', nor (both), nor (neither) is applicable. (And the same applies to those) feelings, perceptions, traits and tendencies, and (forms of) consciousness by which one identifies (him)."

At these words the wanderer Vacchagotta said to the Lord:

"Good Gotama, it is like a great sāl-tree, near to a village or town, whose branches and leaves might perish because of their transient nature, whose bark and young shoots and softwood might (likewise) perish, so that, at a later date, it would be established only in the pith. So it is with the words of the worthy Gotama. Excellent, good Gotama, excellent." (Whereupon the wanderer Vacchagotta took the refuges and sought admission to the Order).

73

Major Discourse with Vacchagotta

489–497

Thus have I heard: once the Lord dwelt near Rājagaha in the Bamboo Grove at the squirrels' feeding place. Then the wanderer Vacchagotta approached the Lord, exchanged greetings and, having conversed in a friendly and polite way, sat down at one side. Said Vacchagotta:

"It is a long time since I spoke with the worthy Gotama. Would that (he) might teach me the skilled and the unskilled in brief."

"I could teach you the skilled and the unskilled in brief or in detail, Vaccha, but I will teach (it) in brief.

Greed is unskilful, Vaccha, lack of greed skilful. Ill-will is unskilful, (its) absence skilful. Delusion is unskilful, lack of delusion skilful. Destruction of life is unskilful, (and so is) taking what is not given, dissolute living, lying, slander, abuse, idle chatter. Abstention (from these things) is skilful. Envy is unskilful, (as are) malice and wrong view. (Freedom from them) is skilful. Thus there are these ten unskilful states and these ten skilful states.

When craving is abandoned by a monk, destroyed at the root, like a torn up palm-tree, annihilated for the future and taking no further hold, that monk is *arahant*, with the distractions rooted out, perfected, having done what was to be done and put down the burden, reaching his goal, and truly freed by knowledge."

"Very well, good Gotama, but is there even one disciple that is a monk or nun who, from the rooting out of the distractions, has reached and experienced the freedom of mind and the freedom of wisdom that is undistracted, having realised it in this life through his own gnosis?"

"Not one, not two, Vaccha, not five hundred – even more (of each)."

"Very well, good Gotama, but is there even one disciple of the worthy Gotama that is a male or female layfollower, a householder dressed in white, a follower of the good life, who has done away with the five fetters that bind (one) to the worldly condition, of spontaneous uprising, achieving *nibbāna* there with no further return from that place?"

"Not one, not two, Vaccha, not five hundred – even more." "Very well, good Gotama, but is there even one (such person still) enjoying worldly pursuits, (but) conforming to the teaching, according with the injunctions, uncertainty left behind, reservations disappeared, and confidence established, who is not dependent on others as regards the Teacher's admonitions?"

"Not one, not two, Vaccha, not five hundred – even more."

"Worthy Gotama, if (you) alone were successful in this *dhamma*, and not monks, this good life would be unfulfilled in that respect, (and if any other of the attainments you have described were lacking) this *dhamma* would be unfulfilled in that respect. (Such not being the case) this *dhamma* is fulfilled in (every) respect.

As the river Ganges, (first) flowing towards the sea, running down to (it), leading into (it), (then) stands pressing against (it), in the same way the worthy Gotama's following, comprising householders and those gone forth, (first) flowing towards *nibbāna*, running down to (it), leading into (it), (then) stands pressing against (it).

Excellent, good Gotama, excellent. It is as though one were to set upright what was overturned, or uncover what was hidden, or show a way to one who was lost, or bring an oil-lamp into a dark place, so that those with eyes might see. Thus, in various ways, is *dhamma* made evident by the worthy Gotama. I go to the worthy Gotama for refuge, and to the *dhamma*, and to the Order of monks. May I obtain the going forth in the worthy Gotama's presence, and (also) ordination."

"Vaccha, anyone who is a former member of another sect and wishes for the going forth in this *dhamma* and discipline, and for ordination, lives on probation for four months. At the end of four months the monks, if they are so minded, permit the going forth and ordination as a monk. Nevertheless differences between individuals are known to me."

"(The Lord speaks of four months, but) I will live on probation for four years and (then) let the monks, if so minded, permit the going forth and ordination as a monk." But the wanderer Vacchagotta obtained the going forth and ordination in the Lord's presence.

Half a month after being ordained venerable Vacchagotta went to the Lord, saluted (him), and sat down at one side. Said Vacchagotta:

"Bhante, I have attained what may be attained through a trainee's knowledge and learning. Let the Lord teach me *dhamma* beyond (this)."

"Well then, Vaccha, cultivate two further states, calm and insight. These two states will engender the comprehension of many conditions. Vaccha, to the extent that you desire (you can wish): 'May I obtain the diverse forms of psychic power. Having been one may I be many, or having been many be one. May I go, visible or invisible, through a wall, a fence, or a mountain as through space; or dive and rise through the ground as though in water; or walk on unbroken waters as though on the ground; or travel cross-legged through the air like a bird on the wing; or touch and stroke with the hand this moon and sun in all their power and splendour; and even as far as the *brahma*-world extend the range of the body.'

To the extent that you desire (you may wish): 'May I hear sounds of both (kinds), be they far or near, with the purified divine ear that transcends the human.'

To the extent that you desire (you may wish): 'May I grasp and comprehend with my mind the minds of other beings and other people. May I know the passionate, the malevolent mind, the deluded mind, the concentrated mind, the mind become great, the unexcelled mind, the composed mind, the mind become free (and all contrary states as such).'

To the extent that you desire (you may wish): 'May I recall various former existences.'

To the extent that you desire (you may wish): 'May I, with the purified divine eye transcending the human, behold the passing away and re-emergence of beings.'

To the extent that you desire (you may wish): 'May I live with the distractions rooted out, reaching and experiencing the freedom of mind and freedom of wisdom that are undistracted, having realised them in this life through my own gnosis.' You will achieve the capacity to be a witness here and there (in all these matters), given the (appropriate) exertion.[1]" Then venerable Vacchagotta, pleased and satisfied at the Lord's words, rose from his place, saluted (him), and with right side towards him, departed.

Whereupon venerable Vacchagotta, living alone and apart, diligent, zealous, and resolute, reached and experienced before long that matchless consummation of the good life, realised in this life from his own gnosis, for which sons of family rightly go forth from home into homelessness. (He knew): "Destroyed is birth, fulfilled the good life, done what was to be done, with no further return to this world." And so venerable Vacchagotta became one of the *arahants*.

Now at that time a large number of monks were going to see the Lord. Venerable Vacchagotta saw (them) coming some way off and approached (them), saying

"Now, where are you going, brethren?"

"We are going to see the Lord, friend."

"Then let the venerable ones pay homage at the Lord's feet with their heads on my behalf saying (that) I honour the Lord, the Adept." (And those monks, on meeting the Lord, told him of their encounter with venerable Vacchagotta). (Said the Lord):

"Already, monks, having grasped and comprehended the mind of the monk Vacchagotta with my mind (I knew): 'The monk Vacchagotta is of threefold knowledge, of great psychic powers, of great eminence.' And *devatās* also told me (this)."

Thus spoke the Lord.

1. Horner – "so long as there is the objective." This comment follows each of the foregoing wishes in the original.

74

With Dīghanakha

497–501

Thus have I heard: once the Lord dwelt at Rājagaha, on Vulture's Peak in the Boar's Cave. Then the wanderer Dīghanakha (of the Aggivessana clan) approached the Lord, exchanged greetings, and having conversed in a friendly and polite way, stood at one side. Said Dīghanakha:

"Good Gotama, I speak like this and hold this view: 'Everything fails to please me.' "

"And this view of yours, Aggivessana – does this also fail to please you?"

"Good Gotama, if this view were pleasing to me, that also would be of such a nature, that would be just like it.[1]"

"Now, Aggivessana, when the majority in the world speak thus: 'That also would be of such a nature, that would be just like it', they do not abandon that same view, and they take hold of a further view. Now when the minority in the world (make such a statement) they *do* abandon that same view, and they do not take hold of a further view.

There are some ascetics and brahmans speaking and thinking like this: 'Everything pleases me.' There are (others) speaking and thinking like this: 'Everything fails to please me.' There are (yet others) speaking and thinking like this: 'Certain (things) please me, certain (things) fail to please me.' In this connection, (and as to the first group), their view approximates to infatuation, to bondage, to enjoyment, to cleaving, to attachment. (As to the second group), their view approximates to non-infatuation, to absence of bondage, to disenchantment, to non-cleaving, to non-attachment."

At these words the wanderer Dīghanakha said to the Lord:

"The worthy Gotama praises my standpoint. (He) extols (it)."

"In this connection, Aggivessana, (and as to the third group), their view approximates (to both the others according to which things are pleasing or fail to please).

Herein an intelligent man reflects about (the first group) as follows: 'If I were to maintain this view – (that) everything pleases me, holding and clinging to it with obstinacy, and declaring (that) this is the truth, all else foolishness, there would be a dispute for me on two fronts – (with those who say the opposite, and with those who take the middle position). In dispute there is contention, in contention there is distress, in distress there is injury.' Considering that dispute, contention, distress, and injury in relation to himself he abandons that same view, and he does not take hold of a further view. (And an intelligent man, reflecting on the other two groups would draw the same conclusion). So, of (all) these views there is the abandonment, of (all) these views there is the rejection.

But this body, Aggivessana, possessed of form, built of the four great elements, born of mother and father, nourished on rice and junket, is a thing worn and chafed, broken and scattered. (It) should be seen as transient, as painful, an illness, an abscess, a dart, a misfortune, an affliction, as alien, as empty, and as devoid of self. Having contemplated this, whatever in regard to the body is delight in (it), affection for (it), companionship with (it), is abandoned.

There are these three (kinds of) feeling, Aggivessana – pleasant feeling, painful feeling, feeling (that is neither). On the occasion when one experiences a pleasant feeling one experiences just (that, not either of the other two kinds of feeling). On the occasion when one experiences a painful feeling one experiences just (that, and likewise for the feeling that is neither pleasant nor painful). Pleasant feelings are transient, composite, dependent on conditions, a wasting thing, a decaying thing, a fading thing, an ending thing, (and so are feelings that are painful, and feelings that are neither pleasant nor painful). Seeing it thus, Aggivessana, the informed *ariyan* disciple turns away from (every kind of) feeling, (and so doing) is freed of passion, being freed of passion is emancipated, and in freedom is freedom's knowledge – destroyed is birth, fulfilled the good life, done what was to be done, with no further return to this world. Thus freed in mind, Aggivessana, a monk does not agree with anyone, and does not dispute with anyone. And whatever is the usage of the world, he expresses himself thereby without taking hold of it."

Now at that time venerable Sāriputta was standing behind the Lord, fanning (him). Whereupon it occurred to (him): "Surely the Lord speaks to us of getting rid of these things through gnosis, (and) of rejecting (them) through gnosis." In this way, and after reflection, venerable Sāriputta's mind was freed from the distractions without any further attachment. But to the wanderer Dīghanakha there came the unblemished, spotless eye of *dhamma* – that whatever is of a nature to arise is of a nature to cease. And seeing, gaining, knowing, immersing himself in *dhamma*, transcending uncertainty, his doubts settled, fully confident of the Teacher's instruction without dependence on another, (he took the refuges and became a lay-follower).

1. This confusing rejoinder presumably follows from the difficulty of replying either "yes" or "no". An affirmative produces a classic paradox, a negative appears like a repudiation of what he has just said.

75

With Māgandiya

501–513

Thus have I heard: once the Lord dwelt among the Kurus, (at) a township of the Kurus called Khammāssadhamma, and on a covering of grass in a heated room belonging to a brahman of the Bhāradvāja clan. Then the Lord, dressing at an early hour, and taking bowl and robe, went into Khammāssadhamma for almsfood. Returning after the meal he went towards a certain jungle-thicket for the afternoon rest and, plunging into (it), sat down at the root of a tree for the afternoon rest.

Then the wanderer Māgandiya, who was given to wandering and roaming about, approached (this) heated room. (He) saw the covering of grass that was made ready, and said to the brahman of the Bhāradvāja clan:

"For whom is this covering of grass made ready – as bedding material for an ascetic perhaps?"

"Good Māgandiya, there is the ascetic Gotama, a son of the Sakyans, gone forth from the Sakya clan, (and a teacher of high renown). For this worthy Gotama the bedding is made ready."

"Good Bhāradvāja, we behold a sorry sight in seeing the bed of the worthy Gotama, the suppressor of life.[1]"

"Watch your words, Māgandiya, watch your words! Many intelligent nobles, brahmans, householders and ascetics have trust in the worthy Gotama, are trained by the *ariyan* method, in *dhamma*, in what is skilful."

"Good Bhāradvāja, we would meet the worthy Gotama face-to-face and say, in his presence: 'The ascetic Gotama is a suppressor of life.' Why so? This is the conclusion of (one of) our discourses.[2]"

"If it is not inconvenient, good Māgandiya, I will tell the ascetic Gotama of this."

"It is immaterial to me whether you tell him what has been said, good Bhāradvāja."

The Lord, with the purified divine ear transcending the human, heard that conversation of the brahman of the Bhāradvāja clan with the wanderer Māgandiya. Then, emerging from seclusion towards evening, (he) approached the heated room of the brahman, and sat down on the covering of grass prepared (for him). Then the brahman went to the Lord, exchanged greetings, and having conversed in a friendly and polite way, sat down at one side. Said the Lord:

"There was some conversation between you and the wanderer Māgandiya concerning this covering of grass."

At these words the Bhāradvāja brahman, stirred and astounded, said to the Lord:

"But it was just this that I wished to tell the worthy Gotama, and then (he) made it unnecessary!"

Now this conversation between the Lord and the brahman was interrupted when the wanderer Māgandiya came into the heated room and approached the Lord. Having exchanged greetings and conversed in a friendly and polite way, he sat down at one side. Said the Lord:

"Māgandiya, the eye delights in, is devoted to, takes pleasure in (physical) form. Tamed, constrained, guarded, and controlled by the Exemplar he teaches *dhamma* for its restraint, (and he deals similarly with the other senses and with the mind itself). Does that account for your statement: 'The ascetic Gotama is a suppressor of life'?"

"That accounts for my statement. Why so? Such is the conclusion of (one of) our discourses."

"What do you think about this, Māgandiya? Imagine someone formerly given over to visible forms, audible sounds (and so on, and to all things) agreeable, pleasant, seductive, attractive, pleasure-laden, exciting. At a later date, having recognised for what it is the origin and disappearance, the satisfaction and disadvantage, and the emancipation from (such things), and having abandoned the craving (for them), dispelling the fever (for them), he might live emptied of thirst, and with a mind inwardly appeased. Māgandiya, what do you have to say of him?"

"Nothing at all, good Gotama."

"Moreover, Māgandiya, when formerly in lay-life, I was possessed of, and provided with the five strands of worldly pursuit, and gave myself over to them (in just such a way). Three palaces were mine, one for the rainy season, one for the winter, and one for the summer. In the four months of the rains, entertained by women musicians, I did not descend from the palace. But, at a later date, having recognised for what it is the origin and disappearance, the satisfaction and disadvantage, and the emancipation from worldly pursuits, I abandoned the craving for (them), dispelled the fever for (them), and lived emptied of thirst, and with a mind inwardly appeased. I observed other beings not without passion for worldly pursuits, eaten up with a craving for (them), burning with a fever for (them), and (therefore) following them. But I did not envy them, did not find pleasure therein. Why so? There is this love that is apart from worldly pursuits and unskilful things, and is directed towards the divine happiness that, once reached, endures. (So) I did not yearn for what is inferior, and found no pleasure in it. One might liken it to a householder or (his) son, rich, very wealthy, and with great possessions, possessed of and provided with the five strands of worldly pursuit, and who might be given over to them. Through proceeding aright in body, word, and thought, he might, on the breaking up of the body at death, achieve a good destiny, a heaven world, and the company of the Devas of the Thirty-Three. There in the Nandana Grove, surrounded by a throng of nymphs, and possessed of and provided with the five strands of worldly pursuit that are divine, he might give himself over to them. He would observe a householder or (his) son, possessed of and provided with the five strands of worldly pursuit, and given over to them. What do you think about that Māgandiya? Would that young *deva*, (in such surroundings), covet (their human pleasures)?"

"Indeed not, good Gotama. Why so? Divine joys are better and more excellent than human joys."

"In the same way, Māgandiya, did I (come to see the matter). Compare it to a leper, his body covered with sores and festering, gnawed at by vermin, scratching at the openings of his wounds with his nails, who scorches his body over a charcoal-pit. His friends, companions, and relatives find him a physician and surgeon, (who) treats him with medicine. Thanks to (it) he is freed from leprosy, well, happy, independent, his own master, going where he wants. He sees another leper (behaving as he had done). What do you think about that Māgandiya? Would he envy the other leper his charcoal-pit and his remedy?"

"Indeed not, good Gotama. Why so? In the case where there is an illness there is need of a remedy. In the case where there is no illness there is (no such need)."

"In the same way, Māgandiya, did I (come to see the matter). Again (with regard to that same leper – suppose, after he is cured), two strong men, taking him by the arms, drag him to the charcoal-pit. What do you think about that, Māgandiya? Wouldn't he writhe this way and that?"

"Certainly, good Gotama. Why so? That fire is painful to the touch, very hot and distressing."

"What do you think about this, Māgandiya? Is this fire (like this) now or was it previously (also of that nature)?"

"(Both now and previously) the fire is painful to the touch, very hot and distressing. But that leper, his faculties impaired, could find an agreeable alteration in his sensations from the painful contact of the fire."

"Just so, Māgandiya, throughout the past, worldly pursuits have been a painful contact, very hot and distressing, (and so it will be, and is now the case). And those beings not without passion for worldly pursuits, eaten up with a craving for (them), burning with a fever for (them) – their faculties being impaired, they could find an agreeable alteration in their sensations by the painful contact of just such worldly pursuits.

(Yet again, Māgandiya, consider the leper) who scorches his body over a charcoal-pit. In so far as he (does this), so those open sores of his become yet more unclean, more evil-smelling and putrid, and there is only a measure of relief and satisfaction from scratching his open sores. Likewise, there is only a measure of relief and satisfaction grounded in the five strands of worldly pursuit.

What do you think about this, Māgandiya? Have you seen or heard of a king, or a king's chief minister, possessed of and provided with the five strands of worldly pursuit and given over to them who, without abandoning the craving for worldly pursuit, and without ridding himself of his fever for (them), has lived, or lives, or will live with a mind emptied of thirst, and inwardly appeased?"

"Not so, good Gotama."

"Well (said), Māgandiya. Neither have I. And such ascetics and brahmans as have lived emptied of thirst, and with a mind inwardly appeased, have all recognised for what it is the origin and disappearance, the satisfaction and disadvantage, and the emancipation from worldly pursuits. (And so it is now and will continue to be)." Then the Lord uttered this verse **Health is the best possession, *nibbāna* the greatest happiness. And of ways, the eightfold it is that leads to security and the deathless.**

At these words the wanderer Māgandiya said to the Lord:

"Excellent, good Gotama, wonderful. How well spoken is this by the worthy Gotama. I, too, have heard this as being spoken by ancient teachers of teachers of wanderers. So there is a correspondence, good Gotama."

"But, as to that which you heard, what is this (that is described as) 'health'? What is this (that is described as) '*nibbāna*'?"

At these words the wanderer Māgandiya simply stroked his own limbs with his hand, saying: "This it is that is 'health'. This it is that is '*nibbāna*'. At this moment I am in good health, and there is nothing wrong with me."

"Māgandiya, it is like a man blind from birth who does not see dark or light shapes, or black or yellow shapes, or red or crimson, does not see the even or uneven, or the stars, or moon and sun. Should he hear a sighted person saying: 'Friend, (this) clean and pure white cloth, perfect in form, is indeed genuine', he might walk about searching for (such a thing). But another man could deceive him with a piece of coarse cloth stained with oil and dust. Having accepted it he might wear it and, in his delight with it, boast (of it in the same terms as the man he had previously heard). What do you think about that, Māgandiya? Would that man blind from birth (be likely to do those things) had he known and seen (what the cloth was really like)?"

"Good Gotama, he would (be likely to do those things only through) not knowing and not seeing (its nature)."

"Likewise, Māgandiya, wanderers of other sects, blind and without eyes, not comprehending 'Health' and not seeing '*nibbāna*', nonetheless speak this verse. This (verse) has now circulated among the masses. Yet this body, a manifestation that is an illness, an abscess, a dart, a misfortune, an affliction – (of this) you say: 'This is health, this is *nibbāna*.' For in you, Māgandiya, there is not the eye of the *ariyan* through which you might know health, and see *nibbāna*."

"I am satisfied that the worthy Gotama can teach me *dhamma*, so that I might know health and see *nibbāna*."

"Māgandiya, it is like a man blind from birth. His friends, associates, and relatives find him a physician and surgeon (who) treats him with medicine, but (that) does not provide him with eyes or restore his sight. What do you think about it? Wouldn't that medical man become exhausted and frustrated (in the attempt)?"

"Yes, good Gotama."

"Likewise, should I teach you *dhamma* (in this matter), you might (still) not know or see, and that would be exhausting and frustrating for me."

"(Still) I am satisfied that the worthy Gotama can teach me *dhamma*, so that I might know health and see *nibbāna*."

"It is like a man blind from birth. Should he hear a sighted person say: 'Friend, (this) clean and pure white cloth, perfect in form, is indeed genuine', he might walk about searching (for such a thing, and obtain a piece of coarse cloth, stained with oil and dirt instead). He wears it. His friends, companions, and relatives find him a physician and surgeon (who) treats him with medicine, and (that) does provide him with eyes, and does restore his sight. His eyesight restored, his enthusiasm and passion for that piece of coarse cloth is abandoned, and he considers that man (who gave him the cloth) as no friend, even as an enemy, and perhaps thinks he ought to kill him.

Likewise, Māgandiya, should I teach you *dhamma* (in this matter), you might know and see. Your eyes opened, enthusiasm and passion with reference to the five embodiments of attachment would be abandoned, and you might think:

'Surely, for a long time I have been cheated, deceived, and overcome by this mind. Taking hold of (physical) form, feeling, perception, traits and tendencies, and consciousness, I was attached to (them). From the condition of taking hold there was (continued) existence for me. From the condition of (continued) existence, there was birth. From birth old age, death, grief, woe, pain, distress, and trouble arise – such is the origin of this entirety of suffering.' "

"(Still) I am satisfied that the worthy Gotama can teach me *dhamma*, so that I might rise from this seat unblinded."

"Now, Māgandiya, you should keep companion with true men. (Thereby) you will hear true *dhamma*. If you hear true *dhamma* you will regulate your life in accordance with *dhamma*. (From that) you will know and see for yourself (that) these ills are abscesses and barbs, and that here (they) can come to an end without remainder. From the cessation of attachment to this is the cessation of (continued) existence, from the cessation of (that in turn) is the cessation of birth, and from the cessation of birth old age and death, grief, woe, pain, distress, and trouble come to an end – and thus there is the fading away of this entirety of suffering."

At these words the wanderer Māgandiya said to the Lord: "Excellent, good Gotama, excellent. It is as though one were to set upright what was overturned, or uncover what was hidden, or show a way to one who was lost, or bring an oil-lamp into a dark place, so that those with eyes might see. Thus, in various ways, is *dhamma* made evident by the worthy Gotama. I go to the worthy Gotama for refuge, and to the *dhamma*, and to the Order of monks. May I obtain the going forth in the worthy Gotama's presence, and (also) ordination."

"Māgandiya, anyone who is a former member of another sect and wishes for the going forth in this *dhamma* and discipline, and for ordination, lives on probation for four months. At the end of four months the monks, if they are so minded, permit the going forth and ordination as a monk. Nevertheless differences between individuals are known to me."

"(The Lord speaks of four months, but) I will live on probation for four years and (then) let the monks, if so minded, permit the going forth and ordination as a monk." But the wanderer Māgandiya obtained the going forth and ordination in the Lord's presence.

Before long, venerable Māgandiya (was) living alone and apart, diligent, zealous, and resolute. Some time later, having realised it from his own gnosis in this life, he reached and experienced that consummation of the good life for which sons of family rightly go forth from home into homelessness. (He knew) "Destroyed is birth, fulfilled the good life, done what was to be done, and no further return to this world." And so venerable Māgandiya became one of the *arahants*.

1. Horner – "the destroyer of growth".
2. There is no further information as to what this might be.

76

With Sandaka

513–524

Thus have I heard: once the Lord dwelt near Kosambī on Ghosita's campus. Now at that time the wanderer Sandaka was living in Fig Tree Cave with a large company of wanderers, some five hundred in number. Then venerable Ānanda, emerging from seclusion towards evening, addressed the monks, saying: "Friends, we will go to Devakaṭa Pool so as to see the cave." And venerable Ānanda went (there) with many monks. At that moment the wanderer Sandaka was sitting with a great company of wanderers, loudly and clamorously proclaiming on a variety of trivial matters such as talk about kings, robbers (and so on).[1] The wanderer Sandaka, seeing venerable Ānanda coming some way off, called his own company to order saying:

"Hush, friends! Don't be noisy. The ascetic Ānanda is coming, a disciple of the ascetic Gotama. Whenever the disciples of the ascetic Gotama live in Kosambī this ascetic Ānanda is among them. These brethren are lovers of quiet, trained to be quiet, and praise (it). Perhaps if he sees a company making little noise he may see fit to approach."

So those wanderers fell silent. Whereupon venerable Ānanda approached the wanderer Sandaka (who) said to (him): "Welcome, good Ānanda, greetings. It is some time since venerable Ānanda took the opportunity to come here. Let venerable Ānanda be seated." Venerable Ānanda sat down in the place prepared (for him whilst) the wanderer Sandaka, taking a low seat, sat at one side. Said Ānanda:

"Of what do you talk, Sandaka, as you sit together at this moment?"

"That conversation is of no consequence, good Ānanda. It will not be difficult to hear about (it) later. It would be well if venerable Ānanda could call to mind some *dhamma*-talk of his own teacher." Venerable Ānanda spoke thus:

"Sandaka, these four ways of not living the good life are declared by the Lord who has known and seen, who is *arahant* and truly enlightened. And four (kinds of) good life that are discouraging are (also) pointed out wherein an intelligent man could not remain, or if remaining, could not procure a true norm, or a skilful condition.

(And what are these four ways of not living the good life?) Herein some teacher speaks and thinks like this: 'There is neither gift, nor offering, nor sacrifice, nor ripening and result of good deeds and bad; neither this world nor another; neither mother nor father nor spontaneous uprising; no ascetics or brahmans living rightly, proceeding rightly, who make known this world and the next, having realised them through their own gnosis.

This man is made up of the four great elements and when he dies the earthy (part)[2] enters and returns to the mass of the earth, the water to the mass of water, the heat to the mass of heat, the air to the mass of air. The faculties are dissipated into space. Taking the corpse, four men carry it on a bier. On the way to the funeral-pyre his characteristics are evident. His bones become grey. Oblations come to nothing. Giving is a fool's doctrine. Those who speak of a profitable doctrine (therein) speak wrongly, falsely, with idle talk.[3] Fools and sages alike are destroyed and perish at the breaking up of the body. After death they are no more.'

With regard to that an intelligent man reflects like this: 'If the words of that worthy teacher are true then what is done is through my not doing it, what is accomplished is through my non-accomplishment. And both of us are equal in this matter as regards an ascetic's achievement, (though) I do not say (that) both of us will be destroyed and perish at the breaking up of the body, (and that) after death we shall be no more. It is superfluous for this worthy teacher to be naked and shaven, to exert himself by squatting, and to pluck out hair and beard, whereas I, living a settled life, surrounded and supported by sons, experiencing Kāsi's sandalwood perfumes, wearing garlands, scents, and cosmetics, and allowing (myself) gold and silver, will come to the same fate as this worthy teacher. (On the basis of) what knowledge and vision would I live the good life under this teacher?'' Recognising this not to be a way of living the good life, he therefore turns away from (it) and departs. This, Sandaka, is the first way of not living the good life.

Then again some teacher speaks and thinks like this: 'From performing or causing action (of whatever kind) no evil is brought about.[4]'

With regard to that an intelligent man reflects (in the same terms).[5] Recognising this not to be a way of living the good life he therefore turns away from (it) and departs. This, Sandaka, is the second way of not living the good life.

Then again some teacher speaks and thinks like this: 'There is no reason, no condition for the corruption of beings.'

With regard to (all) that an intelligent man reflects (in the same terms). Recognising this not to be a way of living the good life he therefore turns away from (it) and departs. This, Sandaka, is the third way of not living the good life.

Then again some teacher speaks and thinks like this: 'These seven forms (of existence) are uncreated, not brought about, not planned, not given a design, sterile, immovable, stable as a pillar, enduring. They do not move, or alter, or injure one another, or (affect) one another's pleasure, pain, or indifference. What seven? – the solid form (of existence), the liquid, the thermal, the aeriform, pleasures, pains, life-principles. In all this there is no one who slays or causes to slay, or hears or causes to hear, or understands or causes to understand. Even someone who severs a head with a sharp sword does not deprive anyone or anything of life, for the sword merely penetrates the interstices between the seven forms (of existence).[6] (And) one cannot say (that) one will bring an undeveloped activity to fruition through conduct, observance, austerity, or living of the good life, or abrogate a developed activity, realising (this by degrees). There is no such thing. In pleasure and pain there is a fixed measure, in transmigration there is (inherent) restriction. There is neither diminution nor increase, neither excellence nor debasement. Like a ball of thread that, when thrown down, runs away unwinding itself – so fools and sages alike, in flowing on and transmigrating, make an end of suffering.'

With regard to (all) that, Sandaka, an intelligent man reflects (in the same terms). Recognising this not to be a way of living the good life he therefore turns away from (it) and departs. This is the fourth way of not living the good life. These, Sandaka, are the four ways of not living the good life wherein an intelligent man could not remain, or if remaining could not procure a true norm, or a skilful condition."

"Excellent, good Ānanda, wonderful! But now what are those four (kinds of) good life that are discouraging, wherein an intelligent man could (likewise feel no satisfaction)?"

"Herein some teacher, all-knowing and all-seeing, claims all-embracing knowledge and vision, saying: 'Whether walking or standing, asleep or awake, knowledge and vision are always and fully available to me.' He enters an empty house. He does not obtain almsfood. A dog bites him. He meets with a fierce elephant and a fierce horse and a fierce bullock. And he asks about the name and clan of a woman or man. And he asks the name and way to a village or town. On being asked: 'How was this?' he says: 'I was bound to enter an empty house, so I (did so). I was bound not to obtain almsfood, so I failed to obtain it. (Someone) had to get bitten by a dog, so I got bitten. (Someone was destined to encounter various fierce animals, and I was the one to do so. Someone was bound to ask questions about people and places, so I asked such questions).'

With regard to (all) that an intelligent man, seeing this (kind of) good life to be discouraging, therefore turns away from (it) and departs. This, Sandaka, is the first (kind of) good life that is discouraging.

Then again, Sandaka, some teacher here is familiar with tradition. He teaches *dhamma* on the basis of successive reports as handed down in the collections. But for (such) a teacher there is both good and bad remembering, both correct and (otherwise).

With regard to that an intelligent man, seeing this (kind of) good life to be discouraging, therefore turns away from (it) and departs. This, Sandaka, is the second (kind of) good life that is discouraging.

Further, some teacher here is a reasoner, an investigator.[7] He teaches a *dhamma* beaten out by logic, associated with investigation, and of his own devising. But for (such) a teacher there is both good and bad investigation, both correct and (otherwise).

With regard to that an intelligent man, seeing this (kind of) good life to be discouraging, therefore turns away from (it) and departs. This, Sandaka, is the third (kind of) good life that is discouraging.

Further, some teacher is dull and stupid. Because of (that), on being asked some question or other, he indulges in pointless talk and prevarication.

With regard to that an intelligent man, seeing this (kind of) good life to be discouraging, therefore turns away from (it) and departs. This, Sandaka, is the fourth (kind of) good life that is discouraging.

These, Sandaka, are the four discouraging (kinds of) good life wherein an intelligent man could not remain, or if remaining, could not procure a true norm or a skilful condition."

"Excellent, good Ānanda, wonderful! But what should a teacher say and proclaim, for an intelligent man to be able to remain in the good life and procure a true norm and a skilful condition?"

"Herein Sandaka, an exemplar arises in the world. Abandoning these five hindrances which blemish the mind and are injurious to wisdom, and remote from worldly pursuits and unskilled states, he reaches and experiences the first, the second, the third, and the fourth (levels of) absorption. In relation to any teacher under whom the disciple comes to this excellent condition, the intelligent man could remain in that (kind of) good life, and could procure a true norm and a skilful condition. (He too may attain these states.)

With a mind composed, perfectly purified, and clear, he turns (it) towards recollection and knowledge of previous existences, to the knowledge of the passing away and re-emergence of other beings, and to the knowledge of the rooting out of the distractions."

"But, good Ānanda, could the monk (thus) freed enjoy worldly pursuits?"

"Sandaka, (such a one) cannot behave in (any of) these five ways: it is impossible for a monk who has rooted out the distractions to intentionally kill a living organism; (or) to take surreptitiously what is not given; (or) to indulge in sexual intercourse; (or) to tell a deliberate lie; (or) to enjoy what is implicit[8] in worldly pursuits, as (he did) formerly in the household state."

"But is the knowledge and vision (that he has) rooted out the distractions always and fully available to him, whether walking or standing, asleep or awake?"

"Now, Sandaka, I will construct a parable for you, for (thereby) some intelligent people grasp the meaning of what has been said. Suppose a man had his hands and feet severed, then, whether walking or standing, asleep or awake, his hands and feet are always and fully cut off, and moreover (he is aware of that). (So it is with a monk who has rooted out the distractions.)"

"But how many great leaders are there in this *dhamma* and discipline, good Ānanda?"

"Not one, not two, Sandaka, not five hundred – even more."

"Excellent, good Ānanda, wonderful! And there will be no exalting of one's own *dhamma* or disparagement of the *dhamma* of others. Both the teaching of *dhamma* in its (full) range and so many leaders are to be seen. But these (other) mendicants are sons without a mother who simply exalt themselves and disparage others, and make evident just three leaders, namely Nanda Vaccha, Kisa Saṅkicca, and Makkhali Gosāla."

Then the wanderer Sandaka addressed his own company, saying: "Go forth brethren! The living of the good life is with the ascetic Gotama, though it is not easy for us to forsake gain, honour, and fame." In such a way did the wanderer Sandaka send his own company to the good life under the Lord.

1. A list of almost thirty topics of mundane conversation is given in a passage which recurs in several discourses.
2. "earth" and "water" elsewhere translated "solid" and "liquid" but the analogy of "ashes to ashes" seems more effective here.
3. Horner – "It is vain, lying, empty talk on their part who profess to say: "There is.' "
4. The second, third, and fourth of the first set of four are abbreviated here. They have been given in full in 60.
5. There are very minor variations between the reflections on the four situations, but I have omitted these since in all cases the point is simply that the teachers concerned postulate realities which cannot be altered and thereby place a question mark against the purpose of their own enterprise.
6. Some numerical classifications have been omitted here which constitute a seeming digression from the point at issue.
7. I take "investigate" to mean purely abstract enquiry in this context.
8. Literally "stored".

77

Major Discourse with Sakuludāyin

1–22

Thus have I heard: once the Lord dwelt near Rājagaha, in the Bamboo Grove at the squirrels' feeding-place. Now at that time many well-known mendicants were staying at the peacocks' feeding-place in the wanderers' park, namely Anugāra, Varadhara, the wanderer Sakuludāyin, and various others. Then the Lord, dressing at an early hour and taking bowl and robe went into Rājagaha for almsfood, (but) it struck him: "It is too early to walk for alms in Rājagaha. Suppose I were to go to the peacocks' feeding-place in the wanderers' park, and approach the wanderer Sakuludāyin." (And he did so).

At that moment the wanderer Sakuludāyin was sitting with a great company of wanderers, loudly and clamorously proclaiming on a variety of trivial matters, such as talk about kings (and so on). The wanderer Sakuludāyin, seeing the Lord coming some way off, called his own company to order, saying:

"Hush, friends! Don't be noisy. The ascetic Gotama is coming, and this venerable one is a lover of quiet and praises (it). Perhaps if he sees a company making little noise he may see fit to approach."

So those wanderers fell silent. Whereupon the Lord approached the wanderer Sakuludāyin (who) said to (him): "Welcome, bhante, greetings. It is some time since the Lord took the opportunity to come here. Let the Lord be seated." The Lord sat down in the place prepared (for him whilst) the wanderer Sakuludāyin, taking a low seat, sat at one side. Said the Lord:

"Of what do you talk, Sakuludāyin, as you sit together at this moment?"

"That conversation is of no consequence, bhante. It will not be difficult to hear about (it) later. Some time ago, among ascetics and brahmans of various sects sitting and assembled together in the debating-hall, this chance conversation came about: 'It is certainly advantageous to the people of Aṅga-Magadha and a great gain (for them) when these ascetics and brahmans, leaders of groups with a following, well-known and renowned, who are founders of sects and highly honoured by the masses – (when such people) visit Rājagaha for the rains retreat. Pūraṇa Kassapa (is such a person, as are) Makkhali Gosāla, Ajita of the hair-blanket, Pakudha Kaccāyana, Sañjaya Belaṭṭhiputta, Nātaputta the Jain – (likewise) the ascetic Gotama. Now who (among these) is esteemed, found worthy of honour, respected and revered by disciples? And how do disciples live (thus) in (such) reliance (on the teacher)?"

Some there thought like this: 'This Pūraṇa Kassapa is leader of a group with a following, is well-known and renowned, and highly honoured by the masses. But he is not esteemed, found worthy of honour, respected and revered by disciples. And disciples do not live in reliance (on him). Once Pūraṇa Kassapa taught *dhamma* to an assembly of several hundreds. A certain disciple there gave voice, saying: "Don't ask Pūraṇa Kassapa about this matter, friends. He does not understand it. We understand it. Ask us about (it). We will explain it." Once Pūraṇa Kassapa, appealing with outstretched arms, was denied the chance to say: "Hush, friends! Don't be noisy. These people are not asking (you), friends. They are asking us. We will explain to them." But many (of his) disciples got the better of him and went away, saying: "You don't understand this *dhamma* and discipline. I understand (it). What do you know of (it)? You are on a wrong course. I am on a right course. I am consistent. You are inconsistent. You say later what should be said first, and first what should be said later. What you failed to think out is (now) altered. You are refuted (and) rebuked. Away with you and your theory, or make yourself clear if you can." So Pūraṅa Kassapa is not esteemed, honoured, respected, or revered by disciples, nor do (they) live in reliance on (him). (He) is, on the contrary, railed against with abuse of his *dhamma*.[1]' Some there thought (the same about) Makkhali Gosāla, Ajita of the hair-blanket, Pakudha Kaccāyana, Sañjaya Belaṭṭhiputta and Nātaputta the Jain.

Some there thought like this: 'This ascetic Gotama is a leader of a group with a following, is well-known and renowned, and highly honoured by the masses. And he is esteemed, honoured, respected and revered by disciples. And disciples do live in reliance (on him). Once the ascetic Gotama was teaching *dhamma* to an assembly of several hundreds. One disciple happened to cough. A companion touched him with the knee, saying: "Hush, brother! Less noise! Our Lord is teaching *dhamma*." When the ascetic Gotama is teaching an assembly of hundreds there is sound neither of spitting nor coughing. Any body of people expecting him are ready, thinking: "We shall hear whatever *dhamma* the Lord may speak." It is like a man at a crossroads who might press out a a small piece of pure honey and, (likewise), any body of people expecting him are ready. Even those disciples of the ascetic Gotama who, having quarrelled with their companions in the good life and abandoned the training, have returned to the worldly condition – even they are praisers of the Teacher, the *Dhamma*, and the Order and blame themselves rather than others, saying: "We were ill-fated, we were of little merit, we who, having gone forth to a *dhamma* and discipline so well-preached, were not able to pursue the good life completely and perfectly for the whole human span." Taking up the five rules of training, they become monastery attendants or lay-followers. So the ascetic Gotama is esteemed, found worthy of honour, respected and revered by disciples. And (they) live in reliance (on him).' "

"But how many things do you perceive in me, Udāyin, as a result of which (they adopt such attitudes)?"

"I perceive five things, bhante. The Lord eats little and praises (that practice). The Lord is content with any kind of robe and praises (such contentment). The Lord is content with any kind of almsfood and praises (such contentment). The Lord is content with any kind of shelter and praises (such contentment). The Lord lives secluded and praises (that state)."

"Udāyin, if disciples were to respect me (on the first count it can be pointed out that) there are disciples of mine living on a bowlful of food, on half a bowlful of food, on a fruit of the vilva-tree, or on half (such) a fruit. But occasionally I both eat fully from the bowl and eat beyond that.

If disciples were to respect me (on the second count it can be pointed out that) there are disciples of mine wearing rags taken from a dust heap, or wearing threadbare robes. Having gathered shreds of cloth from a cemetery, a rubbish dump, or a shop, they make an outer robe and wear it. But occasionally I wear householders' robes, strengthened where threadbare with threads from the white gourd.

If disciples were to respect me (on the third count it can be pointed out that) there are disciples of mine who only eat what is received in the almsbowl, who go on successive[2] almsrounds satisfied with leftovers, who wander between the houses and, on being offered a seat, refuse it. But occasionally, when invited, I eat excellent gruel from which the black grains have been removed, and various soups, various curries.

If disciples were to respect me (on the fourth count it can be pointed out) that there are disciples of mine who are tree-root dwellers out in the open. They don't go under a roof for eight months.[3] But occasionally I live in a gabled house, smeared all round, offering protection from the wind, fastened with bolts, and possessing windows that close.

If disciples were to respect me (on the fifth count it can be pointed out that) there are disciples of mine who are of the forest. They frequent remote forest lodgings in the wilderness, and live there. They return to the midst of the Order every fortnight for the recitation of the obligations. But I occasionally live beset by monks, nuns, lay-people (of both sexes), kings, king's ministers, or by those of other sects and their followers. So, Udāyin, it is not because of these five things that disciples esteeming, honouring, respecting and revering me, live in dependence.

But there are five other things for which (they do). My disciples admire superior levels of conduct, thinking: 'The ascetic Gotama is virtuous and possessed of the highest form of conduct.' This is the first thing. Further, (they) admire superior levels of knowledge and vision, thinking: 'Simply because of knowledge the ascetic Gotama (claims knowledge). Simply because of vision the ascetic Gotama (claims vision). (He) teaches *dhamma* from gnosis, with a foundation, and that is extraordinary.' This is the second thing. Further, they admire the superior levels of wisdom, thinking: 'The ascetic Gotama is wise, possessed of the highest form of wisdom. It cannot be that he will not see a prospective argument, or fail to rebuke with *dhamma* a present challenge deserving rebuke.' What do you think about this, Udāyin? Would my disciples, knowing and seeing this, be likely to interrupt a talk from time to time?"

"Not so, bhante."

"I do not expect instruction from disciples, Udāyin. (They) expect (it) from me. This is the third thing.

Further my disciples, when afflicted and overcome by suffering, come to me and ask about the *ariyan* truth of suffering. I explain. They ask me about the *ariyan* truth as to the origin of suffering, as to its ending, and as to the manner of its ending. I explain. I please the heart with the answer to the question. This is the fourth thing.

Further, Udāyin, I have proclaimed a method for disciples (whereby they) cultivate the four applications of mindfulness. Herein a monk lives observing the body in the body, feelings in the feelings, the mind in the mind, and phenomena in phenomena – zealous, lucid, and mindful that he might remove the longing and distress in the world.

I have proclaimed a method for disciples whereby they cultivate the four right endeavours. Herein a monk generates resolution, strives, puts forth energy, stretches forth and exerts his mind for the non-arising of pernicious states that have not arisen, and for the abandonment of (those that have); for the arising of skilful states that have not arisen and for the continuance, the preservation, the increase, the full development, the cultivation, the consummation of (those that have).

I have proclaimed a method (whereby they) cultivate the four bases of psychic power. Herein a monk cultivates the basis of psychic power endowed with concentrated resolve and concerted effort, with concentrated energy and concerted effort, with concentrated mind and concerted effort, and with concentrated investigation and concerted effort.

I have proclaimed a method (whereby they) cultivate the five faculties and powers.[4] Herein a monk cultivates the five faculties and powers – of faith, of energy, of mindfulness, of concentration, and of wisdom – (all) leading to tranquillity and enlightenment.

I have proclaimed a method (whereby they) cultivate the seven aspects (of enlightenment). Herein a monk cultivates mindfulness, examination of *dhamma*, energy, joy, tranquillity, concentration, and equanimity, (all) being rooted in remoteness, dispassion, cessation, and resulting in renunciation.

I have proclaimed a method (whereby they) cultivate the *ariyan* eightfold way. Herein a monk cultivates right view, aim, speech, action, livelihood, effort, mindfulness, and concentration.

I have proclaimed a method (whereby they) cultivate the eight freedoms. Having form, (a monk) sees forms – this is the first freedom.[5] Perceiving the formless inwardly, he sees forms externally – this is the second freedom. He is intent on beauty[6] – this is the third freedom. By entirely transcending perceptions of form, by the disappearance of perceptions of sensory reaction, and by the disregard of perceptions of diversity, (he is aware of) infinite space. He lives with the realm of infinite space attained – this is the fourth freedom. Entirely transcending the realm of infinite space, he lives with the realm of infinite consciousness attained – this is the fifth freedom.

Entirely transcending the realm of infinite consciousness, he lives with the realm of nothingness attained – this is the sixth freedom. Entirely transcending the realm of nothingness, he lives with the realm of neither perceiving nor not perceiving attained – this is the seventh freedom. Entirely transcending the realm of neither perceiving nor not perceiving, he lives with the cessation of perception and feeling attained – this is the eighth freedom.

I have proclaimed a method (whereby they) cultivate the eight realms of mastery. One who perceives forms internally sees forms externally that are insignificant and fair or foul, and having mastered them perceives: 'I know and see.' This is the first realm of mastery. One who perceives forms internally sees forms externally that are boundless and fair or foul, and having mastered them perceives: 'I know and see.' This is the second realm of mastery. One who perceives the formless internally sees forms externally that are insignificant and fair or foul, and having mastered them perceives: 'I know and see.' This is the third realm of mastery. One who perceives the formless internally sees forms externally that are boundless and fair or foul, and having mastered them, perceives: 'I know and see.' This is the fourth realm of mastery. One who perceives the formless internally sees forms externally that are dark blue (in) colour, appearance, (and) texture, (such as) the flax-blossom; (or) that are yellow, (such as) the kannikara-blossom; (or) that are red, (such as) the bandhujivaka-blossom; (or) that are white, (such as) the star of healing.[7] Having mastered them he perceives: 'I know and see.' (These) are the fifth, sixth, seventh, and eighth realms of mastery.

I have proclaimed a method (whereby they) cultivate the ten *kasina*[8] realms. One is aware of the earth *kasina* – above, below, across, indivisible, immeasurable; of the water *kasina*, the fire *kasina*, the air *kasina*, the blue, yellow, red, and white *kasina*s, the space *kasina*, and the consciousness *kasina* (similarly).

I have proclaimed a method (whereby they) cultivate the four (levels of) absorption.

I have proclaimed a method (whereby they) know: 'This body of mine is possessed of form, built of the four great elements, born of mother and father, nourished on rice and junket, is a thing worn and chafed, broken and scattered. But this consciousness of mine is sited here and bound here. It is like a lapis-lazuli[9] – bright, noble, well-cut in eight facets, gleaming, pure, endowed with every (fine) quality, that might be strung on a thread – blue, yellow, red, white, or orange. And a man possessed of eyes might take it in his hand (and be aware of all this).' Similarly, I have proclaimed a method whereby my disciples (understand this body and this consciousness).

I have proclaimed a method (whereby they) produce another body from this body, endowed with a form that is mind-made, complete in its limbs, and with special faculties. It is as if a man were to pull a sword from its scabbard, knowing: 'This is the sword, this is the scabbard.[10]'

I have proclaimed a method (whereby they) realise the diverse forms of psychic power. It is like a skilled potter who could make any special vessel he might like with well-prepared clay.

I have proclaimed a method (whereby they) hear, with the purified divine ear transcending the human, sounds of both kinds, divine and human, far and near. It is like a powerful conch-blower who, without difficulty, could address himself to the four quarters.

I have proclaimed a method (whereby they) grasp and comprehend the minds of other beings and other people. It is like a woman, or a man, or a youth, used to finery, and beholding (his or her) own face in a perfectly pure and clear mirror or a bowl of sparkling water, (thereby) knowing (whether it has a mole on it or not).

I have proclaimed a method (whereby they) recall a diversity of former habitations. It is like a man who goes from his own village to another village, and might return (recollecting his journeys and what happened to him).

I have proclaimed a method (whereby they), with the purified divine eye transcending the human, behold beings passing away and re-arising. It is as though there were two houses with doors, and a man standing in between were to see people entering, leaving, walking and wandering about.

I have proclaimed a method (whereby), from the rooting out of the distractions, (they) live, reaching and experiencing the freedom of mind and the freedom through wisdom that are undistracted, having realised them in this life from their own gnosis. It is like a lake near the top of a mountain – clear, limpid, and calm – and a man standing on the bank there sees oysters and shells, gravel and pebbles, and shoals of fish swimming about or motionless. With regard to (all these methods) many of my disciples live with the achievement of knowledge, and having reached what is beyond.

This, Udāyin, is the fifth thing for which disciples of mine esteem, honour, respect and revere me, having lived in reliance on me."

Thus spoke the Lord.

1. Horner – "with abuse for his behaviour".
2. Horner – "uninterrupted", i.e. on either translation the greater the scruples the more arduous and prolonged the almsround.
3. i.e. excepting the rains retreat.
4. Two paras in the original but the lists of faculties and powers are identical.
5. A freedom to the extent that he simply lives in the world of forms without being seduced by them.
6. Horner links to the *kasina*-objects that follow particularly the beauty of bright colours.
7. Possibly the planet Venus (PTSD).
8. *Kāsina* is untranslatable, but refers to a meditation device consisting of an external focus of attention, possibly natural, possibly artificial.
9. Horner – "emerald".
10. Multiple analogies are offered in this and ensuing sections.

78

With Samaṇamaṇḍikā's (Son)

22–29

Thus have I heard: once the Lord dwelt near Sāvatthī in the Jeta Grove on Anāthapiṇḍika's campus. Now at that time the wanderer Uggāhamāna, Samaṇamaṇḍikā's son, was staying on Mallikā's campus together with a large company of some three hundred wanderers, and at the One Hall,[1] which was intended for debating and surrounded by tinduka-trees.

Then Pañcakaṅga the carpenter left Sāvatthī at an early hour to see the Lord, (but) it struck him: "It is not yet time to see the Lord. The Lord dwells in seclusion. Nor is it the right moment to see monks engaged in mental development. (They) dwell in seclusion. Suppose I were to go to the One Hall and to Mallikā's park, (where I might see) the wanderer Uggāhamāna." (And he did so.)

Now at that moment the wanderer Uggāhamāna was sitting with a great company of wanderers, loudly and clamorously proclaiming on a variety of trivial matters, such as talk about kings (and so on). Seeing Pañcakaṅga the carpenter coming some way off (he) called his own company to order, saying: "Hush, friends! Don't be noisy. It is a follower of the ascetic Gotama who is coming – Pañcakaṅga the carpenter. These brethren are lovers of quiet and praise (it). Perhaps if he sees a company making little noise he may see fit to approach." So those wanderers fell silent. Whereupon, Pañcakaṅga the carpenter approached the wanderer Uggāhamāna, greeted (him) and, after conversing in a friendly and polite way, sat down at one side. Said Uggāhamāna:

"Carpenter, I declare that an individual endowed with four things is completely and perfectly skilled and of the highest achievement, an invincible ascetic. Herein he does no evil deed with the body, he speaks no evil words, he harbours no evil intentions, he follows no evil mode of living."

Then Pañcakaṅga the carpenter, neither approving nor rejecting what had been said by the wanderer, Uggāhamāna rose from his seat, thinking: "In the Lord's presence I shall understand the meaning of what has been said." Whereupon (he) approached the Lord and, saluting him, sat down at one side. (And he told him what had passed). At these words the Lord said:

"This being the case, carpenter, a small and tender boy lying on his back will be completely and perfectly skilled and of the highest achievement, an invincible ascetic. For (such a one) there is not (the idea of) 'body', so how would he do an evil deed with the body, other than a certain amount of thrashing about? There is not (the idea of) 'words', so how would he speak an evil word, apart from a bit of crying? There is not (the idea of) 'intention', so how would he harbour evil intention, except for some vexation? There is not (the idea of) 'livelihood', so how would he follow an evil mode of living, apart from taking his mother's milk?

Carpenter, I declare that an individual endowed with ten[2] things is completely and perfectly skilled and of the highest achievement, an invincible ascetic. I say that these unskilful modes of conduct are to be recognised in him; that (they) are to be recognised as originating from this (or that); that (they) are to be recognised as ceasing without remainder here;[3] (and) that, for (their) cessation, proceeding in such and such a way is to be recognised (as correct). I say that these skilful modes of conduct, (together with their causes, their cessation, and the manner of their cessation are) to be recognised (similarly). I say that these unskilful intentions (and) these skilful intentions are to be recognised (in the same terms).

And what, carpenter, are unskilful (modes of) conduct? Unskilful bodily (and) verbal activity, evil mode of livelihood – these are termed unskilful modes of conduct. And how are (they) caused? The answer should be that they originate in the mind – but what mind? For the mind is many, various, and manifold. That mind that is imbued with passion, ill-will, and delusion – herein lies the cause of unskilful modes of conduct. And where are these unskilful modes of conduct brought to an end without remainder? Herein a monk abandons bad and cultivates good behaviour in body, word, and thought. Abandoning wrong livelihood, he organises his life in terms of right livelihood. Such is the ceasing of unskilful modes of conduct.

And how does one proceed for the elimination of unskilful modes of conduct? Herein a monk generates resolution, strives, puts forth energy, stretches forth and exerts his mind for the non-arising of pernicious states that have not arisen, and for the abandonment of (those that have); for the arising of skilful states that have not arisen, and for the continuance, the preservation, the increase, the full development, the cultivation, the consummation of (those that have). Such is the proceeding for the cessation of unskilful modes of conduct.

And what, carpenter, are skilful modes of conduct? I say that skilful bodily (and) verbal activity, and purity of livelihood, fall within skilful modes of conduct. And how are (they) caused? The answer should be that they originate in the mind – but what mind? For the mind is many, various, and manifold. That mind that is emptied of passion, ill-will, and delusion – herein lies the cause of skilful modes of conduct. And where are these skilful modes of conduct brought to an end without remainder? Herein a monk is virtuous and wants nothing in virtue, and he knows mental freedom and wisdom's freedom for what they are. In such a manner are (they) brought to an end without remainder.[4]

And what, monks, are unskilful intentions? Worldly intention, malicious intention, intention to injure – these are termed unskilful intentions. And how are (they) caused? The answer should be that they originate in perception – but what perception? For perception is many, various, and manifold. Worldly perception, malicious perception, injurious perception – herein lies the cause of unskilful intentions. And where are the unskilful intentions brought to an end without remainder? Herein a monk, remote from worldly pursuits and from unskilled states, reaches and experiences the first (level of) absorption. Such is the ceasing of unskilled intentions. And how does one proceed for the elimination of unskilled intentions? Herein a monk generates resolution, strives, puts forth energy, stretches forth and exerts his mind for the non-arising of pernicious states that have not arisen, and for the abandonment of (those that have); for the arising of skilful states that have not arisen, and for the continuance, the preservation, the increase, the full development, the cultivation, the consummation of (those that have). Such is the proceeding for the cessation of unskilled intentions.

And what, carpenter, are skilled intentions? Intentions free from worldliness, from malice, from will to injure – these are termed skilled intentions. And how are (they) caused? The answer should be that they originate in perception – but what perception? For perception is many, various, and manifold. Perception free from worldliness, malice, and will to injure – herein lies the cause of skilful intentions. And where are skilful intentions brought to an end without remainder? Herein a monk reaches and experiences the second (level of) absorption. And how does one proceed for the elimination of skilful intentions? Herein a monk generates resolution, strives, puts forth energy, stretches forth and exerts his mind for the non-arising of pernicious states that have not arisen, and for the abandonment of (those that have); for the arising of skilful states that have not arisen, and for the continuance, the preservation, the increase, the full development, the cultivation, the consummation of (those that have). Such is the proceeding for the cessation of skilful intentions.

Carpenter, I declare that an individual endowed with ten things is completely and perfectly skilled and of the highest attainment, an invincible ascetic. As to this, a monk is equipped with the right view of one who is proficient, with (such a person's) right intention, right speech, right action, right livelihood, right effort, right mindfulness, right concentration, true knowledge, and true freedom. These are the ten."

Thus spoke the Lord.

1. Originally the only hall for that purpose – hence the name.
2. Enumerated in the final paragraph.
3. Either in the sense of "at some point" or "here on earth".
4. Omitted – the manner of elimination of skilled states, which is simply a restatement of the elimination of unskilled states, viewed from the standpoint of perfecting skilled states.

79

Minor Discourse with Sakuludāyin

29–39

Thus have I heard: once the Lord dwelt near Rājagaha, in the Bamboo Grove at the squirrels' feeding-place. Now at that time the wanderer Sakuludāyin was staying in the wanderers' park at the peacocks' feeding-place together with a large company of wanderers. Then the Lord, dressing at an early hour and taking bowl and robe, went into Rājagaha for almsfood, (but) it struck him: "It is too early to walk for alms in Rājagaha. Suppose I were to go to the peacocks' feeding-place in the wanderers' park and approach the wanderer Sakuludāyin." (And he did so).

At that moment, the wanderer Sakuludāyin was sitting with a great company of wanderers, loudly and clamorously proclaiming on a variety of trivial matters, such as talk about kings (and so on). The wanderer Sakuludāyin, seeing the Lord coming some way off, called his own company to order, saying:

"Hush, friends! Don't be noisy. The ascetic Gotama is coming, and this venerable one is a lover of quiet and praises (it). Perhaps if he sees a company making little noise he may see fit to approach."

So those wanderers fell silent. Whereupon the Lord approached the wanderer Sakuludāyin (who) said to (him): "Welcome, bhante, greetings. It is some time since the Lord took the opportunity to come here. Let the Lord be seated." The Lord sat down in the place prepared (for him whilst) the wanderer Sakuludāyin, taking a low seat, sat at one side. Said the Lord:

"Of what do you talk, Sakuludāyin, as you sit together at this moment?"

"That conversation is of no consequence, bhante. It will not be difficult to hear about (it) later. Now when I am not come to this company (it) sits talking about a variety of trivial matters. When I am come (it) sits looking into my face and saying: 'Whatever *dhamma* the ascetic Udāyin will tell us that we shall hear.' But when the Lord is come to this assembly then both I and this assembly sit looking into the Lord's face and say 'Whatever *dhamma* the Lord will tell us that we shall hear.'"

"Well then, Udāyin, say to me just what comes into your mind."

"Bhante, some time ago someone who is all-knowing and all-seeing claimed all-embracing knowledge and vision, saying: 'Whether walking or standing, asleep or awake, knowledge and vision is always and fully available to me.' On being asked a question by me about the past he fended it off with another, went off the point, and showed ill-temper, ill-will, and sulkiness. Out of that, joy arose in me regarding the Lord and I thought: 'Truly, it is the Lord, the Adept, who is skilled in these matters'."

"But who was this, Udāyin?"

"Nātaputta the Jain, bhante."

"Udāyin, whoever might recall various previous existences in all their characteristics and detail – either he could ask me a question about the past or I could ask him (such) a question. Either he could convince me with an answer to my question or I could convince with an answer to his. With a purified divine eye transcending the human either he could ask me a question about the future or I could ask him (such) a question. Either he could convince with an answer to my question or I could convince with an answer to his. But never mind the past Udāyin, never mind the future. I will teach you *dhamma*. If this exists that exists. From the arising of this is the arising of that. If this does not exist that does not exist. From the cessation of this is the cessation of that."

"But, bhante, even to the extent that I have realised my own (present) nature, I cannot keep it in mind in all its characteristics and detail. How then should I recall a variety of former existences as does the Lord? (And) indeed I do not now even see a mud-sprite. How then could I behold the passing away and re-emergence of beings with the purified divine eye transcending the human as does the Lord? So when the Lord spoke to me like this: 'Never mind the past, never mind the future. If this exists that exists', (and so on) – that was even more unclear to me. But perhaps I might convince the Lord with the answer to the question of our own teachers."

"So what do your own teachers say, Udāyin?"

"(They) say: 'This is the greatest splendour, this is the greatest splendour'."

"But what is this greatest splendour, Udāyin?"

"There is no other splendour surpassing or excelling this splendour."

"But what is this splendour, Udāyin?"

"There is no other splendour surpassing or excelling this splendour."

"It would take you a long time to amplify this, Udāyin. You speak (thus) but you do not indicate that splendour. It is as though a man might say: 'I seek and desire whoever is the most beautiful girl in this country.' (Someone) might say this to him: 'My good man, do you know (of her whether she is) noblewoman, brahmin, merchant, or artisan; (or whether) she is of such a name and lineage; (or whether) she is tall, or short, or of medium height', (and so on). Thus questioned he (on all counts) replies 'no'. What do you think about this, Udāyin? This being the case, does that man's stupid talk do him any good?"

"Indeed, bhante, such being the case, that man's talk turns out to be stupid."

("And so it is with you, Udāyin, with regard to what you have just said.")

"Bhante, like a precious stone, a lapis-lazuli, bright, noble, well cut in eight facets which, arranged in orange-coloured cloth, shines, and gleams, and sparkles – of just such splendour is the self, free from disease after death."

"What do you think about this, Udāyin? Of these two splendours which is the more surpassing and excellent – the jewel (which you have just described), or the glow-worm or fire-fly in the deep darkness of the night?"

"Of these two, bhante, (the latter) are the more surpassing and excellent."

"And of these two – the glow-worm and fire-fly or an oil-lamp?"

"The oil-lamp, bhante."

"And of these two – an oil-lamp or a great inferno of fire?"

"The great inferno of fire, bhante."

"And of these two – a great inferno of fire or the star of healing in a clear and cloudless sky at dawn?"

"The star of healing, bhante."

"And of these two – the star of healing or the moon at its zenith?"

"The moon at its zenith, bhante?"

"And of these two – the moon at its zenith or the sun at midday in the last month of the rains in autumn?"

"The sun at midday. bhante."

"Greater than these, Udāyin, are those many *devas* who do not partake of the brilliance of moon and sun – that I know. But then I do not say: 'There is no other splendour surpassing or excelling this splendour.' But you speak of a splendour that is inferior to and less than that of the glow-worm and fire-fly, and you do not indicate (it)."

"The Lord has ended the discussion, the Adept has ended the discussion."

"Why do you say (that), Udāyin?"

"Bhante, our teachers say: 'This is the greatest splendour, this is the greatest splendour.' Yet these teachers of ours, on being cross-questioned, asked for reasons, and debated with by the Lord, are empty, vain, and gone wrong."

"But, Udāyin, is there a world that is exclusively happy? Is there a reasonable method for the realisation of (such) a world?"

"Our teachers say (so), bhante."

"And what is (it), Udāyin?"

"Herein someone, having given up the destruction of life, abstains (therefrom), having given up theft, dissolute living, and lying, abstains (therefrom), but proceeds undertaking a certain austerity."

"What do you think about this, Udāyin? At the time when (one) has abandoned (these things) is the self entirely happy, or is it (both) happy and afflicted?"

"(Both) happy and afflicted."

"(And) at the time when one undertakes a certain austerity?"

"(Both) happy and afflicted."

"What do you think about this, Udāyin? Is not the method for the realisation of an exclusively happy world (one in which) happiness and affliction are combined?"

"The Lord has ended the discussion, the Adept has ended the discussion."

"Why do you say that, Udāyin?"

"Bhante, our teachers say there is a world that is exclusively happy and there is a reasonable method for realising (it). Yet these teachers of ours, on being cross-questioned, asked for reasons, and debated with by the Lord, are empty, vain, and gone wrong. But is there (such) a world and (such) a method?"

"There is, Udāyin. Herein a monk reaches and experiences the first, the second, and the third (levels of) absorption. This is a reasonable method for realising a world that is exclusively happy.[1]"

"But this is not (such) a course, bhante. A world that is exclusively happy might have already been realised."

"Indeed, a world exclusively happy could not have already been realised. For just this is the reasonable method for realising (such) a world."

At these words the assembly of the wanderer Sakuludāyin cried out with great noise and clamour: "In this matter our recollection accords with our teachers. We understand nothing further." Then the wanderer Sakuludāyin, quietening those wanderers, said to the Lord:

"But how far might (such) a world be realised?"

"Herein, Udāyin, a monk reaches and experiences the fourth (level of) absorption. As far as *devatās* have come to be in a world that is exclusively happy, he remains, and talks, and holds conversation with (them). (Such) a world could have already been realised."

"Is not the realising of that world which is exclusively happy the reason for following the good life under the Lord?"

"No, Udāyin. There are other things more surpassing and excellent which are the reason for (that)."

"But what are these, bhante?"

"Herein an exemplar arises in the world. Having abandoned the five hindrances that are mental defilements and detracting from wisdom he reaches and experiences the first, the second, the third, and the fourth (levels of) absorption. He turns his mind to the recollection of previous existences. He turns (it) towards the knowledge of the passing away and re-emergence of other beings. He turns (it) towards the rooting out of the distractions. (All these) are things more surpassing and excellent."

At these words the wanderer Sakuludāyin said to the Lord: "Excellent, bhante, excellent." (Whereupon he took the refuges and sought ordination). (But) when he had spoken the assembly said to him: "Do not follow the good life under the ascetic Gotama, friend Udāyin. Do not, having been a teacher, live as a pupil. As a previously good water-pot that has sprung a leak, so would be such a move on the part of friend Udāyin." In this way did the assembly of the wanderer Udayin erect an obstacle for (him) as regards the following of the good life under the Lord.

1. See 119 for the attributes of the various levels of absorption.

80

With Vekhanassa

40–44

Thus have I heard: once the Lord dwelt near Sāvatthī in the Jeta Grove on Anāthapiṇḍika's campus. Then the wanderer Vekhanassa (of the Kaccāna clan) approached the Lord, saluted (him) and, having conversed in a friendly and polite way, stood at one side (where) he gave vent to this utterance:

"This is the greatest splendour, this is the greatest splendour."

"But why do you speak (thus) Kaccāna? What is this greatest splendour?"

"Good Gotama, there is no other splendour surpassing or excelling this splendour. It is the greatest splendour."

"But what is this splendour that is surpassing or more excellent than any other splendour?"

"Good Gotama, there is no other splendour surpassing or excelling this splendour. It is the greatest splendour."

"It would take you a long time to amplify this. You speak (thus) but you do not indicate that splendour. It is as though a man might say:

'I seek and desire whoever is the most beautiful girl in this country'. (Someone) might say this to him: 'My good man, do you know (of her whether she is) noblewoman, brahmin, merchant, or artisan; (or whether) she is of such a name and lineage; (or whether) she is tall, or short, or of medium height', (and so on). Thus questioned, he (on all counts) replies 'no'. What do you think, Kaccāna? This being the case, does that man's stupid talk do him any good?"

"Indeed, bhante, such being the case, that man's talk turns out to be stupid."

("And so it is with you, Kaccāna, with regard to what you have just said.")

"Bhante, like a precious stone, a lapis lazuli, bright, noble, well cut in eight facets which, arranged in orange-coloured cloth, shines, and gleams, and sparkles – of just such splendour is the self, free from disease after death."

"What do you think about this? Of these two splendours which is the more surpassing and excellent – the jewel (which you have just described), or some glow-worm or fire-fly in the deep darkness of the night?"

"Of these two, bhante, (the latter) are the more surpassing and excellent."

"And of these two – the glow-worm and fire-fly or an oil-lamp?"

"The oil-lamp, bhante."

"And of these two – an oil-lamp or a great inferno of fire?"

"The great inferno of fire, bhante."

"And of these two – a great inferno of fire or the star of healing in a clear and cloudless sky at dawn?"

"The star of healing, bhante."

"And of these two – the star of healing or the moon at its zenith?"

"The moon at its zenith, bhante?"

"And of these two – the moon at its zenith or the sun at midday in the last month of the rains in autumn?"

"The sun at midday. bhante."

"Greater than these, Kaccāna, are those many *devas* who do not partake of the brilliance of moon and sun – that I know. But then I do not say: 'There is no other splendour surpassing or excelling this splendour'. But you speak of a splendour that is inferior to and less than that of the glow-worm and fire-fly, and you do not indicate (it).

There are these five strands of worldly pursuit, Kaccāna – visible forms, pleasing, welcome, enticing, voluptuous, pleasure-laden, exciting; (and sounds, tastes, odours, and physical contacts of the same kind). Whatever happiness and delight comes about because of these is called the happiness of worldly pursuits. In this way, through worldly pursuits, there is happiness in worldly pursuits, and the supreme happiness (therein) is proclaimed (as such)."

At these words the wanderer Vekhanassa said:

"Excellent, good Gotama, excellent. Thus far is it well said by the worthy Gotama."

"This is hard for you to understand, Kaccāna, who are of another view, another allegiance, another inclination, another endeavour, another teacher. But those monks who are *arahants*, with the distractions rooted out, who have reached perfection, done what was to be done, their burdens put down, the goal achieved, the thongs of existence entirely destroyed, freed by true knowledge – they might understand it."

At these words the wanderer Vekhanassa, offended and displeased, cursing and reviling even the Lord, said:

"The ascetic Gotama will come to no good. Just so however in this connection, and without knowing the past or seeing the future, have some ascetics and brahmans claimed: 'Destroyed is birth, fulfilled the good life, done what was to be done, and no further return to this world.' Their words prove simply ridiculous, mere talk, empty and vain."

"Kaccāna, such censure for those (who are like this) is only proper. But never mind the past, never mind the future. Let an intelligent man come (along), one who is honest, without guile, and upright, saying: 'I will advise, I will teach *dhamma*.' Proceeding as instructed, soon one will know and see for oneself. Thus there is truly release from the ultimate bondage, namely release from the bondage of ignorance. Kaccāna, it is like a small and tender boy, lying on his back, his throat bound with a fivefold swaddling-band. As he grows and his faculties mature he is set free from these wrappings. (And so it is with this training)."

At these words the wanderer Vekhanassa said to the Lord:

"Excellent, good Gotama, excellent." (Whereupon he took the refuges and became a lay-follower).

81

On Ghaṭīkāra

45–50

Thus have I heard: once the Lord was travelling on foot among the Kosalans together with a large company of monks. Then, descending from the road at a certain point, the Lord smiled. Whereupon venerable Ānanda thought: "Why, and on account of what, does the Lord smile? " Arranging his robe over one shoulder, and saluting the Lord with joined palms, (he) said:

"Why, and on account of what, does the Lord smile?"

"Once upon a time, Ānanda, in this place there was a village township called Vebhaḷiṅga, prosperous, rich, and populous. Kassapa, Lord, *arahant*, truly enlightened, lived dependent on (this) township. Here was (his) campus, here he sat exhorting the Order of monks." Then venerable Ānanda, having spread out a robe folded into four, said:

"Now, let the Lord be seated. Thus the ground at this spot will have been used by two *arahants* who are truly enlightened." After sitting down the Lord said to venerable Ānanda: "Now at Vebhaḷiṅga (in those days), Ānanda, there was a potter called Ghaṭīkāra, who was a supporter, a principal supporter, of Lord Kassapa. A young man called Jotipāla was Ghaṭīkāra's close friend, and (one day) Ghatīkāra said to (him):

'Come, good Jotipāla, we will go and see the Lord Kassapa. I would value highly a sight of (him).' Said Jotipāla: 'Enough, good Ghaṭīkāra. Why bother to see this shaven ascetic?' (And the potter Ghaṭīkāra repeated his request, but the youth Jotipāla would not change his mind).

'Well then, good Jotipāla, we will take a back-scratcher and some bath-powder and go to the river to bathe.' (And Jotipāla agreed to this. When they got there) Ghaṭīkāra said:

'This isn't far from the campus of the Lord Kassapa. Come, good Jotipāla, let us go and see (him).' (But again Jotipāla refused). Then Ānanda, Ghaṭī-kāra the potter, taking hold of the youth Jotipāla by the girdle, (repeated his request yet again, but still Jotipāla would not go with him). So, with Jotipāla having just bathed his head,[1] Ghaṭīkāra took hold of (him) by the hair (and expressed his wish once more). Then, Ānanda, the youth Jotipāla thought:

'Surely it is strange and wonderful, that this potter Ghaṭīkāra, who is of inferior birth, should think to take hold of my hair when I have just bathed my head. This cannot be insignificant.' So he said to Ghaṭīkāra:

'Is it really necessary, good Ghaṭīkāra?'.

'It is, good Jotipāla.'

'Well then, release (my hair) and we will go.' Then (they) approached the Lord Kassapa. Ghaṭīkāra the potter saluted (him) and sat down at one side. But the youth Jotipāla greeted him, and conversed in a friendly and polite way (before doing so). Said Ghaṭīkāra:

'Bhante, this youth Jotipāla is my close friend. Let the Lord teach him *dhamma*.' Whereupon, Ānanda, the Lord Kassapa instructed, aroused, gladdened, and delighted (them both) with *dhamma*-talk. Afterwards, pleased and satisfied, (they) rose from their seats and, saluting, went away keeping their right sides towards (him).

Then Jotipāla said to Ghaṭīkāra:

'Having heard this *dhamma*, why do you not go forth from home into homelessness?'

'Do you not know that I have blind and frail parents to support, good Jotipāla?'

'Well then, good Ghaṭīkāra, I shall go forth from home into homelessness.'

So (they again) approached the Lord Kassapa and, saluting him, sat down at one side. Said Ghaṭīkāra:

'This youth Jotipāla is my close friend. May the Lord let him go forth.' And the youth Jotipāla obtained the going forth and ordination in the presence of the Lord Kassapa.

Not long, some half a month afterwards, Lord Kassapa, having dwelt in Vebhaḷiṅga as long as suited him, set out for Bārāṇasi. Travelling on foot he duly arrived (there). There, Ānanda, (he) dwelt in the deer park. Then Kikī, the king of Kāsi, heard (of his arrival) and, ordering fine carriages to be harnessed, ascended (one of them) and set out for Bārāṇasi with great pomp to see the Lord Kassapa. As far as the terrain permitted he went by carriage then, descending from (it), approached the Lord Kassapa on foot, saluting him and sitting down at one side. The Lord Kassapa instructed, aroused, gladdened, and delighted Kikī, the king of Kāsi, with *dhamma*-talk. Whereupon King Kikī said to (him):

'Let the Lord accept an invitation to a meal with me on the morrow together with the Order of monks.' The Lord Kassapa accepted the invitation in silence. And the king of Kāsi, recognising his consent, rose from his seat and, after saluting, went away keeping his right side towards him.

Then, towards dawn, after having prepared within his own abode abundant foods both hard and soft – dry yellow rices, various curries with the black grains removed, and various condiments – (he) made known the time (of the meal) to the Lord Kassapa.

Then Lord Kassapa, dressing at an early hour, took bowl and robe and went (there), sitting in the place prepared for him along with the Order of monks. And the king of Kāsi satisfied and served with his own hands the order of monks led by the Buddha. When the Lord Kassapa had eaten and put aside the bowl (he) took a low seat and sat down at one side saying:

'Let the Lord accept my rains-residence at Bārāṇasi. There will be care such as this for the Order.'

'Truly sire, I have a rains-residence.' (But King Kikī repeated his request several times, despite further refusals). Then there was wavering and distress for (the king because of this). And (he) said to the Lord Kassapa: 'Bhante, is there someone who is a better supporter of yours than I?'

'Sire, there is a village township called Vebhaḷiṅga, (in which place) is a potter called Ghaṭīkāra. He is a supporter of mine, a principal supporter. But for you sire there is wavering and distress (on account of my refusal). This is not, and cannot be so, for the potter Ghaṭīkāra. Ghaṭīkāra, sire, has taken refuge in the Buddha, in the *Dhamma*, and in the Order of monks. Ghaṭīkāra, sire, abstains from the destruction of life, from taking what is not given, from dissolute living, from lying, and from states of negligence caused by wine, spirits, and (other) intoxicants. Ghaṭīkāra has complete satisfaction with the Buddha, with the *Dhamma*, and the Order of monks. (He) is given to conduct pleasing to the *ariyans*. (He) is sure about suffering, the origin of suffering, the cessation of suffering, and about the way leading (thereto). (He) is one who eats but once a day, is a follower of the good life, virtuous, and fine of character. (He) has divested himself of jewelry and rid himself of gold and silver. (He) does not uproot the earth with a spade or with his own hand. He readily takes away (the soil of) a bank that has been broken up by rats and dogs, and makes a vessel out of that thinking (that) whoever desires, having put down portions of rice-grain, kidney-beans, or chick-peas in this place (by way of exchange, should) take what he wishes.[2] (He) supports blind and frail parents. From the disappearance of the five fetters that bind one to the worldly condition (he) is (destined for) spontaneous uprising, achieving *nibbāna* there, and not for return from that world.

At one time, sire, I was dwelling in the village township of Vebhaḷiṅga. Then, dressing at an early hour, and taking bowl and robe, I approached the parents of Ghaṭīkāra the potter and[3] (asked them where he had gone. They told me he had gone out, saying that I might take boiled rice from the bowl and soup from the cauldron, and enjoy them. Having done so, I went my way. Then Ghaṭīkāra came to his parents and asked them who it was that had eaten and then departed. And they told him). Then, for half a month, Ghaṭīkāra the potter was not without joy and happiness, nor his parents for seven days.

(On another occasion) the hut leaked and I told the monks (to go and) find out whether there (was) grass in the dwelling of Ghaṭīkāra the potter. (They) said to me (that) there (was) no grass (there, but that it had) a grass roof. (Whereupon I told them to go and take that. And they did so). Then (his) parents asked the monks who (was taking it, and the monks told them it was for the hut of the Lord Kassapa, which was leaking. The parents of Ghaṭīkāra bid them take it. And when his parents told Ghaṭīkāra the potter he) was not without joy and happiness for half a month, nor his parents for seven days. And, for all of three months, the house stood open to the sky, but it did not rain. Such a one is Ghaṭīkāra the potter, sire.'

'There is gain, there is good fortune for Ghaṭīkāra the potter in whom the Lord shows (such) confidence.'

Then, Ānanda, Kikī, the king of Kāsi, sent as many as five hundred wagons of rice-grain, dry yellow rice, and curry to Ghaṭīkāra the potter.

Now it may be, Ānanda, that you think that at that time the youth Jotipāla was somebody else. But that is not the way to look at it. I was the youth Jotipāla at that period."

Thus spoke the Lord.

1. Possibly a ritual bathing giving enhanced significance to what happens next.
2. i.e. the potter apparently leaves his wares in the open, unattended, and accepts what others choose to leave him in exchange.
3. There is a large element of close paraphrase in the next two paragraphs so as to avoid the third and fourth levels of inverted commas arising from the use of direct speech in the original.

82

On Raṭṭhapāla

54–74

Thus have I heard: once the Lord, while travelling on foot among the Kurus together with a large company of monks, came to a town of the Kurus called Thullakoṭṭhita. The brahmans and householders (there) heard (that) the ascetic Gotama, a son of the Sakyans gone forth from the Sakya clan (was among them, and that he was of high renown).

Then the brahmans and householders of Thullakoṭṭhita approached the Lord (and greeted him in their various ways)[1] (And) the Lord instructed, aroused, gladdened, and delighted (them) with *dhamma*-talk.

Now on that occasion one Raṭṭhapāla, the son of a family of repute in that (town of) Thullakoṭṭhita was seated in that assembly. And Raṭṭhapāla thought: "However I understand this *dhamma* taught by the Lord, it is not easy for one who inhabits a house to follow the good life completely fulfilled and perfected, polished like mother-of-pearl. Suppose I were to cut off hair and beard, don saffron robes, and go forth from home into homelessness." Then the brahmans and householders of Thullakoṭṭhita, pleased and satisfied at the Lord's words, rose from their place and, having saluted the Lord, went their way, keeping their right sides towards him.

Whereupon Raṭṭhapāla, not long after (their) departure, approached the Lord and, saluting (him) sat down at one side. (And Raṭṭhapāla told the Lord of the thoughts that had occurred to him, saying):

"Let me receive the going forth in the presence of the Lord. Let me receive ordination."

"But do you have your parents' permission, Raṭṭhapāla?"

"(No), bhante."

"Exemplars do not allow the going forth without parental consent, Raṭṭhapāla."

"Bhante, I shall do what is required (to secure it)."

And Raṭṭhapāla, rising from his seat, saluted the Lord and, keeping his right side towards him, (went his way). He approached his parents and (asked their permission). At these words the parents of Raṭṭhapāla said:

"Dear Raṭṭhapāla, you are our only son, loved and cherished, living in comfort and well looked after. You know nothing of suffering. Come – eat, drink, and amuse yourself. In the enjoyment of worldly pursuits and the performance of good works you can find satisfaction. We will not permit you to go forth from home into homelessness. We would be unwillingly deprived in the event of your death. How then should we allow that, still living, you should go forth from home into homelessness." (And, though Raṭṭhapāla repeated his request he continued to get the same answer).

Then Raṭṭhapāla, having failed to get his parents' consent to go forth, simply lay down on the bare ground there, saying: "Here there shall either be my death or the going forth." (But his parents merely repeated what they had said at first). At these words Raṭṭhapāla was silent, (and remained so despite further remonstrations).

Whereupon (his) parents approached (his) friends (and told them how he was behaving. And they asked them to go and speak to Raṭṭhapāla in the same terms as they themselves had done. But the friends, meeting with the same response, returned to the parents, saying:)

"If you do not permit (his) going forth from home into homelessness he will come to his death just there (where he is). But if you do you will see him again. If (he) finds no enjoyment from the going forth what course will remain for him? He will return here. Agree to the going forth."

"(Well then), we consent, dear friends, to the going forth. But after (it) he should come and see his parents." (So his friends returned and told him).

Then Raṭṭhapāla arose and, having recovered his strength, approached the Lord. Saluting (him) he sat down at one side, (and informed him that he now had his parents' consent). And so Raṭṭhapāla received the going forth and ordination in the Lord's presence.

Now, not long after (his) ordination, some half-a-month, the Lord, having lived in Thullakoṭṭhita as long as it pleased him, set off on foot for Sāvatthī and at length came (there). Whilst in Sāvatthī the Lord dwelt in the Jeta Grove on Anāthapiṇḍika's campus. Then venerable Raṭṭhapāla, living alone and apart, diligent, zealous, and resolute, reached and experienced before long that matchless consummation of the good life, realised in this life from his own gnosis, for which sons of family rightly go forth from home into homelessness. (He knew): "Destroyed is birth, fulfilled the good life, done what was to be done, with no further return to this world." And so venerable Raṭṭhapāla became one of the *arahants*.

Whereupon venerable Raṭṭhapāla went to the Lord, saluted him, and sat down at one side. Said Raṭṭhapāla: "I desire to go and see my parents if the Lord permits me." Now the Lord divined with his mind the thoughts of venerable Raṭṭhapāla. When (he) was satisfied (that) it was impossible for (the monk) to repudiate the training and revert to the worldly condition (he) said: "Do whatever you think is now appropriate, Raṭṭhapāla."

Then venerable Raṭṭhapāla, rising from his seat, saluted the Lord and went away keeping his right side towards him. Tidying his lodgings and taking bowl and robe, he set out on foot for Thullakoṭṭhita and at length came (there). There he lived in the deer park of the Kuru king.

Having dressed at an early hour, (he) took bowl and robe and went into Thullakoṭṭhita for almsfood. Walking on successive almsrounds he came to the house of his own father. Now at that moment (his) father was having his hair combed in the middle of a hall with doors. Raṭṭhapāla's father saw (him) coming some way off and said: "Our only son, loved and cherished, has gone forth on account of those shaven ascetics." So venerable Raṭṭhapāla got neither alms nor refusal at his father's house. All he received was reproaches.

Now at that moment the slave-woman of venerable Raṭṭhapāla's relations wanted to throw away the (previous) evening's junket. So venerable Raṭṭhapāla said to her: "If there are leavings, sister, put them in my bowl." (And she did so, but) recognised his hands, his feet, and his voice. So (she) went to Raṭṭhapāla's mother and said:

"Truly mistress, you should know that young master Raṭṭhapāla has returned."

"Glory be – if you speak the truth you are a freed woman." And venerable Raṭṭhapāla's mother went to (his) father (and told him).

Now at that time venerable Raṭṭhapāla was consuming the (food) whilst leaning against a wall. So (his) father approached (him) and said: "Can it be, dear Raṭṭhapāla, that you are eating yesterday evening's junket. Will you not come into your own home?"

"Where is there a home for those of us who have gone forth from home into homelessness. We are without a home, householder. I came to your house, but received neither alms nor a refusal there, just reproaches."

"Come, dear Raṭṭhapāla, we will go to the house."

"Enough, householder, I have done with eating for today."

"Well then, agree to a meal tomorrow." Venerable Raṭṭhapāla consented in silence.

Then (his) father, recognising (his) consent, went (back) to his own dwelling and, getting a large amount of gold and money together, hid it with screens and addressed venerable Raṭṭhapāla's former wives saying: "Go, daughters-in-law, dress yourselves as you used to, with the adornment that made you dear and cherished by master Raṭṭhapāla." Towards dawn, having had prepared within his own dwelling abundant foods, both hard and soft, (he) made known the time (of the meal) to venerable Raṭṭhapāla.

So venerable Raṭṭhapāla, dressing at an early hour, and taking bowl and robe, went to his father's dwelling. Then (his) father had the hoard of gold and money uncovered, and said to (him): "This, dear Raṭṭhapāla, is your mother's wealth, the rest your father's and your paternal grandfather's. It is possible to enjoy wealth and perform good works. Come – repudiate the training and return to the worldly condition."

"Householder, if you were to take my advice, you would load this hoard of gold and money into wagons and drop it in midstream in the river Ganges. Why so? From this source grief and woe, pain, distress, and trouble will come about for you." Then the former wives of venerable Raṭṭhapāla, taking hold of both feet, said to (him): "Of what kind, young master, are those celestial nymphs on account of which you follow the good life."

"Sisters, we do not follow the good life on account of celestial nymphs." Crying: "Young master Raṭṭhapāla addresses us with the word 'Sisters'" they fell down fainting. Then venerable Raṭṭhapāla said to his father: "If food is to be given, householder, give it. Do not insult us."

"Eat, dear Raṭṭhapāla. The meal is ready." And his father served and satisfied venerable Raṭṭhapāla with his own hand, with foods both hard and soft. Then venerable Raṭṭhapāla, after he had eaten, set the bowl aside and, standing upright, spoke these verses:

"See the contrivance of (material) shape, a heap of sores, an assemblage, afflicted, much dwelt on, in which there is no constant state. See the contrivance of form with jewel and ring, the bones covered in skin, endowed with the splendour of clothes, the feet dyed red, the face powdered – enough for the delusion of a fool, but not for one seeking the other shore; hair braided eightfold, eyes anointed with collyrium – enough for the delusion of a fool, but not for one seeking the other shore. Like a new, bright, collyrium box is the foul body when adorned – enough for the delusion of a fool, but not for one seeking the other shore. The deer-hunter set a snare. The deer did not touch the net. Having eaten the bait we depart whilst the deer-stalker laments." Having spoken these lines there where he stood venerable Raṭṭhapāla went to the deer-park of the king of the Kurus, and sat down at the root of a tree for the afternoon rest.

Now the king of the Kurus spoke to a huntsman,[2] saying: "Good huntsman, make a clearing for a pleasure-garden in the deer park. (Then) we will go and look at (it)." (And the man did so and) saw the venerable Raṭṭhapāla sitting (there). Having seen (him) he went (back) to the king of the Kurus and said to (him): "Sire, the deer-park is cleared. But (one) Raṭṭhapāla is there, the son of a family of repute in this (town of) Thullakoṭṭhita, one whom you have often praised."

"Well then, good huntsman, enough for today of the pleasure-garden. We will attend on the worthy Raṭṭhapāla." And (he) said (that) all the hard and soft foods that had been prepared should be given away. Ordering fine carriages to be harnessed, (the king) ascended (one of them) and set out from Thullakoṭthita with great pomp to see venerable Raṭṭhapāla. As far as the terrain permitted he went by carriage, then, descending from (it), approached venerable Raṭṭhapāla on foot. Having exchanged greetings and conversed in a friendly and polite way he stood at one side. Said the king of the Kurus: "Let the worthy Raṭṭhapāla sit here, on the elephant rug." "No, sire. Be seated yourself. I have my own place."

Sitting down, the king of the Kurus said to venerable Raṭṭhapāla: "Good Raṭṭhapāla, there are these four losses because of which some here cut of hair and beard, don saffron robes, and go forth from home into homelessness – loss through old age, loss through illness, loss of possessions, and loss of relations. And what is loss through old age? As to this someone thinks (of himself) as frail, old, venerable, (his) life lived out and having reached the end of (his) days; and (that) it is not easy for (him) to acquire wealth not already acquired nor use to advantage (what) is already possessed. (So, because of that), he goes forth from home into homelessness. That is what is called loss through old age. But the worthy Raṭṭhapāla is still a young man, possessed of the jet black hair of a happy youth, and in his early prime. So there is no such loss through old age for (him).

And what is loss through illness? As to this, someone thinks (of himself as) afflicted with disease, ailing, grievously sick, and (that) it is not easy for (him) to acquire wealth, or use (it) to advantage. (So, because of that), he goes forth from home into homelessness. That is what is called loss through homelessness. But the worthy Raṭṭhapāla is still in good health, without illness, possessed of sound digestion, neither too cold nor too hot. So there is no such loss through illness for (him).

And what is loss of wealth? As to this, someone is rich, of great wealth and possessions, but these are expended in the course of time. He reflects (on this, and thinks that) it is not easy for (him) to acquire wealth not already acquired, nor use to advantage (what) is already possessed. So, because of that, he goes forth from home into homelessness. That is what I term loss of possessions. But the worthy Raṭṭhapāla is the son of a family of repute in Thullakoṭṭhita. So there is no loss of wealth for (him).

And what is loss of relations? As to this, someone has many friends, associates, and relations, but these are lost to him in the course of time. He reflects (on this, and thinks that) it is not easy for (him) to acquire wealth not already acquired, nor use to advantage (what) is already possessed. (So, because of that), he goes forth from home into homelessness. That is what is called loss of relations. But the worthy Raṭṭhapāla has many friends, associates, and relations. So there is no such loss of relations for (him). (In the light of all this) what has (he) known, seen, and heard to have gone forth?"

"Sire, by the Lord who knows and sees, who is *arahant* and truly enlightened, four declarations about *dhamma* have been made. Knowing, seeing, and hearing these, I have gone forth from home into homelessness.

'The inconstant world is carried away' is the first declaration. 'The world is without shelter or protection' is the second. 'The world is not one's own. One must depart, leaving everything' is the third. 'The world is in want, discontented, a slave to craving' is the fourth. These, sire, are the four declarations (because of which) I have gone forth from home into homelessness."

"The worthy Raṭṭhapāla has said: 'The inconstant world is carried away'. But how is the meaning of that statement to be understood?"

"What do you think about this, sire? At twenty or twenty-five years of age could you control an elephant, a horse, a chariot, a bow, and a sword? Were you strong in the thigh and in the arm, competent and at home on the battle-field?"

"Worthy Raṭṭhapāla, (at that age I was all those things). Perhaps at times I was possessed. I saw none with strength like mine."

("And now?")

"By no means, good Raṭṭhapāla. Now I am frail, old, venerable, my life, lived out, with eighty years gone by. At times, thinking (to put my foot in one place), I put it elsewhere."

"It is in this connection, sire, that the Lord (made that first statement)."

"Excellent, good Raṭṭhapāla, wonderful – that this was so well said by that Lord. For there are now in this royal household regiments of elephants, and horses, and chariots, and foot-soldiers, who would come to our defence in case of misfortune. (But) the worthy Raṭṭhapāla has (also) said: 'The world is without shelter or protection.' How is the meaning of that statement to be understood?"

"What do you think about this, sire? Have you any chronic illness?"

"I have a chronic illness of wind. Sometimes friends, associates, and relations stand around me saying (that) the king of the Kurus will now pass away."

"And could you request of your friends, associates, and relations (that they might) share this feeling, so that (you) might experience a more buoyant feeling? Or is it just you that has to experience (it)?"

"I alone have to experience (it)."

"It is in this connection, sire, that the Lord (made that second statement)."

"Excellent, good Raṭṭhapāla, wonderful – that this was so well said by that Lord. Now there exists in this royal household an abundance of gold and money both below and above ground.[3] (But) the worthy Raṭṭhapāla has (also) said: 'The world is not one's own. One must depart leaving everything.' How is the meaning of that statement to be understood?"

"What do you think about this, sire? Whereas you at present enjoy yourself, endowed and equipped with the five strands of worldly pursuit, will you abide in the beyond thinking (that you are still enjoying yourself) like that, or will others occupy themselves with this wealth as you pass on according to your deeds?"

"(The latter), good Raṭṭhapāla."

"It is in this connection, sire, that the Lord (made that third statement)."

"Excellent, good Raṭṭhapāla, wonderful – that this was so well said by that Lord. (But) the worthy Raṭṭhapāla has (also) said: 'The world is in want, discontented, a slave to craving.' How is the meaning of this statement to be understood?"

"What do you think about this, sire? Is this Kuru that you live in prosperous?"

"Yes, good Raṭṭhapāla."

"(And), if a trustworthy and reliable man should come to you here from the east and (tell you of) a great country, wealthy, prosperous, and of vast population (where) there are great regiments of elephants, horses, chariots, and foot soldiers, (and that) there is much ivory there, much gold and money, both worked and unworked, (and) many women; (and that) it can be overcome with appropriate force – what would you do, sire?"

"We should overcome it and live there, good Raṭṭhapāla."

"It is in this connection, sire, that the Lord (made that fourth statement)."

"Excellent, good Raṭṭhapāla, wonderful – that this was so well said by that Lord."

Thus spoke venerable Raṭṭhapāla.

1. As 60.
2. Possibly a gamewarden of some kind.

3. Possibly the old man means that there are secret hoards which others will not be able to find.

83

On Makhādeva

74–83

Thus have I heard: once the Lord dwelt in Mithilā in Makhādeva's Mango-Grove. Then the Lord smiled (when he came to) a certain place. At that, venerable Ānanda thought: "Why, and on account of what, does the Lord smile?" Arranging his robe over one shoulder and saluting the Lord with joined palms, (he) said:

"Why, and on account of what, does the Lord smile?"

"Once upon a time, Ānanda, here in Mithilā, there was a king called Makhādeva, one given over to *dhamma*, a monarch (ruling by) *dhamma*, firm in *dhamma*, a great king who followed *dhamma* in relation to brahmans and householders, townspeople and country people, and who kept observance days on the fourteenth, fifteenth, and eighth days of the half-month. And King Makhādeva, after many years, many hundreds of years, many thousands of years, addressed his barber, saying: 'Good barber, when you see grey hairs growing in my head, you should tell me.' 'Yes Lord', said the barber.

Then, after many years, many hundreds of years, many thousands of years, the barber saw grey hairs growing on the head of the king, and said to (him): 'The messengers of the god (of death) have shown themselves. Grey hairs can be seen growing on your head.' 'Well then, good barber, pull (them) all out with tweezers and wrap them round my finger.' (And the barber did so). Then King Makhādeva, having made the barber the grant of a village (by way of reward), sent for his eldest son and said:

'I have feasted on the worldly pursuits of a human being. Now is the time to seek divine pursuits. Come dear boy, take over this realm. For I shall cut off hair and beard, don the saffron robe, and go forth from home into homelessness. Now when you too see grey hairs growing on your head (do as I have done). Continue this auspicious custom that I have established, and do not be the last man (to do so) after me. In the handing down of the succession in which such an auspicious custom is done away with, (that king) will be the last (of the dynasty).'

Then, Ānanda, King Makhādeva, having duly placed his eldest son on the throne, and having cut off hair and beard in this very mango grove, donned the saffron robe and went forth from home into homelessness. He lived, spreading thoughts joined to goodwill in (all) directions. He lived, spreading (them) everywhere, in every way, to the entire world, abundantly, boundlessly, unrestrictedly, peaceably, benevolently. He lived, spreading thoughts joined to compassion, gladness, and equanimity (in the same way). Indeed, King Makhādeva had indulged boyish amusements for 84,000 years, had been viceroy, (then) king for (similar periods), and was gone forth from home into homelessness here in this very mango grove. Having cultivated the four divine abidings, he arose in the *brahmā*-world on the breaking up of the body at death.

(And his eldest son reigned in his stead and carried out his father's instructions to the letter when his time came). Having cultivated the four divine abidings, he (too) arose in the *brahmā*-world at the breaking up of the body at death. (And his son's descendants maintained this practice also).

Nimi was the last of these kings, one given over to *dhamma*, a monarch (ruling by) *dhamma*, firm in *dhamma*, a great king who followed *dhamma* in relation to brahmans and householders, townspeople and country people, and who adhered to the observance days on the fourteenth, fifteenth, and eighth days of the half-month.

Once upon a time, Ānanda, this conversation arose among the Devas of the Thirty-Three, when they were sitting together, and had come together in the Sudhamma debating-hall: 'It is surely a gain for the Videhas, good fortune for (them, that they have a king such as King Nimi)'. Then, Ānanda, Sakka, lord of the *devas*, said to the Devas of the Thirty- Three: 'Do you wish, gentlemen, to see King Nimi?' 'We do.'

Now at that time King Nimi, having bathed his head on that observance day, the fifteenth, was sitting at the top of his palace. And Sakka, lord of the *devas*, just as a strong man might extend his arm, then bend it back, vanished from among the Devas of the Thirty-Three and appeared before King Nimi, saying:

'For you there is gain, sire, for you there is good fortune (in keeping the observance days and ruling justly). The Devas of the Thirty Three, sire, have a wish to see you. I will send you a carriage harnessed to a thousand thoroughbreds. Climb into the divine carriage without hesitation.' King Nimi consented in silence. (And Sakka, lord of the *devas*, returned to the *brahmā*-world and instructed the divine charioteer Mātali to go to him. Then Mātali the charioteer went to King Nimi and said):

'Climb aboard the divine carriage without hesitation. And by which (route) do I conduct you – the one by which evil deeds come to fruition, or the one by which noble deeds come to fruition?'

'Take me by both, Mātali.' So, Ānanda, Mātali the charioteer brought King Nimi to the Sudhamma debating-hall. Sakka, lord of the *devas*, saw King Nimi coming some way off, and said to (him): 'Welcome, sire! Greetings, sire!' (And he told him of the conversation that had passed among the *devas* and of the praise bestowed upon him).

'Enough, sir! – let me return to Mithilā, there to follow *dhamma* in relation to brahmans and householders, townspeople and country people, and to keep the observance days.' (So King Nimi went back to his realm and maintained the customs of his forbears).

But King Nimi's son was called Kaḷārajanaka. He did not go forth from home into homelessness. He broke with that auspicious custom. He was the last (of the dynasty). Now it may be, Ānanda, that you think that at that time King Makhādeva, who established that auspicious custom, was someone else. But you should not view it thus. I, at that time, was King Makhādeva. I established that auspicious custom. The people who came after kept (it) going. But that auspicious custom did not lead to disenchantment, to dispassion, to cessation, to calm, to knowledge, to enlightenment, to *nibbāna* – only to arising in the *brahmā*-world. However, the auspicious custom that I have now established (does do so). And what is that auspicious custom, Ānanda? It is the *ariyan* eightfold path, namely, right view, aim, speech, action, livelihood, effort, mindfulness, concentration. Of that I say: Maintain this auspicious custom. Do not be the last of the line after me."

Thus spoke the Lord.

84

At Madhurā

83–90

Thus have I heard: once venerable Kaccāna the Great dwelt in the Gundā Grove near Madhurā. Avantiputta, king of Madhurā, heard (of this, and) that a fine reputation circulated (about venerable Kaccāna – that he was) wise, clever, intelligent, well informed, a preacher, articulate, venerable, and *arahant*. (And King Avantiputta thought) it would be good to see (such a person).

Whereupon, ordering fine carriages to be harnessed, (he) ascended (one of them) and set out from Madhurā with great pomp to see venerable Kaccāna the Great. As far as the terrain permitted he went by carriage; then, descending from (it), he approached venerable Kaccāna on foot, greeted (him) and, after conversing in a friendly and polite way, sat down at one side. Said the king:

"Good Kaccāna, brahmans think (that) brahmans are the best caste, others base; (that) brahmans are fair, others dark; (that) brahmans become pure (through cleansing), not others; (and that) brahmans are Brahmā's natural progeny, born of his mouth, sprung from Brahmā, created by Brahmā, inheritors of Brahmā. What does the worthy Kaccāna say about this?"

"Sire, such is mere shouting to the world. What do you think about this, sire? If a nobleman were to prosper in terms of possessions, corn, silver, or gold, might (some other) nobleman be his obedient servant, rising before him and going to bed after him, making himself agreeable and talking pleasantly? (And could a brahman, a merchant, or an artisan also serve in such a capacity)?"

("Yes indeed, good Kaccāna, any of them could do this.")

"What do you think about this, sire? If a brahman, (or) merchant, (or) artisan were to prosper (in these same ways) might (a member of any caste) be his obedient servant (likewise)?"

("Yes indeed, good Kaccāna.")

"That being the case, sire, are these four castes equal (in this respect) or not?"

"That being the case, good Kaccāna, I can see no difference whatsoever therein."

"(Now), what do you think about this, sire? Should (some) nobleman here be a destroyer of life, a taker of what is not given, devoted to dissolute living, a liar, of abusive, slanderous, and frivolous speech, covetous, of corrupt mind and wrong view – would he come to sorrow, to an evil destiny, to ruin, to purgatory, on the breaking up of the body at death – or not? How does the matter strike you?"

"A nobleman (living like that) would come to sorrow, to an evil destiny, to ruin, to purgatory on the breaking up of the body at death. That is how it strikes me, and how I have heard it from (those who are) *arahants*."

"It is well, sire. (And would the same comments be true of a brahman, a merchant, or an artisan who lived in such a way)?"

("Yes, good Kaccāna.")

"That being the case, sire, are these four castes equal (in this respect) or not?"

"That being the case, good Kaccāna, I can see no difference whatsoever therein."

"(Now), what do you think about this, sire? Should a nobleman, a brahman, a merchant, (or) an artisan abstain (from all these things) – would he come to a good destiny, a heaven world, on the breaking up of the body at death? How does the matter strike you?"

"(Such a person, living like that), would come to a good destiny, a heaven world on the breaking up of the body at death. That is how it strikes me and so have I heard it from (those who are) *arahants*."

"That being the case, sire, are these four castes equal (in this respect) or not?"

"That being the case, good Kaccāna, I can see no difference whatsoever therein."

"(Now), what do you think about this, sire?" If a noble, (or) brahman, (or) merchant, (or) artisan breaks into (a dwelling), carries away loot, engages in robbery, waits in ambush, or commits adultery – what do you do to him?"

"We would have him put to death, good Kaccāna, or bring about his ruin or exile, or (otherwise) deal with him as we saw fit. Why so? (Whatever) his former designation, that is finished with. He simply goes by the name of thief."

"That being the case, sire, are these four castes equal (in this respect) or not?"

"That being the case, good Kaccāna, I can see no difference whatsoever therein."

"(Now), what do you think about this, sire? Should a nobleman, a brahman, a merchant, (or) an artisan cut off hair and beard, don the saffron robes, and go forth from home into homelessness, refraining from the destruction of life, from taking what is not given, and from lying; eating once a day and living the good life, virtuous, noble in his conduct – what would you do?"

"We should salute him, rise in respect, or invite him to take a seat; or offer him robes, almsfood, shelter, and medication; or make provision to have him guarded, watched, and protected. Why so? (Whatever) his former designation, that is finished with. He simply goes by the name of ascetic."

"That being the case, sire, are these four castes equal (in this respect) or not?"

"That being the case, good Kaccāna, I can see no difference whatsoever therein."

"In such a way, sire, might such (talk by brahmans) be thought of as mere shouting to the world."

At these words King Avantiputta of Madhurā said to venerable Kaccāna:

"Excellent, good Kaccāna, excellent!" (Whereupon the king of Madhurā took refuge in venerable Kaccāna, in *dhamma*, and in the Order of monks – and became a lay-follower. But venerable Kaccāna said):

"Do not take refuge in me, sire. Go rather for refuge to that Lord to whom I have gone for refuge."

"But where is that Lord who is *arahant* and truly enlightened now dwelling?"

"Sire, that Lord has gone to final *nibbāna*."

"If we were to hear that that Lord were (many miles) distant we should go and see him. Because (however) he has gone to final *nibbāna* we take refuge in (him), in *dhamma*, and in the Order of monks. Let the worthy Kaccāna accept me as a lay-follower from today for the rest of my life."

85

With Prince Bodhi

91–97

Thus have I heard: once the Lord dwelt among the Bhaggas in Bhesakaḷā Grove in the deer-park at Sumsumāragira. Now at that time there was a palace called Kokanada belonging to Prince Bodhi and not long built, which had not been lived in by ascetic or brahman, or any human being whatsoever. Then Prince Bodhi addressed the youth Sañjikāputta saying: "Go, good Sañjikāputta, and approach the Lord. Salute (his) feet with your head in my name and ask whether he is without ailment or sickness, vigorous, strong, and living in comfort. (Then say): 'Let the Lord agree to (attend) a meal on the morrow, together with the Order of monks.' " (And the youth Sañjikāputta did as he was bid). The Lord gave his consent in silence.

So towards dawn Prince Bodhi, having had abundant foods prepared, both hard and soft, had the Kokanada Palace spread with white cloths, even to the last flight of stairs, (and then made known the time of the meal to the Lord). Whereupon the Lord, dressing at an early hour, took bowl and robe and approached the dwelling of Prince Bodhi.

At that time Prince Bodhi was standing waiting for (him) outside the gateway, and seeing (him) some way off went to meet the Lord. After saluting him and paying his respects he went (with him) to the palace. And the Lord stood leaning against the last flight of stairs. Said Prince Bodhi: "Walk on the cloths, bhante. That will be for my profit and wellbeing for many a day." At these words the Lord was silent, (so Prince Bodhi repeated his request). Then the Lord looked at venerable Ānanda (who) said to Prince Bodhi:

"Gather up the cloths, Prince. The Lord will not tread upon a carpeting of cloth. The Exemplar looks towards the people who come after.[1]" So Prince Bodhi had the cloths collected, and had seats prepared at the top of the palace. Then (he) satisfied and served with his own hand the Order of monks led by the Buddha – with abundant foods both hard and soft. When the Lord had eaten and set aside the bowl, Prince Bodhi took a low seat and sat down at one side. Said the Prince;

"Happiness is not to be achieved through happiness. Happiness is to be achieved through suffering."

"Prince, I too, before my enlightenment, being but a *bodhisatta*, thought (like that)." (And the Lord told Prince Bodhi of his early years under two teachers, of his fruitless period of extreme austerities, of his enlightenment, and of the beginnings of the Order).[2]

At these words Prince Bodhi said to the Lord:

"After how long does a monk, taking the Exemplar for his guide, reach and experience that consummation of the good life, realised in this life from his own gnosis, for which sons of family rightly go forth from home into homelessness?"

"Well now, Prince, I will question you on this in turn. Answer as you see fit. Are you a competent rider of elephants, good at using a goad?"

"Yes, bhante."

"What do you think about this, Prince? Suppose a man were to come here (knowing that, and thinking): 'I will train in the art of elephant-riding and goad-handling under (Prince Bodhi).' Were he lacking in faith he could not achieve whatever is to be achieved through faith. Were he in poor health he could not achieve whatever is to be achieved through good health. Were he crafty and deceitful, (or) indolent, (or) weak in wisdom (the same would be true). Could such a man train (successfully) under you in the art of elephant-riding and goad handling?"

"Possessed of such qualities, bhante, (he could not). But what is this talk of five qualities?".

"Likewise, Prince, these are the five qualities for exertion. Herein a monk has faith. He has faith in the enlightenment of the Exemplar thinking: 'This is the Lord, *arahant*, truly enlightened, proficient in knowledge and conduct, adept, seer of worlds, matchless charioteer of men to be tamed, teacher of *devas* and humans, Buddha and Lord.' (The monk) is without ailment or sickness, of sound digestion, neither too cold nor too hot, moderate, persistent in exertion. He is not crafty and deceitful, but reveals himself as he really is to the Teacher, or to intelligent associates in the good life. He lives resolute in energy for the abandonment of unskilled states and the acquisition of skilled states, steadfast, of strong effort, harnessing himself to skilled states. He is wise, possessed of wisdom for the dispelling of appearance and disappearance, and with the *ariyan* discrimination leading to the complete rooting out of suffering. These are the five qualities (necessary) for exertion, Prince. If a monk is possessed of (them) then, taking the Exemplar for his guide, (he may attain the goal of the good life within seven years, and excellence in but a night and day)."[3]

At these words Prince Bodhi said: "A Buddha indeed, a *dhamma* indeed – indeed a *dhamma* well preached (if such be the case!)"

After he had spoken, the youth Sañjikāputta said to Prince Bodhi:

"The worthy Bodhi speaks (like that) but does not add: 'I take refuge in the worthy Gotama, and in *dhamma*, and in the Order of monks.' "

"Do not talk like that, good Sañjikāputta. In my mother's presence I heard and learnt this – on one occasion the Lord dwelt on the Ghosita campus near Kosambī. Then my mother, who was pregnant, went to (him), saluted him, and sat down at one side. saying: 'This that is come into the womb, be it boy or girl, shall take refuge in the Lord, and in *dhamma*, and in the Order of monks. Let the Lord take this lay-follower as gone for refuge henceforth for his whole life.' (And likewise) my wet nurse. carrying me on her hip, (took refuge for me on another occasion). Now, good Sañjikāputta, I take refuge for a third time."

1. Perhaps he viewed it as superstition and wished to discourage its continuance in the future.
2. The account repeats the episodes in discourses 26, 36, and then 26 again.
3. A diminishing list of periods is referred to between these two extremes.

86

With Aṅgulimāla

97–105

Thus have I heard: once the Lord dwelt near Sāvatthī in the Jeta Grove on Anāthapiṇḍika's campus. Now at that time in the realm of King Pasenadi of Kosala there was a bandit called Aṅgulimāla who was fierce, with blood on his hands, given over to injury and slaughter, and with no kindness towards living things. Because of him, villages, towns, and countryside were alike depopulated. Having slain (so many) people he wore a necklace made of their fingers.[1]

Now the Lord, dressing at an early hour, and taking bowl and robe, went into Sāvatthī for almsfood. On his return from the almsround after the meal he tidied his lodging and, taking bowl and robe, set out along the main road in the direction of Aṅgulimāla the bandit. Cowherds, oxherds, ploughmen, and travellers, seeing the Lord going (that way), called out to (him): "Do not take this road, ascetic. On (it) even ten (or more) men setting out together have fallen into (his) hands." At these words the Lord went on in silence.

And Aṅgulimāla the bandit saw the Lord coming some way off and thought to himself: "Astonishing, extraordinary! Even ten (or more) men setting out together have fallen into my hands on this road. Yet this ascetic comes alone and unaccompanied, quite undaunted it seems. What if I were to take (his) life."

So Aṅgulimāla the bandit, seizing his sword and shield, and arming himself with bow and quiver, followed right upon the Lord's heels. Whereupon the Lord performed such a feat of psychic power that, whereas (he) went along at a normal pace, Aṅgulimāla the bandit – proceeding with all haste, was unable to catch (him). Then Aṅgulimāla thought to himself: "Astonishing, extraordinary! – that I who, in the past, have pursued and taken a fleeing elephant, or horse, or chariot, or deer, cannot now overtake this ascetic." Stopping, he called to the Lord:

"Stop, ascetic, stop!"

"I have stopped, Aṅgulimāla. Now you stop."

Then Aṅgulimāla the bandit thought to himself: "These ascetics who are sons of the Sakyans are speakers of truth, acknowledgers of truth. Yet this ascetic, while moving says: 'I have stopped. Now you stop. Suppose I were to question (him).' " So Aṅgulimāla addressed the Lord in verse, saying:

**"You move, ascetic, and say: 'I have stopped.' You call me not stopped, though I stand still. I ask you, ascetic, on this matter. How are you stopped and I not stopped?"

"I have stopped, Aṅgulimāla, ever laying the stick aside for all beings. But you are unrestrained with living beings. Therefore I say you have not stopped."

"Surely it is long since I honoured a great sage. Yet this ascetic has pierced the great thicket. Hearing your *dhamma*-linked verse I shall soon cast out evil." And so the bandit threw his sword and weapons down a pit, a precipice, a chasm, (and) paid homage at the Adept's feet. There he begged for the going forth. The Buddha, the merciful, the great sage, teacher of the world with its *devas* said to him: "Come, monk." Just that gave him the position of monk.**

Then the Lord set out for Sāvatthī with venerable Aṅgulimāla in attendance, (and) arrived (there) in due course. There he dwelt in the Jeta Grove on Anāthapiṇḍika's campus. Now at that time a large group of people had assembled at the palace-gate of King Pasenadi of Kosala, (shouting) noisily and amid great tumult (about the bandit Aṅgulimāla and his reign of terror, and crying): "The King must drive him away."

So King Pasenadi of Kosala, with as many as five hundred horses, went out from Sāvatthī at an early hour and set out towards (Anāthapiṇḍika's campus).[2] As far as the terrain permitted he went by vehicle then, descending from (it), approached the Lord on foot and, after saluting him, sat down at one side. Said the Lord:

"What's the matter, sire? Is King Bimbisāra of Magadha offended with you, or the Licchavis of Vēsalī, or another hostile king?"

"(None of these), bhante. There is, in my realm, a bandit called Aṅgulimāla. Because of him town, village, and countryside are alike depopulated. I shall not be able to drive him away."

"But, sire, if you were to see Aṅgulimāla with hair and beard cut off, having donned the saffron robe, gone forth from home into homelessness and abstaining from the destruction of life, from taking what is not given, from dissolute living, from lying; eating once a day, a follower of the good life, virtuous, and of good conduct – what would you do to him?"

"We should salute him. We should rise from our seat (in respect). We should provide him with robe, almsbowl, shelter, and medicaments. We should appoint a proper (person) to guard, watch, and protect him.[3] But how could such restraint of conduct come about for one who is so villainous and evil in his ways?"

Now at that moment venerable Aṅgulimāla was seated not far from the Lord. And the Lord, with a motion of his right arm, said: "This is Aṅgulimāla, sire." Then King Pasenadi of Kosala was fearful and stupefied, his hair standing on end. And the Lord, seeing (this), said: "Have no fear, sire. There is now no cause for your fear." So the King's fear abated and he went up to venerable Aṅgulimāla and said:

"Bhante, are you truly Aṅgulimāla?"

"Yes, sire."

"What was your father's and mother's name, bhante?"

"Gagga was my father, sire, Mantāṇī my mother."

"Let the son of Gagga and Mantāṇī be at ease. I shall make efforts as regards robe, almsbowl, shelter, and medicaments."

But at that time venerable Aṅgulimāla was forest-gone, taking only food received in the almsbowl, and wearing three robes made from rags taken from a dust heap. And (he) said to the King: "Enough, sire, three robes are sufficient for me." So King Pasenadi of Kosala went (back) to the Lord, saluted (him), and sat down at one side. Said the King:

"Extraordinary, bhante, wonderful! – how the Lord tames the untamed, calms the uncalm, extinguishes (the fires in) the uncool. Him that I could not tame with stick and sword the Lord has tamed without (either). Alas, now we must go. There are many duties and much to be done."

"Do now as you see fit, sire." And King Pasenadi of Kosala, rising from his seat and saluting the Lord, went away keeping his right side towards him.

Then venerable Aṅgulimāla, dressing at an early hour, and taking bowl and robe, went into Sāvatthī for alms. Walking successively for alms he saw a woman in difficult and dangerous labour and thought: "Surely beings are impure". Returning from the almsround after the meal he approached the Lord, saluted (him), and sat down at one side (where he told of his experience).

"Now, Aṅgulimāla, you must go (back) to Sāvatthī and, approaching that woman say (to her): 'Since I was born, sister, I am not aware of having deliberately taken the life of a living being. In that truth let there be safety for you, and for the (contents of) the womb.' "

"But wouldn't that be a conscious lie on my part, bhante? I have deliberately taken the life of many living beings."

"Then say, Aṅgulimāla: 'I have not deliberately taken the life of a living being since I was born into the *ariyan* birth. In that truth let there be safety for you, and for (the contents of) the womb.' (And venerable Aṅgulimāla returned to Sāvatthī and spoke thus to the woman). Then indeed there was safety for the woman, and for the (contents of) the womb.

Then venerable Aṅgulimāla, living alone and apart, diligent, zealous, and resolute, reached and experienced before long that consummation of the good life for which sons of family rightly go forth from home into homelessness, having realised it in this life through his own gnosis. (He knew): "Destroyed is birth, fulfilled the good life, done what was to be done, and no further return to this world." And so venerable Aṅgulimāla was one of the *arahants*.

And venerable Aṅgulimāla, dressing at an early hour, and taking bowl and robe, went into Sāvatthī for almsfood. Now at that time a clod thrown by someone fell on him, together with a stick thrown by another, and gravel by someone else. Then, with (his) head broken and bleeding, and with his bowl smashed and his robe torn, venerable Aṅgulimāla approached the Lord. Seeing him some way off, the Lord said: "Have endurance, brahman.[4] You are experiencing in this life the fruits of deeds for which you might (otherwise) find torment in purgatory for many years, many hundreds of years, many thousands of years." And venerable Aṅgulimāla, finding solitude and immersing himself in meditation, experienced the happiness of freedom.

1. The bandit's name means "finger-necklace".
2. The implication is that he thought first of Gotama, whether to warn him or to seek courage and reassurance.
3. Possibly he feared reprisals against Aṅgulimāla such as occur at the end of the discourse, or continued to be distrustful of him. However, this phrase does occur elsewhere.
4. Used in an ideal exhortatory manner here.

87

On the Products of Affection

106–112

Thus have I heard: once the Lord dwelt near Sāvatthī in the Jeta Grove on Anāthapiṇḍika's campus. Now at that time the small only son of a certain householder, loved and cherished (by him), had just died. Because of the death the father ignored both work and food. He was for ever going to the cemetery and wailing: "Where are you my only son?" Then he approached the Lord, saluted him, and sat down at one side. Said the Lord:

"Householder, is there no capacity in your mind for steadying the faculties? They are disordered."

"How should my faculties not be disordered, bhante! My only son, loved and cherished, is dead. Since his death I can neither work nor eat. I just keep going to the cemetery and saying: 'Where are you my only son?' ".

"So it is, householder. The products of affection, and rooted in affection, are grief, woe, pain, distress, and trouble."

"For whom could this really be so, bhante? For the products of affection, and rooted in affection, are joy and delight." And the householder, displeased with and rejecting the Lord's words, rose from his place and departed.

At that moment a number of gamblers were amusing themselves with dice not far from the Lord. So the householder went up to these gamblers and (told them of the conversation he had just had. Said they):

"So it is householder. The products of affection, and rooted in affection, are joy and delight." And the householder went away (reflecting that the gamblers agreed with him).

Now this topic of conversation found its way in due course into the King's palace. And King Pasenadi of Kosala said to Queen Mallikā:

"Mallikā, it has been said by Gotama the ascetic (that) the products of affection, and rooted in affection, are grief, woe, pain, distress, and trouble."

"If that has been said by the Lord, sire, it is true."

"But however this ascetic Gotama speaks so does Mallikā – to such a degree is she enamoured of him. Indeed, it is like a teacher speaking to a pupil (and gaining meek compliance). Be off Mallikā! Away with you!"

Then Queen Mallikā addressed the brahman Nāḷijaṅgha saying:.

"Go, brahman, approach the Lord and pay homage at (his) feet with your head in my name, and ask whether he is without ailment or sickness, vigorous, strong, and living in comfort. (Then question him as to the meaning of his words). Take in thoroughly whatever the Lord explains to you, and relate it to me. For exemplars do not speak contrary to the truth. (And brahman Nāḷijaṅgha did as he was bid, asking): "Were these the words of the Lord, (that) the products of affection, and rooted in affection, are grief, woe, pain, distress, and trouble."

"That is correct, brahman, (and) this is the way (the matter) should be interpreted. Once upon a time here in Sāvatthī a woman's mother died. Because of his death she went out of her mind, became distraught, and going from street to street, crossroads to crossroads, would say: 'Have you seen my mother? Have you seen my mother?'[1]

(Or again), once upon a time here in Sāvatthī a certain woman went to her relations' family. These relatives, having forcibly separated her from her husband, wanted to give her to another, though she did not wish for that. So (she) said to her husband: 'Those who have torn me from you want to give me to someone else, but I do not wish it.' And that man hacked that woman in twain and then killed himself, thinking (they would) both exist after death. This, too, is the way (what I have said is to be interpreted)."

Then brahman Nāḷijaṅgha, pleased and satisfied with the Lord's words, rose from his place, went to Queen Mallikā, and related his entire conversation with the Lord. And (she in turn) went to (the King) and asked:

"What do you think about this, sire? Is your daughter Vajīrī dear to you?"

"Yes, Mallikā."

"And from alteration and change in your daughter might grief, woe, pain, distress, and trouble arise for you?"

"From (such) alteration there might be a change for me, even for life. How could (such feelings) not come upon me?"[2]

"And what do you think about this, sire? Are the people of Kāsi and Kosala dear to you?"

"Yes, Mallikā. Through (their) greatness we get the sandalwood of Kāsi, we wear garlands, perfumes, and cosmetics."

"And from alteration and change of circumstance for (them) might (such feelings) arise for you?"

"From (such) alteration there might be a change for me, even for life. How could (such feelings) not come upon me?"[3]

"It is in this connection, sire, (that the statement that) the products of affection, and rooted in affection, are grief, woe, pain, distress, and trouble, has been made by the Lord who knows and sees, who is *arahant* and truly enlightened."

"Excellent, Mallikā, wonderful! Thus far does the Lord penetrate and perceive through wisdom. Go, Mallikā, and prepare for washing."[4] And King Pasenadi of Kosala, rising from his place and arranging his robe over one shoulder, made salutation with joined palms to the Lord (going for refuge to him three times).

1. A whole series of bereavements is mentioned.
2. A series of individuals is referred to including the queen herself.
3. Possibly in this case political considerations are also in mind.
4. Presumably a cleansing ritual.

88

The Mantle

112–117

Thus have I heard: once the Lord dwelt near Sāvatthī in the Jeta Grove on Anāthapiṇḍika's campus. Then venerable Ānanda, dressing at an early hour and taking bowl and robe, went into Sāvatthī for almsfood. Having walked in Sāvatthī for alms and returning after the meal, he approached the Migāramātu Palace and the eastern campus for the afternoon rest.

Now at that moment King Pasenadi of Kosala, having climbed on the back of the elephant Ekapuṇḍarīka was leaving Sāvatthī early in the day. (He) saw venerable Ānanda coming some way off, and addressed his chief minister, asking: "Is this not venerable Ānanda, worthy Sirivaḍḍha?" "Yes, sire."

Then King Pasenadi of Kosala said to a certain man: "Approach venerable Ānanda and, in my name, salute (his) feet with your head (and ask him to) wait a moment out of compassion, if he has no pressing engagement." (And the man did as he was bid. Whereupon King Pasenadi of Kosala approached venerable Ānanda and requested him to go to the bank of the river Aciravatī. And venerable Ānanda did so), and sat down in the appointed place,[1] at the root of a tree.

And King Pasenadi of Kosala, having travelled on the elephant as far as the terrain permitted, climbed down (from his back), approached venerable Ānanda, saluted him, and stood at one side. Said (the King):

"Let venerable Ānanda sit on the elephant rug."

"No, sire, be seated. I have my own place." Having seated himself (the King) said to venerable Ānanda:

"Bhante, would the Lord practise the kind of bodily, verbal, or mental activity that would be open to censure by intelligent ascetics and brahmans?"

"Certainly not, sire."

"Excellent, bhante, wonderful![2] When the foolish and inexperienced speak praise or blame without investigation or scrutiny, we do not take that as the essence (of the matter). When the wise, experienced, and intelligent (do so) after investigation and scrutiny, we do take that as the essence (of the matter). But what is the bodily, verbal, and mental activity that is open to censure by intelligent ascetics and brahmans?"

"(That) which is unskilful, sire."

"But what activity is unskilful, bhante?"

"(That) which is faulty, sire."

"But what activity is faulty, bhante?"

"(That) which is injurious, sire."

"But what activity is injurious, bhante?"

"(That) which has painful consequences, sire."

"But what activity is it that has painful consequences, bhante?"

"(That) which leads to hurt to oneself, or to others, or to both, (and) out of which unskilful states increase and skilful states diminish."

"Does the Lord applaud the abandonment of absolutely all unskilled states?"

"Sire, the Exemplar has abandoned all unskilful states, (and) is possessed of skilful states."[3]

"Excellent, bhante, wonderful! We are uplifted and satisfied with venerable Ānanda's well-spoken words, (and) would present (him) with a valuable elephant, and a valuable horse, and an excellent village if he permitted it. However, we know (he would not). This mantle, sent to me by King Ajātasattu of Magadha, son of (the lady) Vedehī, is in length sixteen, in breadth eight (hands). May venerable Ānanda accept it out of compassion."

"No, sire. I am complete as to the three robes."

"Bhante, this river Aciravatī has been seen by venerable Ānanda and by ourselves at a time when the thunder-cloud has poured down rain above the mountain. Then this river Aciravatī races along, overflowing both banks. Just so venerable Ānanda can make three robes for himself from this mantle. His previous three robes he can share out among his companions in the good life. So will this gift of ours go on with an overflow. May venerable Ānanda accept the mantle."

And venerable Ānanda accepted the mantle. Then King Pasenadi of Kosala said to (him): "Alas, now we must be going. We have many duties and there is much to be done." "Do as you now see fit, sire." So King Pasenadi of Kosala, pleased and satisfied with the words of venerable Ānanda, rose from his place, saluted (him), and went away keeping his right side towards him.

And venerable Ānanda, not long after (the King's) departure, approached the Lord, saluted (him), and sat down at one side, (where he related the whole of what had passed), and gave that mantle to the Lord. Whereupon the Lord addressed the monks, saying: "Monks, it is to the gain and the great profit of King Pasenadi of Kosala that he obtained (the opportunity) to see and attend on Ānanda."

Thus spoke the Lord.

1. Usually translated as "the place prepared", but in this case I assume it to mean rather the agreed place.
2. I have omitted a sentence implying that Ānanda has "conveyed in answer to the question what" the King "was not able to convey fully in a question" (Horner). Unless material has been lost this makes no sense as Ānanda has simply replied with a negative.
3. The full text gives parallel discussion of skilful activity at this point.

89

Testimonies to *Dhamma*

118–125

Thus have I heard: once the Lord dwelt among the Sakyans (in) a town (of theirs) called Medaḷumpa. Now at that time King Pasenadi of Kosala had come to Naṅgaraka for some purpose. And he addressed Dīgha Kārāyana, saying:

"Harness fine carriages, good Kārāyana, and we will go to the pleasure-garden and view its pleasant landscape." (And the man did so.) Then King Pasenadi of Kosala climbed aboard (one of the carriages) went out from Naṅgaraka with great pomp, and made for the park. As far as the terrain permitted he went by carriage, then, descending from (it), entered the park on foot. And King Pasenadi, strolling and wandering in the park, saw roots of trees that were pleasant and inviting, quiet and removed from clamour, evoking solitude and far from the crowd, suited to seclusion. Seeing them, recollections of the Lord came upon him, (and he thought): "These (are the sorts of place) where we pay our respects to the Lord who is *arahant* and truly enlightened." And (he) spoke to Dīgha Kārāyana, saying: "Where is the Lord living at the moment, good Kārāyana?"

"(In) Medaḷumpa, sire."

"And how far is Medaḷumpa from Naṅgaraka?"

"Not far, sire – three *yojanas*.[1] It is possible to get there in what remains of the day?"

"Well then, good Kārāyana, we will go and see the Lord."

So King Pasenadi of Kosala set out from Naṅgaraka and, (travelling) for the rest of the day, reached Medaḷumpa, where he made for the park. As far as the terrain permitted he went by carriage, then, descending from it, entered the park.

Now at that time a number of monks were walking about in the open. And King Pasenadi addressed (them), saying: "Where is the Lord who is *arahant* and truly enlightened dwelling at the moment? We desire to see (him)."

"Sire, that is the dwelling. The door is closed. Approach quietly and go as far as the veranda without crossing it. (Then) cough and knock on the door-bolt. The Lord will open the door to you." Then (the King) immediately gave his sword and turban to Dīgha Kārāyana (who) thought: "Now his majesty would be alone. Ought I to remain here?"

(And the king went to the door and the Lord opened it.) Entering (he) bowed his head at the feet of the Lord and covered (them) with kisses, stroked them with his hand, and announced: "Bhante, I am King Pasenadi of Kosala."[2]

"But why, sire, do you make such obeisance to this body, and offer friendship (like this)?"

"Bhante, I draw a conclusion from *dhamma* concerning the Lord – (that he) is truly enlightened, that (his) *dhamma* is well preached, and that (his) order of disciples is proceeding well. (Around) here I see some ascetics and brahmans proceeding within the confines of the good life for ten, twenty, thirty, or forty years. (However), at a later date, well washed and perfumed, with hair and beard trimmed, they amuse themselves with the five strands of worldly pursuit, given over to and possessed by them. But here I see monks following the good life perfectly fulfilled and purified – to the end of their days and their last breath. I do not behold (such a thing elsewhere). Moreover, kings quarrel with kings, nobles with nobles, brahmans with brahmans, householders with householders, mother with son, father with son, brother with brother, brother with sister, and friend with friend. But here I see monks living in harmony, in agreement, not quarrelling, blending as milk and water, and looking on one another with the eye of affection. I do not behold (such a thing elsewhere).

Then again I stroll and wander from park to park, from pleasure-garden to pleasure-garden. I see there some ascetics and brahmans who are lean, coarse, of poor complexion, sallow, their veins showing all over, whom the eye of man might not find appealing. And as to that I think: 'Surely these venerable ones pursue the good life without satisfaction, or else some evil, undisclosed act has been perpetrated (which accounts for their appearance).' So, approaching (them), I (question them on the matter and they reply): 'We have jaundice, sire.'[3]

But here I see monks supremely happy and elated, looking cheerful, joyful at heart, at ease, pacified, interdependent, and living with the mind(s) of wild creature(s). And, as to that, I think: 'Surely these venerable ones perceive the excellent quality in the Lord's teachings from beginning to end (in displaying such an approach).'

And again I, a noble anointed king, can execute those warranting execution, can fine those warranting a fine, exile those warranting exile. In regard to that (people) interrupt the proceedings when I am sitting in judgement (and I have to rebuke them). But here I see monks, (and) when the Lord teaches *dhamma* to various congregations there is no sound of disciples spitting or coughing. (And when this has occasionally happened others have admonished the culprit.)[4] As to that, I thought: 'Excellent, wonderful! – (that) without stick or sword an assembly should be so well trained.' But I do not behold (such a thing elsewhere).

Moreover, I see in these parts some clever nobles, brahmans, householders, and ascetics – subtle and practised in disputing with others, given to hair-splitting – who go about, it seems, destroying opinions with their wisdom. (They seek to refute the ascetic Gotama, yet end up as his disciples.[5])

Then again I see here my equerries Isīdatta and Purāṇā, whose food is mine, whose carriages are mine, and to whom I have provided a livelihood and brought fame. And yet they do not honour me as they do the Lord. Once, whilst marching against an army and testing these (two), I took up residence in cramped quarters. And having passed much of the night in discussion of *dhamma*, they placed their heads towards where they had heard the Lord might be, and lay down to sleep with their feet towards me. From this too I draw a conclusion concerning the Lord.

And again the Lord is a nobleman (and) a Kosalan, the Lord is eighty years old, (and I, too, am all these things). (Therefore) I make obeisance to the Lord, and show (him) friendship. And now we must be going. We have many duties and much to do."

"Sire, do now whatever you think timely."

Then King Pasenadi of Kosala rose from his seat, saluted the Lord, and, keeping his right side towards (him), went his way. And the Lord, not long after (his) departure addressed the monks, saying:

"Monks, King Pasenadi of Kosala, after speaking testimonies to *dhamma*, has risen from his seat and gone his way. Acquire testimonies to *dhamma*. Master (them). Possess testimonies to *dhamma* which are profitable. Testimonies to *dhamma* are profitable, are the starting-point of the good life."

Thus spoke the Lord.

1. About twenty miles.
2. Various parts of the Canon suggest that they were very well known to each other.
3. Horner – "It is an illness that runs in our families".
4. As 77.
5. Previous paragraph much abbreviated. See 27 for detail.

90

At Kaṇṇakatthala

125–133

Thus have I heard: once the Lord dwelt near Ujuññā in the deer-park at Kaṇṇakatthala. Now at that time King Pasenadi of Kosala had come to Ujuññā for some purpose. And (he) told a certain man: "Go and approach the Lord in my name. Salute (his) feet with your head in my name, and ask whether he is without ailment or sickness, vigorous, strong, and living in comfort – and say (that) today after breakfast King Pasenadi of Kosala will come to see the Lord. (And the man did as he was bidden.)

The sisters Somā and Sakulā heard (about the king's intended visit, and) went to (the place) where he was being served with food and said to (him):

"Pray, sire, (tell the Lord that) the sisters Somā and Sakulā salute (his) feet with their heads (and enquire as to his health)." So King Pasenadi of Kosala, having breakfasted, approached the Lord, saluted (him), and sat down at one side, (where he conveyed the greetings of the two sisters).

"But why, sire, did sisters Somā and Sakulā not find some other emissary?"

"Bhante, they heard (about my visit)."

"May the sisters Somā and Sakulā be happy, sire."

Then King Pasenadi said to the Lord:

"I have heard (that you maintain that) there is no ascetic or brahman who is all-knowing, all-seeing, and who has all-embracing knowledge and vision – that this state is not possible. I trust that those (people) speak as the Lord, are not misrepresenting (him) with what is not true, are explaining in accordance with *dhamma*, and that no co-religionist's doctrine gives ground for complaint."

"Sire, those who speak thus do not speak as I do, and do misrepresent me."

Then King Pasenadi of Kosala spoke to (his) general Viḍūḍabha, asking: "Who has put about this report in the palace, general?" 'Sañjaya the brahman, sire, of the Ākāsa clan." (Whereupon the king sent for Sañjaya the brahman.) And King Pasenadi said to the Lord:

"Could it be that, after the Lord has put together words on something else, people have referred back to them in a different way? And in what way is the Lord aware of having spoken (such) words?"

"Sire, I am aware of having (said that) there is no ascetic or brahman who knows and sees everything at one and the same time – that this state is not possible."

"The Lord speaks in terms of a cause and in terms of having a cause (in this matter. But), bhante, there are these four castes – nobles, brahmans, merchants, and artisans. Now might there be a distinction, a diversity among (them)?"

"Of these four castes sire, two – nobles and brahmans – are proclaimed as pre-eminent in terms of respectful greetings, rising from one's seat, salutation with joined palms, and appropriate service."

"I am not asking the Lord about this life. I am asking about a future state."

"Sire, there are these five qualities of exertion. Herein a monk has faith, is without ailment or sickness, is not crafty and deceitful, lives resolute in energy, (and) is wise, possessed of wisdom for the dispelling of appearance and disappearance.[1] Possessed of these five qualities of exertion there is wellbeing and happiness for many a day for (one of any caste)."

"Bhante, there are these four castes. They might be (equally)[2] possessed of these five qualities. But among them might there (still) be a distinction and a diversity?"

"Herein sire, I say there is a difference in the exertion. It is like a pair of elephants, horses, or oxen, that were well tamed and trained – (and others that were not). What do you think about that, sire? Would those that were well tamed and trained give a tamed performance and reached a tamed condition?"

"Certainly, bhante."

"And (the others)?"

"Certainly not."

"Likewise, sire, whatever can be achieved by faith, by health, by not being crafty or deceitful, by resolute energy, by possession of wisdom (cannot be achieved by one who is deficient in these respects)."

"The Lord speaks in terms of a cause and in terms of having a cause. (But) there are these four castes. They might be (equally) possessed of these five qualities, and make proper exertion. But, herein, might there (still) be a distinction and a diversity among them?"

Herein, sire, I maintain there is no diversity among them, that is between freedom and freedom. It is like a man who, taking dry wood from a sāka-tree, makes a fire so that heat is produced; and some other man, taking dry wood from a sāl-tree, a mango-tree, (or) a fig-tree. What do you think about that, sire? From the various woods would any diversity result – between flame and flame, colour and colour, brilliance and brilliance?"

"Not so, bhante."

"Likewise, sire, the heat generated by energy and resulting from exertion – I maintain there is no diversity among them, that is between freedom and freedom."

"The Lord speaks in terms of a cause and having a cause. But – are there *devas*, bhante?"

"How can you ask this, sire?"

"Do *devas* return to this world or (not), bhante?"

"Those that have been malevolent return to this world. Those that have not, do not return to this world."

At these words General Viḍūḍabha said to the Lord: "And are those that have been malevolent able to expel or banish from that place (of theirs) those that are not malevolent?"

Then venerable Ānanda thought to himself: "This general Viḍūḍabha is the son of King Pasenadi of Kosala. I am the Lord's son.[3] This is the moment for a son to talk with a son." So venerable Ānanda addressed General Viḍūḍabha saying: "Now then, general – I will question you in turn on that. Answer as you see fit. Within the bounds of King Pasenadi of Kosala's territory, where he holds sway and sovereignty, could (he) expel or banish an ascetic or brahman, whether possessed of merit (or otherwise), whether a follower of the good life (or not)?"

"Within the bounds of his territory – (yes, of course)."

"(And) where he does not hold sway and sovereignty?"

"(There) he cannot expel or banish (people)."

"What do you think about this, general? Have you heard of the Devas of the Thirty-Three?"

"Yes, and (so has) the worthy king, Pasenadi."

"(And) could King Pasenadi expel or banish them from that place (of theirs)?"

"Friend, King Pasenadi cannot even see the Devas of the Thirty-Three. How then could he expel or banish them?"

"Likewise, general, those *devas* that have been malevolent are not even able to see those that (have not). How then could they expel or banish them?"

Then King Pasenadi of Kosala said to the Lord: "What is the name of this monk, bhante?" "Ānanda, sire."

"Bliss indeed, bliss indeed.[4] Venerable Ānanda speaks in terms of a cause, and in terms of having a cause. But – is there a *brahmā*?"

"How can you ask this, sire?"

"Does this *brahmā* return to this world (or not), bhante?"

"Whoever is a malevolent *brahmā* returns to this world, sire."

(Just) then a man (came and) spoke to (the king) saying: "Sire, Sañjaya the brahman of the Ākāsa clan is come." And King Pasenadi said to Sañjaya the brahman:

"Who has put about this report (regarding the words of the Lord) in the palace?"

"General Viḍūḍabha, sire."

"(But he) says it is Sañjaya the brahman!" Then a man spoke to (the king), saying: "It is time for the carriage, sire." And King Pasenadi said to the Lord:

"We questioned the Lord about omniscience. The Lord explained omniscience, and that (explanation) pleased us, and seemed fitting, so that we are (now) delighted. We questioned the Lord about the purity of the four castes. The Lord explained the purity of the four castes. (Similarly with the celestial *devas* and with *Brahmā*) – just that which we asked about, that the Lord explained. And now we are going. We have much to attend to and many duties."

"Do as now seems fit, sire." And King Pasenadi of Kosala, pleased and satisfied at what the Lord had said, rose from his place, saluted the Lord, and with his right side towards him, went his way.

1. Abbreviated – see 85 for full statement on the five qualities of exertion.
2. "(Equally)" – the king's questions appear designed to elicit a distinction between the castes. All the answers make distinctions which cut across caste.
3. Figuratively – actually his cousin.
4. The literal meaning of "Ānanda".

91

To Brahmāyu

133–146

Thus have I heard: once the Lord was travelling on foot in Videha together with a large company of monks, as many as five hundred. Now at that time the brahman Brahmāyu was living in Mithilā, frail, old, venerable, of great age, his life lived out and having reached the end of his days, one hundred and twenty years of age; versed in the three Vedas, an expert in ritual and vocabulary, phonetics and phonology, with the oral tradition as his fifth (field of knowledge); a grammarian, and fully cognisant of popular philosophy and the attributes of a great man. Brahmāyu the brahman heard that the ascetic Gotama, gone forth from the Sakya clan, (was) travelling in Videha with a large company of monks, (and that he was of high renown). At that time the youth Uttara was a pupil of brahman Brahmāyu and (similarly learned). And brahman Brahmāyu addressed the youth Uttara, saying:

"Go, good Uttara, approach the ascetic Gotama, and find out whether (he) is as reported or otherwise; whether he is of such a character or not. Through you we shall evaluate the worthy Gotama. Good Uttara, handed down in our mantras are the thirty-two attributes of a great man. There are but two destinies open to (one) so endowed. If he remains a householder he becomes a wheel-turning monarch, one given over to *dhamma*, a king (ruling by) *dhamma*, victorious throughout the four quarters, maintaining the safety of the realm, and possessed of the seven royal treasures. These seven treasures of his are: the wheel treasure, the elephant treasure, the horse treasure, the jewel treasure, the woman treasure, the householder treasure, and the adviser treasure as the seventh. He has over a thousand sons who are valiant and heroic (in) defeating hostile armies. He lives conquering the lands girdled by the ocean by means of *dhamma*, not by stick or sword. But if he goes forth from home into homelessness he becomes an *arahant*, truly enlightened, a lifter of the veil of the world. But I am an imparter of mantras, you are a recipient of mantras."

"Very well friend", said the youth Uttara. (Then), rising from his seat and saluting (him), he went away keeping his right side towards him, and set out on foot through Videha (in search of) the Lord. At length (he found him). Approaching the Lord, he exchanged greetings, conversed in a friendly and polite way, and sat down at one side. He looked for the thirty-two marks of a great man in the Lord's body (and) saw all except two. With regard to (these) he was uncertain, perplexed, not settled or assured, (namely) with regard to whether what was hidden by clothing was sheath-cased, and whether the tongue was large. And the Lord (realised what was in the mind of the youth Uttara and) performed a feat of psychic power such that the youth saw that what was hidden by clothing was sheath-cased. And (he) put out his tongue, touching and stroking both ears and both nostrils, and covering the entire dome of his forehead with (it).

Then the youth Uttara thought to himself: "The ascetic Gotama possesses the thirty-two attributes of a great man. Suppose I were to follow (him) and observe his behaviour." So for seven months, like a constant shadow, (he) followed in close attendance on the Lord, (after which) he departed for Mithilā on foot. (Returning there) in due course he went to Brahmāyu the brahman, saluted (him), and sat down at one side (where he described all that he had seen).[1]

After he had spoken, Brahmāyu the brahman, rising from his seat and arranging his robe over one shoulder, saluted the Lord thrice with joined palms and uttered these lines: "In the name of the Lord, (who is) *arahant*, truly enlightened. Surely we shall meet with the worthy Gotama sooner or later. Surely there will be some (opportunity for) conversation."

Now the Lord, travelling about Videha on foot, eventually came to Mithilā. There he lived in Makhādeva's Mango Grove. (And) the brahmans and householders of Mithilā heard (about this and) approached (him). Some saluted him and sat down at one side. Some exchanged greetings and conversed in a friendly and polite way (before doing so), some after saluting with joined palms, some after announcing their names and lineage, some in silence.

Then Brahmāyu the brahman (also) heard (about his arrival and), together with many young men, made for Makhādeva's Mango Grove. And as he neared the mango grove brahman Brahmāyu thought to himself: "It is not proper for me to go and see the ascetic Gotama without being announced first." So (he) addressed a certain youth saying: "Go, young man, approach the ascetic Gotama in my name and ask whether he is without ailment or sickness, strong, and living in comfort. (Tell him who I am and say that), of those brahmans and householders who live in Mithilā, brahman Brahmāyu is reckoned foremost in terms of wealth, in terms of mantras, and in terms of age and reputation." (And the youth did as he was bidden. And the Lord said to the youth): "Young man, let brahman Brahmāyu now do whatever seems fitting."

Whereupon brahman Brahmāyu approached the Lord. That assembly saw (him) coming some way off, and standing to one side, made way for one so well-known and of high repute. And brahman Brahmāyu said to the assembly: "Come friends, resume your places. I shall sit here, next to the ascetic Gotama." And going up to the Lord he exchanged greetings, conversed in a friendly and polite way, and sat down at one side (where) he looked for the thirty-two attributes of a great man. (And, like the youth Uttara he found all but two. So he addressed the Lord in verse regarding these, and the Lord made known his possession of them as before.) Then the Lord addressed brahman Brahmāyu in verse:

These thirty-two marks of a great man, heard of by you, are all on my body. Be not in doubt, brahman. What should be known I know. What should be developed I have developed. What should be cast out I have cast out. Therefore I am *buddha*, brahman. For wellbeing in this life and happiness in the next world ask for the chance (to learn) what you wish."

Then brahman Brahmāyu thought to himself: "The ascetic Gotama has provided me with an opportunity. Shall I question him about what is profitable for this life or what is profitable for the next world?" (But) then (he) thought: "I am skilled as to what is profitable in this life, and others ask me about (it). Suppose I were to question (him) regarding what is profitable for the next world." So (he) addressed the Lord in verse:

"How is there a brahman? How is there a sage? How is there, friend, a threefold knowledge man? Who is called learned? How is there, friend, an *arahant*? How shall one become fully accomplished? How is there, friend, a wise man? And who is proclaimed *buddha*" And the Lord replied to brahman Brahmāyu in verse:

"Whoever knows his former dwelling-place, sees heaven and hell, and achieves the destruction of birth, perfected through gnosis, is a wise man. He knows the pure mind, is entirely released from passion, casting out birth and death, fully accomplished in the good life, gone beyond every condition. Such is proclaimed *buddha*."

At these words brahman Brahmāyu, rising from his seat, bent his head at the Lord's feet, smothered (them) with kisses, stroked them with his hands, and called out his (own) name, saying: "I am Brahmāyu the brahman, friend Gotama." And that assembly gave vent to wonder and astonishment saying (to one another): "Wonderful, astonishing, friend, is the great power and majesty of the ascetic in as much as this brahman Brahmāyu, who is well-known and of high repute, shows such deference." Then the Lord said to Brahmāyu the brahman: "Enough, brahman! As I have pleased your mind, (now) stand up and sit in your own place."

And the Lord conversed with Brahmāyu the brahman on various topics, namely talk about giving, about conduct, about the next world. He explained the disadvantage, the folly, the defilement of worldly pursuit, the value of dispassion. When the Lord knew the mind of Brahmāyu the brahman to be ready, soft, unobstructed, exalted, and reconciled he explained to him the sublime exposition of *dhamma* of the *buddhas* – suffering; its origin; its cessation; and the Way. Just as a clean cloth free from dirt can easily take dye, just so for Brahmāyu the brahman, in that very place, did the spotless, stainless eye of *dhamma* appear, (and he saw) that whatever is of a nature to arise is entirely of a nature to cease. And Brahmāyu the brahman, seeing *dhamma*, reaching *dhamma*, knowing (it), immersing himself in (it), transcending uncertainty, his reservations vanished, and won to confidence in the Teacher's instruction without help from another, said to the Lord:

"Excellent, friend Gotama, excellent!" (And brahman Brahmāyu, having taken the refuges and become a lay-follower, then invited the Lord and the Order of monks to a meal with him on the morrow.) The Lord accepted in silence. So brahman Brahmāyu, comprehending the Lord's silence, rose from his place, saluted, and with right side towards him, departed. Then having had prepared within his own abode abundant foods, both hard and soft, (he) made known the time (of the meal) to the Lord. Then the Lord, dressing at an early hour, took bowl and robe and went (there), sitting in the place prepared for him along with the Order of monks. And brahman Brahmāyu satisfied and served with his own hands the Order of monks led by the Buddha. A week later the Lord departed on his walk through Videha.

Not long afterwards brahman Brahmāyu passed away, and several monks came to the Lord, saluted him, and sat down at one side (where) they told him: "Brahman Brahmāyu is dead. What is his destiny and his future lot?"

"Wise, monks, was brahman Brahmāyu. He pursued the essence of *dhamma* and did not plague me with questions. Brahman Brahmāyu, by completely destroying the five fetters that bind one to the worldly condition, is of spontaneous uprising, achieving *nibbāna* there and without return from that world."

Thus spoke the Lord.

1. Several pages of description about the thirty-two attributes have been omitted.

92

With Sela

Sn 102–112[1]

Thus have I heard: once the Lord, who was travelling on foot among the people of Aṅguttarāpa together with a large company of monks – some twelve hundred and fifty in number – came to a town of theirs called Āpaṅa.

Keṇiya, an ascetic with matted hair, heard (of this). So (he) approached the Lord, greeted (him), and having conversed in a friendly and polite way, sat down at one side. (And) the Lord instructed, roused, gladdened, and delighted (him) with *dhamma*-talk. Then Keṇiya said:

"Let the worthy Gotama consent to (have a) meal with me on the morrow, together with the Order of monks."

Said the Lord:

"Great is the Order of monks, Keṇiya, some twelve hundred and fifty in number, and you are favourably disposed to the brahmans." (However Keṇiya repeated his request, so) the Lord consented in silence.

Whereupon Keṇiya, recognising the Lord's assent, rose from his seat and went to his own hermitage (where) he addressed his friends, companions, and relatives, saying:

"Hear me, good (people). I have invited the ascetic Gotama to a meal on the morrow, together with the Order of monks. (Pray) give me your help." (And they agreed to help him.) Some dug pits (for the fire), some chopped sticks, some washed bowls, some laid out vessels of water, some prepared seats. And Keṇiya himself set up a pavilion.

Now at that time the brahman Sela was living in Āpaṇa.[2] He was engaged in teaching mantras to three hundred youths (and) Keṇiya was well disposed towards him. And Sela, who was given to wandering and strolling about accompanied by the three hundred youths, approached Keṇiyas hermitage (with them). He noticed (the various activities that were going on and) asked Keṇiya:

"Is there to be a marriage or giving in marriage or (some) great sacrifice under preparation, or has King Seniya Bimbisāra of Magadha been invited on the morrow along with his army?"

"No, Sela – (none of these things). The ascetic Gotama, son of the Sakyans, gone forth from the Sakya clan, is come to Āpaṇa with a great company of monks. (He is one of high repute), *buddha* and Lord."

"Did you say "*buddha*", Keṇiya?"

"(Yes), Sela."

Then brahman Sela thought to himself: "Even the very sound '*buddha*' is hard to find in the world. But in our mantras are handed down the thirty-two attributes of a great man."[3] (Then he asked Keṇiya):

"And where is the worthy Gotama now dwelling?"

"By that dark line of trees", said Keṇiya, extending his right arm. So Sela the brahman (and his company) approached the Lord, and (he) addressed (them), saying:

"Proceed quietly, friends. These lords are hard to come upon, like lions that walk alone. When I address the ascetic Gotama do not interrupt the discussion. Wait for me to finish."

Then Sela went up to the Lord, exchanged greetings, and after conversing in a friendly and polite way, stood at one side, (where he) looked for the thirty-two attributes of a great man on the Lord's body, (and eventually found them).[4] And Sela thought to himself:

"The ascetic Gotama is fully possessed of the thirty-two attributes of a great man, but I do not know whether he is *buddha* or not. But I have heard it said by aged and venerable brahmans (that), when praised, those who are *arahant* and truly enlightened reveal themselves. Suppose I were to praise the ascetic Gotama in his presence with appropriate verses." (And he did so. Whereupon the Lord replied with verse of his own, proclaiming the *dhamma*-wheel as set rolling, and exhorting the brahman and his company to faith. Then Sela and his company sought the going forth.)[5] So Sela the brahman together with his assembly received the going forth and ordination in the Lord's presence.

Then, towards dawn, Keṇiya the ascetic with matted hair, having prepared within his own hermitage abundant foods both hard and soft, made known the time (of the meal) to the Lord. Then the Lord, dressing at an early hour and taking bowl and robe, went to Keṇiya's hermitage, where he sat in the place prepared for him together with the Order of monks. And Keṇiya satisfied and served with his own hands the Order of monks led by the Buddha. When the Lord had eaten and set aside the bowl he took a low seat at one side, (where) the Lord thanked him in verse. (Having done so) the Lord rose from his seat and took his leave.

And Sela and his company, living alone and apart, diligent, zealous, and resolute, reached and experienced before long that matchless consummation of the good life, realised in this life from their own gnosis, for which sons of family rightly go forth from home into homelessness. (They knew): "Destroyed is birth, fulfilled the good life, done what was to be done, and no further return to this world." And so venerable Sela and his company became *arahants*.

1. This discourse is identical with one in the *Sutta Nipāta*, and takes its numbering from there.
2. A description of his learning follows, identical with Brahmāyu's in 91.
3. Continues as Brahmāyu's description to Uttara in 91.
4. As for Uttara in 91.
5. Paraphrase of a lengthy verse passage.

93

With Assalāyana

147–157

Thus have I heard: once the Lord dwelt at Sāvatthī in the Jeta Grove on Anāthapiṇḍika's campus. Now at that time some five hundred brahmans from various districts were staying in Sāvatthī. And these brahmans thought: "This ascetic Gotama declares the purity of the four castes. Who can debate this pronouncement with (him)?" In those days there was a youth called Assalāyana living in Sāvatthī, young, shaven-headed, sixteen years old, versed in the three Vedas, an expert in ritual and vocabulary, phonetics and phonology, with the oral tradition as his fifth (field of knowledge); a grammarian, and fully cognisant of popular philosophy and the attributes of a great man. (And those brahmans thought of him.) So (they) approached (him) and said: "This ascetic Gotama has declared the purity of the four castes. Go, good Assalāyana, and debate this pronouncement with (him)."

At these words the youth Assalāyana said to (them): "The ascetic Gotama is truly a speaker of *dhamma*, but speakers of *dhamma* are difficult to debate with. I cannot (do this)." (But they pressed him), saying: "The worthy Assalāyana leads the life of a wanderer. Let (him) not be defeated without a battle."

When they had spoken the youth Assalāyana said to (them): "Friends, I cannot (prevail).[1] Yet I will go at (your) request." Then the Youth Assalāyana, together with a great company of brahmans, approached the Lord, exchanged greetings, and conversed in a friendly and polite way, (after which) he sat down at one side. Said the youth Assalāyana:

"Brahmans say that brahmans are the best caste, others base; that brahmans are fair, others dark;[2] that brahmans are pure, others are not; and that brahmans are Brahmā's natural progeny, born of his mouth, sprung from Brahmā, created by Brahmā, inheritors of Brahmā. What says friend Gotama to this?"

"But, Assalāyana, the wives of brahmans are seen to menstruate, to become pregnant, to give birth, and to give suck. Yet these brahmans, born of the womb (like the rest of us), say brahmans are the best caste (and so on)!"

"However much friend Gotama talks like that, nonetheless brahmans do think (that) brahmans are the best caste."

"What do you think about this, Assalāyana? Have you heard that, in Yona and Kamboja and other adjacent territories, there are just two castes, master and slave; and that, having been a master, one can become a slave (and vice versa)?"

"Yes, friend, I have heard that."

"In this matter, Assalāyana, what is the power, what the confidence of brahmans, (that leads them to say that brahmans are best and so on)?"

"However much friend Gotama talks like that, nonetheless brahmans do think (that) brahmans are the best caste."

"What do you think about this, Assalāyana? Should a noble, a merchant, or an artisan be a destroyer of life, a taker of what is not given, devoted to dissolute living; a liar, of slanderous, abusive, and frivolous speech; covetous, of corrupt mind and wrong view – would (he), at the breaking up of the body at death come to sorrow, to an evil destiny, to ruin, to purgatory, whereas a brahman would not?"

"Not at all, friend Gotama. (The brahman would suffer the same fate as the others.)"

"In this matter, Assalāyana, what is the power, what the confidence of brahmans (that leads them to say that brahmans are best and so on)?"

"However much friend Gotama talks like that, nonetheless brahmans do think (that) brahmans are the best caste."*

"What do you think about this, Assalāyana? Would brahmans who refrain (from such evil behaviour) come to a good destiny, a heaven world – but not nobles, merchants, or artisans?"

"Not at all, good Gotama. (Those of other castes who so refrained would come to a good destiny also.)"

"In this matter, Assalāyana, what is the power, what the confidence of brahmans, (that leads them to say that brahmans are best and so on)?"

"However much friend Gotama talks like that, nonetheless brahmans do think (that) brahmans are the best caste."

"What do you think about this, Assalāyana? Is it only a brahman of this area who can develop amity, freedom from malice, and goodwill, not a noble, a merchant, or an artisan?"

"Not at all, good Gotama. All four castes (can achieve this)."

"In this matter, Assalāyana, what is the power, what the confidence of brahmans, (that leads them to say that brahmans are best and so on)?"

"However much friend Gotama talks like that, nonetheless brahmans do think (that) brahmans are the best caste."

"What do you think about this, Assalāyana? Is it only a brahman who, having taken a back-scratcher and some bath-powder and going to the river, can wash away dust and dirt – not a noble, merchant, or artisan?"

"Not at all, friend Gotama. (The others can do this just as well.)"

"In this matter, Assalāyana, what is the power, what the confidence of brahmans, (that leads them to say that) brahmans are best (and so on)?"

"However much friend Gotama talks like that, nonetheless brahmans do think (that) brahmans are the best caste."

"What do you think about this, Assalāyana? Suppose a noble, anointed king were to assemble a hundred men of various origins and say: 'Come now, good fellows, let those here who are of a noble, brahman, or royal family take good kindlewood from a sāl, a salaḷa, a sandal-tree, or a lotus and light a fire so as to make some heat – but let those who are from a family of outcastes, hunters, workers in bamboo, chariot makers, or refuse collectors take good kindlewood from the trough of a dog, of a pig, of a dyer, or sticks from a castor-oil plant, (and do likewise).' What do you think about that, Assalāyana? Is the fire made (by a member of the first group) brilliant, and multi-coloured, and blazing, and able to perform the function of a fire (in such a way that one produced by a member of the second group is not)?"

"Not at all, friend Gotama. (There is no difference.)"

"In this matter, Assalāyana, what is the power, what the confidence of brahmans, (that leads them to say that brahmans are best and so on)?"

"However much friend Gotama talks like that, nonetheless brahmans do think (that) brahmans are the best caste."

"What do you think about this, Assalāyana? If a youth from the nobility were to have intercourse with a brahman maiden and, as a result, a son were to be born to them – would (he) be like both mother and father, and should he be called both 'noble' and 'brahman'?"

"Friend Gotama, (he) might be like both (parents) and should be called both 'noble' and 'brahman'."

"If a mare were to mate with a donkey and, in consequence of their union, a foal were to be born – would the foal be like both mother and father, and should it be called both 'Horse' and 'donkey'?

"Because of its crossed birth it is a mule. This difference I see in it. But for those others[3] I see no difference at all."

"What do you think about this, Assalāyana? There might be two (brahman) youths, brothers, born of the same uterus, one brought up scholarly and educated, the other (not) – which would brahmans serve first with offerings for the dead, with barley, the brahmanic sacrifice, or with a meal for a guest?"

"The (first), friend Gotama – for what great fruit can come of a gift to an unscholarly, uneducated person?"

"What do you think about this, Assalāyana? There might be two (brahman) youths, brothers, born of the same uterus – one scholarly and educated (but) of bad conduct and evil character, the other unscholarly and uneducated, but upright and of good character. Which would brahmans serve first (in this case)?"

"The (second), good Gotama – for what great fruit can come of a gift to one of bad conduct and evil character?"

"Assalāyana, you began with birth. From birth you went on to mantras,[4] then leaving mantras you returned to the purity of the four castes – which is precisely what I am maintaining."

At these words the youth Assalāyana sat silent and troubled, shoulders drooping, head bent, downcast and bewildered. Then the Lord, observing (this), said:

"Once upon a time, Assalāyana, to seven brahman sages in leaf huts in a forest haunt, came the pernicious opinion (that) brahmans are the best caste, others inferior. The sage Asita Devala heard (about this). So, with hair and beard trimmed, and dressed in crimson garments, (he) put on strong sandals, took a golden staff, and appeared in the hermitage of the seven brahmans. And as he paced up and down (in that place) he said: 'Now where have these seven brahman sages gone?' And the seven brahman sages thought: 'Who is it that, pacing up and down in the hermitage of the seven brahmans like an ox on the threshing-floor, speaks like this? We will put a curse on him.' (And they did so), saying: 'Be reduced to ashes, wretch!'

But the more (they) cursed, the more handsome, good-looking, and agreeable Asita Devala became. So they thought: 'Surely our ascetic practice is futile and our pursuit of the good life fruitless. Previously when we put a curse (of this kind) on someone, (that person) was reduced to ashes. But the more we curse him the more handsome he becomes.' (But Asita Devala said to them):

'Ascetic practice is not futile for the worthy, nor is pursuit of the good life fruitless. But please give up your hostility towards me.'

'We will give up any hostility we may have. But who is our worthy friend?'

'Have you not heard of the sage Asita Devala?'

'Yes, friend.'

'I am he, friends.'

Then the seven brahman sages went up to the sage Asita Devala to pay their respects. And (he) said to (them):

'Truly a pernicious opinion came to seven brahman sages in a leaf hut in a forest haunt. But do my friends know whether their mothers consorted only with brahmans and not with non-brahmans?'

'Not so, friend.'

'(And their fathers?)'

'Not so, friend.'

'And do (they) know how conception occurs?'

'We know, friend, how conception occurs. Herein there is the union of mother and father, the mother is in season, and the *gandhabba*[5] is present. There is conception from the conjunction of these three things.'

'But do (they) not know whether the *gandhabba* is a noble, a brahman, a merchant, or an artisan?'

'No, we don't know (that), friend.'

'This being so, friends, do you know who you are?''

'This being so, friend, we do not.'

So indeed, Assalāyana, did the seven brahman sages, when cross-questioned, debated with, and pressed by the sage Asita Devala fail to explain their own parentage. So how can you now, after being (similarly) pressed by me explain your own parentage – you who have the same teacher as they have, but not the spoon-holder Puṇṇa.[6]''

At these words the youth Assalāyana said: "Excellent, friend Gotama, excellent!" (And Assalāyana took the three refuges and became a lay-follower).

1. The verb means literally "to get" or "obtain". Horner translates "I am not able to argue".
2. Meaning could be figurative, but the earlier Dravidian inhabitants of India were dark as compared with the *ariyan* invaders of the Vedic tradition so some kind of racial insult may be involved.
3. I think this is a reference back to all the preceding examples.
4. Possibly material is missing as this hardly fits what has gone before.
5. The spirit alleged to preside over birth.
6. A benefactor of the seven sages.

94

With Ghoṭamukha

157–163

Thus have I heard: once venerable Udena dwelt near Bārāṇasi in the Khemiya Mango Grove. Now at that time the brahman Ghoṭamukha had arrived in Bārāṇasi on some business. Whilst wandering and roaming about (he) came to the Khemiya Mango Grove. At that moment venerable Udena was walking about in the open. So brahman Ghoṭamukha approached (him), exchanged greetings, and having conversed in a friendly and polite way, kept pace at one side.[1] Said Ghoṭamukha:

"Good ascetic, it seems to me that there is no going forth in (true) *dhamma*, whether because of not seeing such worthies as yourself, or because *dhamma* is not even to be found there.[2]"

At these words venerable Udena descended from where he was walking, entered the dwelling, and sat on a prepared seat. Brahman Ghoṭamukha (did likewise) and stood at one side. Said Udena:

"There are seats, brahman. Sit down if you wish."

And brahman Ghoṭamukha sat down, taking a low seat, (and repeated his comment about the absence of wanderers in true *dhamma*. Said Udena):

"Well now, should you approve what I approve, reject what should be rejected, and question me further concerning those of my words of which you do not understand the meaning – on that basis there might be some conversation herein between us."

("Very well, good Udena.")

"Brahman, there are these four (types of) person to be found in the world. Herein someone is a tormentor of himself, intent on and devoted to (such practices), but someone (else) is (likewise) a tormentor of others. Herein someone is both a tormentor of himself and a tormentor of others, but someone (else) is neither a tormentor of himself nor a tormentor of others. He, satisfied, cooled, and become tranquil in this life, experiences happiness, and lives with a self become like Brahmā. Of these four (types of) person, which pleases your mind?"

"He that lives with a self become like Brahmā – that person pleases my mind."

"But why do these (other) three not please your mind?"

"Bhante, he that is a tormentor of himself (nonetheless) torments a self that is desirous of happiness and averse to pain. He that is a tormentor of others (does likewise, as does) he that is both a tormentor of himself and of others. Therefore (these) do not appeal to my mind."

"There are these two groups,[3] brahman. Herein one group, obsessed with gems and jewelry, seeks for a wife and children, for women and men servants, for land and goods, for gold and silver. But some (other) group, not (thus) obsessed, and having abandoned (all these worldly entanglements), goes forth from home into homelessness.

(Now a certain) person, not self-tormenting, not tormenting others, nor given to the practice (thereof), lives stilled, quenched, become cool in this life, as one experiencing happiness and with a self become like Brahmā. In which group do you see that person for the most part?"

"For the most part I see (him in the second group), worthy Udena."

"But these were your words, brahman: 'Good ascetic, it seems to me that there is no wanderer in (true) *dhamma*, whether because of not seeing such worthies as yourself, or because *dhamma* is not even (to be found) there.' "

"Indeed these words spoken to me by venerable Udena are helpful. It seems to me that there is (after all) a going forth in (true) *dhamma*, and so let venerable Udena understand me. It would be good if, from compassion, the worthy Udena were to analyse in detail for me those four (types of) person (already) spoken of in brief." Said Udena:

"And what is the (kind of) person who is a tormentor of himself, intent on and devoted to (such practices)? Herein someone is unclothed, careless of convention, (given to) mortifying and afflicting the body. This is the (kind of) person who is called a tormentor of himself.

And what is the (kind of) person who is a tormentor of others, intent on and devoted to (such practices)? Herein someone is a sheep-killer, a pig-killer, a fowler, a deerslayer, a huntsman, a fisherman, a robber, a gaoler, an executioner, or (one of) those others who are of bloody occupation. This is the kind of person who is called a tormentor of others.

And what is the (kind of) person who is both a tormentor of himself and a tormentor of others? Herein someone is a noble warrior king, or a brahman with great property. Having brought about the erection of a new conference-hall in the east of the city, he has hair and beard shaved off, dons a rough (antelope) skin, anoints his body with ghee and oil and, scratching his back with a deer-horn, enters the conference hall together with his first consort and chief priest. There he makes his bed on the bare but grass-covered ground. The king sustains himself on the milk in the udder of a cow with a calf of like colour. The first consort sustains herself on the milk from the second udder, the chief priest on the milk from the third udder, and such milk as is in the fourth udder they sacrifice to the fire. The calf lives off the remainder. He talks like this: 'Let so many bulls be slain for the sacrifice, (likewise) so many bullocks, so many heifers, so many goats, so many wethers. Let so many trees be felled, so many bunches of kusa grass reaped for a sacrifice of grass.' Scared of a thrashing and fearful, those termed servants, slaves, and workpeople make the arrangements, tearful and wailing. This is the (kind of) person who is called both a tormentor of himself and a tormentor of others.

And what is the (kind of) person who is neither a tormentor of himself nor a tormentor of others, and is not intent on or devoted to (such practices).

Herein a householder or (his) son hears the *dhamma*, (embraces it, and brings it to fulfilment). This, monks, is the (kind of) person who is called neither a tormentor of himself nor a tormentor of others. He, satisfied, cooled, and become tranquil in this life, experiences happiness and lives with a self become like Brahmā."

At these words brahman Ghoṭamukha said: "Excellent, good Udena, excellent!" (And he sought to take refuge in venerable Udena, in *dhamma*, and in the Order of monks, and become a lay-follower. But venerable Udena said):

"Do not take refuge in me, brahman. Go rather for refuge to that Lord to whom I have gone for refuge."

"But where is that Lord who is *arahant* and truly enlightened now dwelling?"

"Brahman, that Lord has gone to final *nibbāna*."

"If we were to hear that that Lord were (many miles) distant we should go and see him. Because (however) he has gone to final *nibbāna* we take refuge in (him), in *dhamma*, and in the order of monks. Let the worthy Udena accept me as a lay-follower from today for the rest of my life. And the king of Aṅga gives me alms daily on a regular basis, so I am going to give venerable Udena one (such portion)."

"But what does (he) give you, brahman?"

"Five hundred (copper coins).[4]"

"It is not proper for us to accept gold and silver, brahman."

"If that is not proper, then I shall have a dwelling made for the worthy Udena."

"If you wish to have a dwelling made for me, brahman, have an assembly-hall built for the Order at Pāṭaliputta."

"I am very uplifted and satisfied that the good Udena urges me to make the gift to the Order. I shall (do that) from this regular (supply of) alms." (And so it came about.) And now (that hall) is known as the Ghoṭamukhi.

1. Not apparently meaning that he walked along beside him in the normal sense. Possibly the monk was performing some practice involving walking up and down.
2. Effectively seems to be saying that either he has failed to find them or that they do not exist.
3. Normally translates as "assembly", but clearly here refers to a type.
4. A unit of ancient currency is given, for which I have substituted the enclosed phrase.

95

With Caṅkī

164–177

Thus have I heard: once the Lord was travelling on foot among the Kosalans together with a large company of monks, and came to a brahman village of (theirs) called Opasāda. There the Lord stayed to the north of (the village) in the Deva's Grove, the Sāl Grove. Now at that time the brahman Caṅkī was living (as royal official) in Opasāda, a place teeming with life and provided with grass, wood, water, and grain, and granted (to him) by King Pasenadi of Kosala as a royal gift with full powers.

The brahmans and householders of Opasāda heard that the ascetic Gotama, a son of the Sakyans, gone forth from the Sakya clan (was among them, and that he was of high renown). So (they) went forth in throngs, going by the northern entrance to the Deva's Grove, the Sāl Grove. At that time Caṅkī the brahman was reclining during the heat of the day in the upper reaches of the palace. (He) saw the brahmans and householders and (asked a companion where they were going. And the companion told him that they were going to see the Lord. Said brahman Caṅkī):

"Well then approach (them) and say: 'Wait friends – the brahman Caṅkī is going to see the ascetic Gotama.' " (And the man did so.)

Now on that occasion some five hundred brahmans were staying in Opasāda for some purpose, (and) heard (about brahman Caṅkī's proposed visit to the ascetic Gotama). So (they) approached (him) and asked: "Is it really true that the worthy Caṅkī is going to see the ascetic Gotama?"

"That is my intention, friends."

"Don't (do this), worthy Caṅkī. It is not fitting. It is fitting that the ascetic Gotama should come to the worthy Caṅkī to see (him). For the worthy Caṅkī is well-born on both his mother's side and his father's side, and is of pure descent for seven generations back – uninterrupted, irreproachable in terms of parentage. (Moreover), the worthy Caṅkī is rich, of great wealth and possessions. (He) is versed in the three Vedas, expert in ritual and vocabulary, phonetics and phonology, with the oral tradition as his fifth (area of knowledge), a grammarian, and fully cognisant of popular philosophy and the thirty-two attributes of a great man. (He) is handsome, good-looking, and agreeable, possessed of the greatest beauty of complexion, of divine colour and bearing. (He) is upright, and mature in virtue. (He) is of fine conversation and address, given to urbane speech, fluent, clear, well able to articulate his meaning. (He) is a teacher of many teachers, and instructs three hundred youths in mantras. (He) is honoured, respected, esteemed, and revered by King Pasenadi of Kosala (and) by brahman Pokkharasāti. (On these counts) it is not fitting that the worthy Caṅkī should go and see the ascetic Gotama, (but rather the reverse)."

When they had spoken, brahman Caṅkī said to (them): "Well now friends, hear from me (why this is not so. What you have said regarding my birth and parentage is true of him also.) The ascetic Gotama has gone forth renouncing abundant gold and precious things, both under the ground and above it. (He) went forth whilst still young, with jet black hair, youthful, and in his early prime. Though his parents were unwilling, tearful, and lamenting, (he) cut off hair and beard, donned the saffron robe, and went forth from home into homelessness. (He has the same attributes of appearance, virtue, and speech which you claim for me. He) is teacher of many teachers. (He) has rooted out worldly passions and put waywardness behind him. (He) is an advocate of activity (as having consequences), of action (as having an outcome). desiring nothing that might be evil for brahman folk. (He) has gone forth from a noble family of great wealth and possessions. (People) come from distant lands and foreign countries to question (him). Several thousand *devatās* have gone to (him) as a refuge for living things. And a fine reputation is accorded (him, to the effect that) he is *arahant*, truly enlightened, complete as to knowledge and conduct, adept, seer of worlds, matchless charioteer of men to be tamed, teacher of *devas* and humans, *buddha* and lord. (He) is possessed of the thirty-two attributes of a great man. King Seniya Bimbisāra of Magadha has gone to him as a refuge for living things together with his wife and children, (as have) King Pasenadi of Kosala (and) brahman Pokkharasāti.

The ascetic Gotama has reached Opasāda and dwells to the north (of it) in the Deva Grove, the Sāl Grove. But whoever comes to our village neighbourhood, be they ascetics or brahmans, are our guests. And our guests are to be honoured, respected, esteemed and revered. On this count also it is not fitting that the worthy Gotama should come and see us, (but rather the reverse). Thus far have I learnt of the splendour of the worthy Gotama, and this is not the full measure of (it), for (that) is without limit. So it is fitting that we should go and see the worthy Gotama. Well, now we shall all (do that)."

So Caṅkī the brahman, together with a large company of brahmans approached the Lord, exchanged greetings, and having conversed in a friendly and polite way, sat down at one side. And on that occasion the Lord sat talking on various matters with elderly brahmans. But at that time a youth called Kāpaṭhika (of the Bhāradvāja clan), young and with shaven head, some sixteen years old, a master of the three Vedas[1], was sitting in the (surrounding) group. He repeatedly interrupted (their) conversation, whereupon the Lord rebuked him. Then Caṅkī the brahman said to the Lord: "Don't rebuke the youth Kāpaṭhika, friend Gotama. (He) is a man of birth, learned, and capable of debating with friend Gotama on this subject."

Then the Lord thought: "Surely the youth Kāpaṭhika must be proficient in the letter of the threefold knowledge for brahmans to honour him (thus)." And it occurred to the youth Kāpaṭhika: "When the ascetic Gotama glances in my direction I shall ask (him) a question." So the youth Kāpaṭhika said:

"That which is the ancient mantra of brahmans, the oral tradition, through the series of canonical collections, and regarding which brahmans attain certainty, thinking: 'Just this is the truth, all else foolishness' – what has friend Gotama to say about this?"

"But is there, Bhāradvāja, even one brahman who can say: 'I know this, I see this. Just this is the truth, all else foolishness'?"

"Not so, friend Gotama."

"And is there even one teacher of brahmans, one teacher of teachers back through seven generations, who can say (as much)?"

"Not so, friend Gotama."

"And those earlier sages of the brahmans, who were authors and handers down of mantras, and whose ancient way of mantras sung, proclaimed, and composed, that brahmans now praise and repeat, speaking what was spoken, reciting what was recited – namely Aṭṭhaka, Vāmaka, Vāmadeva, Vessāmitta, Yamataggi, Aṅgirasa Bhāradvāja, Vāseṭṭha, Kassapa, and Bhagu – did even they say: 'We know this. We see this. Just this is the truth, all else is foolishness'?"

"Not so, friend Gotama."

"So it is the case that there is not a single brahman who has said (these things either now or in the past). One might compare it to a string of blind men, clinging to one another. The one at the front doesn't see, nor the one in the middle, nor the one at the rear – even so it seems do the sayings of brahmans come out in the likeness of a string of blind men. What do you think about this, Bhāradvāja? Doesn't the faith of brahmans turn out to be without root?"

"But in this matter, friend Gotama, brahmans do not simply pay homage through faith, brahmans also pay homage through tradition."

"Bhāradvāja, you went on about faith, now you talk of tradition. These five things in this life have a twofold outcome – faith, inclination, tradition, careful examination, and approval of opinions.[2] But what is genuinely believed may be empty, vain, and false; what is not genuinely believed may be fact, truth, not otherwise. Or again, what is inclined to may be empty, vain, and false; what is not inclined to may be fact, truth, not otherwise. (And the same applies to the other three states). The preservation of a truth is insufficient for an intelligent man to attain certainty, thinking: 'Just this is the truth, all else foolishness.' "

"But how far, friend Gotama, is there preservation of truth?"

"If a man has faith and says (what it is), he preserves a truth by speaking like that, but does not to that extent achieve the certainty (that entitles him) to say: 'Just this is the truth, all else foolishness.' (And) he preserves a truth, (but does not thereby) achieve certainty (by means of) inclination, tradition, careful examination, (or) approval of opinions."

"To that extent, friend Gotama, there is preservation of truth, and to that extent we behold preservation of truth. But how far is there recognition of truth?"

"Herein, Bhāradvāja, a monk lives with some village or town as his support. A householder or (his) son approaches him, and assesses him with reference to three qualities – greed, ill-will, and delusion. He asks himself: 'Is the venerable one overwhelmed by states of greed such that, without knowing, he might (claim knowledge and), without seeing, he might (claim to see)? Or would he incite someone else to such a condition as would be for the suffering and misfortune of others for many a day?' (Satisfying himself that this is not the case, he concludes): 'The venerable one's bodily and verbal activity is that of one who is not possessed by greed. And (what) the venerable one teaches is profound, hard to perceive, difficult to realise, tranquil, exalted, beyond sophistry, subtle, comprehensible to the wise, not a *dhamma* that might be well taught by one possessed by greed.' Assessing him as pure in terms of states of greed, he then assesses him in reference to states of ill-will and states of delusion (in the same manner). Assessing him as pure (in these respects also) he establishes faith in him. With the arising of faith he draws near, and having drawn near he remains in attendance. (Then, successively), he lends an ear, listens, commits *dhamma* to memory, investigates the meaning of *dhamma* thus remembered, and (these) matters are found satisfactory. (Whereupon) he finds resolve, then is able (to make a beginning, (then) he evaluates, (then) he strives, (then) through resolution reaches the highest truth and, penetrating it, sees by means of wisdom. To that extent, Bhāradvāja, there is recognition of truth."

"To that extent, friend Gotama, there is recognition of truth. But to what extent is there attainment of truth?"

"There is attainment of truth, from the pursuit, development, and constant practice of those things."

"To that extent, friend Gotama, there is attainment of truth. But what is the thing that is most efficacious (in that regard)?"

"For the attainment of truth, exertion is efficacious. If one does not strive for it one will not reach that truth."

"But for exertion, friend Gotama, what thing is efficacious?"

"Evaluation is efficacious for exertion."

"But for evaluation, friend Gotama, what thing is efficacious?"

"Energy is efficacious for evaluation."

"But for energy, friend Gotama, what thing is efficacious?"

"Resolution is efficacious for energy."

"But for resolution, friend Gotama, what thing is efficacious?"

"Approval of *dhamma* is efficacious for resolution."

"But for approval of *dhamma*, friend Gotama, what thing is efficacious."

"Investigation of the meaning is efficacious for approval of *dhamma*."

"But for investigation of the meaning, friend Gotama, what thing is efficacious?"

"Recalling *dhamma* is efficacious for investigation of the meaning."

"But for recalling *dhamma*, friend Gotama, what thing is efficacious?"

"Hearing about *dhamma* is efficacious for recalling *dhamma*."

"But for hearing about *dhamma*, friend Gotama, what thing is efficacious?"

"Giving ear is efficacious for hearing about *dhamma*."

"But for giving ear, friend Gotama, what thing is efficacious?"

"Coming close is efficacious for lending ear."

"But for coming close, friend Gotama, what thing is efficacious?"

"Approaching is efficacious for coming close."

"But for approaching, friend Gotama, what thing is efficacious?"

"For approaching faith is efficacious."

"We asked friend Gotama about the preservation of truth. Friend Gotama explained about the preservation of truth, and it pleased and satisfied us so that we were uplifted. We asked about the recognition and attainment of truth (with the same result). Just what we asked about – that friend Gotama explained. And it pleased and satisfied us so that we were uplifted. Now previously we imagined it thus: 'What are these shaven-headed ascetics, menials, black, scourings of our kinsmen's heals, and who are the ones who know about *dhamma*!' Indeed friend Gotama has inspired in me an ascetic's love of ascetics, satisfaction with ascetics, esteem for ascetics." (Whereupon he took the refuges and became a lay-follower).

1. As for Caṅkī down to " . . . thirty-two attributes of a great man".
2. Literally, "liking one's comprehension of".

96

With Esukārī

177–184

Thus have I heard: once the Lord dwelt near Sāvatthī in the Jeta Grove of Anāthapiṇḍika's campus. Then the brahman Esukārī approached the Lord, exchanged greetings, and having conversed in a friendly and polite way, sat down at one side. Said Esukārī:

"Friend Gotama, brahmans postulate four (kinds of) service. They postulate service for a brahman, for a noble, for a merchant, and for an artisan. As to this (they) hold (that) a brahman may serve a brahman, a noble may serve a brahman, a merchant may serve a brahman, (or) an artisan may serve a brahman. (They hold that) a noble may serve a noble, a merchant may serve a noble, (or) an artisan may serve a noble. They hold (that) a merchant may serve a merchant, (or) an artisan may serve a merchant. (And) they hold (that) an artisan may serve an artisan. For who else could serve an artisan! Herein what has friend Gotama to say?"

"But does everyone concede this to the brahmans?"

"No, friend Gotama."

"Brahman, it is as if there was a man who was a vagrant, impoverished and destitute and, against his will, (people) were to thrust a piece of meat on him, saying: 'You must eat this meat, good fellow, and you must provide money (in return).' Just so do brahmans, with little agreement among ascetics and brahmans, postulate these four (kinds of) service.

I do not say that everyone should be served, or that none should be served. If, on account of the service,[1] evil rather than good might result, there should be no service. If good rather than evil, there should be service. And if one were to ask a noble, a brahman, a merchant, (or) an artisan (in what circumstances he should serve), answering aright he would say: 'I should serve when, as a result of my service, good rather than evil might result.'

I do not say 'better' on account of exalted birth. But neither do I say 'worse' on account of exalted birth. I do not say 'better', (or) 'worse', on account of a fine complexion. I do not say 'better', (or) 'worse', on account of wealth. Herein someone of exalted birth is a destroyer of life, a taker of what is not given, given to dissolute living, a liar, a slanderer, an abuser, a driveller; is envious, of ill-will, (and) wrong view. Therefore I do not say 'better' on account of exalted birth. (But another of exalted birth might be quite the opposite.) Therefore I do not say 'worse' on account of exalted birth. (And the same applies to a fine complexion, or to wealth.) I say that if, in consequence of service, there is growth of faith, (good) conduct, learning, renunciation, (and) of wisdom, then there should be service."

At these words Esukārī the brahman said: "Friend Gotama, brahmans hold that there are four (kinds of) wealth. They lay down wealth for a brahman, a noble, a merchant, (and) an artisan. In this matter they hold that the wealth of a brahman lies in the almsround, and that a brahman who is contemptuous of the almsround is failing in his duties, a guardian appropriating what he has not been given. For a noble in this regard (they) hold that wealth lies in the bow and quiver, and that a noble neglecting these is (similarly) failing in his duties. (They) hold that the wealth of a merchant lies in agriculture and cattle-breeding, and (that) of the artisan in the sickle and pingo, (and that the same judgements apply)."

"But, brahman, does everyone concede this to the brahmans?"

"No, friend Gotama."

"Brahman, it is as if there was a man who was a vagrant, impoverished and destitute and, against his will, (people) were to thrust a piece of meat on him, saying: 'You must eat this meat, good fellow, and you must provide money (in return).' Just so do brahmans, with little agreement among ascetics and brahmans, postulate these four (kinds of) wealth. Now I hold *ariyan* transcendental *dhamma* to be wealth for a man. But, wherever there is the birth of an individual, his ancient maternal and paternal lineage is remembered, and by that he is designated. If there is birth of an individual in a noble family he is designated as noble, (and similarly with the other castes). It is like describing a fire with reference to the material on account of which (it) burns. If (it) burns on account of wood one calls it a wood fire; if because of chips a chip fire, (and so on).

If, brahman, in a noble family, there is one gone forth from home into homelessness and, owing to the *dhamma* and discipline made known by the Exemplar, there is abstention from the destruction of life, from taking what is not given, from the ungodly life, from lying, slander, abuse, and idle chatter, (together with) absence of envy and ill-will, and right view – he is successful in propriety, *dhamma,* and what is skilled. If there is (such a person) in a brahman, merchant, (or) artisan family (the same applies). What do you think about this, brahman? Is only a brahman able to develop amity, freedom from malice, and goodwill – not a noble, a merchant, or an artisan?"

"Not so, friend Gotama. All four castes can (do this).[2] Excellent, friend Gotama, excellent!" (And Esukārī the brahman took the refuges and became a lay-follower.)

1. Rendering of a compound term on which interpretation of the whole passage that follows depends. Literally "cause of serving" but Horner appears to take it as meaning the person serving, thus making the various outcomes relate particularly to the servant.
2. A considerable passage is omitted here which duplicates material in 93.

97

With Dhānañjāni

184–196

Thus have I heard: once the Lord dwelt near Rājagaha, at the squirrels' feeding-place in the Bamboo Grove. Now at that time venerable Sāriputta was travelling on foot on the Southern Mountain together with a large company of monks. Then a certain monk, who had returned after (spending) the rains in Rājagaha, approached venerable Sāriputta, greeted him, and after conversing in a friendly and polite way, sat down at one side. Said Sāriputta:

"I trust, friend, that the Lord is healthy and vigorous."

"The Lord is healthy and vigorous, friend."

"I trust, friend, that the Order of monks is healthy and vigorous."

("That too, friend.")

"Friend, there is a brahman called Dhānañjāni near the Taṇḍulapāla Gateway. I trust that (he, too) is healthy and vigorous."

('That too, friend.")

"And I trust that he is not neglectful of *dhamma*, friend."

"How could there not be negligence (of *dhamma*) on the part of brahman Dhānañjāni. With the King's support (he) robs brahmans and householders. With the support of brahmans and householders (he) robs the King. His wife, who had faith and came from a family with faith, is dead, and (now) he has another wife (who is not like that)."

"Indeed this is bad news that we hear, friend. Surely we shall meet with brahman Dhānañjāni at some time or other, (and) perhaps there will be some conversation."

Whereupon venerable Sāriputta, having dwelt on the Southern Mountain as long as he saw fit, set out on foot for Rājagaha. In due course (he) arrived (there and) dwelt at the squirrels' feeding-place in the Bamboo Grove. Then, dressing at an early hour and taking bowl and robe, (he) went into Rājagaha for almsfood. Now at that time brahman Dhānañjāni was having cows milked in a cow-shed outside the town. And venerable Sāriputta, having walked for alms in Rājagaha and returning after the meal, approached brahman Dhānañjāni. The brahman saw (him) coming some way off and approached (him), saying: "Until it is time for food, worthy Sāriputta, have some milk."

"No, brahman. I have finished eating for today. I shall take the afternoon rest at the foot of a certain tree. You could come there."

"Very well", agreed (the) brahman. Then, having eaten breakfast, (he) approached venerable Sāriputta, exchanged greetings, and having conversed in a friendly and polite way, sat down at one side. Said Sāriputta:

"I trust you are not negligent (of *dhamma*), Dhānañjāni."

"How could I not be negligent, worthy Sāriputta – I who have to support parents, wife and child, servants and work-people; and have to perform tasks for friends, associates, relatives, and guests, for the dead and departed, for *devatās*, and for the King, as well as satisfying and looking after this body."

"What do you think about this, Dhānañjāni? Herein someone, because of his parents (or any of the others you mention, or because of bodily needs), does not live by *dhamma*, but follows a perverse course. (In consequence), the guardians of purgatory drag him off (to that place). Would it profit him to say (that he) took this course on account of his parents? Or would it profit him for his parents to say (that)?"

"Indeed not, worthy Sāriputta. The guardians of purgatory would just hurl him wailing into purgatory."

"What do you think about this, Dhānañjāni? Who is the better – he who, because of his parents (or for any other of these reasons), does not live by *dhamma* and follows a perverse course; or he who, (because of these same considerations), lives by *dhamma* and follows an upright course?"

("The latter, friend Sāriputta.")

"Dhānañjāni, there are other (types of) action – having a cause, grounded in *dhamma*, whereby it is possible to support parents (and others), to perform tasks (for people, and to) satisfy and look after this body – (a way) of not performing evil deeds, and of following a virtuous course."

Then brahman Dhānañjāni, pleased and satisfied at what venerable Sāriputta had said, rose from his seat and departed. But after a time (he) became afflicted, ailing, very ill. And (he) addressed a man, saying:

"Go, good fellow, approach the Lord and, in my name, salute his feet with your head, (and tell him of my affliction. Then approach venerable Sāriputta in the same way), and tell him (that) it would be good of (him) were he, out of compassion, to go to the house of brahman Dhānañjāni." (And the man did as he was bidden.) Venerable Sāriputta consented in silence.

Then venerable Sāriputta dressed and, taking bowl and robe, went to (the) brahman's house. Sitting down, (he) said:

"I trust you are getting better and bearing up, and that the painful feelings are subsiding, not getting worse."

"No, worthy Sāriputta, I am not getting better. Just as a strong man with a sharp sword might cleave one's head, so do severe winds shake my head.[1]"

"What do you think about this, Dhānañjāni? Which is better – purgatory or the womb of an animal?"

"The womb of an animal."

"(And) the womb of an animal or the realm of the dead?"

"The realm of the dead."

"(And) the realm of the dead or the human state?"

"The human state."

"(And) the human state or that of the *devas*."

"(The latter), worthy Sāriputta.[2]"

Then it struck venerable Sāriputta: "These brahmans are devoted to the world of Brahmā. Suppose I were to teach brahman Dhānañjāni the way to companionship with Brahmā." Said Sāriputta:

"And what is the way to companionship with Brahmā? Herein, Dhānañjāni, a monk lives spreading thoughts joined to goodwill in (all) directions. He lives spreading (them) everywhere, in every way, to the entire world, abundantly, boundlessly, unrestrictedly, peaceably, benevolently. He lives spreading thoughts joined to compassion, to gladness, to equanimity (in the same way). This, Dhānañjāni, is the way to companionship with Brahmā."

"Well now, worthy Sāriputta, in my name pay homage at the Lord's feet with your head (and tell him of my affliction)."

So venerable Sāriputta established brahman Dhānañjāni (only) in the inferior world of Brahmā, although there was something further to be done, (after which) he rose from his seat and went his way. And not long after venerable Sāriputta's departure brahman Dhānañjāni passed away. He arose in the world of Brahmā.

Then the Lord addressed the monks, saying: "Monks, Sāriputta established brahman Dhānañjāni (only) in the inferior world of Brahmā, although there was something further to be done."

And venerable Sāriputta approached the Lord (and conveyed the homage and the message of brahman Dhānañjāni). Said the Lord:

"But why, Sāriputta, did you establish brahman Dhānañjāni (only) in the inferior world of Brahmā?"

"It struck me, bhante, (that) brahmans are devoted to the world of Brahmā, (so I thought to teach him) companionship with Brahmā."

"Sāriputta, brahman Dhānañjāni has died and arisen in the *brahmā*-world."

1. Various other metaphors are omitted.
2. Various grades of *devas* are compared.

98

With Vāseṭṭha

Sn 115–123[1]

Thus have I heard: once the Lord dwelt in a jungle-thicket near Icchānaṅkala. Now at that time a large number of notable and affluent brahmans were (also) staying at Icchānaṅkala. And, as the (brahman) youths Vāseṭṭha and Bhāradvāja were strolling and wandering about, the conversation (turned to the question): "How is one a brahman?" Said Bhāradvāja:

"One is a brahman through being well-born on both the mother's and the father's side, back through seven generations." (But) Vāseṭṭha said:

"One is a brahman through being virtuous and punctilious in observance." (And neither could convince the other on the point.) So Vāseṭṭha said to Bhāradvāja:

"There is this ascetic Gotama living in a jungle-thicket near Icchānaṅkala, (and he is a teacher of high renown). We will go and ask (him about this matter and), as he explains, so we shall bear it in mind." So Vāseṭṭha and Bhāradvāja approached the Lord, exchanged greetings and, after conversing in a friendly and polite way, sat down at one side, (where) Vāseṭṭha addressed the Lord in verse (so as to explain their difference of opinion).[2] (The Lord replied in verse):

**"Vāseṭṭha, I shall explain to you the successive grades of living things in accordance with reality, for births are various. Consider the grass and trees. Without even assenting[3] theirs is the mark of good birth, for births are various.[4]

Next the insects – the grasshoppers and ants – theirs is the mark of good birth, for births are various. (Likewise) quadrupeds, small and large; those that use the belly for feet – the snakes, the long of back; the fishes and denizens of water and the sea; the birds, with wings as vehicle, airborne – these, according to their kind, all have the mark of good birth.

There is not (such) individually among men – not in hair, head, ear, or eye (or any other part of the body). Nothing unique (to the individual) is to be found in the human body. Differences among men are given designation (like this). You must know, Vāseṭṭha, that whoever lives by tending cattle is a farmer, not a brahman. Whoever works separately at some craft is a craftsman, not a brahman, (and so on with various occupations).

I do not speak of a brahman in terms of birth from the mother's womb, (or as) one who speaks as a superior, or is a man of means. I call him brahman who has and holds to nothing; that, breaking every bondage, is unexcited, surmounting attachment, unyoked; that, cutting the thong, the strap, the fetter, the bridle, with hindrances removed, is *buddha*; that endures insults, blows, and bonds, uncorrupted and strong in patience; that is without anger, scrupulous in observance, virtuous, unconcerned, restrained, in his last body; that, like water on a lotus-leaf or seed on an arrow-head is not stained by worldly pursuit; that knows the destruction of his own suffering here and now, and is unburdened and unyoked; that, deep in wisdom, intelligent, knowledgeable about the right and wrong paths, has attained the ultimate goal; that, without association with either householders or the homeless, is unworldly and easily satisfied; that withholds the stick from beings whether they be frightened or steadfast, and who neither strikes nor kills; that is unhindered among the obstructed, cool among the violent, among the passionate unattached, and whose passion, ill-will, and pride are fallen, like seed from an arrow-head; that, instructing with mildness, speaks the word of truth that reviles no one; that does not take what is not given, whether long or short, small or large, beautiful or ugly; in whom is found no longing for this world or the next, and is ungrounded and unyoked; in whom no settling-place is found, doubt-free through gnosis, and who is immersed in the deathless; that has passed by the bond of both good and evil, griefless, undefiled, and cleansed; stainless as the moon, cleansed and clear, undisturbed, the life of pleasure extinguished; that has overcome this mire, the hard road, the faring-on, the delusion, crossing over and reaching the further shore absorbed, faultless, emptied of doubt, unattached and cool; that, leaving worldly pursuits and craving behind goes forth to homelessness, extinguishing worldly existence(s) and the life of craving; that, renouncing the human yoke and passing by the divine yoke, is unyoked from every yoke; that, rid of likes and dislikes, is a cooled being, desireless, vanquishing all the worlds, heroic; that comprehends the passing away and re-emergence of all beings without holding on (himself) and is adept, *buddha*; whose course neither *devas* nor men can trace, the distractions rooted out, *arahant*; for whom there is nothing of before and after and in between, having nothing, unattached; a bull, noble, triumphant, consort (of truth), faultless, washen, *buddha*; that knows his previous existence(s) and beholds heaven and hell and, further, brings birth to destruction.

As to the designation of ancestry, begotten in the world, such is (just) convention, arisen here, arranged here. Harbouring so long the viewpoint of incomprehension the uncomprehending proclaim: 'A brahman is by birth'. (But) by birth one is not a brahman. By doing one is a brahman. By doing one is a farmer, craftsman, tradesman, servant, thief, soldier, priest, or king. Thus the wise see the deed, seers of cause and effect, knowledgeable as to the outcome of deeds. The world proceeds by doing. In bondage to deeds are beings, like the axle turned by the (wheel of) the chariot. By self-control, the good life, abstinence, taming – by that one becomes a brahman, (indeed) that produces the ultimate brahman. Attained to the threefold knowledge, done with further renewal, know it thus, Vāseṭṭha. Let Brahmā and Sakka know."[5] **Thus spoke the Lord.

1. As for 92, note 1.
2. The verse includes some ornate courtesies but otherwise merely recounts the situation arrived at.
3. Possibly implying that pollination among plants is apparently random as compared with choice of a mate by animals.
4. Naming of the ensuing biological groups is very tentative, as it must be appreciated that the ancient compilers were not zoologists and terms used are descriptive in a way which allows some latitude of interpretation when translated literally.
5. In fact the piece ends with the usual conversion of the questioners.

99

With Subha

196–209

Thus have I heard: once the Lord dwelt near Sāvatthī in the Jeta Grove on Anāthapiṇḍika's campus. Now at that time the youth Subha, Todeyya's son, was living in the house of a certain householder for some purpose. And (he) said to that householder: "Householder, I have heard (that) Sāvatthī is not devoid of *arahants*. On what ascetic or brahman should we attend today?"

"Bhante,[1] there is) this Lord who dwells in the Jeta Grove of Anāthapiṇḍika's campus. You could attend on (him)." (So) the youth Subha approached the Lord, exchanged greetings, and having conversed in a friendly and polite way, sat down at one side. Said Subha:

"Friend Gotama, brahmans say (that) a householder is successful as to propriety, *dhamma*, and what is skilled, (whereas) one gone forth is not successful in these ways. Herein what does friend Gotama say?"

"On this, young man, I recommend analysis. I have no one position. I praise a wrong course neither in a householder nor in one who has gone forth. In the consequence and condition of pursuing a wrong course (neither one) is successful as to propriety, *dhamma*, nor what is skilled. But a householder or one gone forth is successful (in these ways) from the consequence and condition of pursuing a right course."

"Friend Gotama, brahmans say (that) the pursuits of household life – the many duties, much business, great endeavour, are of great fruit, (whereas) the few pursuits of the life of one gone forth are of little fruit. Herein what does friend Gotama say?"

"On this too, young man, I recommend analysis. I have no one position. There is activity of many pursuits, many duties, much business, and great endeavour – failure in which is of small fruit. There is activity, (equally strenuous), success in which is of great fruit. There is activity involving few pursuits, few duties, little business, small endeavour – failure in which is of small fruit. And there is activity, (equally restricted), success in which is of great fruit.

And what is the (first of these)? Agriculture, young man, is an activity involving many pursuits, many duties, much business, and great endeavour – failure in which is of little fruit. And what is the (second). Agriculture is (such) an activity, success in which is of great fruit.

And what is the (third)? Selling,[2] young man, is an activity of few pursuits, few duties, little business, small endeavour – failure in which is of little fruit. And what is the (fourth)? Selling is (such) an activity, success in which is of great fruit.

Like agriculture (in both respects) are the pursuits of household life. Like selling (in both respects) is the activity of one gone forth."

"Friend Gotama, brahmans declare five things for the performance of a meritorious deed, and for success in what is skilled."

"If it is no trouble, young man, it might be as well for you to tell this company about these five things."

"It is no trouble, friend Gotama. Brahmans declare truth to be the first thing, ascetic practice the second, pursuit of the good life[3] the third, study[4] the fourth, and renunciation the fifth. What does friend Gotama have to say about this?"

"But then, young man, is there even one brahman who has said: 'I proclaim the outcome of these five things, having experienced them from my own gnosis'?"

"Not so, friend Gotama."

"And is there even one teacher of brahmans, one teacher of teachers back through seven generations, who has said (it)?"

"Not so, friend Gotama."

"And those earlier sages of the brahmans who were authors and handers down of mantras as sung, proclaimed, and composed, that brahmans now praise and repeat, speaking what was spoken, reciting what was recited – namely Aṭṭhaka, Vāmaka, Vāmadeva, Vessāmitta, Yamataggi, Aṅgirasa, Bhāradvāja, Vāseṭṭha, Kassapa, Bhagu – did even they (make such a claim)?"

"Not so, friend Gotama."

"So the truth is that there is (no one) who has said: 'I proclaim the outcome of these five things, having realised them from my own gnosis.' One might compare it to a string of blind men, clinging to one another. The one at the front doesn't see, nor the one in the middle, nor the one at the rear – even so, it seems, do the sayings of brahmans come out in the likeness of a string of blind men."

At these words the youth Subha, Todeyya's son, shaken and displeased at being spoken to (like this), cursing and reviling even the Lord, said: "The ascetic Gotama will come to no good. The brahman Pokkharasāti of the Upamañña (clan, and of) the Subhaga forest glade has said: 'Just so do some ascetics and brahmans lay claim to superhuman states, to the truly *ariyan* qualities of knowledge and vision. Their words prove simply ridiculous, mere talk, just empty and vain. For how could a human being know, see, experience, or bring about (such states) – such a thing is impossible'."

"But then does brahman Pokkharasāti encompass with his mind the minds of all ascetics and brahmans?"

"(He) does not even encompass with his mind the mind of Puṇṇika his slave-girl."

"Young man, it is as though a man blind from birth, not seeing dark or light shapes; not seeing green, yellow, red, or crimson shapes; not seeing the even or the uneven; not seeing the forms of the stars, or the moon and sun – (yet) says (that these forms do not exist and concludes): 'I do not know this. I do not see this. Therefore it does not exist.' Would he be speaking aright?"

"Not so, friend Gotama."

"Even so, young man, brahman Pokkharasāti is blind and without eyes (to say what you have just told me). What do you think about this? Which is better for those wealthy brahmans of Kosala; such as brahman(s) Caṅkī, Tārukkha, Pokkharasāti, Jāṇussoṇi, or your father Todeyya – that their words should be of common consent, or not of common consent?"

"Of common consent, friend Gotama."

"(And) that their words should be mantra or non-mantra?"[5]

"Mantra, friend Gotama."

"(And) that their words should be considered or unconsidered?"

"Considered, friend Gotama."

"(And) that their words should be salutary or not salutary?"

"Salutary, friend Gotama."

"What do you think about this, young man? That being so, are the words spoken by brahman Pokkharasati (like that or otherwise)?"

("Otherwise, friend Gotama.")

"There are these five hindrances, young man: worldly pursuits and impulses, ill-will, sloth and torpor, agitation and worry, uncertainty. Brahman Pokkharasāti is veiled, hemmed in, obstructed, and enveloped by these. That he should know, see, experience, or bring about superhuman states, the truly *ariyan* qualities of knowledge and vision – this is impossible.

There are these five strands of worldly pursuit, young man: visible forms, pleasing, welcome, enticing, voluptuous, pleasure-laden, exciting; (and sounds, smells, tastes, and contacts of a similar nature). Brahmān Pokkharasāti is bound, infatuated by these, addicted to them, not seeing their disadvantage or wise as to giving them up. What do you think about this, young man? Which fire is flaming, colourful, and bright – that which one might light with grass and chips as fuel or that which one might light without (them)?"

"If it were possible to light a fire without grass and chips as a fuel that fire would be flaming, colourful, and bright."

"It is not possible, the occasion does not arise, that one might light a fire in the absence of grass and chips – other than through psychic power. Like a fire fuelled by grass and chips – such, young man, I say is that joy that depends on the five strands of worldly pursuit. Like a fire that burns without (any such) fuel – such, young man, I say is that joy that is apart from worldly pursuit and from unskilful things. And what is the joy that is (that) joy? Herein a monk, remote from worldly pursuits and unskilful states, reaches and experiences the first and the second (levels of) absorption. (But) those brahmans who declare five things for the performance of a meritorious deed, and for success in what is skilled – in this what thing do (they) declare the greatest fruit?"

"(They) declare renunciation as the greatest fruit, friend Gotama."

"What do you think about this, young man? Herein a certain brahman might prepare a great sacrifice. Suppose two (other) brahmans come along, thinking: 'We will take part in the sacrifice of brahman so and so.' It might occur to one (of them): 'Surely I can get the best place, the best water, the best food in the refectory.' But it may be that the other brahman (achieves this, and the first one) is shaken and displeased. But what do brahmans hold to be the outcome for him?"

"As to that, friend Gotama, brahmans do not make a gift (with the thought): 'Through this let another be shaken and displeased.' (They do so) just out of compassion."

"That being so, young man, is this a sixth basis for brahmans for the performance of a meritorious deed, namely compassion?"

"That being so, (you are right), friend Gotama."

"These five things that brahmans declare – where do you perceive (them) in abundance, among householders or among those gone forth?"

"Friend Gotama, I perceive them much among those gone forth, little among householders. For a householder, with many pursuits, many duties, much business, great endeavour, is not always and consistently a speaker of truth. (He) is not always and consistently given to ascetic practices, to pursuit of the good life, to study or renunciation – (for the same reasons). But the one gone forth, (not thus occupied), is (more so)."

"Young man, as to those five things laid down by brahmans for the performance of a meritorious deed and for success in what is skilled, I hold these to be mental requisites, that is to say for the development of a mind that is peaceable and free from ill-will. Herein a monk is a truth-speaker (and, knowing it), gains enthusiasm for the goal and for *dhamma*, and the delight associated with *dhamma*. That which is associated with what is skilled I hold to be a mental requisite. Herein a monk is given to ascetic practices, to pursuit of the good life, to study, and to renunciation – (and the same holds good for these)."

At these words the youth Subha said:

"I have heard it said (that) the ascetic Gotama knows a way to companionship with Brahmā."

"What do you think about this – is the village of Naḷakāra near here?"

"Yes, friend."

"What do you think about this? If there were a man who had been born and reared here in Naḷakāra, and had never lived (elsewhere) – would (he), on being asked the way, be obtuse and confused?"

"Not at all, friend Gotama. All the ways to the village of Naḷakāra are well-known to him."

"Indeed there might be (such) obtuseness and confusion, but not for the Exemplar on being asked about the world of Brahmā or the course leading (thereto). I know Brahmā and the *brahmā*-world of the *brahmā*'s, the course leading (thereto), and the arising in the *brahmā*-world in accordance with one's pursuit (of it)."

"I have heard (that) the ascetic Gotama teaches a way to companionship with Brahmā. Would that (he) might teach me (this)." Said the Lord:

"Herein, young man, a monk lives spreading thoughts joined to goodwill in (all) directions. He lives spreading (them) everywhere, in every way, to the entire world, abundantly, boundlessly, unrestrictedly, peaceably, benevolently. When the freedom of mind that is goodwill is cultivated, that is a limited activity which does not remain or linger there. Further, however, a monk lives spreading thoughts joined to compassion, gladness, and equanimity (in the same way, and which are likewise limited).[6] This, young man, is the way to companionship with Brahmā."

At these words the youth Subha said to the Lord:

"Excellent, good Gotama, excellent!" (And he took the refuges and became a lay-follower). "Well now, friend Gotama, we must be going. We have many duties and much business."

"Do now as you see fit, young man."

Then the youth Subha, pleased and satisfied at the Lord's words, rose from his place, saluted (him), and went away keeping his right side towards him. Now at that time brahman Jāṇussoṇi was leaving Sāvatthī early in the day (in a carriage) drawn by white horses. (He) saw the youth Subha coming some way off and said to him: "Now where are (you) coming from so early?"

"I have come from the presence of the ascetic Gotama."

"What do you think of the accomplishment of the ascetic Gotama. Do you find him clever?"

"Who am I, friend, to judge the accomplishment of the ascetic Gotama in wisdom. Surely only one like him would know (about that)."

"The worthy Bhāradvāja truly commends the ascetic Gotama with lavish praise."

"Who am I to praise (him). Praised by the praised is the worthy Gotama, the best among *devas* and humans. And those five things that brahmans lay down for the performance of a meritorious deed and for success in what is skilled, the ascetic Gotama describes as mental requisites, that is to say for cultivating a mind that is peaceable and free from ill-will."

At these words brahman Jāṇussoṇi got down from (his coach), arranging his robe over one shoulder, and made salutation to the Lord with joined palms uttering these words: "Well it is for King Pasenadi of Kosala, in whose territory lives the Exemplar, *arahant*, (and) truly enlightened."

1. Respectful form to a brahman.
2. Horner has "trading".
3. The ancient commentary equates with "chastity".
4. Particularly of the Vedas.
5. In this context possibly meaning "inspired".
6. The Buddhist goal lies beyond them though this is not dwelt on here.

100

With Saṅgārava

209–213

Thus have I heard: once the Lord was travelling on foot among the Kosalans, together with a large company of monks. Now at that time a brahman lady called Dhānañjāni, one devoted to the Buddha, to *dhamma*, and to the Order of monks, was residing in Caṇḍalakappa. Then (that) brahman lady, on stumbling three times, uttered these words: "In the name of the Lord, *arahant*, (and) truly enlightened." Now at that time a youth called Saṅgārava (of the Bhāradvāja clan) (also) lived in Caṇḍalakappa. (He was) versed in the three Vedas, expert in ritual and vocabulary, phonetics and phonology, with the oral tradition as his fifth (area of knowledge), a grammarian, and fully cognisant of popular philosophy and the attributes of a great man. The youth Saṅgārava heard what the brahman lady Dhānañjāni was saying and said to (her):

"It is unworthy and disgraceful of the brahman lady Dhānañjāni that, whilst there are brahmans in existence, she speaks praise of this shaven-headed ascetic."

"But, my good friend, you do not know of the virtue and wisdom of this Lord. If you did you would not think (he) should be abused and censured."

"Well then, lady, when the ascetic Gotama reaches Caṇḍalakappa you might inform me."

Now at length the Lord, travelling on foot among the Kosalans arrived (there, and) dwelt in the grove of the brahmans of Tudi. The brahman lady Dhānañjāni heard (about this and told the youth Saṅgārava), saying: "Now do as you see fit dear friend." (So he) approached the Lord, exchanged greetings, and having conversed in a friendly and polite way, sat down at one side. Said Saṅgārava:

"Friend Gotama, there are some ascetics and brahmans who, (on the basis of) having achieved knowledge and attained perfection in this life, affirm the fundamentals for pursuit of the good life. Among these of what (sort) is friend Gotama."

"I say there is a difference among (such people), Bhāradvāja. There are some ascetics and brahmans, such as the brahmans of the three Vedas, who are traditionalists, who affirm (this) by (reference to) tradition. But there are (others), those given to thought and examination who (do so) entirely through faith. There are (others again) who (do so), having understood *dhamma* for themselves with respect to things previously unheard of. I am (of the third kind), Bhāradvāja. Herein when formerly just a *bodhisatta*, not yet truly enlightened (I went forth from home into homelessness." And the Lord described his own search for enlightenment.)

When he had spoken the youth Saṅgārava said: "Indeed, friend Gotama's exertion was ceaseless, his exertion was that of a true man, such as an *arahant* (who is) truly enlightened. But are there *devas*, friend Gotama?"

"I have grounds for knowing that there are *devas*."

"Even so, friend Gotama, is this not vain and false?"

"If someone says (that) he has grounds for knowing (this), then an intelligent man should conclude that there are *devas*."

"But why did not friend Gotama explain this at the start?"

"There is general agreement that there are *devas*, Bhāradvāja."

At these words, the youth Saṅgārava said: "Excellent, friend Gotama, excellent!" (And he took the refuges and became a lay-follower.)

101

At Devadaha

214–228

Thus have I heard: once the Lord dwelt among the Sakyans (in) a town called Devadaha. There (he) addressed the monks, saying: "There are, monks, some ascetics and brahmans who say and think (that) whatever the individual experiences, whether pleasant, painful, or (neither) – all that is due to what was previously done. Hence from the working out and destruction of former activity (and) the non-performance of new activity, there will be no future effect. Because of (that) there will be a waning of activity. From the waning of activity there will be a waning of suffering. From the waning of suffering there will be a waning of feeling. (And) from the waning of feeling the entirety of suffering will come to an end. So say the Jains, monks. Approaching (them), I say:

'But do you know, friends, (that you) existed in the past?'[1]

'Not so, friend.'

'(Or that you) performed an evil deed in the past?'

'Not so, friend.'

'(Or that you) did not commit an evil deed like this or like that?'

'Not so, friend.'

'Then do you know that so much suffering is finished or is (yet) to be finished, or that in the extinction of so much suffering *all* suffering is to be extinguished?'

'Not so, friend.'

'Then do you understand the abandonment of unskilled states and the acquisition of skilled states in this life?'

'Not so, friend.'

'Well than,it is not fitting for the Jain brethren to (offer such) an exposition, (Only if they knew such things would it be proper to talk like this.) It is as though a man were struck by an arrow thickly smeared with poison. Because of the arrow he is aware of a painful, acute, and severe sensation, (Then) his friends, associates, and relations procure a physician waho is a surgeon, (and who) cuts round the mouth of the wound with a knife. He is (then) aware of a similar sensation because of the knife. (Next) the physician searches for the arrow-(head) with a probe, (and again) he is aware of painful, acute, and severe sensation; (and likewise even after the arrow is withdrawn and the wound dressed). After a time, with the skin healed on the wound, he is well, happy, independent, his own master, going wherever he wishes. (Then he might remember all that has happened.) In the same way, friends, (if you would remember the past so as to answer my questions it would be proper for you to make such an exposition).'

At these words the Jains said to me:

'Natputta the Jain knows all, sees all, (and) affirms all-embracing knowledge, saying: "whether walking or standing asleep or awake, knowledge and vision is always and fully available to me." He says (that) an evil deed committed in the past is to be extinguished through painful austerities (and that), from testraint now in body, speech and thought, there will be no performance of an evil deed in the future. [2] And since that is certainly pleasing to us and approved of by us, we (feel) elevated by it.'

Then I said to the Jains:

'Five things in this life bear fruit in two ways, (namely) conviction, inclination, tradition, reflection on conditions, comprehension and approval of an opinion. In this respect what was the conviction of the Jain brethren about a teacher in the past, what (their) tradition, what (their) reflection on conditions, what (their) comprehension and approval of an opinion?'

When I had said this, monks, I perceived no coherent response in line with their doctrine among the Jains. Again I spoke to (them), saying:

'When you adopt this acute remedy, this acute exertion, do you at that time experience a painful, acute, severe, and sharp sensation? (And) when you (do not act like that is such a sensation absent)?'

'(That is correct), friend Gotama.'

'Well then it is just you yourselves who, through ignorance, stupidity, and infatuation, are made to bear the fruit (though speaking of a remedy).'

When I said this, monks, I again perceived no coherent response among the Jains in line with their doctrine. Yet again, monks, I spoke to (them), saying:

'Is it possible (for that) activity which is experienced in this life to be experienced in a future state (instead), through any remedy or exertion?'

'Not so, friend.'

('Or conversely'?)

'Not so, friend.'

'(Or) is it possible (for that) activity experienced as pleasant to be experienced as painful through any remedy or exertion – (or conversely)?'

'Not so, friend.'

'(Or for that) activity which is experienced as ripening to be experienced as not ripening – (or conversely)?'

'Not so, friend.'

'(Or for that) activity which is to be much experienced as little experienced?'

'Not so, friend.'

'Well then the remedy and exertion of the Jain brethren is without fruit.'

So speak the Jains, monks. The ten sectarian doctrines[3] of Jains who talk thus afford reason for contempt.

Monks, if beings experience happiness and suffering in consequence of previous actions then truly the Jains must have been doers of bad actions in the past to be experiencing sensations in the present that are painful, sharp, and severe. If (they do so) on account of divine dispensation then truly the Jains were produced by a wretched god. If because of destiny then truly the Jains are of evil destiny. If because of their race then truly the Jains are of bad stock. If by reason of their endeavours in this life then surely (their) endeavours are perverse. Even so, monks, is a remedy and an exertion fruitless.

And how, monks, is a remedy and an exertion fruitful? Herein a monk does not soil (his) unstained self with suffering, does not reject rightful happiness, and (yet) is not intoxicated with that happiness. From confronting the nexus (of conditions) at that root of suffering there is dispassion for him in the fight against (it), and accordingly he fights against (it). From looking at the root of suffering with developing equanimity there is detachment for him, and accordingly he develops equanimity. Even so is that suffering brought to an end for him.

Monks, it is like a man devoted and attracted to a woman, eagerly longing and looking (for her). He sees that woman dallying in conversation with another man, laughing and making merry (with him). Seeing (that), might not grief and woe, pain, distress, and trouble be aroused (in him)?"

"Yes, bhante."

"Then that man might think: 'Suppose I were to abandon all desire and passion for (her).' (If he were to achieve that and see her, on another occasion, in dalliance with another man), would (such) feelings) be aroused (in him)?"

"Not so, bhante."

"Even so one does not stain one's unstained mind nor reject rightful happiness. (Yet) one is not intoxicated with that happiness. But further, a monk reflects in this way: 'Living according to my pleasure unskilled states increase, skilled states diminish. But in confronting myself with suffering unskilled states diminish, skilled states increase.' (So he lives adopting that second approach with the result he seeks, but then abandons it.) Why so? Monks, (his) goal is accomplished. It is like a fletcher who heats and scorches a shaft between two firebrands, (and thereby) makes it straight and serviceable. But when (he has done this he has achieved his end and need not continue). Even so a monk (might cease to confront himself with suffering). In such a way also is a remedy and an exertion fruitful.

The Exemplar speaks like this, and his ten doctrines afford reason for praise. If beings experience happiness and suffering because of previous actions, then truly the Exemplar must have been a doer of good actions in the past to be experiencing sensations in the present that are undistracted and happy. If (he does so) on account of divine dispensation then truly (he) was produced by an auspicious god. If because of destiny then (his is a) fine destiny. If because of (his) race then (he) is of fine stock. If because of endeavours in this life then truly (his) are fine endeavours. So speaks the Exemplar, monks, (and his) ten doctrines afford reason for praise."

Thus spoke the Lord.

1. It can be assumed that the ensuing conversation refers both to this and former lives.
2. Continuation as for opening paragraph.
3. The five qualities referred to above multiplied by two, i.e. "remedy" and "exertion".

102

The Threefold Five

228–238

Thus have I heard: once the Lord dwelt near Sāvatthī in the Jeta Grove on Anāthapiṇḍika's campus. There (he) addressed the monks, saying:

"Monks, there are some ascetics and brahmans who theorise and speculate about future states and who express a diversity of opinions (thereof). Some declare (that), after death, the self is unimpaired and endowed with perception; some (that), after death the self is unimpaired but not endowed with perception; some (that it) is unimpaired and is neither with nor without perception. Or they even pronounce the breaking up, destruction, and annihilation of a being. Some proclaim *nibbāna* in this life. So these (views), having been five become three, having been three become five.[1]

As to those who proclaim a self endowed with perception and unimpaired after death – either these worthies assert (such a self) as having form, or as not having form, (or both, or neither); or as perceiving unity or diversity; or what is limited, or what is boundless. Some of them hold that, when the mental aid[2] is transcended, there is the boundless and imperturbable. Saying: 'There is nothingness' some proclaim the realm of nothingness as boundless and imperturbable.[3] Regarding (all) this the Exemplar knows (of it and) which of these perceptions is declared to be purest, highest, best, (and) beyond compare. Regarding what is composite, it is gross. But there is (also) this, (namely) an end to what is composite. Knowing (this), seeing the escape, the Exemplar has transcended it.

As to those who proclaim a self without perception but unimpaired after death, these worthies assert (such a self) as having form, or as not having form, (or both, or neither). Some of them scorn those (others) who assert that, after death, the self is endowed with perception and unimpaired, (saying that) perception is a disease, an abscess, a barb, (whereas) this is good and excellent, namely non-perception. Regarding (all) this the Exemplar knows (of it). Monks, this cannot be – that any ascetic or brahman might say: 'I assert coming or going, or passing away, or arising, or growth, or development, or maturity other than through (physical) form, feeling, perception, traits and tendencies, (or) consciousness.' Regarding what is composite it is gross. But there is (also) this, (namely) an end to what is composite. Knowing (this), seeing the escape, the Exemplar has transcended it.

As to those who proclaim a self neither with nor without perception after death, these worthies assert (such a self) as having form, or as not having form, (or both, or neither). Some of them scorn (the other groups).

(They say that) perception is a disease, an abscess, a barb, (and that) non-perception is a delusion, (but that this on the other hand) is good and excellent, namely neither perceiving nor not-perceiving. Regarding (all) this the Exemplar knows (of it). Now those who proclaim the reaching of that realm merely through what is composed of the visible, the audible, what is otherwise sensed, or the thinkable – (by them) is declared the destruction of that realm through the (very) reaching of it. For this realm is said to be unattainable with any residue of what is composite. Regarding what is composite it is gross. But there is (also) this, (namely) an end to what is composite. Knowing (this), seeing the escape, the Exemplar has transcended it.

As to those who assert the breaking up, destruction, and annihilation of a being, some (of them) scorn (all the other groups). Why so? It is because all these (other) worthies maintain a holding on, saying: 'We will become this hereafter, we will become that hereafter' – just as a merchant gone to trade might say: 'From there I shall have this. From this I shall have that.' Regarding (all) this the Exemplar knows (of these worthies that) they, whilst fearing and despising their own body, move and circle round (it). In the same way might a dog, leashed to a strong stake or post, move and circle round (it). Regarding what is composite it is gross. But there is (also) this, (namely) an end to what is composite. Knowing this, seeing the escape, the Exemplar has transcended it.

Monks, there are some ascetics and brahmans who, (in just the same way), theorise and speculate about the past. Some declare self and the world to be without beginning, (and all contrary views deluded). Some, (similarly), declare self and the world not to be without beginning. Some declare self and the world to be neither (of these alternatives, and) some declare self and the world to be both (of them). (Likewise) some declare an end for self and the world, some no end for self and the world, (and others both or neither). Some assert self and the world as perceiving unity, some as perceiving diversity; some as perceiving what is limited, some as perceiving what is boundless. Some (see them) as entirely happy, some as entirely painful, some as (both), some as (neither).

Monks, as to those who talk and think in such a way, it cannot be that, other than from conviction, from inclination, from tradition, from reflection on conditions, from comprehension and approval of opinion, there will be knowledge that is perfect and pure for each of them. But in the absence of perfect and pure knowledge even that fraction of knowledge that these worthies do purify will be accounted attachment. Regarding what is composite it is gross. But there is (also) this, (namely) an end to what is composite. Knowing (this), seeing the escape, the Exemplar has transcended it.

Monks, some ascetic or brahman, from the casting out of theories about the past and the future, and completely disregarding the bondage of worldly pursuits, reaches and experiences the joy of withdrawal, thinking: 'This is tranquil. This is exalted.' (But), with the ending of (that state) comes sadness, (and) with the ending of sadness comes the joy of withdrawal. Just as the heat of the sun pervades whatever the shade withdraws from, (and) the shade encompasses whatever the sun leaves behind, so it is (with these two states).[4] Regarding (all) this the Exemplar knows (of it). Regarding what is composite it is gross. But there is (also) this, (namely) an end to what is composite. Knowing (this), seeing the escape, the Exemplar has transcended it.

However, monks, some (other) ascetic or brahman, passing beyond the joy of withdrawal, reaches and experiences disinterested happiness, thinking: 'This is tranquil. This is exalted.' With the ending of (that state) comes the joy of withdrawal, and with the ending of the joy of withdrawal comes disinterested happiness. Regarding (all) this the Exemplar knows (of it). Regarding what is composite it is gross. But there is (also) this, (namely) an end to what is composite. Knowing (this), seeing the escape, the Exemplar has transcended it.

Some (other) ascetic or brahman, passing beyond disinterested happiness, reaches and experiences a feeling devoid of either pain or happiness, thinking: 'This is tranquil. This is exalted.' With the ending of (that state) comes disinterested happiness, and with the ending of disinterested happiness comes a feeling devoid of either pain or happiness. Regarding (all this) the Exemplar knows (of it). Regarding what is composite it is gross. But there is (also) this, (namely) an end to what is composite. Knowing (this), seeing the escape, the Exemplar has transcended it.

But some (other) ascetic or brahman, passing beyond the feeling devoid of either sorrow or happiness, perceives: 'I am tranquil. I am at peace. I am without attachment.' Regarding (all) this the Exemplar knows (of it). Regarding what is composite it is gross. But there is (also) this, (namely) an end to what is composite. Knowing (this), seeing the escape, the Exemplar has transcended it.

But now indeed the matchless path to tranquillity has been fully apprehended by the Exemplar in that, having seen the rising and the going down of the satisfaction, the disadvantage, and the giving up of the six sources of experience, there is freedom from attachment."

Thus spoke the Lord.

1. The "five" of the title is the five views summarised in this paragraph, though only the first four are subsequently discussed. The three may mean that views one, two, and three are regarded as variants of one view and that therefore there are only three views in a more fundamental sense.
2. i.e. meditation object.
3. I have transposed this sentence from after the one following for the sake of clarification.
4. The simile is repeated in subsequent paragraphs comparing two states.

103

On "Now What?"

238–243

Thus have I heard: once the Lord dwelt near Kusinārā in the Grove of Oblations. There (he) addressed the monks, saying: "Now what is there for you in me, monks? Does the ascetic Gotama teach *dhamma* as a means to robes, to almsbowls, to lodgings, or for this or that state of being?"[1]

"No, bhante."

"So what is there for you in me, monks?"

"Bhante, there is this for us in the Lord. Seeking the welfare (of beings, he) teaches *dhamma* out of compassion."

"Well then, monks, (as to) those things I have taught you from higher knowledge, namely the four applications of mindfulness, the four right exertions, the fourfold basis of psychic power, the five controlling faculties, the five powers, the seven aspects of enlightenment, and the *ariyan* eightfold way – you should train together in harmony, with satisfaction, and without contention in all (of them).

(But suppose) two (groups of)[2] monks to be in disagreement about the higher realms of *dhamma*. If it occurs to you (that) there is a difference as to the meaning and as to the expression between these brethren, you should approach whichever monk (of the one group) you deem to have spoken the better, (indicating the nature of the disagreement), and saying: 'Let not the brethren fall into contention.' Then you should approach whichever group of the other party you deem to have spoken the better (in the same way).

If it occurs to you (that) there is a difference (of opinion) as to the meaning (but) there is agreement about the expression, (you should proceed in the same way).

If it occurs to you (that) there is agreement as to the meaning, (but) there is a difference (of opinion) about the expression, (you should proceed in the same way), saying: 'This is of little account, namely (form of) expression. Let not the brethren fall into contention concerning what is of little account.'

If it occurs to you (that) there is agreement between these brethren as to the meaning (and) as to the expression, (you should proceed in the same way), saying: 'Let not the brethren fall into contention.'[3] In (all these situations) what is hard to grasp and what is easy to grasp should be remembered (as such), and *dhamma* and discipline spoken of.

Having trained together in these (ways) in harmony, with satisfaction, (and) without contention, suppose there to be an offence, a transgression, on the part of some monk. He is not to be reproved in haste. (That) person is to be examined with the thought: 'There will be no vexation for me or for that other person. Surely (he) is without anger, not of ill-will, not slow-witted, one of true renunciation; and raising (him) from unskilled states I am capable of establishing (him) in what is skilled.' If that is how it appears to you, it is right to speak. If (he is without these desirable traits and) you think: 'There will be no vexation for me, but it will be hurtful for (him). (Nonetheless) raising (him) from unskilled states I am capable of establishing (him) in what is skilled, (and therefore) the hurt (to him) is of little account', it is right to speak. If you think: 'There will be vexation for me, but no hurt for (him). (Nonetheless) raising (him) from unskilled states I am capable of establishing (him) in what is skilled, (and therefore) the vexation (to me) is of little account', it is right to speak. (And the same is true even if there is both vexation for you and hurt for him in such a case.)

But if you think: 'There will be vexation for me and hurt for (him), and I am not capable of raising (him) from unskilled (states) and establishing (him) in what is skilled', equanimity should not be set aside for such a person.

Having trained together in these (ways) in harmony, with satisfaction, (and) without contention, suppose there should arise ways of talking to one another (based on) malicious views, on an angry mind, on dissatisfaction and discontent. Then, approaching whichever monk (of the one party) you deem the easiest to speak with, you should say: 'Friend, having trained together (like this) an ascetic who knew of it would reproach us. But without ridding (ourselves) of this state, is *nibbāna* obtainable?' Answering aright that monk (would agree that it is not). Then you should (deal similarly with the other party).

If others were to ask: 'Through that brother[4] of ours were these monks raised from unskilled states and established in what is skilled?' – answering aright (he) might say: 'Friends, I approached the Lord, (who) taught me *dhamma*. (Then) I spoke it to these monks. (Then) these monks, hearing *dhamma*, were raised from unskilled (states) and established in what is skilled.' Answering in this way a monk truly does not exalt himself, does not disparage others, and explains things according to *dhamma*. And whoever is his comrade in *dhamma* and follows (that) view, gives no cause for reproach."

Thus spoke the Lord.

1. Presumably with reference to worldly status.
2. The text refers to two individuals but this is not compatible with what follows.
3. i.e. either the agreement is unacknowledged, or the admonition must refer to future debates.
4. "that brother" here apparently refers to the arbitrator/peacemaker who is, by implication, the person addressed throughout.

104

At Sāmagāma

243–251

Thus have I heard: once the Lord dwelt among the Sakyans at Sāmagāma. Now at that time Nātaputta the Jain had just died at Pāvā. On his passing away, the Jains fell apart. Dividing, quarrelling, disputing, falling into contention, they lived indulging in mutual recrimination, (saying to one another): "You do not understand this *dhamma* and discipline, (whereas) I do. What can you know about (it)? You are on a wrong course (whereas) I am on a right course. What I say is sensible, what you say is not (so). You say later what should be said first, and first what should be said later. What you failed to think out is (now) altered. You are refuted (and) rebuked. Away with you and your babbling, or make yourself clear if you can." Indeed, destruction was abroad among the Jains who were Nātaputta's pupils. Even the householders clad in white who were his disciples were wearied, displeased, and repelled at a *dhamma* and discipline that were poorly expounded and communicated, not leading (anywhere), not conducive to peace, not proclaimed by one truly enlightened, its support broken and unprotected.

Then Cunda the novice, having spent the rainy season at Pāvā, came to Sāmagāma and approached venerable Ānanda. Saluting (him) and sitting down at one side, Cunda the novice (spoke of the contention among the Jains). When he had spoken venerable Ānanda said: "This news is (something) to see the Lord about. Come, Cunda my friend, we will go to the Lord and relate the matter to (him)."

So venerable Ānanda and Cunda the novice approached the Lord, saluted (him), and sat down at one side. (Then venerable Ānanda told him of the conversation and said):

"It occurs to me, bhante, that we must hope such a conflict does not arise in the Order on the Lord's death – a conflict to the misfortune and unhappiness of the multitude, for the ill of the people, for the disadvantage and suffering of *devas* and humans."

"What do you think about this, Ānanda? These things that I have taught you out of higher knowledge – the four applications of mindfulness, the four right exertions, the fourfold basis of psychic power, the five controlling faculties, the five powers, the seven aspects of enlightenment, (and) the *ariyan* eightfold path – do you see even two monks in disagreement on these matters?"

"(No), bhante. Yet those people who live dependent on the Lord might, on (his) passing away, stir up contention about the mode of livelihood, or the obligations.[1]"

"Dispute about the mode of livelihood or the obligations is of little account, Ānanda. But if dispute should arise in the Order about the Way, that would be for the misfortune and unhappiness of the multitude, for the ill of the people, for the misfortune and suffering of *devas* and humans.

There are these six roots of dissension, Ānanda.[2] In this connection a monk is angry, and bears ill-will. A monk who is (like that) lives lacking respect for, and rebelling against the Teacher, the *Dhamma*, and the Order – and does not fulfil the training. Such a monk sows dissension in the Order. If, Ānanda, you should discern such a source of dissension, either among yourselves or others, you should strive for (its) abandonment (and, failing that), you should pursue a course for (its) non-eruption in the future.

But further, Ānanda, a monk is harsh and unmerciful, envious and greedy, crafty and deceitful, has evil desires and wrong views, looks for worldly gain and is stubborn and obstinate. A monk who is (all these things) sows dissension in the Order. If, Ānanda, you should discern such a source of dissension, either among yourselves or others, you should strive for (its) abandonment (and, failing that), you should pursue a course for its non-eruption in the future.

These, Ānanda, are the six roots of dissension, (and) these are the four procedures – procedures connected with dissension, with censure, with offences, and with the obligations. And there are these seven procedures for settlement – a judgement to be delivered face-to-face, (innocence according to) conscience, restoration (of sanity), the making of an acknowledgement, majority verdict, specific evil, (and) covering (as with) grass.

And what is the face-to-face judgement, Ānanda? As to that, (suppose) monks quarrel (about) *dhamma* or discipline. All those monks should assemble in harmony and thrash out the points at issue. And according to (the outcome of their deliberations), so is the matter to be settled.

And what is the majority verdict, Ānanda? If those monks are unable to settle the matter at that place of residence (they) should go to a place of residence where there are more monks, (and proceed in the same way). So is the matter to be settled.

And what is the judgement of (innocence according to) conscience? As to that, (suppose) the monks reprimand a monk with such a serious offence as warrants expulsion, or verges on (that, but) he says: 'I do not recollect committing a serious offence such as that.' A verdict of (innocence according to) conscience is to be given that monk.

And what is the verdict of restoration (of sanity)? As to that, (suppose) the monks reprimand a monk with a serious offence (but) he, answering this (unsatisfactorily), is pressed, (and they say): 'Now look, brother, consider well.' (Then) he replies: 'I was crazy and of disturbed mind, and I often perpetrated and said much not worthy of a true ascetic. (But) I do not remember whatever was done in (this state of) aberration.' A verdict of restoration (of sanity) is to be given that monk.

And what is the making of an acknowledgement? As to that a monk, whether reprimanded or not, recalls an offence, confesses (and) declares (it). That monk approaches an older monk with his (upper) robe over one shoulder and, after making salutation at (the other's) feet, sits in a squatting position, raising his joined palms. He should say: 'Bhante, having committed such and such an offence I confess it.' (The other) says: 'Do you recognise it'. 'I recognise it.' 'Will you be restrained in future?' 'I will be restrained.'

And what is specific evil? As to that, (suppose) the monks reprimand a monk with such a serious offence as warrants expulsion, or verges on (that, and) he, answering (unsatisfactorily), is pressed, (and they say): 'Now look, brother, consider well.' (Then) he replies: 'I do not remember committing a serious offence such as this. I do remember committing such and such a slight offence. How then could I not admit, when questioned, (to a more serious offence)?' But someone rejoins: 'Indeed, friend, you are not admitting, unasked, to that slight offence! How then would you admit (to a serious offence)!' (Then) he says: 'I do recollect committing a serious offence. (In denying it) I spoke in jest (and) for fun.'

And what is covering (as with) grass? As to that, among monks who live quarrelling, disputing, and falling into contention, there is much perpetrated and said not worthy of a true ascetic. All these monks should assemble in harmony together, and an experienced monk from the one faction, rising from his place and arranging his robe over one shoulder, and saluting with joined palms, should announce to the assembly: 'Let the Order hear me. This (quarrelling of ours) is unworthy of a true ascetic. If the Order concurs I would confess in (its) midst whatever might be the offence of the brethren and of myself. Both for (their) good and for (mine I would do this) for a covering (as with) grass, unless it be a serious fault.' (And then an experienced monk from the other faction should speak in the same terms).

Ānanda, these six memorable things[3] make for conciliation, respect, kindliness, absence of contention, for concord, for unity. As to that, a monk proffers friendly actions to his associates in the good life, both in public and private, (and also) friendly words and thoughts. Moreover whatever is legitimately acquired, even what is put into the alms-bowl – a monk is devoted to sharing the like in common with his worthy associates. Moreover whatever is unbroken, unflawed, untarnished, consistent conduct; producing freedom; praised by the wise, uncorrupted; making for concentration – a monk lives wedded to such (things) in common with his fellows, both in public and private. Moreover such view as is *ariyan*, progressive, leading him that conforms to them to the ultimate destruction of suffering – a monk should live wedded to such a view in common with his fellows, both in public and private.

Ānanda, these six memorable things make for conciliation, respect, kindliness, absence of contention, for concord, for unity. Should you, undertaking (them), mature (in them), do you see any manner of speaking, be it subtle or coarse, that you could not endure?"

"Not so, bhante."

"Then undertake and practise them, Ānanda, and it will be for your wellbeing and happiness for many a day."

Thus spoke the Lord.

1. i.e. minor formal restrictions or matters where a degree of individual choice is proper.
2. The six are anger and the five groups of characteristics separated by commas in the ensuing paragraph.
3. i.e. friendly actions, words, and thoughts plus the three situations introduced by "Moreover".

105

With Sunakkhatta

252–261

Thus have I heard: once the Lord dwelt at Vesālī in the Great Grove in the hall of the Gabled House. Now at that time many monks were claiming gnosis in the Lord's presence, declaring: "We know that birth is destroyed, fulfilled is the good life, what was to be done is done, and there will be no further return to this world." Sunakkhatta, son of a Licchavi (heard about this, approached the Lord, and saluting him, sat down at one side. Said Sunakkhatta:

"I have heard (what some monks are claiming). Did they claim gnosis fairly, or did some there claim (it) from conceit?"

"Sunakkhatta, some claimed gnosis fairly, some claimed (it) from conceit. Regarding those who claimed (it) fairly, that is just how it is for them. But as to those who claim (it) from conceit it occurs to the Exemplar: 'I should teach them *dhamma*.' Then, however, there are some foolish people who approach the Exemplar and ask a prepared question. And again it occurs to the Exemplar: 'I should teach them *dhamma*". It does not occur to him (to think) otherwise.

There are these five strands of worldly pursuit, Sunakkhatta – visible forms, pleasing, welcome, enticing, voluptuous, pleasure-laden, exciting; (and sounds, tastes, odours, and sensations of a similar nature). It is possible, moreover, that some individual in this world is given over to worldly gain. The talk (of such a person) takes a set form, and he reflects and ponders accordingly, associating with that man through whom he gets prosperity,[1] but when there is talk about imperturbability he does not listen or lend an ear, does not devote his mind to (that) knowledge.

Sunakkhatta, suppose that a man long absent from his own village or town sees another man recently come from (that place). He asks (him) about the security, the abundance of food, and the state of health (of those who live there). And that man tells him. What do you think about this, Sunakkhatta. Wouldn't (he) listen, lend and ear, and devote his mind to (that) knowledge?"

"Yes, bhante."

"Even so, Sunakkhatta, it may happen that some individual is given over to worldly gain. But it is (also) possible that some (other) individual in this world is intent on imperturbability. The talk of such a person takes a set form, and he reflects and ponders accordingly, associating with that man through whom he finds happiness. But when there is talk about worldly gain he does not listen, lend an ear, or devote his mind to (that) knowledge.

Sunakkhatta, it is like a withered leaf, separated from its stalk and incapable of becoming green again. Even so, Sunakkhatta, the individual intent on imperturbability, who has distanced himself from the hold of worldliness, should be known (for what he is).

But there is (also) this circumstance – that some individual here is intent on the realm of nothingness. The talk of such a person takes a set form, and he reflects and ponders accordingly, associating with that man through whom he finds happiness, but when there is talk about imperturbability he does not listen, lend an ear, or devote his mind to (that) knowledge. Sunakkhatta, it is like a rock that, split in half and broken, is unmendable. Even so the individual set on nothingness, who has broken the hold of imperturbability, (should be known for what he is).

But it is (also) possible that some individual here is intent on the realm of neither perceiving nor not-perceiving, (and is unconcerned about the realm of nothingness). Sunakkhatta, it is like a man who, after eating a satisfying meal, throws away (the leftovers). Could that man have any further desire for that food?"

"No, bhante. Why so? Surely that food would be disagreeable."

"Just so, Sunakkhatta, the individual intent on the realm of neither perceiving nor not-perceiving throws off the hold of the realm of nothingness, (and) should be known (for what he is).

But it is (also) possible that some individual here is intent on perfect *nibbāna,* (and is unconcerned about the realm of neither perceiving nor not-perceiving). Sunakkhatta, it is like a torn-up palm tree, annihilated for the future, and taking no further hold. Just so, Sunakkhatta, the individual intent on perfect *nibbāna* breaks the hold of the realm of neither perceiving nor not-perceiving, is not liable to re-arise in the future, and should be known (for what he is).

But it is (also) possible that some monk here thinks: 'Craving is spoken of as an arrow by the Ascetic. The poison of ignorance torments through desire, passion, and ill-will. Drawing out that arrow, removing that poison of ignorance, I am intent on perfect *nibbāna*.' Thus he is proud of his current wellbeing. (Because of that) he pursues unsuitable visible forms, (or other sense and mental objects). (Because of that) passion corrupts his mind. Through passion corrupting the mind he comes to death or pain like unto death.

Sunakkhatta, it is like a man struck by an arrow thickly smeared with poison. His friends, associates, and relatives procure a physician who is a surgeon, (and who) cuts round the mouth of the wound with a knife. (Then) he searches for the arrow-(head) with a probe, pulls (it) out, and drains the poison, leaving some residue, though he thinks it all removed. He says: 'My good fellow, the arrow is withdrawn, the poison drained without remainder, and there is no problem for you as long as you eat suitable foods only. (Otherwise) the wound might discharge. You should wash (it) from time to time, and anoint (it, but not in such a way that) the old blood cakes the mouth of the wound. And don't make a habit of going into the wind or heat of the sun. (Otherwise) dust and dirt might infect (it). Continue to guard the wound and (it) will heal.'

(But the wounded man) thinks: 'The arrow is withdrawn, the poison drained without remainder, and there is no problem for me.' (And he takes no heed of the instructions.) Because (of that, and also the noxious poison that remains), the wound swells (so that) he comes to death or pain like unto death. Just so, Sunakkhatta, this circumstance exists, that some monk comes to death, or pain like unto death, through passion corrupting the mind. For this is death in the discipline of the *ariyan*, that one should give up the training and return to the worldly condition. And this is the pain like unto death, that should commit a serious offence.

My example, Sunakkhatta, was to make plain the meaning. 'Wound' is a name for the six inner sources of experience. 'Poison' is a name for ignorance, 'arrow' for craving, 'probe' for mindfulness, 'knife' for the *ariyan* wisdom, 'physician who is a surgeon' for the Exemplar.

Truly, Sunakkhatta, the monk who exercises restraint with regard to the six sourcess of experience thinking: 'Attachment is the root of suffering' is, understanding it so, freed by the destruction of attachment. It cannot be that he should concentrate his body on attachment, or devote his mind to it. It is like a venomous snake (to which) a man comes along desiring life, not wanting death, desiring happiness, averse to suffering. What do you think about this? Would that man offer hand or toe to the snake knowing (the likely outcome)?"

"Not so, bhante."

"It is likewise, Sunakkhatta, for the monk who exercises restraint with regard to the six sources of experience."

Thus spoke the Lord.

1. Horner translates as "felicity". The Pali term might cover anything from erotic pleasure to profitable trade.

106

Helpful Imperturbability

261–266

Thus have I heard: once the Lord dwelt among the Kurus (in) a town called Kammāssadhamma. There (he) addressed the monks, saying:

"Transient, monks, are worldly pursuits – vain, false, of no value. Born of deception is common speech. Those worldly pursuits and perceptions of (them) that are of this world (or) of the next world, are under Māra's sway, are Māra's realm, Māra's portion, Māra's field. There these evil, unskilled intentions lead to envy, ill-will, and destruction, and these form an obstacle in the training of the *ariyan* disciple.

The *ariyan* disciple reflects: 'Suppose I were to live with a great and expanded mind, overcoming the world, and with resolute thoughts. (Then those) evil, unskilled intentions, and that envy, ill-will, and destruction, will not come into being. And through the abandonment of them my mind will become unbounded, immeasurable, and well-developed.' This, monks, is proclaimed as the first course in helpful imperturbability.

The *ariyan* disciple reflects: 'There are those worldly pursuits and perceptions of (them) that are of this world (and) of the next world, and whatever has form (consists of) the four great elements, and is derived from (them).' This, monks, is proclaimed as the second course in helpful imperturbability.

The *ariyan* disciple reflects (that all worldly and other-worldly states are transient, and that) what is transient is not worth rejoicing in, not worth welcoming, not worth holding on to. This, monks, is proclaimed as the third course in helpful imperturbability.

The mind of him that practises and is living fully (in any of these ways) is peaceful in that realm and, being at peace, either enters the imperturbable now or is set on wisdom. On the breaking up of the body at death it is possible for that evolving consciousness to reach the imperturbable.

But further, monks, the *ariyan* disciple reflects (that where all these things, even the perception of beneficial imperturbability), dissolve without remainder, that is tranquil, that is exalted, namely the realm of nothingness. This, monks, is proclaimed as the first course in the helpful realm of nothingness

The *ariyan* disciple gone to the forest, or to the root of a tree, reflects: 'Empty is this of self or of what belongs to self.' This, monks, is proclaimed as the second course in the helpful realm of nothingness.

But further, monks, the *ariyan* disciple reflects: 'I am nothing, no one's, and nowhere, nor is there anything of mine that is anything or anywhere.'

This, monks, is proclaimed as the third course in the helpful realm of nothingness.

The mind of him that practises and is living fully (in any of these ways) is peaceful in that realm and is at peace, either entering the realm of nothingness now or being set on wisdom. On the breaking up of the body at death it is possible for that evolving consciousness to reach the realm of nothingness.

But further, monks, the *ariyan* disciple reflects (that, where even the perception of the realm of nothingness) dissolves without remainder – that is tranquil, that is exalted, namely the realm of neither perceiving nor not-perceiving.

The mind of him that practises and is living fully thus is peaceful in that realm and, being at peace, either enters the realm of neither perceiving nor not-perceiving now or is set on wisdom. On the breaking up of the body at death it is possible for that evolving consciousness to reach the realm of neither perceiving nor not-perceiving. This, monks, is proclaimed as the helpful realm of neither perceiving nor not-perceiving."

At these words venerable Ānanda said to the Lord:

"Bhante, (suppose) a monk here is proceeding with the thought: 'If (this) were not it would not be mine. It shall not be, and will not be mine. What is and what has been, that I renounce.' Thus he gains equanimity. Does that monk reach final *nibbāna*."

"As to that, Ānanda, one monk may, another may not."

"Bhante, what is the cause, what the condition of (that)?"

"As to that, Ānanda, (suppose) a monk is proceeding (in such a way). He rejoices, welcomes, and abides holding on to that equanimity. (But) such consciousness is dependent. It is an attachment. The monk who has attachment does not gain final *nibbāna*, Ānanda."

"But where, bhante, does the monk who is attached take hold?"

"The realm of neither perceiving nor not-perceiving, Ānanda."

"Truly, bhante, (he) takes hold of the best attachment."

"(Certainly) that is the best attachment, Ānanda. (But another) monk proceeds with the thought: 'If (this) were not it would not be mine. It shall not be, and will not be mine. What is and what has been, that I renounce.' Thus he gains equanimity. He does not rejoice, or welcome, or abide holding on to that equanimity, (and such) consciousness is not dependent, and is without attachment. The monk who has no attachment attains final *nibbāna*, Ānanda."

"Strange, bhante, wonderful! Truly by such means is the crossing of the flood proclaimed to us by the Lord. But which (of these) is the *ariyan* freedom?"

"As to that, Ānanda, the *ariyan* disciple reflects: 'There are those worldly pursuits and those (material) forms that are of this world, or of the next, (and the perceptions that accompany them), and perceptions of the realm of nothingness, and of the realm of neither perceiving nor not-perceiving, and that one's body is just one's body. (But) this is the deathless, namely freedom of the mind from attachment.' And so, Ānanda, I have taught the course in (all these things). What a teacher seeking the wellbeing of disciples may do out of compassion, that I have done for you. Here are roots of trees, here are empty places. Meditate, Ānanda, be not slothful, do not be remorseful later. This is our instruction to you.''

Thus spoke the Lord.

107

With Gaṇaka-Moggallāna

1–7

Thus have I heard: once the Lord dwelt near Sāvatthī at the Migāramātu Palace on the Eastern Campus. Then brahman Gaṇaka-Moggallāna approached the Lord, exchanged greetings, and having conversed in a friendly and polite way, sat down at one side. Said (the) brahman:

"Friend Gotama, just as, in the Migāramātu Palace, a gradual training, a gradual performance, a gradual method can be seen, in fact as far as the last flight of stairs – likewise for these brahmans with regard to study; for archers with regard to archery; likewise for we who live by calculation with respect to accountancy. For, when we get a pupil we make him reckon – one one, two twos, three threes, four fours (and so on). We make him reckon a hundred in all. Is it not possible to lay down (such a course) in this *dhamma* and discipline?"

"Brahman, it is possible to lay down a gradual training, a gradual performance, a gradual method in this *dhamma* and discipline. As a skilful horse-trainer, on acquiring a fine thoroughbred, first just imposes the bit, then additional work – so the Exemplar, on getting a trainee, firstly instructs him thus: 'Come monk, be virtuous, live governed by the restraint of the obligations, successful in the field of conduct, fearful of slight faults and, shouldering the precepts, persevere (with them).'

When the monk is (thus skilful) the Exemplar enjoins him further, saying: 'Guard the doors of the faculties, (and) seeing a form with the eye, be not infatuated with the appearance nor with the attributes. For longing and distress, (and) wretched and unskilled states, may intrude on the eye that is wayward. So proceed with restraint, guard the eye, undergo the discipline of the eye; (and likewise of the ear, the nose, the tongue, the tactile sense, and mental images).'

Once the monk is a guarder of the faculties the Exemplar again exhorts him, saying: 'Be moderate in eating, reflecting thoroughly. You may take food not for sport, not for indulgence, not for finery, not for ornament, but in the measure needed for the endurance and sustenance of the body; for its protection, and for furtherance of the good life, (thinking that you) will make an end of old feeling, and not create new feeling, and (that) there shall be continuance, and blamelessness, and comfort for (you).'

As soon as the monk is moderate in eating the Exemplar enjoins him further, saying: 'Live set on vigilance. In a day of walking about and sitting down clear the mind of obstructive states. In the first watch of the night (do likewise). In the middle watch of the night lie down on the right side in the lion posture, with one foot resting on the other, mindful and lucid, attending to the thought of getting up. In the last watch of the night arise (and continue as before).'

(When vigilance has been attained by the monk) the Exemplar once more exhorts, saying: 'Be mindful and lucid – in coming and going; in looking forward and looking round; in bending and stretching; in carrying cloak, or almsbowl, or robe; in eating and drinking, in chewing and tasting; in excreting and urinating; in walking, standing, sitting, sleeping, waking, speaking, and remaining silent.'

(Finally) the Exemplar instructs him, saying: 'Resort to a solitary abode in a forest, at the root of a tree, on a rock, in a glen, a mountain cave, a cemetery, a woodland grove, in the open, or on a heap of straw.'

On returning from the almsround after the meal the monk sits down cross-legged, with body upright, establishing mindfulness before him as his aim. Abandoning longing for the world he lives with a mind purged (thereof). Abandoning the taint of ill-will he lives without malevolence, and with friendship and mercy to all living things. Abandoning sloth and torpor he lives emptied (thereof), perceiving light, mindful and lucid. Abandoning agitation and worry he lives inwardly calm and composed. Abandoning perplexity he lives beyond doubt, untroubled as to skilful things.

Abandoning those five hindrances which blemish the mind and are injurious to wisdom, and remote from worldly pursuits and unskilled states, he reaches and experiences the first, second, third, and fourth (levels of) absorption. Such is the form of my teaching, brahman, for trainee monks of unfulfilled purpose, who live longing for the matchless haven from bondage. But as to those monks who are *arahants*, with the distractions rooted out, fulfilled ones who have done what needs to be done, have shed the burden, reached their goal, finally broken the thongs of existence, and are released by true freedom – for them these things lead to a state of happiness in this life, to mindfulness and lucidity."

At these words brahman Gaṇaka-Moggallāna said: 'On being advised and instructed thus, do all friend Gotama's followers achieve the perennial goal of *nibbāna*, or do some not reach it?"

"Some of my followers achieve (it), brahman, some not."

"What then is the cause, what the condition (for this), since *nibbāna* exists, the way to *nibbāna* exists, and friend Gotama is there as adviser?"

"Well, brahman, I will now put this question in return. Answer as you please. What do you think about this? Are you knowledgeable regarding the way to Rājagaha?"

"Certainly, friend."

"Then what do you think about this? A man comes along wishing to go to Rājagaha, (and asks you the way). You tell him: 'This road leads to Rājagaha. Follow it for a short while. (Then) you will see a village. (Continue further, then) you will see a market town. (Continue again, then) you will behold Rājagaha with its lovely parks, woods, fields, and lakes.' (Following) your advice and instructions he might (nevertheless) take the wrong road, and go westwards. Then a second man comes along (and is given the same information). He might get to Rājagaha safely. What then is the cause, what the condition (for this), since Rājagaha exists, the way leading to Rājagaha exists, and you are there as adviser?"

"What have I to do with that, friend Gotama? I am (just) the teller of the way."

"Likewise, brahman, (when) some achieve the perennial goal of *nibbāna*, (whilst) others do not, what have I to do with that? The Exemplar is (just) the teller of the way."

At these words (the) brahman said: 'Those people who have gone forth from home into homelessness without faith, through lack of a livelihood, crafty, hypocritical, deceitful, pretentious, haughty, garrulous, of loose talk, not guarding the doors of the faculties, heedlessly immoderate in eating, unconcerned about vigilance, without feeling for the life of the ascetic or eager enthusiasm for the training, lavish, lax, soon lapsed, shirking the responsibility of solitude, indolent, of feeble energy, of unaroused mindfulness, not lucid, inattentive, of wayward mind, stupid, incoherent – friend Gotama has no association with them. Just as black gum is declared to be pre-eminent among scented roots, red sandalwood (similarly) among pith scents, (and) jasmine among fragrant flowers, so are friend Gotama's admonitions first among the teachings of our time. Excellent, friend Gotama, excellent!" (And brahman Gaṇaka-Moggallāna took the refuges and became a lay-follower).

108

With Gopaka-Moggallāna

7–15

Thus have I heard: once, not long after the Lord's final *nibbāna* (venerable) Ānanda was living near Rājagaha, at the squirrels' feeding-place in the Bamboo Grove. At that time King Ajātasattu of Magadha, the son of (the lady) Videha, was having Rājagaha strengthened from fear of King Pajjota. Then venerable Ānanda, dressing at an early hour, and taking bowl and robe, went into Rājagaha for almsfood. But it struck (him): "It is too early to walk in Rājagaha for alms. Suppose I were to approach brahman Gopaka-Moggallāna at his work-place." (And he did so.)

Brahman Gopaka-Moggallāna saw (him) coming some way off and said: "Welcome, good Ānanda, greetings. It is some time since the worthy Ānanda took the opportunity to come here. Let (him) be seated. This seat is ready." Venerable Ānanda sat down in the place prepared (for him and the) brahman took a low seat. Said Gopaka-Moggallāna:

"Ānanda, is there even one monk wholly and completely in possession of those things possessed by the worthy Gotama, who was *arahant* and truly enlightened?"

"(No), brahman. For the Lord was the originator of a way not (previously) come into being, the parent of a way (previously) unconceived, the teller of a way (previously) untold. Now, however, the disciples are followers of the Way in his wake."

Now this conversation was interrupted (when) brahman Vassakāra, the chief minister of Magadha in Rājagaha, who was visiting the works (there), approached venerable Ānanda. Having exchanged greetings and conversed in a friendly and polite way he sat down at one side. Said brahman Vassakāra:

"What were you talking about as you were seated here and what conversation have I interrupted?" (And venerable Ānanda told him. Said the brahman):

"Yet is there even one monk designated by the worthy Gotama (to the effect that), after (his) decease, (that person) should be your refuge, and to whom you might now turn?"

"There is not, brahman."

"Then is there even one monk satisfactory to the Order, and designated by a number of elder monks (for this purpose)?"

"There is not, brahman."

"But, without such refuge, good Ānanda, what is the basis of your unity?"

"We are not without refuge, brahman. *Dhamma* is the refuge."

"You say (that) *dhamma* is the refuge, but what meaning should be attributed to those words?"

"Brahman, by that Lord who has known and seen, *arahant* and truly enlightened, a rule of training was laid down, and an obligation indicated. In so far as we live relying on a single village neighbourhood we congregate on each observance day and enquire what has befallen each one (of us). If, in such a recital, there is an offence or transgression on the part of a monk, we deal with that according to *dhamma* and as instructed. Truly it is *dhamma*, not the brethren, that deals with us."

"Is there, good Ānanda, even one monk whom you honour, respect, esteem, and revere and, (so doing), live in reliance (on him)?"

"There is, brahman."

"You say there is one monk on whom (you) live in reliance, but what meaning should be attributed to those words (in the light of what you said earlier)?"

Brahman, ten inspiring things have been declared by that Lord who has known and seen, *arahant* and truly enlightened.[1] Herein a monk is virtuous, lives governed by the restraint of the obligations, successful in the field of behaviour, and perceiving danger in the smallest faults. Undertaking them, he trains (himself) in regard to the precepts. He is well-informed, remembering and retaining what he has heard. Those things that are auspicious at the outset, in the progress, and in the consummation, and that proclaim in the meaning and expression a good life wholly fulfilled and purified – he is well-informed about such things, (and they are) kept in mind, given utterance to, augmented, pondered over, and properly penetrated by (right) view. He is content with the requisites of robe, almsfood, shelter, and medicines for the sick. He is one who, when he wishes, and without difficulty or trouble, achieves the four (levels of) absorption that are dependent on the clearest consciousness and are the dwelling-place of happiness in this life. He experiences the various forms of psychic power. With the purified divine eye transcending the human, he hears sounds of both kinds, divine and human, far and near. He knows with his mind the minds of other beings and individuals. He recalls a variety of previous existences. With the divine eye transcending the human he beholds beings passing away and re-emerging according to the consequences of their deeds. Rooting out the distractions he lives undistracted, having reached and experienced freedom of mind and the freedom of wisdom that are undistracted through his own gnosis in this life. These, brahman, are the ten inspiring things declared by that Lord who has known and seen, *arahant*, truly enlightened. We honour, respect, esteem, and revere him in whom these ten things are found."

At these words brahman Vassakāra, chief minister of Magadha addressed General Upananda, saying: 'What do you think about this, general? When these worthies thus honour, respect, esteem, and revere (one who should be so treated they behave rightly). For should (they) not honour (such a person thus), whom indeed could they live in reliance on?" Then (he) spoke to venerable Ānanda:

"But where is the worthy Ānanda living at present?"

"I am now living in the Bamboo Grove, brahman."

"I trust, good Ānanda, that the Bamboo Grove is pleasant, with little noise and clamour, and protected from the winds, unfrequented, and ideal for seclusion."

"Yes indeed, brahman, (it is all these things), as (might be expected) with a custodian and guardian such as yourself."

"(And) indeed as (befits) brethren who are meditating and have the habit of meditation. On one occasion, good Ānanda, the worthy Gotama lived near Vesālī in the Great Grove in the hall of the Gabled House. And I approached (him there, where) he conversed in various ways about meditation. The worthy Gotama was a meditator and given to the practice of meditation. Moreover he praised all meditation."

"Not so, brahman. The Lord did not praise all meditation. So what kind of meditation did (he) not praise? Herein someone lives with a mind possessed by worldly pursuits and passions, overcome by (them) and does not understand, for what it is, the escape from (these things). Having made worldly pursuits and passions an obstacle, he meditates, is consumed, frets, and ponders (thereon). (Or) he lives with a mind possessed by ill-will, sloth and torpor, agitation and worry, or perplexity (in the same way). The Lord did not praise such meditation. And what kind did he praise? Herein a monk, remote from worldly pursuits and unskilled states, reaches and experiences the first, the second, the third, and the fourth (levels of) absorption. Such meditation (he) praised."

"Truly the worthy Gotama condemned base (forms of) meditation, and praised praiseworthy (forms). Well, good Ānanda, we must be going. We have much to attend to and many duties."

"Do now as you see fit, brahman."

Then brahman Vassakāra, chief minister of Magadha, pleased and satisfied with the words of venerable Ānanda, rose from his seat and went his way. And brahman Gopaka-Moggallāna, not long after (his) departure, said to venerable Ānanda:

"What we asked the worthy Ānanda, that (he) has not (yet) explained."

"Did we not say to you, brahman, (that) there is not even one monk wholly and completely possessed of those things possessed by that Lord who has known and seen, *arahant* and truly enlightened. For the Lord was an originator of a way not (previously) come into being, the parent of a way (previously) unconceived, the teller of a way (previously) untold. Now, however, the disciples are followers of the Way in (his) wake."

1. 'The following section is much abbreviated after the first item, the other nine being given in detail in identical sections elsewhere.

109

Major Discourse at the Time of the Full Moon

15–20

Thus have I heard: once the Lord dwelt near Sāvatthī at the Migāramātu Palace on the Eastern Campus. Now on the night of the full moon on the fifteenth, an observance day, the Lord was seated in the open, surrounded by a group of monks. Then a certain monk rose from his place, arranged his robe over one shoulder, and saluted with joined palms, saying: "I would like the chance to question the Lord on a certain point."

"Very well, monk. Be seated and ask whatever you wish."

Said the monk, sitting down (again): "Bhante, are there not these five embodiments of attachment, namely (physical) form, feeling, perception, traits and tendencies, and consciousness?"

"Indeed, monk, those are the five embodiments of attachment."

"Then, bhante, what is (their) root?"

"(Their) root is desire, monk."

"So is attachment just these five embodiments of attachment, bhante, or is there attachment apart from (them)?"

"In fact, monk, attachment is not just these five, but neither is there any attachment apart from (them)."

"May it be, however, bhante, that diversity exists in the desire and passion for the five embodiments?"

"That may be, monk", said the Lord. "For instance, someone thinks: 'May (physical) form be thus in the fullness of time, may feeling be thus in the fullness of time (and so on).' In that way there is (such) diversity."

"But to what extent, bhante, can the embodiments be designated?"

"Monk, whatever is (physical) form in the past, the future, or the present, be it internal or external, gross or subtle, fair or foul, far or near, that is the embodiment (comprising physical) form, (and the same is true of the other four). Thus far, monk, can (they) be designated."

"But what, bhante, is the cause, what the condition, for the discovery of the embodiment (comprising physical) form (and each of the others)?"

"The four great elements, monk, are the cause and condition for the discovery of (physical) form. (Response to) a stimulus is the cause and condition for the discovery of feeling, perception, and traits and tendencies. Individuality and form is the cause and condition for the discovery of consciousness."

"But how, bhante, (are the embodiments) seen as one's own?"

"As to that, monk, some uninformed person is heedless of the *ariyans*, untrained in the *dhamma* of true men, (and) regards (physical) form as self, or self as having (physical) form, or (physical) form as within self, or self as within (physical) form. (Or he regards) feeling, perception, traits and tendencies, (or) consciousness (in any of these ways)."

"And how, bhante, are (they) not seen as one's own?"

"In that case, monk, an informed disciple of the *ariyans* does not regard body, feeling, perception, traits and tendencies, (or) consciousness (in any of these ways)."

"And what, bhante, is the satisfaction, what the disadvantage, what is freedom with respect to (each of them)?"

"Monk, wherever happiness and delight arise because of (physical) form, that is the satisfaction in (physical) form. That which is the transience, the pain, the mutability of (physical) form is (its) disadvantage. Whatever is the driving out,- the abandonment of desire and passion for (physical) form, that is freedom from (it). (And the same is true of the others)."

"But how (can) it be known and seen, bhante, that there is no lurking conceit of: 'I the doer, mine the deed', with regard to this mind-imbued body and all external manifestations?"

"Whatever is (physical) form in the past, the future, or the present, be it internal or external, gross or subtle, fair or foul, far or near – (that one must not think of) as mine, as me, as myself, (but) see it as it is with deepest wisdom. (And) whatever is feeling, perception, traits and tendencies, (and) consciousness (must be viewed similarly)."

At that point a thought occurred to a certain monk: "So, one gathers that (physical) form is not self, (nor) feeling, (nor) perception, (nor) traits and tendencies, (nor) consciousness. (Then) what self is affected by the deeds of (that which is) not self?"

Then the Lord, knowing the thought in the mind of that monk, addressed the monks, saying: "It is the case that some foolish man here, unknowing, ignorant, his mind in the grip of craving, may think to go beyond the Teacher's instruction. Monks, you have been trained by me to look for conditions here and there, in regard to one thing and another. What do you think – is (physical) form enduring or transient?"

"Transient, bhante."

"And that which is transient – is it painful or pleasant?"

"Painful, bhante."

"But is the transient, the painful, the mutable, fitly perceived thus: 'This is mine, I am this, this is myself'?"

"Not so, bhante."

"(And) feeling, perception, traits and tendencies, consciousness?"

"Transient, bhante."

"Wherefore, monks, seeing it thus, the informed disciple of the *ariyans* turns away from (physical) form, turns away (too) from feeling, perception, traits and tendencies, (and) consciousness. Turning away, he experiences detachment. Through detachment he becomes free. In freedom there is freedom's knowledge and he knows: 'Destroyed is birth, fulfilled the good life, done what was to be done, and there will be no more return to this world.' "

Thus spoke the Lord.

110

Minor Discourse at the Time of the Full Moon

20–24

Thus have I heard: once the Lord dwelt near Sāvatthī, at the Migāramātu Palace on the Eastern Campus. Now on the night of the full moon on the fifteenth, an observance day, the Lord was seated in the open, surrounded by a group of monks. Then, as the assembly became silent, (he) looked round and addressed (them), saying:

"Monks, is it possible for an evil man to know an evil man (for what he is)?"

"Not so, bhante."

"Agreed, monks. This cannot be, this is impossible. But is it possible for an evil man to know a good man (for what he is)?"

"Not so, bhante."

"Agreed, monks. This too cannot be, this is impossible. An evil man is consumed with evil states of mind, is companion to evil men, thinks like (one), speaks like (one), behaves like (one), shares (their) views, makes a gift like (one).

An evil man is faithless, unscrupulous, reckless, ill-informed, indolent, careless, unwise. Thus is the evil man consumed with evil states of mind.

Ascetics and brahmans (of evil thoughts and ways) are his friends and associates. Thus is the evil man companion to evil men.

He thinks and advises (so as to bring) harm to himself, harm to others, harm to both. Thus the evil man thinks and advises like an evil man.

He is a liar, a slanderer, an abuser, a driveller. Thus the evil man speaks like an evil man.

He is a taker of life, a thief, a libertine. Thus the evil man behaves like an evil man.

(Thinking): 'There is neither gift, nor offering, nor sacrifice, nor ripening and result of good deeds and bad; neither this world nor another; neither mother nor father, nor spontaneous uprising; no ascetics or brahmans living rightly, proceeding rightly, who make known this world and the next, having realised them through their own gnosis.' – thus does the evil man share the views of evil men.

He gives carelessly, not with his own hand, without esteem, discarding (what he no longer wants), regardless of the future. Thus an evil man makes a gift like an evil man.

Monks, that evil man, on the disintegration of the body at death, finds an existence (fitting) for evil men – purgatory or the bestial state.

(Now), is it possible for a good man to know a good man (for what he is)?"

"Yes, bhante."

"Agreed, monks, that is possible. But is it possible for a good man to know an evil man (for what he is)?"

"Yes, bhante."

"Agreed, monks. This too is possible.[1] Monks, the good man, on the disintegration of the body at death finds an existence (fitting) for good men – greatness in heaven, or greatness in the world of men."

Thus spoke the Lord.

1. A reverse statement follows for all the above points.

111

The Continuous

25–29

Thus have I heard: once the Lord dwelt near Sāvatthī in the Jeta Grove on Anāthapiṇḍika's campus. There (he) addressed the monks, saying:

"Monks, clever is Sāriputta. Of great and broad wisdom is Sāriputta. Of bright, swift, sharp, and penetrating wisdom is Sāriputta. For half a month Sāriputta enjoyed continuous insight into *dhamma*.

(Because of this), he reaches and experiences the first (level of) absorption, remote from worldly pursuits and unskilled states, and linked to thought and investigation, born of remoteness, joyful and happy. And those things which belong to the first (level of) absorption[1] are established by him continuously. Known to him they arise. Known to him they appear. Known to him (they) dissolve. Unattached, unrepelled by these states, not relying on them, not bound to them, freed and unharnessed from them, he experiences an unrestricted mind. He knows (that) there is a further outcome, (and) practises zealously.

Consequently, monks, from the suppression of thought and investigation, and with mind inwardly tranquillised and focused, Sāriputta reaches and experiences the second (level of) absorption, born of concentration, joyful, and happy. And those things which belong to the second (level of) absorption are established by him continuously. Known to him they arise. Known to him they appear. Known to him they dissolve. Unattached, unrepelled by these states, not relying on them, not bound to them, freed and unharnessed from them, he experiences an unrestricted mind. He knows (that) there is a further outcome, and practises zealously.

Consequently, monks, from the fading away of joy Sāriputta experiences equanimity, is mindful and lucid, and feels in his body that happiness described by the *ariyan*s. He reaches and experiences the third (level of) absorption. And those things which belong to the third (level of) absorption are established by him continuously. Known to him they arise. Known to him they appear. Known to him they dissolve. Unattached, unrepelled by these states, not relying on them, not bound to them, freed and unharnessed from them, he experiences an unrestricted mind. He knows (that) there is a further outcome, and practises zealously.

Consequently, monks, from the giving up of happiness and suffering, from the going down of former delights and sorrows, Sāriputta reaches and experiences the fourth (level of) absorption, entirely purified by equanimity and mindfulness. And those things which belong to the fourth (level of) absorption are established by him continuously. Known to him they arise.

Known to him they appear. Known to him they dissolve. Unattached, unrepelled by these states, not relying on them, not bound to them, freed and unharnessed from them, he experiences an unrestricted mind. He knows (that) there is a further outcome, and practises zealously.

Consequently, monks, by completely transcending the perception of (physical) form, by the waning of the perception of sensory response, and by disregarding the perception of diversity, Sāriputta reaches and experiences the realm of infinite space. And those things which belong to the realm of infinite space are established by him continuously. Known to him they arise. Known to him they appear. Known to him they dissolve. Unattached, unrepelled by these states, not relying on them, not bound to them, freed and unharnessed from them, he experiences an unrestricted mind. He knows (that) there is a further outcome, and practises zealously.

Consequently, monks, by completely transcending the realm of infinite space, Sāriputta reaches and experiences the realm of infinite consciousness. And those things which belong to the realm of infinite consciousness are established by him continuously. Known to him they arise. Known to him they appear. Known to him they dissolve. Unattached, unrepelled by these states, not relying on them, not bound to them, freed and unharnessed from them, he experiences an unrestricted mind. He knows (that) there is a further outcome, and practises zealously.

Consequently, monks, by completely transcending the realm of infinite consciousness, Sāriputta reaches and experiences the realm of nothingness. And those things which belong to the realm of nothingness are established by him continuously. Known to him they arise. Known to him they appear. Known to him they dissolve. Unattached, unrepelled by these states, not relying on them, not bound to them, freed and unharnessed from them, he experiences an unrestricted mind. He knows (that) there is a further outcome, and practises zealously.

Consequently, monks, by completely transcending the realm of nothingness, Sāriputta reaches and experiences the realm where there is neither perceiving nor not-perceiving. He emerges, mindful, from that (level of) attainment, regarding those states (that) are past, ceased, and changed (as such). Unattached, unrepelled by (them), not relying on them, not bound to them, freed and unharnessed from them, he experiences an unrestricted mind. He knows (that) there is a further outcome, and practises zealously.

Consequently, monks, by completely transcending the realm where there is neither perceiving nor not-perceiving, Sāriputta reaches and experiences the realm of the cessation of perception and feeling. And to him, through wisdom, comes the final rooting out of the distractions. He emerges, mindful, from that level of attainment, regarding the states (that) are past, ceased, and changed (as such). Unattached, unrepelled by (them), not relying on them, not bound to them, freed and unharnessed from them, he experiences an unrestricted mind. He knows (that) there is no further outcome.

Monks, one can rightly say (of Sāriputta that) his is the mastery, the perfection of *ariyan* conduct, *ariyan* concentration, *ariyan* wisdom, *ariyan* freedom.

Monks, one can rightly say (of Sāriputta that) he is the Lord's own son, born from his mouth, born of *dhamma,* inheriting *dhamma,* not the things of the flesh. Sāriputta, monks, truly keeps rolling the matchless wheel of *dhamma* set in motion by the Exemplar."

Thus spoke the Lord.

1. A list is given at this point in each paragraph, but many of the terms (such as feeling and attention) are obvious and the progression is best understood by reference to the attributes successively discarded

112

The Sixfold Cleansing

29–37

Thus have I heard: once the Lord dwelt near Sāvatthī in the Jeta Grove on Anāthapiṇḍika's campus. There (he) addressed the monks saying:

"Suppose a monk claims gnosis, saying: 'Destroyed is birth, fulfilled the good life, done what was to be done, and there is no further return to this world.' You should neither approve nor scorn (his) words. You should put the question: 'Friend, these four types of statement are correctly set forth by the Lord – to say of what is seen that it is seen, of what is heard that it is heard, of what is (otherwise) sensed (similarly), and of what is cognised that it is cognised. But in terms of these how has the venerable one known and seen his mind to be freed from the distractions, (and) without attachment?"

Monks, for an answer in accordance with *dhamma* (one might expect) this of a monk who has rooted out the distractions, fulfilled the life, done what was to be done, shed the burden, reached the goal, finally broken the thongs of existence, and is released by true knowledge: 'Friends, with regard to things seen there is neither attraction, nor revulsion, nor reliance on them, nor bondage to them (on my part). Free and unyoked from them I experience an unrestricted mind; (likewise) with things heard, (otherwise) sensed, and with things cognised.' Monks, you should approve and be pleased with the words of that monk. (Then) you should put a further question:

'Friend, these five embodiments of attachment are correctly set forth by the Lord – (physical) form, feeling, perception, traits and tendencies, and consciousness. But in terms of these how has the venerable one known and seen his mind to be freed from the distractions, (and) without attachment?'

Monks, for an answer in accordance with *dhamma* (one might expect) this of a monk who has rooted out the distractions: 'Friends, having found (physical) form to be weak, perishable, and comfortless, attachment to such forms being a compulsion, a predilection, an (innate) bias of the mind, I know freedom of mind in the rooting out, perishing, cessation, renunciation, and rejection of these (tendencies. And the same is true of feeling, perception, traits and tendencies, and consciousness.) 'Monks, you should approve and be pleased with the words of that monk. (Then) you should put a further question:

'Friend, these six elements are correctly set forth by the Lord – the solid, liquid, thermal, (and) aeriform elements, (together with) space and consciousness. But in terms of these how has the venerable one known and seen his mind to be freed from the distractions, (and) without attachment?'

Monks, for an answer in accordance with *dhamma* (one might expect) this of a monk who has rooted out the distractions: 'Friends, I approached solidity (and each of the other elements) as not self and self as not dependent on solidity, the dependence on and attachment to solidity being a compulsion, a predilection, an (innate) bias of the mind. I know freedom of mind in (its) rooting out, perishing, cessation, renunciation, and rejection.' Monks, you should approve and be pleased with the words of that monk. (Then) you should put a further question:

'Friend, six inner and outer sources (of experience) are correctly set forth by the Lord – the eye and shapes, the ear and sounds, the nose and odours, the tongue and savours, the body and physical contacts, thought and objects (of thought). But in terms of these how has the venerable one known and seen his mind to be freed from the distractions, (and) without attachment?'

Monks, for an answer in accordance with *dhamma* (one might expect) this of a monk who has rooted out the distractions: 'Whatever, friends, is resolve, passion, delight, or craving for the eye, for shape, for visual consciousness, for the visible – attachment to these being a compulsion, a predilection, an (innate) bias of the mind – I know freedom of mind in (its) rooting out, perishing, cessation, renunciation, and rejection. (And the same applies to the other sources of experience.) 'Monks, you should approve and be pleased with the words of that monk. (Then) you should put a further question:

'But in what way has the venerable one known and seen the lurking conceit of: "I the doer, mine the deed", in respect of this mind-imbued body and all external manifestations, to have been eradicated?' Monks, for an answer in accordance with *dhamma* (one might expect) this of a monk who has rooted out the distractions: 'Formerly, friends, as a householder I was ignorant, (but) the Exemplar or (his) disciple taught me *dhamma*. When I had heard *dhamma* I found conviction. (Then) I reflected (that) the household life is confined and dusty, open to the skies (that) of the ascetic, (and that) the living of the good life, wholly fulfilled, purified, and polished like a conch shell, is not easy for the householder. So, after a while, renouncing possessions small and great, (together with) my circle of relatives, I cut off hair and beard, donned the saffron robe, and went forth from home into homelessness.

Entering on the training and life of monks I lived having renounced the destruction of life, and with the stick thrown aside, weapon-free, scrupulous, compassionate, friendly and kind of heart towards all living things. Renouncing and abstaining from theft I lived with self become pure, taking and seeking only what was given. Renouncing depraved living mine was the good, the solitary life, divorced from dealings with women. Renouncing and abstaining from lies I was a truth-teller, at one with truth, trustworthy, dependable, honest with the world. Renouncing and abstaining from slander I was not one to proclaim what I had heard elsewhere (so as to sow) dissension. Hence I was a reconciler of discords, an effector of unions, a speaker of words (showing) fondness for peace, devotion to peace, pleasure in peace, and making for peace. Renouncing and abstaining from abuse I was a speaker of words that were gentle, agreeable, amiable, (appealing) to the heart, urbane, of service, and pleasant to the multitude. Renouncing and abstaining from drivel I was a speaker of words that were timely, factual, useful, on *dhamma* and discipline, worth remembering, that being timely were to the point, were purposeful and salutary.

I avoided injury to the growth of seeds and plants. I ate one meal a day, desisting from eating at night, or at a wrong time.[1] I was content with robes to protect the body, and with almsfood to sustain the stomach. Wherever I went I went conforming to (these principles), like a bird transporting its wings wherever it flies. Through possession of these *ariyan* principles I knew inwardly the happiness of being without fault.

Seeing a form with the eye I was not infatuated with the appearance nor with the attributes. For longing and distress, and wretched and unskilled states, may intrude on the eye that is wayward. Thus I proceeded with restraint, guarding the eye, undergoing the discipline of the eye, (and likewise of the other faculties). Through possession of the *ariyan* control of the faculties I knew, inwardly, unalloyed happiness. I was mindful and lucid – in coming and going; in looking forward and looking round; in bending and stretching; in carrying cloak or almsbowl, or robe; in eating, drinking, chewing, tasting; in excreting and urinating; in walking, standing, sitting, sleeping, waking, speaking, and remaining silent.

Possessed of the *ariyan* principles of mindfulness and lucidity I made solitary abode in the forest, at the root of a tree, on a rock, (or elsewhere). Returning from the almsround after the meal I would sit down cross-legged, with body upright, establishing mindfulness before me as my aim. Abandoning longing for the world I lived with a mind purged (thereof). Abandoning the taint of ill-will I lived without malevolence, and with friendship and mercy to all living things. Abandoning sloth and torpor I lived emptied thereof, perceiving light, mindful and lucid. Abandoning agitation and worry I lived with a mind inwardly calm and composed. Abandoning uncertainty I lived beyond doubt, untroubled as to skilful things.

From the abandonment of these five hindrances, which blemish the mind and are injurious to wisdom, remote from worldly pursuits and from unskilled states, I reached and experienced the first, second, third, and fourth (levels of) absorption. And so, with a mind that was firm, pure, clear, and unblemished; with impurities vanished – malleable, workable, stable, immovable – I directed (it) to knowledge of the rooting out of the distractions. I knew as it is: "This is suffering, this the origin of suffering, this the cessation of suffering, this the way leading to (that) cessation."

Having known and seen this, my mind was freed from the distraction of worldly pursuits, from the distraction of (continued) existence, from the distraction of ignorance. In freedom was freedom's knowledge – destroyed is birth, fulfilled the good life, done what was to be done, and there is no further return to this world. And so, friends, is it known and seen that the lurking conceit of: "I the doer, mine the deed", is eradicated in respect of this mind-imbued body and all external manifestations.'

Monks, you should approve, and be pleased with the words of that monk, saying: 'Yours is the gain, well it is for you, friend, that we see such an exponent of the good life as the venerable one.' "

Thus spoke the Lord.

1. Omitted – sections on abstinence from watching shows of various kinds, use of perfumes, "finery" and "high beds' plus non-acceptance of gold and silver, raw foodstuffs of various kinds, women, slaves, and various animals.

113

The Good Man

37–45

Thus have I heard: once the Lord dwelt near Sāvatthī in the Jeta Grove on Anāthapiṇḍika's campus. There (he) addressed the monks, saying:

"Monks, (suppose) an evil man has gone forth from a noble, great, rich, (or) eminent family.[1] Because of (that) he exalts himself, whilst disparaging others. (On the other hand) a good man reflects thus: 'It is not through (the nature of one's) family that states of greed, ill-will, and delusion come to an end. For even if one has not gone forth from (an important) family one can live in accordance with *dhamma,* and correctly, and hence be honoured and praised.' Making his object simply the practice, he neither exalts himself nor disparages others (on account of family). This is the *dhamma* of good men.

Further, monks, (suppose) an evil man is well-known, (or) well-informed, (or) an expert in the monastic rules, (or) a speaker on *dhamma,* (or) a forest-dweller, (or) a wearer of robes taken from a dust-heap, (or is pre-eminent in any other form of austerity). Because of (that) he exalts himself, whilst disparaging others. (On the other hand) a good man reflects thus: 'It is not through (any of these things) that states of greed, ill-will, and delusion come to an end. For even if one (is not any of these things) one can live in accordance with *dhamma,* and correctly, and hence be honoured and praised.' Making his object simply the practice, he neither exalts himself nor disparages others (in regard to the externals of the good life). This too is the *dhamma* of good men.

Further, monks, (suppose) an evil man reaches and experiences the first, second, third, and fourth (levels of) absorption, (and) the realms of infinite space, infinite consciousness, nothingness, (and) neither perceiving nor not-perceiving. Because of (that) he exalts himself, whilst disparaging others. (On the other hand) a good man reflects thus: 'Lack of desire even for (these states) is spoken of by the Lord. For whatever (people) imagine (them) to be, (they are) otherwise.' Making his object just the absence of desire, he neither exalts himself nor disparages others (in regard to spiritual attainments). This too is the *dhamma* of good men.

The good man, by completely transcending the realm of neither perceiving nor not-perceiving, reaches and experiences the realm of the cessation of perception and feeling. And (thus) to him through wisdom comes the final rooting out of the distractions. And that monk does not imagine that he is anything, or anywhere, or anywise."

Thus spoke the Lord.

1. This discourse is particularly condensed, since the factors listed at the beginning of this and subsequent paragraphs are given analogous sections each in the original. I have found it possible to group the various criteria into three, though a few trivial factors have been omitted altogether.

114

What Should and Should Not be Resorted To[1]

45–61

Thus have I heard: once the Lord dwelt near Sāvatthī in the Jeta Grove on Anāthapiṇḍika's campus. There (he) addressed the monks saying:

"Monks, I say that bodily, verbal, and mental activity (are each) of two sorts. What should and should not be resorted to – such (are the) alternative (forms. And) I say that the emergence of thought, the acquiring of perceptions, of views, and of one's (form of) existence is (also) of two sorts. What should and should not be resorted to – such (are the) alternative (forms.)"

At these words venerable Sāriputta said to the Lord:

"I understand the detailed meaning of what the Lord has (only) spoken of briefly like this. In so far as unskilled states increase and skilled states diminish when bodily activity is resorted to, that is the kind not to be followed. In so far as (the reverse is true), that is the kind to be followed.

(And) from resorting to what kind of bodily activity do unskilled states increase and skilled states diminish? Herein someone is a taker of life, cruel, with blood on his hands, set on injuring and overcoming. He is a thief, (and) whether gone to a village or to the forest, takes by stealth what is not given him. He is a libertine, (and) has intercourse with (girls) who are under the protection of mother, or father, or brother, or sister, or (some other) relative, or who have husbands, or even who are garlanded (for betrothal).

(And) from resorting to what kind of verbal activity do unskilled states increase and skilled states diminish? Herein someone is a liar. Called upon to testify, whether in an assembly, or in a crowd, or amid his relations, or in a guild or the king's court (he is told): 'Say what you know, friend.' Not knowing, he replies: 'I know.' Knowing, he replies: 'I do not know'. Not seeing, he replies: 'I saw.' Seeing, he replies: 'I did not see.' So a deliberate lie is told, either on his own account, or someone else's, or for some gain. Also he is a slanderer. Hearing (something) in one place, he relates it elsewhere to sow dissension. So he is a breaker of harmony and a bringer about of disagreements, delighting in discord, intent on discord, finding enjoyment (therein), with discord as the motive for his speech. He is abusive, and his words are insolent, hard, bitter towards others, cursing others, close to anger, not conducive to concentration. He is a driveller, of untimely speech, at variance with reality, an unprofitable speaker, a talker about what is not *dhamma*, not discipline. He speaks words that are not worth bearing in mind, that being untimely are pointless, undiscriminating, useless.

(And) from resorting to what kind of mental activity do unskilled states increase and skilled states diminish? Herein someone is covetous, thinking: 'Would that that which belongs to another might be mine.' He is maliciously disposed, corrupt in thought and character, thinking: 'Let these beings be killed, destroyed, exterminated, made to perish and not to be.'

(And) from resorting to what kind of emergence of thought (and) acquiring of perception, do unskilled states increase and skilled states diminish? Herein someone is covetous, living with a mind imbued with envy, (or is similarly affected by) malevolence, (or will to) injure.

(And) from resorting to what kind of acquisition of views do unskilled states increase and skilled states diminish? Herein someone thinks like this: 'There is neither gift, nor offering, nor sacrifice, nor ripening and result of good deeds and bad; neither this world nor another; neither mother nor father nor spontaneous uprising; no ascetics or brahmans living rightly, proceeding rightly, who make known this world and the next, having realised them through their own gnosis.'

(And) from resorting to what kind of acquisition of one's existence do unskilled states increase and skilled states diminish? The acquisition of one's existence that is injurious because of the imperfection of reproduction (is of such a nature).[2]

Thus do I understand the detailed meaning of that which the Lord has (only) spoken of briefly."

"It is well, Sāriputta, that you understand (the matter) thus. Sāriputta, I say that visible form, audible sound, (and cognisable odours, savours, sensations, and mental states) are (similarly) of two sorts, (namely those) which should and should not be resorted to.[3] (And the same applies to the acquisition of requisites, to the places where one may stay, and to the people with whom one may associate).

If all nobles, brahmans, merchants, (and) artisans; if the world with its *devas*, its *māra*s, its *brahmās*, its ascetics and brahmans, if the living universe with its *devas* and humans, were to understand this, the detailed meaning of that which I have (only) spoken of briefly, it would be for their wellbeing and happiness for many a day."

Thus spoke the Lord.

1. This discourse incorporates three of the main forms of repetition which this abridgement attempts to deal with. Of the various factors discussed several, e.g. bodily, verbal, and mental activity are described in the same way (serial repetitions). Hence, as elsewhere, I have telescoped the variables into the same paragraph so as not to repeat identical descriptions. The preferred conditions that are paired with each of those criticised, i.e. those for which skilled states increase, are also omitted, as the attached descriptions are merely the reverse of the ones for the paired terms (reverse repetitions). Finally Gotama confirms Sāriputta's expanded discussion verbatim. Cases like this, where something already stated is referred back to I have called "parenthetical repetitions".

2. Apparently not a reference to congenital defects.
3. No specific descriptions are attached to these remaining factors. They are merely indicated as subject to the general criteria referred to throughout.

115

The Manifold Elements

61–67

Thus have I heard: once the Lord dwelt near Sāvatthī in the Jeta Grove on Anāthapiṇḍika's campus. There (he) addressed the monks, saying:

"Monks, whatever fears, distress, (or) troubles arise – all arise for the foolish, just as flames from a house thatched with rushes or grass set fire to the upper stories.[1] There is neither fear, nor distress, nor trouble for the wise. So you must train yourselves thinking: 'By investigating we will become wise.' "

At these words venerable Ānanda said: "Bhante, how far can it be truly said that by investigating, a monk is wise?"

"From the time, Ānanda, when the monk is skilled as to the elements, skilled as to the sources (of experience), skilled as to cause and effect, and skilled as to the impossible."

"But how far can it be said, bhante, that a monk is skilled as to the elements?"

"Ānanda, there are these eighteen elements. The eye, shapes, and consciousness of seeing; the ear, sounds, and consciousness of hearing; the nose, odours, and consciousness of smelling; the tongue, flavours, and consciousness of taste; the body, physical contact, and physical sensation; the mind, (its) states, and consciousness of thinking. From the time when he knows and sees these it can truly be said (that) a monk is skilled as to the elements."

"But might there be another way by which (this) can truly be said?"

"There might, Ānanda. There are these six elements – the solid, liquid, thermal, and aeriform elements, (together with) space and consciousness. From the time when he knows and sees these it can truly be said (that) a monk is skilled as to the elements."

"But might there be another way by which (this) can truly be said?"

"There might, Ānanda. There are these six elements – pleasure and pain, happiness and unhappiness, equanimity and ignorance. From the time when he knows and sees these it can truly be said (that) a monk is skilled as to the elements."

"But might there be another way by which (this) can truly be said?"

"There might, Ānanda. There are these six elements – worldly pursuit and (its) absence, malevolence and benevolence, harming and non-harming. From the time when he knows and sees these it can truly be said (that) a monk is skilled as to the elements."

"But might there be another way by which (this) can truly be said?"

"There might, Ānanda. There are these three elements – worldly pursuits, form, and the formless. From the time when he knows and sees these it can truly be said (that) a monk is skilled as to the elements."

"But might there be another way by which (this) can truly be said?"

"There might, Ānanda. There are these two elements – the compounded and the uncompounded. From the time when he knows and sees these it can truly be said (that) a monk is skilled as to the elements."

"But, bhante, how far can it be said (that) the monk is skilled as to the sources (of experience)?"

"Ānanda, there are these six internal and external sources (of experience) – the eye and shape, the ear and sound, the nose and odour, the tongue and savour, the body and physical contact, the mind and (mental) objects. From the time when he knows and sees these, it can truly be said (that) a monk is skilled as to the elements."

"But, bhante, how far can it truly be said (that) a monk is skilled as to cause and effect?"

"As to that, Ānanda, a monk knows: '(Where) *that* is *this* comes to be. *That* having arisen, *this* arises. (Where) *that* is not *this* is not. From the stopping of *that* is the stopping of *this*. Namely, with ignorance as pre-condition, formative tendencies; with formative tendencies as pre-condition, consciousness; with consciousness as pre-condition, individuality and form; with individuality and form as pre-condition, the six sources (of experience); with the six sources (of experience) as pre-condition, (response to) a stimulus; with (response to) a stimulus as pre-condition, feeling; with feeling as pre-condition, craving; with craving as pre-condition, attachment; with attachment as pre-condition, (continued) existence; with (continued) existence as pre-condition, birth. With birth as pre-condition old age and death, grief and woe, pain, distress, and trouble (all) come into being. Such is the origin of suffering in its entirety.

But from the complete waning and ending of ignorance is the ending of formative tendencies; from the ending of formative tendencies the ending of consciousness; from the ending of consciousness the ending of individuality and form; from the ending of individuality and form the ending of the six sources (of experience); from the ending of the six sources (of experience) the ending of (response to) a stimulus; from the ending of (response to) a stimulus the ending of feeling; from the ending of feeling the ending of craving; from the ending of craving the ending of attachment; from the ending of attachment the ending of (continued) existence; from the ending of (continued) existence the ending of birth; from the ending of birth the ending of old age and death, grief and woe, pain, distress, and trouble. Such is the ending of suffering in its entirety.' At that point it can truly be said (that) a monk is skilled as to cause and effect."

"But, bhante, how far can it truly be said (that) a monk is skilled as to the impossible?"

"As to that, Ānanda, it is impossible, it cannot be, that a man of (right) view should treat any compounded thing as permanent, should treat any compounded state as happy, should treat any compounded thing as self.

It is impossible, it cannot be, that a man of (right) view should take his mother's life, his father's life, (or) with murderous intent spill the blood of an Exemplar. It is impossible, it cannot be, that one of (right) view should create schism in the Order, or proclaim another teacher. It is impossible, it cannot be, that from evil living in body, speech, or thought, an enjoyable result should emerge. It is impossible, it cannot be, that one of evil ways in body, speech, or thought should, from such an origin and condition come to a good destiny, a heaven world, on the disintegration of his body at death.[2]"

Thus spoke the Lord.

1. The metaphor is slightly modified and abbreviated.
2. Omitted impossibles – that two *buddha*s or two wheel-turning kings should arise simultaneously, or that an enlightened woman (or various grades of spirit) can be either.

116

At Isigili

68–71

(This discourse is little more than a catalogue of names of *buddha*s of earlier eras, and is omitted.)

117

The Great Forty

71–78

Thus have I heard: once the Lord dwelt near Sāvatthī in the Jeta Grove on Anāthapiṇḍika's campus. There (he) addressed the monks, saying:

"I will teach you the *ariyan* right concentration, monks, along with its causes and concomitants. (They are) right view, aim, speech, conduct, livelihood, effort, (and) mindfulness. Whatever focusing of the mind has these seven concomitants is called the *ariyan* right concentration.

Right view comes first. If one knows wrong view (as such) and right view (as such), that is one's right view. And what, monks, is right view? I say that (it) is twofold. There is right view imbued with the distractions (but) possessing virtue, which results in attachment. There is (also) right view that is *ariyan*, free of the distractions, sublime, a part of the Way.

And what is the right view that is imbued with the distractions? – that there is (result) of gift, offering, and sacrifice; that there is ripening and fruition for good deeds and bad; that there is this world and another world; that there is (benefit of serving) mother and father; that there are spontaneously arisen beings; that there are ascetics and brahmins living and proceeding rightly who make known this world and the next, having realised them through their own gnosis. Such is right view imbued with the distractions.

And what is right view freed from the distractions? Whatever is wisdom, the faculty and power of wisdom, the investigation of *dhamma* that is an element of enlightenment in one who, having cultivated the *ariyan* way, is of *ariyan* thought – that is right view freed from the distractions.

Whoever strives to be rid of wrong view and to bring about right view – that is his right effort. Mindful, he forsakes wrong view; mindful, he lives embracing right view. That is his right mindfulness. So these three things move round and engage with right view, namely right view, right effort, right mindfulness.

Right view comes first. If one knows wrong aims (as such) and right aims (as such), that is one's right view. And what is right aim? I say that (it) is twofold. There are right aims imbued with the distractions (but) possessing virtue, which result in attachment. There are (also) right aims that are *ariyan*, free of the distractions, sublime, a part of the Way.

And what is right aim that is imbued with the distractions? – the aim of renunciation, benevolence, harmlessness, is right aim imbued with the distractions.

And what is right aim that is free from the distractions? Whatever is reasoning and reflection, purpose, (and) speech, through the directing and focusing of the mind in one who, having cultivated the *ariyan* way, is of *ariyan* thought – that is right aim free from the distractions.

Whoever strives to be rid of wrong aims and to bring about right aims – that is his right effort. Mindful, he forsakes wrong aims; mindful, he lives embracing right aims. That is his right mindfulness. So these three things move round and engage with right view, namely right view, right effort, right mindfulness.

Right view comes first. If one knows wrong speech (as such) and right speech (as such), that is one's right view. And what is right speech? I say that (it) is twofold. There is right speech that is imbued with the distractions (but) possessing virtue, which results in attachment. There is (also) right speech that is *ariyan*, free of the distractions, sublime, a part of the Way.

And what is right speech imbued with the distractions? Abstention from lies, from slander, from abuse, from (idle) prattle – that is right speech imbued with the distractions.

And what is right speech free from the distractions? Whatever is abstention from the four deviant modes of speech in one who, having cultivated the *ariyan* way, is of *ariyan* thought – that is right speech free from the distractions.

Whoever strives to be rid of wrong speech and to bring about right speech – that is his right effort. Mindful, he forsakes wrong speech; mindful, he lives embracing right speech. That is his right mindfulness. So these three things move round and engage with right view, namely right view, right effort, right mindfulness.

Right view comes first. If one knows misconduct (as such) and right conduct (as such), that is one's right view. And what is right conduct? I say that (it) is twofold. There is right conduct that is imbued with the distractions (but) possessing virtue, that results in attachment. There is (also) right conduct that is *ariyan*, free from the distractions, sublime, a part of the Way.

And what is right conduct imbued with the distractions? Abstention from taking life, from theft. from dissolute living – that is the conduct that is imbued with the distractions.

And what is right conduct free from the distractions? Whatever is avoidance of the three deviant modes of conduct in one who, having cultivated the *ariyan* way, is of *ariyan* thought – that is right conduct, free from the distractions.

Whoever strives to be rid of misconduct and to bring about right conduct – that is his right effort. Mindful, he forsakes misconduct; mindful, he lives embracing right conduct. That is his right mindfulness. So these three things move round and engage with right view, namely right view, right effort, right mindfulness.

Right view comes first. If one knows wrong livelihood (as such) and right livelihood (as such), that is one's right view. And what is right livelihood? I say that (it) is twofold. There is right livelihood that is imbued with the distractions (but) possessing virtue, which results in attachment. There is (also) right livelihood that is *ariyan*, free from the distractions, sublime, a part of the Way.

And what is right livelihood imbued with the distractions? Abstention from fraud, begging-talk, prognostication, jugglery, profiteering, rapacity[1] – that is right livelihood imbued with the distractions.

And what is right livelihood free from the distractions? Whatever is avoidance of wrong livelihood in one who, having cultivated the *ariyan* way, is of *ariyan* thought – that is right livelihood free from the distractions.

Whoever strives to be rid of wrong livelihood and to bring about right livelihood – that is his right effort. Mindful, he forsakes wrong livelihood; mindful, he lives embracing right livelihood. That is his right mindfulness. So these three things move round and engage with right view, namely right view, right effort, right mindfulness.

Right view comes first. And how, monks, does right view come first? Right aim proceeds from right view; right speech from right aim; right conduct from right speech; right livelihood from right conduct; right effort from right livelihood; right mindfulness from right effort; right concentration from right mindfulness; true knowledge from right concentration; true freedom from true knowledge. Herein the trainee's progress has eight parts, the *arahant*'s ten.

Right view comes first. And how, monks, does right view come first? In one of right view the various evil states that arise from a condition of wrong view (and all other wrong approaches to life) are overcome, and the various skilled states with right view as their pre-condition progress to fulfilment.

So, monks, there are twenty skilful aspects and twenty unskilful aspects. The discourse on the great forty (now) set going is not to be rolled back by ascetic, or brahman, or deva, or *māra*, or brahmā, or by anyone in the world.[2]"

Thus spoke the Lord.

1. This list occurs in the previous para. in the original. I have transposed it to the same position as for the other elements of the Way. The exact meaning of several of these terms is very arguable. Horner has "trickery, cajolery, insinuating, dissembling, rapacity".
2. The discourse ends with a rambling comment on those who reject or approve the foregoing. This adds virtually nothing of substance and has been omitted.

118

Mindfulness of Breathing In and Out

78–88

Thus have I heard: once the Lord dwelt near Sāvatthī at the Migāramātu Palace on the Eastern Campus, along with many well-known elders and disciples – venerable Sāriputta, Moggallāna, Kassapa, Kaccāna, Koṭṭhita, Anuruddha, Revata, Ānanda, (and various others). The monks who were elders advised and instructed the novice monks, (who) were conscious of excellent progress. Now, on the night of the full moon, an observance day, after the Pavāraṇā (ceremony), the Lord was seated in the open, surrounded by a group of monks. As the assembly became silent (he) looked round and addressed them, saying:

"I am well content with this course of training, monks. So make abundant effort to attain the unattained, to find the undiscovered, to realise the unrealised. Now I shall wait here in Sāvatthī for the Komudī (festival) in the fourth month." Monks dwelling in the countryside heard (of the Lord's presence there and) visited Sāvatthī to see the Lord.

(Then, once more) on an observance day, the Lord addressed the monks, saying:

"This assembly is not given to (idle) prattle, monks. It is established in the pure essence (of things). An Order of monks such as this is an assembly worthy of veneration, of hospitality, of gifts, of salutation with joined palms, (and to be seen as) an unsurpassed field of merit for the world. (It) is an assembly to which, if a little is given, it becomes much, (and) if much is given it becomes even more. (It) is an assembly seldom seen in the world. (It) is an assembly worth going many a mile[1] to see, foodbag on shoulder.

There are monks in this Order who are *arahants*, with the distractions rooted out, fulfilled ones, who have done what was to be done, who have shed the burden, reached their goal, finally broken the thongs of existence, (and are) released by true knowledge. There are monks in this Order for whom the five fetters that bind to the worldly condition are entirely done away with, who are of spontaneous uprising, finding final *nibbāna* hereafter (and) returning no more to this world. There are monks in this Order for whom the three fetters are done away with, and who, with passion, ill-will, and delusion vanished, returning once to this world, will make an end of suffering. There are monks in this Order for whom the three fetters are done away with, enterers of the stream (of *dhamma*), not on the road to ruin, assured, proceeding towards enlightenment. There are monks in this Order who live given over to cultivation of the four applications of mindfulness, the four right exertions, the four bases of psychic power, the five controlling faculties, the five powers, the seven aspects of enlightenment, the *ariyan* eightfold path, to goodwill, compassion, gladness, and equanimity. There are monks in this assembly given over to cultivating (meditation on) things unpleasant, on the perception of transience, (and) on breathing in and out.

Mindfulness of breathing in and out, monks, if developed and made much of, is of great fruit and profit. (It) brings to fulfilment the four applications of mindfulness.[2] And how is (it) developed and made much of? As to that, a monk is gone to the forest, or the root of a tree, or an empty place, (where he) sits down cross-legged, with body upright, establishing mindfulness before him as his aim. Mindful, he breathes out; mindful, he breathes in. Exhaling a long breath, he is aware (of it). Inhaling a long breath, he is aware (of it). Exhaling a short breath, he is aware (of it). Inhaling a short breath, he is aware (of it). He trains himself, thinking: 'I will breath out (then) in, experiencing the whole body'. Or he trains himself, thinking: 'I will breath out then in, pacifying the body's tendencies, (or) experiencing joy, (or) experiencing happiness, (or) experiencing the mind's tendencies, (or) pacifying the mind's tendencies, (or) experiencing the mind, (or) rejoicing in the mind, (or) composing the mind, (or) emancipating the mind, (or) observing transience, (or) observing dispassion, (or) observing cessation, (or) observing renunciation.' Monks, mindfulness of breathing in and out, if developed (and) made much of, is of great fruit and great profit.

And how, (in these ways), are the four applications of mindfulness brought to fulfilment? When a monk, exhaling or inhaling a long (or) a short breath, is aware (of it and) trains thus experiencing the whole body, or pacifying the body's tendencies – at that time, observing the body in the body, he lives zealous, lucid, and mindful, for the giving up of longing and distress in regard to the world. I declare, monks, that in terms of bodies this is a body, namely breathing in and out.

When a monk trains (thus), experiencing joy, (or) experiencing happiness, (or) experiencing the mind's tendencies, (or) pacifying the mind's tendencies – at that time, observing feeling in feeling, he lives zealous, lucid, and mindful, for the giving up of longing and distress with regard to the world. I declare, monks, that in terms of feelings this is a feeling, namely proper attention to breathing in and out.

When a monk trains (thus), experiencing the mind, rejoicing in the mind, composing the mind, emancipating the mind – at that time, observing the mind in the mind, he lives zealous, lucid, and mindful, for the giving up of longing and distress with regard to the world. I declare, monks, that cultivation of breathing in and out is not for the unmindful or inattentive.

When a monk trains (thus), observing transience, equanimity, cessation, (or) renunciation – at that time, observing phenomena in phenomena, he lives zealous, lucid, and mindful, for the giving up of longing and distress with regard to the world. (In achieving this) through wisdom he is one who contemplates properly. Thus developed, thus made much of, breathing in and out brings to fulfilment the four applications of mindfulness.

And how do the four applications of mindfulness bring to fulfilment the seven aspects of enlightenment? When a monk lives observing the body in the body, zealous, lucid, and mindful, for the giving up of longing and distress with regard to the world – at that time unclouded mindfulness is established, developed, and consummated in him.[3] Living mindfully he examines, investigates, produces something for enquiry by means of wisdom. (In) examining something by means of wisdom active exertion is aroused. From the arousal of exertion disinterested joy arises. The body and mind of the one who is joyful is pacified. When the body and mind of one who is joyful is pacified serenity is aroused. In one whose body is pacified and happy the mind is concentrated. (In achieving) such mental composure (the monk) contemplates properly, (and thereby) the aspect of enlightenment that is detachment is aroused, developed, consummated. And so, monks, do the four applications of mindfulness bring to fulfilment the seven aspects of enlightenment.

And how, monks, do the seven aspects of enlightenment bring freedom (gained) through knowledge to fulfilment? As to that, the monk develops (each) aspect of enlightenment with dependence on seclusion, detachment, and cessation, terminating in abandonment."

Thus spoke the Lord.

1. The unit of distance employed does not equate with a mile but the sense is the same i.e. a long way.
2. These in turn promote the seven aspects of enlightenment, as explained subsequently.
3. The three verbs are repeated for each aspect.

119

Mindfulness of Body

88–99

Thus have I heard: once the Lord dwelt near Sāvatthī in the Jeta Grove on Anāthapiṇḍika's campus. Then there arose this conversation among a number of monks returned from the almsround after the meal, and seated together in the assembly hall:

"How strange and wonderful, friends, that mindfulness of body, when developed and made much of, is of great fruit and profit, as described by the Lord who has known and seen." But this conversation remained unfinished, for the Lord, returning from seclusion towards evening, came to the assembly hall and sat down in the place prepared (for him). (Then he) addressed (them), saying:

"What have you been discussing, monks, as you sat here together?" (And they told him.)

"How then, monks, is mindfulness of body, when developed and much practised of great fruit and profit? As to that, a monk is gone to the forest, or to the root of a tree, or an empty place, (where he) sits down cross-legged with body upright, establishing mindfulness before him as his aim. Mindful, he breathes out; mindful, he breathes in. Exhaling a long breath, he is aware (of it). Inhaling a long breath, he is aware (of it). Exhaling a short breath, he is aware (of it). Inhaling a short breath, he is aware (of it). He trains himself, thinking: 'I will breath out (then in), experiencing the whole body.' Or he trains himself, thinking: 'I will breath out then in, pacifying the body's tendencies.'

Further, a monk, when walking, is aware (of it); when standing still, is aware (of it); when seated, is aware (of it); when lying down, is aware (of it). Hence, in whatever way the body is disposed he knows it to be so.

A monk is lucid in (his) comings and goings; in looking forward and looking round; in bending and stretching; in carrying cloak, or almsbowl, or robe; in eating and drinking, chewing and tasting; in excreting and urinating; in walking, standing, sitting, sleeping, waking, speaking, and keeping silent.

A monk contemplates this very body, upwards from the soles of the feet, downwards from the hair of the head, encased by skin and full of various impurities, thinking: 'There is in this body hair of head and of body, nails, teeth, skin, flesh, muscles, bones, marrow, kidneys, heart, liver, membranes, spleen, lungs, intestines, mesentery, stomach, excrement, bile, phlegm, pus, blood, sweat, fat, tears, grease, saliva, mucus, synovic fluid, urine'. Just like a double-mouthed provision bag, full of various kinds of grain such as rice, paddy, kidney-beans, sesame, (and so on),[1] (which) a man might contemplate on pouring them out – so does a monk contemplate this very body, upwards from the soles of the feet, downwards from the hair of the head.

A monk contemplates this very body as regards its placement and control in terms of the elements, thinking: 'There (are) in this body solid, liquid, thermal, and aeriform elements.' Just as a skilled butcher, having slaughtered a cow, might sit at the crossroads chopping it into pieces – so does a monk contemplate this very body as regards its placement and control in terms of the elements.

And, just as a monk might see a corpse; one, two, or three days dead; thrown away in a cemetery; swollen, discoloured, and festering – so he focuses on this very body, thinking: 'This body, too, is such a thing, has such a nature, cannot escape such (an end).'[1]

A monk, aloof from worldly pursuits and from unskilled states, reaches and experiences the first (level of) absorption, linked to thought and investigation, born of remoteness, joyful, and happy[2] – just as a skilled bath attendant might knead bath-powder in a bronze vessel, whilst sprinkling it repeatedly with water (until it is saturated).

From the suppression of thought and investigation, and with mind inwardly tranquillised and focused, (he) reaches and experiences the second (level of) absorption. He suffuses this very body with the joy and happiness born of concentration – like a lake with water welling up (from below), but with no inlets from (any) side.

From the fading away of joy (he) experiences equanimity, is mindful and lucid, and feels in his body that happiness described by the *ariyans*. He reaches and experiences the third (level of) absorption. He suffuses this very body with the happiness that is without joy – just as in a pond lotuses (of many colours) are born in the water, grown in the water, their limbs immersed in (it), nourished by (it), and from top to root are drenched by (it).

From the giving up of pleasure and pain, from the going down of former delight and sorrow, (he) reaches and experiences the fourth (level of) absorption, purified by equanimity and mindfulness. He sits having pervaded this very body with a mind that is clear and pure – just like a man sitting swathed in white clothing right to the head.

The worldly memories and aspirations of one who has lived diligent, zealous, and resolute in (all these ways) are given up and, being rid of them, the mind is inwardly settled, composed, focused, and concentrated. So it is that, (in all these ways), a monk cultivates mindfulness of body.

Monks, the skilled states conducive to knowledge are present in whoever has developed and made much of mindfulness of body – like streams flowing into an ocean. (But) Māra finds the opportunity and the means (to disturb) whoever (is lacking) – just as a man might drop a heavy round stone in a wet heap of clay.

Monks, anyone at all who cultivates and makes much of mindfulness of body turns his mind, through the realisation of gnosis to whatever state may be (so realised), and (thereby) achieves the role of a witness in this or that realm of mindfulness.

These ten advantages are to be expected from practising, cultivating, and making much of mindfulness of body. One quells likes and dislikes. One overcomes fear and dismay. One endures the contact of heat and cold, hunger and thirst, gadfly and mosquito, wind and sun, crawling things, disreputable and unwelcome ways of speaking. One is of a character to bear the onset of feelings that are painful, disagreeable, deadly. At will, and without difficulty or trouble, one obtains the four (levels of) absorption that are dependent on clearest consciousness, and are the abode of happiness in this life. One realises the diverse forms of psychic power.[3] With the purified divine ear transcending the human one hears sounds of both kinds, divine and human, far and near. One's mind grasps and comprehends that of other beings and people – one knows the hating, the deluded, the disturbed mind, the mind become great, the unexcelled mind, the composed mind, the mind that is freed. One recalls a variety of previous existences together with their attributes and detail. With the purified divine eye transcending the human one beholds beings passing away, and re-emerging in accordance with their deeds. Such, monks, are the ten advantages to be expected from practising, cultivating, and making much of mindfulness of body."

Thus spoke the Lord.

1. Three ensuing sections on this theme are omitted. They refer to seeing the corpse eaten by wild animals, to a skeleton, and to a heap of bones.
2. Many parables are used from this point on to characterise each state. I have abbreviated some and omitted others.
3. Detail of psychic powers given in 12.

120

On Arising Through (Mental) Characteristics

99–103

Thus have I heard: once the Lord dwelt near Sāvatthī in the Jeta Grove on Anāthapiṇḍika's campus. There (he) addressed the monks, saying:

"A monk is endowed with faith, with (right) conduct, with the Word, with renunciation, with wisdom. It occurs to him: 'O that I might arise in the company of wealthy nobles, brahmans, or merchants; or with *devas* or *brahmās*[1] on the breaking up of the body at death.' He addresses his mind to that, fixes his attention on it, wills it. Those (mental) characteristics and projections, (when) developed and made much of, are conducive to arising (in those places).

Further, a monk is endowed with faith, with (right) conduct, with the Word, with renunciation, with wisdom. It occurs to him: 'O that, with the distractions rooted out, I might reach and experience mental freedom and the freedom of wisdom that are undistracted, having realised them through my own gnosis in this life.' (And he brings that about.) That monk arises nowhere and in no place."

Thus spoke the Lord.

1. Various grades of celestial beings and their attractions are mentioned.

121

Minor Discourse on Emptiness

104–109

Thus have I heard: once the Lord dwelt near Sāvatthī at the Migāramātu Palace on the Eastern Campus. Then venerable Ānanda, emerging from seclusion towards evening, approached the Lord, saluted (him), and sat down at one side. Said Ānanda:

"There was an occasion when the Lord dwelt among the Sakyans (in a) town called Nagaraka. There I heard the Lord say: 'Ānanda, through dwelling on emptiness I now experience (its) abundance.' Did I hear and grasp this aright, bhante?"

"Indeed you did hear and grasp this aright, Ānanda. And now, too, I experience abundance through dwelling on emptiness, as formerly. As this Migāramātu Palace is empty of elephants, cows, horses, and mares; empty of gold and silver; empty of gatherings of men and women; and there is only this that is not emptiness, namely solitude rooted in the Order of monks – even so, Ānanda, a monk, ignoring perception of the village and of people, pays attention to solitude rooted in perception of the forest. His mind is pleased and satisfied, settled and freed by perception of the forest. He is aware: 'Such cares as might be derived from perception of the village and of people do not exist here. And there are only such cares as derive from solitude rooted in perception of the forest.' He is aware: 'This perceiving is empty of the perception of the village and of people. And only that which is solitude derived from perception of the forest is not emptiness.' So he regards it as empty of what is not there. But, as to what remains, he is aware: 'That being, this is.' This then comes to be a true, uncorrupt, and pure realisation of emptiness for him. Further, Ānanda, a monk, ignoring perception of the forest, pays attention to solitude rooted in perception of the earth. His mind is pleased and satisfied, settled and freed by perception of the earth – like a bull-hide well stretched by means of a hundred pegs, its strength subjugated. Even so, a monk, ignoring all upon this earth – highland and lowland; hard-to cross rivers and swamps; (plants) with stakes and thorns; mountains and inaccessible places – pays attention to solitude rooted in (just) perception of the earth. He is aware: 'Such cares as might be derived from perception of the forest do not exist here. And there are only such cares as derive from solitude rooted in perception of the earth.' He is aware: 'This perceiving is empty of the perception of the forest. And only that which is solitude derived from perception of the earth is not emptiness.' So he regards it as empty of what is not there. But, as to what remains, he is aware: 'That being, this is.' This then comes to be a true, uncorrupt, and pure realisation of emptiness for him.

A monk, ignoring perception of the earth, pays attention to solitude rooted in perception of the realm of infinite space; ignoring perception of the realm of infinite space pays attention to solitude rooted in perception of the realm of infinite consciousness; ignoring perception of the realm of infinite consciousness, pays attention to solitude rooted in perception of the realm of nothingness; ignoring perception of the realm of nothingness, pays attention to solitude rooted in perception of the realm of neither perceiving nor not-perceiving.

Further, a monk, ignoring perception of the realm of neither perceiving nor not-perceiving, pays attention to solitude rooted in the concentration of mind that is without attributes. His mind is pleased and satisfied, settled and composed (in that) concentration. He is aware: 'Such cares as might be derived from perception of the realm of neither perceiving nor not-perceiving do not exist here. And there are only such cares as derive from the six sources (of experience which are) dependent on the life-principle and rooted in this body.' He is aware: 'This perceiving is empty of the perception of the realm of neither perceiving nor not-perceiving. And only that which is the six sources (of experience), dependent on the life principle and rooted in this body, is not emptiness.' So he regards it as empty of what is not there. But, as to what remains, he is aware: 'That being, this is.' This then comes to be a true, uncorrupt, and pure realisation of emptiness for him.

And again (he) is aware: 'This concentration of mind that is devoid of attributes is prepared and planned. But whatever is prepared and planned is transient, a thing (bound) to (come to an) end.' Knowing and seeing this, his mind is freed from the distractions – from the distraction(s) of worldly pursuits, (continued) existence, (and) ignorance. In freedom is freedom's knowledge, and he knows: 'Destroyed is birth, fulfilled the good life, done what was to be done, and (there is) no further return to this world.' He is aware: 'Such cares as are rooted in the distraction(s) of worldly pursuits, (continued) existence, and ignorance do not exist here. And there are only such distractions as derive from the six sources (of experience), dependent on the life-principle and rooted in this body.' He is aware: 'This perceiving is empty of distractions. And only that which is the six sources (of experience) dependent on the life principle and rooted in this body is not emptiness.' So he regards it as empty of what is not there. But, as to what remains, he is aware: 'That being, this is.' This then comes to be a true, uncorrupt, and pure realisation of emptiness for him.

Ānanda, all those ascetics and brahmans who, throughout the past, reached and experienced (such) emptiness, who in the fullness of future time will (do so), or are now (doing so) experience just this emptiness. This is how you (too) must train yourself."

Thus spoke the Lord.

122

Major Discourse on Emptiness

109–118

Thus have I heard: once the Lord dwelt among the Sakyans on Nigrodha's campus at Kapilavatthu. Then, dressing at an early hour and taking bowl and robe, (he) went into Kapilavatthu for almsfood. Returning from the almsround after the meal, he approached the dwelling of the Sakyan Kāḷakhemaka for the afternoon rest. Now at that time many lodgings were prepared in (this) dwelling. The Lord saw (these) and wondered: "Are many monks staying here?"

Now at that time venerable Ānanda, along with many monks, was making robes in the dwelling of Ghaṭāya the Sakyan. And the Lord, emerging from seclusion towards evening, went there, sat down, and addressed venerable Ānanda, saying:

"Many lodgings are prepared in the dwelling of Kāḷakhemaka the Sakyan, Ānanda. Are many monks staying there?"

"(Yes), bhante. It is the time when our robe-making takes place."

"Ānanda, a monk does not excel who takes pleasure in (the company of) his own (or any other) group. Indeed it cannot be that (such) a monk, at will, and without difficulty or trouble, should obtain the happiness of renunciation, or seclusion, or calm, or enlightenment. (Nor) will (he) reach and experience freedom of mind, (whether it be) temporal and pleasant, or timeless and sure. But this may come about – that a monk who dwells alone, remote from the multitude, may be expected (to do so). Ānanda, I see not a single (material) form wherein is (vested) delight and fondness, that will not give rise to grief and woe, pain, distress, and trouble, from its liability to change and become otherwise.

However this experience is fully understood by the Exemplar, namely the reaching and experiencing of inner emptiness through ignoring every attribute. And if, as the Exemplar abides in (it), he is approached by monks and nuns, by male and female lay-followers – then, with a mind entirely inclined towards detachment, withdrawn, devoted to renunciation, and with the basis of the distractions completely obliterated – his talk is confined to encouragement.[1]

So, if a monk should wish (to) reach and experience inner emptiness, Ānanda, (he) should settle, calm, focus, and concentrate his mind inwardly. And how does a monk (achieve this)? As to that, (he) reaches and experiences the first, second, third, (and) fourth (levels) of absorption. In this way a monk settles, calms, focuses, and concentrates his mind inwardly.

He pays attention to inner emptiness, (but perhaps) his mind is not satisfied, purified, settled, nor freed inwardly (thereby). That being so, Ānanda, the monk is aware (of it). He pays attention to external emptiness. He pays attention to internal and external emptiness. He pays attention to imperturbability, (but perhaps) his mind is not satisfied, purified, settled, or freed by reference to imperturbability. That being so, Ānanda, the monk is aware (of it). He should settle, calm, focus, and concentrate his mind on just that earlier attribute of concentration. He pays attention to inner emptiness. His mind is (now) pleased, satisfied, settled, and freed. That being so, Ānanda, the monk is aware (of it). He (once more) pays attention to inner emptiness, (then) to external emptiness, (then) to internal and external emptiness, (then) to imperturbability. His mind is (now) satisfied, purified, settled, and freed (thereby). That being so, Ānanda, the monk is aware (of it).

If, in the course of that experience, the monk turns his mind to pacing up and down he (does so with the thought): 'Whilst I walk up and down like this, longing and distress, wretched and unskilled states, shall not intrude upon me.' So he is clearly aware of that.

If, in the course of (any of these experiences), the monk turns his mind to speaking, he (does so with the thought): 'I will not converse in ways that are base, common, vulgar, *unariyan*, unprofitable; that are unconnected with disenchantment, dispassion, calm, gnosis, cessation, and enlightenment, or are not conducive to *nibbāna* – namely about kings, robbers (and so on).' So he is clearly aware of that.

If, in the course of (any of these experiences), the monk turns his mind to thinking, he (does so with the thought): 'I will not think in ways that are base, common, vulgar, *unariyan*, unprofitable; that are unconnected with disenchantment, dispassion, calm, gnosis, cessation, and enlightenment, or are not conducive to *nibbāna* – (those linked to) worldly pursuits, malevolence, or harming.' So he is clearly aware of that.

Ānanda, there are these five strands of worldly pursuit – visible forms that are pleasing, welcome, enticing, voluptuous, pleasure-laden, exciting; (and sounds, odours, savours, and sensations of a similar nature). In this connection a monk should continually consider his own mind, asking: 'Does any predilection arise in my mind for this or that realm of the five strands of worldly pursuit.' If, on consideration, (he) is aware (that there does, then he knows): 'That which is desire and passion in me for this or that realm of the five strands of worldly pursuit has not been abandoned.' So he is clearly aware of that.

Ānanda, there are these five embodiments of attachment. As to these, they are to be destroyed through a monk's observing their waxing and waning (thus): 'Here is a (physical) form, here (its) emergence, here (its) disappearance. Here is a feeling, here (its) emergence, here (its) disappearance. Here is a perception, here (its) emergence, here (its) disappearance. Here is a trait or tendency, here (its) emergence, here (its) disappearance.

Here is a (manifestation of) consciousness, here (its) emergence, here (its) disappearance.' In this observation of the waxing and waning of the five embodiments of attachment is his abandonment of any conceit of: 'I am.' That being so, the monk is aware (of it). These *ariyan* states, Ānanda, concerned with entrance to what is wholly skilled, are supermundane, inaccessible to the Malign One.

Ānanda, it is not fitting that a disciple should follow a teacher for the sake of an exposition of discourses in prose and verse. Why so? Because for a long time (such) things have been heard, learnt by heart, spoken, mentally scrutinised, (and) well worked through by considered theory. But the talk that is austere, a help to opening up the mind, conducive to disenchantment, dispassion, cessation, calm, gnosis, enlightenment, *nibbāna* – such as talk of frugality, contentment, solitude, aloofness, the generation of energy, (right) conduct, concentration, wisdom, freedom, (and) the comprehension and vision of freedom – for talk of that kind it is fitting that a disciple should follow a teacher, even to the point of shadowing[2] him.

(However), Ānanda, this being so, there is misfortune for a teacher, for a pupil, for a liver of the good life. And how is there misfortune for a teacher? As to that some teacher resorts to a solitary abode in a forest, at the root of a tree, on a rock, in a glen, in a mountain cave, a cemetery, a woodland grove, in the open, or on a heap of straw. While he is living in such seclusion brahmans and householders, townspeople and country people, crowd in on him. (When this happens) he becomes infatuated, he conceives desire, he becomes envious, and reverts to (worldly) abundance. Ānanda, this is what is meant by an unfortunate teacher. Because of (it) wretched and unskilled states afflict him, (states) tending to corruption and continued (unhappy) existence, states that are fearful, resulting in suffering and future birth, decay, and death. Such is the misfortune of a teacher.

And how is there misfortune for a pupil? As to that, the teacher's follower, devoting himself to detachment, (imitates the teacher). While he is living in such seclusion (he, too, is accosted by various people, and he, too, reverts to worldly abundance). Such is the misfortune of a pupil.

And how is there misfortune for a liver of the good life? As to that, an exemplar arises in the world, *arahant*, truly enlightened, complete in knowledge and conduct, adept, seer of worlds, matchless charioteer of men to be tamed., teacher of *devas* and men, *buddha* and lord. He resorts to a solitary abode. While he is living in such seclusion (various people) crowd in on him. (When this happens) he does not become infatuated, or conceive desire, or become envious, and does not revert to (worldly) abundance. However, a disciple of this teacher, devoted to aloofness, (imitates the teacher). While he is living in seclusion (he in turn is accosted by brahmans and householders, and others). He become infatuated, he conceives desire, he becomes envious, and reverts to (worldly) abundance. Ānanda, this is what is meant by an unfortunate liver of the good life. But this misfortune is productive of more suffering, and is more severe in its result than (that which befalls other) teachers or (their) pupils. And it leads to ruin.

So treat me with friendship, Ānanda, not with hostility, and that will be for your wellbeing and happiness for many a day. And how do disciples treat a teacher (thus)? As to that, a teacher teaches *dhamma* to disciples, compassionate and seeking their welfare. And his disciples listen, lend an ear, prepare their minds for knowledge and, undeviating, do not stray from the teacher's instruction. Even so do disciples treat a teacher with friendship, not with hostility. (Do likewise), Ānanda, and there will be wellbeing and happiness for you for many a day. And I will not deal with you like a potter with an unbaked (vessel) which is not fully dry. I will speak constantly reproving, constantly cleansing. What belongs to the essence[3] will endure."

1. Horner draws attention to ambiguity in this passage, since the word translated encouragement may also mean dismissal. The possible inference is that he addresses them briefly, giving encouragement only.
2. Horner has, "even though he is being repulsed", but PTSD indicates that the relevant verb normally refers to harnessing or yoking to something.
3. "essence" here translates a word which refers to the pith, or hardest part of a tree. The assumed meaning is that the truest part of the disciple will survive the training.

123

Strange and Wonderful Attributes

118–124

Thus have I heard: once the Lord dwelt near Sāvatthī in the Jeta Grove on Anāthapiṇḍika's campus. Then there arose this conversation among the monks as they were seated together in the assembly-hall, having returned from the almsround after the meal:

"Strange, friends, wonderful, is the great power and majesty of the Exemplar, in that concerning earlier *buddhas* who are in final *nibbāna*, their obstacles and paths terminated, their rounds (of existence) finished, all suffering spent – (he) should know (that their) births, names, lineages, conduct, mental states, wisdom, attainments, and freedom were thus (and thus)."

At these words venerable Ānanda said to (them): "Wonderful indeed are exemplars, and possessed of wonderful attributes." Such was the conversation between the monks that was interrupted (as) the Lord, emerging from seclusion towards evening, came into the assembly-hall and sat down on the place prepared (for him. Then he) addressed the monks, saying:

"What were you discussing as you sat here together?" (And they told him.) Whereupon the Lord addressed venerable Ānanda, saying: "Then bring to mind in greater measure the wonderful and remarkable attributes of an exemplar, Ānanda.[1]"

"In the Lord's presence I have heard and learnt (how) the *bodhisatta* arose, mindful and lucid, in the (heaven of) the Tusita group; (how he) remained (there) for a lifetime; (and how), mindful and lucid, (he) entered the mother's womb, having passed out of (that heaven. Then) a boundless and noble radiance beyond the majesty of the *devas* manifested itself in the world with its *devas*, *māras*, and *brahmās*, its ascetics and brahmans, and in the living universe with its *devas* and humans. And even those limbos between worlds, dark, opaque, and black, where even the sun and moon, for all their power and majesty, do not penetrate – there, too, (it) was evident. And those beings that had arisen there perceived one another (and knew of one another's existence). And this ten-thousand-world-system shook, trembled, and was agitated.

When the *bodhisatta* has entered the mother's womb four sons of *devas* come to her so as to protect the four quarters, saying: 'Let neither human nor non-human, nor any (being) whatever, annoy the *bodhisatta* or (his) mother'.

The *bodhisatta's* mother, (at this time), is virtuous by nature, shunning the destruction of life, theft, dissolute living, lies, (and all) intoxicants productive of indolence. There is no thought (in her) of the five strands of worldly pursuit in relation to men. (At this time she, otherwise) possessed of the five strands of worldly pursuit, diverts herself (with them. She) incurs no illness, being at ease through a body that does not weary. And (she) sees the *bodhisatta* leaving the womb, with perfect limbs and enhanced[2] faculties. It is like a lapis-lazuli, bright, noble, well-cut in eight facets, which might be strung on a thread – blue, yellow, red, white, or orange. And a man possessed of eyes might take it in his hand (and be aware of all this). Just so the *bodhisatta's* mother sees (him) leaving the womb, with perfect limbs and enhanced faculties.

Whereas other women give birth after shelter of the foetus in the womb for nine or ten months, the *bodhisatta's* mother (does so after) exactly ten months. (And) whilst other women give birth sitting or lying down, (she does so) standing.

When the *bodhisatta* issues forth from the womb *devas* receive him first, humans afterwards. (He) does not reach the ground. The four sons of *devas*, having caught him, place him before his mother, saying: 'Be uplifted, lady. The son you have gained is of great authority.'

(He) issues forth clean, unstained by fluid, phlegm, blood, or any impurity. It is like a precious stone set in cloth of Bārāṇasi. The cloth does not soil the precious stone, nor the precious stone the cloth. Why so? – both are clean, (and) likewise (the *bodhisatta* and his mother's womb). Two streams of water appear from the sky, one cool, one hot, and make a water-libation for (child) and mother.

The newly-born *bodhisatta*, standing firmly on both feet, and turning towards the north, takes seven strides where, under a white canopy brought up behind him, he scans every quarter and speaks boldly, saying: 'I am the foremost, the best, the first in the world. This is the final birth. Now there will be no further renewal of existence.' Seven days after (his) birth the *bodhisatta's* mother dies and arises in the (heaven of) the Tusita group.[3]

(All these manifestations) I recognise as the strange and wonderful attribute(s) of an exemplar."

"Then recognise this also as a wonderful and remarkable attribute of an exemplar, Ānanda. Known to the Exemplar feelings arise, linger, and depart. Perceptions are (likewise) known. Known to the Exemplar thoughts arise, persist, and vanish."

Thus spoke venerable Ānanda (and) the Teacher approved.

1. In the full text all the subsequent material is divided into paragraphs repeating the subsequent statement and Ānanda's final comment. The words are put into the Lord's mouth by Ānanda, using direct speech.
2. Possibly implying psychic powers.

3. I have transposed this final statement from earlier in the passage to what seems its most logical position.

124

By Bakkula

124–128

Thus have I heard: once venerable Bakkula dwelt near Rājagaha in the Bamboo Grove at the squirrels' feeding-ground. Then Kassapa the naked (ascetic), formerly (his) friend in lay life, approached (him), exchanged greetings, and having conversed in a friendly and polite way, sat down at one side. Said Kassapa:

"How long is it since you became a wanderer, friend Bakkula?"

"Eighty years, friend."

"And during those eighty years, friend Bakkula, how many times have you indulged in sexual intercourse?"

"Do not put the question thus, friend Kassapa, (but rather ask): 'How many times during those eighty years have perceptions of sensuality arisen for you?' "

"And how many times (is that)?"

"I am not aware (of any such perception, nor of) perception of ill-will, or (desire to) injure in me, (nor any) thought (thereof).

(Moreover) during that eighty years I am not aware of having made use of householder's robe(-material), of having cut (such) with a knife, or sewn (it) with a needle, or dyed (it) with a dye, (or) of having sewn (it) on a frame. I am not aware of being occupied with making robes for companions in the good life, of accepting an invitation (to a meal or desiring such), of sitting between houses, or of eating (in such a place). I am not aware of being pre-occupied with the detailed characteristics of womenfolk, of having taught (them) *dhamma*, even by means of a verse of four sentences, of having gone to the dwelling of the nuns, of having taught *dhamma* to a nun, a (female) probationer, or a female novice. I am not aware of having brought about (anyone's) going forth, (or their) ordination, or of giving (them) help, (or) of keeping a novice in attendance. I am not aware of having washed in a (hot) bathroom, (or) with chunam (soap-powder), (or) of getting companions in the good life to massage my limbs. I am not aware of incurring any illness, (or) of carrying medicines about, even bits of the yellow myrobalan tree. I am not aware of leaning against a backrest, (or) of lying down, (or) of seeking shelter in the neighbourhood of a village during the rains. For just seven days I ate the country's almsfood, being (yet) imperfect. Then, on the eighth, gnosis arose (for me)."

"Friend Bakkula, may I obtain the going forth in this *dhamma* and discipline, and may I obtain ordination." And Kassapa the naked (ascetic) obtained the going forth and ordination.

Before long, venerable Kassapa (was) living alone and apart, diligent, zealous, and resolute. Sometime later he reached and experienced that matchless consummation of the good life, realised in this life from his own gnosis, for which sons of family rightly go forth from home into homelessness. (He knew): "Destroyed is birth, fulfilled the good life, done what was to be done, and (there is) no more of this world." And so venerable Kassapa became one of the *arahants*.

Then venerable Bakkula, taking his key, and going from dwelling to dwelling, said: "Proceed, brethren, proceed![1] Today is my final *nibbāna*." And, seated in the midst of the Order of monks, (so it was for him).

1. The verb used also means to approach

125

The Tamed State

128–137

Thus have I heard: once the Lord dwelt near Rājagaha, in the Bamboo Grove at the squirrels' feeding-place. Now at that time the novice Aciravata (of the Aggivessana clan) was staying in the Forest Hut. Then Prince Jayasena, whilst walking and strolling about, came up to Aciravata. Having exchanged greetings and conversed in a friendly and polite way, he sat down at one side. Said the Prince:

"I have heard, friend Aggivessana, that here (in the present existence) a monk might attain the focusing of the mind if he lives diligent, zealous, and resolute."

"That is so, Prince."

"It would be well if venerable Aggivessana were to teach me *dhamma* as he has heard and remembered it."

"I cannot teach you *dhamma* as I have heard and remembered it, Prince. Were I to (do so) you might not understand the meaning, (and) that would be wearisome and annoying for me."

"Let venerable Aggivessana teach me *dhamma*. Perhaps I would understand the meaning."

"Should I teach you *dhamma*, Prince, and you were to understand it that would be good, but if you do not (do so) let it be. Do not (then) question me further."

Then the novice Aciravata taught Prince Jayasena *dhamma* as he had heard and remembered it. After he had spoken (the) Prince said: "It is impossible, it cannot be, that a monk, by living diligent, zealous, and resolute, should attain the focusing of the mind." Then Prince Jayasena, declaring (this), rose from his seat and went his way.

Whereupon Aciravata the novice, not long after (the) Prince's departure, approached the Lord, saluted (him), and sat down at one side, (where) he related the whole of (his) conversation. Said the Lord:

"What can come of this, Aggivessana? It is impossible that Prince Jayasena, living surrounded by and enjoying worldly pursuits, consumed with thoughts (thereof), burning with fever, active in the search (for such things), should know, see, or realise for himself, or produce what is (achieved) through renunciation. It is like a pair of elephants, horses, or oxen, (that were) well tamed and trained, (and others that were not). What do you think, Aggivessana? Would those that were tamed give a tamed performance and reach a tamed condition?"

"Certainly, bhante."

"And the others?"

"Certainly not, bhante."

"Just so, Aggivessana, is it impossible that Prince Jayasena should realise what is to be realised through renunciation. It is as though there were a great rock near a village or town. Two friends coming from that village or town approach (it), hand in hand. One remains at the foot, the other climbs to the top. And the (first calls to the second): 'What do you see as you stand at the top?' 'I see beautiful parks, and woods, and planes, and ponds.' (But his friend does not believe this, so the other descends and brings him to the top of the rock, where he asks): 'What do you see as you stand (here)?' 'I see beautiful parks, and woods, and planes, and ponds.' (Whereupon the other reminds him of what he said at first.)

'That was because, screened by this great rock, I did not see what was there to be seen.'

Likewise, Aggivessana, but to a greater extent, is Prince Jayasena shut off, enveloped, obstructed, and covered over by basic ignorance. If these two similes (had been used in reply to the) Prince, (he) would have immediately trusted you and acted (accordingly)."

"But how could they have been used in reply, bhante, (having just occurred to the Lord)?"

"Aggivessana, it is like an elephant tamer who, mounting a king's elephant, goes into the forest, (and finds) a forest elephant. (Then) he ties (him) to the neck of the king's elephant, (who) takes him out into the open. But the forest elephant has a longing for the elephant-forest.

(So) the elephant-tamer, driving a great post into the ground, ties the forest elephant to it by the neck, in order to subdue his forest ways, memories, and aims; his distress, fatigue, and fever (for it); and so as to make him happy, and instruct him in human ways. (He) uses whatever form of words is gentle, agreeable, kind, to the heart, urbane, pleasant, and enjoyable to the multitude.

The forest elephant listens, lends an ear, and prepares his mind for knowledge. Next, the elephant-tamer supplies him with grass, fodder, and water. When the forest-elephant has accepted (this) the elephant tamer thinks: 'Now the king's elephant will remain alive.' Next (he) imposes a further task, saying: 'Pick up' (or), 'Put down', then 'Advance', (or) 'Retreat', then 'Get up', (or) 'Sit down.' When the king's elephant is obedient (in all these ways) the elephant-tamer imposes a further task called 'being immovable'. He binds a shield to the great animal's trunk. A man holding a spear sits on his neck, and (others) with spears stand all around him. The elephant-tamer, grasping a lance with a long shaft, stands in front of him. (The elephant) does not move the front or the rear foot, the fore or the hind part of his body; does not move head, ear, tusk, tail, or trunk. The king's elephant is hardened to the blow of spear, sword, arrow, hatchet, noise and din of drum and kettle-drum, conch, and tam-tam, and he is (like) purified gold, purged of all its dross and impurities, fit for a king, a royal possession, and reckoned as a regal emblem.

Just so, Aggivessana, an exemplar arises here in the world, *arahant*, truly enlightened. A householder or a householder's son hears (his) *dhamma*. Having heard (it) he finds conviction. Then he reflects: 'Confined and dusty is the household life, open to the skies (that) of the ascetic. The living of the good life, wholly fulfilled, purified, and polished like a conch shell, is not easy for the householder.' (And so he goes forth from home into homelessness.)[1] In such measure does the *ariyan* disciple (too) get out into the open. But *devas* and men have a longing for the five strands of worldly pursuit. (So the Exemplar exhorts him to the practice of *dhamma* and discipline.)[2] (Thereafter) he is able to endure the contact of heat and cold, hunger and thirst, gadfly and mosquito, wind and sun, crawling things, disreputable and unwelcome ways of speaking. He is of a character to bear the onset of feelings that are painful, acute, severe, and purged of all the dross and impurities of passion, hatred, and delusion. He is worthy of respect, hospitality, gifts, and salutation with joined palms, an unsurpassed field of merit in the world.

Aggivessana, if a monk dies without rooting out the distractions he is reckoned as one who has died untamed."

Thus spoke the Lord.

1. Detail as 27.
2. Detail as 107.

126

With Bhūmija

138–144

Thus have I heard: once the Lord dwelt near Rājagaha, in the Bamboo Grove at the squirrels' feeding-place. Then venerable Bhūmija, dressing at an early hour and taking bowl and robe, approached the dwelling of Prince Jayasena, (where) he sat down in the place prepared (for him). Prince Jayasena came up to (him), exchanged greetings, and having conversed in a friendly and polite way, sat down at one side. Said (the) Prince:

"There are some ascetics and brahmans, friend Bhūmija, who talk and theorise thus, saying (that) if one leads the good life with expectation one cannot gain the fruit; and if one leads the good life without expectation one cannot gain the fruit; and if one leads (it) both with and without expectation, (or) neither with nor without expectations, one cannot gain the fruit. What does friend Bhūmija's teacher say and declare regarding this (question)?"

"Prince, I have not seen or heard about this in the Lord's presence, but it is possible that the Lord might explain it (by saying that), if one leads the good life injudiciously, one cannot gain the fruit (whether expecting it or not). And if one leads the good life judiciously one can (whatever one's expectations)."

"If friend Bhūmija's teacher speaks and declares (it) thus he surely overshadows all the other ascetics and brahmans." Then Prince Jayasena offered venerable Bhūmija his own dish of rice cooked in milk.

Returning from the almsround after the meal venerable Bhūmija approached the Lord, saluted (him), and sat down at one side. (Having related the conversation he said:)

"Bhante, I wonder whether, replying as I did, I was speaking as would the Lord, and not misrepresenting (him). (I wonder whether) I was answering in accordance with *dhamma,* and no co-religionist's doctrine gives ground for complaint."

"Indeed, Bhūmija, you were not misrepresenting me, (nor does such a view) incur blame. If those ascetics and brahmans who are of wrong view, aim, speech, action, livelihood, effort, mindfulness, and concentration lead the good life with expectation, they cannot gain the fruit. And if they lead the good life without expectation, they cannot gain the fruit. And if they lead the good life both with and without, (or) neither with nor without expectation, they cannot gain the fruit. Why so? Bhūmija, this is not the way to gain the fruit.

It is like a man in need of oil, seeking for oil, travelling around in search of (it, who) scatters sand in a trough and, sprinkling water all over, presses it down. If he does (this) with expectation, he cannot obtain oil. If he does (it) without expectation, (or) with and without, (or) neither with nor without expectation, he cannot obtain oil. Why so? Bhūmija, this is not the way to obtain oil.

(But) if those ascetics and brahmans who are of right view, aim, speech, action, livelihood, effort, mindfulness, and concentration lead the good life with expectation, they can gain the fruit. And if they lead the good life without expectation they can gain the fruit. And if they lead the good life both with and without, (or) neither with nor without expectation they can gain the fruit. Why so? Bhūmija, this is the way to gain the fruit.

It is like a man in need of oil, seeking for oil, travelling around in search of (it, who) scatters oil-seeds in a trough and, sprinkling water all over, crushes them. If he does this with expectation, without expectation, (or both or neither), he can obtain oil. Why so? Bhūmija, this is the way to obtain oil.[1]

If (that) simile (had been used in reply to the) Prince, he would have immediately trusted you, and would have acted (accordingly)."

Thus spoke the Lord.

1. Three other similes are used but add nothing of substance.

127

By Anuruddha

144–152

Thus have I heard: once the Lord dwelt near Sāvatthī in the Jeta Grove on Anāthapiṇḍika's campus. Then Pañcakanga the carpenter said to a certain man: "Go, good fellow, approach venerable Anuruddha and, in my name, salute (his) feet with your head saying: 'Let venerable Anuruddha and three others[1] agree to take a meal with Pañcakanga the carpenter on the morrow, and let (him) come early as Pañcakanga the carpenter is busy, and has much to attend to in work for the king." (And the man did as he was bidden.)

The following morning[2] venerable Anuruddha, dressing at an early hour, and taking bowl and robe, approached the house of Pañcakaṅga the carpenter, and sat in the place provided (for him). Then Pañcakaṅga the carpenter served and satisfied venerable Anuruddha by his own hand with abundant food, both hard and soft. When venerable Anuruddha had set the bowl aside (Pacakanga) took a low seat at one side. Said Pañcakaṅga:

"Elder monks have approached me and said: 'Householder, cultivate the freedom of mind that is without limit.' Some elders say: 'Householder, cultivate the freedom of mind that is widely disseminated.' Are these states different in both meaning and expression? Or are they one as to meaning, but different as to expression?"

"Well now, householder, speak your own mind on the matter so as to get at the truth."

"Bhante, I think (that) these states are one as to meaning, but different as to expression."

"(No), householder. These states are different both as to meaning and as to expression. And what, householder, is the freedom of mind that is without limit? Herein a monk lives spreading thoughts joined to goodwill in all directions. He lives spreading them everywhere, in every way, to the entire world, abundantly, boundlessly, unrestrictedly, peaceably, benevolently. He lives spreading thoughts joined to compassion, to gladness, and to equanimity (in the same way).

And what, householder, is the freedom of mind that is widely disseminated? Herein a monk lives spreading and manifesting (his practice as) disseminated like one, two, or three tree-roots; like one, two, or three village-fields; like one, two, or three great kingdoms. In such a manner is it to be understood that these states are different in both meaning and expression.

Householder, there are these four ways of renewing existence. Herein someone lives spreading and intent on (a mind of) restricted light. On the breaking up of the body at death he arises in the company of the *devas* of restricted light. Herein someone (else) lives spreading and intent on (a mind of) light without limit. On the breaking up of the body at death he arises in the company of the *devas* of light without limit. Herein someone (else) lives spreading and intent on (a mind of) defiled light. On the breaking up of the body at death he arises in the company of the *devas* of defiled light. Herein someone (else) lives spreading and intent on (a mind of) pure light. On the breaking up of the body at death he arises in the company of the *devas* of pure light.

There is a time when *devatās* assemble together. When they are (thus) assembled a variety of colours is evident but not a variation of light. It is like a man who enters a house with several oil-lamps and, (in so doing), various flames can be seen but not a difference in light. There is a time when *devatās* go away from that place and, (in so doing), both various colours and a difference of light can be seen, (as when the man takes the oil-lamps out of the house). Those *devatās* do not think: 'This is a permanent, constant, and perpetual (state of affairs) for us.' Further, just where those *devatās* alight, just there they take their pleasure, like flies carried along on a pingo or basket."

At these words venerable Abhiya Kaccāna said to venerable Anuruddha: "It is well, bhante, but I have a further question to put on this matter. Are all *devatās* of restricted light or are some of light without limit?"

"According to circumstances some *devatās* are of restricted light, some of light without limit."

"Bhante, what is the reason, what the condition (that brings this about)?"

"Now, friend Kaccāna, I will put a question to you about this in turn. (Which of these two developments of the mind is more widely disseminated – that disseminated like one tree-root, or like three great kingdoms?")[3] "(The latter), bhante."

"This is the reason and the condition that, of those *devatās* that have arisen in one group of *devatās* some are *devatās* of restricted light, some of light without limit."

"It is well, bhante, but I have a further question to put on this matter. As regards *devatās* of light, are they all *devatās* of defiled light or are some of pure light?"

"According to circumstances some *devatās* are of defiled light, some of pure light."

"Bhante, what is the reason, what the condition (that brings this about)?"

"Now, friend Kaccāna, I will construct a parable for you. An intelligent man may understand the meaning of what is said (by such means). It is as though the oil burnt by an oil-lamp were impure and the wick dirty. Both from the impurity of the oil and the dirtiness of the wick, it burns only dimly. Herein some monk lives spreading and manifesting defiled light. His bodily passions are not well subdued, sloth and torpor are not removed, agitation and worry not expelled. (Thus) he burns only dimly. On the breaking up of the body at death he arises in the company of the *devas* of defiled light. (But some other monk deals successfully with these hindrances.) On the breaking up of the body at death he arises in the company of the *devas* of pure light. Friend Kaccāna, this is the reason and the condition whereby some *devatās* are of defiled light, some of pure light."

When he had spoken, venerable Abhiya Kaccāna said to venerable Anuruddha: "It is well, bhante. Venerable Anuruddha did not speak like this saying: 'Thus have I heard', or 'It should happen thus.' Instead (he) just said: 'These *devas* here are thus, those *devas* are thus.' Surely venerable Anuruddha has mingled with, conversed with, and come upon these *devas* previously."

"Indeed, friend Kaccāna, these words verge on a challenge. (So) I will explain to you further (that) for a long period I did (do so)."

At these words Abhiya Kaccāna said to Pañcakaṅga the carpenter: 'Yours is the gain and the profit, householder, that you have abandoned your state of doubt, and also gained the opportunity to hear this exposition of *dhamma*."

1. Literally "with self as fourth".
2. Elsewhere translated "towards dawn".
3. The comparisons are tediously drawn out into a series of pairings. They have here been telescoped into one.

128

Corruptions

152–162

Thus have I heard: once the Lord dwelt near Kosambī on Ghosita's campus. But at that time the monks of Kosambī lived disputing, quarrelsome, disputing, and contentious, indulging in mutual recrimination. Then a certain monk came to the Lord and saluted (him) saying: "It would be well for the Lord, out of compassion, to approach those monks." (And the Lord did so), and said: "Enough monks! Desist from disputes, quarrels, and strife." At these words one monk said to (him): "Let the *dhamma*-master wait. Let the Lord live unconcerned, and intent on experiencing happiness in this life. For it is we who will be held accountable." (Then a second and a third time the Lord admonished those monks, and that monk gave him the same answer.)[1]

(Some time after) the Lord approached the Eastern Bamboo Grove (where) venerable Anuruddha, venerable Nandiya, and venerable Kimbila were living. The keeper of the grove saw (him) coming some way off, and said: "Ascetic, do not enter this grove. There are three young men of good family dwelling here desiring (to know) the nature of self. Do not inconvenience them." But venerable Anuruddha heard the keeper of the grove, and said (to him): "Do not hinder the Lord, friend. It is our teacher who comes." Then venerable Anuruddha went to (the other monks) and said: "Come hither, brethren. Our teacher has arrived". So (they) went to meet (him), one taking his bowl and robe, one providing a seat, one supplying water for his feet. The Lord sat down (and) washed his feet. Said the Lord: "I hope all is well with you, that you are bearing up, and do not go short of almsfood."

"All is (indeed) well with us, Lord; we are bearing up, and do not go short of almsfood."

"(And) I hope you live in harmony, on friendly terms, without contention, becoming as milk and water, and viewing one another with affection."

"Yes, indeed, bhante, we do (live together in that way)."

"And how then do you (succeed in living like that)?"

(Said Anuruddha): "Bhante, it seemed to me (that) there is gain and advantage for me in living with such companions in the good life. Because of it I have (the opportunity) to offer (them) friendly deeds, friendly words, friendly thoughts, both in public and private. I thought: 'Let me proceed under the influence of (their) minds, having surrendered my own.' Bhante, we are different in our bodies, but our minds are as one." And venerable Nandiya and venerable Kimbila (also answered the Lord in these terms).

"That is good. And I hope you are living diligent, zealous, and resolute."

"Yes indeed, bhante."

"And how then do you (succeed in living like that)?"

"Whichever of us returns first from going to the village for alms prepares seats and gets drinking and washing water ready, (as well as) a refuse bowl. Whoever returns later eats any remaining food, should he so desire. If not he throws it away in a place without grass, or into water where there are no living things. He puts (everything) away, having washed the refuse bowl, and sweeps the eating area.[2] And every fifth night we settle down for a discussion on *dhamma*. This is how we live diligent, zealous, and resolute."

"That is good. But have you achieved superhuman states, the truly *ariyan* qualities of knowledge and vision, a state of ease?"

"Bhante, we perceive light and a vision of forms. But soon (they) vanish from us. And we do not comprehend the reason."

"But the reason should be comprehended. I too, before my enlightenment, being still a *bodhisatta*, perceived light and a vision of forms. But soon (they) vanished from me. (So) I asked myself: 'What is the reason, what the condition by which (they) vanish?' And it struck me: 'Uncertainty has arisen in me, and because of (that) concentration has fallen away. When concentration falls away (they) vanish. So I will act in such a way that uncertainty does not arise in me again.' And living diligent, zealous, and resolute, I perceived light and a vision of forms. But soon (they) vanished from me. (Then) it occurred to me: 'Inattention has arisen in me and, because of (that), concentration has fallen away. When concentration falls away (they) vanish. So I will act in such a way that neither uncertainty nor inattention arise in me again.' And living diligent, zealous, and resolute, I perceived light and a vision of forms. But soon (they) vanished from me. (Then) it occurred to me: 'sloth and torpor has arisen in me and, because of (that), concentration has fallen away. So I will act in such a way that neither uncertainty, not inattention, nor sloth and torpor arise in me again.' And living diligent, zealous, and resolute, I perceived light and a vision of forms. But soon (they) vanished from me. (Then, in succession) it occurred to me that, (first), consternation, (then) elation, (then) evil (thoughts, then) over- (or) under-exertion, (then) perception of the variety of things, (then) excessive absorption in form, (were the cause of their disappearance). And, finding (all these things) to be corruptions of the mind, I got rid of (them).

So, living diligent, zealous, and resolute, I perceived light, and did not behold forms. Then, for a whole night and a whole day, I saw forms, but did not perceive light. (Then) I asked myself: 'What is the reason, what the condition, that I perceived (first one, then the other).' Then it struck me: 'It was when I ignored the reflex-image of forms, but attended to (that) of light, that I perceived light. It was when I ignored the the reflex-image of light but attended to (that) of forms, that I beheld forms.'

(Then) it occurred to me: 'Whatever is a corruption of the mind I have (now) got rid of. So now I develop a threefold concentration.' And I developed concentration linked to thought and investigation; without thought and linked only to investigation; without (either); linked to joy;

without joy; accompanied by the pleasurable; accompanied by equanimity. When (these experiences had been attained), then knowledge and vision arose in me, (and I knew): 'Unshakable is release. This is the ultimate birth. Now there will be no renewal of existence.' "

Thus spoke the Lord.

1. A verse passage intervenes in which the Lord reflects on the folly of such discord. Then he visits a monk called Bhagu, but no discussion of significance takes place.
2. A further, obscure, sentence expanding on these mundane activities is omitted.

129

The Foolish and the Wise

165–178

Thus have I heard: once the Lord dwelt near Sāvatthī on the Jeta Grove of Anāthapiṇḍika's campus. There (he) addressed the monks, saying:

"Monks, there are these three marks, characteristics, and attributes of the fool. The fool is a thinker of mistaken thoughts, a speaker of mistaken words, a doer of mistaken deeds. If (this were not so) how could the wise know him (for what he is)?

The fool experiences three kinds of suffering and distress in this life. Suppose (he) is sitting in an assembly-hall, by a carriage-road, or at a crossroads. Suppose people there make appropriate judgements about him. Suppose him to be a destroyer of life, a thief, a libertine, a liar, or a drunkard. Then it occurs to (him): 'People make appropriate judgements – these things are in me, and I do engage in these things.' Such, monks, is the first kind of suffering and distress experienced by the fool in this life.

Then again the fool sees kings who, on catching a thief, a malefactor, mete out various punishments, (such as flogging, sprinkling with hot metal or boiling oil, feeding to dogs, impaling alive on a stake, or decapitation with a sword.)[1] So it occurs to (him): 'Evil deeds of such a kind are the reason why kings mete out (such punishments). So if kings knew about me (they) might catch me, (and wreak those punishments on me also).' Such, monks, is the second kind of suffering and distress experienced by the fool in this life.

Then again his mistaken deeds, words, and thoughts of earlier days rest upon the fool, cling to him, hang over him, while he is on a chair, or a bed, or lying on the ground. As the shadows of great mountain peaks at evening rest on, cling to, and hang over the earth, so do (these things) rest upon the fool. Then it occurs to (him): 'Truly I have not done what is noble, or skilful, or made a shelter against fear, (but) I have done what is evil, what is cruel, what is corrupt. To the extent that there is a destiny for those (who live like this), that will be my destiny hereafter.' He mourns, he grieves, he laments, he beats his breast, he wails, he shows bewilderment. Such, monks, is the third kind of suffering and distress experienced by the fool in this life.

He who has lived mistakenly in body, word, and thought, comes to sorrow, to an evil destiny, to ruin, to purgatory on the breaking up of the body at death. One might rightly say of purgatory that it is thoroughly undesirable, disagreeable, and unpleasing. Such are the sufferings of purgatory that a parable is not easy."

At these words a certain monk said to the Lord: "But is it possible to construct a parable for me, bhante?"

"It is possible, monk. It is as if (people) were to catch a thief, a malefactor, and then explain (the matter) to the king, saying: 'Sire, prescribe a punishment as you see fit.' The king might say this: 'Depart friends, (and) pierce this man with a hundred spears in the early morning.' Then at midday the king might ask: 'What about that man?' 'He is still alive, sire.' (So) the king (might repeat his order a second and a third time on receiving that answer). What do you think about that, monks? Would not that man experience suffering and distress?"

"Bhante, even from one spear (he) would (do so). How much more from three hundred!"

Then the Lord, taking a small stone the size of his hand said: "Which is the greater – (this), or the Himalaya, king of mountains?"

"Bhante, this small stone is insignificant compared with Himalaya, king of mountains. It cannot be calculated, it does not approach a millionth part. There (simply) is no comparison."

"Just so, monks, the suffering and distress felt by the man pierced by three hundred arrows does not approach a millionth part as compared with (that of) purgatory.[2]

Monks, there are animals, living things, that are grass-eaters, (others) that are dung-eaters, (others) that (live) in darkness, (or) in water, (or putrefaction).[3] That fool who, in earlier days, tasted pleasure in this world after committing evil deeds, comes into the company of these beings on the breaking-up of the body at death. Monks, I could speak of animal birth by many characterisations but, such are (its) sufferings that it is not easy to convey them by means of a parable.

It is as though a man might throw a yoke with one hole in it into the sea. The east wind would take it westwards, the west wind eastwards, the north southwards, and the south wind would drive it to the north. Suppose there to be a blind turtle that might come to the surface once in a hundred years. What do you think about this, monks? Would that blind turtle poke his neck through that yoke with one hole in it?"

"If at all, bhante, then only once in a very long time."

"Yet harder to come by (than this) I say, is (return to) the human state by the fool who has gone to destruction. What is the reason for that? Monks, there is no living by *dhamma* there, no even course, no skilled or meritorious conduct. There is mutual devouring, living on the weak. If the fool, once in a very long time, returned to the human state, he would be born to a humble, a low-born family; to a family of hunters, of bamboo-workers, of chariot-makers, of refuse-collectors; in the kind of family that is impoverished, and where nourishment and clothing are obtained with difficulty. And he would be ill-favoured, ugly, stunted, sickly, deformed, lame, blind, or paralysed.[4]

Monks, it is like a gambler who, at the first losing throw, might lose his son, his wife, his entire property, and moreover experience imprisonment. Greater than this is the losing throw (whereby) the fool comes to sorrow, to an evil destiny, to ruin, to purgatory. Such, fulfilled in its entirety, is the career of the fool.

There are these three marks, characteristics, and attributes of the wise man. The wise man is a thinker of true thoughts, a speaker of true words, a doer of true deeds. If (this were not so) how could the wise know a wise man (for what he is)?

The wise man experiences three kinds of happiness and delight in this life. Suppose (he) is sitting in an assembly-hall, by a carriage-road, or at a crossroads. Suppose people there make appropriate judgements about him. Suppose he (is one who) refrains from the destruction of life, from theft, from dissolute living, from lies, from drunkenness. Then it occurs to (him): 'People make appropriate judgements – these things are in me, and I do engage in such things.' Such, monks, is the first kind of happiness and delight experienced by the wise man in this world.

Then again the wise man sees kings who, on seizing a thief, mete out various punishments. It occurs to (him): 'These states do not occur in me, nor do I engage in these things.' Such, monks, is the second kind of happiness and delight experienced by the wise man in this life.

Then again his true deeds, words, and thoughts of earlier days rest upon the wise man, cling to him, hang over him. Such, monks, is the third happiness and delight experienced by the wise man in this life. He who has lived rightly in body, speech, and thought, comes to a good destiny, a heaven world, on the breaking-up of the body at death. One might rightly say of heaven that it is thoroughly desirable, agreeable, and pleasing. Such is the happiness of heaven that a parable is not easy."

At these words a certain monk said to the Lord: 'But is it possible to construct a parable for me, bhante?"

"It is possible, monks. It is like a wheel-turning king who, possessing seven treasures and four powers, experiences happiness and delight for that reason. What are (his) seven treasures?

As to that, when the noble anointed king has bathed his head on an observance-day, the fifteenth, and has gone to the upper storey of the royal palace, the celestial wheel-treasure appears, with its thousand spokes, its rim, its hub, and every part complete. On seeing it (he) thinks: 'May I be a wheel-turning king.'

Then, rising from his seat, (he) takes a ceremonial water-jar with his left hand and, with his right, sprinkles water upon the wheel, saying: 'May the wheel-treasure roll on. May the wheel-treasure triumph." Then the wheel rolls eastwards and, behind it (goes) the wheel-turning king, with an army of four divisions.[5] And in whatever place the wheel comes to rest, there the king makes his home. And rival kings of the east come to (him) and say: 'Greetings great king, welcome. All is yours. Advise (us).' The wheel-turning king says to them: 'Life is not to be destroyed, what is not given is not to be taken, dissolute living is not to be pursued, lies are not to be told, strong liquor is not to be drunk, and (eat) only according to need.' And those rival kings of the east become (his) vassals.

Then the wheel-treasure, plunging into the eastern sea and rising out (of it again), rolls on southwards, westwards, northwards. And in whatever place the wheel comes to rest, there the wheel-turning king takes up his residence. (And the rival kings in all these quarters become his vassals.) Then, when the wheel-treasure has overcome the sea-encircled earth and returned to the royal city, it stands as if fixed by the axle, at the palace-gate. In such a way does the wheel-treasure appear to the wheel-turning king.

Next the elephant-treasure appears (to him), all-white, sevenfold-firm, crossing the sky by psychic power, an elephant-king called Uposatha. On seeing him the wheel-turning king is pleased at heart, and he thinks: 'An auspicious possession is the elephant-vehicle, should he submit to training.' Then, monks, the elephant, like a thoroughbred, submits to taming. Once upon a time the king mounted (him) early one morning and, in trying him out, crossed the sea-encircled earth and, returning even to the royal city, took his morning meal. In such a way does the elephant-treasure appear to the wheel-turning king.

Next the horse-treasure appears to (him in the same way, and with the same outcome)

Next the jewel-treasure appears (to him) – a lapis-lazuli, bright, noble, well cut in eight facets. And the light of that jewel is shed around for many a mile. Once upon a time the king, trying (it) out, and having assembled an army of four divisions, set out in the darkness of the night, with the royal jewel raised aloft at the top of his standard. And the villagers roundabout set about their business by its radiance, believing it to be daytime. In such a way does the jewel-treasure appeal to the wheel-turning king.

Next the woman-treasure appears (to him), perfect of form, and fair to behold, charming, and possessed of a lovely complexion; neither too tall nor too short; neither too thin nor too fat; neither too dark nor too pale; surpassing human beauty, though of less than divine beauty. And the touch of the body of the woman is like tufts of cotton or thistledown. (Her) limbs are warm when it is cool, and cool when it is hot. From (her) body comes the breath of sandalwood, from (her) mouth that of lotuses. (She) rises before the king and retires after (him), ministering to his pleasures, and conversing affably. Moreover, that woman is never unfaithful in thought – how then in body? In such a way does the woman-treasure appear to the wheel-turning king.

Next the householder-treasure appears (to him). As a result of his (former) behaviour the divine eye appears by which he sees treasure both with and without an owner. He comes to the wheel-turning king, and says: 'Rest content, sire. Through the medium of your wealth I will do what should be done with wealth.' Once upon a time the king, trying (him) out, climbed aboard a boat and sailed it through the stream to the middle of the river Ganges, (where) he said to (him): 'Householder, (give) me prosperity through gold and money.' Then, monks, that householder, plunging both hands in the water, drew up a pot full of gold and money, and said to the king: 'Is this suitable great king? Is this enough great king? Are you served?' 'This is (indeed) suitable (and) enough. I am (well) served, householder.'

In such a way does the householder-treasure appear to the wheel-turning king.

Next the adviser-treasure appear to (him) – wise, accomplished, intelligent, competent in providing the wheel-turning king with what is to be provided, removing what is to be removed, saving what is to be saved. He comes to (him) and says: 'Rest content, sire. I will instruct (you).' In such a way does the adviser-treasure appear to the wheel-turning king. The wheel-turning king, monks, is possessed of seven treasures.

And with what four powers? As to that, the wheel-turning king is perfect of form, handsome to behold, charming, and endowed with beauty of complexion. Then again, (he) has longevity beyond that of other men. Then again (he) has little illness, does not get sick, and possesses good digestion. Then again (he) is dear and beloved to brahmans and householders. Just as fathers are dear to sons so is (he) to (them). The wheel-turning king is possessed of these four powers.

What do you think about this, monks? Does not a wheel-turning king possessed of (all these things) experience happiness and delight?"

"Bhante, even from one – how much more from (all)!"

Then the Lord, taking a small stone the size of his hand, said: "Which is the greater – (this) or the Himalaya, king of mountains?"

"Bhante, this small stone is insignificant compared with Himalaya, king of mountains. It cannot be calculated, it does not approach a millionth part. There (simply) is no comparison."

"(And likewise, monks, there is no comparison between this happiness and the happiness of the wise.) Monks, it is like a gambler who, at the first winning throw, might acquire great possessions. Greater than this is the winning throw whereby the wise man comes to a good destiny, to a heaven world, on the breaking-up of the body at death. Such, fulfilled in its entirety, is the career of the wise man.[6]"

Thus spoke the Lord.

1. The list of tortures and punishments is abbreviated.
2. An extended section on the torments of purgatory is omitted.
3. Five paragraphs are devoted to the five groups mentioned here. The first and fourth mention specific herbivores and aquatic animals, the second various scavengers and farmyard animals. The third refers to earthworms and, (apparently), ground-living insects, the description probably indicating a subterranean habitat. The fifth group does not name any particular type of animal, though the modern reference would presumably be to bacteria.
4. And he is likely to return to purgatory again.
5. Elephants, chariots, cavalry, and infantry.
6. The discourse ends with a description of the wise man's rebirth in exactly opposite terms to those stated earlier for the fool.

130

The Divine Messengers

178–187

Thus have I heard: once the Lord dwelt near Sāvatthī in the Jeta Grove on Anāthapiṇḍika's campus. There (he) addressed the monks saying:

"Monks, suppose there were two houses with doors, and a man standing between them (who) might see people entering a house, leaving it, or walking and wandering about (between them). Likewise with the divine eye of superhuman clarity do I see beings passing away, and re-arising according to the consequences of their deeds – beings base or exalted, beautiful or ugly, of good or ill destiny. I think: 'Truly these worthy beings that are possessed of right living in body, word, and thought, not finding fault with the *ariyans*, of right view, and acquiring the activities (based on) right view, come to a good destiny, a heaven world, on the breaking-up of the body at death, (or they) arise among men.

Those worthy beings of wrong view, and acquiring the activities (based on) wrong view, come to be among departed spirits. (Others) of wrong view come to be among animals, (or) to sorrow, to an evil destiny, to ruin, to purgatory.'

Monks, the guardians of purgatory seize such a person and show him to King Yama, saying: 'Sire, this man is without respect for mother or father, ascetic or brahman, or for the elders of the clan. Decree a punishment for him, sire.'

Then King Yama questions, interrogates, speaks to him concerning the divine messenger(s), saying:[1]

'Good fellow, did you not see the first divine messenger who appeared among men?'

'I did not, bhante.'

'(But) did you not see a young baby boy, prostrate, and lying in his own excrement?'

'I saw (this), bhante.'

'Did it not occur to you, who are intelligent, and ripe in years (that you) too were liable to birth, (and would do well to strive for good)?'

'I was not able, bhante. I was negligent.'

'(So), out of negligence you did (nothing) good. Truly (others) will act towards you as befits that negligence. That evil was done by you. You will experience its fruit.

Good fellow, did you not see the second divine messenger who appeared among men?'

'I did not, bhante.'

'(But) did you not see among men a woman or a man that was eighty, ninety, or a hundred years old – senile, crooked as a rafter, bent, leaning on a stick, going along palsied, sick, (long) past youth, with teeth broken, with thin grey hair and (going) bald, wrinkled, and with limbs discoloured?'

'I saw (this), bhante.'

'Did it not occur to you that you) too were liable to old age, (and would do well to strive for good)?'

'I was not able, bhante. I was negligent.'

'(So), out of negligence you did (nothing) good. Good fellow, did you not see the third divine messenger who appeared among men?'

'I did not, bhante.'

'(But) did you not see among men a woman or a man affected with illness, ailing, very enfeebled, and lying in his own excrement, rising and getting to bed (only) with the help (of others)?'

'I saw (this), bhante.'

'Did it not occur to you (that you) too were liable to sickness, (and would do well to strive for good)?'

'I was not able, bhante. I was negligent.'

'(So), out of negligence you did (nothing) good. Good fellow, did you not see the fourth divine messenger who appeared among men?'

'I did not see (this), bhante.'

'(But) did you not see among men kings who, on catching a thief, a malefactor, meted out various punishments?'

'I saw (this), bhante.'

'Did it not occur to you (that your) evil deeds were subject to punishment, (and that you would do well to strive for good)?'

'I was not able, bhante. I was negligent.'

'(So), out of negligence you did (nothing) good. Good fellow, did you not see the fifth divine messenger who appeared among men?'

'I did not see (this), bhante.'

'(But) did you not see among men a woman or a man dead for one, two, or three days bloated, discoloured, festering?''

'I saw (this), bhante.'

'Did it not occur to you (that you) too were liable to death, and would do well to strive for good)?'

'I was not able, bhante. I was negligent.'

'(So), out of negligence you did (nothing) good. Truly (others) will act towards you as befits that negligence. That evil was done by you. You will experience its fruit.'

(Whereupon King Yama returns him to the guardians, who subject him to all the torments of purgatory by way of punishment.)[2]

Once upon a time it occurred to King Yama: 'Truly those who perpetrate evil deeds are subjected to various punishments such as these. Would that I might acquire human status and that an exemplar, *arahant*, truly enlightened, might arise in the world. (Would that) I might do homage to that Lord, (that) he might teach me *dhamma*, and I might learn (it).'

Monks, I speak of that which I have heard from no other ascetic or brahman."

Thus spoke the Lord.

1. The foregoing statement recurs five times i.e. for each visitation in the full text.
2. A lengthy section describing these is omitted.

131

On What is Timely

187–189

Thus have I heard: once the Lord dwelt near Sāvatthī in the Jeta Grove on Anāthapiṇḍika's campus. There (he) addressed the monks, saying:

"Monks, I will teach you the exposition and analysis of what is timely. **The past should not be pursued, nor the future longed for. What is past is left behind and the future is unobtained. But whoever has insight here and there into the present state, let him cultivate the mind, knowing that (attainment) to be unconquerable and immovable. Exercise zeal this very day. For who knows whether death may come to-morrow? With the great hosts of death there is no compact. Living zealously in such a way, unwearying day and night – such a one is called timely and described as a tranquil sage.**

And how, monks, does someone pursue the past? He thinks: 'I had a certain physical form in past times', and he finds pleasure therein. (Or he thinks likewise about his feelings, perceptions, traits and tendencies, or form of consciousness.) In such a way does someone pursue the past.

And how, monks, does someone not pursue the past? He thinks: 'I had a certain physical form in past times', but does not find pleasure therein. (Or he thinks likewise about his feelings, perceptions, traits and tendencies, or form of consciousness.) In such a way does someone not pursue the past.

And how, monks, does someone long for the future? He thinks: 'I may have a certain physical form in the fullness of time', and he finds pleasure therein. (Or he thinks likewise about his feelings, perceptions, traits and tendencies, or form of consciousness.) In such a way does someone long for the future.

And how, monks, does someone not long for the future? He thinks: 'I may have a certain physical form in the fullness of time', but does not find pleasure therein. (Or he thinks likewise about his feelings, perceptions, tendencies, disposition, or state of consciousness.) In such a way does someone long for the future.

And how, monks, is someone caught up in the present? In this connection some uninformed person is heedless of the *ariyans*, untrained in the *dhamma* of good men, (and) regards (physical) form as self, or self as having (physical) form, or (physical) form as in self, or self as in (physical) form. (Or he thinks likewise about his feelings, perceptions, traits and tendencies, or form of consciousness.) In such a way is someone caught up in the present.

And how, monks, is someone not caught up in the present. In this case an informed disciple, trained in the *dhamma* of good men, does not regard (physical) form, feeling, perception, traits and tendencies, or consciousness (in any of these ways).

It was in reference to this (that I said): 'Monks, I will teach you the exposition and analysis of what is timely?' "

Thus spoke the Lord.

132

Ānanda on What is Timely

189–191

(Omitted – this discourse is virtually identical in content to 131, except that it is related at second hand by Ānanda.)

133

Kaccāna the Great on What is Timely

192–199

Thus have I heard: once the Lord dwelt near Rājagaha On Tapoda Campus. Then venerable Samiddhi, rising before dawn, went to Tapoda (lake) for a bathe. Having bathed, he stood in one robe drying his limbs. Then, towards dawn, a certain *devatā* of great beauty, shedding a radiance over the whole of Tapoda came to venerable Samiddhi and stood at one side, saying:

"Monk, do you call to mind the exposition and analysis concerning what is timely?"

"(No), friend. Do you?"

"(No), monk. But do you call to mind the verses concerning what is timely?"

"(No), friend. Do you?"

"(No), monk. Monk, acquire, learn, and bear in mind the exposition and analysis of what is timely. (It) is advantageous, and the starting-point of the good life."

Thus spoke the *devatā*, and vanished from that spot. And venerable Samiddhi approached the Lord when morning had broken and, having saluted (him), sat down at one side, (where he related his experience). Said the Lord:

"The past should not be pursued, nor the future longed for. What is past is left behind and the future is unobtained. But whoever has insight here and there into the present state, let him cultivate the mind, knowing that (attainment) to be unconquerable and immovable. Exercise zeal this very day. Who knows whether death may come to-morrow? With the great hosts of death there is no compact. Living zealously in such a way, unwearying day and night – such a one is called timely and described as a tranquil sage." Saying this, the Lord, the Adept, rose from his seat and entered the dwelling-place. And, shortly after (his) departure, these monks (asked themselves): "Who can elucidate in full the meaning of that exposition set forth by the Lord in brief? The venerable Kaccāna the Great can (do so). Suppose we were to approach (him)."

Whereupon (they did so) and, having greeted (him) and conversed in a friendly and polite way, sat down at one side. (Then they explained the question that had arisen for them). (Said Kaccāna):

"Friends, like a man who walks around in need of the pith, wanting the pith, seeking the pith of a great, enduring, and pithy tree – who, passing by the root and the trunk, thinks that the pith is to be looked for in the branches and foliage – such is the brethren's behaviour in that, having been in the Teacher's presence, you pass (him) by and think to question me on the matter. Now friends, the Lord knows what is known, sees what is seen. (He) is vision-born, knowledge-born, *dhamma*-born, *brahmā*-born, enunciator, expounder, dispenser of meaning, giver of the deathless, *dhamma*-master, exemplar. This was your opportunity to question (him)."

"Certainly, friend Kaccāna. But venerable Kaccāna is praised by the Teacher, and has the esteem of intelligent companions in the good life. Let (him) deal with (the question), if it is not inconvenient."

"Friends, I understand the full meaning of that exposition set forth by the Lord in brief like this. How does one pursue the past? Thinking: 'Such was sight and (visual) forms (or any other kind of experience) for me long ago', one's consciousness is held there by resolve and passion. (From that) one gets enjoyment, (and so) one pursues the past. And how does one not pursue the past? (Whatever experience related to the past arises one's consciousness is not thus) held by resolve and passion.

And how does one long for the future? Thinking: 'Sight and (visual) forms (or any other kind of experience) may be such for me in the fullness of time', one directs the mind to gaining what is not (yet) gained. (From that) one gets enjoyment, (and so) one longs for the future. And how does one not long for the future? (Whatever thought of the future arises) one does not direct the mind (in such a way).

And how is one caught up in the present? When sight and (visual) forms, (or any other conjunction of faculty and object), are both manifested one's consciousness is held (thereto) in resolve and passion. (From that) one gets enjoyment (and so) one is caught up in the present. And how does one not get caught up in the present? (Whatever experience arises in the present), one's consciousness is not held (thereto) in resolve and passion.

That is how I understand the meaning of that exposition set forth in brief by the Lord. But if you so wish, brethren, approach and question the Lord on the matter."

Then those monks, pleased and satisfied at what the venerable Kaccāna the Great had said, rose from their seats and approached the Lord. Having saluted (him) they sat down at one side (and told him of their conversation with venerable Kaccāna).

"Monks, clever and of great wisdom is Kaccāna. If you had questioned me on the matter I too would have explained (it) exactly thus."

Thus spoke the Lord.

134

With Lomasakaṅgiya on What is Timely

199–202

Thus have I heard: once the Lord dwelt near Sāvatthī in the Jeta Grove on Anāthapiṇḍika's campus. Now at that time venerable Lomasakaṅgiya lived among the Sakyans on Nigrodha's campus at Kapilavatthu. Then Candana, son of a deva, and of great beauty, shedding a radiance over the whole of Nigrodha's campus towards dawn, came to (him) and stood at one side, saying:

"Monk, do you call to mind the exposition and analysis concerning what is timely?"

"(No), friend. Do you?"

"(No), monk. But do you call to mind the verses concerning what is timely?"

"(No), friend. Do you?"

"I do call to mind the verses concerning what is timely."

"And in what manner do you (do so)?"

"On that occasion the Lord dwelt among the Devas of the Thirty-Three, at the foot of the Coral Tree, on the Stone of the Red Blanket. There (he) spoke the exposition and analysis concerning what is timely, (namely), **'The past should not be pursued, nor the future longed for. What is past is left behind and the future is unobtained. But whoever has insight here and there into the present state, let him cultivate the mind, knowing that (attainment) to be unconquerable and immovable. Exercise zeal this very day. Who knows whether death may come to-morrow? With the great hosts of death there is no compact. Living zealously in such a way, unwearying day and night – such a one is called timely and described as a tranquil sage.'** Monk, acquire, learn, and bear in mind the exposition and analysis of what is auspicious. (It) is advantageous, and the starting-point of the good life." Thus spoke Candana the son of a *deva*, and vanished from that spot.

When morning had broken, venerable Lomasakaṅgiya tidied his lodgings and, taking bowl and robe, set out on foot for Sāvatthī. At length he (came there, and) went to the Jeta Grove of Anāthapiṇḍika's park and the Lord. Saluting (him), he sat down at one side, (telling what had passed. Said the Lord):

"But do you know that son of a *deva*, monk?"

"(No), bhante."

"That son of a *deva*, monk, is called Candana. With application and attention, and concentrating his entire mind, he listens to *dhamma*.

And how, monks, does someone pursue the past? He thinks: 'I had a certain (physical) form in past times', and he finds pleasure therein. (Or he thinks likewise about his feelings, perceptions, traits and tendencies, or form of consciousness.) In such a way does someone pursue the past.

And how, monks, does someone not pursue the past? He thinks: 'I had a certain (physical) form in past times', but does not find pleasure therein. (Or he thinks likewise about his feelings, perceptions, traits and tendencies, or form of consciousness.) In such a way does someone not pursue the past.

And how, monks, does someone long for the future? He thinks: 'I may have a certain (physical) form in the fullness of time', and he finds pleasure therein. (Or he thinks likewise about his feelings, perceptions, traits and tendencies, or form of consciousness.) In such a way does someone long for the future.

And how, monks, does someone not long for the future? He thinks: 'I may have a certain (physical) form in the fullness of time', but does not find pleasure therein. (Or he thinks likewise about his feelings, perceptions, traits and tendencies, or form of consciousness.) In such a way does someone long for the future.

And how, monks, is someone caught up in the present? In this connection some uninformed person is heedless of the *ariyan*s, untrained in the *dhamma* of good men, (and) regards (physical) form as self, or self as having (physical) form, or (physical) form as in self, or self as in (physical) form. (Or he thinks likewise about his feelings, perceptions, traits and tendencies, or form of consciousness.) In such a way is someone caught up in the present.

And how, monks, is someone not caught up in the present. In this case an informed disciple, trained in the *dhamma* of good men, does not regard (physical) form, feeling, perception, traits and tendencies, or consciousness (in any of these ways)."

Thus spoke the Lord

135

The Minor Analysis of Behaviour[1]

202–206

Thus have I heard: once the Lord dwelt near Sāvatthī in the Jeta Grove on Anāthapiṇḍika's campus. Then the youth Subha, Todeyya's son, approached the Lord, exchanged greetings, and having conversed in a friendly and polite way, sat down at one side. Said Subha:

"Friend Gotama, what is the reason, what the condition, whereby (both) inferiority and excellence are seen among men, while (they) are in human form? For they are seen to be short- or long-lived; much- or little-oppressed; ugly or comely; weak or powerful; impoverished or wealthy; of humble or noble family; deficient in or possessed of wisdom. Friend Gotama, what is the reason, what the condition of that?"

"One's own behaviour, young man – beings are inheritors of their behaviour. Behaviour is the womb, the kinsman, the assistant. Behaviour distinguishes beings as regards inferiority or excellence."

"I do not entirely understand the meaning of that which friend Gotama has referred to briefly, but not explained in full. Would that (he) might teach me."

"Well then, listen and attend carefully. Some woman or man is a destroyer of life, cruel, with blood on his hands, bent on killing and injury, devoid of kindness to living things. Through performing and taking upon himself such activity (that person) comes to sorrow, to an evil destiny, to ruin, to purgatory on the breaking-up of the body at death. (But if this does not happen), and he comes (back) to the human state – (then), wherever he is born again, he is short-lived. This course is conducive to shortness of life, namely being a destroyer of life.

Or again some woman or man is of a nature to be hurtful to (other) beings with hand, or clod of earth, or stick, or sword. Through performing and taking upon himself such activity (that person) comes to sorrow, to an evil destiny, to ruin, to purgatory on the breaking-up of the body at death. (But if this does not happen), and he comes (back) to the human state – (then), wherever he is born again, he is oppressed (by others). This course is conducive to being oppressed, namely being of a nature to be hurtful to (other) beings.

Or again some woman or man is wrathful, greatly incensed, when even trifling (matters) are spoken of – he curses, gets agitated, disagrees, is obdurate. He evinces anger, hatred, and dissatisfaction. Through performing and taking upon himself such activity (that person) comes to sorrow, to an evil destiny, to ruin, to purgatory on the breaking-up of the body at death. (But if this does not happen), and he comes (back) to the human state – (then), wherever he is born again, he is ugly. This course is conducive to ugliness, namely wrathfulness.

Or again some woman or man is envious – of the property of others, their fame, and with regard to acts of respect and honour paid to them. Through performing and taking upon himself such activity (that person) comes to sorrow, to an evil destiny, to ruin, to purgatory on the breaking-up of the body at death. (But if this does not happen), and he comes (back) to the human state – (then), wherever he is born again, he is of little account. This course is conducive to being of little account, namely being envious.

Or again some woman or man is not a giver of food, drink, clothing, vehicle, garlands, perfume, ointment, bed, lodging, or light to ascetic or brahman. Through performing and taking upon himself such activity (that person) comes to sorrow, to an evil destiny, to ruin, to purgatory on the breaking-up of the body at death. (But if this does not happen), and he comes (back) to the human state – (then), wherever he is born again, he is impoverished. This course is conducive to impoverishment, namely not being a giver.

Or again some woman or man is stubborn and proud, not saluting one worthy of salutation, not giving up a seat or giving way, not honouring (one worthy of honour). Through performing and taking upon himself such activity (that person) comes to sorrow, to an evil destiny, to ruin, to purgatory on the breaking-up of the body at death. (But if this does not happen), and if he comes (back) to the human state – (then), wherever he is born again, he is of humble family. This course is conducive to being of humble family, namely not honouring one who should be honoured.

Or again some woman or man, on approaching an ascetic or brahman, does not interrogate him asking: 'Bhante, what is skilled, what unskilled; what blameworthy, what praiseworthy; what is to be practised, what not to be practised; what might be done by me that makes for harm and suffering, or for wellbeing and happiness for many a day.' Through performing and taking upon himself such activity (that person) comes to sorrow, to an evil destiny, to ruin, to purgatory on the breaking-up of the body at death. (But if this does not happen), and he comes (back) to the human state – (then), wherever he is born again he is deficient in wisdom. This course is conducive to deficiency in wisdom, namely not being one who interrogates.

Behaviour is one's own. Beings are inheritors of their behaviour. Behaviour is the womb, the kinsman, the assistant. Behaviour distinguishes beings as regards inferiority or excellence."

At these words Subha, Todeyya's son, said to the Lord: "Excellent, excellent, friend Gotama." (And Subha took the refuges and became a lay-follower.)

1. The same Pali term is translated both as "behaviour" and "activity" in this discourse and the next.

136

The Major Analysis of Behaviour

207–215

Thus have I heard: once the Lord dwelt near Rājagaha, in the Bamboo Grove at the squirrels' feeding-place. Now at that time venerable Samiddhi was living in a forest-hut. Then Potaliputta the wanderer, who was walking and strolling about, came up to (him). Having exchanged greetings and conversed in a friendly and polite way, he sat down at one side. Said Potaliputta:

"Friend Samiddhi, in the presence of the ascetic Gotama I have heard and understood that physical (and) verbal activity (are) illusory;[1] only mental activity is real. And there is that attainment, on reaching (which) one feels nothing."

"Don't say that, friend Potaliputta. Don't misrepresent the Lord. Misrepresentation of the Lord is not good, nor would (he) say (these things)."

"How long is it since you went forth, friend Samiddhi?"

"Not long friend – three years."

"Now why do we address monks who are elders, when a novice monk thinks the Teacher should be defended in this way.[2] Friend Samiddhi, when intended activity is performed by the body, through speech, or mentally – what does one experience?"

"One experiences suffering, friend Potaliputta." Whereupon the wanderer Potaliputta, neither approving nor scorning what venerable Samiddhi had said, rose form his seat and went his way.

Not long afterwards venerable Samiddhi approached venerable Ānanda. Having exchanged greetings and conversed in a friendly and polite way,he sat down at one side, (where) he related the whole of the conversation with the wanderer Potaliputta. When he had spoken venerable Ānanda said:

"Friend Samiddhi, this is a conversation that should be drawn to the Lord's attention. As the Lord explains (the matter) to us, so we should bear it in mind."

Then, having approached and saluted the Lord they sat down at one side, (and) venerable Ānanda (told him of venerable Samiddhi's conversation). At these words the Lord said:

"I am not even aware of the wanderer Potaliputta's viewpoint, how then of such a conversation (as this). Surely, Ānanda, the question was answered one-sidedly by this foolish man Samiddhi, (though) requiring an analysis."

At these words venerable Udāyin said to the Lord: "But if, bhante, that was the import of what was said by venerable Samiddhi then, whatever is felt, that is suffering."

Then the Lord addressed venerable Ānanda, saying:

"Ānanda, see the wrong approach of this foolish man Udāyin. I knew that (he) would intervene to no purpose. The wanderer Potaliputta really asked about the three feelings. If that foolish man Samiddhi had replied (by saying that), having performed activity of body, speech, or mind intending pleasure one feels pleasure; intending suffering one feels suffering; (and) intending neither one experiences neither – he would have answered aright. Moreover, Ānanda, wanderers of other sects who are uninformed and inexperienced will gain knowledge of the Exemplar's great analysis of behaviour if you listen (whilst I expound it).

Ānanda, there are these four (types of) individual to be found in the world. Someone is a destroyer of life, a thief, a libertine, a liar, a slanderer, an abuser, a driveller; is covetous, of corrupted mind, and wrong view. On the breaking-up of the body at death he comes to sorrow, to an evil destiny, to ruin, to purgatory. (Or) someone (behaves in such a way but), on the breaking-up of the body at death, comes to a good destiny, a heaven world. (Or) someone abstaining from (this wrong behaviour) is of right view. At death he comes to a good destiny, a heaven world. (Or) someone abstaining (thus, nevertheless) comes to sorrow, to an evil destiny, to ruin, to purgatory.

Herein, Ānanda, some ascetic or brahman, in consequence of zeal, of exertion, of application, of conscientiousness, of right attention, attains such concentration of mind that, in (his) mental composure, he beholds (the first kind of evil doer and his evil destiny) with the purified divine eye transcending the human. He thinks: 'Truly there are evil deeds, and bad living bears fruit. Whoever is (like this) comes to sorrow, to an evil destiny, to ruin, to purgatory, on the breaking-up of the body at death. Those who know thus know truly.' Thus obstinately seizing and adhering to simply that which is his own knowledge, his own view, his own discovery he decides: 'Just this is the truth, all else is foolishness.'

However, Ānanda, some (other) ascetic or brahman beholds (the second kind of evil doer and his good destiny by the same means). He thinks: 'Truly there are no evil deeds, and bad living bears no fruit. Whoever is (like this) comes to a good destiny, a heaven world, on the breaking-up of the body at death. Those who know thus know truly.' Thus obstinately seizing and adhering to simply that which is his own knowledge, his own view, his own discovery, he decides: 'Just this is the truth, all else is foolishness'.

(And those ascetics and brahmans who behold the two other kinds of person draw conclusions in the same way.)

In regard to (all) this, Ānanda, whatever ascetic or brahman says (that) there are bad deeds, and (that) bad living bears fruit, or (that) there are good deeds, and (that) good living bears fruit – that I concede him.[3] (But) whatever ascetic or brahman says (that) there are no fruits (of either) – that I do not concede him.

(Or again) whatever ascetic or brahman says this: 'Moreover I saw an individual (who was an evil doer) come to sorrow, to an evil destiny, to ruin, to purgatory, on the breaking-up of the body at death' – that, too, I concede him. (Or if he says): 'I saw (such a person) come to a good destiny, a heaven world;' (or if he says): 'I saw (a good person) come to a good destiny, (or) to an evil destiny' – that I concede him. But if he says this: 'Whoever (is an evil doer) comes to a (particular) destiny', (or) 'Whoever (is not an evil doer) comes to a (particular) destiny' – that I do not concede him. Why so? The Exemplar's great analysis of activity is otherwise.

Ānanda, anyone there might be (who is an evil doer and) comes to sorrow, to an evil destiny, to ruin, to purgatory on the breaking-up of the body at death – he has performed an evil deed (at some time),[4] to be experienced (later) as suffering. Or he has seized on, and taken up, a wrong view at the time of death.

(But) anyone there might be (who is an evil doer and) comes to a good destiny, a heaven world, on the breaking-up of the body at death – he has performed a good deed (at some time), to be experienced (later) as happiness. Or he has seized on, and taken up, a right view at the time of death. (And anyone there might be who is not an evil doer comes to his destiny in like manner.)

So, Ānanda, there is futile behaviour with the appearance of futility[5] (as regards the outcome, or otherwise; and) there is efficacious behaviour with the appearance of effectiveness (or otherwise)."

Thus spoke the Lord.

1. The nuances of interpretation are a matter for speculation – "illusory" and "real" could possibly have the force of "ineffective" and "effective".
2. Sarcasm seems possible.
3. This and the ensuing paragraph involve some re-arrangement of the material. In the original the detail of the next paragraph follows each of the general statements given here.
4. "(at some time)" – the full text refers to "earlier" or "later" without further explanation.
5. Horner translates the key terms here as "inoperative" and "operative".

137

Analysis of the Six Sources (of Experience)

215–222

Thus have I heard: once the Lord dwelt near Sāvatthī in the Jeta Grove on Anāthapiṇḍika's campus. There (he) addressed the monks, saying:

"I will teach you the analysis of the six sources (of experience).[1] Six inner sources are to be known (and) six outer sources; six bodies of consciousness (and) six bodies of stimuli; eighteen mental discriminations; thirty-six modes for beings; (how to) abandon this because of that.[2] (Also) there are three applications of mindfulness which the *ariyan* practises, (and is thereby) worthy to be a teacher who instructs a group, (so that) among trainers he is called an incomparable charioteer of men to be tamed. Such is the outline of the analysis of the six sources (of experience).

In regard to what is it said (that) six inner sources of experience are to be known? – (in regard to) the sources of the eye, the ear, the nose, the tongue, the body, (and) the mind.

In regard to what is it said (that) six outer sources of experience are to be known? – (in regard to) the sources of (visible) form, sound, odour, flavour, (physical) contact, (and cognised) phenomena.

In regard to what is it said (that) six bodies of consciousness are to be known? – (in regard to) consciousness of seeing, hearing, smelling, tasting, of body, and of thought.

In regard to what is it said (that) six bodies of stimuli are to be known? – (in regard to) a stimulus for the eye, ear, nose, tongue, body, and mind.

In regard to what is it said (that) eighteen mental discriminations are to be known? – (with regard to the fact that), seeing a form with the eye, one discriminates the form giving rise to delight, the form giving rise to distress, the form giving rise to equanimity; (and similarly with regard to the other five sources). So there is a sixfold discrimination for delight, for distress, for equanimity.

In regard to what is it said (that) there are thirty-six modes for beings? – (with regard to) the six delights of household life, the six delights of renunciation, (and the corresponding experiences of distress and equanimity within each)."

So, what are the six delights of the household life? There is the delight of obtaining and observing the acquisition of agreeable, enjoyable, pleasant, and seductive forms, connected with worldly gain and previously perceived, or of recollecting (what was) formerly obtained (that is) past, vanished, (or) altered.[3] Delight of such a nature (in each of the six sources of experience) is called a delight of the household life.

Now, what are the six delights of renunciation? Having observed the transience of forms, their mutability, fading away, and vanishing – both in the past and now, delight arises in seeing this as it is in accord with true wisdom. Delight of such a nature (in each of the six sources of experience) is called the delight of renunciation.

And what are the six (kinds of) distress of household life? There is the distress of not obtaining (what is pleasant), or of recollecting (what was) formerly not obtained.[4] Distress of such a nature (in each of the six sources of experience) is called the distress of the household life.

And what are the six (kinds of) distress of renunciation? Having observed the transience of forms, their mutability, fading away, and vanishing – both in the past and now, and seeing this as it is in accord with true wisdom – one conceives a thirst for incomparable freedom, and asks oneself: 'When might I reach and experience that realm even now reached and experienced by the *ariyans*?' Thus, distress arises based on (that) thirst. Distress of such a nature (in each of the six sources of experience) is called the distress of renunciation.

And what are the six (kinds of) equanimity of household life? Having recognised a form there is equanimity for the foolish, errant, worldling, who has not overcome (that which defiles), who has not overcome the results (of activity), who sees no disadvantage. This kind of equanimity does not pass beyond (phenomena). Therefore this is called the equanimity of household life (in each of the six sources of experience).

And what are the six (kinds of) equanimity of renunciation? Having observed the transience of forms, their mutability, fading away, and vanishing – both in the past and now, and seeing this as it is in accord with true wisdom, equanimity arises. This kind of equanimity passes beyond (phenomena). Therefore, this is called the equanimity of renunciation (in each of the six sources of experience).

In regard to what is it said (that one might) abandon this because of that? Now monks, because of these six delights of renunciation, with reference to them, abandon and transcend those six delights of the household life. Because of these six (kinds of) distress of renunciation, with reference to them, abandon and transcend those six (kinds of) distress of the household life. Because of these six (kinds of) equanimity of renunciation, with reference to them, abandon and transcend those six (kinds of) equanimity of the household life.

There is, monks, equanimity that is a diversity, and based on diversity. There is (also) equanimity that is a unity, and based on unity. And what is the equanimity that is a diversity? There is equanimity with regard to (visible) forms, sounds, odours, flavours, (and) physical contacts. And what is the equanimity that is a unity? It is the equanimity based on the realm of infinite space, of infinite consciousness, of nothingness, (or) of neither perceiving nor not-perceiving. Now monks, because of the equanimity that is a unity, with reference to it, abandon and transcend the equanimity that is a diversity. (In these various ways) is it said (that one should) abandon this because of that.

With regard to what is it said (that) there are three applications of mindfulness which the *ariyan* practises, (and is thereby) worthy to be a teacher who instructs a group? Now monks, a teacher who is compassionate instructs disciples in *dhamma*, seeking their wellbeing. (But) his disciples do not listen, do not lend an ear, do not prepare their minds for knowledge and, turning aside, desert the teaching. With regard to that, the Exemplar is not pleased, but (nonetheless) lives untroubled, mindful, and lucid. Or again some disciples do not listen, lend and ear, or prepare their minds for knowledge (whilst others do so). With regard to that, the Exemplar is neither pleased nor displeased, and lives untroubled, mindful, and lucid. Or again the disciples (of that teacher) do listen, do lend an ear, do prepare their minds for knowledge. With regard to that the Exemplar is indeed pleased, but (nonetheless) lives untroubled, mindful, and lucid.

With regard to what is it said (that), among trainers, one is an incomparable charioteer? When, monks, an elephant to be tamed is driven by an elephant-tamer, he goes towards just one region – whether eastwards, westwards, or to north or south. When the trainee is driven by the Exemplar he travels to eight regions.

Possessing form he beholds (physical) forms. That is the first. Not perceiving forms inwardly he perceives them externally. That is the second. He directs himself to only what is beautiful. That is the third. Through completely transcending perception of forms, through the laying to rest of sensory response, through ignoring the perception, (and recognising) the infinity of space, he reaches and experiences the realm of infinite space. That is the fourth. Completely transcending the realm of infinite space, he reaches and experiences the realm of infinite consciousness. That is the fifth. Completely transcending the realm of infinite consciousness he reaches and experiences the realm of nothingness. That is the sixth. Completely transcending the realm of nothingness he reaches and experiences the realm of neither perceiving nor not-perceiving. That is the seventh. Completely transcending the realm of neither perceiving nor not-perceiving he reaches and experiences a realm where there is the cessation of perception and feeling. That is the eighth. Monks, when the trainee is driven by the Exemplar who is *arahant*, truly enlightened, he travels to those eight regions."

Thus spoke the Lord.

1. Horner translates "sense-fields", but I have avoided this phrase on the grounds that the mind is not a sixth sense.
2. The original uses the imperative.
3. The second part of this sentence could be read as satisfaction with the fact that unpleasant past experiences have vanished, but in the light of the parallel statement in the next paragraph, I think the words at the end are merely the usual emphasis on the transient character of worldly pleasure.

4. This sentence is filled out in the same way as the comparable one in the earlier paragraph though here abbreviated.

138

An Outline and Analysis

223–229

Thus have I heard: once the Lord dwelt near Sāvatthī in the Jeta Grove on Anāthapiṇḍika's campus. There (he) addressed the monks, saying:

"Monks, a monk should investigate in such a way that, (having done so), he is unagitated by attachment, (with) his consciousness undistracted and not diffuse regarding externals, and not internally unsettled. With consciousness (in that state) there is no future emergence and production of birth, old age, and death (for him)." Saying this, the Lord, the Adept, rose from his seat and entered the dwelling-place. And, shortly after (his) departure, these monks (asked themselves): 'Who can elucidate in full the meaning of that exposition set forth by the Lord in brief? The venerable Kaccāna the Great can (do so). Suppose we were to approach him."

Whereupon (they did so) and, having greeted (him) and conversed in a friendly and polite way, sat down at one side. (Then they explained the question that had arisen for them). (Said Kaccāna):

"Friends, like a man who walks around in need of the pith, wanting the pith, seeking the pith of a great, enduring, and pithy tree – who, passing by the root and the trunk, thinks that the pith is to be looked for in the branches and foliage – such is the brethren's behaviour in that, having been in the Teacher's presence, you pass (him) by and think to question me on the matter. Now friends, the Lord knows what is known, sees what is seen. (He) is vision-born, knowledge-born, *dhamma*-born, *brahmā*-born, enunciator, expounder, dispenser of meaning, giver of the deathless, *dhamma*-master, exemplar. This was your opportunity to question (him)."

"Certainly, friend Kaccāna. But the venerable Kaccāna is praised by the Teacher, and has the esteem of intelligent companions in the good life. Let (him) deal with (the question), if it is not inconvenient."

"Friends, I understand the full meaning of that exposition set forth by the Lord in brief like this. How is consciousness said to be distracted and diffuse regarding externals? Herein, friends, for a monk who has seen a form with the eye, (his) consciousness pursues (its) attributes, is enslaved, bound, fettered by satisfaction with (them). (Thereby) his consciousness is said to be distracted and diffuse regarding externals. (And the same applies for the other senses, and for mental phenomena.)

And how is consciousness said to be internally unsettled? Herein a monk, remote from worldly pursuits, and from unskilled states, reaches and experiences the first (level of) absorption. His consciousness pursues the joy and happiness produced by that remoteness, is enslaved, bound, fettered by satisfaction (with that attainment). (Thereby) his mind is said to be internally unsettled. Or again he reaches and experiences the second (level of) absorption. His consciousness pursues the joy and happiness produced by concentration, is enslaved, bound, fettered by satisfaction (with that attainment). (Thereby) his mind is said to be internally unsettled. Or again he reaches and experiences the third (level of) absorption. His consciousness pursues equanimity, is enslaved, bound, fettered by satisfaction with (that) equanimity and (its associated) happiness. (Thereby) his mind is said to be internally unsettled. Or again he reaches and experiences the fourth (level of) absorption. His consciousness pursues the absence of delight or distress, is enslaved, bound, fettered by satisfaction (with that attainment). (Thereby) his mind is said to be internally unsettled.

And how is there agitation on account of attachment? Herein, friends, an uninformed person, heedless of the *ariyans*, untrained in the *dhamma* of true men, perceives (physical) form as self, or self as possessed of (physical) form, or (physical) form as in self, or self as in (physical) form. (But) that (physical) form of his alters and is something else, and (his) consciousness is preoccupied with (such) alteration. From (this in turn) there is agitation, and the states that arise overwhelm the mind and remain (there). Due to that overwhelming of the mind, he is fearful, annoyed, and consumed by desire; and through (such) attachment he is agitated. (Or he approaches feeling, perception, traits and tendencies, or consciousness in the same way and with the same result.)

That is how I understand the meaning of that exposition set forth in brief by the Lord. But if you so wish, brethren, approach and question the Lord on the matter."

Then those monks, pleased and satisfied at what venerable Kaccāna had said, rose from their seats and approached the Lord. Having saluted (him) they sat down at one side (and told him of their conversation with venerable Kaccāna).

"Monks, clever and of great wisdom is Kaccāna. If you had questioned me on the matter I too would have explained (it) exactly thus."

Thus spoke the Lord.

139

The Analysis of Peace

230–237

Thus have I heard: once the Lord dwelt near Sāvatthī in the Jeta Grove on Anāthapiṇḍika's campus. There (he) addressed the monks, saying:

"Monks, I will teach you the analysis of peace. One should not be addicted to the worldly happiness (that is) base, vulgar, plebeian, un*ariyan*, unprofitable. Nor should one be addicted to the practice of self-mortification, (that is) painful, un*ariyan*, and unprofitable. Not involving either extreme is the middle course, fully comprehended by the Exemplar, productive of vision and knowledge and leading to calm, gnosis, true wisdom, (and) to *nibbāna*. One should know praise and disparagement and, knowing (them), should neither praise nor disparage, but simply teach *dhamma*. One should know how to recognise happiness and, knowing (it), one should be intent on inner happiness. One should not talk covertly (about people).[1] Face-to-face (with them) one should not talk provocatively. One should speak without haste, not hurriedly. One should not adhere to local dialect, and one should not go beyond recognised parlance. This exposition constitutes the analysis of peace.

One should not be addicted to the worldly happiness (that is) base, (nor) to the practice of self-mortification? Whatever is connected with worldly happiness (through) the practice of a delight that is base, is a condition of suffering, injury, trouble, and fever – a bad course (to take). (But) whatever is connected with a worldly happiness (that is not like this), is a good course (to take). Whatever is the practice of self-mortification that is painful, is a condition of suffering, injury, trouble, and fever – a bad course (to take).

There is a middle course, not involving either extreme, and fully comprehended by the Exemplar? (It is) the *ariyan* eightfold way, namely right view, aim, speech, action, livelihood, effort, mindfulness, and concentration.

One should know praise and disparagement and, knowing (them), should neither praise nor disparage, but simply teach *dhamma*. (Well) monks, what is praise and disparagement (that is) not the teaching of *dhamma*? One disparages some in this world, saying (that) all those who find worldly happiness in pursuing the practice of a delight that is base, are living wrongly. (At the same time) one praises (others who do not), saying that they are living rightly. (And one approaches self-mortification in the same way.)

And what, monks, is neither praise nor disparagement, but (just) the teaching of *dhamma*? One (does not make judgements about people in any of these ways). One just teaches *dhamma*, saying (that such and such a practice) is a condition without suffering, injury, trouble, and fever, a good way of living (and that the reverse is bad).

One should know how to recognise happiness and, knowing (it), should pursue inner happiness. (As to that) monks, there are these five strands of worldly pursuit – forms visible to the eye, agreeable, pleasing, enticing, sensuous, exciting; and sounds, odours, flavours, and physical contacts (that have the same effect). The happiness and delight that comes about because of these is called worldly happiness, vile, plebeian, and *unariyan*. I say of this that it is not to be pursued, not to be cultivated, not to be made much of, (but) to be feared. Regarding that a monk, remote from worldly pursuits and from unskilled states, reaches and experiences the first, second, third, and fourth (levels of) absorption. Such is called the happiness of renunciation, of solitude, of tranquillity, and true wisdom. Of this happiness I say that that it is to be pursued, cultivated, made much of, not to be feared.

One should not talk covertly (about people and), face-to-face (with them), one should not speak provocatively. As to that, monks, knowing covert talk to be untrue, unjustified, and unprofitable, one should not speak it (of others) as far as possible. If one knows that (it) is true (and) justified, (but) unprofitable, one should train oneself not to speak it. If one knows that it is true, justified, and profitable, one should know the right time to tell (it).[2] (In the same way) if one knows that provocative words (spoken) face-to-face are untrue, unjustified, and unprofitable; (or) true and justified (but) unprofitable, one should not speak them. If one knows (them to be) true, justified, and profitable, one should know the right time to speak.

One should speak without haste, not hurriedly. As to that, monks, from speaking hastily the body tires and thought suffers (together with) the voice. The throat is affected, and hurried speech is indistinct and incomprehensible.

(And) with reference to what is it said (that) one should not adhere to local[3] dialect, (and) one should not deviate from recognised parlance? (Well) monks, what is adherence to local dialect, (and) deviation from recognised parlance? As to that, monks, in some districts (they know one word for bowl and elsewhere they recognise others). So however they know it in some region or other, (some)one expresses (the matter) with stubborn dogmatism and tenacity, saying: 'Just this is the truth, all else foolishness.' And what, monks, (is the alternative to this)? In whatever way they know it in some region or other, one expresses (the matter) undogmatically, saying: 'Regarding the brethren they definitely express it thus.' Such, monks, is (the avoidance) of adherence to (a given) local dialect, and of deviation from recognised parlance.

So, monks, (whichever of these is a wrong course), that is a disturbed condition, (but whichever of these is a right course), that is a peaceful condition. Therefore, monks, (thinking in each case): 'I will know the disturbed condition, and I will know the peaceful condition and, knowing (both), I will pursue the peaceful course' – thus, monks, must you train yourselves."

Thus spoke the Lord.

1. Horner – "One should not utter a secret speech"
2. There is some ambiguity in the preceding passage as it is not entirely clear whether the telling of the "covert talk" might be to the party implicated, to others, or both.
3. Horner "of the countryside"

140

Analysis of the Elements

237–247

Thus have I heard: once the Lord, whilst travelling on foot among the Magadhians arrived in Rājagaha, (where) he approached Bhaggava the potter, saying: "If it is not inconvenient to you Bhaggava, I would spend a night in your house."

"It is not convenient, bhante. There is one gone forth who has already come. But, if he assents, stay at your pleasure."

Now at that time a son of family called Pukkusāti had gone forth from home to the homeless life out of faith on account of the Lord. It was he that was already come to the potter's house. And the Lord approached venerable Pukkusāti, saying: "If it is not inconvenient to you, monk, I would spend a night in this house."

"The potter's house is large, friend. Let the venerable one stay at his pleasure." Then the Lord, entering the potter's house, and having prepared a grass covering at one side, sat down, establishing mindfulness before him as his aim. Seated (thus) the Lord passed a large part of the night. Venerable Pukkusāti also spent much of the night seated. Then the Lord asked himself: "Is this son of family getting along alright? Suppose I were to question him." So (he) said to venerable Pukkusāti: "Monk, on account of whom have you gone forth? Who is your teacher? Whose *dhamma* do you approve?"

"Friend, there is an ascetic, (one) Gotama, a son of the Sakyans, gone forth from the Sakya clan (who is of high renown). I am gone forth on account of (him). (He) is my teacher. It is (his) *dhamma* I approve."

"But where might this Lord be dwelling at this moment?"

"There is a town called Sāvatthī in the north of the country, friend. (He) is currently living there."

"But have you ever seen (him, or) having seen, would you know (him again)?"

"No, I have never seen, (nor) would I know (him)."

Then the Lord said to himself: "This young man of family has gone forth on account of me. Suppose I were to teach him *dhamma*." So (he) addressed venerable Pukkusāti, saying:

"I will teach you *dhamma*, monk. This man consists of six elements, six sources of stimulation, eighteen mental distinctions, four resolves.

This man consists of six elements, but what is the basis for this statement? The solid, liquid, thermal, and aeriform elements (together with) space and consciousness – this is the basis for the statement.

This man consists of six sources of stimulation, but what is the basis for this statement? The sources of stimulation that belong to the eye, the ear, the nose, the tongue, the body, and the mind – this is the basis for the statement.

This man consists of eighteen mental distinctions, but what is the basis for this statement? Having seen a form with the eye he distinguishes the form furnishing delight, furnishing distress, (and) furnishing equanimity (or, similarly, in terms of the other sources of experience) – this is the basis for the statement.

This man consists of four resolves, but what is the basis for this statement? Resolve for wisdom, for truth, for renunciation, for tranquillity – this is the basis for the statement.

Whatever (belongs to the four great elements, namely whatever is the internal or external solid, liquid, thermal, or aeriform elements)[1], is to be seen with true wisdom for what it is (in terms of): 'This is not mine. I am not this. This is not my self"; and (likewise with regard to whatever) is the element of space.

The space element may be internal or external. And what is the internal space element? Whatever is internally, individually space, become space, and of a secondary nature, namely the ear and nasal orifice, the mouth opening, and that by which one swallows what is eaten, drunk, consumed, and tasted, (the place) where one contains (it), and that by which (it) is evacuated from the lower part of the body; or whatever else, internal to the individual, is the space element, or converted to space (and) is of a secondary nature. Seeing it thus one turns away from (all the elements), one purges the mind of (them).

Then just consciousness remains, pure (and) cleansed. (It is) through this consciousness one knows anything. One discriminates pleasure, one discriminates pain, one discriminates what is neither. A pleasant feeling arises in consequence of experiencing a pleasant stimulus. On experiencing a pleasant feeling one knows (that one does so). From the cessation of that stimulus experienced as pleasant, one knows (that) the pleasant feeling dependent on (it also) ceases and is extinguished. (And the same is true of painful and neutral feelings.)

Monk, as from the contact and friction of two sticks heat arises and light results, and from (their) separation and laying aside the corresponding heat ceases and is dissipated – so it is (with the relationship between stimulus and feeling).

Then just equanimity remains, pure (and) cleansed, soft, workable, and bright. Monk, it is like a skilled goldsmith or (his) apprentice who, after preparing a furnace, ignites a smelting-pot and, seizing the pure metal with forceps, places it in the smelting-pot. From time to time he might blow on it, might sprinkle it with water, might look carefully at it. That pure metal – blown, purified, cleansed, and removed free from dross; soft, workable, and bright for whatever kind of ornament one wishes – is suitable for that purpose, whether for ring, earring, necklace, or golden garland. Likewise just equanimity remains, pure (and) cleansed, soft, workable, and bright.

Hence one knows: 'If I focus this equanimity on the realm of infinite space, (or) of infinite consciousness, (or) of nothingness, (or) of neither perceiving nor not-perceiving, and develop the mind in accordance with that condition, then this equanimity might thereby stand supported and nourished in me for a long time.'

(Then) one comprehends: 'If I focus this equanimity on (levels of experience such as these), that is (something) contrived.' (So) one does not prepare or plan for existence or separation from existence. Not preparing or planning (thus) one clings to nothing in the world. Not clinging one is untormented, (and from that) one comes of oneself to final *nibbāna*. One knows: 'Destroyed is birth, fulfilled the good life, done what was to be done, and no further return to this world.' One knows that, if one experiences a pleasant, painful, or neutral feeling, it is transient, not to be held on to, not to be rejoiced at. Experiencing a feeling limited by the body (or) bounded by the lifespan, (one comprehends it as such). One knows that, on the breaking-up of the body at the end of one's lifespan, all enjoyable experiences here will become cool.

Monk, as an oil-lamp burns because of the oil and the wick, but goes out from (their) consumption, given no replenishment – so it is with (such worldly experience). Possessed of that (knowledge) a monk is possessed of the highest resolve for wisdom. For this, monk, is the highest *ariyan* wisdom, namely gnosis regarding the elimination of suffering in its entirety. His freedom, resting on truth, is enduring and unshakable. For that is deceptive which is of a nature to be deceptive, (whereas) that truth that is undeceptive by nature is *nibbāna*. Possessed of this (knowledge) a monk is possessed of the highest resolve for truth.

Truly his former foolish attachments are brought to an end and broken up. They are abandoned and cut off for him at the foundation, like an uprooted palm-tree incapable of growth and with no future existence. Possessed of that (knowledge), a monk is possessed of the highest resolve for renunciation. For this, monk, is the highest *ariyan* renunciation, namely the relinquishing of all attachment. Truly, one's former foolish coveting was passionate desire, one's former foolish hostility was malevolence and corruption, one's former blind ignorance was a delusion and a corruption. They are abandoned and cut off for him. Possessed of that (knowledge) a monk is possessed of the highest resolve for tranquillity. For this, monk, is the highest *ariyan* tranquillity, namely the tranquillizing of passion, ill-will, and delusion. (So) one should not neglect wisdom. One should preserve truth. One should practise abandonment. One should train oneself in tranquillity. (These are the four resolves).

Where there is steadfastness the flow of opinion does not persist and (thereby) the sage is said to be calmed. But what is the basis for saying this? 'I am. I am this. I shall be. I shall not be. I shall have form. I shall be formless. I shall have perception. I shall not have perception. I neither shall nor shall not have perception.' (All such are opinions.) Opinion, monk, is an illness, an abcess, a barb. From the surmounting of all opinions the sage is said to be calmed. Indeed the sage who is calmed is not born, does not age, is not agitated, desires nothing. Since there is not that for him by which he can come to birth how can he age? Not ageing how can he die? Not dying how can he be agitated? Not being agitated how can he want anything? Such is my analysis into the six elements, monk, put briefly. Bear it in mind."

Then venerable Pukkusāti thought: "Surely it is the Teacher who has come to me. Surely it is the Adept who has come to me. Surely it is the Truly Enlightened One who has come to me." Then, rising from his seat, arranging his robe over one shoulder, and bowing his head at the Lord's feet he spoke thus to the Lord:

"I am at fault, bhante, in that ignorant, erring, and unskilled I thought to address the Lord by the term 'friend'. May the Lord acknowledge the fault as a fault, that there may be restraint in the future."

"Indeed, monk, you were at fault. But since, seeing the fault as a fault, you confess it in accordance with *dhamma,* we acknowledge it for you. For this is growth, monk, in the *ariyan* discipline."

"Bhante, may I receive ordination in the Lord's presence?"

"But have you obtained bowl and robe, monk?"

"(No), bhante."

"The Exemplar does not ordain one without bowl and robe."

Then venerable Pukkusāti, pleased and satisfied at the Lord's words, rose from his seat and after saluting (him) went away keeping his right side towards him, and in search of bowl and robe. But then venerable Pukkusāti, whilst (so doing) was killed when a cow ran amok.

Subsequently a number of monks approached the Lord, saluted (him), and sat down at one side. Said (they): "The young man of family called Pukkusāti, whom the Lord instructed in brief, is dead. What is his destiny, what his future state?"

"Intelligent, monks, was the young man of family Pukkusāti. He sought the essence of *dhamma,* and did not plague me with questions. By the destruction of the five fetters that bind one to the worldly condition Pukkusāti is one of spontaneous arising, not destined for return (from the other world), and whose final *nibbāna* is there."

Thus spoke the Lord.

1. Much condensed – detail of the four elements as in other discourses.

141

Analysis of the Truths

248–252

Thus have I heard: once the Lord dwelt near Bārāṇasi in the Isipatana deer-park. There (he) addressed the monks, saying:

"Monks, (here) in the Isipatana deer-park of Bārāṇasi by the Exemplar, who is *arahant* and truly enlightened, has been set rolling the matchless wheel of *dhamma* that is not to be turned back by ascetic, or brahman, or *deva*, or *mārā*, or *brahmā*, or anyone in the world – namely the proclamation, preaching, disclosure, setting forth, revelation, analysing, and unfolding of the four *ariyan* truths – of suffering, the origin of suffering, the cessation of suffering, and the course leading (thereto).

Monks, associate with Sāriputta and Moggallāna, resort to (them), the clever monks who are helpmates of those of the the good life. Like a mother – such is Sāriputta. Like a child's foster-mother – such is Moggallāna. Sāriputta instructs regarding the fruits of entering the stream (of *dhamma*), Moggallāna as to the ultimate goal. Sāriputta is able to proclaim, preach, disclose, set forth, reveal, analyse, and unfold the four *ariyan* truths in detail."

Thus spoke the Lord, and having spoken the Adept rose from his seat and entered the dwelling-place. Shortly after the Lord's departure venerable Sāriputta addressed the monks in this connection, saying:

"And what, friends, is the *ariyan* truth of suffering? Birth is suffering. Old age is suffering. Death is suffering. Grief, woe, pain, distress, and trouble are suffering. Failing to get what one wants is suffering. In short the five embodiments of attachment are suffering.

And what, friends, is birth? The production, appearance, entry, coming into being, rebirth in this or that realm of beings, the manifestation of the basic components (of existence), the taking-up of the sources (of experience) – that is called birth.

And what, friends, is old age? Whatever in this or that realm of beings is old age, decrepitude, broken teeth, grey hair, wrinkled skin, the lessening of the life-span, and the decay of the faculties – that is called old age.

And what, friends, is death? Passing away, removal, breaking-up, disappearance, dying, the completion of one's time (on earth), the breaking-up of the basic components (of existence), the discarding of the carcase – that is called death.

And what, friends, is grief? The grief, sorrow, sorrowfulness, inner grief and anguish of one beset by some misfortune or other, (and) affected by some painful state or other – that is called grief.

And what, friends, is woe? The crying, lamenting, wailing, bewailing, the states (thereof in such a person) – that is called woe.

And what, friends, is pain? Bodily suffering, what is physically disagreeable and born of a painful bodily stimulus that is felt to be unpleasant – that is called pain.

And what, friends, is distress? Whatever is mental suffering, mentally disagreeable and born of a painful mental stimulus that is felt to be unpleasant – that is called distress.

And what, friends, is trouble? The depression and trouble, the states (thereof) of one beset by some misfortune or other, (and) affected by some painful state or other – that is called trouble.

And what, friends, is (the suffering of not getting what one wants)? For beings of a nature to be born there arises a longing: 'Would that we were not of a nature to be born, to grow old, (or) to die.' But this (situation) is not obtained by wishing (for it).

And what, friends, are the five embodiments of attachment? (They are) as follows – (physical) form, feeling, perception, traits and tendencies, and consciousness – those, in short, are the five embodiments of attachment.

And what, friends, is the *ariyan* truth of the origin of suffering? The craving for renewal, associated with enjoyment and passion, finding pleasure here and there, namely craving for worldly pursuits, for existence, for non-existence – that is called the *ariyan* truth of the origin of suffering.

And what, friends, is the *ariyan* truth of the cessation of suffering? The passionless cessation without remainder of just that craving, its giving up and forsaking, freedom from and non-adherence to it – that is called the *ariyan* truth of the cessation of suffering.

And what, friends, is the *ariyan* truth of the course leading to the cessation of suffering? It is just this *ariyan* eightfold way, namely right view, aim, speech, action, livelihood, effort, mindfulness, and concentration.

And what, friends, is right view? Whatever is knowledge of (the four *ariyan* truths) – that is called right view.

And what, friends, is right aim? The aim of renunciation, of not being malevolent, of not harming – that is called right aim.

And what, friends, is right speech? Abstaining from lies, slander, abuse, and idle chatter – that is called right speech.

And what, friends, is right action? Refraining from the destruction of life, from theft, from dissolute living – that is called right action.

And what, friends, is right livelihood? Herein the *ariyan* disciple, abandoning wrong livelihood, earns a living through right livelihood. That is called right livelihood.

And what, friends, is right effort? Herein a monk puts forth resolve, strives, arouses energy, extends and takes hold of the mind for the non-arising of evil and unskilled states that have not arisen, (and) for the abandonment of (those that have); (and likewise) for the arising of skilled states that have not arisen, and for the maintenance, non-corruption, increase, abundance, cultivation, and perfection of (those that have). That is called right effort.

And what, friends, is right mindfulness? Herein a monk lives observing the body in the body, feelings in feelings, the mind in the mind, and phenomena in phenomena – zealous, lucid, and mindful – in order that he might remove the longing and distress in the world. This is called right mindfulness.

And what, friends, is right concentration? Herein a monk, remote from worldly pursuits and from unskilled states, reaches and experiences the first, second, third, and fourth (levels of) absorption. This is called right concentration, (and these eight factors together are) called the *ariyan* truth of the way leading to the cessation of suffering.

Friends, (here) in the Isipatana deer-park of Bārāṇasi by the Exemplar, who is *arahant* and truly enlightened, has been set rolling the matchless wheel of *dhamma* that is not to be turned back by ascetic or brahman, *deva*, or *māra*, or *brahmā*, or anyone in the world – namely the proclamation, preaching, disclosure, setting forth, revelation, analysing, and unfolding of the four *ariyan* truths – of suffering, the origin of suffering, the cessation of suffering, and the course leading (thereto)."

142

The Analysis of Offerings

253–257

Thus have I heard: once the Lord dwelt among the Sakyans on Nigrodha's campus near Kapilavatthu. Then Mahāpajāpati Gotami approached the Lord bringing a set of new garments and, saluting (him), sat down at one side, (saying):

"This new set of garments was made and woven by me especially for the Lord. May (he) accept it out of compassion."

At these words the Lord said: "Give it to the Order, Gotami. If it is given to the Order both I and the Order will be honoured." (And a second and third time Mahāpajāpati Gotami repeated her request and received the same answer.)

(Then) venerable Ānanda addressed the Lord, saying:

"Let the Lord receive the new set of garments. Mahāpajāpati Gotami has been of great service to the Lord. (She is his) maternal aunt, his foster-mother who nursed him, gave him milk, and suckled him for (his) dead mother. It is due to the Lord that (she) has taken refuge in the Buddha, in *dhamma*, and in the Order. It is on account of the Lord that (she) is one who refrains from the destruction of life, from theft, from dissolute living, from lying, (and) from intoxicants that occasion sloth. (She) is possessed of unwavering confidence in the Buddha, in *dhamma*, in the Order, and of the conduct dear to the *ariyan*s. It is due to the Lord that (she) is emptied of doubt concerning suffering, the origin of suffering, the cessation of suffering, (and) the course leading (thereto). Bhante, Mahāpajāpati Gotami has been of great service to the Lord."

"That is so, Ānanda, that is so. I say there can be no adequate return by an individual to that (other) person because of whom (all these things came about) – neither through making welcome, standing up (out of respect), salutation with joined palms, (nor) through doing the right thing as regards furnishing robes, almsfood, lodging and medicines for the sick.

However there are these fourteen offerings, Ānanda, in terms of the individuals (who receive them) – to an exemplar who is *arahant* and truly enlightened; to one who is independently enlightened;[1] to the disciple of an exemplar who is *arahant*; to one on course for realising the fruits (thereof); to a non-returner, a once-returner, (or) one who has entered the stream (of *dhamma*); (those on course for such attainments); to one who is beyond and emptied of worldly passions; to an ordinary person of upright conduct; to an ordinary person deficient in conduct; (or) to an animal. These are the fourteen offerings in terms of the individuals (who receive them).

With reference to these, Ānanda, the gift to an animal may be expected (to ripen) a hundredfold, to an ordinary person a thousandfold (or more). To one who has entered the stream (of *dhamma* the ripening) is incalculable and immeasurable.[2]

And there are these seven offerings to the Order – to both Orders with the Buddha at their head; to both orders after the Buddha has entered final *nibbāna*; to the Order of monks; to the Order of nuns; (or), saying: 'May a given number of (both) monks and nuns, (or either) monks (or) nuns be specified for me by the Order.' These are the seven offerings to the Order.

However, in the fullness of time, Ānanda, there will be those of the lineage, the saffron robe about their necks, (but) of evil conduct and bad habits, (and people) will make a gift to the Order on account of these malefactors. I declare that a gift to the Order at such a time is incalculable and immeasurable, and I do not say that a gift in terms of individuals is of greater fruit than any manner of offering to the Order.[3]

Ānanda, there are these four sanctifications of an offering. There is the offering sanctified in the giving, but not in the receiving, (and vice versa. There is the offering sanctified in both respects and in neither.) As to that, the giver (may be) one of upright conduct and virtuous habit, but not the receiver. (Or) the receiver may be (such) but not the giver, (or both or neither). These are the four sanctifications of an offering."

Thus spoke the Lord.

1. Higher in status than an *arahant*, because self-enlightened, but not a great teacher after the manner of an exemplar.
2. Full text gives fourteen ripenings to correspond with the previous para.
3. An enigmatic passage, possibly implying that a gift in these circumstances requires greater faith, and distinguishing the worthiness of the Order from the worthiness of some of its members.

143

Counsel for Anāthapiṇḍika

258–263

Thus have I heard: once the Lord dwelt near Sāvatthī in the Jeta Grove on Anāthapiṇḍika's campus. Now at that time the householder Anāthapiṇḍika was a sick man, suffering and grievously ill. And (he) addressed a certain man, saying: "Go, good fellow, approach the Lord, and in my name salute (his) feet with your head. (Tell him of my affliction and then approach venerable Sāriputta in the same way." And the man did as he was bidden, and then said to venerable Sāriputta):

"Would that venerable Sāriputta might come to the dwelling of Anāthapiṇḍika out of compassion." Venerable Sāriputta consented in silence. Then (he) dressed and, taking bowl and robe and with venerable Ānanda in attendance, approached the dwelling of the householder Anāthapiṇḍika, (where) he sat on the seat provided. Said Sāriputta:

"I trust you are getting better, householder, that you are bearing up, and that the painful feelings are subsiding, not getting worse."

"(No), worthy Sāriputta, I am not getting better. Just as a strong man with a sharp sword might cleave one's head, so do extreme winds shake my head."

"Then you should train yourself thus, householder, thinking: 'I shall not cleave to the eye, the ear, the nose, the tongue, the body, the mind, (or the corresponding objects of sense and cognition), and there will be no consciousness for me that is dependent on (any of these).'

(And) you should train yourself, thinking: 'I shall not cleave to visual consciousness, (or to consciousness linked to any other sense, or to mental phenomena, and) I shall not cleave to the stimulus (that gives rise to such consciousness, nor to) the feeling produced (thereby), nor will there be consciousness for me dependent (on any of these).'

(And) you should train yourself, thinking: 'I shall not cleave to the solid, liquid, thermal, aeriform, or spatial elements, and there will be no consciousness for me dependent (thereon).'

(And) you should train yourself, thinking: 'I shall not cleave to (physical) form, feeling, perception, traits and tendencies, or consciousness, and there will be no consciousness for me dependent (thereon).'

(And) you should train yourself, thinking: 'I shall not cleave to the realm of infinite space, of infinite consciousness, of nothingness, (or) of neither perceiving nor not-perceiving, and there will be no consciousness for me dependent (thereon).'

(And) you should train yourself, thinking: 'I shall not cleave to this world, (nor) the next world, and there will be no consciousness for me dependent (thereon).'

(And) you should train yourself, thinking: 'I shall not cleave to what is seen, heard, (otherwise) sensed, recognised, investigated, or reflected on by the mind, and there will be no consciousness for me dependent (thereon).' "

At these words the householder Anāthapiṇḍika cried out, and shed tears. Whereupon venerable Ānanda said to (him):

"Are you holding fast, householder, or are you sinking?"

"I am not holding fast, bhante, I am sinking. Although the Teacher and monks developing their minds have visited me over a long period, I have not before heard such *dhamma*-talk."

"Such *dhamma*-talk is not (generally) made evident for (the benefit of) householders in white, (but only) for those gone forth."

"Well, bhante Sāriputta, let it be made evident for (the benefit of) householders in white. There are young men of family who are little sullied and who, from not hearing *dhamma*, are coming to ruin. They could become learners of *dhamma*."

Then venerable Sāriputta and venerable Ānanda, having counselled the householder Anāthapiṇḍika (like that), rose from their seats and departed. And shortly after, on the breaking-up of his body at death, the householder Anāthapiṇḍika arose in the Tusita group (of *devas*). Then Anāthapiṇḍika, son of *devas*, shedding a radiance through the entire Jeta Grove towards dawn approached the Lord, saluted (him), and stood at one side, (where he) addressed the Lord in verse, saying:

"This friendly Jeta Grove, enjoyed by the company of sages, inhabited by the King of *Dhamma*, is the bringer of my joy. Action, knowledge, and *dhamma*, (right) conduct and living in the highest (degree) – by these mortals are cleansed, not by lineage or wealth. Therefore the intelligent man, considering his own goal, in the thorough investigation of *dhamma* thus becomes pure therein. Like Sāriputta in wisdom, virtue, and tranquillity, let the monk gone to the further (shore) be supreme in these."

So spoke Anāthapiṇḍika, son of *devas*, and the Teacher approved. Then Anāthapiṇḍika, saluting the Lord and with his right side towards him, vanished from that spot. And the Lord addressed the monks the next morning, (and told them of the occurrence, but not the *deva's* name.)

When he had spoken, venerable Ānanda said: 'Now surely this will be Anāthapiṇḍika, son of *devas*, bhante, who had complete trust in venerable Sāriputta."

"Correct, Ānanda. In so far as reasoning can reach (the truth of the matter), you have reached (it). It was Anāthapiṇḍika, son of *devas*, none other."

Thus spoke the Lord.

144

Counsel for Channa

263–266

Thus have I heard: once the Lord dwelt near Rājagaha in the Bamboo Grove at the squirrels' feeding-place. Now at that time venerable Sāriputta, Cunda the Great, and Channa were living on the mountain of Vulture's Peak. Venerable Channa was a sick man, suffering, and grievously ill. Then venerable Sāriputta, emerging from seclusion towards evening, approached venerable Cunda and said:

"Come, friend Cunda, let us go to venerable Channa and ask about his illness." (And they did so.) After greeting him, and conversing in a friendly and polite way, they sat down at one side. Said Sāriputta:

"I trust you are getting better, friend Channa, that you are bearing up, and that the painful feelings are subsiding, not getting worse."

"No, friend Sāriputta, I am not getting better. Just as a strong man with a sharp sword might cleave one's head, so do extreme winds shake my head. I shall take the knife (to myself). I have no wish to go on living."

"Do not take the knife. Let venerable Channa keep going. We want (him to do so). If venerable Channa is in want of proper foods (or) medicines I will seek (them) out. If (he) has no suitable attendant I shall attend (to him)."

"Friend Sāriputta, (these things are not lacking). Moreover, for many a day I have attended satisfactorily on the Teacher.[1] For it is fitting that a disciple (should do so). The monk Channa will take the knife free from fault. Bear that in mind, friend Sāriputta."

"We would ask venerable Channa about something if (he) will give us the chance to put a question."

"Ask, friend Sāriputta. On hearing (you) we shall know (how to reply)."

"Friend Channa, do you regard the eye, visual consciousness, and things visible to the eye, (or their counterparts in the other senses and the mind) in terms of: 'This is mine. I am this. This is my self'?"

"(No, I do not), friend Sāriputta."

"(And) having seen what, and through knowing what in respect of (all these phenomena) do you say: 'This is not mine. I am not this. This is not my self'?"

"Having seen, and through knowing cessation in relation to (all these phenomena) I say: 'This is not mine. I am not this. This is not my self.' "

At these words venerable Cunda the Great said:

"And therefore, friend Channa, the Lord's teaching deserves to be continually born in mind.[2] Wavering is for the dependent (person). There is no wavering for the (one who is) not dependent. In the absence of wavering there is the presence of serenity. In the presence of serenity there is the absence of inclination. In the absence of inclination there is no coming and going. In the absence of coming and going there is no passing away or re-emergence. In the absence of passing away and re-emergence there is not even here or hereafter, or what is in between both. Just this is the end of suffering."

Then venerable Sāriputta and venerable Cunda the Great, having counselled venerable Channa (like that), rose from their seats and departed. And shortly after venerable Channa took the knife (to himself). Then venerable Sāriputta approached the Lord, saluted (him), and sat down at one side. Said Sāriputta:

"Bhante, venerable Channa has taken the knife (to himself). What is his destiny and future state?"

"Sāriputta, did not venerable Channa, in your presence, declare himself to be without fault?"

"Bhante, there is a village of the Vajjis called Pubbajira. There are families there, friendly and well-disposed to venerable Channa, families that are at fault.[3]"

"(There were such) families, Sāriputta. But I do not say that, to that extent, he was at fault. Anyone who gets rid of this body and grasps at another body I declare to be at fault.[4] The monk Channa did not do this, (and) took the knife (to himself) without blame."

Thus spoke the Lord.

1. Horner assumes this to mean satisfactorily to the Teacher rather than to himself.
2. In the ensuing passage Cunda may be indirectly querying whether Channa's action will constitute grasping at non-existence.
3. Sāriputta's rejoinder appears to question whether Channa has been on too familiar terms with these families, and thereby at fault.
4. i.e. suicide is blameworthy if undertaken as an attempt to obtain a better incarnation.

145

A Talk with Puṇṇa

267–270

Thus have I heard: once the Lord dwelt near Sāvatthī in the Jeta Grove on Anāthapiṇḍika's campus. Then venerable Puṇṇa, emerging from seclusion towards evening, approached the Lord, saluted (him), and sat down at one side, (saying):

"Would that the Lord might instruct me briefly so that, having heard *dhamma*, I might live alone, secluded, content with little, zealous, and resolute."

"Puṇṇa, there are forms (visible) to the eye that are agreeable, enjoyable, and attractive, beloved, pleasurable, and enticing. If a monk rejoices in them, makes them welcome, ties himself to them, delight arises for him. I declare, Puṇṇa, that from the arising of delight comes the arising of suffering. (And so it is with the other senses, and with mental states.) (But) if a monk does not rejoice in them, make them welcome, (or) tie himself to them, delight wanes. I say, Puṇṇa, that from the ceasing of delight comes the ceasing of suffering. In what area will you stay Puṇṇa, now that you have been briefly instructed?"

"There is a district called Sunāparanta, bhante. I shall live there."

"The people of Sunāparanta are fierce, Puṇṇa. (They) are rough. If (they) abuse and revile you how will it be for you?"

"Bhante, (if they do so I shall think): 'It is good of them not to strike me with their hands.' "

"But if they should strike you with their hands how will it be for you?"

"Bhante, (I shall think): 'It is good of them not to strike me with clods of earth, with a stick, or with a knife.[1]' "

"(And if they do that?)"

"(I shall think): 'It is good of them not to take my life.' "

"But if (they) should take your life, Puṇṇa, how will it be for you?"

"If (they) take my life it will be thus for me – there are disciples of the Lord who, incommoded and disgusted by the body and by life, look about for a knife. Yet that very knife will have come to me without my looking for it."

"It is well, Puṇṇa. Endowed with such self-control and tranquillity you will be able to live in the Sunāparanta country. Now do as you see fit."

Whereupon venerable Puṇṇa, pleased and satisfied with the Lord's words, rose from his seat and saluted (him, and departed) keeping his right side towards him. Having tidied his lodgings and taking bowl and robe he set off walking towards the Sunāparanta country, (and duly arrived there).

And during that same rainy season venerable Puṇṇa converted as many as five hundred lay-people (of each sex),[2] and realised in himself the threefold knowledge. Then sometime afterwards (he) passed away into final *nibbāna*.

Then a number of monks approached the Lord, saluted (him), and sat down at one side (saying):

"Bhante, the young man of family called Puṇṇa, who was given brief instruction by the Lord, is dead. What is his destiny, what his future state?"

"Monks, Puṇṇa was intelligent. He pursued the essence of *dhamma*, and did not plague me with questions. Monks, Puṇṇa the young man of family has entered final *nibbāna*."

Thus spoke the Lord

1. The full text gives these as successive statements.
2. I have avoided the "lay devotee/female lay devotee" translation which is normal, since a convert is a "devotee" by definition.

146

Counsel from Nandaka

270–277

Thus have I heard: once the Lord dwelt near Sāvatthī in the Jeta Grove on Anāthapiṇḍika's campus. Then Mahāpajāpati Gotami came to the Lord together with some five hundred nuns and, saluting (him), stood at one side. Said Mahāpajāpati Gotami:

"Let the Lord give counsel to the nuns, (and) instruct (them). Let the Lord provide *dhamma*-talk for (them)."

Now at that time the elder monks were counselling the nuns by turn. But venerable Nandaka did not wish to (engage in this). Then the Lord addressed venerable Ānanda saying:

"Whose turn is it to counsel the nuns today, Ānanda?"

"It is the turn of Nandaka, bhante, (but he) does not wish to (do so)."

Whereupon the Lord addressed venerable Nandaka, saying:

"Give counsel to the nuns, Nandaka, (and) instruct (them). Provide *dhamma*-talk for the nuns, brahman."[1]

(So) venerable Nandaka, dressing at an early hour and taking bowl and robe, went into Sāvatthī for alms. Having walked in Sāvatthī, and returning after the meal, he approached King's Park unaccompanied. The nuns saw venerable Nandaka coming some way off, and made ready a seat and provided water for the feet. Venerable Nandaka sat down and washed his feet, (whilst) those nuns, saluting (him), sat down at one side. Said Nandaka:

"There will be a talk with questions, sisters. Let those who understand say (so), and (likewise) those who do not (in each case). But I should be questioned by anyone in doubt or perplexity."

"Thus far we are uplifted and satisfied with what the worthy Nandaka offers us."

"What do you think about this, sisters. Is the eye, (or any other sense-organ), enduring or transient?"

"Transient, bhante."

"And is the transient pleasant or painful?"

"Painful, bhante."

"But is the transient, the painful, the mutable fitly perceived thus: 'This is mine. I am this. This is my self'?"

"Not so, bhante. Why so? This has already been well-perceived in true wisdom by us for what it is. These six internal sources are transient."

"Agreed, sisters. (Now) what do you think about this? Are (visible) forms, (or any other external object of sense or the mind) enduring or transient?"

"Transient, bhante."

"And is the transient pleasant or painful?"

"Painful, bhante."

"But is the transient, the painful, the mutable fitly perceived thus: 'This is mine. I am this. This is my self'?"

"Not so, bhante. Why so? This has already been well-perceived in true wisdom by us for what it is. These six external sources are transient."

"Agreed, sisters. Now what do you think about this? Is visual consciousness (or any other area of consciousness) enduring or transient?"

"Transient, bhante."

"And is the transient pleasant or painful?"

"Painful, bhante."

"But is the transient, the painful, the mutable fitly perceived thus: 'This is mine. I am this. This is my self'?"

"Not so, bhante. Why so? This has already been well-perceived in true wisdom by us for what it is. These six bodies of consciousness are transient."

"Agreed, sisters. It is like the oil burnt by an oil-lamp (which), together with the wick, the flame, and the luminescence, is a transient and mutable thing. If anyone should say that the oil, the wick, and the flame were (like that, but) that the luminescence was an enduring, constant, perpetual, and immutable state, would he be speaking aright?"

"Not so, bhante. Why so? The oil, the wick, and the flame (being like that), how much more the luminescence."

"Likewise, sisters, were someone to say: 'These six inner sources (of experience) are transient, but the pleasure, pain, or (neutral feelings) which I undergo dependent on the six sources is an enduring, constant, perpetual, and immutable state, would they be speaking aright?' "

"Not so, bhante. Why so? Those (various) feelings come about (only) on such a condition. From the cessation of that condition those feelings disappear."

"Agreed, sisters. It is like a skilful butcher who, having slaughtered a cow, carves, slices, and cuts around the adjoining tendons, sinews, and joints with a sharp knife, (but) without injuring the internal flesh or the external hide. Having done (that), and having removed the external hide, he (then) covers that cow with that hide (again) and says: 'That cow is connected to that hide.' Would he be speaking aright?"

"Not so, bhante. That cow is not connected to that hide.[2]"

"Sisters, I have constructed this parable for clarification of the meaning. Just this is its meaning. 'The flesh within' is a reference to the six inner sources (of experience); 'the external hide' to the six outer sources (of experience); 'the adjoining tendons, sinews, and joints' to enjoyment and passion; 'the butcher's sharp knife' to the *ariyan* wisdom by which one carves, slices, and cuts around the adjoining depravity, enslavement, and bondage.

These, sisters, are the seven aspects of enlightenment, from the cultivation and furtherance of which a monk reaches and experiences the freedom of mind and the freedom of wisdom that are undistracted, having realised them in this life through his own gnosis. What seven? Herein a monk cultivates mindfulness, examination of *dhamma*, energy, joy, tranquillity, concentration, and equanimity, (all) being rooted in remoteness, dispassion, cessation, and resulting in renunciation. These, sisters, are the seven aspects of enlightenment."

And with that counsel venerable Nandaka took leave of those nuns, saying: "Go, sisters. It is time." Whereupon, pleased and satisfied with (his) words, (they) rose from their seats, saluted him, and with their right sides towards (venerable Nandaka) approached and saluted the Lord, (who in turn dismissed them).

And not long after (their) departure the Lord addressed the monks, saying: "Just as on an observance day, a fourteenth, there is no doubt or perplexity among the people as to whether the moon is less than full or full, for the moon is then not full – so those nuns were just uplifted by Nandaka's teaching of *dhamma*, but not fulfilled in their aims." Then the Lord addressed venerable Nandaka, saying:

"Now, Nandaka, give that (same) counsel again to-morrow." (And venerable Nandaka did so.) And shortly after those nuns had departed the Lord addressed the monks saying: "Just as on an observance day, a fifteenth, there is no doubt or perplexity among the people as to whether the moon is less than full or full, for the moon is then full – so those nuns were both uplifted by Nandaka's teaching of *dhamma*, and fulfilled in their aims. Whoever is the last of those five hundred nuns is an enterer of the stream (of *dhamma*), not liable to destruction, certain (of truth), and destined for enlightenment."

Thus spoke the Lord.

1. A term of commendation in this context.
2. A second parable has been omitted.

147

A Talk with Rāhula

277–280

Thus have I heard: once the Lord dwelt near Sāvatthī in the Jeta Grove on Anāthapiṇḍika's campus. Then to the Lord in solitude and seclusion came the thought: "In Rāhula the conditions for the development of freedom are (now) mature. What if I were to give (him) further guidance with regard to the rooting out of the distractions." Then, dressing at an early hour, and taking bowl and robe, the Lord entered Sāvatthī for alms. Returning from the almsround after the meal he spoke to venerable Rāhula, saying: "Take your cloth for sitting on, Rāhula. We will go to the Blind Mens' Grove for the afternoon rest." Assenting, venerable Rāhula took up his cloth and followed on the Lord's heels. Then the Lord, entering Blind Mens' Grove, sat down at the foot of a tree, (saying):

"Now what do you think about this, Rāhula – is the eye enduring or transient?"

"Transient, bhante."

"And that which is transient – is it painful or pleasant?"

"Painful, bhante."

"But is the transient, the painful, the mutable fitly perceived thus: "This is mine. I am this. This is my self'?"

"Not so, bhante."

"(And) the forms (seen by the eye)?"

"Transient, bhante."

"(And) visual consciousness (itself)?"

"Transient, bhante."

"(And) the visual stimulus?"

"Transient, bhante."

"(And) that which arises because of a visual stimulus by way of feeling, perception, traits and tendencies, or consciousness?"

"Transient, bhante."

"(And so it is with the other senses, and with mental phenomena in these respects.) Recognising it as such, Rāhula, the informed *ariyan* disciple wearies of (the senses and the mind, and their related attributes). Being wearied, he becomes dispassionate. In dispassion there is freedom, and in that freedom is freedom's knowledge: 'Destroyed is birth, fulfilled the good life, done what was to be done, and there is no further return to this world.' " Thus spoke the Lord. Venerable Rāhula was pleased at his words. And during that explanation (his) mind was freed from the distractions (and left) without attachment.

148

The Six Sixes

280–287

Thus have I heard: once the Lord dwelt near Sāvatthī in the Jeta Grove on Anāthapiṇḍika's campus. There (he) addressed the monks, saying:

"Monks, I will teach you a *dhamma* that is auspicious at the outset, auspicious in its progress, and auspicious in its consummation, and shall proclaim (both) the meaning and the expression of the good life, wholly fulfilled and purified.

Six inner sources (of experience) are to be known (and) six outer sources; six bodies of consciousness (and) six bodies of stimuli; six bodies of feeling (and) six bodies of craving.

Regarding what is it said (that) six inner sources of experience are to be known? – (in regard to) the sources of the eye, the ear, the nose, the tongue, the body, (and) the mind. This is the first six.

Regarding what is it said (that) six outer sources of experience are to be known? – (in regard to) the sources of (visible) form, sound, odour, flavour, (physical) contact, (and cognised) phenomena. This is the second six.

Regarding what is it said (that) six bodies of consciousness are to be known? On account of the eye and with reference to (visible) forms visual consciousness arises, (and correspondingly with the other senses). With the mind and (cognised) phenomena as basis, ideas arise. This is the third six.

Regarding what is it said (that) six bodies of stimuli are to be known? Eyes, (visible) forms, visual consciousness – the meeting of the three constitutes a stimulus, (and correspondingly with the other senses). The mind, cognised phenomena, ideas – the meeting of the three constitutes a stimulus. This is the fourth six.

Regarding what is it said (that) six bodies of feeling are to be known? Conditioned by a stimulus, feeling (arises). This is the fifth six.'

Regarding what is it said (that) six bodies of craving are to be known? With a feeling as pre-condition, craving (arises). This is the sixth six.

If anyone should say: 'The eye, (or visible) forms, (or) visual consciousness, (or) a visual stimulus, (or) a feeling (or) craving (derived therefrom) is self' – that is not the case. For it is evident that there is manifestation and disappearance (for all these phenomena). Whoever recognises this is reduced to saying: 'There is manifestation and disappearance for me of self.' So whoever says (that any of these) is self – that is not the case. If anyone should (speak similarly of the other senses) – that is not the case. If anyone should say (that) mind is self, cognised phenomena are self, ideas are self, a mental stimulus is self, (or) a feeling (or) craving (derived therefrom) – that is not the case.

But, monks, the way (the idea of) the body as one's own arises is this. With regard to the eye, or (visible) forms, or visual consciousness, (or any of the other things referred to, one thinks): 'This is mine, I am this, this is my self.' And, monks, the way (the idea of) the body as one's own ceases (is in not thinking any of these things).

Monks, on account of the eye and with reference to (visible) forms, visual consciousness arises. The meeting of the three constitutes a stimulus. Conditioned by a stimulus an experience arises which is either pleasant, or painful, or (neither). On being affected by a pleasant feeling one (may) rejoice in it, make it welcome, tie oneself to it. (If so) one's propensity for passion persists. On being affected by a painful feeling, one (may) grieve, be troubled, lament, beat one's breast, show bewilderment. (If so) one's propensity for revulsion persists. On being affected by a feeling that is neither pleasant nor painful, one (may be) in truth unaware[1] of its manifestation or disappearance, its satisfaction, disadvantage, or driving out. (If so) one's propensity for ignorance persists. Truly, monks, that one should make an end of suffering in this life without abandoning one's passion for pleasant feeling, without dispelling one's revulsion for painful feeling, without removing one's ignorance regarding feeling which is neither pleasant nor painful – such a thing cannot be.

Recognising it thus the informed *ariyan* disciple wearies of (the senses and the mind, and their related attributes). Being wearied, he becomes dispassionate. In dispassion there is freedom, and in that freedom is freedom's knowledge: 'Destroyed is birth, fulfilled the good life, done what was to be done, and there is no further return to this world.' "

Thus spoke the Lord.

1. Horner has, "does not comprehend". It is a moot point how far we are talking about failure to apprehend the presence of such a state as against failure to understand its nature.

149

The Six Great Sources (of Experience)

287–290

Thus have I heard: once the Lord dwelt near Sāvatthī in the Jeta Grove on Anāthapiṇḍika's campus. There (he) addressed the monks, saying:

"I will teach you the six great sources (of experience). In not knowing, not seeing the eye, (or visible) forms, (or) visual consciousness for what they are, one (becomes) attached (to them). In not knowing, not seeing for what it is that which arises conditioned by a visual stimulus, and is experienced as pleasant, painful, (or) neither – to that, too, one (becomes) attached. The five embodiments of attachment drive on to a future harvest in one who has lived enamoured, fettered, infatuated, (and) finding satisfaction (in such ways). And one's craving increases – leading to rebirth, accompanied by delight and passion, finding enjoyment here and there. Then, too, physical and mental discomfort, torment and fever, increase. One experiences suffering both of the body, and of the mind. (And so it is with the other senses and mental states and phenomena.)

(But if one knows and sees these things for what they are) craving abates, physical and mental discomfort, torment and fever, abate. One experiences happiness both in the body and in the mind. Seeing things as they are is one's right view. Aspiring for what truly is, is one's right aim. Striving for what truly is, is one's right effort. Mindfulness of what is, is one's right mindfulness. Concentration on what truly is, is one's right concentration. (In that way), one's former physical activity, verbal activity, (and) livelihood are well purified. Thus does this *ariyan* eightfold way proceed to its complete development (and thereby) the four applications of mindfulness, the four right exertions, the four bases of psychic power, the five faculties, the five powers, (and) the seven aspects of enlightenment. (And) these two things move in conjunction – calm and insight. One discovers those things discoverable through gnosis. One abandons those things to be abandoned through gnosis. One develops those things to be developed through gnosis. One realises those things to be realised through gnosis. And what, monks, are the things to be discovered? The answer is the five embodiments of attachment, namely attachment to (physical) form, to feeling, to perception, to traits and tendencies, (and) to consciousness. And what, monks, are the things to be abandoned? Ignorance, and craving for (continued) existence – these are the things to be abandoned. And what, monks, are the things to be developed? Calm and insight – these are the things to be developed. And what, monks, are the things to be realised? Knowledge and freedom – these are the things to be realised."

Thus spoke the Lord.

150

To The People of Nagaravinda

290–293

Thus have I heard: once the Lord, whilst travelling on foot among the Kosalans together with a large group of monks, came to Nagaravinda, a brahman village of Kosala.

Then the brahman householders[1] of Nagaravinda approached the Lord, exchanged greetings, and having conversed in a friendly and polite way, some sat down at one side. Others (did so) after saluting (him) with joined palms, others after making known their names and lineage, others in silence. Said the Lord:

"If, householders, wanderers of other sects ask you what kinds of ascetics and brahmans should not be treated with respect, not esteemed, not revered, not honoured, you might answer as follows: 'Those ascetics and brahmans who are not empty of passion, ill-will, and delusion with respect to visible forms (and other sense objects), not inwardly tranquil, proceeding sometimes temperately, sometimes intemperately[2] in body, speech, and thought, should not (be so treated). Why so? Though we (are like this and) proceed sometimes temperately, sometimes intemperately, yet they fail to see that our temperate course is the better.[3]'

If (they next) ask you what kinds of ascetics and brahmans should be treated with respect, esteemed, revered, honoured, you might answer as follows: 'Those ascetics and brahmans who are empty of passion, hatred, and delusion with respect to visible forms (and other sense objects), inwardly tranquil, and proceeding temperately in body, speech, and thought should (be so treated). Why so? Though we (are not like this and) proceed sometimes temperately, sometimes intemperately, yet they do see that our temperate course is the better.'

If (they next) ask you: 'What are the grounds, what the authority whereby (you say that) these venerable ones are either empty of passion, ill-will, and delusion, or on course for (their) removal?' you might answer: 'These venerable ones keep solitary dwelling in the deepest jungle. Yet there are no visible forms (or other sense objects) there, (the continual experience of which) could delight them. These are the grounds, this the authority whereby we say (this).' Thus might you answer them."

At these words the brahman householders of Nagaravinda said to the

Lord: "Excellent, worthy Gotama, excellent." (Whereupon they took the refuges and became lay-followers.)

1. A compound term more usually translatable as brahmans *and* householders, but this is stated to be a brahman village.
2. Horner – "now evenly, now unevenly."
3. i.e. declaring their faith in the better part of their own nature.

151

Purification of the Almsround

293–297

Thus have I heard: once the Lord dwelt near Rājagaha in the Bamboo Grove at the squirrels' feeding-place. Then venerable Sāriputta, emerging from seclusion towards evening, approached the Lord, saluted (him), and sat down at one side. Said the Lord:

"Your faculties are bright, your complexion clear and clean, Sāriputta. In what (field of) experience are you now immersed?"

"In the experience of emptiness, bhante."

"It is well, Sāriputta. Truly you are now living immersed in what is experienced by great human beings. So, if a monk should aspire (to that, the matter) should be considered (by him) in this way: 'On the road by which I entered the village for alms, in the place where I walked for (it), on the road by which I left the village – was there in my mind any resolve, or passion, or ill-will, or delusion, or mental reaction in respect of visible forms (or any other kind of sensation or idea)?' If a monk, on reflection, realises (that there was, he) should strive for the abandonment of those evil, unskilled states, but if he realises (that there was not), he can put them behind him with joy and delight, training day and night in the states that are skilled.

And again, Sāriputta, a monk should consider the five strands of worldly pursuit and the five hindrances (in the same terms).

And again, Sāriputta, a monk should consider thus: 'Do I thoroughly understand the fivefold basis of attachment? Have I developed the four applications of mindfulness, the four right exertions, the four bases of psychic power, the five faculties, the five powers, the seven aspects of enlightenment, the *ariyan* eightfold way, together with calm and insight? Have I realised knowledge and freedom?'

If a monk, on reflection, realises (that he has not, he) should strive (for those attainments), but if he realises (that he has), he can put them behind him with joy and delight, training day and night in the states that are skilled. Sāriputta, all those ascetics and brahmans who, throughout the past, purified the almsround, did so only after repeated reflection in these ways. (And so it will be with those who do so) in the fullness of future time, (or) in the present."

Thus spoke the Lord.

152

Development of the Faculties

298–302

Thus have I heard: once the Lord dwelt near Kajaṅgalā in the Mukhelu Grove. Then the youth Uttara, a pupil of Pārāsariya, approached, exchanged greetings, and having conversed in a friendly and polite way, sat down at one side. Said the Lord:

"Uttara, does Pārāsariya the brahman teach the development of his disciples' faculties?"

"(He does), friend Gotama."

"But in what way does (he) teach (it), Uttara?"

"(He) teaches (that) one does not see (visible) form by means of the eye, (nor) hear sound by means of the ear."

"If that is the case, Uttara, the blind (and) the deaf will become of developed faculties according to (him). For the blind man does not see by means of the eye, (nor) the deaf man hear by means of the ear."

At these words, Uttara, the pupil of Pārāsariya, sat silent and troubled, with shoulders drooping and head bent, downcast and bewildered. Whereupon the Lord, aware of (this), spoke to venerable Ānanda, saying:

"Ānanda, Pārāsariya the brahman teaches the development of the faculties to (his) disciples in one way. But, in the discipline of the *ariyans* the utmost development of the faculties is otherwise. But what is the discipline of the *ariyans* (in this matter)? As to that a form that is attractive, or unattractive, or (both), arises, as perceived by the eye (or any other sense organ). One (should) know it thus: 'That which has arisen for me that is attractive, unattractive, or (both), is compounded and coarse because of its (mode of) production, (but) this is pure and exalted, namely equanimity.' For (such a person these various likes and dislikes) abate, (and) equanimity remains. Ānanda, as a man might open or close his eyes – just as rapidly, just as quickly, and with as little trouble, whatever has arisen abates for (such a person and) equanimity remains.[1]

Further, Ānanda, something that is attractive, unattractive, or (both) arises in the mind. One (should) know it thus: 'That which has arisen for me that is attractive, unattractive, or (both), is compounded and coarse, because of its (mode of) production, (but) this is pure and exalted, namely equanimity.' For (such a person these various likes and dislikes) abate, (and) equanimity remains. It is as though a man might let fall two or three drops of water daily on a red-hot iron vessel. Slow though the dropping had been they would quickly meet their end, and be consumed. It is this that, in the discipline of the *ariyans*, is spoken of as the utmost development of the faculties.

And what is the learner's course, Ānanda? As to that, one is worried, depressed, disgusted by the arising of what is attractive, unattractive, or (both). And how is an *ariyan* of developed faculty? If he aspires, thinking: 'Let me live perceiving the repulsive in the agreeable', then he lives (like that). If he aspires, thinking (to) perceive the agreeable in the repulsive, then he lives (like that). If he aspires thinking (to) perceive the agreeable in (both), or the repulsive in (both), he lives (like that). If he aspires, thinking: 'Ridding myself of both the agreeable and the repulsive let me live tranquil, mindful, and lucid', then he lives (like that).

And so I have taught the learner's course, and the *ariyan*'s developed faculty. What a teacher seeking the wellbeing of disciples may do out of compassion, that I have done for you. Here are roots of trees, here are empty places. Meditate, Ānanda, be not slothful, do not be remorseful later. This is our instruction to you."

Thus spoke the Lord.

1. The full text repeats the preceding for each sense, with varying similes. I have retained only the final one for the mind in the next paragraph.